D0809318

Beginning 3D Game Development with Unity 4:

All-in-One, Multi-Platform Game Development

Sue Blackman

Apress·

Beginning 3D Game Development with Unity 4: All-in-One, Multi-Platform Game Development

Copyright © 2013 by Sue Blackman

All rights reserved. No part of this work may be reproduced or transmitted in any form or by any means, electronic or mechanical, including photocopying, recording, or by any information storage or retrieval system, without the prior written permission of the copyright owner and the publisher.

LucasArts and the LucasArts logo are registered trademarks of Lucasfilm Ltd. © 1992-1998 Lucasfilm Entertainment Company Ltd. or Lucasfilm Ltd. & ® TM, as indicated. All rights reserved.

ISBN-13 (pbk): 978-1-4302-4899-6

ISBN-13 (electronic): 978-1-4302-4900-9

Trademarked names, logos, and images may appear in this book. Rather than use a trademark symbol with every occurrence of a trademarked name, logo, or image, we use the names, logos, and images only in an editorial fashion and to the benefit of the trademark owner, with no intention of infringement of the trademark.

The use in this publication of trade names, trademarks, service marks, and similar terms, even if they are not identified as such, is not to be taken as an expression of opinion as to whether or not they are subject to proprietary rights.

President and Publisher: Paul Manning
Lead Editor: Michelle Lowman
Development Editor: Douglas Pundick
Technical Reviewer: Robert Reed
Editorial Board: Steve Anglin, Mark Beckner, Ewan Buckingham, Gary Cornell, Jonathan Gennick, Jonathan Hassell, Michelle Lowman, James Markham, Matthew Moodie, Jeff Olson, Jeffrey Pepper, Douglas Pundick, Ben Renow-Clarke, Dominic Shakeshaft, Tom Welsh
Coordinating Editor: Christine Ricketts
Copy Editor: Michael G. Laraque
Compositor: SPi Global
Indexer: SPi Global
Artist: SPi Global
Cover Designer: Anna Ishchenko

Distributed to the book trade worldwide by Springer Science+Business Media, LLC, 233 Spring Street, 6th Floor, New York, NY 10013. Phone 1-800-SPRINGER, fax (201) 348-4505, e-mail orders-ny@springer-sbm.com, or visit www.springeronline.com.

For information on translations, please e-mail rights@apress.com, or visit www.apress.com.

Apress and friends of ED books may be purchased in bulk for academic, corporate, or promotional use. eBook versions and licenses are also available for most titles. For more information, reference our Special Bulk Sales–eBook Licensing web page at www.apress.com/bulk-sales.

The information in this book is distributed on an "as is" basis, without warranty. Although every precaution has been taken in the preparation of this work, neither the author(s) nor Apress shall have any liability to any person or entity with respect to any loss or damage caused or alleged to be caused directly or indirectly by the information contained in this work.

The source code for this book is available to readers at www.apress.com. You will be required to answer questions pertaining to this book in order to successfully download the code.

For Phillip, who kept reminding me about how long I had been talking about writing this book.

Contents at a Glance

Contents

About the Author

Sue Blackman is a 3D artist and interactive applications author and instructor based in Southern California. She has taught 3ds Max and game classes for artists for well over ten years in top-rated community colleges and private schools, such as The Art Institute of California, and has been lead 3D artist on games for Activision, through one of its subsidiaries. Blackman has worked in the industry for several years, helping to train Fortune 1000 companies, such as Boeing, Raytheon, and Northrop Grumman, to create serious games and training applications with game-based formats. She has been involved with the commercial development of real-time 3D engines for more than ten years and has authored multiple training-video courses for the Unity engine for Lynda.com. She is an avid tutorial writer and has created both tutorials, as a contributing author, and artwork for various 3ds Max books over the years, as well as training manuals for 3D authoring applications for serious games. She has also written for ACM Siggraph on serious games, one of her favorite topics. You can visit Blackman's web site at www.3dadventurous.com or contact her through the Unity Forum.

About the Technical Reviewer

 **Robert Reed,** who currently resides in Phoenix, Arizona, where he attained a bachelor's degree in game design from Collins College, was first introduced to the Unity3D game engine in 2010, when trying to decide what to use for his graduation game project, and he has used it ever since. JavaScript is his primary language when using the Unity3D game engine, but in addition to JavaScript, he has become a bit proficient in a few other programming and scripting languages, including Java, C, C++, C#, ActionScript 3.0, and Lua.

Acknowledgments

Thanks go out to Gabriel Acosta and Jenny Wang, who helped brainstorm much of the game play for the book's project. I owe special thanks to Jenny for the start menu design and stele idea, as well as the 3DAventurous web site.

Thanks also to Bryan Taylor and Sean McCurry of Binary Sonata Studios for the temple music and camera match code.

Thanks are also in order for Evalyn Hernandez, Zach Sarachman, Rosendo Rojas, Mario Im, and Pablo Ortega, who got roped into recording some of the character dialogue. A special thanks goes out to Erik Toraason, who channeled his "inner Yoda" for the Gimbok character.

Thank you all for taking time out from your own game projects to contribute to mine. Your assets, ideas, and enthusiasms were much appreciated.

Introduction

Why Write This Book

Real-time 3D games have been around for well over ten years now. We've all played them, created assets in the style of our favorites, and maybe even "mod"ed a few of them. But with the Unity game engine leaping ahead in its effort to provide a free or low-cost means of authoring for desktop, mobile, or console games, the only barrier left to creating your own games is your level of commitment and the number of hours you are willing or able to devote.

Times have changed. 3D has become affordable not only in the movie industry, as seen by the number of titles featuring CG (computer graphics), but also in the game industry, where we've seen a shift in casual games from 2D to a 3D format. With Unity's bold move to offer a robustly featured free version of its engine, a radical change in the pricing models of the high-end engines has rocked the industry. The cost of the engine is no longer a barrier to taking your game from a nebulous idea to a working prototype and even on to a marketable product.

Whether your interest is in casual games or you have more ambitious aims, if you have no previous scripting experience but are eager to bring your art assets and story to life, this may be just the book to get you under way. In today's modern game engines, the heavy programming is handled by the engine itself, so the logic and game play can be scripted by those with more creativity than traditional programming knowledge.

In this book, I will approach game creation and design decisions from a 3D artist's view, taking the logic and scripting in small pieces, while introducing artists, budding game designers, and novice programmers to real-time game engine concepts at the same time.

This book is written in a project-based format, so you will not only end up with a playable game and scripting resources you can reuse for other games, but you will experience typical design decisions that have to be addressed throughout the process. You will create your game by starting with the basics and refining it as you add functionality; I will explain the logic behind certain choices and real-time game concepts as you go along.

The project for this book is based on a first-person point-and-click adventure game, complete with inventory, state management, load/save functionality, and a strong emphasis on the visual aspects of game creation. Even if you are more of a first-person-shooter-type game enthusiast, you will be able to see how including entertaining or interesting tasks and features can enhance your favorite genre.

The aim of this project is to introduce you to a logical progression of design decisions and problem solving that will be of value well beyond the scope of the adventure game genre. It provides a framework and a methodology for creating and, more important, *finishing* your own game. You will be going beyond the basic Unity functionality and use of standard assets to investigate topics rarely covered in online tutorials or books. All of the necessary art assets to complete the project are provided.

Author's Note

Several years ago, after taking my class through a race game, a first-person shooter, and a platform jumper, I decided that the last mini-project would be a classic adventure game. Much to my surprise, the class got quite motivated with all of the design decisions and logic involved. As there were no existing tutorials on this genre at the time, we created the game from the ground up, borrowing scripts from the previous projects, creating several of our own, and drawing heavily on the knowledge base of the Unity community. This book grew out of that experience, both to fill a need and to share the adventure with others.

Contemporary Adventure Games

For this project, you will be creating a variation on the classic point-and-click adventure game. The adventure genre, of which there are many variations, is an ideal starting place for artists and others with little or no scripting experience. The story, art assets, and animation are major components of this type of game, and the slower pace allows more freedom from script optimization, as split-second player reaction time is not required. If your only goal is to create a first-person-shooter-type game, this book may not be for you. Conversely, if your tastes are more eclectic, you may find all sorts of information that can be applied to your current genre of choice.

With Unity 4.0, the addition of Mecanim provides an ideal opportunity to introduce another common feature of the adventure genre—characters and dialogue trees. That you can do so without being an expert on character animation makes it even more fun. The more substantial incorporation of physics and various special effects this time around has also contributed to pushing this edition of the book's project from "classic" to "contemporary."

One of the most enjoyable components of the adventure game is the collection and use of an odd assortment of objects. Because of the importance of inventory and state management, several chapters are dedicated to their design and implementation. Neophyte Unity developers often ask how to implement these features in community forums, but they rarely receive answers, owing to the scope of the topic. By the end of this book, you will be armed with the scripts, concepts, and experience to be able to take the knowledge beyond this genre.

Interactive adventure games are also ideal for indie developers, and they appeal to a broad range of players. FireProof Games' *The Room*, authored in Unity, was one of the top-rated mobile games of the year, proving that Unity has taken its commitment to the mobile and casual gaming community very seriously.

About the Unity Game Engine

Unity is the perfect choice for small studios, indie developers, and those of us who have always wanted to make our own games. Its large user base (more than 1.2 million in the summer of 2013) and extremely active user community allows everyone from newbies to seasoned veterans to get answers and share information quickly.

Unity provides an excellent entry point into game development, balancing features and functionality with price point. The free version of Unity allows people to experiment, learn, develop, and sell games before committing any of their hard-earned cash. Unity's very affordable, feature-packed Pro version is royaltyfree, allowing people to make and sell games with the very low overhead essential to the casual games market.

The market for multi-platform games—especially casual games for iPhone and Android—is extremely popular at the moment, and Unity's commitment to cross-platform delivery is well proven. Originally a Mac-based authoring application that could publish to Mac and Windows, Unity unveiled its Windows version in spring 2009. As expected, it has opened opportunities for PC-based developers and artists. Since that time, Unity has continued to add support for iPhone, Android, iPad, and Wii and is developing support for Xbox 360 and PS3. In spring 2013, Unity Technologies revealed its latest surprise: for Unity free users, the license for iOS, Android, Windows 8 mobile, and Blackberry is now, or will shortly be, free as well.

Early adapters of the Unity engine tended to migrate from Flash and Director, making the scripting environment easily adoptable. While many Unity users have an ActionScript background in making Flash games, it is by no means a prerequisite. There is a lot of material for creating games in Unity, including first-person shooters, racing games, platform jumpers, and the like. Even if your interest lies elsewhere, there are plenty of helpful tips and tricks to be gleaned from even the most unlikely sources. Don't be afraid to take advantage of the resources available on the Unity web site (www.Unity3D.com), the Unity Forum (forum.unity3d.com), Wiki (www.unifycommunity.com/wiki), UnityAnswers (answers.unity3d.com), and numerous private-party web sites devoted to the Unity engine.

Unity documentation also contains a wealth of valuable information, but, as with any technology that has a unique vocabulary, it's sometimes hard to find just what you're looking for. Prefacing your query with Unity or Unity3D and searching the Internet is often the easiest way to find elusive concepts or functionality. You can make use of them via the Help menu, but it is often quicker to take advantage of the online version.

Qty	Item		Location		Condition	Price

Beginning 3D Game Development with Unity 4: All-in-One, Multi... Profe (Technology in Action)
Blackman, Sue
ASIN: B00A0000074838
ISBN: 1430248998 - Books

1 H13/2014 00000038718 Good $11.20
Matthew Fagan
Standard
1015746
Amazon US

Subtotal
Shipping $6.99
Total Tax: $0.00

Total

UNITED STATES
Washington, DC 20019

Thanks for your order!

If you have any questions or concerns regarding this order, please contact us at...

To: Matthew Fagan

jason@jason-c-shepp-operator.com
UNITED STATES
Shepherdsville, KY 40129
192 Davis Rd
The Book Factor, LLC

UNITED STATES
Shepherdsville, KY 40129
192 Davis Rd
The Book Factor LLC

Notes:

Will I Have to Learn to Script?

You don't have to be a programmer to make your own game with Unity, but you *will* have to be able to understand enough of what the scripts do to know what can be tweaked to your advantage or decide if a particular script will suit your needs.

Most game play has to be scripted in Unity, but there are hundreds of scripts already available that can be readily reused. Unity ships with several of the most useful. More can be found by searching the Unity Forum, Wiki, or UnityAnswers. Many forum members will even write bits of script for less adept users. In the Collaboration section of the forum, you can even find scripters looking to trade for art assets. By the end of this book, you should know enough to be able to take advantage of the wealth of material available from the Unity community.

Games, by their very definition, are about interaction; even in games that are largely controlled by physics, logic-driven cause and effect is what differentiates them from linear plot-driven passive media. Even the most "artist friendly" game engines require scripting to move beyond simple environmental walk-throughs. This book's aim is to familiarize you with scripting a few lines at a time, while providing visual feedback as often as possible. The assumption is that you have not yet decided to *learn* to script but are happy enough to participate in its creation in a more passive manner.

Scripting Is More About Logic Than Syntax

While many people worry that learning a new language will be difficult and intimidating, think of it this way: most people under the age of 35 are quite fluent in texting, which is a valid subset of our native language. To a certain extent, it has its own vocabulary and syntax, and it is very similar to scripting languages, in that it is more of a subset than an entirely new language.

The difference mainly lies in the method used to acquire the "language." In texting, as with our native language, one doesn't set out to study and *learn* the language. Instead, one absorbs, experiments, and eventually becomes competent through repeated contact, trial and error, and a host of other passive means, rather than rote memorization and stressful examination. This book, because it's about the *logic* behind game design and creation, treats scripting as an immersive experience that is a sideline to the game-development process. You are free to choose your own amount of involvement with the scripting. Whatever you choose, the main scripts developed in the book will enable you to create or expand upon the final output of the book, the game, with your own ideas and art assets.

That being said, there are only a few important concepts and a handful of keywords you need to know in order to get an idea of what's being done in a script. Fortunately, most scripters are quite good at including comments explaining what the code is doing, thus making complicated scripts much less daunting to investigate.

Scripts developed in this book will be provided on a per-chapter basis, and the logic behind them explained in the chapters, but I hope that you will display classic adventurer curiosity and take advantage of the scripting explanations to do some experimenting on your own.

What About Math?

One of the most common things we hear people say in the 3D industry is, "If I'd known math was going to be so useful, I would have paid more attention in class." Be that as it may, most artists and designers are not going to want to invest any time in brushing up on their math skills. Don't worry! My primary goal is to help you create a game. Some of the functionality you will scavenge for your game is easy to use without even knowing how it works. Most of us are quite happy to drive cars without having extensive knowledge of the internal combustion engine. Don't be afraid to treat scripting the same way!

Assumptions and Prerequisites

This book assumes that you are at least somewhat familiar with 3D assets and 3D space, but it does have a short review of the concepts and plenty of tips and tricks throughout.

It assumes that you will not have had much scripting experience (if any at all) but that you'll be willing to work through it in order to bring your stories to life.

It assumes that, as of yet, you have little or no experience with using the Unity game engine.

It also assumes that you are fairly new to the game-making process but have a strong desire to create your own real-time 3D game.

Additionally, this book assumes that if you want to explore genres other than classic point-and-click adventure games, you will work through the book with a goal of thinking about how to apply the various techniques to get results related to the other genre. In the casual game market, combining elements of adventure games, first-person shooters, and other genres is not only acceptable but makes for some very entertaining results.

What This Book Doesn't Cover

This book is not about conventional game design; it is more of a precursor, getting you into the habit of analyzing needs and weighing choices. Not only is creating a massive design document intimidating when you are the one who will have to implement everything, but it is likely to be unrealistic until you are more familiar with the engine and your own capabilities. You're going to build your game up a little bit at a time, prototyping ideas and functionality as you go along.

This is not a book on how to become a programmer, still less on programming best practices. The scripting in this book is designed to ease a non-programmer into the process by providing instant visual feedback as often as possible. While there are usually several ways to attain the same goal, the scripting choices made in this book are the easiest to read and understand from an artist's or designer's point of view. In this book, scripting is presented in the way a native speaker learns his or her own language. He or she is surrounded by it, immersed in it, and allowed to tinker with it to slowly gain a basic working knowledge of it. Don't worry about remembering it all. Some things you will use throughout the project, and others you will be encouraged to take note of for future reference.

Conventions Used in This Book

1. Instructions look like this.

▓ **Tip**   Follow this format.

```
Code looks like this.
```

Platform

This book was written using Unity 4.x in a Windows 7 and a Windows 8 environment. Differences for shortcut keys and operating system file storage with Unity on a Mac will be noted throughout the book and are also available through the help files.

CHAPTER 1

▓ ▓ ▓

Introduction to Game Development

In the first edition of this book, the classic point-and-click adventure genre provided not only a forgiving environment in which to create a game, but it also allowed readers to explore tips, tricks, and techniques often ignored in other beginning Unity game books. This edition updates the classic adventure game to its modernized counterpart, the contemporary adventure game. A 3D world, physics, real-time special effects, and 3D characters enhance the player's experience as he goes through the world acquiring objects of questionable use and solving puzzles, both physical and logic-based.

Coupled with the fact that it appeals to a wide range of players, including many who have never played a first-person-shooter type game, it also becomes an ideal vehicle for the casual games market. And in case your idea of adventure still includes gratuitous use of weaponry, you will even get an introduction to that as well, as the book progresses. As with any project, how to begin is with a bit of research. Critical thinking and investigation at the start will save time in the long run.

The Adventure Genre

If you are old enough to have been around during much of the adventure game's history, you've probably gotten ideas for your own game, based on the most successful and entertaining features of the classics. If you are younger, you may have discovered them through various web sites dedicated to their preservation. Either way, there are lots of good ideas to be found, especially as changes in technology open new avenues for game content to take advantage of.

Text Adventure Games

"You are standing at the end of a road..."

The granddaddy of all adventure games is arguably *Adventure*, the text-based game originally design by Will Crowther in the mid-1970s. In an era where computer games were dominated by *Pong* and *PacMan*, the text-based game that catered to those with a dexterous mind rather than dexterous fingers was a revelation. In the earliest version, also known as *Colossal Cave*, Crowther set the scene for intrepid adventurers to explore a great underground cave system, collecting loot and dealing with the occasional monster. It was reportedly fashioned after the Mammoth Cave system in Kentucky, where Crowther had developed a vector-based map in conjunction with his own explorations and existing surveys.

Adventure set the stage for the genre, where the prose was always beautifully descriptive and often highly entertaining, due in part to the vocabulary and parsing of the users' input.

Infocom's *Zork* series, introduced us to the Great Underground Empire, the Flathead dynasty, and the coin of the realm, the zorkmid. They spawned several memorable lines, such as "Your lamp is getting dim," "You can't get there from here," and many running jokes. Anyone who knows what a grue is can tell you that when your lamp goes out, you are in danger of being eaten by one.

Graphical Adventure

With the advent of computer graphics, the text-based adventure-game genre waned, as graphic quality and resolution slowly improved. Eventually, the text-based predecessor gave way to the still-image format, or graphical adventure genre, pioneered by Sierra Online's *King's Quest*, a host of LucasArts offerings, and Infocom's later *Zork* titles.

The graphical format spelled the end of players typing in their instructions or questions, relying instead on a short predefined list of verbs activated by mouse picks. Gone was a large part of the charm of the early text adventures, where one could type in just about anything to see if the authors had allowed for it, no matter how ridiculous or risqué.

As far as creating material for the new genre, it now required more than just a writer and programmer. It introduced the artist as a major part of the production pipeline. As resolution increased, so did the art assets required. Unlike levels in today's first-person shooters, where the player faces enemies that are increasingly more difficult to overcome in each successive level, the worlds in adventure games continue to be strongly differentiated by theme, visual style, color scheme, and music. The reward for gaining access to the various worlds is the discovery of new and intriguing environments, designed to stimulate the senses and draw the player into the fantasy.

In the early 1990s, Rand and Robyn Miller's *Myst* twisted the usual format to introduce the concept of using game play to reveal the story itself. Acquisition and inventory was practically nonexistent, but interaction and task- or puzzle-solving was visually breathtaking for the times (Figure 1-1). Among the first to incorporate 3D graphics instead of traditional artwork, they introduced another shift in the genre. Now, not only did one require artists to produce a game, a good number of them had to be able to create artwork in the fledgling 3D programs.

Figure 1-1. *Myst, one of the first adventure games to make use of 3D graphics. (Myst [TM] is the sole property of Cyan Worlds, Inc. Copyright 1993, 2001. Cyan Worlds, Inc. All rights reserved. Used with permission.)*

LucasArts Titles

Undoubtedly a force in the early days of the graphical adventure game genre was LucasArts. With an army of professional film personnel from which to draw, LucasArts titles gained a huge reputation for outstanding storytelling, top-notch graphics, and marvelous soundtracks. Of note is the *Monkey Island* series. As with several other titles, such as *Sam and Max* and *Day of the Tentacle*, the entertainment is heavily driven by humor, references to pop culture, and a hearty sense of the ridiculous.

Monkey Island III, The Curse of Monkey Island was one of the last LucasArts titles to use traditional hand-painted backdrops and cell animation. Apart from low resolution by today's standards, its style and execution continue to stand the test of time.

Fast Forward to Real Time

The next paradigm shift in the game industry came with the introduction of real-time environments and navigation. By now, adventure-game enthusiasts expected stunning high-end graphics, such as those in *Myst*'s sequel, *Riven* (Figure 1-2). The difficulty of staying oriented in a beautiful pre-rendered world was still preferable to the low resolution, minimalistic environments of real-time navigation. While it allowed the graphical adventure genre to hold on a bit longer, the latest threat to the pre-rendered format's existence became economic. In the early 1990s, the big publishers found larger markets with real-time first-person shooters, such ID's *Doom* and its successor, *Quake,* at a fraction of the production cost.

Figure 1-2. Cyan's Riven, the pinnacle of the pre-rendered adventure game (Riven [TM] is the sole property of Cyan Worlds, Inc. Copyright 1997, 2003 Cyan Worlds, Inc. All rights reserved. Used with permission.)

Now, well over a decade later, graphics quality is finally beginning to approach pre-rendered standards, and once again the adventure-game genre is making a comeback, but not in the expected venue. As major publishers (as well as software companies) have grown larger, they are less inclined to spend money on developing games that will not sell millions of copies. Other genres that traditionally might sell only 70,000 to 150,000 units each slowly disappeared from the shelves, as did the stores and shelves themselves.

The two biggest factors in the revival of not only the adventure-game genre but other specialty genres are the shift to online buying of products, enabling developers to bypass the big publishers, and the ease and affordability of the software required to author and produce games. The ensuing casual games market, blown wide open with the advent of the iPhone and other mobile platforms, has enabled small studios to enjoy success and motivated individuals to break into the industry as never before.

Modern Successes of the Genre

Not surprisingly, the current reincarnation of the adventure game often uses a non-photorealistic style, thereby allowing studios to concentrate on story, game play, and content that does not require the income of a small country to produce. Adventure games have become increasingly popular with independent studios, as they are able to cut out the extra overhead of the big publishers and do well, without having to sell more than a million copies to recoup their outlay.

Also instrumental in the continued interest in the adventure-game genre is the burgeoning casual games market. Coupled with the latest trend in releasing chapters, as opposed to entire traditional-length games, production times and costs can be better managed, which allows developers to keep the cost to consumers in the realm of impulse purchases. The traditional format of four worlds translates perfectly into the chapter or installment format. That TellTales Games's

Tales of Monkey Island was one of the most successful casual games a few years ago is a testament to the ongoing popularity of the genre.

More recently, *The Room*, a classic puzzle game designed for the mobile market by Fireproof Games, has garnered an impressive number of awards. Winner of the GDC 2013 iPad Game of the Year and developed using the Unity game engine, *The Room* (Figure 1-3) has proven that the adventure game is still alive and well.

Figure 1-3. *Screenshots from The Room, an award-winning classic puzzle/adventure game created in Unity (courtesy of Fireproof Games, 2013)*

Another Unity-authored game of interest is Lionel "Seith" Gallat's *Ghost of a Tale* (Figure 1-4). Due out in 2014, the game recently raised funding through Indiegogo, where a goal of private donations was more than met by the set date. As a crossover, "action-adventure with a hint of RPG," this game is a prime example of what an artist with a dream is capable of creating in Unity. After "struggling for almost a year with a 3D engine famous for its amazing visuals," Gallat discovered Unity and, within a couple of months, was able to create an alpha version of his game as a proof of concept—both to himself and to future contributors. And that included learning C# for the scripting.

Figure 1-4. *Screenshot from Ghost of a Tale, a funded action-adventure game created in Unity and due out in 2014 (courtesy of SeithCG, 2013)*

What Draws People to This Genre?

The repeated revival of the adventure-game genre proves that there is a continuing demand for this type of entertainment. While it would be fairly easy to copy its puzzle format without understanding the underlying principles, the resulting game would probably be less than satisfying. If, on the other hand, you take the time to start with a list of people's motivations for playing adventure games, it will take a lot of the guesswork out of the design process. Once identified, you will be surprised at how quickly the design and development will progress.

To begin with, we can surmise that the audience for adventure games is not looking for a way to let off steam, challenge themselves with physical dexterity, or develop an online persona for a social network. As a broad generalization, it could be said that people play adventure games in order to escape to a world more interesting and stimulating than their own reality. While this observation is probably too generic to be of much use, it provides a starting point.

New Experiences

We may be seeking experiences that we don't have the time or money to pursue ourselves. *Monkey Island* becomes the Caribbean vacation that is always just out of reach. Rather than risking thousands of dollars hoping the real experience will provide the unexpected, we know that, with our help, Guybrush Threepwood will bumble through cultural faux pas, discover local points of interest, and land in plenty of sticky situations.

Suspension of Consequences

In games, we are also allowed virtual experience, without physical or social accountability. Fox Network's *House, M.D.* series once touted House as the "doctor you love to hate." Far from hating House, most of us envy his lack of adherence to social norms. In adventure games, we are at liberty, and often required, to forego the social niceties in pursuit of the game's goal. Trespassing, grand theft, and a host of misdemeanors are often part and parcel of the required actions to complete the game.

Intellectual Stimulus

Intellectual stimulus is another of the factors that appeals strongly to the adventure-game enthusiast. Without a doubt, it is one of the main advantages that interactive games have over the passive media of films and TV. Recent studies have shown how important it is to exercise and challenge the brain in order to slow its aging process. That game companies such as Nintendo have been highly successful with their brain teasers, brain training, and brain fitness games validates peoples' requirement for cerebral exercise.

No Dexterity Required

Adventure-game enthusiasts are not afraid of admitting to being couch or computer potatoes. Unlike fans of first-person shooters, we have no illusions that complicated keyboard and mouse sequences will prove our own physical prowess. That doesn't mean that battling monsters to get to a particular place in the storyline is verboten; it merely means two or three attempts should provide the probability that allows us to be victorious and move on. The achievement of physical tasks should be aimed at making the story more interesting, rather than merely posing problems to be solved by dexterous use of keyboard, mouse, or other input device.

Visual Interest

Unlike first-person shooters, where one is usually moving through the scene too fast to appreciate the surroundings, a big draw for the adventure genre is the visual richness of the environment itself. Although *Riven* raised the bar to almost impossible heights, real-time visual quality is finally getting close enough to be acceptable for realistic environments. Visual richness is not, however, limited to photorealism. Even in the cartoon-styled games, such as the later *Monkey Island* episodes, our suspension of disbelief is maintained by unfamiliar vegetation, whimsical buildings, and Rube Goldberg–type contraptions. As long as the environment is full of interesting content, the artistic style can be considered a separate component.

Story

The story also tends to be of greater weight in adventure games, as it can often be the only clue to solving several of the tasks or puzzles. A formal story-driven plot, versus the goal being revealed as you advance through the game, will also set the scene for the style of game play. Without a clear plot at the outset, successful short-term goals move the game forward by being intriguing and challenging in their own right, drawing us into the game, as we tinker with the intractable objects. Conversely, with plot-driven games, we work through the game in anticipation of having all of the pieces finally fall into place, in hopes of a clever twist on the expected results.

It is no surprise that many games in this genre are based upon books or stories by conventional authors. As with books and, to a lesser extent, films, associating with the main character is a good portion of why we enjoy playing any kind of immersive game. Additionally, the mechanism of controlling a character in the story, whether as first person or third person, draws us in even deeper. In the games where character interaction is minimal, we become the protagonist in first-person format, being responsible for his actions and decisions as the story unfolds. Successful adventure games that rely heavily on interaction with characters of any type, on the other hand, tend to include and develop quirky regulars that appear throughout subsequent additions to the series.

Designing Your Game

With a better idea of why people like playing games, let's consider the implications. Assuming you do not have a fifty-artist team and two years to produce your game, you will have to make some smart design decisions, to enable a good chance of success. Story line, concept art, interaction, and, to some extent, functionality can proceed independently of the game engine. At some point, however, you will find that technology, regardless of how many man-hours you have allotted for the art assets, will not allow for everything you can envision. The toughest part for the artist is deciding what can be sacrificed. At the design stage, with some forethought, you can make the process less painful, as you visualize the intriguing locations and entertaining solutions (see Figure 1-5).

Figure 1-5. I don't think we're in Kansas anymore. (Triberian Oasis, Sue Blackman, 2002)

The movie *Avatar*—and, more recently, Blue Sky's *The Crudes*—has raised the bar on our expectations of virtual worlds. With a massive amount of geometry and special effects, even a single frame of the Avatar world took a reported 30–50 *hours* to render. In real time, we hope to have at least 30 frames *per second*. Obviously, something must be sacrificed.

Figure 1-6 depicts a world that, in 2003, was pre-rendered only with 1.5 million polygons and special effects. Today, in real time, this scene easily achieves a high enough frame rate to be used as a game environment—even before optimization.

Figure 1-6. *What was once only possible in pre-rendered scenes may now be reproducable in real time. (Swamp Scene, Sue Blackman, 2003)*

Visual quality in real time *can* be achieved with clever application of a lot of "smoke and mirrors," thanks to today's shaders and the graphics cards they are designed to communicate with. Unfortunately, the time and resources required to build large, stunning, photorealistic environments are generally not within reach of casual or budding game developers. Don't despair. Rather than falling short of the realism you are trying to achieve, you can sidestep the problem with a few easy-to-implement design decisions.

Defining a Style

By clearly defining a style for your environment, you can prevent people from expecting impractical levels of realism. It can be as overt as using a cartoon, anime, or other well-defined visual language, or it can be more subtle, by placing the world itself in a fantasy or alien realm. Shortcomings in photorealism are much harder to detect when the mind has nothing with which to compare. When you decide upon a style, start by listing its most distinctive features for colors, motifs, lighting, and anything else that visually defines it. Whatever style you choose, be careful to keep continuity throughout the assets, wherever appropriate. Just for fun, let's use the classic adventurer's companion, the lantern (Figure 1-7), to illustrate a few different styles. The two basic requirements of a lantern are that it must be a light source and it must be readily portable.

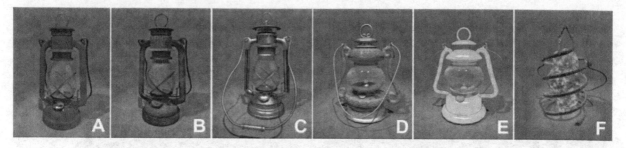

Figure 1-7. The lantern, a mainstay of adventure games and a good indicator of artistic style

New, but classic, design (Figure 1-7, A): This lantern could be bought at any hardware store or through any catalogue at any time in the past 150 years. Its lack of wear and tear could indicate that your protagonist is embarking on a first adventure in a world that is fairly contemporary. Colors should reflect the period chosen.

Dust and rust (Figure 1-7, B): This is the same lantern after a century or so of neglect. This could signal a chance encounter, as your protagonist explores an unexpected find, or it could be part of a story set in a post-apocalyptic world where everything is rusted. Colors would be muted, mostly grays and browns, and broken bits of technology would litter the scenes.

Steampunk (Figure 1-7, C): In the Mechanical Age, metals and fabricating were an art form and in high use. Motif was in the form of functional detail, more than particular designs. This style can be cutting-edge of its era, or it can be combined with a healthy dose of grunge, for interesting environments. Colors are muted, except for brass, copper, iron, and polished steel.

Fantasy, magic, and imagination (Figure 1-7, D): Ornamentation and use of gold trim and colors such as magenta, cyan, and the like are prevalent in this style. Shapes tend to be flowing and whimsical. Mechanical details can be left out.

"Toon" (Figure 1-7, E): Primary or secondary colors and simplified or whimsical shapes define this style. With today's shaders, you can also combine "toon" style with realism for a hybrid style, as shown in this variation of the adventurer's lantern.

Alien (Figure 1-7, F): Anything goes in this style, so long as there is a reasonable connection to the physical constraints of the world. Think like a native and make use of what you "find." In this variation on the lantern, I distilled the two basic requirements—it must be a light source and readily portable—and then I built it with "native" materials.

Compartmentalizing Environments

Any given game engine, in conjunction with the machine it is running on, can only draw so many objects onscreen at any one time. Additionally, machines or devices can only hold so many textures and meshes in memory at any one time. When asked why there are game levels, a room full of gamers will give any number of reasons—the primary one being as a measure of accomplishment. While that is a valid reason as far as game play and story goes, the real truth is that the technology becomes the limiting factor.

Although streaming data may become more prevalent in the future, at this time, we will soon hit a limit as to how much geometry and textures can be loaded into memory. Obviously, the amount will vary with the platform and graphics card, so the first decision is the minimum platform your game should be able to run on. That will serve as a basis for determining how vast each level can be.

Think in terms of creating towns or areas of interaction inside box canyons (see Figure 1-8). The steepness and height of the walls will block the view of neighboring clusters of settlements or whatever the assets are. Twisting entries to the areas can block line of sight to other polygon-heavy areas and make occlusion culling possible.

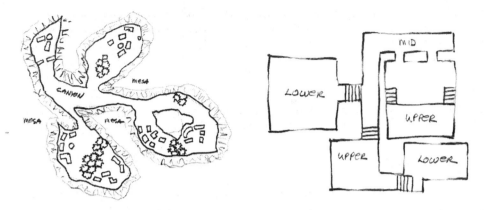

Figure 1-8. Exterior and interior environments designed for occlusion culling

Designing structures works in much the same way. Long, straight vistas where everything must be rendered are far less economical than creating hallways and passages that block the view of all but the immediate area. If you can effectively narrow visibility to smaller spaces, you are free to fill those spaces with more objects, to increase the visual sophistication of the area.

First-Person or Third?

The next topic in the decision-making process is halfway between technical considerations and artistic decisions. The adventure genre is split between first-person and third-person delivery. While third-person provides the opportunity to do a lot of character development, it comes with technical drawbacks in the form of camera control and character animation.

Unlike first-person shooters, where characters may be limited to a small set of standard behaviors (idle, walk, run, shoot, jump, die), the third-person format requires a different collection of behaviors to deal with object interaction and conversation scenarios. Besides the animation requirements, you will also want to engage voice actors to record all of the dialogue. You could, of course, get around this by using conversation that takes place in dialogue bubbles and have the character assume a neutral position instead of speaking.

With first-person, the technical challenges are much less restrictive and, therefore, a better way to go for your first adventure game. A player is free to enter and exit buildings and other tight spaces without worrying about the camera passing through walls or other geometry. And an entire game can be designed so that the player never has to interact directly with any other human beings. Crucial clues can be delivered in written or pictorial form, when necessary.

For the best of both, while keeping your first game from getting too out of hand, you have a third option. You can go with first-person, but introduce characters with whom the player must converse to move the game forward. It requires some character animation, but that could be limited to a simple idle animation and an optional talking animation. It will also, depending on how complex the conversation will be, require a system to manage the conversation. Unlike camera control, a dialogue tree is more about logic than high-level math. The upside with this scenario is that it will allow you to do some character development that can greatly enhance the story and game play, without getting too deep into the mechanics of character animation.

Animation

In many cases, animation can make up for realism. An object that has less sophisticated materials and lower poly count than its pre-rendered counterpart can be far more believable with a well-done animation. Be aware that the human brain is just as quick to pick up animations that "just don't look right" in mechanical sequences as it is with organic or character-type animation. To be believable and compelling, they must be of the highest quality. Fortunately, top-notch animation generally takes up the same amount of resources as poorly executed animation.

If you plan on doing your own nonorganic animation, remember to think about the physics involved. If two objects collide, there will be a transfer of energy. A little bump, jiggle, or compression goes a long way in making your animation not only more believable but more interesting as well.

Content

With the technical considerations addressed, you can start thinking about the actual content you would like to have in your game. As with anything else, it bears some critical thinking, if you want your game to be a success.

Challenges, Tasks, and Puzzles

While the technical considerations are a good basis for generic game design in several different genres, content is much more specialized for the adventure genre, where interaction and problem solving are among the key features.

Designing challenges that are gratifying to solve is not enough in itself, because what is difficult and fulfilling for one person may be easy and trivial for someone else. The resulting sequence should be compelling, entertaining, and interesting, whenever possible. Here we can also learn from the comedy of Peter Sellers or the suspense of Alfred Hitchcock: if the solution seems obvious, do something extra, and use anticipation to your advantage. Add something unexpected to the mix. The *Monkey Island* series, carried on by TellTale Games, has mastered the art. Many objects, once found, immediately suggest their purpose, but when used, tend to surprise the player with something unexpectedly entertaining, in addition to the anticipated result.

As the aim is to reward the player for correct behavior or actions, it is also a good idea to avoid frustrating him. For enjoyable game play, the character can certainly bumble into sticky situations, but he should be able to get himself out with cleverness, ingenuity, and a dollop of luck. In short, avoid setting the player up for failure. If you plan on making it so that the obvious will not work, at least give the player hints beforehand.

What Basic Human Characteristics Make for Fun?

Above all, we play games for entertainment. Unlike passively watching a movie on television, an interactive game takes commitment. If it's not enjoyable or challenging, we'll turn it off and walk away. Even with the games that are more serious than tongue-in-cheek, the basic characteristics that make us human prompt us to behave in predictable patterns. A short list of characteristics is as follows:

- **Ferengi Rules of Acquisition:** Like the Ferengi of *Star Trek: The Next Generation*, we like to collect things, especially if they don't belong to us. Call it a survival trait from our distant past; if it isn't nailed down, our instinct is to collect it and stash it for a rainy day. Bumper stickers that read "He who dies with the most toys wins" echo the sentiment in a more modern-day context.

- **Naughty or nice:** We like to fantasize about doing things deemed naughty or somewhat socially unacceptable. In games, we can act on our baser instincts without having to worry about the censure of our peers. Often, it is even a requirement to move the game forward.

- **Superpowers:** We like to fantasize about having physical prowess or skills that may involve danger or years of training, but unlike the gamers who play first-person shooters, we feel no compulsion to master complicated or dexterous key and mouse sequences to perform such feats.

- **Consequences:** We like to be able to see what happens when we hold that bomb or grenade too long, because in this type of genre, we expect the unexpected and entertaining to happen.

Managing Your Project

Everyone has a story or game idea, and chances are if you find someone else to work with, their idea will be different from yours. Even if you establish yourself as the leader, conflicts will arise, and the probability of splitting up increases (unless, of course, you are able to pay them a reasonable wage).

Typically, first-time authors are not in the position to be able to pay employees. With non-funded collaboration comes the likelihood that the game will never get finished if the team falls apart. By accepting that you will be solely responsible, you can get on with the creation and development. Even if your skills will take you only as far as a proof of concept, the completion of that version will establish your credibility. A working prototype proves both intent and the ability to see a project through. At that point, looking for funding to create a commercial product, or just looking for volunteers to take the project to the next level, takes on a whole different aspect.

Multiple Roles

The biggest drawback to being the sole author of your first game is the necessity of wearing three different hats during the process. The first, designing game play, story, and style, is within reach of most people, though perhaps more suited to the artistic type. The second, creation of art assets for the game, is clearly an artist task, but there are plenty of free assets to be found on the Web for the art-challenged. The problem for nonartists becomes creating continuity. The third component of game creation is the scripting. In high-end commercial engines, this was traditionally the realm of hard-core programmers, but today's authoring engines have redesigned the scripting process to allow artists to readily use pre-scripted animations and component scripts to achieve their visions.

This book is specifically written with the goal of helping the artist or designer become familiar with the scripting process, in order to produce a reasonably sophisticated game or proof of concept. With the examples and concepts you will discover in this book, it is hoped you can realize your dream, or at least take the first step in that direction.

The bottom line is that a lot of people talk about making games. Very few, however, actually do it. This book aims to remove barriers and lessen the learning curve, so that you will have the opportunity to fulfill your ambition to create a game. This book is not just about learning to use the Unity game engine. A good part of it is about the process of creating and completing a game and the decision-making process that involves.

Choosing the Game Engine

In the past, game-authoring engines were either fully featured commercial offerings, such as the UnReal and Crytek engines, that were licensed on a per-game basis or proprietary in-house engines that by necessity only did what the game required. With the advent of the casual game, the Unity engine has moved to the forefront as the engine of choice for small studios and individuals.

The Unity engine is ideal for a first serious effort at game creation in that it offers a lot of high-end features, has a free version and low-cost Pro version, runs on either a Mac or a PC, and has the capability of authoring to several different platforms. Additionally, for those of you interested in the mobile market, Unity has now made the iOS and Android licenses free for Unity free-version users. Free Blackberry 10 and Windows 8 mobile authoring is promised as well.

The Requirements

Having weighed the various technical, artistic, and production considerations, you are probably anxious to get down to details. This is a good time, however, to make a rough list of the basic requirements and decide what is optional and what is mandatory before you get started.

- **Entertaining:** Above all, the adventure game should be entertaining. Whether it comes from humorous interaction, intriguing animation sequences, or intellectual conundrums, game play and environment must draw the player in and keep him engaged.

- **Story/Goal:** The game is not a Big Book of Puzzles. The tasks or puzzles should at least have a logical, mechanical, or physical tie to the world's defined properties (as in the case of magic being part of its description) and, preferably, tie in with the premise of the story.

- **Object interaction:** Interaction with objects is one of the defining features in all aspects of the genre. Whether the player is allowed to gather objects or must only work with what is immediately at hand, the typical point-and-click functionality is a mainstay.

- **Object-to-object interactivity:** A big part of the task-solving component of adventure games is the player's ability to combine multiple objects to attain the key that lets him solve a problem or repair a mechanism in order to move the game forward. While this is not always present in all adventure games, it is a common feature.

- **Conversations:** Player dialogue with NPCs (non-player characters) definitely falls under the bells-and-whistles category, but can be a great addition to your game. Keep in mind that you don't want the player to miss any clues within them. For topic choices that don't contain clues or pertinent information, be sure to make the replies entertaining, so the player will be rewarded for his diligence.

- **Inventory:** Also not a requirement but a much loved component is the inventory system. In order to allow the player to collect everything that is not nailed down, the game must keep it all readily available for use. Sophisticated or large games should also provide a means of scrolling through the player's stash, in case the onscreen representation of the contents of the inventory is limited.

- **Save/Restore:** Unlike many of today's casual games, even the shorter chapter-style adventure games are rarely played from start to finish in one sitting. Players may devote an hour or so in an evening to playing the game, stopping when they are stuck and starting up again when their mind is fresh. Saving the game is a necessity when the game is expected to give the player several hours of enjoyment over a period of days or weeks.

- **Music and sound effects:** As defined by the early graphical games, sound effects helped reinforce and enhance object interaction. Music not only sets the mood for the individual worlds or environments but is also commonly used as part of the solution to puzzles or tasks in game.

- **Action objects:** Also common to the various derivations of the adventure genre is a means of identifying interactive objects. In the original text adventures, the interactive objects were always listed after the general room description. With the shift to graphical adventures, the player was often forced to search a still image pixel by pixel to find the available objects. Occasionally, objects could be identified by their lack of anti-aliasing, but with advancing technology and higher resolution, it became common to change the cursor or highlight the cursor/action object when the mouse moved over it.

Tips for Completing Your First Game

Even at its simplest, the game-creation process is not trivial. For those of you who have taken game-design courses where you were required to create a 20+ page design document, it's time to come back to reality. Unless you have unlimited funds and a well-seasoned game studio at your beck and call, implementing your grand plan is probably not going to be realistic. Lock it away and hide the key. Until you know what the engine, your programming skills, and your art skills are capable of, consider that you are building a prototype. Getting stuck on finish details near the start of the process will at best turn out to be a waste of time and at worst stop the project completely. Changes in design are inevitable. The goal is to make the big changes earlier in the project, before time has been spent on details. For more on this philosophy, check out Bill Buxton on Sketching.

As you work to create your first game, you may want to keep a few of these tips and tricks in mind:

- **Rule #1.** Don't waste your best ideas on your first game. Work out the technology, but consider your first project a learning experience.

- **Keep a log of the hours you spend on everything.** Break it down into researching, documenting, scripting, modeling, mapping, animating, and testing. This will give you a good idea of how long things take, so you will eventually be able to make realistic time schedules, access coworkers or employees, and most important, meet milestones.

- **Don't bite off more than you can chew.** Most creative people tend to get carried away when they design things. When a project gets too big and complicated, its chances of reaching completion diminish drastically. Plan for levels of completeness, to allow you to reach attainable goals. Instead of organizing your milestones into the separate game levels or worlds, organize the *entire game* into levels of completeness or sophistication. Think in terms of the base amount that must be accomplished first. Then add a list of extra features or improved assets you'd like to have, if you had more time. And, finally, have a list of refinements, features, and improvements you would add if time and money were no object. This way, you will always be able to fall back on a less sophisticated level and still have something to show for your efforts.

- **Entertaining or tedious?** Ask yourself this question before implementing an idea for a task or game play. As text adventures became more sophisticated, the player was required to eat and drink during his explorations, or he would become faint and eventually die. While having to keep your lamp full of lamp oil could make for an interesting turn in the game, failing to eat or drink was merely tedious.

- **Feasible?** It doesn't have to be real if it's logical and your world permits it. Just make sure the premise of the world and the population's culture is clearly defined.

- **The path of least resistance.** Good design choices can speed up production. The development of color schemes, design motifs, and "local" building materials early on will allow for faster design of individual assets, as well as provide continuity of visual environment. For instance, if the local environment is short on wood and has long-established settlements where the culture symbolized their faith with an equilateral triangle, you might expect to see the majority of buildings made of stone and utilizing a triangular motif throughout. Wood might be reserved for precious objects. A particular plant indigenous to the area might figure largely in the production of cloth, and the color might dominate the settlement. Aside from making design decisions much quicker, you will also find that you can reuse a good number of the assets throughout the environment. Even if the player is not informed of the underlying reasons, his subconscious will find the world more believable.

- **Bait and switch.** Don't be afraid to use stunt doubles for multiple tasks. It is often much quicker to create a duplicate for a different task than trying to complicate the original to perform both.

- **Assets: freebees, purchase, or build from scratch?** Weigh the costs in time and money carefully. If an object is so generic as to look the same no matter who creates it, consider using one that's readily available. Conversely, sometimes the time spent in preparing and repairing a purchased object outweighs its cost. If the object is unique to your game or world, then plan on creating it yourself. Sometimes new and unique mapping and a small bit of tweaking of an existing asset will do the job. The same goes for scripts. If it's free, or you can afford it and it saves a lot of time, don't feel you have to reinvent the wheel by writing it all from scratch. The Unity Asset Store is a good place to start, especially if you are at the stage where proxy objects are useful.

- **Technical considerations.** Decide at the start whether your game will require cutting-edge technology, mid-range technology, or if it will be able to run on older hardware. If you are developing on faster, better equipped machines, test your progress regularly on a target machine, until you get a feel for the frame rate and limitations required. The same goes for deployment on mobile platforms.

- **Available features.** Don't design with the hopes that a crucial bit of technology will be available by the time you require it, unless you have a viable substitute.

- **Design alternatives.** Be flexible, in case the functionality you want is not feasible for the current software technology or your target machines. Don't waste time on trying to make high-end features work, when you know frame rate or hardware will not properly support them.

- **Platform restrictions.** If you are creating your game for a mobile platform, or plan on porting a desktop version of it to mobile, research the restrictions and limitations thoroughly. Be aware of image size and format required, audio type, and polygon count for scene and characters. Be aware that there are size restrictions for uploaded games and asset packages for your game's extensions.

- **Plan and test first.** Know where you are going and what you will require *before* you start out. Don't get bogged down in details until the basics have been sorted out and you have a clear understanding of what is required.

- **Paper design.** Sketch ideas, environment maps, and other ideas before starting on the permanent 3D assets, environments, textures, and other artwork.

- **Proxy objects.** Create proxies and stand-ins for mock-ups, tests, and early proof of concepts. Make sure of the functionality before spending time on the final assets. Inability to get a particular idea working may change the asset requirements drastically.

- **Consistency.** Research ideas for styles, worlds, and content. Choose a theme, define a world, a style, a mood, and color scheme, and then stick to it faithfully.

- **Beta testers.** Don't tell everyone about your clever ideas; you will require beta testers that come to it fresh. Don't stand over them and provide hints and instructions. Watch to see what they do without knowing the critical path to follow.

- **Interactivity.** Create flowcharts or other diagrams until you have mapped out exactly how each object should act and react, before you start working on the actual functionality.

New to Real Time vs. Pre-render

Even the most seasoned 3D artists will be confronted with a multitude of concepts, restrictions, and issues unique to real time when they first delve into creating their own game. While many of the words and phrases may already be familiar, dealing with them can be challenging. As an artist, the compromise between the asset in all its glory and the physical requirements to keep the game running at an acceptable frame rate can be extremely frustrating.

The most common misconception is that poly count is the main factor in frame rate. In reality, almost everything costs. Besides poly count, frame rate is also affected by the number of lights in a scene, the complexity of materials or shaders, the amount of memory taken up by both textures and meshes, physics, animations, particle systems, and just about everything else. Most of the concepts new (or at least more visible) to real time are used mainly to help improve frame rate.

Terms and Concepts

This section provides a short description of many of these terms, but more important, briefly explains why and how they work to increase frame rate.

DCC (Digital Content Creation applications): These programs include 3ds Max, Maya Cinema4D, Blender, and many others. While a few have an associated real-time engine, most are geared toward creating assets for real-time applications or pre-rendered still shots or movies for their final output.

Frame rate: The human eye does not see much beyond 30 frames per second. In DCC applications, an animation, the finished product, is usually viewed at 24 or 30 frames per second, depending on whether it is for film or video. In DCC applications, when you animate an object, you keyframe according to the frame rate used by the target media. In real time, frame rate takes on a whole new meaning. Real-time engines render frames constantly during runtime. Depending on what is in the scene and visible, what is animating, using physics, being lit, or any of the other myriad factors, the frame rate will be *constantly changing*. Add processor speed and graphics card into the mix and you can easily see why keeping frame rate as fast as possible for the target audience becomes important.

In a studio situation where game development may be spread out over two years for a ΛΛΛ title, if you start development on a cutting-edge machine at the beginning of the project, that machine will probably be mainstream by release time. Indy developers, on the other hand, may have development times of two to six months per title and should plan accordingly. Thirty frames per second is a good low-end range to aim for, unless your game is more of a training application, where 20 fps (frames per second) is generally acceptable. As a rule of thumb, if you are authoring on a fairly fast machine, you will probably want to set a low-end limit of 100 to 150 fps. If possible, you will want to try some benchmarking tests to solidify your frame rate targets on your working machine. Be aware of your target market and their typical hardware for your game, from the start of the project.

Navigation: One of the big differences between DCC and real time is scene navigation. A big part of games is the method of navigating through the 3D environment. Far from being standardized after near 20 years of real-time games, in a room full of 20 budding game artists and designers, you will get at least 20 different opinions on the best controls for a game. Obviously, the type of game plays a big part in the choice, but, additionally, the skill level of the player also dictates the choices. Many games allow the key controls to be remapped or assigned by the player, while others strive to make navigation as invisible to the user as possible, by allowing a mixture of controls.

Collision: Another important concept in real time is that of collision. Once players are allowed to travel wherever they wish in a 3D world, physical constraints must be set to prevent them from traveling through walls, yet allowing them to move over uneven terrain, stairs, and other obstacles. In a 3D engine, typically, the constraints will be invisible primitive objects, or they may be derived from the mesh object's geometry directly. The former are the most economical, as far as frame rate goes. With complicated meshes, one often creates a lower poly stand-in for collision. Many game engines will do this for you.

Poly (short for polygon): This term is used in many different ways, depending on the application. In real time, we are generally talking about a triangular face of a mesh object. Poly count refers to the number of polygons or "tris" in a mesh object or in an entire scene. People new to the game-development process almost always ask how many polys their characters should be. The answer is always dependent on whatever else is happening in the scene. If you have a scene with a lot of geometry that is drawn at the same time in every frame, the number would be a lot lower than if the character was always alone in a desert with a couple of rock formations. Another important concept is how important the object is, or how close it will be viewed. If the object is secondary to the plot or game play, it probably doesn't warrant a high poly count. If the player will never see the object larger than 200×200 pixels worth of screen space, there's a good chance that high poly detail will be wasted resources, both in creation time and CPU usage.

When importing models to a game engine, you may notice a difference in vertex count. Figure 1-9 shows three spheres with 48 tris. The first sphere is smoothed where vertices are shared between multiple faces. The middle sphere has hard edges, so only vertices on co-planar faces can be shared. The last sphere is smoothed but has been unwrapped. Because the same vertex cannot exist in multiple places on the unwrap texture, vertex numbers are also higher than the smooth sphere, with no mapping coordinates.

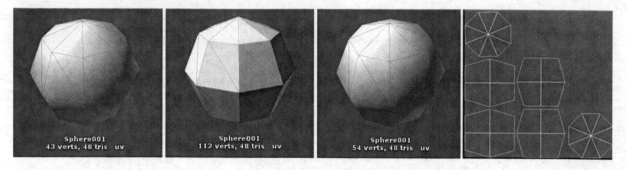

Figure 1-9. *The same sphere with shared vertices, (left), no vertex sharing, (center), and sharing, but unwrapped, (left)*

Simple primitives vs. mesh objects: A primitive is an object that is parametrically defined by a set of parameters. A sphere, for example, can be described by its radius and height and width segments. A mesh object is defined by giving the exact location, or offset, of its vertices in relation to the object's transform axis. Most engines will have at least a few primitive objects for simple-use cases. They are most useful for experimentation and, occasionally, projectiles. While a primitive object is smaller on disk, once in the game, it will go into memory, just as any mesh-type object.

LOD or Level of Detail (Figure 1-10): If an object will be seen up close and requires lots of detail at some point in the game, but it will be far enough away at other times to needlessly tax the engine, one often uses an LOD stand-in. At a particular distance, the high poly object is hidden, and the low poly stunt double is shown in its place, to improve frame rate. With some engines, this may be handled by the engine itself creating the lower poly version and swapping out at a pre-determined distance. In other engines, or with important meshes, the artists will provide the LOD version or versions.

Figure 1-10. *LOD example showing poly count of the different versions of an object*

The lowest poly version is often an alpha channel–using image. In its static form, two planes containing the image are crossed to form an X configuration. Occasionally, three planes are used. The image is always fully self-illuminated. The dynamic version consists of a single plane containing the image that is always turned to face the camera. This technique is called billboarding (see Figure 1-11).

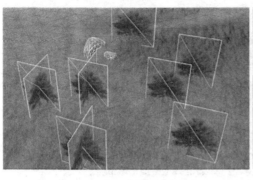

Figure 1-11. *X-trees and billboarded trees using the same image*

Distance culling: Related to LOD, distance culling means that at a particular distance, the object will no longer be drawn in the scene. When a high-poly-count object takes only a few pixels onscreen, it is wasting resources. Typically, one might use a low-poly stand-in at a particular distance, then use distance cull to stop drawing the low-poly stand-in at some point.

Fog: Besides being visually more interesting for an environment, fog works well with distance culling, by allowing the objects to be culled sooner as they disappear into the fog. Fog can be of two types: vertex fog, where the vertex color of an object is affected more as the object recedes, and pixel fog, which gives more consistent results but uses more resources.

Clipping planes (Figure 1-12): Cameras have near and far clipping planes. Objects are not rendered if they are closer than the near clipping plane or beyond the far clipping plane. When used in conjunction with fog, clipping planes present a quick and efficient means of limiting the rendering of objects in the scene. If any part of an object's bounding box is within the view frustum (the part of the screen you see) and the camera clipping planes, then each face of the object has to go through the checking process, to see if it will have to be rendered.

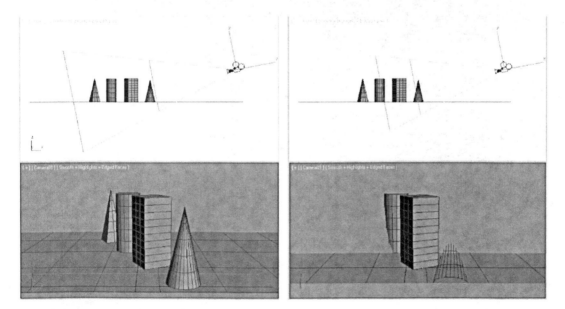

Figure 1-12. *Camera clipping planes*

Draw order: When a scene is rendered, objects are drawn into that scene one at a time. Depending on how an engine is set up, it may also draw certain types of objects before or after other objects. If the objects are drawn in the order they were added to the scene, it's possible that you will see alpha draw order issues. This happens when an object with partial transparency is drawn sooner than objects that lie behind it. During drawing, if an object is partially occluded, that part is not drawn. The check for occlusion does not check the opacity of all of the occluding objects; it's either occluded or not. To ensure that objects are drawn behind transparent objects, the semitransparent objects are drawn last.

In some engines, the scene is parsed at start time in order to determine locations of semitransparent objects, so that it knows the order in which to draw them, thereby avoiding draw-order issues. The downside of this method is that draw order may be adversely affected when a semitransparent object is animated out of its starting position.

In engines that draw objects into the scene in a predictable order, you can have fun with draw order, by creating an x-ray machine. In other engines, you may be able to use special shaders to achieve the same effect.

Occlusion culling: Occlusion culling is another means of increasing frame rate by not rendering certain objects in a scene. With automatic occlusion culling, data is created with the scene objects, in order to be able to check large blocks of objects. In the example where towns or settlements are located in box canyons, you know that when you are in one canyon, the others by definition will be occluded. Rather than having to check objects one at a time to see if they are visible from a particular vantage point, the entire contents of the town can be skipped.

Good game design can make occlusion culling possible and help to increase frame rate. Manual occlusion culling can easily be done by organizing objects in groups or marking tags. When the player crosses in or out of zones, all objects that will not be seen can be turned off or on.

Lighting: In 3D, basic, non-GI (global illumination) is performed on a per-vertex basis. Each vertex has what is called a vertex normal, a vector that determines how the face or triangle will be lit (Figure 1-13). A ray is traced from the light to the vertex, and the angle between the two, the angle of incidence, is used to calculate the percentage of that light received by that vertex. The light received by each vertex is averaged between each. The smaller the angle, the more light the vertex receives.

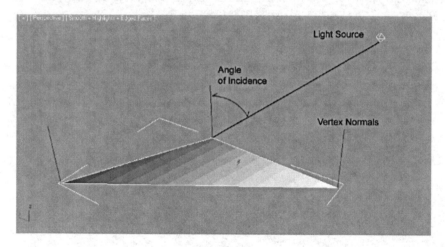

Figure 1-13. *Basic lighting on a single face*

Shared or averaged vertices (Figure 1-14): Whether adjacent faces share vertices or use an average of their vertex normals, the result will be a soft, or smoothed, result. When vertices are not shared or their normals averaged, a hard edge is perceived, because the amount of light is calculated for each vertex. Most DCC applications hide the true number of vertices, to make modeling easier. This is why the cube that had eight vertices when you modeled it is suddenly shown as having twenty-four vertices after import into real-time engine.

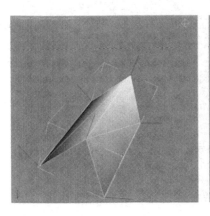

Figure 1-14. *Smoothed (shared vertices) vs. hard edges(not shared)*

Vertex vs. pixel lighting: The previous examples use what is called vertex lighting. It is the fastest type of lighting and is quite efficient with lower polygon models. Unfortunately, with low-poly models, the averaging of the light between vertices can leave splotchy, irregular results. As expected, higher poly count makes for more even lighting, but at the cost required to calculate lighting on more vertices. Pixel lights, on the other hand, perform more calculations on the mesh, depending on its current onscreen size. A close object receives more extra render time than the same mesh farther back in the scene.

Pixel lighting also allows for other affects, such as shadows, cookies (projected masks), and normal maps—all at a cost, of course. While these features are assumed in DCC programs, they are each responsible for using additional resources and slowing frame rate in real time. In the Unity game engine, if a graphics card does not support pixel lights, the lights will automatically be dropped back down to vertex lights.

Normal mapping (Figure 1-15): Normal mapping works by simulating surface details on a mesh, so that lighting can be performed as if the detail were actually in the mesh. While this doesn't save much in resources for rendering, the overhead of high poly meshes can be greatly reduced. The trade-off is in extra storage for the normal map, which can be quite large, if it represents a lot of detail. While most people are familiar with images of low-res monster heads with normal mapped detail, it is noteworthy to be aware that normal maps are quite good at providing detail for nonorganic objects as well.

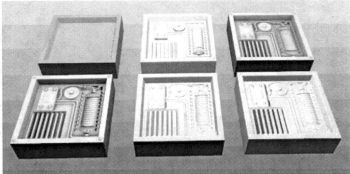

Figure 1-15. *Normal map (left): the distinctive blue/cyan/magenta colors represent the directional topology of the original mesh. The lighting pass is made from this information, rather than the lower poly mesh's vertex normals. Normal maps (right): The low-poly mesh (top left); the high-poly mesh (top middle); the low-poly mesh with the resulting lightmap (top right); the low-poly mesh with the lightmap and a high res normal map (bottom left); the low-poly mesh with a low res normal map (bottom middle); and the low poly mesh with a high res normal map and no lightmap (bottom right)*

Shaders: In 3D, after you create a mesh object, you assign a material to it that contains all the properties required to visually describe its surface properties. These can be color, texture or pattern, smoothness, reflectivity, emissive qualities, and many more. Traditionally, the render was handled generically and limited to only a handful of properties. As graphics cards have improved, they have taken over more of the tasks involved in describing the object's surface, so now you have specific bits of code called Shaders that tell the graphics card what to do for each material. Shaders, as with lights, can be written for vertex rendering or pixel rendering. As before, vertex shaders are more efficient than pixel shaders, while pixel shaders have much higher visual quality and are able to portray many more effects.

Boundaries, real and invisible: An important design consideration for real-time games is how to stop the user from leaving the game area. Physically, it is only necessary to create invisible collision walls. Visually, there are several common methods of defining the player boundaries. The two most common outdoor solutions are to set the scene either on an island surrounded by water, in a plane, or in a valley surrounded by mountains. City environments may be blocked by walls, road blocks, and blind alleys. In games where the environment or story permits, swamps or mine fields could provide reasonable barricades.

Terrain generators: Most modern game engines contain terrain-generating modules. The author is allowed to paint the shape of the terrain, creating hills, valleys, lakes, and more with an internal displacement map. Actual geological data, in the form of a displacement map, can also be used. Once the mesh is in place, most engines allow the user to paint textures onto the terrain with various brush types. A mask is internally created for each texture, and the result layered together to provide a rich and varied terrain.

Some terrain generators also provide the option to paint trees, foliage, and other meshes around the terrain. Trees and small scrubs or grasses can often be affected by wind and will generally contain an automatic LOD mechanism.

Dynamic tessellation (Figure 1-16): In addition to terrain generators, the resulting terrain mesh is often dynamically tessellated, to provide more detail up close, where the player is focused, and less farther away, where higher detail can be an unnecessary waste of resources.

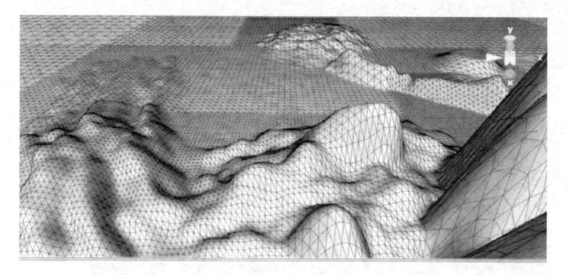

Figure 1-16. *Tessellation of a terrain mesh*

Summary

In this chapter, you reviewed the history of the adventure game from its roots as interactive text through the early graphical adventures and on into the 3D rendered era that eventually gave way to the real-time formats of today. Along the way, you identified the elements of the genre that persist through the changes in style and format. Intrepid adventurers want to play in worlds that are more interesting and stimulating than their own reality. With no special computer skills, they want to have the fantasy of physical prowess and experience, while they collect everything that is not nailed down and solve intellectual conundrums without the baggage of social accountability.

You looked at design elements for developing your game from physical issues such as environmental layout to the conceptual considerations of what is fun to the technical specifications that ultimately influence your final decisions. Then you explored the pros and cons of the first-person format versus the third-person format and found a compromise suitable for a first game, first-person with some NPC conversation. You then checked out a list of good practices for first-time game creators.

And, finally, you started to look at 3D from the perspective of real-time engines, as opposed to pre-rendered DCC applications, such as 3ds Max, Maya, Cinema4D, and Blender. You found that the frame rate required to run a successful game depends on a multitude of factors, such as poly count, lighting types, materials, and culling of various types. The navigation so unique to real time, with its interaction with floor and wall collision, will present you with a variety of challenges that will be revealed as you continue through the book.

In the next chapter, you will get your feet wet in Unity, discovering (or reviewing) basic functionality of transforms, viewports, and asset management, followed by a short section on 3D in general.

■ ■ ■

CHAPTER 2

Unity UI Basics—Getting Started

As you are probably pretty anxious to get started creating something in Unity, the introduction to Unity's UI (user interface) will be kept rather brief. You will explore and investigate it more fully as the need arises, but for now, you can get a basic feel for the layout options and concepts. If you'd like to delve further into the UI before moving on, the Unity help files include a very good section on getting started.

Installing Unity and Starting Up

Download Unity from http://unity3d.com/unity/download/ and install it. The Unity icon will appear on your desktop when the installation is complete (Figure 2-1). When you run it for the first time, you'll have to register the product by following the prompts. Registration can be done quickly online from any machine, even if the machine you've installed Unity on isn't connected to the Internet. If your machine is connected, you'll be taken directly to the registration page. A 30-day trial of the Pro version is available from Unity3D. As you will be introduced to a few of the Pro features in the last few chapters, you may wish to try the Pro version at that time.

Figure 2-1. *The Unity icon*

To start Unity, you can click the desktop icon or choose it from the Windows Start menu ➤ Programs ➤ Unity and, on the Mac, Applications ➤ Unity.

Loading or Creating a New Project or Scene

To work with Unity, you must always start with a project.

■ **Tip** The folder you create or select for your project *is* the project. When you open a project through the Project Wizard, you select the folder.

When you create a new project, a directory or folder is created, with sub-folders containing the required files. Be sure to note where the project is installed or use the Browse button to select a different location. You will be asked to choose which asset packages you want to include with your project. Earlier versions of Unity had generic Pro and Standard packages as the choices. Now, however, the packages have been split into component parts, so you can reduce clutter for specific game types. In the book, you will use most of the packages, so you can get a feel for what is available.

1. Open Unity.

If you have downloaded the demo project, Unity will open it to start. If there is no project, the Project Wizard dialog opens, prompting you to select a project.

2. If Unity has opened an existing project, from File, select Open New Project.

3. Select the Create New Project tab, as shown in Figure 2-2.

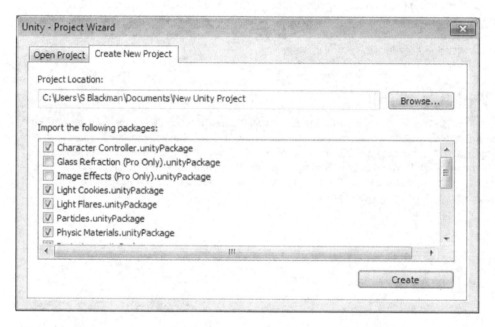

Figure 2-2. *Project Wizard Packages*

■ **Tip**   If Unity is already open, choose New Project from the File menu.

---

4. Click Browse and navigate to where you'll keep your Unity projects, then create a New Folder for the book project.

5. Name the folder **BookProject**

6. Select Character Controller, Light Cookies, Light Flares, Particles, Physics Materials, Projectors, Scripts, Skyboxes, Terrains, and Water(Basic).

■ **Note** This book will make optional use of several Pro features, but the project will not rely on them to achieve a finished result. Should you decide to upgrade to Unity Pro or try the 30-day trial midway through the project, you can import the Pro packages easily, through the Assets menu, under Import Package.

7. Click Create.

Unity closes and reopens to show your new project—BookProject.

Unity Pro ships with the "dark" UI, as shown in Figure 2-3. As many readers of this book will be using the free version, screenshots will reflect the original, lighter version of the UI.

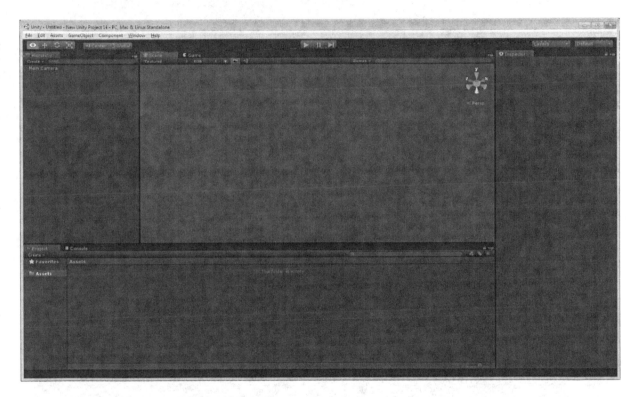

Figure 2-3. *The default Unity Pro "Dark" Skin*

If you have Pro, you may choose between the two skins through the Preferences dialogfrom the Edit menu, as shown in Figure 2-4.

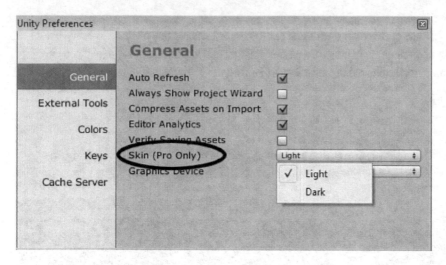

Figure 2-4. The Unity Preferences dialog

In your new scene, you will see a camera in the Hierarchy view and several items in the Project view (see Figure 2-5). When you create a new project, a folder called Assets is created in your machine's file system; its contents are displayed in the Project view. The top section contains filters to help you locate assets quickly, and in the lower section, you will see the Assets folder and its subfolders. In the right-hand column, you can see the contents of the selected folder.

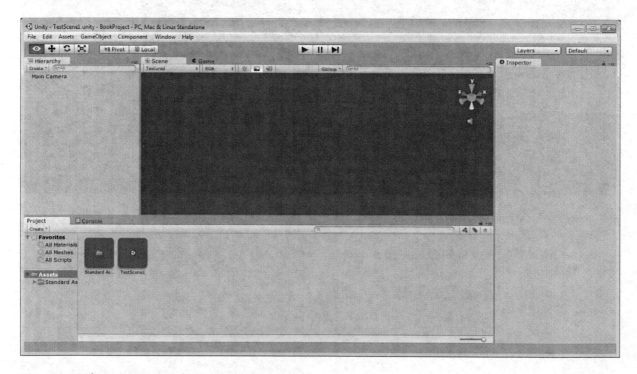

Figure 2-5. The new project in the main editor window

▪ **Important!**   Once an asset has been added to your scene, *never* rearrange or organize it using the OS, i.e., Explorer (Windows) or Finder (Mac), as that will break internal paths and metadata in the scene.

Before going any further, you will save the *scene*. Think of scenes as levels. A project can contain several scenes. Some may be actual levels, while others may be menus, splash screens, and so forth.

8.   From the File menu, choose Save Scene, and save the scene as **TestScene1**.

As a default, the new scene is saved in the root Assets folder, one of the folders automatically created every time you start a new project. In Unity, it appears in the Project view with the Unity game icon next to its name in the One Column Layout, or in the second column if you are using the Two Columns Layout as shown in Figure 2-5.

You will eventually give the scenes a sub-folder of their own, but for now, the scene is easily visible. When you open a project, you will often have to select a scene before anything shows up in the Hierarchy view.

The Layout

There are many ways to rearrange the layout of the Unity UI. For this book, it is assumed that you will be using the standard 2×3 layout, as shown in Figure 2-6, because it allows you to have access to the Scene view when you are in Play mode. You can change the layout by selecting from the Layout drop-down in the upper right area of the application window, as shown in Figure 2-7. If you have the screen real estate, you may even want to tear off the various views into floating windows.

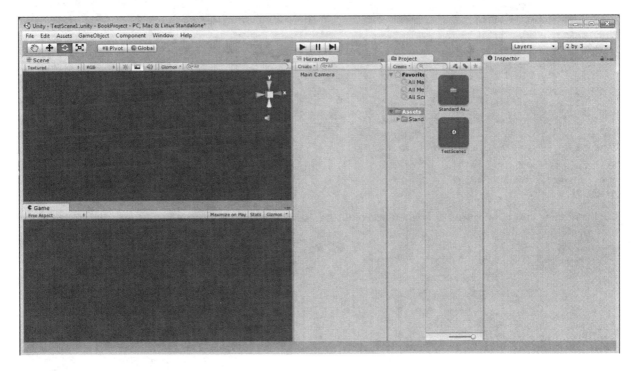

Figure 2-6. *Unity's UI—the 2×3 layout*

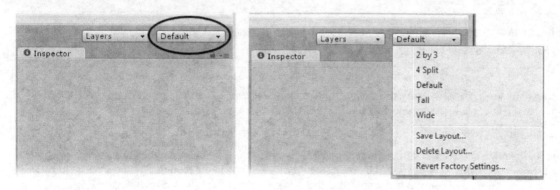

Figure 2-7. *Reconfiguring the UI using the Layout drop-down*

Unity 4.0 introduced a new split-column Project view. It's great for inspecting new assets in unfamiliar projects, but many people feel it introduces unnecessary clutter in their own projects. You are free to use whichever you prefer, but for the book, most instructions and screenshots will assume you are using the one-column Project view. You can select the Project-view layout of your choice by right-clicking over the Project tab and choosing either One Column Layout or Two Columns Layout, as in Figure 2-8.

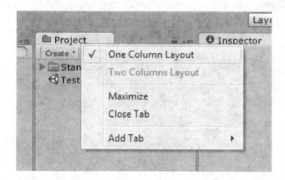

Figure 2-8. *Selecting the One Column Layout*

Scene View

The Scene view shown in Figure 2-9, is where you build the visual aspects of your scene—where you plan and execute your ideas.

Figure 2-9. *The Scene view, showing the camera icon and the grid*

■ **Tip** To show the grid in the Scene view, toggle off the Game Overlay button (Figure 2-9).

Game Window

The Game window, shown in Figure 2-10, is where you test your game before building it in the runtime environment. You can't select objects in this view and, unlike the Scene view, it has no default lighting. You'll have to use the Main Camera to see objects in the Game window.

Figure 2-10. *The Game window*

Hierarchy View

The Hierarchy view (Figure 2-11) shows what's in the currently active scene. GameObjects that are dynamically added and removed from the scene during runtime will appear here when they are active in the scene.

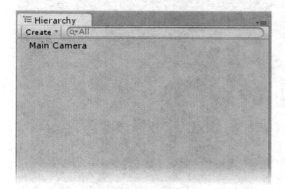

Figure 2-11. *The Hierarchy view, showing the only object in the scene, the Main Camera*

Project View

The Project view, shown in Figure 2-12, contains all the assets available to the current project, as well as all scenes or levels available for the finished game or application. It is a mirror of the Assets folder in the directory where the project resides. Removing assets from this location deletes them from the hard drive! Removing assets from the directory in Explorer removes them from the Project view and could break the scene.

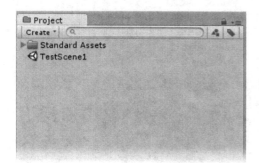 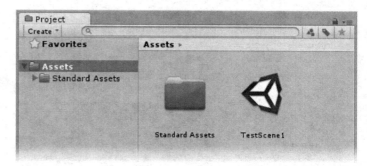

Figure 2-12. *The Project view , One Column Layout (left) vs. Two Columns Layout (right)*

Inspector

You use the Inspector to access various properties and components for objects you've selected in either the Hierarchy or Project views. You can also access other scene-related information here. Select the only object that's in the scene now, the Main Camera, from the Hierarchy view, and then take a look at the Inspector, as shown in Figure 2-13.

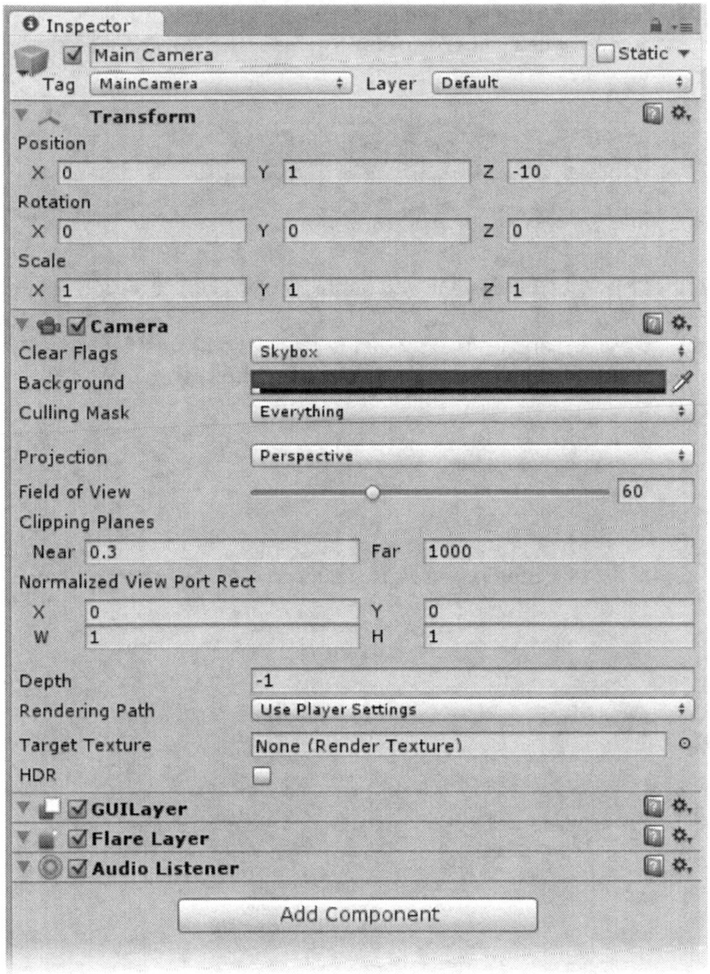

Figure 2-13. *The Inspector, with the Main Camera selected in the Hierarchy view*

Toolbar

Below the menu bar is the toolbar (see Figure 2-14), which contains five different controls.

Figure 2-14. *The toolbar*

The Transform tools, shown in Figure 2-15, provide functionality for navigating the scene and transforming objects. The button on the far left, the pan tool, can also become orbit and zoom tools for navigating and adjusting the Scene view. You can click and drag to move the view around (to pan). To orbit the current viewport center, hold the Alt key down, while clicking and dragging. And to zoom, hold the Alt key (Windows) or the Cmd key (Mac), plus the right mouse button. There are other ways to perform these tasks, as you'll see when you add an object to the scene. But don't test the navigation until you have an object to work with.

Figure 2-15. *Scene navigation tools, pan, orbit, and zoom, (far left of each of the transform buttons)*

The remaining three buttons are for transforming objects in the scene in edit mode. The available transforms are move, rotate, and scale.

Objects can be transformed in different coordinate systems and from different pivot points. The next set of controls, to the right of the Navigation tools, shown in Figure 2-16, let you toggle between the choices.

Figure 2-16. *Pivot point and coordinate system tools*

The center controls, those shown in Figure 2-17, are the Play mode controls that allow you to see how the game will work in real time, as if you were the player.

Figure 2-17. *The Play mode controls*

To the right of the Play controls, you'll find the Layers drop-down (Figure 2-18). Layers are used in Unity for controlling which objects are rendered by which cameras or lit by which lights.

Figure 2-18. *The Layers control*

You already tried the Layout drop-down (Figure 2-19), when you set it to use the 2×3 split layout. You can rearrange and customize most of Unity's UI. The Layers drop-down lets you quickly get back to several default or predefined layouts.

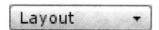

Figure 2-19. *The Layout control*

Menus

Along with the usual file-handling options, there are many concepts and features that are specific to Unity. Most are found in the menus, as shown in Figure 2-20. Menus items also show the keyboard shortcuts for those who prefer them.

File   Edit   Assets   GameObject   Component   Window   Help

Figure 2-20. *The Unity Menu bar*

File

In the File menu, you can load, create, and save scenes and projects. It is also where you build your game as an executable or other deployment type.

Edit

The Edit menu (Figure 2-21) contains the expected Cut, Copy, Paste, Duplicate, and Delete commands, as well as several runtime commands. The actual editing of assets, however, is done in the Inspector. Of particular value here are the keyboard shortcuts shown next to the commands.

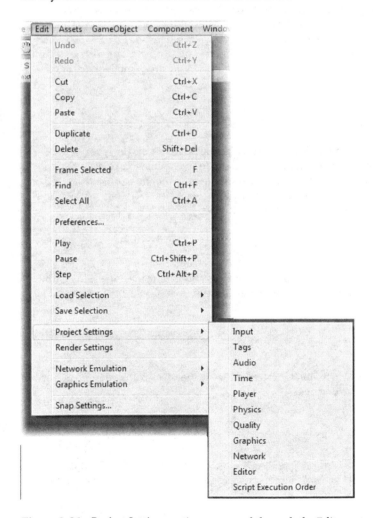

Figure 2-21. *Project Settings options accessed through the Edit menu*

There are several scene settings that are not accessed through the Hierarchy or Projects views. Besides the Render Settings, the Project Settings (Figure 2-21) are where you'll access many of your scenes' attributes. When you choose an option, the information will show up in the Inspector view.

Assets

In the Assets menu, you will find the Create submenu. This is where you can create the type of assets that generally can't be imported from DCC programs, such as non-mesh special effects, physics materials, and scripts. It is also the place to define custom fonts and organize the project with folders and prefabs. You can also reach this menu by right-clicking in the Project view.

GameObject

The GameObject menu lets you create an empty GameObject. The GameObject is the base container for objects, scripts, and other components in Unity. Like a group, it has its own transform and, so, is a logical means of organizing similar objects or meshes. At its simplest, a GameObject contains its transforms (location and orientation) and a few other properties. With the addition of various components, it can become almost anything you need. GameObjects are invaluable when used as a parent group or "folder" to keep multiple scene objects organized.

You can create various objects, such as lights, particle systems, GUI 2D objects, and Unity primitive objects from scratch with Components or find them ready-made in the Create Other submenu. Unlike many modeling programs, you cannot change the number of segments in Unity's primitive objects.

Component

The Component menu gives you access to items associated with objects, such as meshes, rendering types, sound, scripts, and colliders, as well as those that create or extend functionality with predefined behaviors or even editors. Components let you add physics characteristics to imported meshes, function-curve animation to objects, and all of the interactive intelligence that drives games and other, more serious applications via scripts. They are the building blocks that are added to the GameObject foundation to create almost everything in your scenes.

Window

As you'd guess, this menu displays the commands for managing various windows and editors in Unity, along with their keyboard shortcuts. It is also the way you must access Unity's Asset Store, a place where you can find or purchase assets of all sorts for your project.

Help

The Help menu provides access to the various Unity help manuals, as well as to the massively supported Unity Forum, Unity Answers, release notes, and instructions for reporting bugs.

Creating Simple Objects

It always helps to have something in the scene when you're going to experiment with navigation in a 3D application. Though you will import most of the assets for your games, you'll find many uses for the primitive objects available in the Unity game engine.

1. From the Create Other option in the GameObject menu, select Cube, as in Figure 2-22.

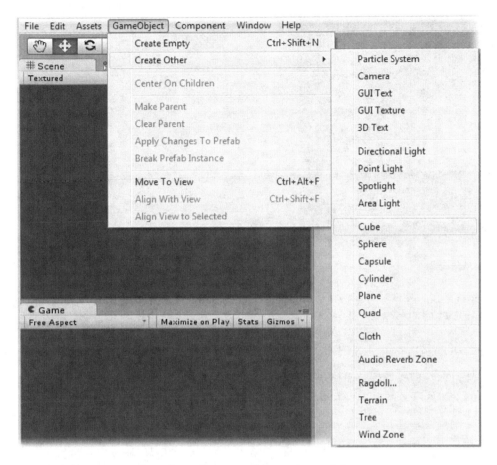

Figure 2-22. *Choosing the Cube in the GameObject ➤ Create Other menu*

A cube is created in the center of the Scene viewport. It may be little more than a speck at this point, if you've played with the viewport navigation tools. You may also see it as a small dark square in the Game window.

■ **Tip** If you have not navigated the viewport yet, the Move button will be active in the Navigation toolbar, and you will see the cube's transform gizmo.

---

2. To zoom, use the middle mouse roller or the Cmd button on the Mac. Zoom in and out on the new cube in the Scene view, as shown in Figure 2-23.

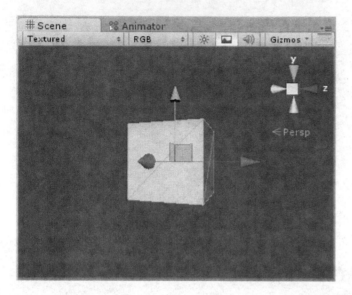

Figure 2-23. *The newly created cube*

To see the cube properly in the Game view, you have to move the camera. Rather than fussing with moving and rotating the camera, you can set the camera to match the Scene view, where you've already adjusted the preferred view of the cube.

3. Select the Main Camera in the Hierarchy view.

4. From the GameObject menu, choose Align with View.

The cube is now visible in the Game view and the camera Preview inset in the Scene view (see Figure 2-24).

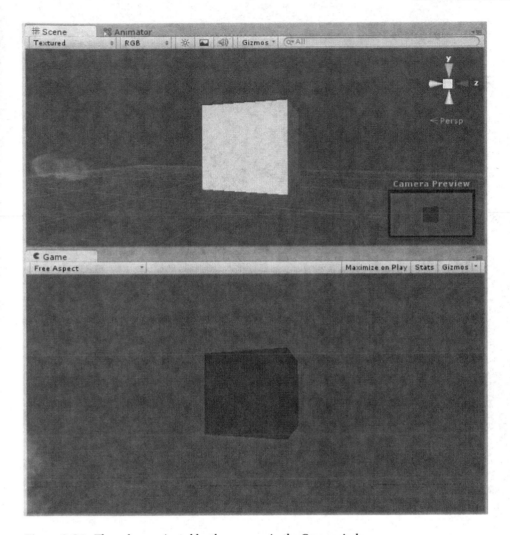

Figure 2-24. *The cube, as viewed by the camera in the Game window*

When the Light button is off, the Scene window is lit with default lighting, a single light pointing straight into the viewport. This assures that the object in focus is always well lit.

5.   Toggle the built-in lighting off and the scene lighting on, by clicking the light button.

The cube is now lit only with the scene ambient light, as in the Game window (Figure 2-25).

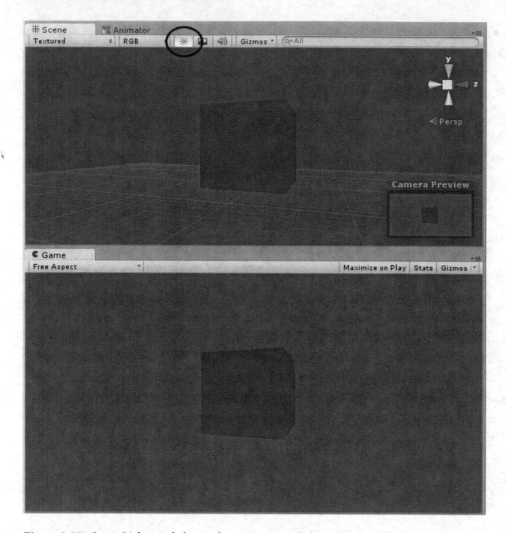

Figure 2-25. *Scene Light toggled on—there is no scene light yet*

Navigating the Scene viewport does not affect the camera. You can also zoom in and out by positioning the cursor in the viewport, holding the Alt key down, and holding the right mouse button down and moving the mouse back and forth. On a Mac, hold down the Cmd key while clicking and dragging to zoom.

Don't pan the viewport yet.

6. Toggle the scene lighting back off in the Scene view.

7. Slowly zoom out from the cube in the Scene view until a large camera icon blocks the cube.

8. Continue to zoom out, then zoom back in.

The icon changes size as you zoom in and out.

9. Click Gizmos above the Scene view and uncheck 3D to supress icon scaling (Figure 2-26).

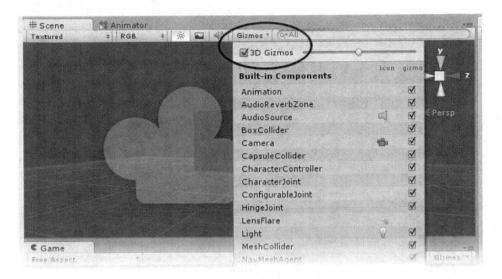

Figure 2-26. *Gizmo options for the Scene view*

10. Deselect the camera by clicking in a blank area of the Hierarchy view.

11. Toggle off the scene Light button.

12. To orbit the viewport around the cube, position the cursor in the viewport, hold down the Alt key and the left mouse button, and move the mouse around.

The view pivots around the center of the viewport's focal point. The cube itself is not rotated, as you can see by watching the cube in the Game view.

You can pan the viewport by clicking the Pan button and then holding the left mouse button down and dragging in the viewport. You can also position the cursor in the Scene window, hold the middle mouse roller down, and move the mouse.

13. Pan the viewport so the cube is no longer centered.

14. Use the Alt key again and orbit, to see how the view still orbits its current center point, *not the cube* (Figure 2-27).

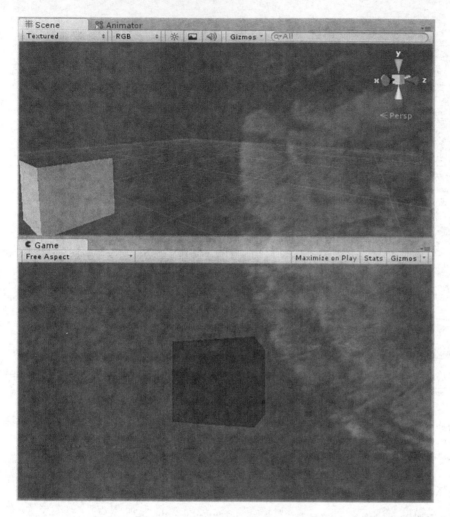

Figure 2-27. *The cube is no longer focused in the Scene view. Note that adjusting the view in the Scene view does not affect the camera's view, as seen in the Game window*

Selecting and Focusing

One of the most important navigation concepts in Unity is that of quickly zooming in to specific objects or areas. To focus the viewport back to the cube, or to "find" the cube, do the following:

1. Make sure the cube is selected in the Hierarchy view.

2. Put the cursor *over the Scene window.*

3. Press the F key on your keyboard.

The view shifts to the center of the cube.

Also note that the edges of the selected object show in pale green. Using the View mode drop-down, shown in Figure 2-28, you can view scene objects in several other modes.

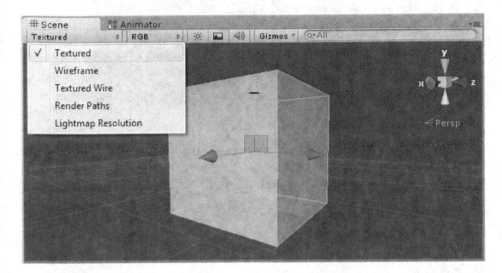

Figure 2-28. *The View mode drop-down*

4. Try the Wireframe mode.

The object shows only the object edges.

5. Try the Texured Wire.

The Textured Wire mode shows the solid object with the edges, but unlike the selected object in Texture mode, all of the scene objects will also be shown textured and edged.

6. Return the view mode to Textured.

Transforming Objects

In 3D space, you use what is called the Cartesian coordinate system. If you come from Autodesk products, you will be used to Z representing "up" in the world. This derived from traditional drafting, where the paper coordinates on the drafting table were X and Y, so Z became up. In Unity, Y is up, harking back to the early days of 2D monitor space, where X is horizontal and Y is vertical. With the advent of 3D space on computers, Z was assigned as back or forward from the monitor. Z depth is an important concept in real-time applications, as it is used to determine the order objects are drawn into the scene.

No matter which way is up, the directions are color-coded, with red, green, blue (RGB) corresponding to X, Y, Z. Objects imported from applications using Z up will retain their original orientation, regardless of coordinate system.

Objects can be transformed (moved, rotated, scaled) around the scene with the rest of the tools on the upper left toolbar (Figure 2-29).

Figure 2-29. *Translate(Move), Rotate, and Scale Tool gizmos*

1. Select the cube from the Hierarchy view or by picking it in the Scene view.

2. Select the Move button.

A Transform axis appears for the cube.

3. Click and drag on any of the three axes.

The active direction turns yellow, and the movement is confined to that arrow's direction. The object also moves in the Game window, as Figure 2-30 shows.

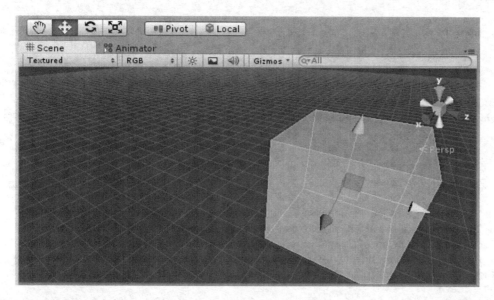

Figure 2-30. *The translated (moved) cube. Note that the camera has not moved, but the cube has, as is reflected in the Game window*

4. Next choose the Rotate icon.

The gizmo consists of circles, once again color-coded.

5. Click and drag the red, green, and blue circles to see what happens.

The gray outer circle will rotate the object to the current 2D screen coordinates, no matter which way you orbit the view.

In the Inspector, you can set the object's transforms manually (see Figure 2-31).

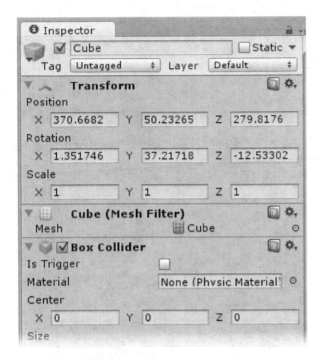

Figure 2-31. Performing transforms on the cube, as shown in the Inspector

6. In the Transform section for the cube, set the Y Position to **0**, the X Position to **20**, and the Z Position to **10**.

7. Use the F key to focus the viewport to the cube's new position, but remember to position the cursor in the Scene window first.

■ **Tip**   In Unity, a single unit is generally considered to be 1 meter. As with most 3D apps, though, scale is really quite arbitrary. You will, however, find that elements such as lights and physics typically have default settings that will require quite a bit of tweaking if you stray too far from the norm.

The transforms are all floating point numbers; that is, they can have fractions, as indicated by the decimal points.

You can also adjust the values by positioning the cursor over the axis label, pressing the left mouse button, and dragging.

8. Position the mouse over the Y Scale label and drag.

The cube is scaled on its Local axis, and the values change accordingly in the Inspector.

The small center gray rectangle allows you to adjust more than one axis at the same time. With the Scale gizmo, it will cause the object to be uniformly scaled on all three axes.

9. Select the Scale tool.

10. Test the uniform scale by clicking and dragging within the small gray cube at the center of the Scale gizmo.

11. Set the X, Y, and Z Rotations and Positions to **0**.

12. Set the Scale X, Y, and Z to **1**.

13. Use the F key to focus the viewport again.

Snaps

Besides manually moving objects in the Scene view or adjusting their transforms in the Inspector, you can snap objects by incremental amounts, or to each other, by vertex.

1. From the bottom of the Edit menu, open the Snap settings dialog, shown in Figure 2-32.

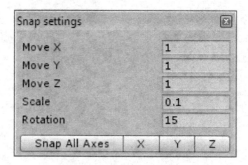

Figure 2-32. *The Snap settings dialog*

Note that Move X, Move Y, and Move Z are all set to 1, and the Rotation snap is set to 15 degrees. To use the increment snap, hold down the Ctrl (Windows) or Cmd (Mac) key while transforming the object.

2. Select the cube.

3. Make sure the Transform tool is active.

4. Hold down the Ctrl or Cmd key and move the cube slowly in the Scene window.

Ever so subtly, the cube moves in one-unit increments, as you can see by watching the Inspector.

5. Zoom out a bit, using either Alt + the right mouse button or the mouse roller, if you have one.

6. In the Snap settings dialog, change the Move amounts from 1 to 5.

7. With the Ctrl or Cmd key still down, move the cube again.

8. Set the Move amounts back to **1**.

This time, the snap is more noticeable.

Rotation snaps can be very useful when changing an object's orientation. Rotation snaps work the same way as the position snaps.

1. Select the cube.

2. Make sure the Rotation tool is active.

3. Hold down the Ctrl or Cmd key and rotate the cube slowly in the Scene window.

The cube snaps in 15-degree increments.

4. Close the Snap settings dialog.

Vertex Snaps

As well as the increment snaps, you can also snap objects using their vertices as registration points. While this may not be terribly useful in an organic environment, it can be invaluable for snapping objects such as platforms, walls, roads, and tracks together.

1. Activate the Move tool.

2. Select the cube.

3. Use Ctrl+D to duplicate the cube.

4. Select one of the cubes and move it away from the other.

5. Hold down the V key (for Vertex) and slowly move the cursor over the repositioned cube.

The transform gizmo snaps to the cube's vertices as you move the cursor, as shown in Figure 2-33.

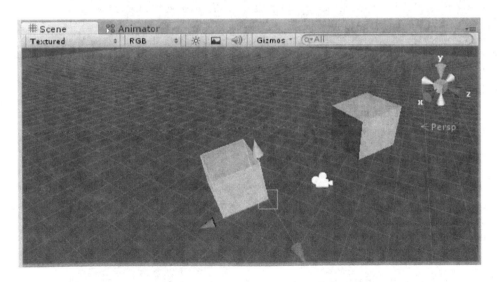

Figure 2-33. *The transform gizmo, snapped to one of the cube's vertices*

6. Continuing to hold the V key down, press and hold the left mouse button and move the cube toward the other cube, until it snaps to the desired vertex on the other cube.

7. Delete the extra cube by using the Delete key on the keyboard or right-clicking the cube in the Hierarchy view and selecting Delete from the menu.

For more information on positioning objects with the snaps, see "Positioning GameObjects" in the manual.

Scene Gizmo

So far, you have adjusted the viewport and transformed the object in a Perspective viewport. While this is useful when you know the exact location, or don't need to be exact at all, it can be challenging and slow to continually rotate the view and adjust the object with more accuracy. The Scene Gizmo icon, shown in Figure 2-34, lets you switch between Perspective and Iso views by clicking on the view label. You can also quickly change the viewing direction by clicking on the gizmo's cones. The cones point in the viewing direction. Orthographic views, Front, Back, Top, Bottom, when using Iso projection, allow you to judge position and scalar relationships without the distortion of perspective.

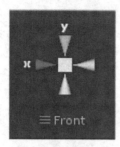

Figure 2-34. *Scene Gizmo, showing a perspective view (left) and an iso Front view (right)*

1. Click the Y cone on the Scene Gizmo icon.

You are now in a Top viewport. At this point, the screen-space transform gizmo makes more sense.

2. Select the cube and activate the Rotate tool.

3. Rotate the cube about 20 or 30 degrees with the outer circle, until it is no longer in an orthographic orientation.

4. Activate the Move tool.

5. Toggle the coordinate system from Global to Local (see Figure 2-35).

Figure 2-35. *Global to Local Coordinate system and object pivot to object center toggles*

The local coordinate system allows you to transform the object relative to its own local coordinates, as opposed to the fixed scene or World coordinates. You may also wish to use the object Center instead of the object's creation Pivot.

6. Now, move the box in its local X direction.

7. Set the cube's rotations back to **0** in the Inspector.

You may have noticed a small gray square in the middle of the Move gizmo. It allows two-axis movement and is very useful in orthographic-iso views.

Non-Snap Alignment

To align an object with another, you can once again use the options in the GameObject menu.

1. Click the gray center box of the Scene Gizmo to get back to a Perspective viewport.

2. Select the cube and use the F key to focus or find it.

3. From the GameObject menu, choose Create Other ➤ Create a Sphere.

4. Activate the Scale tool.

5. Scale the sphere using the center yellow cube on the gizmo to uniformly scale it, so it shows through the cube (see Figure 2-36).

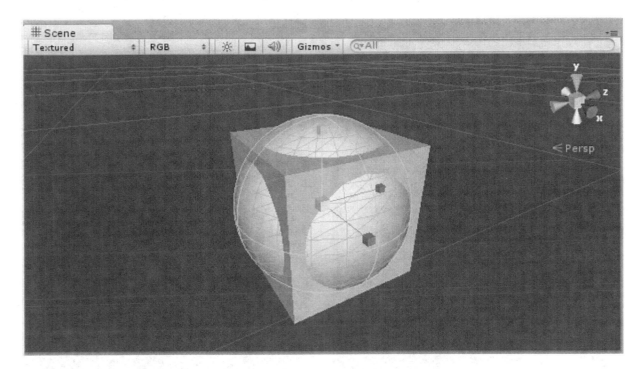

Figure 2-36. *The sphere is created in the same position as the cube*

The sphere is created in the same spot as the cube.
To align existing objects, you can use the third alignment option from the GameObject menu.

1. Select the Move tool.

2. Move the sphere away from the cube.

3. Select the cube and focus the view to it.

4. Select the sphere.

5. From the GameObjects menu, select Move to View.

The sphere is positioned at the cube once again, because the cube was focused to the center of the view.

6. Delete the sphere by selecting it in the Hierarchy view, then pressing the Delete key, or by selecting Delete from the Edit menu, or by pressing Shift+Delete.

Lights

In the Game window, the cube is dark, illumined only by ambient scene lighting, but in the Scene window, it is lit. When you pressed the Lighting button at the top of the window, it toggled the built-in lighting off, so you could see the scene lighting. Because there are no lights in the viewport yet, it went dark, just as in the Game window.

1. Focus the Scene view on the cube again and zoom out a bit.

2. From the GameObject menu, choose Create Other ➤ Create a Directional Light.

Directional lights emit parallel rays, no matter where they are in the scene.

3. Move the light up and out of the way of the cube.

4. Rotate it in the Scene window until the cube is lit nicely in the Game window, as shown in Figure 2-37.

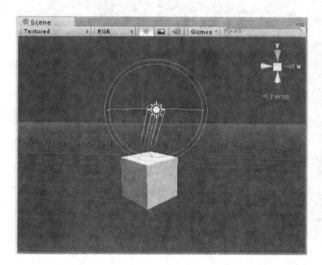 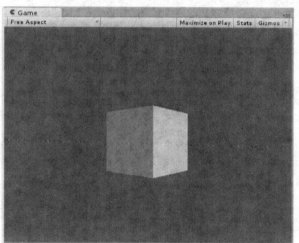

Figure 2-37. *The Directional light oriented to light the cube*

5. Using Alt + the left mouse button, drag/orbit the viewport so that you are facing the unlit side of the cube, as shown in Figure 2-38, left.

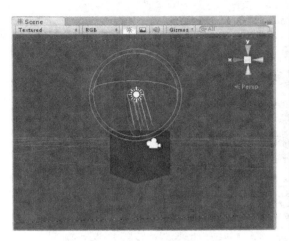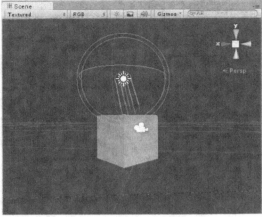

Figure 2-38. *The unlit side of the cube (left) and the Light button toggled off (right)*

The details disappear.

6.   Toggle the scene lighting back off with the light icon (Figure 2-38, right).

The default lighting shines directly into the viewport, ensuring objects are easy to see, regardless of viewpoint in the Scene window.

As you create your scene, you will probably toggle the Scene lighting off and on regularly.

Now is a good time to take a peek at the light in the Inspector (see Figure 2-39). The light object is simply a gameObject with a Light component.

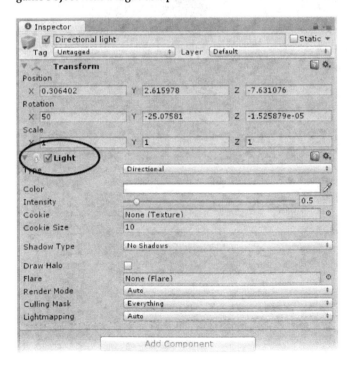

Figure 2-39. *Light component selected in the Inspector*

7. With the light selected, uncheck then check the box next to the Light component's label (Figure 2-39).

The light turns off then on.

8. Click on the color swatch next to the Color label.

The floating Color dialog opens, as shown in Figure 2-40.

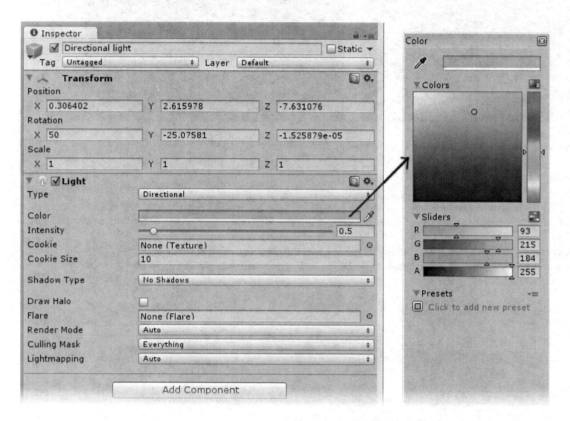

Figure 2-40. *The Color dialog, accesed through the Light's Color parameter*

9. Click and drag in the Color's image/color swatch and watch the light's color on the cube change.

10. Choose something subtle.

11. Close the dialog.

Next, you will add a new material to the cube to replace the default.

1. In the Inspector, select the Cube.

2. In the Mesh Renderer section, click to open the Materials array list (see Figure 2-41).

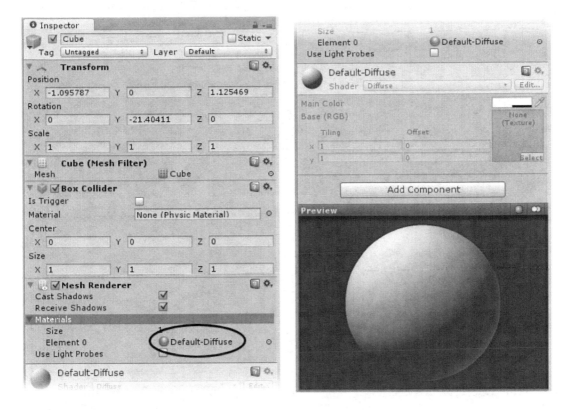

Figure 2-41. The cube's default material

It has a single material, Element 0, named Default-Diffuse. The material is shown at the bottom of the Inspector.

Most of the ready-made materials from the standard assets package are specialty materials, so you will be creating your own. You will begin by creating a new folder to keep them organized.

3.   From the Assets menu, choose Create ➤ Folder (Figure 2-42).

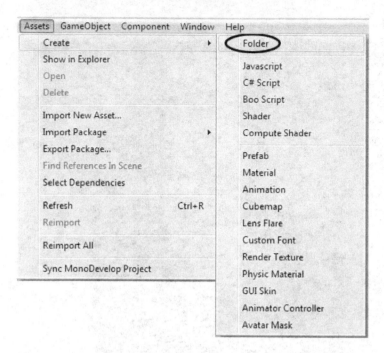

Figure 2-42. Creating a new folder

4.   Rename the folder **My Materials**.

■ **Tip**   As you create new assets for a game, it becomes important to stay organized and keep the Project view uncluttered. You will be creating several folders for that purpose throughout the book.

You can access the same menu directly in the Projects view.

5.   Right-click the new My Materials folder and, from the same Create submenu, choose Material (Figure 2-43).

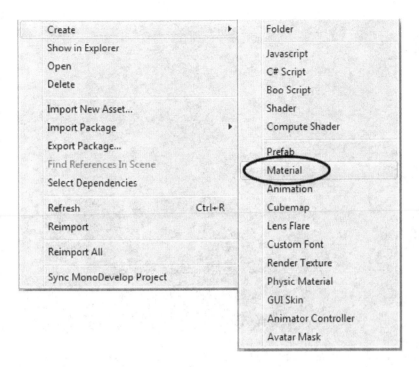

Figure 2-43. *Creating a new material*

A New Material entry appears in the Inspector.

6. Name the new material **TestBark**.

7. Drag and drop the material from the folder onto the cube in the Scene window.

8. In the Texture thumbnail window (not the Preview window), pick the Select button (Figure 2-44) and, with the preview slider all the way to the left in the Asset Selector (Figure 2-45), choose Palm Bark Diffuse.

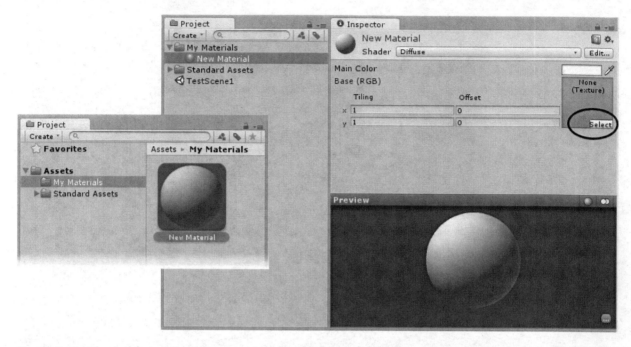

Figure 2-44. *The new material in the Project view and in the Inspector. The inset shows what the Project view looks like when using the the two-column layout*

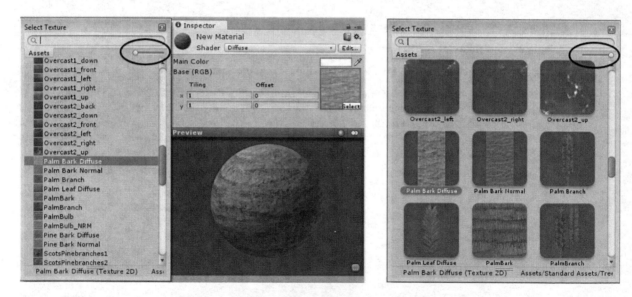

Figure 2-45. *Selecting Palm Bark Diffuse texture in the Select Texture dialog(left). The browser with small icons (left) and with large icons (right)*

▮ **Tip** The Asset Selector is one way to load images, animation clips, and sound clips into components, shaders, or other parameters in your scene. It has the advantage of filtering for only the correct asset type, but the disadvantage is that it shows *all* available assets of that type. Later in the project, you will also drag assets directly from the Project view into the target parameters.

The cube now has a more interesting texture.
The default shader is a simple Diffuse shader.

9. Click the down arrow and select the Specular shader.

10. Try adjusting the Shininess slider.

Note the texture is retained as you experiment with different shaders.
Now that your simple test scene has a few objects in it, you should save it.

11. From the File menu, select Save Scene, then repeat to Save Project.

▮ **Tip** While it is not always necessary to save the project as well as the scene, it is a safe habit to get into. You won't be reminded to save often, but you should do so regularly to prevent data loss in case of mishaps. Changes in the Hierarchy, whether directly or in scene object parameters, require a scene save. Changes in project settings or asset parameters in the Inspector generally require a project save.

3D Objects

This book is generally aimed toward artists and designers looking to become familiar with the Unity engine and game-engine concepts in general. However, as a review for those already familiar with 3D, as well as a short primer for those with a 2D art background, you will look at 3D from a slightly different viewpoint, to see how several concepts relate to real-time and game-associated issues.

Most people these days are quite familiar with the end-product of 3D, through film or games. Many have watched several "Making of" documentaries and already possess a basic knowledge of many of the concepts. As you have already experimented with transforms and viewport navigation in the previous sections, this time, you will look at the objects themselves.

Meshes

While outwardly they appear no different from the primitive objects you've been using as test subjects so far, meshes are stored quite differently. Instead of being stored as a list of parameters used to create a 3D object, meshes are stored as a collection of points in space. As such, they can take on an endless variety of shapes but tend to take up a lot of hard drive space. In runtime memory, both types of objects take up the same amount of space, so storage, and download time, become more important issues when deciding if it is easier to create simple meshes in Unity or import them as collapsed meshes.

Sub-Objects of a Mesh

Unity does not provide easy access to the sub-objects of a mesh, but you *can* affect them through scripting, so it is worth looking into what makes a mesh.

- **Vertex:** A vertex is the smallest sub-object, a point in space. Since vertices are little more than locations, they are not drawn. They can, however, contain information about color, opacity, and lighting, for example.

- **Edges:** Edges are the straight lines between vertices. It is worth noting that in most 3D applications, the rendered result does not contain true curved lines or surfaces; rather, they are approximations of curves created by a large number of smaller straight lines.

- **Faces:** The face, also referred to as a triangle (see Figure 2-46), is the smallest renderable part of a mesh. It is defined by three vertices, the edges that connect them, and the surface between them. A face also has what is called a normal, to tell the engine on which side to render the face. Unless you're using a shader that specifically indicates that a face should be rendered on both sides, a face is drawn only on one side.

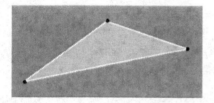

Figure 2-46. *Anatomy of a face*

Faces are often treated differently in DCC applications. In 3ds Max, for example, you can work with backfaces "turned on," but at render time and export time, they are not calculated. In Maya, the default actually creates backfaces that render and export. This increases the amount of information contained in a mesh, as well as taking extra time to cull the hidden faces at render time—a step to be avoided in real-time engines. A good practice is to get in the habit of turning off backfaces when you are modeling assets for your game.

The face normal is not to be confused with the vertex normal. Vertex normals are used to calculate the light a face will receive. A vector is traced from the light to the vertex normal, and the angle of incidence, the angle between the two, is used to calculate the amount of light received at that vertex. The smaller the angle of incidence, the higher the percentage of light it receives. A vertex with a light directly over its normal would have an angle of incidence of 0 degrees and receive the full amount of light.

Occasionally, you'll see faces with either the face normal flipped or the vertex normals flipped, giving very odd results, as shown in Figure 2-47. CAD data used for meshes often has no face normal information at all. As it tends always to be drawn double-sided, when normals are created for it, they are often mixed up.

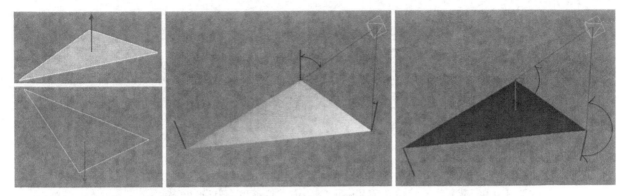

Figure 2-47. *Faces and their face normals and vertex normals. Left: The face normal determines which side the face is drawn on. Think of a perpendicular line that indicates the "up" side (top). The face normal pointing down (the face is not drawn [bottom]). Center and right: The vertex normals and angles of incidence. Note the large angle of incidence on the face, with its vertex normals pointing away from the light. The smaller the angle of incidence, the higher the percentage of light received at that vertex. The amount is blended across the face from vertex to vertex. Face normal and vertex normals pointing up, small angles of incidence (left). Face normal pointing up, but vertex normals pointing down (right)*

Mapping

Whenever an object uses a texture, or image, as part of its material, it needs mapping coordinates, to tell the renderer how to apply the image to the object's faces. Mapping can be as straightforward as a simple planar projection or as complicated as multiple UV unwraps.

Mapping coordinates are referred to as U, V, and W, where U represents one side of the map and V represents the other edge, as in Figure 2-48. W is the axis of a face normal and is of use when rotating the map about that axis.

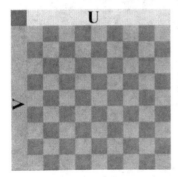

Figure 2-48. *U, V, W coordinates*

The four most common mapping types are planar, box, cylindrical, and spherical, as shown in Figure 2-49.

Figure 2-49. *The four most common mapping types*

- **Planar:** The image is projected from the chosen direction, through the mesh.

- **Box:** Planar projections of the image are put on each side of the object in a cube fashion. Some applications project only three sides, leaving the "back" side inside out.

- **Cylindrical:** The image is wrapped into a cylinder and projected inward and outward onto the mesh. This mapping type requires a map that tiles at the edges, so the seam won't be noticeable, or that the position of the seam is never seen. The caps are often mapped using planar projection.

- **Spherical:** The image is wrapped into a cylinder and then gathered at top and bottom. This also usually requires seamless tiling.

An object can have a combination of mapping types, as with the sign shown in Figure 2-50. The posts are cylindrical; the sign is box-mapped; and the finials are spherical mapping type.

Figure 2-50. *Compound mapping on an object. The sign's geometry (far left); the sign with box, cylindrical, and spherical mapping (center left); the mapped sign with a single texture (center right); the mapped sign with multiple materials (far right)*

When a single texture is painted for an object, as opposed to using separate materials for its sub-objects, it is considered "unwrapped." The mapping is arranged (packed) to fit within a specific aspect ratio, usually 1:1, a square, and the pieces are often hand-painted to achieve a more customized texture. The tricky part about unwrapping is the compromise between less distortion but hard to paint (lots of small pieces) and more distortion but easier to paint (large pieces), as shown in Figure 2-51.

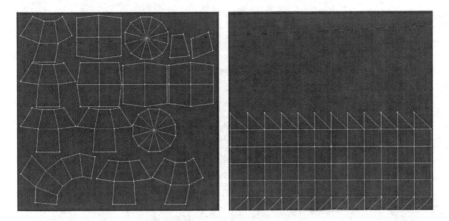

Figure 2-51. *Unwrap compromise with a sphere. Little distortion (left) and ease of painting (right)*

Using a single texture image instead of several is another trade-off. The downside is that you generally forfeit resolution in favor of custom detail. The upside is that for one-off objects, a single material is far easier to manage in the game engine. Additionally, in Unity, separate objects are internally combined, or *batched,* when they use the same material and are below a certain vertex count, for more efficient handling.

When the object is structural rather than organic, you can save the hand-painting step by rendering the conventional mapping and materials into the unwrap map, as shown in Figure 2-52. This can be touched up or altered in your painting program or used as is.

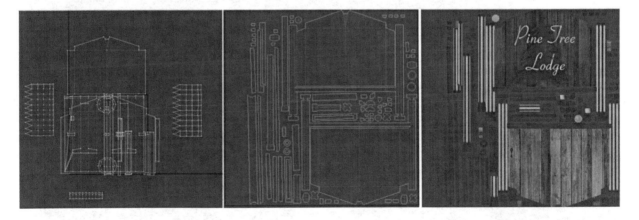

Figure 2-52. *The sign, original mapping, mapping unwrapped, packed and rendered out using the pre-existing materials and original mapping rendered to the new unwrap channel—materials "baked" together*

Typically, you also include lighting information in static objects. This is known as *baked lighting.* It can be actual scene lighting or serve as grunge or *ambient occlusion* (the darkness in nooks and crannies), as shown in Figure 2-53.

Figure 2-53. *The sign with lighting baked in (left) and fully self-illuminated, no lighting (right)*

One problem with lightmaps is that you can't have any pieces overlapping. This means that parts of the mesh that are identical or mirrored now have to be separated. The pieces all must be normalized, or shrunk to fit within the map, causing a loss of resolution.

One solution to this problem is to use two sets of UV maps—one for the diffuse texture and one for the lightmap (see Figure 2-54). Although this does take a bit more time to render, it allows for much higher resolution of the diffuse textures, as they can be tiled and/or overlapped. The lightmap doesn't require the same amount of detail and is added in at render time. The lightmap is "modulated" with the texture map, so that white is ignored and black is blended in. The Photoshop layer-type Multiply is an example of this functionality. Typically, buildings and other structures with large areas of the same physical material are handled this way, where a large lightmap will service an entire structure, and a single detailed texture map is tiled across all. It is also quite useful for terrains, where parts of the baked shadow map are swapped out at runtime for real-time shadows, and also for games and configurators that let the player customize textures in the game or application.

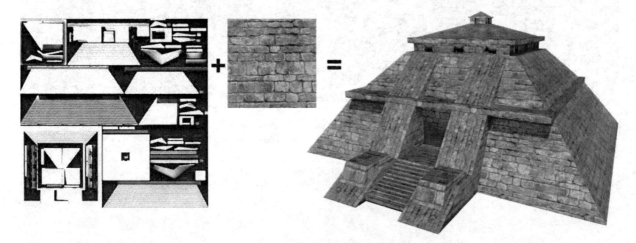

Figure 2-54. *A structure using separate diffuse and lightmaps and the resulting combination of the tiled diffuse modulated with the normalized lightmap*

Materials

Materials are generally different in real-time engines than in their DCC counterparts. At best, simple materials with a diffuse texture will import intact. Plan on spending time rebuilding materials with their shader counterparts, once they're in the engine. Most game engines have a particular process for best practices when dealing with imported textures.

Modern engines have shaders for many uses, so you can use your textures and masks to duplicate the more complex materials from your DCC application.

Summary

In this chapter, you got your first look at using Unity. You started by creating a new project, then took a quick look at each of the five main views: Scene view, where you edit and arrange your assets; Hierarchy view, where the assets in the current scene are listed; Project view, where all of the assets available to the project reside; the Game window, where you can see and interact as the player; and the Inspector, where you can access asset parameters, components, and scene or project settings. The most important takeaway from this section is that you should never rearrange the contents of the project's Assets folder from the operating system's file manager.

Next, you took a brief look at some of the menus, to get an idea of what they contain, noting especially the Help menu, with its link to the Unity Forum and Unity Answers.

You created your first object, a simple cube, in Unity and used it as a test subject to explore viewport navigation, object finding or focusing, and object transforms (move, rotate, and scale). You were able to create a directional light and also match a camera to the Scene view, so you could view your test object in the Game window. You found that selected objects displayed their parameters and other information in the Inspector and that you could modify their transforms more accurately by changing their values in the Inspector. And, finally, you learned how to create a new folder in the Project view and a new material asset to go inside it.

Having gotten a start (or perhaps a review) on exploring the 3D space of viewports, objects, and transforms, you delved a bit deeper into concepts uniquely 3D and looked at the sub-objects that make up a 3D mesh. You saw how light is calculated and why 3D faces have a front and back side. You then looked at the mapping of 3D objects, starting with simple mapping types and working your way up to fully unwrapped and light-mapped treatments, and the logic behind deciding which type to use for various objects. To finish, you found that most materials will probably require a bit of attention to get the best results after importing your meshes.

In the next chapter, you will look at scripting in Unity. You will start by creating very simple scripts to make your objects perform on cue, then deconstruct a couple of Unity's most useful standard asset scripts to start getting a feel for the syntax.

CHAPTER 3

■ ■ ■

Scripting: Getting Your Feet Wet

The heart of interactivity is scripting. In Unity, pretty much everything needs to be scripted. Fortunately, there are ready-made scripts from a multitude of sources. Unity ships with a large collection of useful scripts to get you up and running. The Help section is full of examples and snippets of script; it also includes a full Scripting section. The Unity3D Wiki, Unity Forum, and Unity Answers are other good sources. Another useful place to find what you need is in the tutorials that you can download from the Unity web site. Most of the tutorial resources do a very good job of explaining what the code does. Note that while Unity scripts can be written in JavaScript, C#, and Boo, most official Unity tutorials and help examples are written in JavaScript, so I will follow suit in this book.

While the purpose of this book is not necessarily to *teach* you to script, you will be able to do more with Unity if you can at least learn to read through the scripts and have a basic understanding of what each part does. Many scripts are well-commented, but others are not, so you will examine key parts as you develop the game functionality, adding to your knowledge as painlessly as possible. Keep in mind that scripting is as much about *logic* as it is about *syntax*—and logic is what drives interaction.

What Is a Script?

Think of a script as a set of instructions. Let's say you're going to your great-aunt Mildred's farmhouse for a party this weekend. You might use Google or MapQuest to get the directions and print them out, taking advantage of the easy-to-follow instructions. You volunteered to bring chips and a dip to the gathering, so you might also make a note to yourself at the top of the directions to remember to stop by the supermarket and get the items. Your sister tells you to park your car on the far side of the barn, so there will be room for everyone. Your brother warns that if you drive your motorcycle instead of your car, you should bring a cover to put over it to keep the chickens from trying to roost on it. Realizing that you are likely to forget something, you add the extra instructions to the back of the driving directions, so everything pertaining to the party will be in one place. If you have written your notes on different pieces of paper, you might staple them all together and write "Aunt Mildred's Party" across the top.

Scripts, then, can contain any amount of information and instruction. It will be up to you to keep your scripts organized, so the game engine will know how and when to use the information.

Another scripting challenge is deciding where to put the scripts. With some scripts, such as the instructions to open and close a door, the choice will be easy. In this case, the script can go on any door in the scene that needs to be functional. Likewise, the script that causes an alligator to rush out and snap at the player's character will more than likely belong on the alligator. Other scripts, however, may not be associated with anything in particular, such as a script that changes day into night. It may control the state of several objects in the scene, but it may be dependent on time, rather than player interaction, to know when to execute the instructions. In this case, you would probably make an empty GameObject for the express purpose of holding that particular script and name it accordingly.

In Unity, objects can be manipulated by any number of scripts in the scene. A script can reside on the GameObject it will manipulate, or, as in the case of a light switch, it could trigger an action on a different object, such as a light. Scripts can be simple and very reusable, complex and very specialized, and anywhere partway between.

Before your head starts spinning from too much scripting theory, let's simplify the process and just start building some simple scripts.

Components of a Script

Scripts consist of three main types of components: *variables*, *functions*, and *comments*. Variables hold values that can be anything from numbers to text. Functions do something, generally with variables and mathematical equations. Comments are ignored when the code is executed, allowing you to make notes about what the code is or should be doing or even to temporarily disable the code. Let's start by looking at Unity's default script "template" and investigating the functions.

Functions

Functions in Unity can be roughly grouped in three types: game-related (system, input, network), object-specific, and user-defined.

If you are reopening Unity for this chapter, open the scene you were working on in Chapter 2, TestScene1.

1. Click on TestScene1 in the Project view.

2. Create a New Folder in the Project view using the right-click menu or the Assets menu in the menu bar.

3. Name the new folder **My Scripts**.

4. With the new folder selected, right-click it to bring up the contents of the right-click menu. Select JavaScript from the Create submenu.

■ **Rule** Any time you are asked to create a new script for this book, assume that it will be a JavaScript script.

A new script called NewBehaviourScript is added to your folder. You can see its contents in the Inspector (see Figure 3-1), but you can't edit it from there.

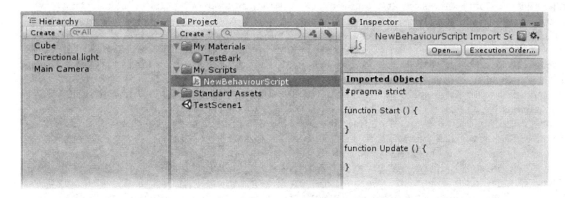

Figure 3-1. *The new script in the [One Column Layout] Project view and the Inspector*

■ **Tip** Always rename the newly created script before editing it.

---

5. Change its name by clicking the name in the Project view and waiting for it to go into rename mode.

6. Name this script **SimpleRotate** and press Enter to finish.

7. To open the MonoDevelop script editor (as shown in Figure 3-2), either double-click the script's name in the Project view or click the Edit button at the top of the Inspector.

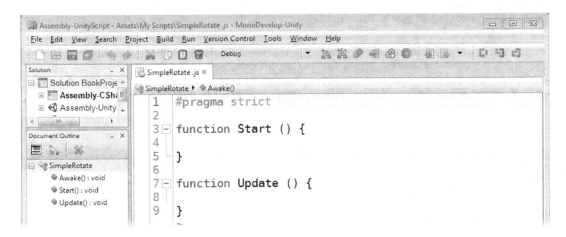

Figure 3-2. *The new script opened in the MonoDevelop script editor*

As you can see in the preceding figure, the new script already has some code in it—something called #pragma strict, an empty Start function, and an empty Update function.

```
#pragma strict

function Start () {

}
function Update () {

}
```

Ignore the for now. You'll revisit it later, when you start adding variables.

Anatomy of a Function

Now that you've got a couple of empty functions to look at, let's investigate their component parts.

What they are: function. It is in lowercase and is blue, because it is a reserved word. A function carries out a set of instructions.

Their names: Start, Update. In JavaScript, function names are *always capitalized*.

Arguments: (). Information that gets passed to the function when it is called. In these two cases, there is nothing being passed, so the parentheses remain empty.

Content: {}. The content, or instructions, goes inside the curly brackets. There are no instructions as of yet in these two functions.

The Update function is one of the most important functions in any game engine. This system function is checked at least *every frame* during runtime to see if anything needs to be executed. It can make a transform such as a rotation continuously loop, check to see if a particular condition is met, and many other things. The Start function is only called once as the scene is started and is a good place to initialize values that don't exist until the game has been loaded. Both of these functions are optional. Throughout the book, as you create new scripts, feel free to delete them when they are not used.

1. Delete the Start function.

2. Position the cursor after the open curly bracket and press Enter a few times to make room for some code.

3. From inside the remaining function, Update (inside the curly brackets), tab over once, and add the following:

```
transform.Rotate(0,5,0);
```

Tip Indenting or tabbing over is not a required part of the syntax, but it will make it easier to read your scripts as you add more functionality.

The parts of this line of code mean the following:

- transform is part of a set of definitions that control how an object can behave.

- Rotate is the Rotate function (note that its first letter is capitalized) for a specific operation from the transform class.

- (0,5,0) refers to the X, Y, and Z rotations parameters that are needed by the Rotate function.

- ; indicates the end of the operation or line.

This line of code also employs *dot notation* (see Figure 3-3), which is the way to access functions and variables (parameters) available to various objects and operations.

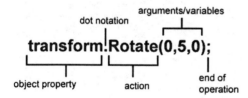

Figure 3-3. *Dot notation*

Because the script will be put on your cube, you can assume that the object that will be rotated is the object that the script resides on, so you don't have to preface the line with the object itself.

your little bit of code is inside the Update function, the object will be rotated 5 degrees each frame, every time the scene is drawn to the Game window.

4. Save the script by clicking the Save icon or through the File menu, Save.

The script is updated in the Inspector as soon as you change focus to the Unity application.

5. Minimize (don't close) the script editor, then drag the script from the Project view onto the Cube, either in the Hierarchy view or in the Scene view.

6. Select the Cube in the Hierarchy view and look for the SimpleRotate script in the Inspector.

It will be directly above the material (which is always listed last), as shown in Figure 3-4.

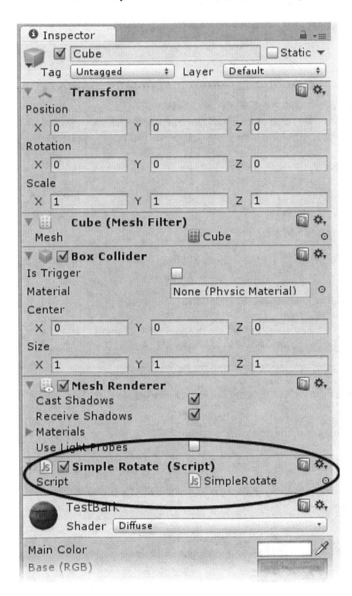

Figure 3-4. *Locating the script*

7. Click the Play button at the top of the editor.

The editor goes slightly darker, and the cube spins in both the Scene and the Game views.

8. Maximize the script editor again and change the **5** to a **1**, like so:

```
transform.Rotate(0,1,0);
```

9. Save the change and click the editor again to resume focus.

10. The cube rotates slower.Click the Play button again to stop Play mode.

Because the rotation is set to occur every frame, everyone will see a different speed, depending on the frame rate on their machine.

Time.deltaTime

The next important concept in Unity scripting is `Time.deltaTime`. `Time.deltaTime` allows you to animate things on a per-second basis rather than per frame, so animations will be consistent across machines and their varying frame rates. `Time.deltaTime` is a variable that returns the amount of time that has passed since the last call to the `Update` function.

1. Change the line to read

```
transform.Rotate(0,5 * Time.deltaTime,0);
```

Now, instead of rotating 5 degrees *per frame*, it will rotate 5 degrees *per second*.

2. Click Play.

The speed is radically different.

3. Change the degrees from **5** to about **50** and save again to see a nice effect.

■ **Tip** Remember to save the script after each change, to see its effects.

Let's add a `Translate` (move) and see what happens if your syntax is not correct. Note the lowercase *t* on `translate`.

1. Add the following inside the `Update` function, just below the `Rotate` line:

```
transform.translate(2 * Time.deltaTime,0,0);
```

As soon as you save your addition, an error immediately pops up in the status line below the Game view (see Figure 3-5). You can click on it to open the console (see Figure 3-6).

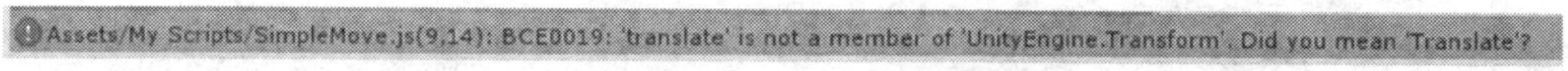

Assets/My Scripts/SimpleMove.js(9,14): BCE0019: 'translate' is not a member of 'UnityEngine.Transform'. Did you mean 'Translate'?

Figure 3-5. *The error reported on the status line*

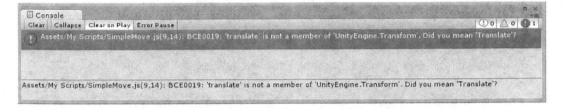

Figure 3-6. *The console and error message*

In this case, the error was easily recognized, and a suggestion was made.

2. Change the lowercase *t* to uppercase *T* and re-save the script.

3. Click on the console to move focus back to Unity.

The error message goes away, and the console is cleared.

4. Close the console.

5. Save the changes and click Play.

The script now tells the cube to move at 2 meters per second, but the cube may or may not behave as you expected. Apparently, the rotate is evaluated first, and the move/translate is evaluated second on the cube's local axis.

If you want the cube to rotate while traveling in a straight line in the X direction, you can enlist the help of a GameObject. In Unity, the GameObject is used to order functionality, organize assets in the scene, hold all sorts of components, and for other useful purposes. You will often see it referred to as the GO.

Before you set up the GameObject, you will be separating your two operations into different scripts.

1. Click the Play button to stop play mode.

2. From the script editor's File menu in the script editor, choose Save As and name the clone **SimpleMove.js**; see Figure 3-7.

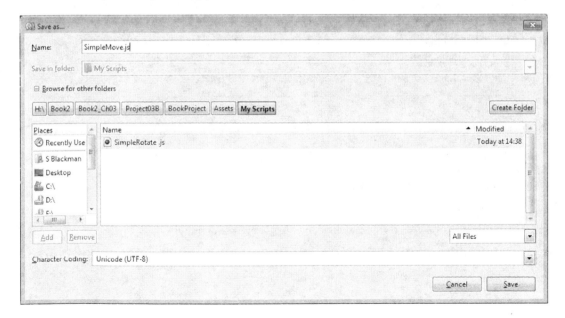

Figure 3-7. *Saving the script from the MonoDevelop script editor*

Because SimpleRotate was renamed, you will need to reopen the original in the script editor. You will now see both scripts in the Project view, so you can open it from there.

    3.   Open the SimpleRotate.js script.

You should now have a tab for each script in the editor, as you can see in Figure 3-8.

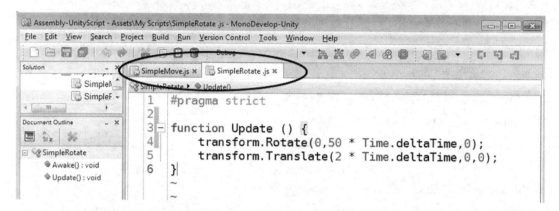

Figure 3-8. *The two scripts in the editor*

    4.   In the SimpleRotate.js script, add two backslashes to the beginning of the line with the translate operation, as follows:

```
//transform.Translate(2 * Time.deltaTime,0,0);
```

The line should turn green and appear in a different font, indicating that it has been *commented out* and should be ignored.

■ **Tip** You just used the comment mechanism to prevent code from being executed while you experiment. You will also be using it to make actual comments about what the code does. This makes it easier for you to remember what the code should do. Comments also make it easier for another user to understand the code.

---

    5.   Repeat the process for the SimpleMove.js script, commenting out the rotate operation like so:

```
//transform.Rotate(0,50 * Time.deltaTime,0);
```

    6.   Be sure to save the changes for both scripts.

    7.   Minimize the script editor.

    8.   Back in the regular editor, from the GameObject menu, select CreateEmpty.

    9.   Name the new GameObject **Cube Parent**, as shown in Figure 3-9, left.

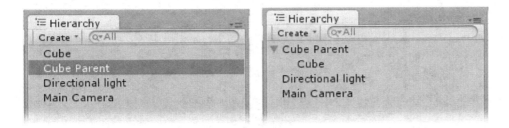

Figure 3-9. The new GameObject, Cube Parent (left), and after the Cube has been dropped on it (right)

10. Drag and drop the Cube onto the Cube Parent in the Hierarchy view, see Figure 3-9, right.

11. Drag and drop the SimpleMove.Js script from the Project view onto the Cube Parent object in the Hierarchy view.

The SimpleMove script appears in the Inspector when you select the Cube Parent (see Figure 3-10).

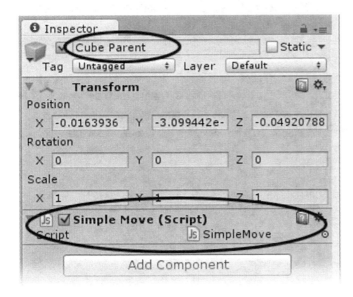

Figure 3-10. The Cube Parent and the Simple Move script in the Inspector

12. Click Play.

The cube rotates slowly as it heads off in its local X direction. You may need to zoom out in the Scene view to see the action more clearly.

Variables

Until now, most of the changes have been made to scripts, which need to be saved before they can be tested. As you have just made several changes to the *scene*, now would be a good time to save it.

1. Use Ctrl+S to save or Save from the File menu.

About now, you may be feeling a bit intimidated about handling animations by *hardcoding* them into the game. Don't worry! You will be using different methods to animate the actual game objects. Scripting the transforms just provides obvious feedback for your first efforts at scripting.

Let's look next at variables. Variables provide a means to keep track of states, values, text, and more. Variables are a mechanism for storing information. In Unity, those variables can be exposed to the Inspector, so you no longer have to open a script to make changes. This also lets you keep the scripts generic, so the same script can be used on several different objects while allowing for custom settings for each individual object.

As it stands right now, when you want to change the speed of the cube's rotation, you need to change the number inside the rotate operation. Let's switch it to a variable.

■ **Tip** Give your variables meaningful names, but keep them short. You can—and should—add comments for a fuller explanation.

■ **Rule** Variable names must not start with a numeric digit or with certain special characters and must not include spaces. Also, there are several reserved words you should not use as names. While not strictly necessary, it is good scripting practice to begin each variable name with a lowercase character. When words in the variable name are capitalized, a space will appear in the Inspector.

---

2. Change the code in the SimpleRotate script to the following (leave #pragma strict as is):

```
var myDegrees = 50;
function Update () {
    transform.Rotate(0,myDegrees * Time.deltaTime,0);
}
```

3. Save the script.

4. Click the Cube Parent to open the group and gain access to its child, Cube.

5. Select the Cube and look in the Inspector to see the new variable exposed (see Figure 3-11).

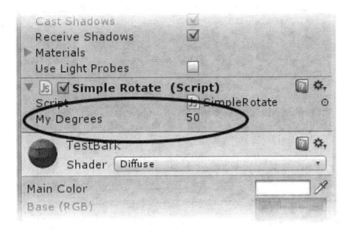

Figure 3-11. *The newly exposed variable, My Degrees, and its value, 50*

Note that where a character in the variable name was capitalized, there is now a space in the name, making it easier to read in the Inspector. The first character has also been capitalized.

6. Click Play and note that nothing looks any different.

7. In the SimpleMove script, change the **2** to **0.5** to slow down the move animation so the cube is visible in the scene window for a longer period of time.

8. Save the script and select the Cube if it is not already selected.

9. Click Play.

10. In the Inspector, not the script editor, change the My Degrees parameter from **50** to **200**.

The cube spins faster.

11. Click Play again to stop the game.

Note that the value has been reset to 50.

■ **Rule**   In Unity, most changes made in the Inspector during runtime **will be lost.** While this allows you to experiment and direct feedback without breaking anything, it also means you must return to Edit mode before you can make permanent changes.

---

12. In the script editor for the SimpleRotate script, change the variable's value to **100** and save the script.

Note that the original value of 50 remains in the Inspector.

13. Click Play.

The rotation uses the slower value from the Inspector. The value in the Inspector *always* overrides the value initialized in the script itself.

■ **Rule**   Once a variable has been exposed to the Inspector, it will always override the original value in the script where the variable was declared and/or initialized.

14. Stop Play mode.

15. Now that you are no longer in Play mode, change the value of your parameter in the Inspector to **200**.

16. Click Play.

The rotation is fast, as expected.

■ **Caution**   If you set the rotation on an object too fast, it may strobe or appear to go slower or even backward on slower machines that can't deliver a fast frame rate.

There are a few other things you ought to know about variables. As mentioned, there are a few different types. In the rotate script, when you declared myDegrees to equal 50, it automatically interpreted the number to be of type int (integer, a whole number). If you had used 50.0, it would have assumed a float (floating point, a fractional number). Many variables are only declared for their type, waiting to have their values assigned or initialized at a later time. Let's add a couple of new variables to the SimpleMove script.

1. Below the #pragma strict at the top of the SimpleMove script, add the following:

```
var mySpeed : float;
var someString : String = "This is a test";
var someSetting : boolean = true;
var someObject : GameObject;
```

2. Save the script and select the Cube Parent to see the new additions in the Inspector (see Figure 3-12).

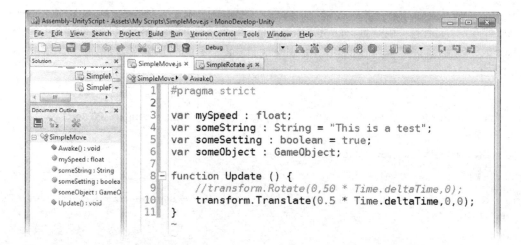

Figure 3-12. *The newly added variables*

Let's get a closer look.

var mySpeed : float; declares a variable of type *float* but doesn't initialize a value.

var someString : String = "This is a test"; declares and initializes a variable of type *String*. Strings are always surrounded by quotation marks and appear magenta in the MonoDevelop script editor. *String* is short for *character string*, a string of characters. Numbers inside quotation marks are also characters and have no value unless converted.

Caution   If you copy and paste the quotation marks from a word processor, the characters may be different than the editor expects. If you get an error, try retyping the quotation marks manually in the editor.

---

var someSetting : boolean = true; declares a variable of type *Boolean* (true or false) and initializes it as true. In the Inspector, a Boolean variable is depicted as a checkbox. In Unity's JavaScript, *boolean* is not capitalized.

Tip   In JavaScript, as long as the value of the variable is an obvious type, declaring the type is optional. If you declare the type, you save the engine from trying to decide automatically what the type should be. For mobile platforms, such as iOS or Android, you *must* declare type. The code at the top of new scripts, #pragma strict, checks to make sure the type can be determined when the code is started. For best practices, you will be declaring the type from now on.

Note that all of the variables start with *var*. In Unity's version of JavaScript, *var* is assumed to be a *public* variable. In other words, it will be exposed to the Inspector and can be accessed by other scripts. Originally, *private* would allow you access to another script's variables without exposing them to the Inspector. Be aware that Unity no longer allows that functionality. Now, if you want to keep a variable from showing in the Inspector, while still allowing other scripts to access it, you will need to use the keyword *internal*.

3.   Try changing someSetting to internal var instead of just var:

internal var someSetting : boolean = true;

4.   Save the script.

5.   Select the Cube Parent.

6.   Pick in the editor to change the focus and update the Inspector.

The someSetting parameter no longer appears in the Inspector.
Let's look at another variable type:

var someObject : GameObject;

In addition to the usual types seen in most programming languages, Unity lets you define a variable type as being something as broad as a top-level GameObject, down to as specific as its transform or other property, or even component type (such as Camera or Light).

For a script even to have access to another object's variables and functions, it must be declared as the value of a variable itself. Here's the tricky part: because an object's name is just one of its properties, the object must be accessed in a more abstract manner.

7. Try dragging the light or the camera in your scene from the Hierarchy view into the Some Object parameter in the Inspector.

Once assigned, your script has access to that object's parameters and those of its children and components.

8. Save your scene and project.

■ **Tip** Changes in the Hierarchy view are saved with Save Scene. Changes in the Project view are changes in the computer's file system and don't have to be saved. Changes made in the Inspector may need Save Project when they are not directly related to the current scene. Changing both scene and project is the safest way to ensure nothing is lost. Be sure to save regularly.

Picking an Object in the Game

While you are digesting your first taste of scripting, let's stop a moment to consider one of the big differences between first-person shooters and classic point-and-click adventure games. In the former, interaction is generally proximity-based: You bump into an elevator button with your weapon, and the doors open. You get within range of an enemy, and it turns and starts firing on you. Or, you shoot a pile of crates with a missile launcher, and the missile, with the help of physics, scatters the unfortunate crates.

In classic point-and-click adventure games, generally, the cursor becomes the means of interaction, rather than collisions, physics, and ray casting.

1. Open the scripting Help (Help ➤ Scripting Reference).

2. Do a search for "On Mouse Down."

You will see about 57 matches. Glancing through them, you can see that the fifth is the most likely candidate.

3. Click on MonoBehavior.OnMouseDown.

Let's create a new JavaScript for it. You could add it to one of the existing scripts, but you may decide to move it around.

4. Select the MyScripts folder, right-click and create a new JavaScript.

5. Name the new script **MousePick** and open it in the script editor.

6. Delete the Start function.

You don't need the Update function for this script, so rename it OnMouseDown, after the function you found in the Scripting Reference.

The sample in the Scripting Reference shows the code loading a new scene, but you only have to see if the pick registers. Unlike the Update function, the OnMouseDown function is only called when that event, a mouse button down, occurs.

Printing to the Console

A typical way to check for the expected functionality is to have the program print a message to the console. In the scripting Help, do a search for "print to console." A quick glance through the offered results suggests that Debug.Log will log a message to the console. Pick it to see what the syntax looks like. It should be fairly straightforward. Also, take note of MonoBehaviour.print for later use, as it produces the same results as Debug.Log and is easier to remember.

1. Add the following line inside the OnMouseDown function:

   Debug.Log("This object was picked");

2. Save the script.

Note that the description says the function "is called when the user has pressed the mouse button while over the GUIElement or Collider." You don't have any GUI (Graphical User Interface) elements in your simple scene, so you need a Collider.

3. Select the Cube.

In the Inspector, you will see that it already has a Box Collider component.

■ **Tip**   Primitive objects created in Unity are assigned a Collider component on creation.

To make the cube easier to pick, you can disable the SimpleMove script on the Cube Parent so it doesn't escape the Game view.

4. Select the Cube Parent.

5. Uncheck the SimpleMove script so it is no longer enabled (see Figure 3-13).

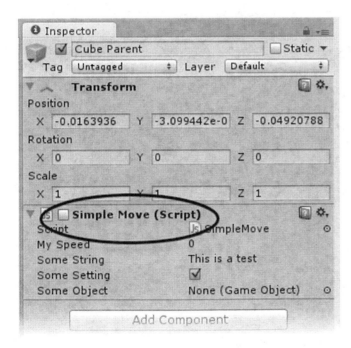

Figure 3-13. *The disabled SimpleMove component*

■ **Tip** GameObjects are *Activated* and *Deactivated* at the top of the Inspector. Components are *Disabled* or *Enabled* at the checkbox next to their names in the Inspector. The terminology will follow through to scripting.

---

6. Now drag and drop the MousePick script onto the Cube in the Hierarchy view.

7. Click Play and pick the Cube.

The message appears on the status line (see Figure 3-14).

This object was picked

Figure 3-14. The Debug.Log message on the status line

■ **Tip** If nothing happens when you pick the Cube, make sure you put the MousePick script on the Cube, not on the Cube Parent. This is because the parent doesn't have a collider.

---

8. Open the console by clicking the status line.

Each time you click the Cube, the message is output to the console (see Figure 3-15).

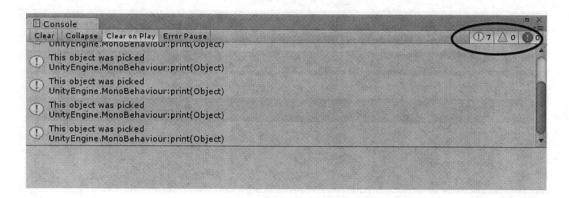

Figure 3-15. The console after picking the object seven times

Objects don't have to be visible or rendered to be pickable. This allows you to get very creative in a game environment.

9. Select the Cube and note where it is in the Game window.

10. In the Inspector, uncheck Mesh Renderer to disable it.

The cube disappears from the Game view. In the Scene view, though, you can still see the green bounding box of the cube (see Figure 3-16).

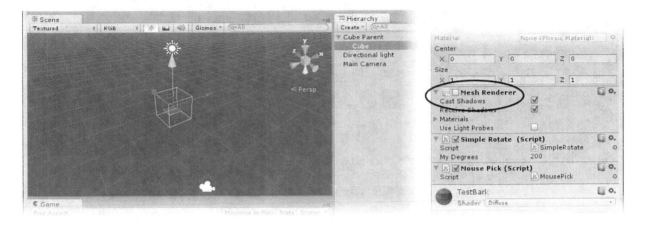

Figure 3-16. The Cube's disabled Mesh Renderer

11. Pick the area in the Game view where the cube used to be.

A pick is still registered in the console.

12. Turn the Mesh Renderer back on.

13. This time, deactivate the entire object by unchecking the checkbox at the top of the
     Inspector (see Figure 3-17).

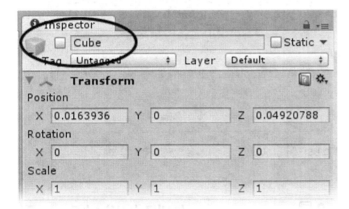

Figure 3-17. The deactivated Cube in the Inspector

Note that the collider no longer shows in the Scene view, and the object is grayed out in the Hierarchy
(see Figure 3-18).

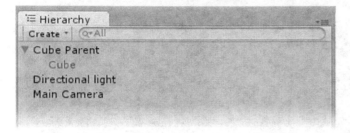

Figure 3-18. *The deactivated Cube grayed out in the Hierarchy*

14. Try to pick where the cube should be in the Game view.

Nothing happens.

15. Reactivate the Cube and, this time, disable its Box Collider.

16. Try to pick the cube again.

Nothing happens because its collider is no longer enabled.

17. Stop playback and close the console.

Counting Mouse Picks

In your point-and-click adventure game, some objects will have to be picked more than once to advance the object to its next state or behavior. This time, you will add a variable of type *integer* (whole number) to keep track of how many times the object has been picked.

1. Open the MousePick script in the script editor.

2. At the top of the MousePick script, below #pragma strict, add the following line:

```
private var pickNum : int = 0;
```

■ **Rule**   When you are instructed to add something "to the top of the script," this means you should add it below the #pragma strict.

Next, you have to add a line inside the OnMouseDown function to increment the pickNum every time the function is called.

3. Add the following line above the Debug.Log line:

```
pickNum = pickNum + 1; // increment the number of times the object was picked
```

Note the use of the comment to remind you what the line does; everything after the // is ignored.

You can also get the Debug.Log to report the number to you. Let's go ahead and start using the print syntax to achieve the same output. Note that *print* is not capitalized, because it is not really a JavaScript function. Also, note that to add a variable to the message, you will have to separate the strings (the text within the quotation marks) with plus signs.

4. Rewrite the Debug.Log line as follows:

```
print("This object was picked " + pickNum + " times.");
```

5. Save the script.

6. Click Play and start picking the cube.

The message updates every time to show the latest number of clicks (see Figure 3-19).

```
This object was picked 17 times.
```

Figure 3-19. *The status line reporting the number of mouse picks*

Sometimes you may see an abbreviated syntax for incrementing a variable. The `pickNum = pickNum + 1;` can be written as `pickNum += 1` and reduced even further to `pickNum++`, if you are only incrementing by 1.

7. Substitute the abbreviated version for the original, as follows:

```
pickNum += 1; // increment the number of times the object was picked
```

8. Save the script.

9. Click Play and test.

10. Try the third option:

```
pickNum++; // increment the number of times the object was picked by 1
```

The results are the same.

Conditionals and State

The key to engaging interaction is being able to specify conditions under which various alternative scenarios play out. Even in a traditional shooter game, an object may need to be hit a certain number of times before it switches to its destroyed state. Each time it is hit, the program must check to see if certain conditions have been met before it knows what to trigger. Each of these conditions can also be thought of as a *state*.

In a classic point-and-click game, state becomes even more important. Typically, almost everything you can interact with needs to be aware of its state. When you click on a door, it has to know if it is locked or unlocked, closed or open, before the correct response can be triggered.

Continuing with your simple cube, let's set up a basic two-state system to turn the rotation off and on. Because you want to control the rotation, you will add an `OnMouseDown` function to the rotation script.

You will use an internal var, so it will not be exposed to the Inspector. Theoretically, because it only has two states (on/off or true/false), you could use a *Boolean* type for your variable, to use less memory. However, because many action objects will have more than two states, it doesn't hurt to start thinking of states in terms of numbers. So, for this variable, you will be using integers.

1. Open the SimpleRotate script.

2. Add the following variable and its comment at the top of the script:

```
internal var rotationState : int = 1; // this variable keeps track of the state of the
rotation- whether it is off or on- 1 is on, 0 is off
```

■ **Tip** The order that variables and functions are listed in the script is not crucial, but one generally organizes public variables at the top (because they will appear in the Inspector), followed by private vars. Because the book is not showing the entire script, each time it gives an instruction, you will generally be told to add new code above or below existing code. The finished scripts for each chapter can be downloaded from the book's page on the Apress web site.

---

3. Add the following function beneath the Update function:

```
function OnMouseDown () {
   if (rotationState == 1) {
      rotationState = 0; // set it to 0
   }
   else if (rotationState == 0) {
      rotationState = 1; // set it to 1
   }
   print("State = " + rotationState);
}
```

4. Save the altered script as SimpleRotateToggle.js.

Rather than removing the existing SimpleRotate script component and adding the new version, you can reassign the script in the Inspector. This method has the advantage of retaining variable values that have been assigned in the Inspector.

1. Open the Cube Parent in the Hierarchy view and select the Cube.

2. Click the Browse icon next to the loaded script in the Inspector (see Figure 3-20).

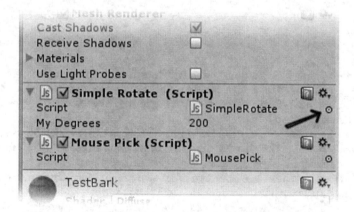

Figure 3-20. *Replacing an existing script component*

The Asset browser lists the scripts available for your project (see Figure 3-21).

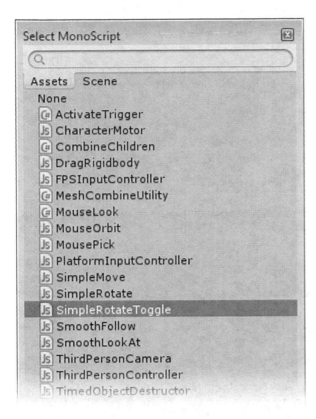

Figure 3-21. *The available scripts*

    3.   Select the SimpleRotateToggle script.

The SimpleRotate script is replaced, and the MyDegrees setting remains intact.

Deconstructing the Conditional

Next, you will be taking a closer look at the conditional, if (rotationState == 1).Within the parenthesis is the expression whose condition must be met in order to do what is inside the curly brackets. Of note is the double equal sign; this is the *equivalency operator,* and it checks to see if the variable rotationState currently holds the value of 1. If so, inside the curly brackets, it updates the value of rotationState to 0, so now rotationState = 0 (the single equal sign being the *assignment operator*). Otherwise, you get else if (rotationState == 0), the rotationState is currently 0, so set it to 1, rotationState = 1. After the state has been identified and updated, you will have it printed out to the console, as in print("State = " + rotationState).

    If you were to click Play and test the functionality right now, you would have to open the console to see the results, because the message output by the MousePick script is being output after your state message. Instead of opening the console, you can disable the print line in the MousePick script instead.

    1.   Open the MousePick script and comment out the print line by prefacing it with two backslashes, like so:

```
// print("State = " + rotationState);
```

2. Save the script.

3. Click Play and test the functionality.

The state toggles between 1 and 0 as you pick the cube. Now that you know that the state tracking mechanism works, you can turn the rotation off and on.

4. Open the SimpleRotateToggle script.

5. In the Update function, change the code to the following:

```
function Update () {
    if (rotationState == 1) { // if the state is 1, rotate
        transform.Rotate(0, myDegrees * Time.deltaTime, 0);
    }
}
```

6. Save the script.

7. Click Play and test the functionality.

The cube starts and stops its rotation nicely, depending on what state it is in.

8. Save the scene and the project.

Order of Evaluation

In scripting, the order of evaluation is generally the same as in mathematical equations. Multiplication and division are evaluated first, then addition and subtraction, and, finally, comparisons (and/or). Contents of parentheses are evaluated from the innermost nested to the outermost.

Summary

In this chapter, you got your first taste of controlling a 3D object with scripting in Unity's implementation of JavaScript. You found out that scripts have *functions* for carrying out instructions, use *variables* to allow for both storing and changing values, and that *comments* can both disable instructions as well as provide a commentary about what the script is doing.

You learned about the Update function, a system function that is called every frame during runtime, and that objects can be transformed (using a move, rotate or scale) on a per-second basis rather than per frame by using Time.deltaTime. You also found that the order of evaluation between moves and rotates can be controlled by parenting objects.

You discovered that case (capitalization) is generally critical in the scripting syntax but that, sometimes, the error message in the console will help by suggesting the correct case for the offending command. You also discovered that you could tell the console to print out information on the state of your variables, whether the code is being read in a particular function or other uses.

To pick an object in the scene, you found that it needed to have a Collider to be able to register the pick, but that the object did not actually have to be drawn by the Mesh Renderer. If you deactivated an object in the Inspector, it was no longer available for use in the scene.

Variables, you found, can be of different *types:* integers, character strings, Booleans, and floats, to name a few. By using an addition operation to increment the value of an integer type variable, you could count how many times an object had been picked. This led to the introduction of two of the most important concepts in game development: *state* and the *conditional.* You learned that different sets of instructions could be carried out, depending on the results of the expression being evaluated or the state it represented.

CHAPTER 4

■ ■ ■

Terrain Generation: Creating a Test Environment

One feature common to many game engines is a terrain editor. It allows you not only to sculpt your idea into being but to populate it with foliage, from grass to bushes to trees, via paint textures.

In Unity's Terrain Engine many things are handled for you, such as LOD (level of detail), distance culling, and animations. While this makes it extremely easy to get up and running around a terrain, as with anything that does a lot of the work for you, it also comes with limitations. For more in-depth information on the terrain editor, go to the Reference Manual ➤ Terrain Engine Guide.

In this chapter, you will create a basic terrain to test more functionality than is strictly necessary for a classic point-and-click adventure game. During the process of developing the functionality and logic sequences for your game, you will quickly discover the need to keep everything in a fairly small area. Having to travel halfway across the terrain to find an object will get old fast. For that reason, you only need a smallish area to work in, until everything not related directly to the topography is up and running.

Creating Environments

As long as you are still in test mode, go ahead and create a new scene from the Files menu.

1. Open Unity if you have not already done so.

It should open the BookProject project by default, unless you have opened other projects since the last time you saved it. If it does not open the BookProject from the File menu, choose Open Project and select it from the Open Project tab. You may also use the version available in the Chapter 4 folder from the book's downloadable package.

■ **Note**   You may import terrains created in DCC programs(digital content creation applications such as 3ds Max, Maya, Blender, etc.) to use as the ground, but you will not be able to paint trees, grasses, and other detail meshes that respond to wind and scene lighting. A compromise would be to create a height map from your external terrain and then load it into a Unity terrain, instead of painting the topography.

---

2. If the project opened with TestScene1 loaded, go to File ➤ New Scene.

3. From File ➤ Save Scene, save it as ➤**TerrainTest**.

4. In the Project view, create a new folder and name it **Scenes**.

■ **Tip** During the project, you will be creating and importing many assets. You will soon be buried under folder upon folder, so it is good practice to stay organized. Even those of us who are inclined to be organizationally impaired will soon be forced to admit that organization is an important requirement of making even smaller games. As Unity's file system is based on dependencies, you must always remember to implement your housekeeping chores inside the Project view and never out in the OS's Finder or Explorer.

5.   Drag both the TestScene1 and TerrainTest scenes into the new folder.

Creating a Terrain Object

With your folders tidied up, it's time to create your first terrain.

1.   From the GameObject menu, CreateOther, near the bottom of the list, select Terrain, as shown in Figure 4-1.

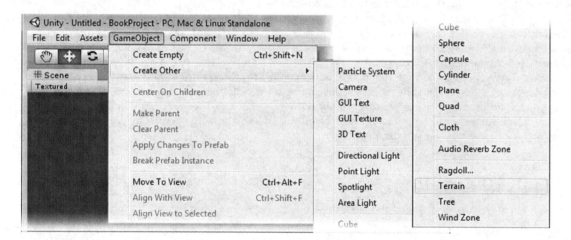

Figure 4-1. *Create Terrain in the Terrain menu*

You will see that a Terrain object has been added to both the Scene and the Hierarchy views, with one of its corners at 0,0,0, as shown in Figure 4-2.

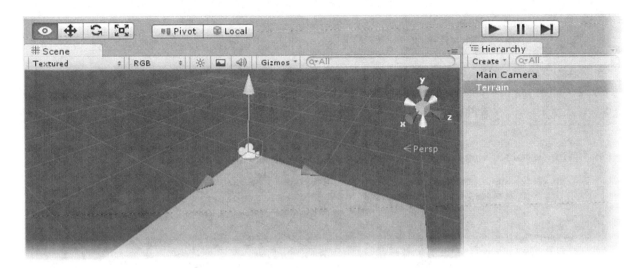

Figure 4-2. The new terrain object, with its corner at 0,0,0

In the Inspector, with the Terrain object selected, you will see its properties and the tools available for refining it, as shown in Figure 4-3.

Figure 4-3. The Terrain tools in the Inspector

2. Make sure you are using default, rather than Scene, lighting in the Scene view.

▀ **Tip** Scene lighting can be toggled off and on using the Scene Lighting button, ⬚☼⬚, at the top of the Scene view. It's a sure bet that you will often find yourself toggling this critter off and on throughout the project, depending on the objects with which you are working.

Before experimenting with the tools, you need to set the other parameters of the terrain.

1. In the Inspector, select the Terrain Settings tool to access the Resolution parameters near the bottom of the panel as shown in Figure 4-4.

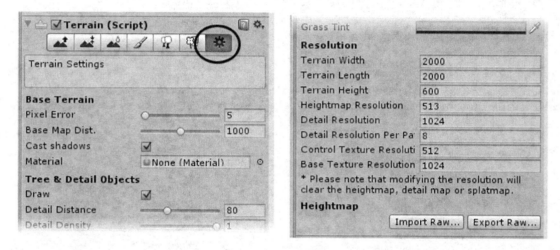

Figure 4-4. *The Resolution section of the Terrain Settings tool*

2. Take note of the "modifying the resolution will clear the heightmap, detail map or splatmap" warning.

This means that if you change the resolution of your terrain after creating it, you will lose many of your modifications.

▀ **Tip** A *splatmap* is another name for the Terrain texture map/mask. Once you have begun painting your terrain, you will be able to see that it is basically a grayscale mask on steroids; it uses RGBA, and each color channel is used to mask a different texture.

---

3. Set the Terrain Width and Length to 500 meters and the Height to 200 meters.

This size is still overkill for what you will need during the development process, but it will allow for lots of practice with the terrain tools. Don't stress over making it perfect.

Because you can sculpt the terrain up or down, you will have to set the base height to allow for maximum depth where you may want to paint the terrain lower (see Figure 4-5).

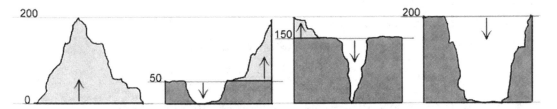

Figure 4-5. *Terrain base height shifted to allow painting of depressions for lakes, crevasses, etc.*

4. In the Inspector, select Paint Height as shown in Figure 4-6.

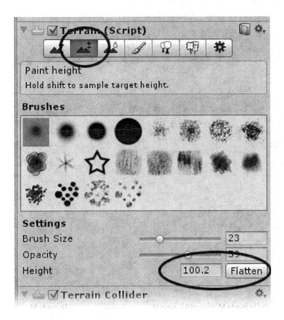

Figure 4-6. *The Flatten button for the Height section in the Inspector*

5. Set the Height to **50** to give you 25% of your terrain's total height below sea level.

6. Click Flatten.

The terrain may drop out of sight in the Scene view.

Before you sculpt, take a few minutes to experiment with the navigation tools; there are subtle differences in how they work with terrains because of the scale involved.

1. Select the Terrain in the Hierarchy view.

2. Double-click the Terrain in the Hierarchy view.

The viewport is zoomed all the way out, so you can see the extents of the terrain object, as shown in Figure 4-7.

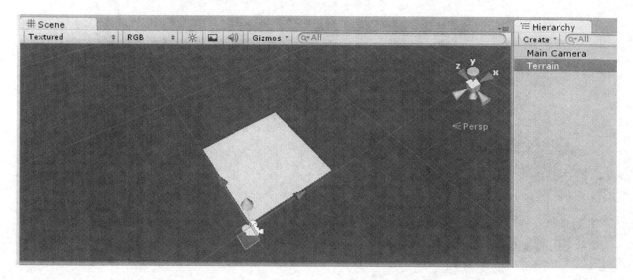

Figure 4-7. The full terrain found or focused in the Scene view

Using the F key to focus or find the terrain has different functionality, depending on how much terrain is showing in the viewport. If you are already zoomed in, the F key will attempt to zoom closer to where your cursor is. If not, it will perform the usual zoom extents.

Flythrough Scene Navigation

You can also use flythrough type navigation in your scene. This becomes useful when creating terrains because it allows you to travel through the scene in the direction you are looking, as if you were a bird or even a caped superhero.

1. Zoom in close to an edge of the terrain.

2. Click and hold the right mouse button.

3. Use the WASD keys to move left/right, forward/backward.

4. Use the Q and E keys to move up and down.

5. Hold the Shift key down to move faster.

The Terrain Engine

A flat terrain is pretty boring. So, next, you will get some hands-on experience with Unity's terrain editing tools, which will enable you to add various kinds of features to your new terrain.

Topology

It's time to do some damage to your terrain, so let's start with some mountains.

1. Zoom out, so more of the terrain is visible.

2. In the Inspector, choose the first tool: Raise/Lower Terrain.

Note the user instructions immediately beneath the Terrain tools toolbar when you select a tool; they may seem cryptic at first, but once you get under way, they will start making sense.

3. Select a Brush.

4. Click and drag or use your favorite pressure pen to create mountains around the terrain, as shown in Figure 4-8.

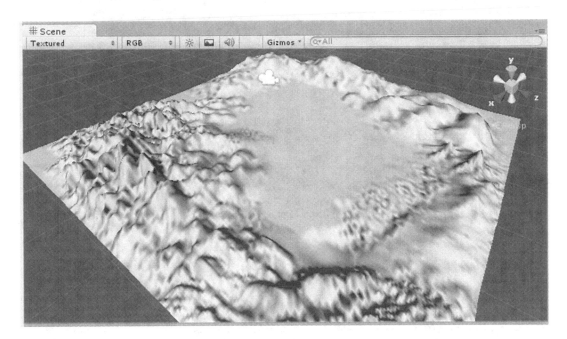

Figure 4-8. *Mountains created on the terrain*

■ **Tip** You can undo the last action with Ctrl+Z. Unity allows a large number of undos, but as with any program, you should not count on going back too far. Inevitably, an action you want to get rid of will be one more than the limit.

Note that as you paint, if you have zoomed out to view the entire terrain, you will see it at its highest resolution in an area around the cursor. One of the great benefits of using Unity's terrain engine is that it has a built-in LOD (level of detail) mechanism. As soon as you let go, the terrain reverts to its LOD resolution for the far distance (see Figure 4-9). While this can be frustrating, remember that it is just terrain, and the scale is such that once in play, it is likely not going to be crucial. You will be able to adjust the LOD distance later, should you wish, in the Terrain Settings' Detail Distance parameter.

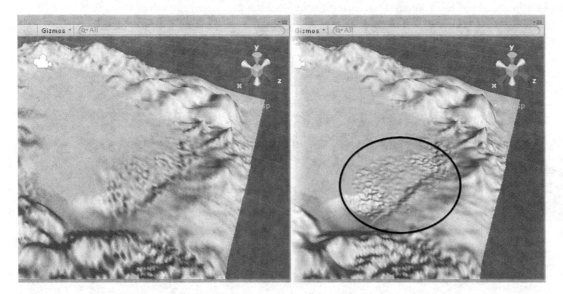

Figure 4-9. *True LOD resolution, on the left, and the temporary higher resolution, or detail where you are painting, on the right*

For now, just experiment with the Brush type, Brush Size, and Opacity (strength). The brush size will be depicted in blue in the Scene view.

■ **Tip** With this tool, you may paint over existing topography to increase it to the maximum set in the Set Resolution dialog (in your case, 200).

---

5.   Hold the Shift key down while painting to lower the ground, as shown in Figure 4-10.

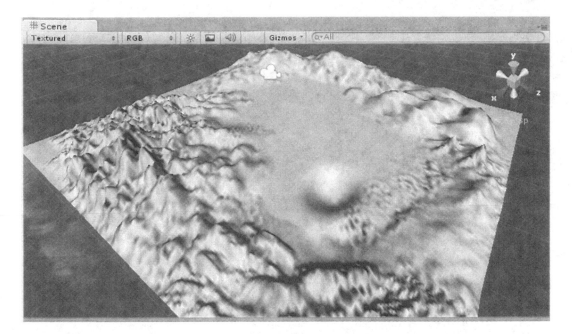

Figure 4-10. *A depression made in the terrain by holding the Shift key down while painting*

Because you set the Flatten Height to 50, that is as deep as the terrain can be displaced when you paint. You will deal with the hard edge later. You may also use the Shift key to lower mountain peaks that are too high, but there is a better tool for that coming up.

The next tool to try is the Paint Height tool. This tool *specifies* a height to work to, so the amount you set dictates whether you will be painting up or down. The most important thing about this tool is that it allows you to create flat areas, such as building pads, plateaus, mesas, sink holes, or anything else where the surface is superficially flat, at specific heights.

Remember that your default height is set to 50, so the height you set here will determine whether painting adds or subtracts to the terrain.

6. Select the Paint Height tool ![icon] .

7. Set the Height to **40** and paint in a default flat area until the hole bottoms out at 40.

8. Now set the Height to **60** and paint an area so the height tops out at 60 (see Figure 4-11).

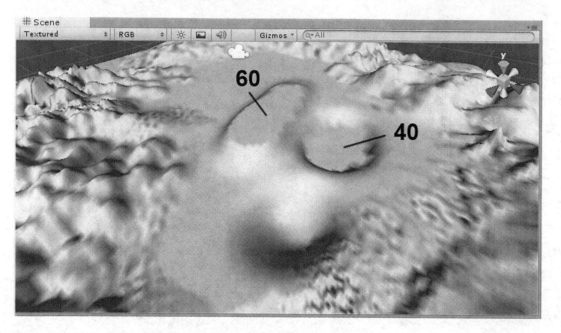

Figure 4-11. *The Paint Height results from 40 (right) and 60 (left)*

If you want to be extremely clever, write down the height of areas you plan to place structures on at some point. This way, rather than manually moving the object up and down until it looks sort of okay, you can type in the Y position in the Inspector and move on. As anyone who has worked with 3D for any length of time can tell you, deciding when an object is "on the ground" can be challenging. If you are using Unity Pro with dynamic shadows, the task is somewhat easier, but shadows are not a silver bullet. Numbers are still your friend.

To get rid of the nasty looking sharp edges where the tools have bottomed out or caused a crease, you can use the next tool in the collection. Smooth Height relaxes the terrain to give it a more natural look or adds a bit of weathering, for example, to your jagged mountains.

9. Zoom in to the area where you painted the Height.

10. Select the Smooth Height tool .

11. Smooth the hard edges left over from the Paint Height tool (see Figure 4-12).

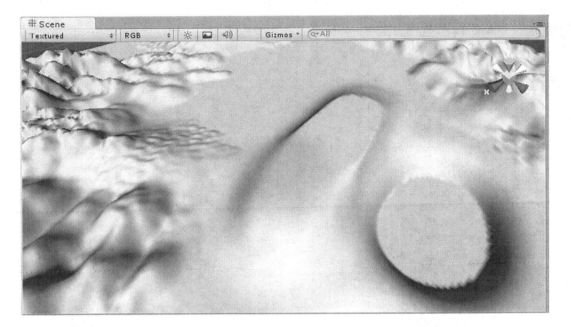

Figure 4-12. *The half-smoothed topology*

12. Experiment with the three Height tools until you are comfortable with your efforts.

13. Save your scene and project.

Painting Textures

With the topology in place, it's time to put some textures on the terrain, so that it looks less like something from a government survey site (see Figure 4-13).

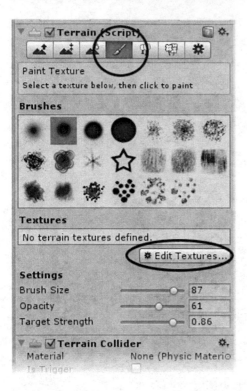

Figure 4-13. *Paint Texture and Edit Textures buttons in the Inspector*

1. Click the Paint Texture button ![paint brush icon].

Before you can begin painting the terrain, you will have to set up some textures. The first texture you load will fill the entire terrain, so choose a texture that will make the most sense as a base texture.

2. To load textures for painting, click the Edit Textures button and choose Add Texture (see Figure 4-14).

Figure 4-14. *Add Texture*

A dialog box appears, and you are prompted to select a texture. You can do this by either clicking the Select button and choosing from the asset list (double-click it), or you can drag and drop a texture into it directly from the Project view. To finish the addition, you must click the Add button at the bottom of the dialog (see Figure 4-15). This is also the place to add the matching normal maps to your terrain textures. Calculating bump for the textures will cost overhead, so choose wisely.

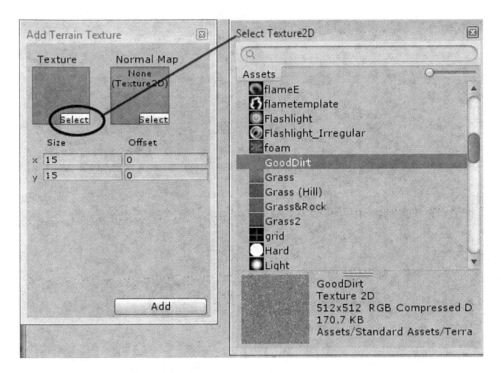

Figure 4-15. *Adding a texture*

Tiling parameters indicate the size of the tiling, not the number of tiles. Smaller numbers will increase the number of tiles, while larger numbers will decrease the tiling. At this point, you probably have no idea of the scale, so you may adjust the tiling parameters later by clicking Edit Texture then selecting Edit Textures.

    3.   Add a few more textures to your palette. The active texture has a blue underline (see Figure 4-16).

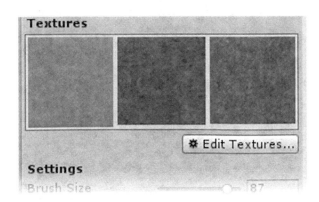

Figure 4-16. *More textures for the terrain: GoodDirt, Grass(Hill), Grass&Rock*

    4.   Using the various Brushes, paint the textures onto the terrain, as shown in Figure 4-17.

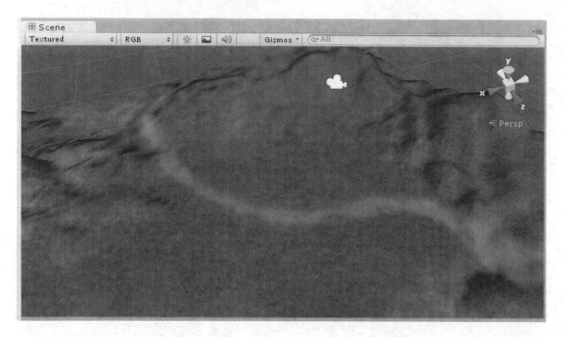

Figure 4-17. The terrain painted

As with any of the other terrain tools, you can access and adjust or change any of your terrain elements whenever you wish.

■ **Tip**   Remember, you can zoom to an area by moving the cursor to the spot you want and then pressing the F key. Pressing the mouse scroll wheel down will also get you closer, but can give unexpected results.

To view the splatmap created while you painted the various textures onto the terrain, you can look at the Terrain asset in the Project view.

5.   Save the scene to make the splatmap show up in the Project view.

6.   Open the Terrain asset in the Project view.

7.   Select the SplatAlpha 0 object.

The splatmap shows in the Inspector (see Figure 4-18). Note that it uses the Red, Green, Blue, and Alpha channels as a mask for the various textures.

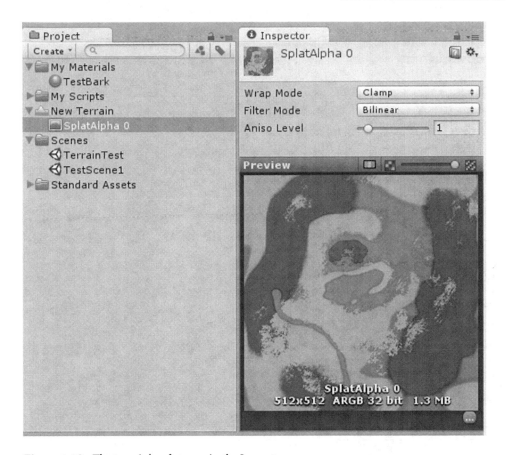

Figure 4-18. *The terrain's splatmap in the Inspector*

Trees

An important part of the terrain editing tools is the Place Trees tool. While you could create and place your own trees, using the terrain editing tools to populate your scene provides several advantages. As you might expect, it also has some limitations.

> **Pros:** Trees generated by the Terrain Engine can be animated to sway in the breeze. They also have automatic LOD: At a certain distance, the full mesh tree is swapped for a billboard plane with the tree's image, and at a far distance, the billboard object is not drawn at all, or *distance culled*. These distances can be set in the Inspector for the Place Trees tool, but more important, the engine will automatically reduce the distances to ensure acceptable frame rate on slower machines. *Shadowing* is automatically generated for the trees. If a tree is on the shadowed side of a mountain, the trunk and leaves will be darkened.

> **Cons:** Trees used for the Place Trees tool should not be above 2,000 polygons. Anything larger may not load properly in the Terrain Engine. Trees for the Terrain Engine can't use more than two materials. The materials used are limited to a few specialty shaders. If you don't use the Nature-Ambient Occlusion shaders in their materials, the lighting and the billboard will not be generated. In sparse areas, the transition between LOD models may be too noticeable.

■ **Rules**   Imported trees used for the Terrain Engine should be no more than 2,000 polygonsand have no more than two materials, and these materials must use the Nature-Soft Occlusion shaders. The trees must also be in a folder named Trees Ambient-Occlusion.

1.   Select the Place Trees tool 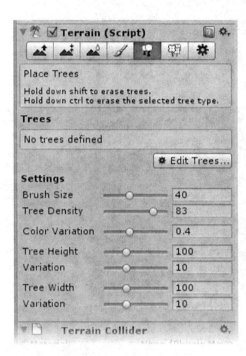 shown in Figure 4-19.

Figure 4-19.   The Place Trees tool

Just like textures, trees must be loaded before they can be used.

2.   Click the Edit Trees button and choose Add Tree (see Figure 4-20).

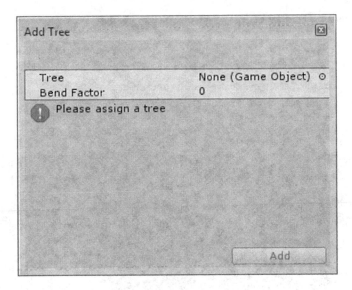

Figure 4-20. *The Add Tree dialog*

3. In the dialog, click the Browser icon and select the Palm asset (see Figure 4-21), but do not click Add yet.

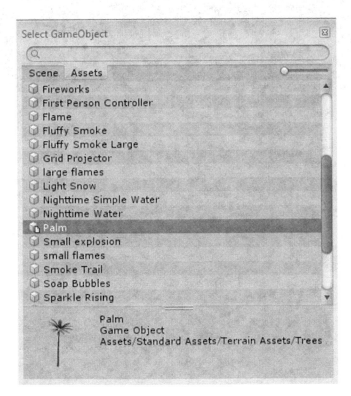

Figure 4-21. *The Palm asset*

Bend Factor is the parameter that controls the amount of wind effect the trees receive.

4. Set the Bend Factor to **0.5**.

5. Click Add.

6. Paint some trees on the terrain, experimenting with the various parameters, as shown in Figure 4-22.

Figure 4-22. *The palm trees added to the terrain*

7. Navigate the Scene view until you are close enough to see the mesh trees, rather than just their billboard LOD versions, as shown in Figure 4-23.

Figure 4-23. *A closer view of the palm trees*

To get a better view of the trees in the Game view, you need to do a few more things. Just as in the first cube experiments, you have to match the camera to the view you want, then you will want to add a directional light. Additionally, because this is a real outdoor environment, you ought to add a sky.

1.   Select the Main Camera.

2.   From the GameObject menu, choose Align with View.

The camera matches the Scene view, and the view appears in the Game view.

3.   From the GameObject menu ➤ Create Other, create a Directional light.

4.   Rotate the light until the palm trees are well lit, as shown in Figure 4-24.

Figure 4-24. *The trees lit and seen in the Game view*

5. Toggle the coordinate system to Global rather than Local and move the light up, out of the way.

6. In the Scene view, toggle on the Scene Lighting button, so the lighting looks the same in both views.

■ **Tip** You will find that it will be necessary to toggle the Scene Lighting off and on throughout the project, depending on what you are doing.

---

7. If you have Pro, set the light's Shadow Type parameter to Soft Shadows and set the Strength at about **0.7**.

Now that you can see the trees more clearly in the Game view, you may notice that their trunks particularly look very rough. In the default settings of Good Editor Quality, anti-aliasing is turned off.

ANTI-ALIASING

When an object is drawn against an existing background or other objects, its edges will appear jagged. In render-type DCC applications, anti-aliasing is performed on an object basis with a variety of anti-aliasing algorithms, depending on the desired effect and style.

In real time, however, where speed is of the utmost importance, that type of anti-aliasing is too slow. Instead, it is performed by what is known as super-sampling, where the scene is rendered out two, four, six, or eight times (depending on the capabilities of the graphics card) the size of the render window, then sized down to the final dimensions. The scaling produces a reasonable softening of the edges in a fraction of the time of traditional anti-aliasing.

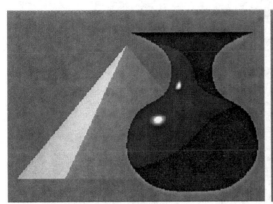 

Non-anti-aliased edges (the "jaggies"), on the left, and traditional anti-aliasing (fuzzy), on the right

Super-sampling (sharp but smooth)

8. From the Edit menu ➤ Project Settings, select Quality.

9. Open the Good preset, as shown in Figure 4-25.

Note that anti-aliasing is turned off in this preset.

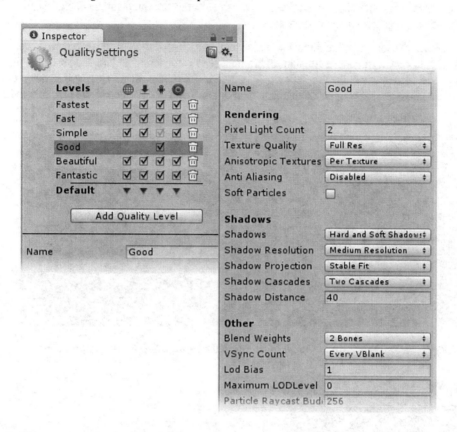

Figure 4-25. *The Quality settings*

10. If your graphics card is fairly good, change the editor quality to Beautiful or Fantastic to see the difference, as shown in Figure 4-26.

Figure 4-26. *The scene with Fantastic quality turned on in the editor and soft shadows (Pro only)*

Both choices use 2 × Multi-Sampling so the trees should appear much smoother.

■ **Tip** You can set the Default Standalone Qualities here, but the player will have the option to change them when first starting the game. Unity will automatically drop down to a setting that is supported by the player's graphics card.

Sky

As long as you are taking a brief sidetrack to improve the overall look of things, let's add a sky to the scene. Skies can be added to regular geometry, as in the case of a skydome, or, in Unity, you can employ a shader that uses a six-sided cubic map to do the job, as shown in Figure 4-27.

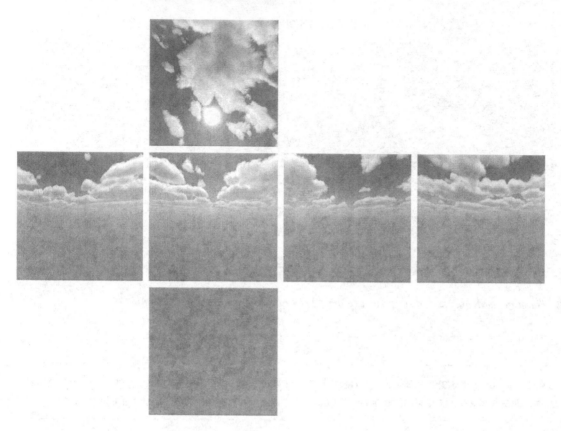

Figure 4-27. The six images used for a cubic sky map

A traditional skydome would have the advantage of working on systems that do not have much shader support, but because it generally uses simple spherical mapping, it's prone to distortion at the top. Take care to use an image that avoids the problem as much as possible. Skydomes also have the disadvantage of finite geometry. If they are too close, you will see where they intersect the regular scene geometry. If they are too far, they extend the camera clipping plane and increase the possibility of Z order fighting where two surfaces are too close to each other.

Because you are creating your game to play on traditional computers, you will go ahead and use the built-in shader type sky for your scene. Unity has two shader options for skies: one that uses six separate maps and one that is able to use some preformatted cube maps. If you are using an external cube map, it may need to be broken into the six images using the RenderFX/Skybox. The advantage of component parts means you can make adjustments to size and quality via the import settings.

1. In the Project view, open the Standard Assets folder and open the Skyboxes folder.

2. Select the skybox info text asset and quickly read through it.

It gives information about skyboxes in Unity.

3. Click each of the materials (sphere icons) to look at the choices.

4. Expand the Textures folder and open the Sunny3 folder.

This is where the images used to generate the materials reside and where you would go to reimport them using different settings.

5. Select the Sunny3 Skybox material, as shown in Figure 4-28.

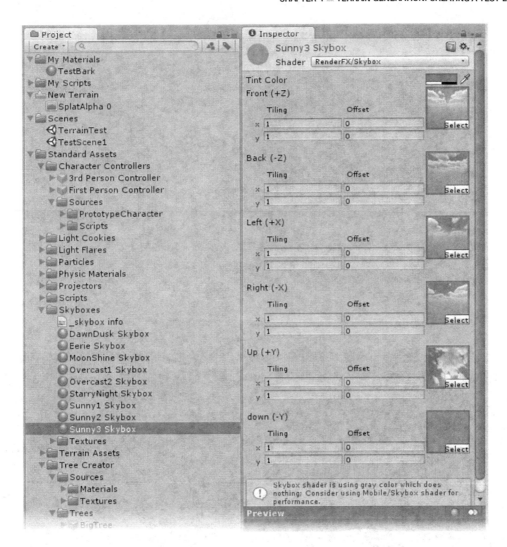

Figure 4-28. *The Sunny3 Skybox material in the Inspector*

Each of its component images is shown.
To load a skybox into your scene, you will access Render Settings from the Edit menu.

■ **Tip** You can also load a skybox into a camera directly in the Component/Rendering menu.

---

6. From the Edit menu, select Render Settings.

7. Drag the Sunny3 Skybox texture into the Skybox Material slot, or pick the asset browser icon to the far right and select it from the list (see Figure 4-29).

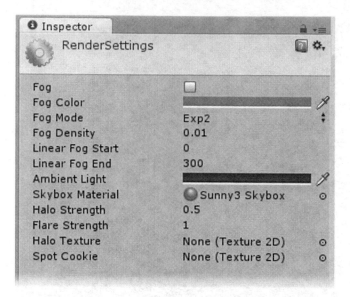

Figure 4-29. *The Sunny3 Skybox loaded into the RenderSettings' Skybox Material setting*

Figure 4-30. *The skybox in the Game view*

■ **Tip** You can turn the skybox on in the Scene view by toggling on the Game Overlay ⬜ icon next to the Scene Lighting button.

Back to the Trees

Now that your environment is looking better, you can continue with the terrain editing tools.

1. From the GameObject menu, Create Other, create a Wind Zone.

2. Set its Wind Pulse Frequency to **1**.

3. Click Play.

The trees sway gently in the breeze.

4. Select the Terrain object in the Hierarchy view once again.

5. In the Inspector, select the Place Tree tool again.

6. Select the Palm tree and choose Edit Trees to change the Bend Factor to **5**.

7. Set the WindZone's Wind Turbulance to **0.1** to reduce the jerkiness of the sway.

The nearer trees bend with a vengance, but the billboard versions further back in the view are unaffected.

8. Click Play again to exit Play mode, set the palms' Bend Factor back to **0.5**, and make the WindZone change permanent.

■ **Tip**   Changes made to the terrain editing tools during runtime will **not** be lost when you stop playback, so you can freely adjust parameters animation while getting instant feedback.

Once loaded, the billboard version of the tree (an image with an alpha channel) will show in the editor. The currently active tree's alpha area will appear gray, and the selected tree image will be outlined in blue, when it is selected for use.

9. Click Edit Trees, Add Tree and select Big Tree this time.

10. Reduce the Density and paint the new tree around the scene.

11. Select the Big Tree in the Project view (see Figure 4-31).

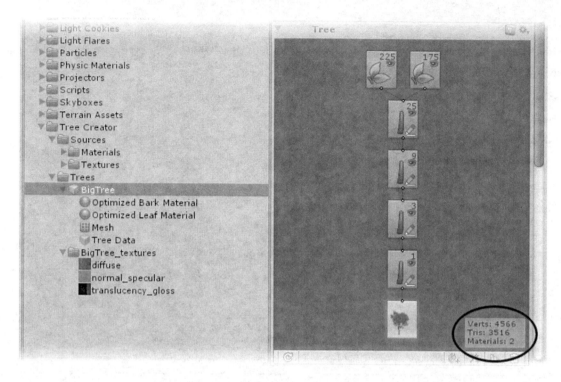

Figure 4-31. *The Big Tree selected in the Project view*

The Big Tree is an asset created with the Tree Creator. It has almost twice the recomended polygons or tris (see Figure 4-31), so use it spareingly. The Tree Creator is well-covered in the Unity docs, if you feel like creating your own trees.

If you are using Pro and soft shadows, you may have noticed another problem. The leaf opacity is not being used in the views.

1. Save the scene and save the project (the next few steps may cause a crash).

2. Select a top Leaf node, then re-select the base tree node (see Figure 4-32).

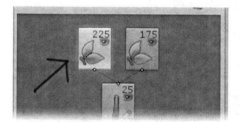 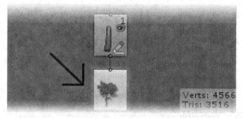

Figure 4-32. *Re-initializing the Big Tree asset*

There is a brief pause while assets are re-initialized, and the scene Big Trees shift slightly. If you were to drag the Big Tree asset directly into the viewport, you would see that its leaves now respect opacity (see Figure 4-33). To update the terrain versions, you will have to refresh them from the Terrain menu.

Figure 4-33. *Shadow opacity recovered*

3. From the Terrain menu, select Refresh Tree and Detail proto types.

■ **Tip** In case you got a bit heavy-handed with the brush, you can erase trees by holding down the Shift key. Any tree, in addition to the currently selected tree, will be removed. Holding down the Ctrl key will selectively remove the currently selected tree.

Importing UnityPackages

You are probably getting tired of palm trees by now. Let's see how to go about reusing assets from another scene.

Importing trees for use with the terrain involves more than just bringing in a textured mesh. Unity makes good use of what are called *prefabs*, prefabricated game objects that can contain all kinds of information, child objects, scripts, and other components. In the case of trees, they will need the special Nature shaders, and if thicker than saplings, they will probably need colliders.

You've seen colliders used before to "catch" mouse events. The more obvious use for colliders, of course, is to prevent the player from going through what should be solid objects. To that end, larger trees will need collider components.

1. Locate the Palm tree in the Project view and drag it into the Scene view.

If you scroll through its components in the Inspector (see Figure 4-34), you will see that it does not have a collider. At runtime, you would be able to move through it. Testing for collision does use resources, so not all trees will or should have colliders. In the case of the palm trees, it will be less frustrating for the player if you let him go through them. As a side note, you probably wondered about the Animation component. It is a casualty of Unity's long-term plan to merge legacy animation with the newer Mechanim system. Feel free to right-click the component name and Remove Component.

113

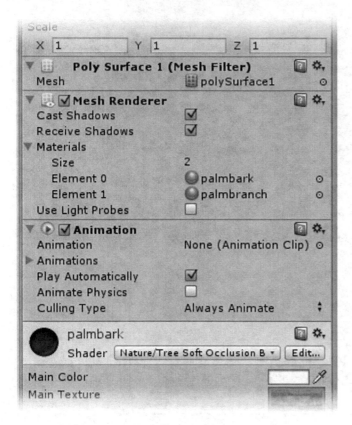

Figure 4-34. *The Palm asset's components in the Inspector*

2.   Delete the Palm from the Hierarchy view.

■ **Tip**   An empty prefab is represented by a white cube. As soon as you add scripts

or meshes to it, the cube becomes blue, and the Prefab icon receives an addition: .

If you use Import Asset to import a tree, only the GameObject (the parent group), the mesh, and the materials and textures will come in. The textures will need to be reassigned and the shaders changed to the Nature shaders.

By copying the whole folder into the scene's Assets folder via the OS (Explorer for Windows), there will be less to repair, but you'll certainly lose some connections. The safest way to transfer assets from one scene to the other is to save them as packages.

Packages are collections of assets that, for the most part, can be imported into a project without losing important connections or dependencies. In the following section, you will be making use of an asset package created for this book. You may also wish to experiment with an asset package available for download from the Unity3D Asset Store, TerrainAssets.unitypackage. This package contains several useful textures, trees, and other terrain-related assets.

■ **Tip**   You can access the Unity Asset Store directly through the Window menu in the Unity editor.

3.   From the Assets menu, select Import Package, Custom Package.

4.   Navigate to the Book Assets folder, Ch04, Assets04, and select
      ExtraTerrainAssets.unitypackage.

5.   Click Open.

The package is decompressed, and you are presented with a dialog that allows you to select the assets you wish.
They should all be checked by default, as shown in Figure 4-35.

Figure 4-35.   *The Importing Package dialog*

6.   Click Import.

7.   A new folder with the name of the package's original folder name is added to the
      Project view.

8.   Open the ExtraTerrainAssets folder\.

9.   Open the Trees Ambient-Occlusion folder.

■ **Tip**   In order for trees to cast and receive shadows, they must be in a folder named Trees Ambient-Occlusion and
make use of the Nature shaders.

10.   Select BanyanOld.

As an imported mesh object, it does not yet have a collider. Because it is probably larger than a meter in diameter in real life, you really ought to prevent the player from going through it. Before you add the collider, you should make sure the import scale is correct. Let's load the new tree into the Terrain Engine and try it out to see how the scale looks.

1. Select the Terrain object in the Hierarchy view.

2. Select the Place Trees tool in the Inspector.

3. Click Edit Trees and Add Tree.

4. Select the BanyanOld.

5. Choose an empty area near the palm trees (so you will be able to judge the scale) and paint some banyan trees on the terrain.

6. If you see no results, zoom in very close to the ground where you painted the trees.

As you paint the banyan, you will be seeing tiny little trees on the ground where you expected a great spreading behemoth (see Figure 4-36). You probably pictured them bigger!

Figure 4-36. Tiny trees

On import, meshes are scaled and often need their scale value adjusted.

7. Select the BanyanOld in the Project view.

8. In the Inspector, in the Model section, change the Scale Factor to **1** and click the Apply button, as shown in Figure 4-37.

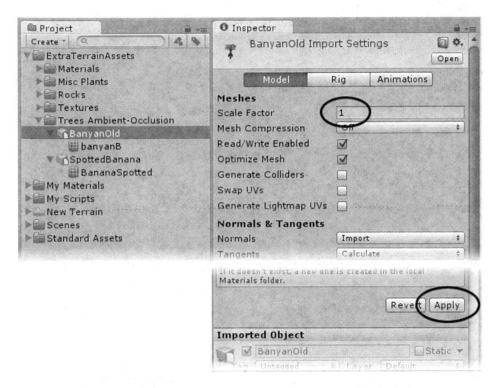

Figure 4-37. The Apply button

The banyans grow dramatically (you may need to click in the viewports to get them to update).

■ **Tip** In a perfect world, you may be able to control the scale the imported assets are using in the original DCC program so that they always come in the same. It is probably more realistic to assume you will end up scrounging assets from several different sources and will need to adjust the Scale Factor. Fortunately, Unity is very good with scale adjustments, even skinned meshes.

---

9.   Rotate the view to examine the newly scaled trees.

Depending on your view, you may notice the billboard versions are still small. Any time you make changes to assets used in the Terrain Engine, you need to update them to make sure the automatically generated features are updated as well.

10.   In the Terrain menu, select Refresh Tree and Detail Prototypes.

■ **Tip** Refresh Tree and Detail Prototypes updates light maps, LOD billboards, materials, etc.

---

11.   Select the Banyan and use Ctrl and paint to remove only the banyan trees.

Before repainting the trees, you need to add a collider. With the exception of the materials, imported assets cannot be directly affected in the Project view. To add a collider, you will need to instantiate a copy of the tree directly into the scene, add the collider, and then use it to create a prefab, which can then be used in the Terrain Engine.

1. Select BanyanOld in the Project view from the ExtraTerrainAssets folder's Trees Ambient-Occlusion folder.

2. Drag it directly into the Hierarchy view.

It turns up at 0,0,0, where it was located in the file it came from.

3. From the Component menu ➤ Physics, select Capsule Collider, as shown in Figure 4-38.

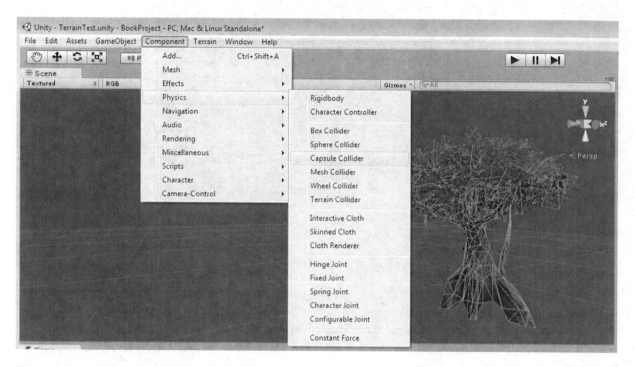

Figure 4-38. *Adding a Capsule Collider*

A collider is added to the tree, encompassing the entire tree.

4. In the Inspector, click to open or expand the Capsule Collider component.

5. Set the collider's radius to about **1.75** and adjust the Center parameters to align the collider with the trunk and smaller trunk extension, as shown in Figure 4-39.

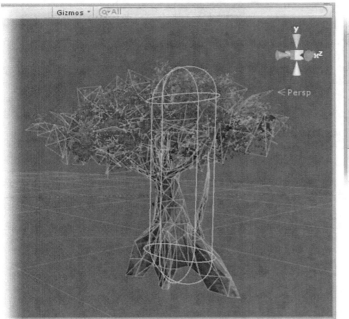
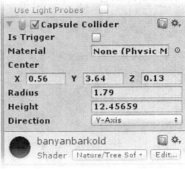

Figure 4-39. *The adjusted collider in the Scene view and the Inspector*

The tree is now ready to be *prefabbed*.

6. Select the ExtraTerrainAssets folder.

7. Create a new folder in it and name it **Prefabs**.

8. Select the new folder.

9. Right-click folder, select Create ➤ Prefab, as shown in Figure 4-40.

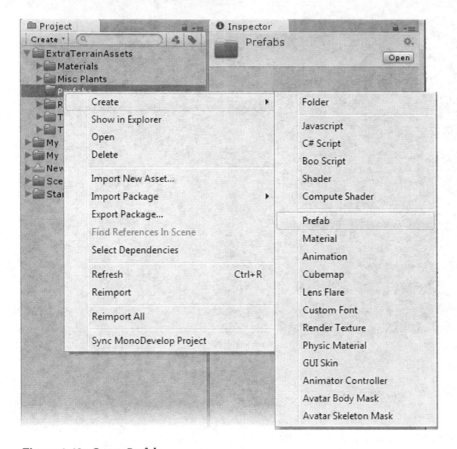

Figure 4-40. *Create Prefab*

■ **Tip** Alternatively, you can access the Create submenu from the Assets menu.

---

10. Name it **BanyanTree**.

11. Drag the BanyanOld object from the Hierarchy into the new prefab.

Once the prefab has been created, you can delete the altered original from the Hierarchy view. The prefab does not need to be in the Trees Ambient-Occlusion folder because it references the original BanyanOld from there. The white cube icon for the prefab turns blue once an asset is added to it.

12. Select the BanyanOld in the Hierarchy view and delete it.

13. Select the Main Camera.

14. From the GameObject menu, use Align View to Selected to get back to where you were last planting trees.

15. Select the Terrain and activate the Place Tree tool in the Inspector.

Now that you have a replacement tree with a collider, you need to delete the currently loaded version of the Banyan.

16. Select the currently loaded banyan.

17. From the Edit Trees menu, select Edit Tree.

18. Replace the BanyanOld with the BanyanTree prefab.

19. Adjust the Density and repaint them where you want them.

You may wish to adjust the banyan's bark material a bit.

20. Select the BanyanBarkOld material in the Extra Terrain Assets folder's Materials folder.

21. Experiment with the Base Light and Ambient Occlusion sliders (see Figure 4-41).

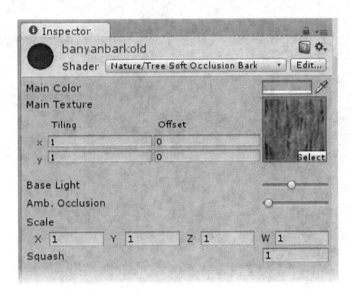

Figure 4-41. *The bark material*

22. In the Terrain menu, select Refresh Tree and Detail Prototypes after each adjustment, if you are not seeing the results (see Figure 4-42).

    -+-0.
    +

Figure 4-42. The adjusted bark

■ **Tip** If the trees need to be a little larger and you do not wish to adjust the import size further, you can increase the Tree Height and other settings in the Place Trees parameters.

Sometimes it's easier to remove trees from a densely populated area than to paint them manually where you want them. You can populate your entire terrain all at once to make things quicker. To mass place trees, select Mass Place Trees from the Terrain menu. You may set the amount of trees. All trees currently loaded in the editor will be used, but you can't specify the percentages. Once populated, you can remove trees from unwanted areas by using the Shift key while painting.

Terrain Extras

With the trees handled and the terrain texture painted, you are probably thinking your terrain is still missing something. Everything between the trees and ground is added with Paint Details (see Figure 4-43). This includes gresses, bushes, and even rocks or other small mesh-based objects.

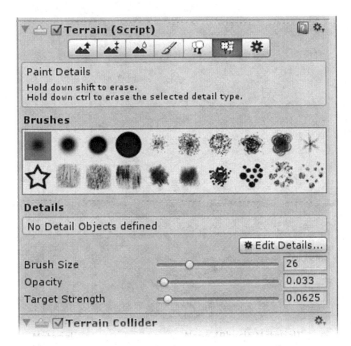

Figure 4-43. *Paint Details*

This feature lets you paint grasses, scrub, rocks, and other details. There are two main types of details: grasses and meshes. Grasses are simple planes that are billboarded (they always face the camera) and can be set to animate to sway in the breeze. When you set up grasses, you will select only an alpha channel-using texture.

1. Select the Paint Details tool .

2. Pick Edit Details and Add Grass Texture, as shown in Figure 4-44.

Figure 4-44. *Add Texture*

3. Select Grass, as shown in Figure 4-45.

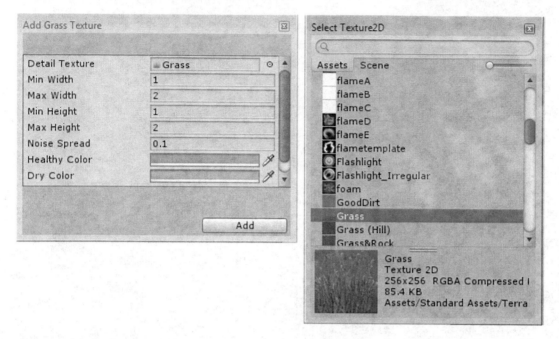

Figure 4-45. *The Grass asset*

4. Paint the grass around the scene, as shown in Figure 4-46.

Figure 4-46. *Grass added to the terrain*

Note the color variation provided by the Dry Color and Healthy Color textures. Also, if you are using Pro and have soft shadows, you will see that the painted grass receives shadows just like the terrain.

■ **Tip** Take care when painting grasses and detail meshes. If you are too far away when you are painting, the grass will automatically be distance culled, so you may not see the results of your work until you zoom in closer, at which point you may find you have a lot more than you planned.

Unlike trees that have a Bend Factor, it is assumed that grass will bend and sway in the wind. Bend Factor isn't what makes the trees sway back and forth, it just dictates how stiff or bendy the tree is. Wind speed for the detail grasses and meshes, along with several other parameters, can be found in the Terrain Settings tool.

1. Click Play and watch the wind act on the grass.

2. Use Edit Tree to add or adjust the Bend amount for the trees if you wish.

In addition to grasses, the Texture Grass detail mesh is good for many annual flowers and weeds. There's a nice section in the docs on prepping images. In the Manual's FAQ, Graphics Questions, look for "How do I Import Alpha Textures?" The remaining Detail type is a mesh object. This is where you will add 3D meshes, such as rocks and mesh plants. The detail meshes are like grasses in that they have color ranges with Healthy and Dry. They can also be animated to move in the wind with Render Type. Grass will let them be affected by wind; Vertex Lit will keep them static. The downside of Vertex Lit is that the mesh will not respect texture alpha channel. Noise Spread is the size variation.

1. Add the SpottedBanana as a detail mesh and set it to Grass Render Mode, so it will sway in the wind.

2. Try adjusting several of the Spotted Banana's parameters before you start painting.

3. Carefully click to place the plants, as shown in Figure 4-47.

Figure 4-47. *A few more plants*

You will probably have to adjust the material's Base Light and Ambient Occlusion. Remember to Refresh Tree and Detail Prototypes after each adjustment, to see the results.

Next, add the rock as a static mesh in Details.

1. Click Edit Details and select Add Detail Mesh this time (Figure 4-48).

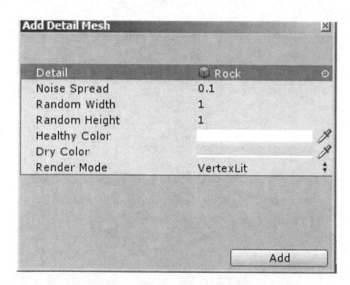

Figure 4-48. *The Rock asset assigned as a Detail mesh*

2. Add the Rock by dragging it from the Rocks folder or selecting it from the browser.

3. Change the Healthy and Dry Colors to something more subtle.

4. Since rocks shouldn't sway in the wind, set the Render Type to Vertex Lit.

5. Adjust the Random Width and Height to **2** to get a nice size variation on the rocks.

You may be tempted to populate your terrain with boulders using detail meshes.

6. Try increasing the height of your rocks, then zooming in and out (Figure 4-49).

Figure 4-49. *A good size for rocks that will be distance culled*

Unlike the trees, detail meshes are not replaced with lower poly replacements at distance; they are merely distance culled.

7. Remove the boulders.

8. Edit the Noise Spread to something smaller. As with the other terrain assets, you will need to select the icon in the Inspector, select the Edit button, and choose Edit from the list of options.

For large plants, you may be better off adding the mesh to the tree section. Do be aware that only one billboard tree image is made from the mesh, and trees all face the same direction, so asymmetrical meshes will not work well in sparsely populated areas. Also, detail meshes may not have colliders. As with all painted terrain assets, they will disappear at the culling distance, so think carefully when deciding what to place manually and what to paint.

Creating Your Own Terrain Assets

Assuming you may want to try your hand at creating your own terrain assets, there are a few things to keep in mind.

Options

There are four main ways to bring plant-type objects into your scene. Each has advantages and disadvantages. Several of the issues are due to shaders with the express purpose of faster frame rate. Let's use the Stripey Plant asset as a test case (see Figure 4-50).

Figure 4-50. *Plant options: Detail Mesh-Vertex Lit (far left), Detail Mesh-Grass (left), gameObject (right), Terrain Engine tree (far right)*

- *Regular GameObject:* Allows the best control for placement because each object has to be manually placed. Can cast and receive shadows, but LOD is not managed for you. Can use any material. Does not react to wind.

- *Terrain Tree:* Can be painted onto terrain, have its Bend adjusted, and has automatic LOD handling. Is limited in materials and poly count. Density is controlled by object bounding box.

- *Detail Mesh, Vertex Lit:* Can be painted onto terrain, has automatic LOD handling. Is not affected by wind. Does not respect texture opacity. Receives but does not cast shadows. Material is overwritten with terrain shaders.

- *Detail Mesh, Grass type:* Can be painted onto terrain, has automatic LOD handling. Is affected by wind according to vertex alpha values. Respects texture opacity. Receives but does not cast shadows. Material is overwritten with terrain shaders.

Trees

As mentioned before, trees and plants require the Nature shaders, Tree Soft Occlusion Bark, and Tree Soft Occlusion Leaves to receive shadows and color tints. The shadowing color on trees is created with vertex color, as are the Healthy/Dry variations in Detail Meshes, and is added to the color set by the texture and shader Main Color.

In addition to keeping the tree under 2,000 faces, it must also use no more than two materials. Careful unwrapping and texturing can do much to make up for this limitation. The banyan tree, using a derivation from the TerrainAssets package, has a texture with full leaves, a bare branch, and a vine of some sort, all using the alpha channel.

Orientation

If you create your assets in 3ds Max or another application that uses Z as up rather than Y, you will have to orient the objects so that they appear up in the top viewport (see Figure 4-51).

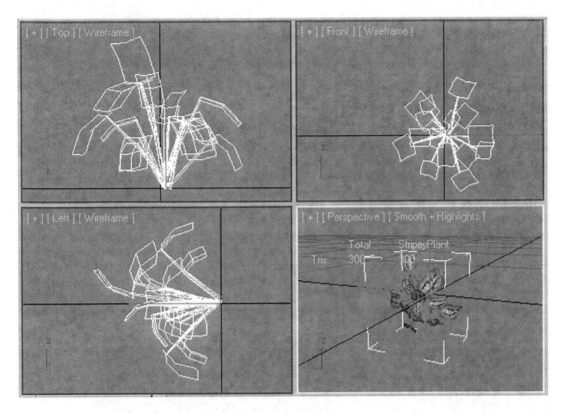

Figure 4-51. *Orientation in 3ds Max*

Unlike the regular imports that are able to convert their native orientation, terrain assets must be correct before import. To ensure the transform is baked in, create a plane in the top viewport, attach (from the Edit Mesh modifier) the terrain asset to it, then remove the plane with sub-object element, as shown in Figure 4-52.

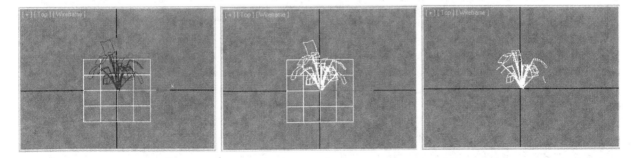

Figure 4-52. *Getting a clean transform matrix in 3ds Max*

1. Create a plane in the top viewport.

2. Collapse the plane to an editable mesh and attach the plant to it.

3. In sub-object element, select the plane and delete it.

4. Name the object and export.

If you plan on making mesh objects that will utilize the wind setting, you should know that the amount of bend on the object is dictated by the values from alpha channel information stored on vertices. Ideally, you will want the base of your plant to use black, no bend, and the top to use gray to white, depending on how much movement you want. DCC programs tend to handle vertex painting differently, so you may have to do a bit of research.

Bend for Detail Meshes

You've seen how the Grass and Vertex Lit versions of the Detail Mesh objects behave. With Grass Detail Meshes, alpha channel on the texture is used, but the mesh is subject to wind from the Terrain Settings section of the Terrain Engine. If you've already downloaded some of the free terrain asset packages from the Unity Asset Store, you may have run into some problems. Occasionally, plants using alpha channel transparencies on simple planes wander back and forth across the terrain when wind is enabled for the Detail Meshes. Let's investigate what controls bend.

Unity supports a few types of vertex information. The typical and default uses are for vertex color, where the color is used to tint the texture. Another supported bit of information is an alpha value. In Unity, the shader used for Vertex Lit Detail Meshes uses the alpha value to determine bend amount. Black is no bend, and white is full bend. Typically, plants will have black at the base and white to dark gray at the top, depending on how much bend is desired. The problem comes with assets that have no alpha vertex information. If none is found, it uses a default color—white. Since white is full bend, the entire plant will wander back and forth across the terrain when set as a Vertex Lit Detail Mesh. While entertaining, it is rarely the effect you will want to see. Figure 4-53 shows one of the extra terrain assets, the Stripey Plant, and its use of vertex color and alpha channel.

Figure 4-53. *Vertex information on the Stripey Plant: texture only (left), vertex color (middle), vertex alpha (right)*

The important thing to know about the vertex information is that even if you only want the alpha, to control the bend, you will have to include the color channel, to prevent the alpha being misinterpreted.

Terrain Settings

The last icon on the terrain editing tools, ![icon], deals with Terrain Settings. This allows you to change distances for LOD and distance culling for trees and details, as well as to adjust wind strength.

1. Select the Terrain object.

2. Select the Terrain Settings tool in the Inspector.

3. Click Play.

4. Adjust the wind settings, speed, size, and bending until it looks good—a value of about 0.25 for each works well.

You can turn off the trees and Detail Meshes to make editing terrain easier. This is also the place to affect terrain mesh density.

5. Under Terain and Detail Objects, uncheck Draw.

The trees and plants disappear.

6. In the Scene view, Change the display from Textured to Wireframe.

7. Under Base Terrain, make note of the Pixel Error value, then try changing the slider to see the terrain mesh density changed (see Figure 4-54).

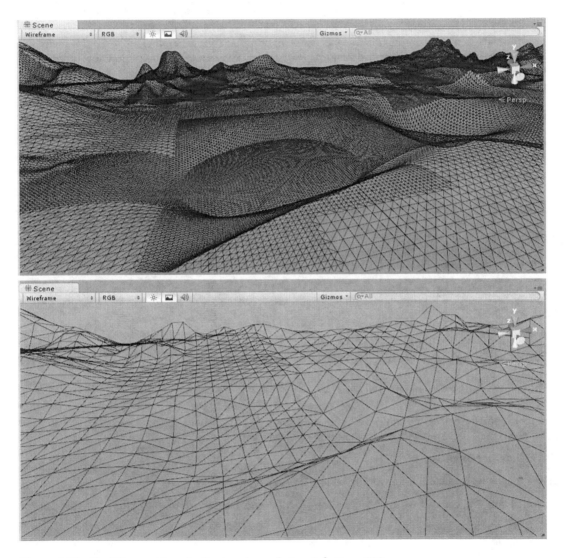

Figure 4-54. *Pixel Error settings for the terrain mesh: top, 0, bottom, 200*

8. Return the Pixel Error to its original value.

9. Return the view to Textured.

10. Check Draw to get the trees and detail objects to appear.

Finally, not part of the terrain editing tools but close enough to take a quick look at is the Terrain Collider component. Note that it has a Create Tree Colliders option. Similar to the Cast Shadows option in the Base Terrain section, this one only works on objects that already have a collider.

Shadows

Next, let's bake some shadows into the terrain. Because terrains can be quite large, generating lightmaps for them can take a great deal of time and use a lot of texture memory. *Baked* shadows can add nice definition to your scene but don't allow for objects that are dynamic or will animate. Dynamic shadows will track animated objects but can lack the subtlety obtained with large numbers of carefully set lights and global illumination (where light bounces are calculated).

If you are using Unity Pro, you can have the best of both. You can bake the shadows into the terrain and have dynamic shadows as well, with the dual lightmap system. Two lightmaps are created: one with all shadows included, Far, and one with only the indirect lighting shadows, Near. Within a specified range, the Shadow Distance, the Near map is used, and real-time shadows calculated. Beyond that range, the Far shadow map is used (see Figure 4-55). You will be visiting Beast later in the project.

Figure 4-55. *No shadows (left), baked shadows (middle), and dynamic, real-time shadows (right)*

In your test scene, you have only one light, the Directional light, and its Lightmapping parameter is set to Auto, so you should be good to go. Let's start with a brief look at the Lightmapping dialog.

1. Select the Directional light in the Hierarchy view.

2. In the Inspector, select Soft Shadows for Shadow Type.

If you are using Unity Pro, you will see dynamic shadows in the scene to a distance of 150 meters from the camera (as set in the Quality settings).

3. Select the Terrain object.

4. From the Window menu, select Lightmapping, as shown in Figure 4-56.

Figure 4-56. *The Lightmap Display in the lower right corner of the Scene view after starting the Beast lightmapper, the Terrain object currently selected with Pro's dynamic shadows showing*

The first thing of note is the Static check box. Because this is a terrain and will not be animating, it is automatically set to Static. Later, when you import assets that are not used with the Terrain Engine, you will have to remember to set the objects as Static or not, depending on whether they will be animating. Only Static objects will be included in lightmapping. If you are using with Unity pro, you will have more available lightmapping options (see Figures 4-57 and 4-58).

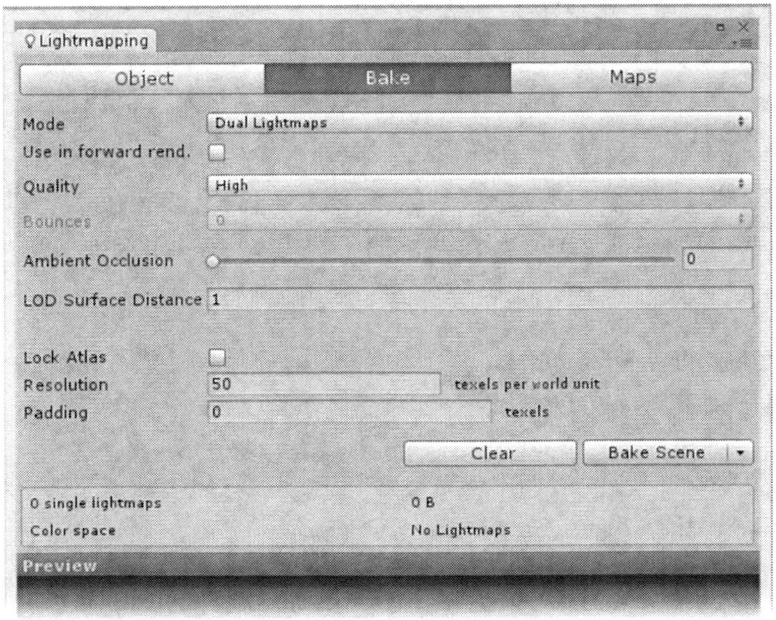

Figure 4-57. *Beast in the free version of Unity. No Bounces or Global Illumination options*

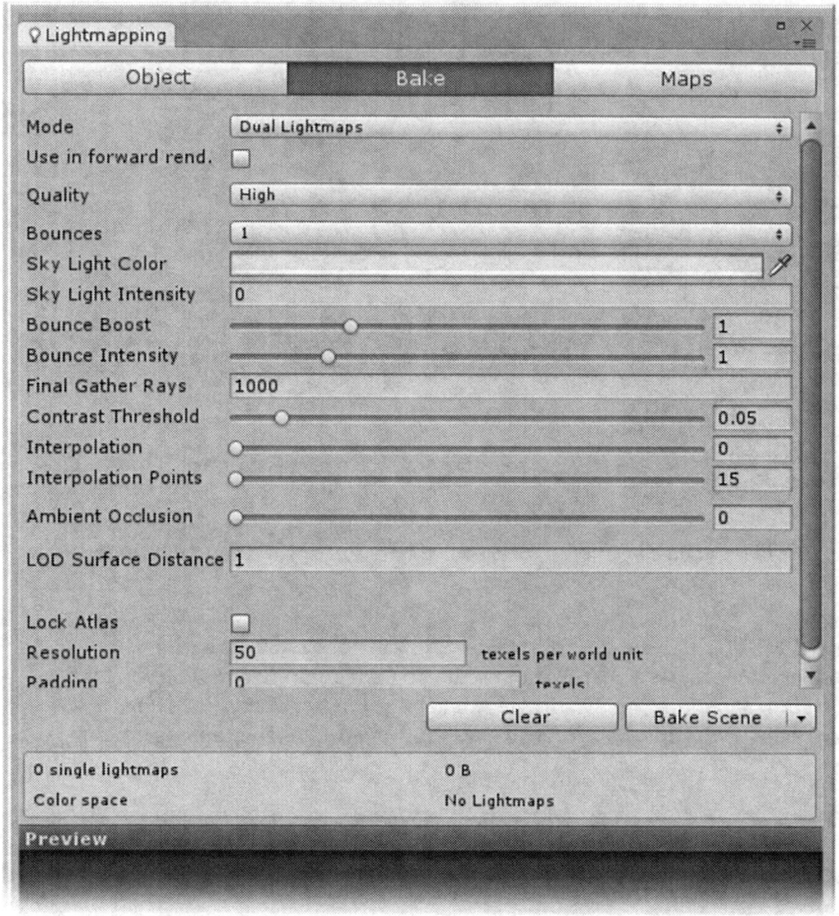

Figure 4-58. Beast in Unity Pro. More settings to use Global Illumination

Let's start by baking out a couple of different sized lightmaps, just to see the difference. Because you will be adding objects to the scene throughout the development of a game, the lightmap will need regular updating, so there is no need to spend much time on it at this stage.

1.   If you are using Unity Pro, set the Bounces to 0.

2.   Set Mode to Single Lightmaps if you are not using Unity Pro.

3.   With the Terrain selected, pick the Bake Scene button.

The status line, bottom, far right, will show the progress as the light is baked. A thumbnail of the resulting map (or maps) is shown in the Preview window.

4.   Note the time it took to render the map[(s) and the memory it (they) will use, as shown in Figure 4-59.

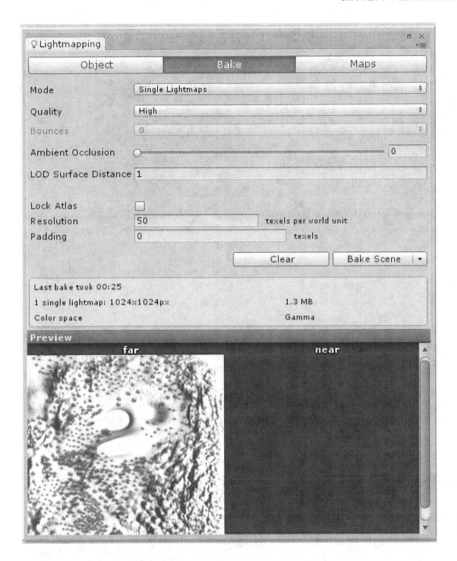

Figure 4-59. *The first bake of the Terrain*

For comparison, you will bake the same settings to a smaller map size. The default size for the Terrain map is 1024; try one at 256 to see the difference (see Figure 4-60).

Figure 4-60. *The results of the two map sizes, 1024 (left) and 256 (right)*

1. From the Object tab, change the Lightmap Size to **256**.

2. Click Bake Scene.

As you can see in the preceding figure, the smaller map produces soft, indistinct shadows. Note that the smaller map takes up 85.3KB instead of 1.3MB.

3. If you are using Unity Pro, set the Bounces back to the default of 1 Bounce and render the 1024 map size again.

There may be a slight lightening of the shadows from light that could bounce back off the tree trunks, but at this point, it is not worth the extra render time (see Figure 4-61). Bounced light will become more important with the addition of structures. For this book, since it is not assumed that everyone will have Unity Pro, the structures will contain prebaked lightmaps.

Figure 4-61. *Terrain using Pro's dual lightmap system: the foreground shows dynamic shadows plus ambient lightmap; the middle ground and background use full lightmap*

If you are using Unity Pro, note that dynamic shadows are no longer in effect, because you baked the shadows to a single lightmap. To make use of the dual lightmap system, you will need to switch from Forward to Deferred Lighting in the Player Settings. You will revist lightmaps and shadows at various times throughout the book.

Fog

As a final touch for your test scene, you can add a bit of fog for some environmental perspective. Fog is fairly cheap and will help promote the feel of a moist tropical jungle.

1. From the Edit menu, select Render Settings.

2. Check Fog, as shown in Figure 4-62.

Figure 4-62. Render Settings with Fog activated, using Exponential2 mode

3. Change the fog color to a greenish blue to simulate light filtering through the forest with high humidity, as shown in Figure 4-63.

Figure 4-63. *The fog in the Game view*

For the game, you will be importing a package that already contains its own terrain. Feel free to create your own version.

4.   Save the scene and save the project.

Summary

In this chapter, you learned how to use Unity's built-in Terrain Engine to create the basis for your outdoor environment. Using the Raise/Lower Height, Paint Height, and Smooth Height tools, you were able to sculpt mountains, lakes, and valleys, as well as create building pads and other areas of interest. You learned that focusing on a terrain object is different than for regular objects, but that the flythrough mode of scene navigation is quite useful.

You were able to paint multiple textures on the terrain using the variety of brushes available in the editor. You also learned how to add grass and mesh objects with the option to sway in the wind. Trees were added the same way, but you discovered that to prevent the player from going right through the trunks, you needed to create a prefab containing a collider. You discovered how to import packages of prepared assets and learned a few tips for creating your own terrain assets. Finally, you learned how to bake shadows into the terrain at a few different settings and then to add a bit of fog for some environmental perspective.

In the next chapter, you will learn how to navigate through your environment and start customizing the existing scripts to fit the needs of your adventure game.

CHAPTER 5

■ ■ ■

Navigation and Functionality

So far, you have explored the terrain in the Scene view with zoom, pan, orbit, and flythrough navigation. Every environment artist's dream is to be able to experience his or her creation firsthand. And while "holodeck" technology is not quite here yet, being able to travel through your environment in first-person mode for the first time is, for many of us, one of the best parts of making real-time games. To make your environment into an actual game environment, you will need to be able to travel around inside the world, responding to terrain topography and large objects during runtime. Only by doing this can you tell if scale, layout, color scheme, and all the rest of the design have come together to create the mood you intend. Even though what you're creating here is just a temporary test scene, the effect is the basis for every entertainment author's goal: suspension of disbelief.

Navigation

Fortunately, Unity provides a prefab for a first-person shooter-type controller. It consists of a Capsule Collider to provide physical interaction with the scene, a camera to provide the viewpoint, and scripts to allow the user to control them through keyboard and mouse.

Anyone who has ever played 3D games, even of the same genre, is well aware that there are many different means of controlling the character or the first person. Moreover, if you get a group of 20 people together in the same room and ask them what the best controls are, you would most likely get a different answer from every person, depending on the game he is currently playing or his all-time favorite game.

You will be tweaking a bit of the First Person Controller as you develop the game, but it is extremely useful to be able to jump right in and travel around the scene right away.

1. Open the Project as you left it in the previous chapter, to the TerrainTest scene.

2. Locate or create a clearing on level ground, as shown in Figure 5-1.

Figure 5-1. *The clearing*

3. Toggle the Overlays button off in the Scene view to hide the fog and sky and turn the fog off in the Render Settings for now.

4. From the Character Controllers folder in the Standard Assets directory, drag the First Person Controller into the Scene view.

Because the First Person Controller is a prefab, its text appears blue in the Hierarchy view, instead of the usual black (see Figure 5-2).

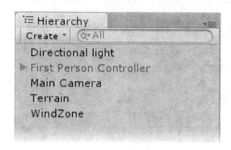

Figure 5-2. *The new First Person Controller in the Hierarchy view (left) and the single-column Project view (right)*

■ **Tip**   You can add an object into the scene in a few different ways. Previously, we focused the view and added the object to the Hierarchy so it appears at the focus spot. This time, we added the object directly into the scene. If you know the object's position will need to be changed, you can simply drag it directly into the Scene view and get on with the repositioning.

5. From the GameObject menu, choose Align with View, to move it near the existing view.

6. Use the Scene Gizmo to select the Top view (Y), then click the SceneGizmo label to change it from a top perspective view to an orthographic (no perspective) view (see Figure 5-3).

Figure 5-3. *Top view, perspective (left) and orthographic (right)*

The icon next to the label goes from wedge-shaped (perspective) to three short parallel lines (orthographic).

7. Select the First Person Controller in the Hierarchy view.

8. Zoom out to see the area better.

9. Select the Move tool.

10. Using the gray rectangle from the Transform Gizmo, adjust the position of the First Person Controller, if necessary, to center it in the clearing.

■ **Tip**   The First Person Controller contains its own camera, which overrides the existing Main Camera object, so you will now see its view in the Game view.

Because the default height was set to 50, the prefab may be beneath the terrain surface, if you modified it in that area.

11. Use the F key to focus the view on the First Person Controller prefab.

12. Click the label again to put the Scene view back to a perspective view, then use Alt+Left mouse to orbit the view back down.

13. Move the First Person Controller up or down in the viewport by dragging its Y arrow up until you can see the ground in the Game view.

14. Use F to focus the First Person Controller prefab again.

15. Adjust its height until the capsule is slightly above ground level (see Figure 5-4).

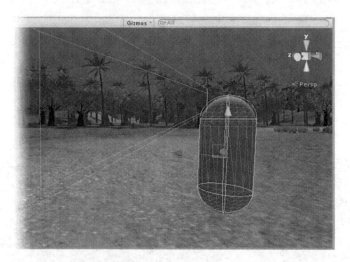

Figure 5-4. The First Person Controller in the Scene view

Before you head off to experience your scene in first-person mode, let's take a quick look at what the prefab contains.

1. Select the First Person Controller in the Hierarchy view and click the arrow to the left of the name to open the group (or GameObject), as shown in Figure 5-5.

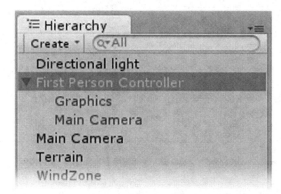

Figure 5-5. The contents of the First Person Controller

It has two children—something called Graphics and Main Camera.

Graphics, as you probably guessed, contains the mesh for the capsule. If you check and uncheck Mesh Renderer in the Inspector (see Figure 5-6), you can see that it affects whether or not the capsule is drawn in the Scene view. Note that neither Cast Shadows nor Receive Shadows is checked. If you are using Unity Pro, you will be able to see what happens if they are checked.

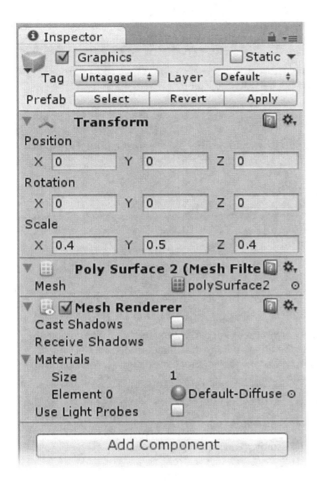

Figure 5-6. The Graphics object in the Inspector

Because the camera object is inside the capsule and you are looking out through the back side of the mesh's faces, you will not see it in the Game view. Remember that faces are only drawn on the side that their normals are pointing—in this case, the outside of the capsule.

    2.   Click Play.

You may notice that the Console status line is telling you there are two Audio Listeners in the scene. (See Figure 5-7.)

⊙ There are 2 audio listeners in the scene. Please ensure there is always exactly one audio listener in the scene.

Figure 5-7. The status line warning

    3.   Stop the scene by clicking the Play button again.

As you may surmise, this has to do with enabling audio, but you should have only one per scene. Because every scene must have at least one camera, the default camera comes supplied with that component, as does the Main Camera present in the First Person Controller.

Eventually, you'll have to add and animate other cameras to show the player when and where some particularly important event happens, but for now, just remember to delete the default Main Camera whenever you add the First Person Controller prefab.

4. Select the original scene Main Camera, right-click, and delete it.

The remaining Main Camera object will be referenced by name by various other objects throughout this project, as well as by any other games that use the scripts you'll be creating. Do not rename this object!

5. Click Play.

6. Move around the scene, using W to go forward, S to go backward, A to strafe left, and D to strafe right.

7. Move the mouse around to look up and down or to turn left or right.

8. Use the spacebar to jump.

9. Try running into one of the banyan trees.

10. The collider prevents you from going through it.

If you experimented with tiling on the terrain textures, you may want to select the Terrain object and change the tiling on some of them. Remember, a smaller number increases the tiling, making the image smaller on the terrain.

If you added large rocks to the scene as Detail Meshes, you will notice they do not have colliders; you can move right through them.

11. Select the First Person Controller in the Inspector.

12. You will find three script components and one other component.

13. Take a look at the variables exposed to the Character Motor script (see Figure 5-8).

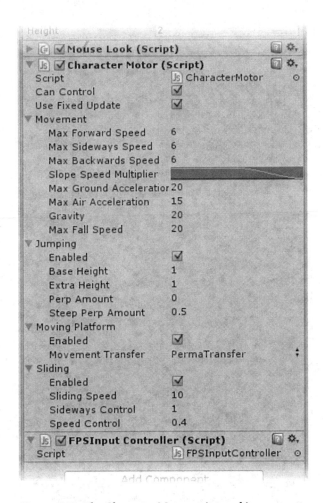

Figure 5-8. *The Character Motor script and its parameters*

As long as you are in Play mode, you can make changes to speed, jump speed, and gravity that will not be permanent.

■ **Tip** To remove focus from the Game view, click outside of it before trying to access other parts of the editor. This will stop the view from spinning wildly.

Opening the script in the editor is somewhat overwhelming. Fortunately, you can just accept that it does lots of nice things to help you travel around the scene and leave it at that. Movement and Jumping are pretty self-explanatory, even if a few of the parameters are not. Moving Platform is an option in the First Person Controller system that you will experiment with a bit later. Sliding is whether the character sticks or slides back down steep slopes when jumping.

The First Person Controller is basically a first-person shooter-type control, with some attributes that will be useful and some that will not. The quickest way to find out what controls what is to turn off scripts and see what happens—or in this case, no longer happens.

1. Select the First Person Controller.

2. Disable the MouseLook script.

3. Test the restricted functionality.

You'll find that you can still go forward and sideways, but you can't turn left or right; you can only strafe with the left and right arrows or A and D keys.

You can still look up and down, however. A bit of investigation shows that the Main Camera also has a MouseLook script, but that its rotation Axes is set to work on the X axis rather than the Y axis, such as the one on the main group or GameObject (see Figure 5-9). This means that to turn to look, the whole object is turned. When the object goes forward, it will always go in the direction it is facing. When it has to look up or down, only the camera is rotated, leaving the forward direction correct.

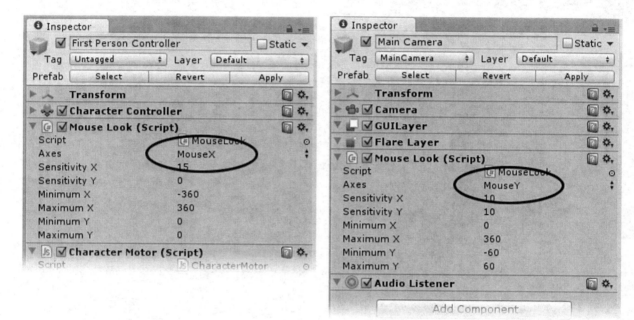

Figure 5-9. *The MouseLook script on the First Person Controller (left) and the MouseLook on the Main Camera (right)*

4. Disable (uncheck) the MouseLook script on the Main Camera object.

5. Test the restricted functionality.

Now you can only go forward, backward, or sideways. On the positive side, you now have full use of the cursor for your point-and-click adventure.

6. Stop Play mode.

Arrow Navigation and Input

Typically, people who are not avid shooter-type game players are more comfortable using the arrow keys to travel and turn. Ideally, you want to cater to both types of users as transparently as possible. To do so, you have to do a bit of tinkering with the Input system.

Unity's Input system lets you assign different input types to a named functionality. This enables two important things: it lets you reference the name of a behavior rather than specifically calling each key or mouse control the behavior can use, and it lets users change or re-map the keys according to their preferred configuration. Because you will be making the two control types work together, you will not allow the user to re-map the keys. You can, however, still make use of the naming benefits when you set up the functionality for the game.

Let's see how the re-mapping works. Jump has only a positive key assigned: the spacebar, or space. It's easy to temporarily change this input assignment.

1. From Edit ➤ Project Settings, choose Input.

2. Click the down arrow next to Axes to see the assignments.

There are currently 17 presets.

3. In the Jump preset, select the Positive Button's entry field (see Figure 5-10).

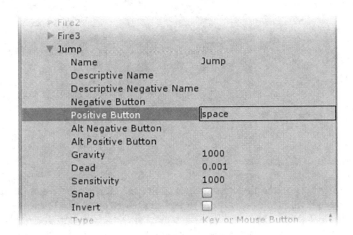

Figure 5-10. *Re-mapping the Jump key*

4. Change space to a different key (in lowercase).

5. Click Play and test.

The jump function now works from the newly assigned key. This means you could eventually let the user re-map or assign the keys without having to change any of your scripts.

6. Stop Play mode and change the Positive Button back to space.

■ **Tip** See Appendix B for the names of the keyboard keys to use in scripts.

Let's get started altering the default First Person Controller navigation.
The first thing to do is turn off strafing for the left and right arrows, leaving that capability strictly to the A and D keys.

7. Open the first Horizontal and Vertical sets (there are duplicates of both further down the list), as shown in Figure 5-11.

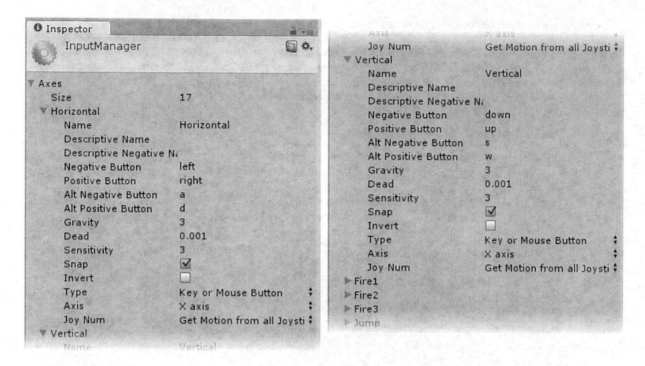

Figure 5-11. *The Input Manager, Horizontal, and Vertical opened in the Inspector*

A good portion of the parameter assignments are handled internally, so you can safely ignore them. Of interest to us are the button assignments: Negative, Positive, Alt Negative, and Alt Positive. Horizontal and Vertical are misleading, if you're used to a 3D world. Vertical is not up and down, as you'd assume, but forward and backward. Horizontal is a strafe (sideways move) left or right. At first glance, these don't make much sense in your 3D world, but if you picture early 2D games played on screen, you can see how the left and right arrows would move the cursor left and right on the horizontal X axis and the up and down arrows would move it up and down on the vertical Y axis. Tip the whole thing down to make the ground plane, and you can see why some 3D packages use Z as the up axis and why Unity calls its axes Vertical and Horizontal (see Figure 5-12).

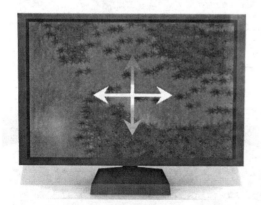 

Figure 5-12. *The origin of Unity navigation terminology. Left: The overhead view of a world where Vertical (on the monitor) moves you forward through the scene. Right: The directions tilted down to use in a 3D world*

The Vertical preset is perfect for our use, employing either the W and S keys or the up and down arrows to move forward or backward. The Horizontal preset needs a bit of modifying to disable the left and right arrow keys.

8. In Horizontal, delete the left and right entries for both the Negative Button and the Positive Button (see Figure 5-13).

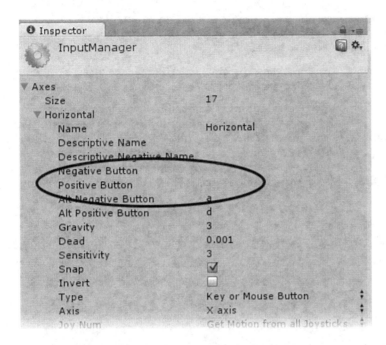

Figure 5-13. Left and right removed from the Horizontal preset

9. Click Play and test the left and right arrows.

The arrows no longer strafe.

10. Stop Play mode.

11. At the top of the Inspector, change the Size to **18**.

A duplicate of the last preset, Jump, is created.

12. Open the new preset and change its Name to **Turn**.

13. Change its Negative Button to **left** and its Positive Button to **right**.

14. Change its Sensitivity to **3**.

15. Because you just changed the game settings, now is a good time to save the project.

Now you have to see if the engine will recognize input from the new virtual key. The most logical place to test your new input preset is in the FPS Input Controller script. This is the script that processes the input from the player.

16. Select the FPS Input Controller script in the Project view ➤Standard Assets ➤ Character Controllers ➤ Sources ➤ Scripts. Use Ctrl+D (Cmd+D on the Mac) to duplicate the script.

17. Rename it to **FPAdventurerInputController**.

18. Double-click it to open it in the editor.

149

At line 4, you'll see a new function called Awake. It is a system function and is one of the very first to be evaluated when a game is started. Objects are created first, then scripts. Once the scripts exist, Awake is the first function to be called. You will make use of it in several of the later chapters.

Lines 36 and 37 are an oddity; they begin with an @ and don't end with a semicolon. These lines are not JavaScript, and their functions differ.

- The first, @script RequireComponent, checks to make sure a certain component is attached to the GameObject. If that component is missing, the RequireComponent attribute will add it, if it is missing when the script is first added to the object.

- The second, @script AddComponentMenu, adds this script to the Component menu, so you can easily access it when you want to add it to a new GameObject.

Fortunately, by definition, the whole purpose of @script lines is to do things for you, so you don't have to worry about them.

A familiar item in the script should be the Update function at line 9. Most of the script's contents, however, seem to be dealing with more vector math than you probably care to analyze. Traditionally, Unity books started with an in-depth analysis of the navigation scripts. Since the newer character controller scripts are three or four times larger and more complicated than their predecessors and this book is written more for artists, feel free to accept its functionality as is and be grateful for it.

■ **Important Concept**   You don't necessarily have to understand something to use it. People who get bogged down trying to understand every little detail rarely finish their first game. Don't expect the game to be perfect; you can always revisit it and make improvements as your understanding grows. In this project, we will be constantly improving and refining the scripts and functionality.

There should be a few more features that strike you as being vaguely familiar. Since you were just tweaking the Input settings, Input.GetAxis("Horizontal") and Input.GetAxis("Vertical") should stand out. While you shouldn't interfere with either of these, they should provide a clue as to how to check for input from your new preset, Turn.

Let's start with something simple.

1. Under the var directionVector = new Vector3 line, add the following:

    ```
    if (Input.GetAxis("Turn")) print  ("turning");
    ```

■ **Tip**   You can also use Debug.Log instead of print. This has the advantage of giving you more information, which may make more sense as you become more familiar with scripting.

---

2. Save the new script via the Editor's Save button or through the File menu.

3. Select the First Person Controller in the Hierarchy view.

4. In the Inspector, with the First Person Controller selected, click the browse icon next to the FPS Input Controller script and select our new version of it, FPAdventurerController.

■ **Tip** Replacing a script this way preserves the current values exposed in the Inspector, as long as the variable names have stayed the same.

5. Because you are changing the First Person Controller prefab in the Hierarchy, you may receive a warning about losing the prefab connection. If so, press Continue and click Play.

6. Click in the Game view and then try the arrow keys.

As soon as you press either the left or right key, the "turning" message appears in the status line. You haven't yet told the First Person Controller to turn, but at least you know it reads your code.

You can get a bit more information from Input.GetAxis. It returns a value between –1 and 1 as you press the two arrow keys.

7. Change that line to the following:

```
if (Input.GetAxis("Turn")) print ("turning " + Input.GetAxis("Turn"));
```

8. Save the script.

9. Click in the Game view and test the keys again.

The left arrow returns a value less than 0, and the right arrow returns a value greater than 0. This tells you which direction to turn. You will add the turn functionality next, but instead of adding it to the Update function, which is frame-dependent, you will use another system function, the FixedUpdate function. The FixedUpdate function is called at fixed intervals rather than every frame. While this function is primarily used for physics operations, it is handy for other functionality that needs to be consistent across different systems and throughout the game. This way, the turn speed should be about the same on an old machine as on the latest cutting-edge gaming system.

10. Delete the **if (Input.GetAxis("Turn"))** line you added to the script.

You are ready for the real functionality now. (Caution: scary math follows).

11. Add the following function above the // Require a character controller line at the bottom of the script:

```
//this is for the arrow turn functionality
function FixedUpdate () {

    if (Input.GetAxis("Turn")) {      // the left or right arrow key is being pressed
        // the rotation = direction * speed * sensitivity
        var rotation : float = ( Input.GetAxis("Turn") ) * rotationSpeed * rotationSensitivity ;
        // add the rotation to the current orientation amount
        rotation = rotation + transform.eulerAngles.y ;
        // convert degrees to quaternion for the up axis, Y
        transform.localRotation = Quaternion.AngleAxis ( rotation, Vector3.up ) ;

    }
}
```

12. Near the top of the script, just beneath the motor variable declaration, add the two variables needed to go along with the arrow turn code:

```
//add these for arrow turn
var rotationSpeed : float = 20.0;
internal var rotationSensitivity = 0.1 ; // This makes rotationSpeed more managable.
```

13. Save the script.

■ **Tip** When you are having trouble making a bit of code work, you can often get the help you need on the Unity forums. If you have more complex issues and not enough time to work them out on your own, you might consider trading art assets for code. One of the great things about the Unity forums is the Collaboration section. To get the rotation functionality nailed down quickly for a few key features of our game, I enlisted the help of the team at Binary Sonata Studios. Thanks guys!

---

14. Click in the Game window and test the keys again.

The left and right arrow keys now allow you to turn left and right in the scene.

15. Stop Play mode.

16. Save the scene and save the project.

Rotation math can be very complicated. Euler angles allow us to change rotations on X, Y, and Z axes independently, but they are subject to gimbal lock, which is when the camera is watching a target and must flip to continue. In Figure 5-14, the character on the left can watch the sphere as it goes around him by rotating around his vertical axis with no problems. The figure on the right rotates his head on a horizontal axis, but when the sphere goes overhead, he must turn 180 degrees on his vertical axis to continue watching it once it has passed overhead. With Euler angles, if a rotation involves multiple axes, it needs to be handled one axis at a time. Deciding which axis to solve first is often problematic.

Figure 5-14. Depiction of gimbal lock

Quaternions (complex numbers used to represent rotations) are not subject to gimbal lock but are more confusing to use without a good background in vector math (which is akin to voodoo for many of us). Quaternions use vectors to point in a given direction, so they can always rotate the objects on all axes simultaneously to get to the desired new vector with efficiency and stability.

On top of all of this, objects have both local (object space) and global (world space) rotation possibilities. To further complicate matters, transforms can be permanently changed, as in the editor, or temporarily changed, as in game animations.

When you see `transform.rotation` in a Unity script, it is referring to quaternions. When you see `transform.eulerAngles`, it is dealing with degrees. The numbers we see in the Inspector's Transform component for rotation show us `localEulerAngles`. Internally, Unity uses quaternions, but in scripting, you will see both used.

Bottom line: feel free to accept the navigation code as is (with no shame), so that you can continue with the game.

If you are still curious about rotation, try looking up "Quaternions and spatial rotation" in Wikipedia. While you are there, check out "gimbal" to see the origin of the term and a nice example of one in action.

Tweaking the Mouse Look

Before we change the existing `MouseLook` script, we need to define the required functionality. At the top of the functionality list is preventing it from working all the time. There's nothing worse than having the view spinning wildly as you try to position the cursor on an object in the scene for picking. The first thing the script will need is a conditional to tell it when it can be used. We will start with the basics and add to them.

1. Stop Play mode.

2. Select the `MouseLook` script in the Project view ➤ Standard Assets ➤ Character Controllers ➤ Sources ➤ Scripts.

3. Duplicate the script using Ctrl+D (Cmd+D on the Mac).

4. Rename it **MouseLookRestricted**.

Note the `.cs` extension. The `MouseLook` script looks a bit different as it is written in C# instead of JavaScript. The syntax is close enough in many cases for making minor adjustments. All of the other scripts you will create or deal with in this project are JavaScript.

5. Replace the `MouseLook` script for both the First Person Controller and the Main Camera with the new `MouseLookRestricted` in the Inspector, through the browser.

6. Double-check to make sure the First Person Controller is using the Mouse X axis and the Main Camera is using the Mouse Y axis (Figure 5-15).

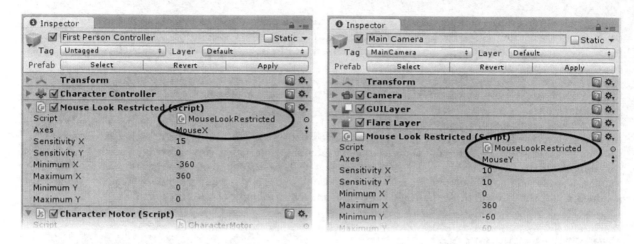

Figure 5-15. *The correct axes for the First Person Controller and Main Camera*

7. Turn on the MouseLookRestricted script on the Main Camera.

8. Open the MouseLookRestricted script in the script editor.

9. Inside the Update function (void Update ( )), just beneath the open curly bracket, add the condition so that it looks like this:

```
void Update ()
    {
    // only do mouse look if right mouse button is down
    if (Input.GetMouseButton ( 1 ) ) {
```

You can use curly brackets inline, as with the line containing the if conditional, or on a different line altogether, such as with the void Update ( ) line. Feel free to use whichever makes the script easier to read. The important point to remember is that, just as with parentheses, if you have an open one, you must have a closed one to match.

■ **Tip** In the MonoDevelop script editor, you can find the closing curly bracket that goes with an opening bracket by clicking just before or just after the opening bracket. The corresponding closing bracket will be highlighted a pale gray.

In this case, we are putting the entire contents of the Update function within the conditional, so the closing curly bracket will go right above the Update function's closing curly bracket.

10. Add the closing curly bracket one line above the curly bracket that closes the Update function (the only thing left below that in the script is a short Start function).

The final four lines of the Update function are as follows:

```
    transform.localEulerAngles = new Vector3(-rotationY, transform.localEulerAngles.y, 0);
    }
    } // add this to close the conditional
}
```

11. Select the original contents, right-click, and select Indent Select from the right-click menu.

Indenting text inside the conditional or other types of code blocks will make reading easier and help ensure parentheses and curly brackets match.

12. Save the script.

You should get an error on the status line, as shown in Figure 5-16.

⊘ Assets/Standard Assets/Character Controllers/Sources/Scripts/MouseLookRestricted.cs(18,14): error CS0101: The namespace `global::` already contains a definition for `MouseLook`

Figure 5-16. *One of many possible errors reported in the Console*

The status line tells us that the namespace global::' already contains a definition. Or if you are using a Mac, you may see "The class defined in script file named 'MouseLookRestricted' does not match the file name!" A quick look through the script shows that the script is referred to by name somewhere around lines 17 and 18.

13. Change those lines to reflect the new name.

```
[AddComponentMenu("Camera-Control/Mouse Look Restricted")]
public class MouseLookRestricted : MonoBehaviour {
```

14. Save the script.

The Console should clear itself of error messages.
Line 17 is interesting in that it shows how scripts can add to the Component menu for easy access.

15. From the Component menu ➤ Camera-Control, observe the new entry, Mouse Look Restricted, shown in Figure 5-17.

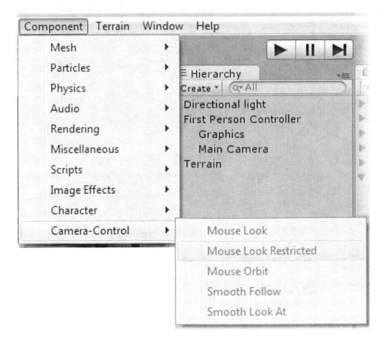

Figure 5-17. *The new menu item*

16. Stop Play mode.

17. Click Play and test.

■ **Tip** If you do a search in the Scripting Reference for `Input.GetMouseButton`, you will see that it "Returns whether the given mouse button is held down. /button/ values are 0 for left button, 1 for right button, 2 for the middle button."

You should now be able to mouse look when the right mouse button is held down ... unless you don't have a right mouse button!

If you are developing on a Mac or just want your executable to run on either a Mac or a PC, you'll need to add another option for the conditional. This time, we'll select a key that must be held down to enable mouse look.

To do this, we will need to introduce the or operator in the condition that must be met. The *or* operator uses two pipe characters, || (the shift character of the \ key).

1. Change the `if` line to include a check for the left Shift key:

```
if (Input.GetMouseButton ( 1 ) || Input.GetKey ("left shift") ) {
```

Note that the key name is all lowercase characters. The Scripting Reference indicates that `Input.GetKey()` "Returns true while the user holds down the key identified by name." In contrast, `Input.GetKeyDown()` "Returns true during the frame the user starts pressing down the key identified by name." This function represents a single event and, therefore, is not the one you need to use.

2. Save the script and test.

Now, mouse-button-impaired users can also take advantage of mouse look.

■ **Tip** See Appendix B for the names of the keyboard keys for use in scripts or search for Input Manager in the Unity Manual.

If the user tries to use the right Shift key instead of left Shift, she will find that it doesn't work. You should probably add the right Shift to round out the choices.

3. Add the right Shift option:

```
if (Input.GetMouseButton (1) || Input.GetKey ("left shift") ||
    Input.GetKey ("right shift")){
```

4. Save the script and test.

By now you're probably getting some idea about controlling input. A nice touch for WASD users would be to allow automatic mouse look while navigating the scene. You know when the player is navigating the scene because of the keys mapped out for this. To cover all of the possibilities, the conditional would be something like the following:

```
if (Input.GetKey ("up") || Input.GetKey ("down") ||Input.GetKey ("d") ||
    Input.GetKey ("s") || Input.GetKey ("w") || Input.GetKey ("a") || Input.GetKey
    ("left shift") || Input.GetKey ("right shift") || Input.GetMouseButton ( 1 ) ) {
```

Though this will certainly work as expected, it hardcodes the keys that must be used, some of which already have virtual counterparts in the Input Manager.

You have used `Input.GetAxis()` to get movement from the virtual buttons, but you will need something that returns a Boolean value (true or false) to check to see if our virtual buttons are being held down. That will be `Input.GetButton()`, which "Returns true while the virtual button identified by `buttonName` is held down."

Now you can simplify the condition by using the virtual buttons.

5. Change the `if` line to the following:

```
if (Input.GetMouseButton ( 1 ) || Input.GetKey ("left shift") ||
    Input.GetKey ("right shift") || Input.GetButton("Horizontal") ||
    Input.GetButton("Vertical") ) {
```

■ **Tip**   Make sure there is a || between each of the conditions and the code is all on one line, or you will get several errors.

---

6. Save the script and test.

Now, when the player is navigating the scene, the mouse look works automatically, as with regular shooter controls, but as soon as the player stops, the cursor can be moved around the scene without the world spinning dizzily.

At this point, it may have occurred to you that if you could create a virtual button for any keys that need to be held down when the user is not navigating, you could simplify things even more and consider yourself quite clever in the process. Let's create a new virtual button called ML Enable (Mouse Look Enable).

1. Stop Play mode.

■ **Tip**   As you experimented with the code in the `MouseLookRestricted` script, you were able to keep Unity in Play mode because saving the script re-compiled it, and the changes were picked up immediately in the `Update` function. If you had added changes to the `Start` function, you would have needed to restart Unity after each save so the new content could be used. `Awake` and `Start` are evaluated only at startup.

---

2. From Edit ➤ Project Settings, select Input.

3. Increase the array size to **19**.

4. Open the new Turn duplicate and name it **ML Enable**.

5. Add the shift keys and right mouse button into the Negative, Positive, and Alt Negative Button fields (see Figure 5-18).

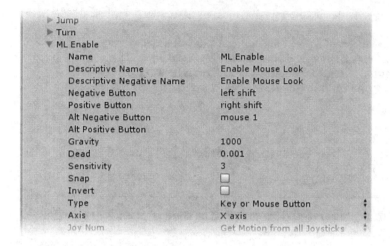

Figure 5-18. *The new ML Enable virtual button*

6.   Set the Descriptive Name to **Enable Mouse Look**.

Because the settings were inherited from the previous entry, yours may be different if you tweaked any of them. Now you can simplify the `if` conditional in the `MouseLookRestricted` script. At the same time,

7.   Change the line to the following:

```
if (Input.GetButton ("ML Enable") || Input.GetButton("Horizontal") ||
    Input.GetButton("Vertical") ) {
```

8.   Save the script.

9.   Click Play and test.

10. Save the project so you don't lose the new input assignment.

The functionality should remain the same.

As a final refinement, you can allow mouse look only on the X axis when the left or right arrows are pressed, so the player can mouse look up and down. The tricky part about this functionality is that the same script is used on the camera for X-axis rotation and on the First Person Controller for the Y-axis rotation. Because the left and right arrow keys rotate the first person on the Y axis, you must avoid multiple, possibly conflicting, input on the Y.

The script uses a variable named axes that lets the author choose the axis to rotate. Of the three choices, `RotationAxes.MouseXAndY`, `RotationAxes.MouseX`, and `RotationAxes.MouseY`, the only one that does not allow Y to rotate is `RotationAxes.MouseX`. The condition that must be met if the mouse look is allowed will be if either the Turn virtual button is pressed and the value of the axes variable is `RotationAxes.MouseX`. To ensure that the entire condition is evaluated together, you will wrap it in parentheses. The *and* in the conditional is written as a double ampersand, &&.

11. Finally, change the `if` line to the following:

```
if (Input. GetButton ("ML Enable") || Input.GetButton("Horizontal") ||
    Input.GetButton("Vertical") ||
    (Input.GetButton("Turn") && axes == RotationAxes.MouseY) ) {
```

12. Save the script.

13. Click Play and test the functionality.

The navigation for the game is now ready to use.

Now that you've altered a few scripts, you should start organizing your scripts for the game before they get out of hand.

1. Create a new folder in the Project view.

2. Name it **Adventure Scripts**.

3. From the Standard Assets ➤ Character Controllers ➤Sources ➤ Scripts folder, move the `FPAdventurerInputController.js` script into the new folder.

The `MouseLookRestricted` script is C# rather than JavaScript and needs to be left where it is. Unity compiles scripts according to where they are located, which can affect access to the scripts by other scripts. JavaScript is more forgiving, so you can move the other scripts where you please. All of the remaining scripts you'll work with or create are JavaScript.

4. Save the scene and save the project.

■ **Tip** You added three keys to be represented by your virtual ML Enable button, using three of the four button slots in the preset. If you need more than four keys or mouse buttons, you could add another preset using the same name.

At this point, you need to make an executive decision—a design decision. The other navigation inputs are handled only if the Collider is on the ground. If you want the player to be able to turn only while on the ground, you must add your code inside the `if (grounded)` conditional. If, however, you want the player to be able to "turn his head," or even "twist his body around," while in midair, the code should not be inside the conditional. Because the purpose of the game is entertainment, let's go with the latter.

Fun with Platforms

As a reward for getting through the navigation code, let's have a bit of fun using one of the features of the Character Motor script—the Platform functionality. Unless you are an experienced platform-jumper player, the thought of trying to navigate several fast-moving platforms may be intimidating. For an adventure game, however, you might want to make use of platforms that aren't challenging to use but add interest to navigating the environment. Many graphical adventure games of the pre-rendered era featured rendered sequences where the player was taken on wild rides through tunnels or on skyways. The book's game will feature a simple raft to allow the player access to a grotto behind a waterfall.

1. Select the First Person Controller.

2. Set its Y Rotation to **270** in the Inspector.

■ **Tip** This last step is optional, but will make the next couple of sections easier to follow. If you prefer to keep your First Person Controller looking in a different direction, just try to keep your scene looking similar to the screen shots.

---

3. Select the Main Camera from the First Person Controller object.

4. Use Align View to Selected to set the Scene view.

5. Create a Cube and name it **Platform**.

6. Change its Scale to **2** on the X, **0.3** on the Y, and **6** on the Z (see Figure 5-19).

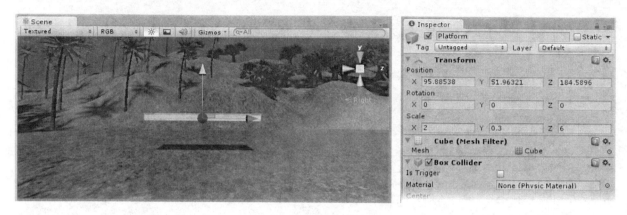

Figure 5-19. *The new Platform settings*

7. Move it down, so it just intersects with the ground.

8. Add a material, such as TestBark, to it (see Figure 5-20).

Figure 5-20. *The new platform*

Next, you will need to build a simple script to move the platform. You could feed numbers into it, but it will be easier to set up if you just create a couple of target objects to move between. I have borrowed the code from a script in an old Unity tutorial.

9. Select the Adventure Scripts folder.

10. Create a new JavaScript in it.

11. Name the script **PlatformMover**.

12. Open the script in the editor.

13. Replace the default functions with the following:

```
var targetA : GameObject;
var targetB : GameObject;

var speed : float = 0.1;

function FixedUpdate () {
        var weight = Mathf.Cos(Time.time * speed * 2 * Mathf.PI) * 0.5 + 0.5;
        transform.position = targetA.transform.position * weight +
                        targetB.transform.position * (1-weight);
}
```

■ **Tip**   Just in case the math for that last bit of code made your head hurt, you should know it originated from the 2D Gameplay tutorial. While it is currently not available through the Asset Store, a search of the forums should help you find a link to it. As recommended at the start, you can find all manner of useful code in tutorials for all different genres. Don't be afraid to copy, paste, and tweak—you never know what will prove useful in your game!

---

14. Save the script.

Plan Ahead

In the early stages of prototyping your game or even just testing techniques for functionality, it is tempting to go with the simplest solution. When you are dealing with animating objects, however, it is well worth a couple of extra steps to create a GameObject to hold the mesh and then put the animation on it instead of the mesh. This gives you the freedom to swap out early proxy objects with the final versions or add more objects to the group without having to redo the animation or triggers.

1. Focus the scene on the Platform by double-clicking the Platform in the Hierarchy view.

2. Create an Empty GameObject; it should be created in the same place as the Platform.

If the GameObject is not in the same place (especially the Y axis), you can copy the x, y, and z coordinates from the Platform's Transform component at the top of the Inspector to the new Empty GameObject's x, y and z.

3. Name it **Platform Group**.

4. Drag the `PlatformMover` script from the Project view onto the Platform Group object.

5. Drag the Platform into the Platform Group.

This script uses two target objects for its transforms. The variables that will hold them are defined as type GameObject. After you create a couple of targets, you'll have to drag the target objects onto the variables' value fields in the Inspector (see Figure 5-21).

Figure 5-21. *The Target A and B variables in the Inspector, waiting for GameObjects*

The Speed variable allows you to adjust the speed with which the platform will move between the targets.

Because you want the speed to be consistent regardless of frame rate or computers, it uses a FixedUpdate function.

Inside the FixedUpdate function, a cosine function is used in conjunction with the speed and target positions to move the platform between the targets (see Figure 5-22)

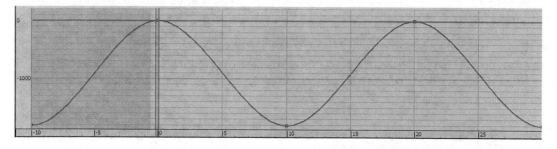

Figure 5-22. *A cosine function curve. With time on the horizontal and position on the vertical, you can see how the platform slows to a stop before reversing direction*

Theoretically, all you have to use for your target objects are a couple of empty GameObjects. The problem is that it would be difficult to get them positioned correctly without any geometry. As an alternative, you can clone the original platform, position it, and then remove its renderer and collider components.

6. Select the Platform object.

7. Use Ctrl+D (Cmd+D on the Mac) to make a duplicate of it.

8. Name it **PlatformMesh** and drag it out of the Platform Group.

9. Locate its Box Collider component in the Inspector.

10. Right-click the component label and choose Remove Component, as shown in Figure 5-23.

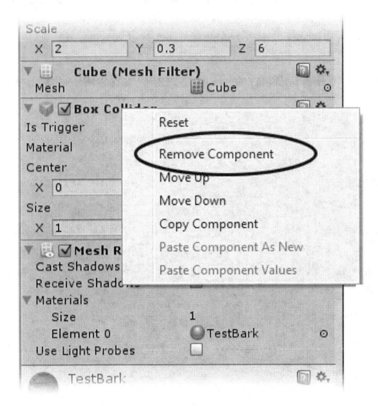

Figure 5-23. *Remove Component*

11. In the Mesh Renderer component, uncheck Cast Shadows and Receive Shadows.

At this point, you could clone the platform and finish the platform functionality, but in the spirit of getting in the habit of using an important Unity concept, let's create a prefab for extended use.

1. Create a new folder.

2. Name it **Adventure Prefabs**.

3. Select the new folder.

4. Right-click on top of it and create a new prefab.

5. Name the prefab **Platform Target**.

6. Drag the PlatformMesh object from the Hierarchy view onto the Platform Target prefab in the Project view.

The PlatformMesh is now an instance of the Platform Target prefab, and its white cube icon has turned blue.

7. Rename the PlatformMesh to **Target A**.

Because it is already in the same place as the original platform, you can leave it in place and use it as one of the target positions.

8. Drag the Platform Target prefab from the Project view into the Hierarchy view.

9. Name this one **Target B**.

10. In the Scene view, move Target B away from the platform in the Z direction (see Figure 5-24).

Figure 5-24. *The two target platforms (A is in place, over the original platform.)*

11. Select the Platform Group object.

12. Drag Target A and Target B from the Hierarchy view onto their target parameters in the Inspector, as shown in Figure 5-25.

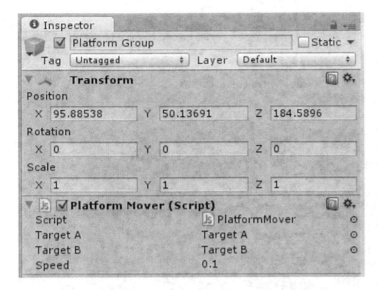

Figure 5-25. *The PlatformMover script with both targets loaded*

13. Click Play.

The PlatformGroup moves smoothly between the two targets.

Having positioned the targets, we can now turn off their MeshRenderers, so they will not be rendered in the scene. One of the beauties of the prefab is that by turning off *its* Mesh Renderer, it will be turned off in both of its children.

1. Stop Play mode.

2. Select the PlatformTarget prefab in the Project view.

3. Uncheck the Mesh Renderer component (see Figure 5-26).

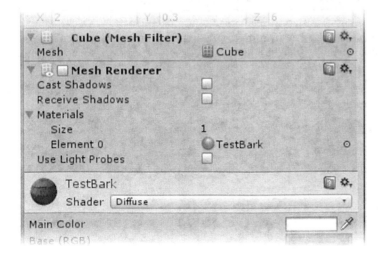

Figure 5-26. *Disabling the Mesh Renderer*

The two target platforms are no longer rendered in the scene.

4. Click Play.

5. Drive the First Person Controller onto the platform.

If your platform is low enough to drive onto, the First Person Controller gets taken for a ride. If not, use the spacebar to jump up onto your platform, or lower it so the First Person Controller can climb aboard (see Figure 5-27).

Figure 5-27. *Going for a ride*

The default platform functionality is only a starting point for serious platform jumpers. We don't need more than the basics for our game, so we just need to be aware of what it can and can't do. Let's investigate.

6. Drive off the platform and position the First Person Controller in the path of the platform.

Depending on your platform height, the platform may push the First Person Controller out of the way, or it may just go through it, occasionally picking it up and taking it for a ride. The important thing to note here is that the results are not consistent. You should investigate functionality fully, so you know its pros and cons before deciding to add it to your game and spending time on asset creation.

Let's see what happens if the platform is taller.

7. While still in Play mode, select the Platform object and change its Y Scale to **1**.

Half of the platform goes lower, but there's still have about half a meter aboveground.

8. Move into the path of the moving platform again.

This time, the platform passes through the First Person Controller every time, as shown in Figure 5-28.

Figure 5-28. *The taller platform ignores the First Person Controller*

9. As the platform approaches again, press the spacebar to jump on to it as it gets close.

You should now be riding the platform again.

If you drive at the taller platform, the First Person Controller might be stopped, but unless it is in motion, collision is not detected. While there are things you can do to overcome this effect, they are generally costly and not within the scope of this adventure game.

If you do want to use a moving platform in your game, you'll need to set up a system to prevent the player from getting near the platform while it is in motion. This could be a toll gate or barricade that the player can only enter at certain times. It could require the player to insert a token into a receptacle to activate the platform. You'd also need a means of preventing the player from jumping off the platform, which, of course, you'd have to disable to allow him to get off and on at the correct times. All of this is possible and would indeed increase player enjoyment of the game, but you should always be aware of the work involved.

1. Stop Play mode.

2. Select the PlatformTarget object in the Project view and turn its Mesh Renderer back on.

3. Select the Target B object and move it up about 10 meters in the Scene view.

4. Turn off the PlatformTarget's Mesh Renderer.

5. Click Play.

6. Take a ride on the lifting platform (see Figure 5-29).

Figure 5-29. *View from the top*

The First Person Controller is carried up to the new vantage point.

7. While you are up near the top, drive off the platform.

The First Person Controller falls gracefully to the ground.

Clearly, you will need to design carefully to deal with the various aspects of the functionality. While you might be happy to let the player jump off a funicular while it is in motion, you'd want to prevent him from landing where it will be able to pass through him on the way back down. As this is a more complicated problem to solve, you can leave it for now and tackle walls instead.

8. Stop Play mode.

9. Save your scene and save the project.

Collision Walls

In traveling around your terrain, you've had firsthand experience with the topography of both the terrain and the moving platform. You've also had a run-in or two with the collider on the banyan tree. You need colliders on anything you don't want the player to be able to pass through. Unity can generate Mesh Colliders for imported meshes, such as buildings, and offers several primitive colliders as well for more efficient collision detection.

As with the platform, walls in Unity have some peculiarities that need to be investigated.

1. Select the First Person Controller.

2. Use Align View to Selected from the GameObject menu.

3. Create a cube and position it in front of the First Person Controller but closer than the platform.

4. Name it **Wall.**

5. Set its Scale parameters to **0.3** for X, **5** for Y, and **6** for Z.

6. Move the wall up in the Y direction, so only a small bit intersects the ground.

7. Rotate it about **5** degrees on the Y, so it does not face the viewport exactly and the First Person Controller will approach it at a slight angle.

8. Drag the TestBark material onto it.

9. Zoom back in the viewport until you can see quite a bit above it (see Figure 5-30).

Figure 5-30. *The wall object and adjusted Scene view*

The green bounding box you see in the Scene view is the collider that was automatically generated when the cube was created. In the Inspector, you'll see that it is a simple Box Collider.

10. Click Play and drive into the wall.

The First Person Controller is stopped.

11. Use the spacebar to jump as you try to move forward.

It does not get you any farther.

12. Stop Play mode.

13. In the Inspector, rotate the wall to **20** degrees on its Z axis.

14. Click Play and drive at the wall again.

The First Person Controller may slide left or right along the wall as you continue to try to go forward, but it does not climb the wall.

15. Once again, use the spacebar to jump while trying to move forward.

This time, you can easily scale the wall and go over the top if you move at a bit of an angle.

While this may be quite entertaining, it means that your players can probably get to places you'd prefer they do not. You could turn off jumping altogether in the Motor script, but it does make navigation more interesting when allowed.

16.   Stop Play mode.

17.   Select the First Person Controller.

18.   In the Inspector, in the Jumping section of the Character Motor component, set the Base Height to **0.5** and the Extra Height to **0**.

19.   Click Play and attempt to climb or jump the wall again.

It is more difficult, but tenacious gamers may discover that moving sideways a bit as they jump and move forward will eventually allow them to reach the top.

■ **Tip**   Always assume that if something can be done, it will be done, regardless of how pointless it seems to you as the author of the game.

So far, you know that a player will not be able to scale a fully perpendicular wall. Anything with even a small degree of slope, however, is subject to abuse. Because Unity does not differentiate between floor and wall collision surfaces, you will need a way to prevent unwanted climbing of some buildings or other artifacts. Rather than getting deep into the Character Motor code and worrying about up vectors and the like, you will take the artist's way out and simply block access with a nonrendering planar object.

1.   Stop Play mode.

2.   Again, in the Character Motor component, temporarily set the Base Height to **3** and the Extra Height back to **1**.

3.   Create a Plane object and position it about three-quarters of the way up the wall.

4.   Adjust its size and position to make it an effective barrier, as shown in Figure 5-31.

Figure 5-31. *The plane in position as a ceiling*

5.   Click Play and test the new barricade.

The First Person Controller still gets through it.

6.   Select the plane.

7.   Rotate the Scene view until you can see underneath the plane (see Figure 5-32).

Figure 5-32. *The underside of the plane*

And nothing shows!

In the Inspector, you'll see that the plane has a Mesh Collider. Because there are no faces on the backside of the plane, no collision detection is taking place. The other collider types (Box, Sphere, and Capsule) use only the primitive shape of their collider and are not dependent on the object mesh for collision.

It would seem you could solve the problem by flipping the plane over.

8.   Set the plane's X rotation to **180**, as shown in Figure 5-33.

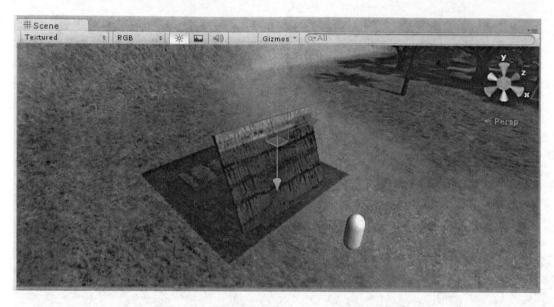

Figure 5-33. The plane flipped upside down. Note the orientation of the Transform Gizmo and also, if you are using Unity Pro, that shadows are cast regardless of the plane's orientation

9. Make sure the coordinate system is set to Local.

10. Click Play and try to jump over the wall again.

This time, the First Person Controller hits the ceiling and falls back down.

Since you can now see the plane from the underside, you need to either turn off its Mesh Renderer or remove that component altogether.

11. Stop Play mode.

12. Select the Plane.

13. Right-click over the Mesh Renderer component and Remove it.

The plane is no longer drawn in the Game view, but the Mesh Collider is drawn in the Scene view (see Figure 5-34).

Figure 5-34. *The Plane's Mesh Collider showing now that the Mesh Renderer has been removed*

Another experiment worth trying is to see what happens to the First Person Controller when the platform rises through it.

14. Move the plane so it is in the path of the rising platform.

15. Click Play and jump onto the platform.

When the First Person Controller gets to the plane, it is pushed down through the platform. Apparently, the First Person Controller is inheriting the movement from the platform, and collision detection against the plane is registered.

A final test might provide the means for keeping the player from jumping off a moving platform.

16. Set the Z rotation of the plane to **90** degrees in the Inspector (see Figure 5-35).

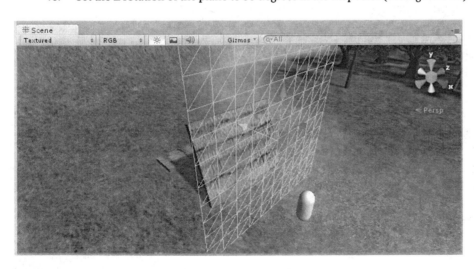

Figure 5-35. *The Plane as an invisible wall*

17.   Click Play and try to drive through the invisible plane.

You will find that you can pass through it from the back side but not the front side.

If you surround the platform with planes for collision, you could allow the player to get onto the platform, but not off, thereby preventing him from jumping off midway.

The problem then becomes how to let him disembark when he reaches the plane's destination.

18.   Stop Play mode.

19.   Select the plane.

20.   In the Inspector, in the Plane's Mesh Collider component, check Is Trigger.

21.   Click Play.

22.   Now try going through the plane from both sides.

The collider no longer acts as a barrier.

Let's create a simple script to toggle the `IsTrigger` variable off and on with a key press. Before assuming that a particular functionality will work, you should always test first.

23.   Select the My Scripts folder.

24.   Create a new JavaScript.

25.   Name it **ToggleIsTrigger**.

26.   Open it in the script editor.

In this script, you will watch for a key down in the `Update` function. When one is detected, you will call another function that you will create—a user-defined function. If you think that you'll use a particular procedure over and over and call it from different places or objects, it may be worth putting in its own function. An example might be a three-way light switch. Three separate switches can toggle the light off and on, but only the light contains the code to handle the functionality. Each of the switches would call the light's on/off function. In the case of the `IsTrigger` toggle, you might test it with a key press, but later you might have to press a button to toggle it or even let it be triggered by some other event. You will name the function `ToggleTrigger`.

27.   Change the `Update` function as follows:

```
function Update () {

    // call the ToggleTrigger function if the player presses the t key
    if (Input.GetKeyDown ("t")) ToggleTrigger();

}
```

■ **Tip**   When a method or object-specific function returns a Boolean value, true or false, there is no need use the `==` operator. In the conditional you just wrote, the `if(Input.GetKeyDown("t"))` could also be written as `if(Input.GetKeyDown("t") == true)` and produce the same results.

Now, let's create the `ToggleTrigger` function. You'll need to check the state of the collider's `isTrigger` variable and then reset it, depending on the result. At its simplest, you could write it in just a few lines.

28.   Add the following somewhere below the Update function:

```
function ToggleTrigger () {

    if (collider.isTrigger == true) collider.isTrigger = false;
    else collider.isTrigger = true;

}
```

When you are first testing code and functionality, it's worth adding some print statements, so you can see what's happening. Note that the if conditional doesn't require curly brackets as long as only one command is given, if the condition evaluates to true (the if), or only one is specified, when the condition does not evaluate to true (the else).

Think of the if and else as hands that can each hold only one object. The curly brackets are like a shopping bag—the hands still hold a single object (the shopping bag), but the bag can contain lots of objects.

29.   Change the ToggleTrigger function to include a couple of print statements:

```
function ToggleTrigger () {

        if (collider.isTrigger == true) {
                collider.isTrigger = false;
                print ("Closed");
        }
        else {
                collider.isTrigger = true;
                print ("Opened");
        }
}
```

30.   Save the script.

■ **Tip**   Function names always start with a capital letter. Like variable names, function names may not contain spaces, start with numbers or special characters, or be reserved words. To make the names easier to read, you will often see underscores instead of spaces, or the first letter of each word capitalized.

---

31.   Drag the ToggleIsTrigger script onto the Plane object.

32.   Click Play.

33.   Select the Plane, then click in the Game window to change focus.

34.   Watch its Is Trigger parameter in the Inspector.

35.   Press the t key to toggle the Is Trigger off and on. Try driving forward and backward through the invisible plane.

You should be able to drive through from both sides when Is Trigger is turned on, but only from the back side if Is Trigger is off.

So far, you have used the IsTrigger parameter for one of its side effects—to turn off physical collision. Its intended purpose is to allow an object, such as the First Person Controller, to trigger an event or action by passing into or out of a (frequently) non-rendered object containing a collider.

Returning to our hypothetical light example, picture a long hallway with sensor lights. Each light has a zone that when entered turns the light on and when exited turns the light off. The zones are Box colliders, and you can use the OnTriggerEnter and OnTriggerExit functions to trap the events and send the message to the light.

Without going to the trouble of creating collision walls for the platform, you can still get a feel for how you can use a collider to manipulate the isTrigger parameter of other colliders. Let's set up a GameObject that will turn the isTrigger parameter of the plane off and on when the platform enters and exits its collider.

36. Stop Play mode.

37. Deactivate the Wall object by unchecking the box at the top of the Inspector (see Figure 5-36).

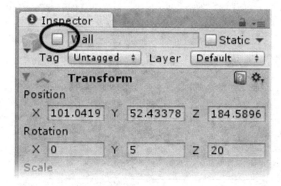

Figure 5-36. *The activate checkbox for the Wall object*

■ **Tip** Deactivating an object not only prevents it from being drawn in the scene, it also disables its collider and any other components. Note that the object's name is grayed out in the Hierarchy. You will make good use of the Active property of GameObjects when you start adding interactive objects as the game progresses.

---

1. Select the PlatformTarget in the Project view and turn on the Mesh Renderer.

2. Create an Empty GameObject.

3. Name it **TheTrigger**.

4. With TheTrigger still selected, choose Physics from the Components menu and add a Box Collider.

5. Scale the collider by using the X, Y, and Z Size parameters in the Box Collider component in the Inspector.

6. Position the collider so it is high enough off the ground to prevent the First Person Controller from running into it and so it is stretched between the two platform targets as shown in Figure 5-37.

Figure 5-37. *The Trigger's collider sized and positioned*

Make sure to check the collider in a Top view for alignment and position (see Figure 5-38).

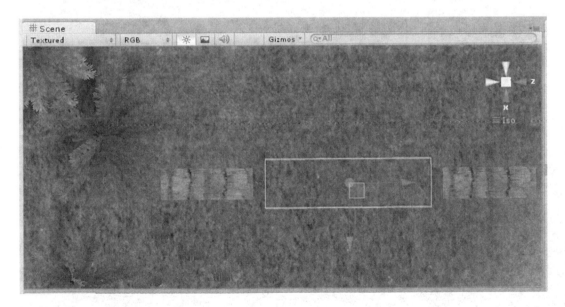

Figure 5-38. *The Top view of the collider*

7. Make sure TheTrigger is selected, so you can see the collider in the Scene view.

8. Click Play.

9. Move the First Person Controller onto the moving platform.

The First Person Controller is pushed off the platform as the platform moves into the collider (see Figure 5-39).

Figure 5-39. *First Person Controller being pushed off the platform*

10. Stop Play mode.

11. Check the Is Trigger parameter in the Inspector.

12. Click Play and test.

The First Person Controller no longer gets pushed off the platform (see Figure 5-40).

Figure 5-40. *The First Person Controller is no longer affected by the collider*

Now, you need to create a script that sends a message to the plane to tell it to toggle its Is Trigger parameter.

1. Stop Play mode.

2. Select the My Scripts folder.

3. Create a new JavaScript.

4. Name it **SendMessageOnTrigger** .

5. Open it in the editor.

6. Delete the default functions and add the following:

```
var sendToObject  : GameObject;

function OnTriggerEnter (object : Collider) {

        // call the function on the specified object
    sendToObject.SendMessage("ToggleTrigger");
}
```

Let's see what is happening with this function. The variable sendToObject is defined as a GameObject type, but the value is not yet provided. SendToObject will be the object that contains the script with the ToggleTrigger function you need to call. As with the platform targets, you will have to drag and drop the actual object into it in the Inspector. The reason you can't specify the object when you declare the variable is that variables are read into the system before any of the scene objects are loaded and, therefore, do not yet exist.

The OnTriggerEnter function is an event-type function that is called when another object's collider first enters its collider. With the argument object : Collider, the colliding object is returned in case you need to do any condition-checking with it. The argument, the local variable object, is declared as a Collider type. It gets its value, the colliding object's collider, when the event happens. Because it is a local variable, it is destroyed as soon as the function is finished, thereby freeing memory. You don't have to use the word *var* because it is understood that the argument is a variable.

The guts of the function, SendToObject.SendMessage("ToggleTrigger"), looks through the sendToObject's scripts for one with a function named ToggleTrigger. When it finds one, it calls that script.

1. Stop Play mode.

2. Save the script.

3. Drag it onto TheTrigger.

4. Drag the Plane object onto its Send To Object parameter in the Inspector.

5. Click Play and watch the status line to see when the plane is "opened" or "closed."

Nothing appears to be happening.

6. Drive the First Person Controller onto the platform and let it go for a ride.

Now, the status line reports when the plane's Is Trigger parameter is being toggled.

The Scripting Reference for OnTriggerEnter tells us that "trigger events are only sent if one of the colliders also has a rigidbody attached." You can't see it, but the First Person Controller has its own simplified version of a rigidbody. To make the platform trigger the OnTriggerEnter event, you will have to add a rigidbody component to it.

7. Stop Play mode.

8. Select the Platform Group object.

9. From the Component menu ➤ Physics, select Rigidbody.

10. Click Play.

The intersection with TheTrigger is now registering, but the platform is sinking lower and interacting with the ground.

1. Stop Play mode.

2. Uncheck the Rigidbody's Use Gravity parameter in the Inspector.

3. Click Play.

The Platform triggers the intersection and no longer sinks.
Let's not forget to test it with the First Person Controller.

4. Drive the First Person Controller to the platform and jump aboard.

If the First Person Controller doesn't jump cleanly onto the platform, the platform skews wildly and the First Person Controller eventually falls off. There seems to be a small problem . . . .

5. Stop Play mode.

6. In the Rigidbody component, check Is Kinematic.

7. Click Play and take the First Person Controller for a ride on the platform again.

Everything works as expected now. While the Rigidbody is marked isKinematic, it will not be affected by collisions, forces, or any other part of physX. Is Kinematic tells the engine not to use any of the regular physics parameters but allows collision testing to be more efficient.

■ **Rule** A Static Collider is a GameObject that has a Collider but not a Rigidbody. You should never move a Static Collider on a frame-by-frame basis. Moving Static Colliders will cause an internal recomputation in PhysX that is quite expensive and which will result in a big drop in performance. On top of that, the behavior of waking up other Rigidbodies based on a Static Collider is undefined. Colliders that move should always be Kinematic Rigidbodies, if you do not want any physics calculations performed.

---

8. Select the PlatformTarget prefab in the Project view and deactivate its Mesh Renderer.

Now that you've had a first look at triggering events, let's get back to the SendMessageOnTrigger script. The script toggles the plane's Is Trigger parameter only when the collider is entered. If you were using the script to affect collision walls around the platform, you would want the exit event to toggle the plane's Is Trigger as well. As you might guess, there is an OnTriggerExit function.

1. Copy the OnTriggerEnter function and paste it below the original.

2. Change Enter in the name to **Exit**.

3. Save the script.

4. Watch the status line.

The message from the Plane's ToggleTrigger function shows that it is now being called when the platform enters the collider and exits it.
Let's not forget the First Person Controller.
Jump the First Person Controller onto the platform and watch the status line.

Now both objects, the First Person Controller and the platform, trigger the function call, so the messages change quickly or don't appear to change at all. If you open the Console, you'll see that the function is working. (The Console can be opened through the Window menu or by the keyboard shortcut found there.) It is now overworking, in fact. This is where the argument that reports the colliding object comes in handy.

5. Inside both `OnTrigger` functions, just above the `sendToObject.SendMessage` line, add the following line:

```
print (object.name); // this is the name of the object triggered the event
```

6. Save the script and watch the results in the Console (see Figure 5-41).

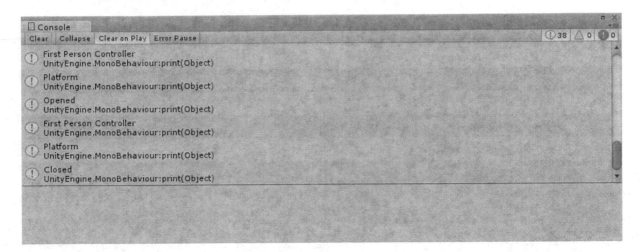

Figure 5-41. *The triggering objects being reported in the Console*

Object Names

The most important concept to understand here is that an object's name does not represent the object. The name is only another parameter of the object. This is another reason why you can't type an object name as the value of a variable. The name is of type String. It is just a string of characters and does not represent the actual object.

For the script, you need to determine if the colliding object is the one you are interested in. In a shooter-type game, you're less interested in the colliding object specifically and more interested in generalities. If the object is a projectile, it needs to send a message to whatever it hit to take damage points or even be destroyed. For this adventure game, you need to be more specific. Let's add a variable that holds the only object we want to trigger the send message. You may be thinking that the Platform Group is the collider, because that was what we added the rigidbody to, but a check of the Console printout shows us that the Platform itself is what has the collider and was passed in as an argument (another good reason to print out the colliding objects).

1. In the `SendMessageOnTrigger` script, add the following variable beneath the `var sendToObject` line at the top of the script:

```
var correctObject: GameObject; //this is the only object we allow to trigger the event
```

2. Save the script.

3. Drag the Platform object onto the Correct Object parameter in the Inspector (see Figure 5-42).

Figure 5-42. *The loaded parameters*

4. Change the `sendToObject.SendMessage` line in both `OnTrigger` functions to the following to add the conditional:

`if(object == correctObject.collider) sendToObject.SendMessage("ToggleTrigger");`

5. Now, the only time the `ToggleTrigger` function will be called is when the argument (a collider object) that is passed in on intersection matches the collider component of the object you specified as the correct object. Comment out or delete the two print statements.

6. Save the scene and save the project.

Your First Build

Now that you can travel around the environment and interact with some of it, you may as well try your first build. Because the project already contains three scenes, you'll need to specify which one you want.

1. From the File menu, select Build Settings (see Figure 5-43).

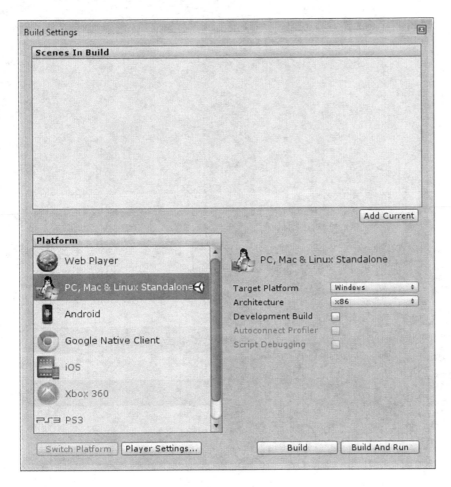

Figure 5-43. *The Build Settings window*

2. Click the Add Current button at the lower right of the Scenes In Build window (see Figure 5-44).

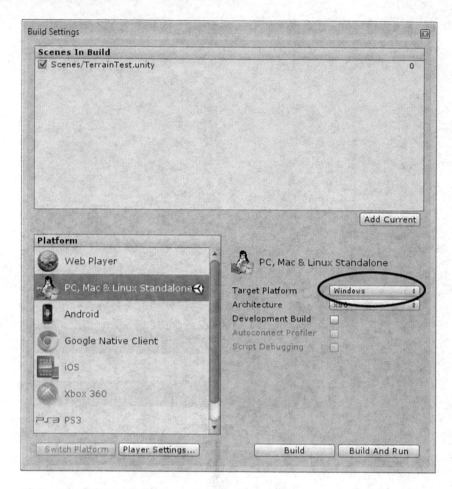

Figure 5-44. *The Build Settings window with the current scene loaded*

3.   If there are any other scenes there that are checked, uncheck them.

4.   Select your Target Platform as Windows or Mac.

5.   Click Build and Run.

You will be prompted to give a file name and location.

6.   Name your scene **Chapter5Navigation.exe**.

As indicated by the button name, the game will be built and then immediately run.

The first thing you'll see is the configuration window (see Figure 5-45), where the user can choose screen resolution and see or change the keyboard and mouse mapping. You will learn how to suppress this dialog to prevent the player from setting up conflicting keyboard controls later on.

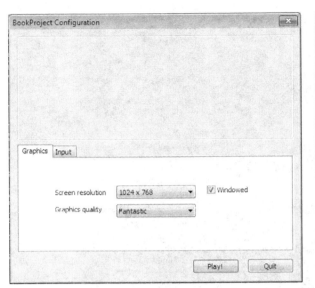
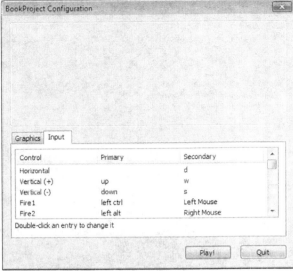

Figure 5-45. The configuration and Input windows in Windows (It will be slightly different on a Mac.)

    7.   Click the Input tab.

A pruned-down version of the Input Manager appears with all of the key assignments (see Figure 5-45).

When creating a Unity .exe for Windows deployment, you will have the .exe file and a folder of the same name that contains the data (see Figure 5-46). If you wish to share your file at that stage, you will need to distribute both the folder and the .exe. For Mac deployment, you'll get one package with everything in it.

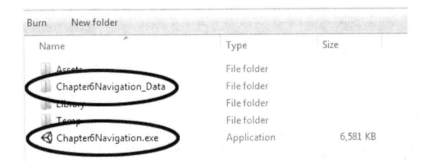

Figure 5-46. The files associated with the runtime application in Windows

    8.   Click Play and test the scene (see Figure 5-47).

Figure 5-47. *The scene running as an .exe*

Don't forget the invisible wall: the platform will toggle it off and on, or you can use the t key.

Defining Boundaries

You may have discovered that you can fall off the edge of the world. Even with steep mountains around the edges, you can still use the jump technique to climb to the top and then jump off. If you think about what you've learned about collisions walls, you know you need something perfectly perpendicular to foil those pesky jumpers and climbers. You've seen a planar object used to provide a collision wall, but you've no doubt noticed that there's no Plane Collider, so you can assume it's not very economical. The best choice is a Box Collider for each side.

1. Use the Scene Gizmo to get to a Top view of the scene.

2. Zoom out in the Scene view until you can see the edges of the terrain, as shown in Figure 5-48.

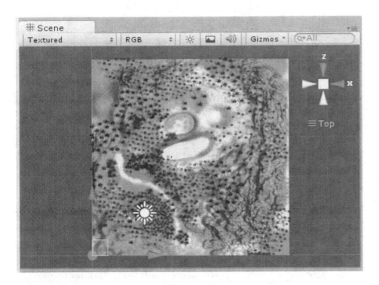

Figure 5-48. *The edges of the known world*

3. Create an Empty GameObject.

4. Name it **Terrain Boundaries**.

5. Create another Empty GameObject.

6. Name it **Boundary1**.

7. Add a Box Collider to Boundary1.

8. Adjust the Collider's Size to create a thin wall at the edge of the terrain.

9. Drag it into the Terrain Boundaries object.

10. Clone Boundary1 to create the remaining three sides (see Figure 5-49).

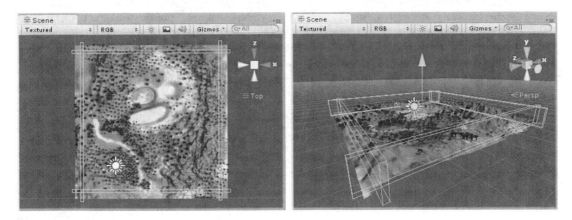

Figure 5-49. *The scene boundaries*

11. Save the scene and save the project.

Summary

In this chapter, you added player navigation to your test terrain by starting with the First Person Controller prefab and making a few changes. With the help of the Input Manager, you modified the shooter-type controls, WASD, to allow less-experienced gamers to use the arrow keys to turn instead of strafe. Next, you added the code for arrow turning in the FPS Input Controller script to create your own version of the script, the FPAdventurerController. Because the arrow turns needed to be frame rate–independent, you added that code to the FixedUpdate function rather than the regular Update function, as FixedUpdate is checked at set intervals rather than every frame.

In your version of the MouseLook script, MouseLookRestricted, you restricted mouse look to require the shift keys, the right mouse button, or any of the regular navigation keys. The restriction on the mouse look functionality will enable your player to interact with or pick objects in the scene without having the view spin wildly as he or she tries to put the cursor over a particular object.

By using the concept of the virtual buttons created in the Input Manager, you were able to use Input.GetButton after creating your own virtual buttons, instead of hardcoding each individual key or mouse button with Input.GetKey and Input.GetMouseButton. You used the logical and, &&, and the logical or, ||, to expand your conditional statements to check for multiple conditionals.

From another component of the First Person Controller, the CharacterMotor script, you found where you could fine-tune navigation speeds and functionality. As one of the options was to enable platform functionality, you experimented with a simple moving platform to explore its capabilities and limitations. You discovered that your platform didn't exhibit behavior sufficiently consistent to use without a lot of extra thought and design.

With the platform targets, you learned to create prefabs for objects that would have multiple instances in a scene, to allow for more economical handling. You found you could remove or disable components such as the Mesh Renderer or Colliders to streamline the functionality of your objects.

This introduced the concept of collision walls to block the player from going through objects. You discovered that a fully perpendicular wall will stop the First Person Controller from getting through an object with a collider, but that if the wall was not perpendicular, the player could possibly use the jump action to climb the wall. Rather than delving into mathematical calculations to prevent this, you found that a simple plane object with its Mesh Collider would effectively block the action.

During your experiments with the plane object, you found that a collider's Is Trigger parameter would let you pass through an object and even trigger an event, as long as one of the objects, or its children, also contained a rigidbody component. You learned that an object that moves without the help of physics should contain a rigidbody marked as Is Kinematic. With the help of the SendMessage function, you learned how to call functions when intersection was caught by the OnTriggerEnter and OnTriggerExit event functions. You also found that a GameObject's name was merely a parameter of the object, of type String, and did not represent the GameObject itself. Finally, you built your first .exe of the scene, only to discover you still needed to create collision walls around the perimeter of the terrain.

In the next chapter, you will be developing the cursor functionality so that you can have full control over its behavior. Cursors, after all, are key to the point-and-click adventure genre.

CHAPTER 6

■ ■ ■

Cursor Control

In point-and-click games, cursors are a large part of the user experience. Besides showing the user where the cursor pick point is, they often give the user clues as to when they are over an action object and even the type of interaction expected. If it's done well, cursor functionality in games is taken for granted by the player. Surprisingly, there are a lot of design decisions you will have to make to achieve that level of invisibility. In this chapter, you will be confronting many of the issues and testing various solutions, as you find out how they are handled in the Unity game engine.

Currently, Unity has a few different systems for creating GUI (graphical user interface) elements. The older system uses gameObjects that live in 2D space on the screen. The other system is fully script-based and doesn't exist until you are in Play mode. A third system is under development and was not yet available for beta when this book was being updated. To make the decision more difficult, in 4.0, Unity provided a means of replacing hardware cursors with your own images. While this solves a lot of issues, the size is limited to 32×32 pixels on some operating systems. You will be experimenting with a few different options.

As with most problem solving, it is usually best to start simple and then add more or better functionality a little at a time. You will start by manipulating the default operating system cursor.

Cursor Visibility

One of the more confusing problems when first learning to script in Unity is knowing where to put the bit of code shown in the Scripting Reference or other sample source for testing. Because the cursor is not related to a particular object in the scene, the code to control it could go in any script's Update function, because it must be checked every frame. For this test, you will create an empty GameObject to hold your small test script.

1. Open the TerrainTest scene in Unity that you created in the previous chapter.

2. Save the scene as **CursorControl** in the Scenes folder.

3. Deactivate the Plane, the Wall, and TheTrigger at the top of the Inspector.

4. Save the scene.

Before going any further, let's also turn the print statement on a script that stays active.

5. In the FPAdventureController script, delete or comment out the
   if(Input.GetAxis("Turn")) print... line.

6. Save the script.

Now you're ready for some more tests.

7. Create an empty GameObject.

8. Name it **ScriptHolder**.

9. In the My Scripts folder, create a new JavaScript.

10. Name it **HideCursor**.

11. Open it in the script editor.

It's time for a design decision. You know you don't want the cursor to appear when the player is navigating the scene, so you have to check for the virtual buttons involved in navigation: Horizontal, Vertical, and Turn. If any of them is being pressed, the cursor should be hidden. The decision is whether to have it show during mouse look, while the player is stationary. Because looking is a type of navigation, let's include the virtual ML Enable button in the conditional (but you may leave it out if you wish).

1. To hide the operating system cursor, add the following lines inside the Update function:

```
if (Input. GetButton ("Horizontal") || Input. GetButton ("Vertical") ||
   Input. GetButton ("Turn") || Input.GetButton("ML Enable") ){
   // a navigation key is being pressed, so hide the cursor
   Screen.showCursor = false; // hide the operating system cursor
   }
```

2. Just above the last curly bracket of the Update function, add:

```
else {
// no navigation keys are being pressed, so show the cursor again
Screen.showCursor = true; // hide the operating system cursor
}
```

3. Save the script.

_____

■ **Note** In your conditional, you have used Input.GetButton, because it returns a true-or-false value when the virtual button or key is down. You could also use Input.GetAxis, even though it returns numbers, which may be less intuitive at this stage but slightly more efficient. If you eventually plan on creating apps for iPhone or iPad, Input.GetAxis is the one to use, because mobiles have no mouse button functionality!

_____

4. Drag it onto the ScriptHolder object in the Hierarchy view.

5. Click Play and test navigation.

The cursor may or may not disappear as expected. If not, it should in maximize mode.

6. Turn off Play mode.

7. At the top of the Game window, turn on Maximize on Play (Figure 6-1).

Figure 6-1. *Maximize on Play*

8. Now click Play.

The Game view window is maximized (Figure 6-2), and now the cursor behaves as expected: it disappears when you are moving.

Figure 6-2. *The maximized game window*

9. Turn off Play mode and turn off Maximize on Play.

Let's see what happens when the First Person Controller is riding on the platform.

10. Click Play again.

11. Drive the First Person Controller onto the platform.

The cursor is visible while the First Person Controller is passively riding the platform. On the off chance you want to have an action object that the player must interact with while en route, such as picking an orchid off a rocky cliff face or stealing an egg out of a bird's nest, you can consider it acceptable.

12. Stop playback.

Custom Cursors

As mentioned, a big part of point-and-click adventure games is the cursor. In the first-person variety, when navigation stops, the user is free to scan the objects in the view, or frustum, to see if any objects are action objects.

■ **Tip** The viewing *frustum* is the area of the 3D world that can be seen within the game's viewport at runtime or in Play mode. If the player turns, and an object is no longer visible in the scene, it is considered "out of the frustum." The state of an object in respect to the frustum is important in that any manner of things can be done to improve frame rate, such as stopping calculations on looping animations.

For your purposes, you will consider an action object something that can be put into inventory or will animate when picked; it's something that is a critical part of the game/story.

Typically, to identify an action object, the cursor might change color or appearance. In more stylized games, the action object itself might change color or tint. Once the cursor picks an object, it will usually either be turned off while the object animates or, if the object is an inventory object, it (or a 2D icon representing it) could become the cursor. One of the fun features of adventure games is finding out which items can be combined to make a new, more useful object.

In Unity, 2D sprites and GUI (Graphical User Interface) objects are handled quite differently than 3D mesh objects. Unity's camera-layering system allows you to overlay mesh objects onto your 3D world space, but the mesh objects rarely appear scaled to fit the objects with which you wish to interact, depending on the player's location in the scene. Using 2D textures as cursors will involve a little work but provides a great amount of flexibility, especially if you wish to use cursors larger than 32×32 pixels.

Cameras have a built-in GUI layer that automatically draws 2D objects into 2D screen space, layered on top of the 3D world. UnityGUI is a purely scripted means of drawing 2D objects onto the screen; it's handy for menus and controls but is less intuitive for artists and designers with no scripting experience. To start, you'll experiment with a tangible object that can be seen and manipulated from the Hierarchy view.

GUI Texture Cursor

1. In the Project view, create a new folder.

2. Name it **Adventure Textures**.

3. From the Assets menu, select Import New Asset.

4.   From the book's Chapter 6 Assets folder, select GamePointer.tif (Figure 6-3).

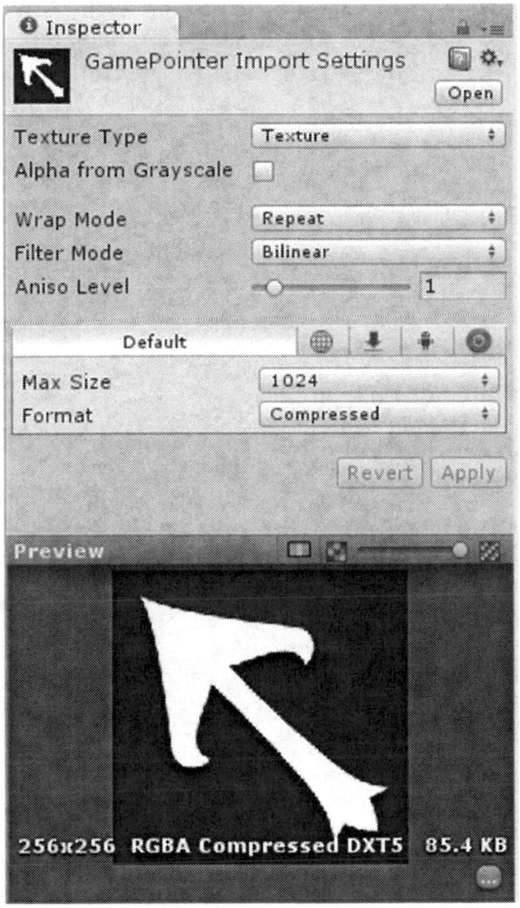

Figure 6-3. *The GamePointer image in the Inspector*

5.   Select the image in the Project view.

Texture Importer

The Texture Importer comes with several handy presets, as well as the Advanced option for full control. Let's take a quick look at it, just to see the possibilities.

1.   In the Texture Type drop-down at the top of the Texture Importer, select Advanced (Figure 6-4).

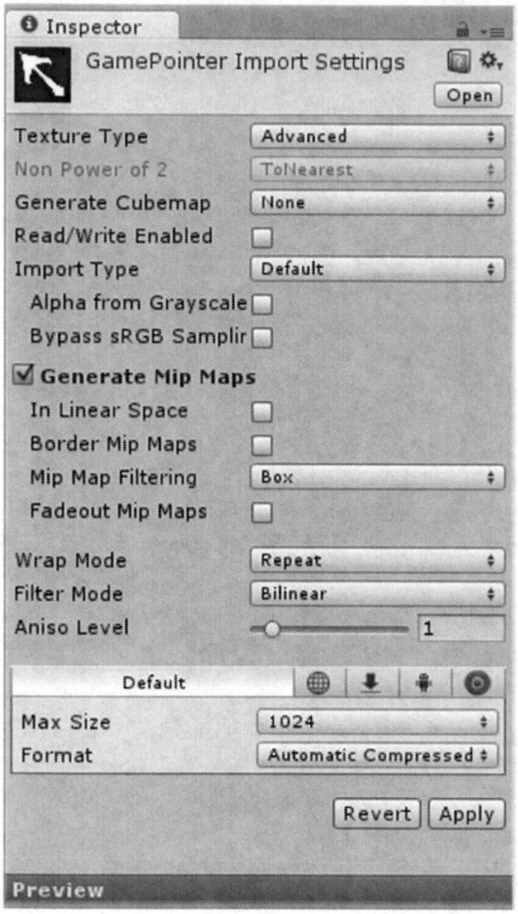

Figure 6-4. *The advanced parameters*

Take a look at the parameters in the Inspector (see preceding Figure 6-4). Because the texture will only be used as a cursor in 2D screen space, it doesn't have to be Mip mapped. This will save memory.

MIP MAPPING

Mip mapping is when an image is copied and reduced in size and clarity to provide blurrier images at greater distances. This reduces the nasty flickering as the view is changed. As an example, picture a black-and-white checker texture. As the texture gets farther back into 3D space, there are fewer and fewer pixels to represent the black checkers and the white checkers. At some point, it is a tossup as to whether the pixel will be black or white. In one frame, it may be black, but in the next, it may be white. This causes a flickering known as *artifacting*. By scaling the image down by powers of two, the successive images are blurrier and blurrier, eliminating or greatly reducing artifacting.

Mip Maps for a checker texture at 256, 128, 64, and 32

You may also notice in the Preview window that the image is shown as an RGBA Compressed DXT5 image. Unity converts image formats to the .dds format, so feel free to use larger file size images, such as .tif, .psd, and others.

▓ **Tip** Unity automatically updates images when changes are made to them, so you may indulge yourself and leave them in a layered format in the Assets folder.

Fortunately, your needs for the GamePointer image are simple, so you can use a preset.

2.   From the Texture Type drop-down, select GUI.

3.   Just above the Preview window, click Apply.

The image is ready to use (Figure 6-5).

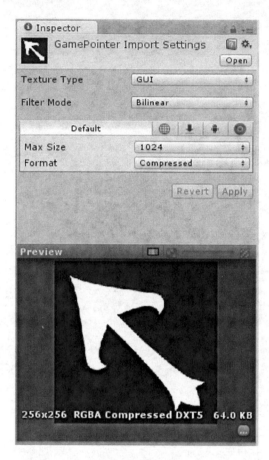

Figure 6-5. The texture as GUI import type

4. With the image still selected in the Project view, from the GameObject menu ➤ Create Other, select GUI Texture (Figure 6-6).

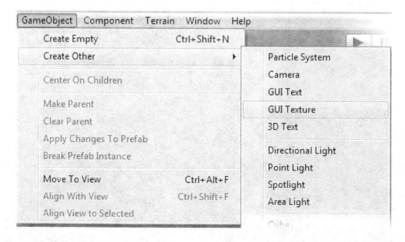

Figure 6-6. New GUI Texture

The image appears in the middle of the Game view (Figure 6-7).

Figure 6-7. *The new GUI Texture in the Game view*

When created by selecting the texture first, the new GUI Texture object is given the name of the texture.

   5.   If you choose to use your own texture, rename the new GUI Texture object GamePointer.

■ **Tip**   When an image is selected before the GUI Texture gameObject is created, the sprite, or screen blit, will be made the exact size of the image and will be given the image's name as well.

A bit of history: The term *blit* originated as an acronym (Berryman Logical Image Technique), whereby copying a rectangle on the screen and *blitting* it into another position on a computer screen was an early means of 2D animation.

---

   6.   Click in the Game view to move the focus to that window.

   7.   Press the spacebar to toggle the view to maximum.

Note that the GUI Texture remains the same size.

   8.   Toggle the view back and adjust the Game view window size by hovering the cursor over the edge until you get a resize icon, then drag the window smaller (Figure 6-8).

Figure 6-8. The squashed Game window

The pointer image remains the same size.

Before you can decide how big the GUI Texture object should be, you need to decide on the size of the window when the game is published. As you may remember from the Configuration window that popped up before your test game was played, the user can be allowed to change the screen size. As you may have guessed, because 2D UI objects do not scale to keep their size relative to the screen size, allowing the user to change it would mean a lot of extra scripting on your part. While you may choose to go that route eventually, for now you'll look into constraining the resolution and preventing the player from making changes.

> **Note** Later on, you'll see that you can force screen mode and screen size in the Player Settings, but this gives you a good way to learn about the Screen functions that are useful throughout the project, so let's experiment with them.

If you do a search for resolution in the scripting help, you will see several useful resolution related topics. Let's start with Screen.SetResolution.

The code and description looks pretty straightforward. You feed it an x and a y dimension and use a Boolean true/false to tell it to use full screen or not. The question is the usual, if you are new to scripting and/or Unity: where to use the code and what function to put it under.

Since this is something that should be handled at the start, when the game is loaded, let's create an object just for holding scene settings.

1. From the GameObject menu, create a new Empty GameObject.

2. Name it **Control Center**.

3. In the Adventure Scripts folder, create a new JavaScript and name it **GameManager**.

4. Open it in the editor.

The GameManager object will be referenced by name by various other objects throughout this project and any other games where you use these scripts. You may not rename this object.

So far, you have put code in the Update function, so it will be evaluated every frame, or the FixedUpdate function, when it needs to be evaluated at a constant rate. For the starting settings, however, you need to look at two new functions: the Awake function and the Start function.

The Awake function is used to initialize any variables or scene states before the game starts but after all objects have been created. It is always called before the Start function. The Start function is where you can pass variables to scripts that will need them. As with Update, any script can have its own Awake and Start functions, so theoretically, you could set the size of the game window anywhere. Logically, you will want to be able to find the scene settings script or scripts quickly, hence the creation of the GameManager script.

A published exe file will allow the user to change the screen resolution on startup. If you have a HUD or other GUI elements that could be impacted by view resolution, you may have to add code to internally compensate for screen resolution. For now, however, you'll just force a resolution override. You may wish to comment it out after you have tested it. Unity defaults to using pixel size and location with its GUI elements but allows you to position parent groups from the sides or center, so this may not impact the visual layout of your GUI as the screen is resized.

1. In the GameManager script, change the Start function to an Awake function.

2. Add the following line inside its curly brackets, so it looks as follows:

```
function Awake () {

    Screen.SetResolution (1280, 800, false); // false means not full screen, used windowed
}
```

3. Save the script.

4. Drag it onto the Control Center object.

5. At the top of the Game view, click the left-most button.

There is no option for the new resolution, just screen ratios. To get the desired size to show up for the Game view you will have to change the project settings.

6. From Edit, Project Settings, Player, in the Resolution and Presentation section, set the Default Width and Height to **1280×800**.

7. Now you can choose the Standalone (1280×800) option (Figure 6-9).

Figure 6-9. *Game view settings*

8. Toggle Maximize on Play (Figure 6-10).

Figure 6-10. *The window at game resolution and/or aspect ratio*

9. Click Play.

Now you can see how big the cursor will appear. In your case, it happily occupies a large portion of your Game window. Obviously, you must make some adjustments. These can be made in either the Import settings, where you can specify a maximum size, or in the GUI Texture's parameters.

10. Stop playback.

11. Select the GamePointer texture in the Project view.

12. Set its Max Size to **32** and click Apply.

The newly resized image is stretched up to fit the original Width and Height.

13. Select the GamePointer object.

14. In the Inspector, set the Pixel Inset's Height and Width to **32**.

15. Set the X and Y Pixel Inset values to **-16** (half the texture size) to center it again (see Figure 6-11, left).

Figure 6-11. *The resized GUI Texture object*

As you can see in the Game view image of Figure 6-11, allowing some program (such as a game engine) to scale an image down may yield less than desirable results: note that the edges are jagged and nasty looking.

1. Select the Adventure Textures folder in the Project view.

2. From the Assets menu, select Import New Asset.

3. Import GamePointerSm from the Chapter 6 Assets folder.

4. In the Inspector, change its Texture Type to GUI.

5. Click Apply (you will be prompted to do so if you forget).

6. Select the GamePointer in the Hierarchy view.

7. Drag the GamePointerSm texture onto the Texture field or use the Browse icon next to the currently loaded GamePointer texture to select it from the Asset browser.

The new cursor image does not appear as jagged as its shrunken predecessor did (Figure 6-12).

Figure 6-12. *The smaller version of the GamePointer texture*

BASE 2

If you are at all familiar with game texture assets, you may recognize that most are in powers of two. This is because computer memory is arranged in base-two sized blocks. Images in pixel sizes that are powers of two fill the block entirely. An example would be an image that is 256×256 pixels. If that image were just one pixel larger in each direction, it would use up a 512×512 sized block—nearly four times as much memory! Therefore, whenever possible, the final image should be made in sizes such as 2, 4, 8, 16, 32, 64, 128, 256, 512, 1024, 2048, etc.

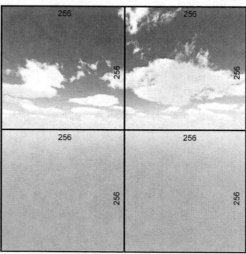

Memory usage

The image on the left takes up the same amount of memory as the image on the right. As soon as the image is even 1 pixel larger than the base-two size, it uses the next chunk of memory.

8.   Set the Game window back to Free Aspect.

9.   Turn off Maximize on Play.

10.   Save your scene and project.

Color Cues

Now that you have shrunk your cursor into an acceptable size, let's try a few experiments on the cursor texture or image.

1.   Select the GamePointer object in the Hierarchy view.

2.   In the Inspector, find the Color parameter in the GUITexture section and click on the color swatch to bring up the Color dialog.

3.   Change the color while watching the results in the Game view (Figure 6-13).

Figure 6-13. *Changing the cursor color*

Cursor Position

In Unity, in order to use a custom texture as a cursor, you have to turn off the OS (operating system) cursor, then track its position and feed it to your custom GUI Texture. Because there are several tasks that must be managed with your cursor, it makes sense to create a script for that very purpose. Vector2 type variable holds an x and a y value.

1. Create a new JavaScript in your My Scripts folder.

2. Name it **CustomCursor**.

3. Open it in the script editor.

Getting and assigning a cursor position is obviously something that needs to be done at least every frame, so it belongs inside the Update function. You will also add offsets to put the corner of the pointer in the correct position.

4. Add the following code inside the Update function so it looks as follows:

```
function Update () {
    // gets the current cursor position as a Vector2 type variable
    var pos = Input.mousePosition;

    // feed its x and y positions back into the GUI Texture object's parameters
    guiTexture.pixelInset.x = pos.x;
    guiTexture.pixelInset.y = pos.y - 32; // offset to top
}
```

5. Save the script.

6. Drag it onto the GamePointer object.

7. Click Play and move the cursor to the middle of the Game view.

Your brand-new cursor may not show up.

8. Move the cursor to the bottom left of the view.

The custom cursor now comes to the center of the viewport. It looks like you've got an offset issue.

9. Stop playback.

10. At the top of the Inspector, look at the values for the GamePointer's X and Y Position transforms.

They are both 0.5, which explains the large offset. For a GUI Texture object, the Position is in normalized screen space; 1.0 equates to 100% of the length or width.

1. Set them both to **0.0**, to line the custom cursor up with the OS cursor.

■ **Tip** GUI transforms are shown as a percentage of screen; full width and height is 1.0.

---

2. Click Play and test again.

If curiosity has gotten the best of you, and you have tweaked the X and Y Pixel Inset, you will have discovered that it reflects the screen position offset from the transforms.

3. Toggle off Maximize on Play.

4. Click Play again.

5. Move the cursor about the viewport, watching the Pixel Inset values change in the Inspector.

6. Stop Play mode.

If you are seeing a bit of ghosted operating system cursor, you will notice a bit of lag. On the positive side, changing the color of the texture will be easy.

Hardware Cursor

Let's take a minute to access the lag issue. In an adventure-type game, this probably isn't an issue. In other game genres, however, it could be a problem. In this section, you will give up the option to have a cursor larger than 32×32 pixels, in favor of allowing the operating system to take care of the cursor for you. A good feature of a hardware cursor is always drawn on top of everything else in the scene.

1. Select the GamePointer object and deactivate it in the Inspector.

Before you can assign a texture for the hardware cursor, you will have to change its Texture Type.

2. Select the GamePointerSm texture in the Project view.

3. Change the Texture Type to Cursor and click Apply.

4. From the Edit menu, select Game Settings, Player and load the GamePointerSm texture into the Default Cursor (Figure 6-14).

Figure 6-14. *Assigning a hardware cursor*

5. Move the cursor into the Game view, to see it using the new cursor texture.

6. Click Play and try navigating the scene.

As expected, this one is turned off by the Hide Cursor script when the player moves through the scene. The downside to the hardware cursor is that there is no way to quickly change its color. You could change the texture for a mouseover stand-in during runtime, but that would mean making duplicates for all of the textures that will eventually be used as cursors. It would also leave you without an easy way to let the player choose the mouseover color. It is also limited to 32×32 pixels on some operating systems, which will be small for representing action objects as cursors.

UnityGUI Cursor

A third option for the cursor is to use a scripted-only cursor. It has the advantage of always drawing on top of GUI Texture objects and can easily be set to draw on top of other UnityGUI elements (including text). The earlier GUI Texture object method will eventually be useful when you create the 2D inventory screen, but the cursor draw order issue means that you will need a better solution for your cursor. A downside of the UnityGUI cursor is that it exists only in code, so there is nothing tangible to work within the Hierarchy or other views.

Without delving deeply into UnityGUI for the time being, you can at least get a simple cursor up and running. Because the code for the cursor could theoretically be put anywhere, let's go ahead and put it on the GameManager script, so it can always be easily found.

UnityGUI elements are created in their own function, the OnGUI function. To start, you will need a couple of variables to store the default texture, and since the cursor will eventually change, the current cursor texture.

1. Open the GameManager script in the editor.

2. Add the following variables:

    ```
    var defaultCursor : Texture;         // the default cursor texture, the arrow
    internal var currentCursor : Texture; // the current cursor texture
    ```

3. In the Start function, assign the default cursor as the current cursor:

    ```
    function Start () {

            currentCursor = defaultCursor; // assign the default as the current cursor
    }
    ```

4. Create the OnGUI function:

    ```
    function OnGUI () {

        GUI.DrawTexture (Rect(Screen.width/2, Screen.height/2,64,64), currentCursor);
    // draw the cursor in the middle of the screen
        }
    ```

5. Save the script.

■ **Tip** Function order in the script generally doesn't matter, but it's traditional to list the functions in the order that they are used. After the script's variables, an Awake function would be first, then the Start function, followed by the Update, the FixedUpdate, and then event-based and user-defined functions.

Before you can see anything, you will have to assign the texture and then click Play. But let's look at the GUI.DrawTexture line first. It starts by defining the size and position of a rectangle on the screen, then tells it which texture to put in the rectangle. Note that the size is set to 64×64 pixels. The arrow cursor is fine at 32×32, but when you have inventory objects used as cursors, you will want to use a bigger image. Rather than constantly scaling the rect up and down, it will make more sense to put the small arrow texture on a larger texture. The texture you will use is 128×128, but it will automatically be scaled down to f it the rectangle's space.

6. Select the Adventure Textures folder, right-click and select Import New Asset.

7. Bring in the GamePointerOffset texture from the Chapter 6 Assets folder.

8. In the Inspector, set its Texture Type to GUI and click Apply (Figure 6-15).

Figure 6-15. *The offset cursor texture*

9. Select the Control Center object in the Hierarchy view and drag the GamePointerOffset texture onto the GameManager's Default Cursor parameter.

10. Click Play.

The cursor image, or the upper-left corner of it to be exact, appears in the center of the viewport. Next, it needs to be matched to the operating system's location, just as you did with the GUI Texture version. As before, there will be some lag, but in this type of game, the pros outweigh the cons. Note how the pos variable, a Vector2 Type, uses dot notation to access its two values.

11. In the OnGUI function, change the DrawTexture line to the following:

```
var pos : Vector2 = Input.mousePosition; //get the location of the cursor
GUI.DrawTexture (Rect(pos.x, Screen.height - pos.y,64,64), currentCursor);
// draw the cursor there
```

12. Save the script, click Play, and test the new cursor.

In the Game view, with the hardware system cursor now matching the UnityGUI cursor, it's hard to tell how well it is working.

1. Stop Play mode.

2. From the Edit menu, select Game Settings, Player and click the Settings button on the Default Cursor thumbnail.

3. Select None from the top of the texture list.

Now when you see the ghosting in the Game view, you can tell that it is the hardware or operating system cursor. You will see that the hardware cursor disappears when you are navigating the scene, but your new custom cursor does not. Thinking back, you may remember that you added code to your ScriptHolder script to hide and show the operating system cursor. Let's start by turning off the hardware cursor at startup.

4. At the top of the Start function, turn off the operating system cursor:

```
Screen.showCursor = false; // hide the operating system cursor
```

Now you will have to use part of the hide code from the earlier HideCursor script. Unlike regular objects, UnityGUI code is not enabled or activated, so it will require a conditional to allow it to be skipped over when not needed. You will run the conditional in the Update function as before, but will only switch a flag with it.

5. Add the flag variable for the navigating conditional:

```
var navigating : boolean;    //flag for navigation state
```

6. Add the code to set the flag in the Update function:

```
if (Input.GetAxis("Horizontal") || Input. GetAxis ("Vertical") ||
   Input. GetAxis ("Turn") || Input.GetButton("ML Enable") ){
 // a navigation key is being pressed
navigating = true; // player is moving
 }
```

7. Just above the last curly bracket of the Update function, add:

```
else {
// no navigation keys are being pressed
navigating = false; // player is stationary
}
```

8. Wrap the DrawTexture code into the navigation conditional:

```
if (!navigating) { // if not navigating
    var pos : Vector2 = Input.mousePosition; //get the location of the cursor
    GUI.DrawTexture (Rect(pos.x, Screen.height - pos.y,64,64), currentCursor);
    // draw the cursor }
```

9. Save the script.

10. Click Play and test.

■ **Tip** Flags are merely variables whose values are watched for use in conditionals. A variable named `doorLocked` could be considered a flag; if `doorLocked` is true, the user will not be able to interact with the doorknob to open the door. If `doorLocked` is false, not only could the user open it, but other events (such as randomly spawned monsters coming through the door) could be generated as well.

Flags can track more than simple true/false states. A sidewalk café might need a flag for the weather. If it is sunny and hot, the variable weather = 0; if it is raining, weather = 1; and if it is overcast, weather = 2. If weather < 2, the umbrellas need to be put out. The weather constantly changes.

If you are still seeing the occasional flicker from the hardware cursor, there's one more trick you can use. Having the ability to assign your own texture means you can give it an almost fully alpha channel. A single pixel, not quite black, does the trick.

1. Select the Adventure Textures folder, right-click and select Import New Asset.

2. Bring in the AlmostBlankAlpha texture from the Chapter 6 Assets folder.

3. Set its Texture Type to **Cursor** and click Apply.

4. Load it in as the hardware cursor.

The hardware cursor is no longer showing, and the new cursor hides during navigation, so you are good to go.

Object-to-Object Communication

Now comes the tricky part and one of the most crucial concepts to understand in Unity: how to access one object's variables from another object's scripts. This will enable all of the individual objects to access generic settings, allow events on one object to trigger events on other objects, and generally tie all the game information together.

As mentioned, you can gain access to parents and children of GameObjects without too much trouble, but in order to allow "unrelated" objects to communicate, you must "introduce" them to each other first.

Hardcoding the objects into each other's code will require the object to exist in the scene; otherwise, you will get an error. Your game will have a few objects that must be named correctly, in order for them to be accessed this way. Hopefully, you have been heeding the warning about which object names you may not change. In this section, you will set up the functionality to keep track of whether the player is currently navigating through the scene or not in the GameManager script. This way, the action objects can access it whenever their scripts are activated.

While you could just duplicate the check-for-navigation keys being pressed in each script that needs that information, having the same condition checked in multiple scripts every frame (remember, it's inside an Update function) is a waste of resources and could slow frame rate. As it turns out, you've already done that twice (once for the HideCursor and once for the MouseLookRestricted), so you really ought only to calculate it once, if possible, and have whatever scripts need it access it from a single location.

FRAME RATE

When asked what affects frame rate (the number of frames per second that the engine can output), most people are quick to reply "poly count" (the number of polygons in the scene). While this is certainly a major contributor, in reality, almost everything contributes: the number of scripts being evaluated, the objects that are animating, the physics solutions being calculated, the GUI elements being rendered and monitored, the amount of textures stored in memory, the number of polygons within the view frustum at any one time, the network communications being sent back and forth, the shadows and shaders being calculated, and just about everything else. Unity Pro's Profiler is a great help in finding where resources are bottlenecking and can help you streamline your code for games that need high frame rates or need to run well on mobile platforms, where resources are more limited.

As you get deeper into your game creation, you will find other tasks and variables that will have to be accessed by multiple scripts, so you may as well use your GameManager script for that purpose.

GLOBAL VARIABLES

Some of you may already be familiar with the concept of global variables. Global variables in Unity are, at best, only global to the object they are on. While this makes it necessary for you to do a lot more work to access the variables from other objects, it makes it possible for the game to make better use of multiple processors and multithreading.

■ **Tip** Different scripts may use the same variable name, but it does not follow that the variables share the same value. To do so, one or both must update the other.

Vars and internal vars can share the same name as variables in other scripts. Even when they contain the same information, because they live in different scripts; they are not the same entity. Think of it as two people named John Smith. They both have the same name but live in different houses. John Smith on Maple Lane constantly checks with John Smith on Sixth Street to see if he is in his house or out traveling about. Depending on the latter's status, the former will take appropriate action.

In most cases, you can't refer to an object by name when declaring a variable. You *can*, however, drag and drop an object into the value field for the variable in the Inspector. While this may seem like an easy solution, when you start adding action objects to the game, it will quickly become tedious, dragging the same objects over and over.

It turns out that once the GameObjects have been loaded, you *can* find them by name, as long as they haven't been deactivated.

Mouseover Cursor Changes

Before you start working on mouseover events, you must have an understanding of how mouseover works. The most important concept is that rather than the cursor constantly firing rays into the scene and then evaluating what it's over, an object can report when the cursor is over it. While it is safe to say you will only want a limited number of objects to trigger the mouseover event, it will be well worth your while to make one generic reusable script that will handle interactions. Because this script will get larger as you progress through the functionality of your game, let's start by defining some of your own functions, in order to keep things tidier.

Your first order of business is to work out the mechanics of your cursor color change. By definition, if you're going to change the color, you will have to define the default color, so you'll know what to return it to on mouseoff. As long as you're in the design process, you may as well plan on letting the author (and possibly the player, at some point) choose the mouseover color, rather than hardcode it in. Because that should be an option in the game, let's add it to the GameManager script.

1. Open the GameManager script.

2. At the top of the script add:

```
var mouseOverColor : Color = Color.green;  // mouse over color for the cursor
```

Note the use of a prepackaged color, `Color.green`. If you do a search through the scripting help for color and select the top choice, Color, you will see the other class variables.

Now you can easily change the color manually in the Inspector to the color of your choice at any time (Figure 6-16).

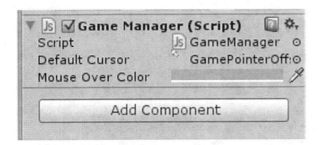

Figure 6-16. *The new mouseover color parameter*

You may decide to use your own cursor image, and that image may be more than just black-and-white. The best choice for the default color is white, so let's consider white the default color, as it will not interfere with the texture's image.

Now that the GameManager script knows what color to use for mouseover, you have to create your own function that can be called from other objects to change the cursor color when the mouse goes over and off the object. As you have seen before, user-defined functions look the same as the system and event functions, except that you can choose their names. You'll call this function `CursorColorChange`. It will be a simple toggle to switch back and forth between the default white color and the specified mouseover color.

Let's also look at a new concept, that of passing an *argument* or value to a variable. You used this with the `OnTriggerEnter` function when it reported the object that intersected with it, but this time, you'll be in charge of passing the argument as well as receiving it. You will start by putting the name of the variable or argument and its type inside the function's parentheses.

For the argument, you'll tell the function what state the cursor is in when you call the function, so it will know which color to set it to next. To change the color of a UnityGUI element, you'll need a variable to keep track of the current cursor color.

1. In the GameManager script, add the following variable:

```
internal var currentCursorColor : Color; // current tint color of cursor
```

2. Initialize the variable in the Start function:

```
currentCursorColor = Color.white; // start color to white
```

3. Add the following below the Update function:

```
function CursorColorChange (colorize: boolean) {

    if (colorize)  currentCursorColor = mouseOverColor;

    else  currentCursorColor = Color.white;
}
```

Unlike a regular gameObject, tinting UnityGUI elements changes all elements after the color change. First, you will assign the current color above the GUI.DrawTexture line, then you will change it back

4. Inside the OnGUI function, add the following above the GUI.DrawTexture line:

```
GUI.color = currentCursorColor; // set the cursor color to current
```

5. Below the GUI.DrawTexture line, add:

```
GUI.color = Color.white; // set the cursor color back to default
```

6. Save the script.

In using a Boolean type for the value that you pass into your function, you don't really have to think of it as true or false; it's just as useful to think of it as 0 or 1. The cursor is either white or the mouseover color, one of two states. Let's consider the default color, white, to be state 0 and the mouseover color to be state 1. Reading through the function, if it was passed a false (0), it will change the color to the mouseover color; otherwise (else), it was passed a true (1), so it will turn it back to white. Note that you don't have to tell it the argument is a variable, but you do have to define its Type.

You have had no control over the functions you have previously used; Awake and Start are called when you first start the game, and Update and FixedUpdate are called every frame or at least are dependent on frame rate. A user-defined function, in contrast, can be called whenever you wish.

You will be calling the CursorColorChange function from inside a couple of system functions, OnMouseEnter and OnMouseExit. But you first have to make a very generic script to put on every action object.

1. In the Adventurer Scripts folder, create a new JavaScript.

2. Name it **Interactor** and open it in the script editor.

3. Delete the default Update function.

This script will have to talk to the Control Center object to call the function you just created, so it needs to be "introduced" first. In the SendMessageOnTrigger script you created, you had to manually drag the target object onto its parameter in the Inspector. While that's fine for a one-off situation, you'll quickly get tired of repeating the same setup task for multiple objects. This time, you will be having the code do the assignment for you, using Find.

Rather than having to drag and drop it into the script every time you add it to a new action object, you can let Unity search the scene and Find it for you by name. Because Find searches the entire scene, it shouldn't be used in the Update function or any other place where it can adversely affect frame rate. Using it once in the Start function, you won't be slowing the rest of the game down.

4. Add the following variable declaration:

```
// Gain access to these objects
internal var controlCenter : GameObject; // the Control Center object
```

5. Find and assign the Control Center in the Start function:

```
controlCenter = GameObject.Find("Control Center"); // locate by name and assign the
object to the var
```

Next, you'll trigger the color change function on the GameManager script using a SendMessage when the cursor mouses over the object that holds the Interactor script.

6. Add the following function below the Start function:

```
function OnMouseEnter () {

    controlCenter.SendMessage("CursorColorChange", true); // colorize the pointer
}
```

7. Save the script.

OnMouseEnter and OnMouseExit are similar to the OnTriggerEnter and OnTriggerExit functions you used in the previous chapter. They are all event-type functions. As with their OnTrigger cousins, the OnMouse functions also require that the object has a Collider, before they will work.

When you used the SendMessage function or method in the previous chapter, the only thing you sent was the name of the function you wanted to call. This time, separated by a comma, you send the argument that your function is expecting, a type Boolean.

■ **Tip** User-defined functions can hold as many arguments as needed. SendMessage, however, can only send a single argument with the message.

Before you can see the fruits of all your labor, you'll have to create a test object to mouse over.

1. From the GameObject menu, Create Other, select Sphere.

2. Move the sphere in the Scene view until you can see it in the Game view (Figure 6-17).

Figure 6-17. *The sphere in view*

3. Drag the Interactor script onto the Sphere.

4. Select the Sphere.

5. Click Play and test the functionality.

The cursor changes color as it moves over the sphere, proving that the sphere was in contact with the Control Center object and sent the message that activated the color change function.

Next, you'll want to revert the color when the cursor moves off the object.

6. Add the following code to the Interactor script beneath the `OnMouseEnter` function:

```
function OnMouseExit () {

    controlCenter.SendMessage("CursorColorChange", false); // turn the pointer white

}
```

7. Save the script.

This function, as you would expect, is called when the cursor passes off the action object. Because your `CursorColorChange` function can handle either state, you send it a false this time, to tell it to carry out the `else` clause.

8. Click Play and test the mouseover functionality.

Everything works as expected (Figure 6-18).

Figure 6-18. *The mouseover color change*

Now comes the fun part. This is where you see the beauty of making scripts that can be used by multiple and distinct objects.

1. From the GameObject menu, create a Cube and a cylinder near the Sphere.

2. Select the Sphere and in the Inspector, right-click over the Interactor script component's name and choose Copy Component.

3. Select the Cube and the Cylinder; position the cursor over any component name (Transform will work fine); right-click and choose Paste Component As New.

The Interactor component, with its current parameter settings and assignments, is copied to the two other objects.

4. Click Play and test the mouseover functionality with the new objects (Figure 6-19).

Figure 6-19. *The three action objects*

While the other scripts you have built will be reusable in future games, the Interactor script is a specialized script that will be applied to every action item in this particular game.

By exposing variables to the Inspector, you can customize the events associated with the individual action object, without changing the actual Interactor script. An example of this is an informative (or entertaining) message on mouseover, where the message differs for each object ("It is a solid-looking cube, approximately 1 meter square" or "It is a featureless sphere suspended in thin air"). Eventually, the Interactor script will contain the functionality to deal with all types of interaction, no matter what action object it resides on.

Because the same script is on all three objects, when you make a change to it, all objects using it are updated.

5.   Back in the Game view, move backward from the objects you have added until they are only a few pixels in the viewport.

6.   Stop and test the mouseover functionality.

It still works (Figure 6-20), which is probably not something you want.

Figure 6-20. *Mouseover triggered from far, far away…*

Distance Check

In the early days of point-and-click adventures, the game was based on a series of beautifully rendered high-resolution still shots (Cyan's Riven) or hand-painted toon-style backgrounds (LucasArts' Curse of Money Island). Hotspots (the area on the image where the item was in the picture) were created manually for each still shot.

In real-time 3D, the action object itself, because of its collider, becomes the hotspot, whether it is near or far. As you have discovered, this allows for the possibility of opening doors or picking up buckets, while several hundred meters away. While this could be part of the design in a game, to prevent your player from triggering things he or she can't even see, you'll have to limit the distance within which the player can interact with an object.

First, you'll have to calculate the distance the First Person Controller is from the action object, and then you'll check to see if it is within mouseover range. If it isn't within range, you must skip the mouseover functionality.

Let's start by creating a function that will calculate the distance from the object to the camera. This is a very typical user-defined function; it can be found in almost any game with enemies that can turn to face you (and shoot, if you are within range). This one uses some vector math, the dot product, to calculate the distance the camera is from the action object the script is on. The nice thing is that you don't have to understand the math that makes the script work to reap the benefit.

■ **Tip**   It pays to watch or read through tutorials for other game genres (even if they don't interest you), because they may contain intriguing functionality that you can use in your game.

---

1. In the Interactor script, add the following user-defined function:

```
function DistanceFromCamera () {

    // get the direction the camera is heading so you only process stuff in the line of sight
    var heading : Vector3 = transform.position - cam.transform.position;
    //calculate the distance from the camera to the object
    var distance : float = Vector3.Dot(heading, cam.transform.forward);
    return distance;
}
```

■ **Note** In this function, you see the use of a Vector3 type variable. It expects a three-part value, such as (X,Y,Z) or (R,G,B). A Vector2 might expect (X,Y), and a Vector4 might expect (R,G,B,A).

There's something else that's new in this function: it *returns* a value. When you look at how the function is called, you will notice that the value returned by the function is being assigned directly to a variable.

Before you can get this working, however, you will have to define cam, the camera it is referencing.

2. Add the following internal variable beneath the controlCenter variable declaration:

```
internal var cam : GameObject; // the main camera on the first person controller
```

3. Then add the following to the Start:

```
cam = GameObject.Find("Main Camera"); // find and assign the Main Camera to this variable
```

The last line inside the DistanceFromCamera function says return distance. The variable distance was declared and assigned a value in the previous line, so that is nothing new. But the word *return* is a reserved word.

Variables declared inside functions are *local* to that particular function. They are not accessible outside the function and are cleared on completion of the function. So in order to be able to access the distance variable, it would either have to be declared up with the regular script variables, or its value passed back out to whoever called the function in the first place.

On its own, *return* simply tells you to leave the function (and that will be useful very shortly). But when coupled with a variable, it sends the value of that variable back to where the function was called, before the local variable is cleared.

Right now, you want to check the distance from the camera, before you allow the cursor color change to happen.

1. Add the following lines of code *above* the controlCenter.SendMessage line inside the OnMouseEnter function:

```
if (DistanceFromCamera() > 7) return;
```

You call the function with DistanceFromCamera(), and it returns the distance it calculated in the function. You then immediately check to see if that returned value or distance is less than 7 meters. If not, the return bumps you out of the OnMouseEnter function before the color change function can be called. If it's evaluated as less than 7 meters, the rest of the contents of the OnMouseEnter function are carried out, and your cursor's color is changed.

You may decide that 7 meters is not the optimal distance for the mouseover to work. Rather than digging through the code each time to change it, it would make sense to create a variable to hold the distance you want to declare. Creating a variable near the top of the script will make it easier to change, as you add more functionality to your script, but if you expose it to the Inspector, it will also allow you to change the distance on an individual action object basis, which could possibly be beneficial.

2. Add the following line up at the top, above the other public variables:

```
// Pick and Mouseover Info
internal var triggerDistance : float = 7.0; // distance the camera must be to
the object before mouse over
```

3. Change the line in the OnMouseEnter function to use the variable, instead of the hardcoded value:

```
if (DistanceFromCamera() > triggerDistance) return;
```

You may decide that manually changing the trigger distance is a tedious way to hone in on the optimal distance. If you temporarily have the distance print out to the console, you can decide very quickly what it ought to be.

4. Add the following line above the if clause in the OnMouseEnter function:

```
print (DistanceFromCamera());
```

5. Save the Script.

6. Click Play.

7. Experiment with the trigger distance (Figure 6-21), by watching the results in the status line.

Figure 6-21. *Reporting distance on mouseover*

8. When you are happy with it, change the `triggerDistance` variable to your optimal value and remove `internal`, so the variable is exposed to the Inspector.

9. Remove or comment out the print line.

10. Save the script again.

11. Exit Play mode.

■ **Tip** As soon as you change a value in the Inspector, it will always override the value initialized in the script. If you change the value in the script and want to reset the value in the Inspector, you can change the variable to internal, then change it back again. This will effectively reset the default value in the Inspector.

This is also the first place to check, if you are changing the value of a variable inside the script but seeing no effect. Make sure that variable is set to internal.

Quick Publish

At this point, you may be getting itchy to see how everything runs, so let's take a few minutes to build an executable and try it out.

Because you are now using a different scene, CursorControl, you will have to Add Current in the Scenes to Build and uncheck TerrainTest.

1. Save the scene and the project.

2. From the File menu, select Build Settings.

3. Click Add Current.

4. Uncheck the other scenes in the Scenes in Build window (Figure 6-22).

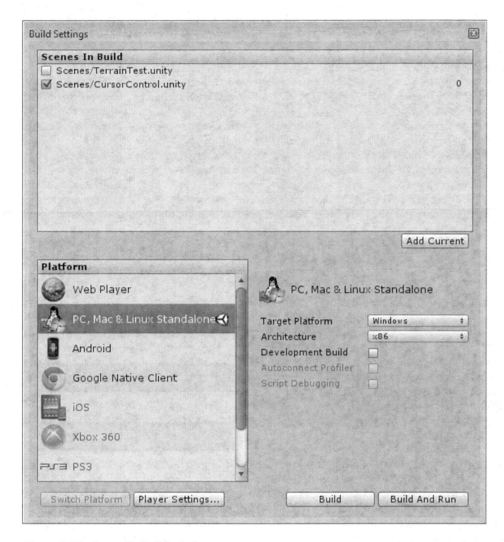

Figure 6-22. *Scenes in Build window*

5. Click Build And Run and save this exe as CursorControl.exe.

6. Test the build.

With the cursor responding to objects in the scene, your little scene is starting to look like a real game.

7. Close the Build Settings dialog.

Object Reaction to Mouseover

Another means of action-object identification, often seen in more stylized point-and-click adventures, such as Tales of Monkey Island, is to have the object itself change color. This method is particularly advantageous on mobile devices, such as phones, where the screen is small, as it provides an additional visual cue.

Owing to the need to include new features in the second version of this book, I have removed the section on color changes in action objects with a mouseover event.

If you are interested in attempting this functionality on your own at some point, you will have to get the object's material with: `GetComponent(MeshRenderer).material;`.

Substituting a new material on mouseover, you will realize that you could probably use the same material for all of the objects and merely change the texture. You can find the texture with: `GetComponent(MeshRenderer).material. mainTexture;`.

Using a Vertex Lit shader for the mouseover material will allow you to turn the Emissive value of the shader up, so the object is no longer affected by scene lighting, making it stand out nicely.

As long as each action item has a single material that has a main texture, the scripting stays fairly simple. If, however, only some objects and their materials meet the requirements, you will have to script around the differences. Another issue is that not every object has a MeshRenderer. Characters, for example, have a SkinnedMeshRenderer, and interactive cloth has a ClothRenderer. So you would have to find out which kind of renderer an action object had before you could get its material . . . or materials. You can see how the logic behind the object color change can get quite complicated.

Summary

In this chapter, you experimented with cursor control, finding that you could hide the operating system's cursor with a simple `Screen.showCursor = false`. After creating a variable called `navigating`, which checked your virtual buttons to see if any were active, you were able turn the cursor off while moving and back on as soon as you stopped.

To allow for more artistic license, you substituted a GUITexture object as a cursor with the help of the Texture Importer presets. You learned that GUI objects in Unity are not sized relevant to screen size and, so, explored forcing screen resolution via scripting. By getting the operating system's cursor's position with `Input.mousePosition`, you were able to set your own cursor's Pixel Inset values with `guiTexture.pixelInset.x` and `guiTexture.pixelInset.y`.

A downside to the GUI Texture cursor was a bit of lag, so you next tried using your own texture for the operating system or hardware cursor. It had great responsiveness and was guaranteed to draw on top of everything else in the scene but was too limited in size and color options.

Your final cursor test involved a purely scripted cursor, using the UnityGUI system. It also replaced the operating system cursor, so there was a bit of lag, but it had the ability to have its color and size adjusted, as needed. You learned that it will be able to draw on top of the rest of the scene with no problems.

Next, you started designing a script that would hold and manage the master game information and be able to communicate with other object's scripts. You found that after creating a variable to hold a GameObject, you could either drag one into it in the Inspector or use `GameObject.Find` in the `Start` function to locate the object you wanted to communicate with. Names, you discovered, are only properties of objects, materials, and components and representatives of their objects. The same variable names used in different scripts don't store the same values, unless you specifically update them.

With the introduction of `OnMouseEnter` and `OnMouseExit`, you were able to instigate color changes for your cursor, as it passed over and off your action objects. By using `GetComponent`, you found you could access variables from the script components you created, allowing you to keep important data on a single script that could be accessed by all.

In the next chapter, you'll work with imported objects and their animations and start to get them acting like actual game assets.

CHAPTER 7

■ ■ ■

Imported Assets

Having made a good start on the cursor, now you are probably thinking about adding action objects, some of which will animate. Obviously, the handful of primitive objects available in Unity won't go very far for creating most games, so you'll have to look into one of the more challenging aspects of game creation—importing assets built in other programs. As anyone familiar with creating games or other 3D content can tell you, every game engine or 3D application handles the import process differently. Some handle it more gracefully than others, but there are always going to be issues and gotchas. Adding animations to the mix complicates it even further.

3D Art Assets

Unity was originally designed primarily to create first-person shooters, where imports are most likely characters or static buildings and other structures. A classic point-and-click adventure game, on the other hand, features the animation of a multitude of different objects, many of which animate together to play out complicated sequences as a reward for the player's cleverness in hitting upon the correct solution.

You will start by learning how to handle imported animations, because there are always going to be sequences that are better off imported. Then you'll delve into Unity's Animation view and create a few animations directly in Unity. Characters will be introduced later in the book, because their animation will use the newer Mecanim system and is handled quite differently.

Whether you'll be creating your objects in a Digital Content Creation (DCC) program such as 3ds Max, Maya, C4D, or Blender, or taking advantage of Unity's Asset Store, you will have to start with the import settings. For this book, you are using assets created in 3ds Max and exported in FBX format.

Unity supports the file types of 3ds Max, Maya, C4D, and Blender by converting them internally into FBX format, once they are in the Assets folder. You can still work on them and resave them, and they will be automatically updated on scene load. If you are creating assets for someone else, you should get in the habit of saving as FBX, so they have maximum portability.

For this project, you'll be importing two types of objects: non-animated objects and pre-animated objects. You may think of the former as static objects, such as structures and large environmental objects, but the latter can also be structural as well as animated.

What about materials? Unity attempts to create materials similar to what the object had in the DCC app, but because there are few correlations between regular materials and shaders, you can pretty well count on redoing them all. That being the case, keep materials as basic as possible, as you'll almost always have to rebuild after import, to take advantage of anything other than the apparently default Diffuse shader. And before you go getting all excited about using Diffuse Parallax Reflective Bump shaders on everything, remember that everything affects frame rate—use the fancy stuff sparingly.

■ **Tip** If Unity can't find the textures at the time of import, it will create generic Diffuse materials, and you'll have to set them all up manually once you've loaded the textures. When saving a new DCC file directly to the Assets folder, it's safest to load the textures first, so the materials will be generated with them when the meshes are loaded.

TIPS FOR CREATING YOUR OWN ASSETS

- Name all objects.

- Use naming conventions for your textures. Unity will create only a base Diffuse texture for your objects on import; you will have to add bump, shininess, height, and other specialty maps.

- Two objects using the same material in your DCC app will also share the material in Unity.

- If your modeling application allows, collapse objects to editable mesh, not editable poly, to prevent edge errors. FBX does not support turned edges, so your model could change on export.

- Expect to go back and make adjustments to your files. Real-time renderers and navigation will show errors and mistakes that you may miss in your DCC app.

- When exporting the FBX, make sure to check Animations, if you have them. Y is up in Unity (you can keep the original Z from Max, if you wish, with the latest FBX exporters), and note the scale: it can be changed in Unity, but it is worth noting.

- Keep complex animation hierarchies in orthogonal orientation until after importing into Unity. FBX doesn't support non-orthogonal rotation matrices.

- Unity does not currently support vertex animation, e.g., morph targets. Any animation that affects objects on a vertex basis must be done with bones. Morph target technology is under development, so this tip will eventually be obsolete.

- If you are using 3ds Max, you can use the Resource Collector to copy your textures into the Assets folder before you export the FBX.

Importing the Art Assets

There are several ways to bring assets into your Unity project. You will start by bringing supported file types directly into the project and will eventually learn to import and export Unity Packages.

As with any asset in Unity, once the asset has been imported or added to the Assets folder through the OS, you must only move the file around inside the Project view (expect to be reminded of this regularly—it is crucial!). If you delete it from the Assets folder, it will be deleted for good. If you make your own assets, always have a reference scene in your program's native format stored elsewhere on your hard drive that you can go back to, should you forget and delete something by mistake.

1. Open the CursorControl scene.

2. Delete all but the Control Center, Directional Light, First Person Controller, Terrain, Terrain Boundaries, and WindZone.

3. Save the scene as **ImportedAnimations**.

4. Move it to the Scenes folder in the Project view, if you didn't save it there.

5. Locate the Chapter 7 Assets folder in the downloaded book assets.

6. Copy the Animation Tests folder into the Assets folder in your project folder, via Explorer (Windows) or Finder (Mac).

The folder has both the FBX files and the textures in it, so it should import nicely.

Unity will take a few moments to process the assets, adding internal IDs and mapping out connections between the meshes and materials, as well as generating Unity-specific parameters for the Inspector. When Unity finishes loading, you should see the new Animation Tests folder in the Project view.

1. Open the new Animation Tests folder and inspect the contents, as shown in Figure 7-1.

 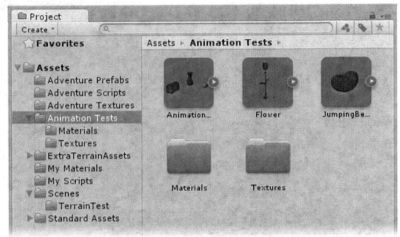

Figure 7-1. *The contents of the Animation Tests folder in the One Column Layout (left) and the Two Columns Layout (right)*

When importing assets that someone else created, you may wish to get an overview of what you've got. For that, you can switch to the Two-Columns Layout for the Project view. It takes up a lot of screen space but is a quick way to look at what you've just brought in.

■ **Tip**   If you've forgotten how to change the layout, right-click over the Project label and select the layout you want. You can adjust the size of the icons from the slider at the bottom of the view. The book will continue to use the One Column Layout for screen shots, but you may use the option you prefer.

Unity has made a prefab to hold each FBX file and, using the preexisting Textures folder, has generated a Materials folder with the materials for each object.

2. Open the AnimationObjects asset (Figure 7-2). In the Two Columns Layout, you will have to click the small arrow on the right side of the thumbnail.

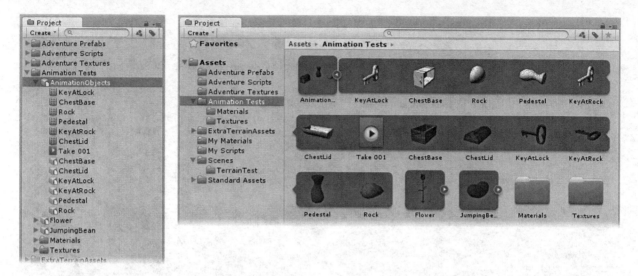

Figure 7-2. *The contents of AnimationObjects in the One Column Layout (left) and the Two Column Layout (right)*

Inside the AnimationObjects, you'll find a prefab for each individual mesh to hold its properties, the original mesh, and something called Take 001.

3. Click one of the mesh objects, ▦, to see it in the Preview window (Figure 7-3).

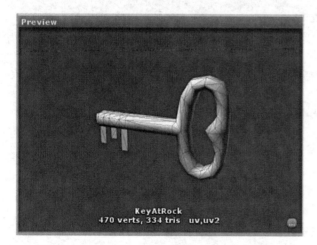

Figure 7-3. *One of the meshes from the scene*

The mesh is shown with edges, and the vertex and triangle ("tris") count is shown. You can also orbit the Preview window to see the mesh from all directions.

4. Select each item to see its preview in the Inspector.

If an object has animation, you can preview it in the Inspector as well.

5. Select and open the AnimationObjects asset.

6. Select its Take 001 asset—the animation clip.

7. In the Preview window, click the Play button and view the animation (Figure 7-4).

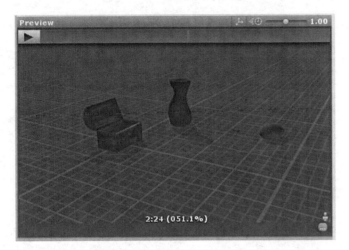

Figure 7-4. The collection of objects run through their animations

8. Check out the Take 001 clips for each of the imported object groups.

The Preview window was designed to show character animation and is only marginally useful for animated inorganic objects. It has a camera that is targeted to the root object of the animations. In the case of the AnimationObjects asset, the group itself does not animate, so the rock quickly moves out of frame, and the small keys barely show.

You might want a bit more practice with the Two Columns Layout. Let's do a bit of experimenting.

1. Right-click the Project tab at the top of the panel; select Two Columns Layout, if you are not already using it.

2. Adjust the spacing and, at the bottom of the second column, move the slider all the way to the right, to see full-sized icons.

Icons are shown for the contents of the Animation Tests folder, including the already opened AnimationObjects.

3. Close the AnimationObjects by clicking its arrow.

4. Experiment with the icon-size slider, to see the viewing options.

■ **Tip** Double-clicking the mesh's GameObject counterparts will open the files in your default FBX app. You may not rename the imported objects in the Project folder.

To keep things less cluttered and allow more screen space for the Scene and Game windows, you will be switching back to the single column. Feel free, however, to switch back and forth on your own, when you find it helpful.

5. Right-click the Project tab and select One Column Layout.

Import Settings

When you bring mesh assets into Unity, they are processed through the importer, for settings that will dictate how the model appears, what system controls its animation, and how the animated clips are defined and interpreted. The three parts of the l are Model, Rig, and Animation.

Import Settings: Model

The first of the import settings is in the Model section. Let's start by selecting one of the newly imported assets.

1. Select the AnimationObjects asset and select the Model section (Figure 7-5).

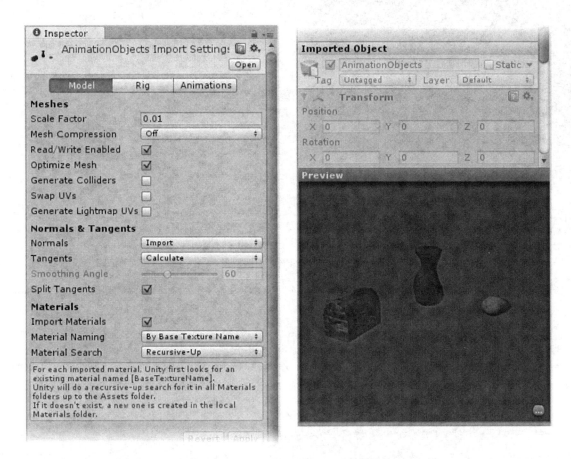

Figure 7-5. *The top and bottom of the Model section of the Import Settings*

The top setting is Scale Factor, but until you have the objects in the scene, you will have no way to tell whether it is good or not.

2. Drag the AnimationObjects asset into the Scene view, in front of the First Person Controller (Figure 7-6).

Figure 7-6. The AnimationObjects asset in the scene, scale unknown

While your own imported meshes are likely to have a consistent scale, you may occasionally come across scenes where that's not the case. Scaling 3D objects in Unity is simple. The unit of measure in Unity is a meter, which is approximately three feet. A newly created Cube is 1 meter cubed and makes a good means of assessing scale. It's not essential that the scale be perfectly correct, only that it be believable.

1. Create a new cube in the scene.

2. Move the cube near the chest to assess the scale (see Figure 7-7).

***Figure 7-7.** Imported object and cube for scale comparison*

If the cube is 1 cubic meter, the chest is about the size of a compact car. It looks like the imported objects could stand to be much smaller. While you could scale it in the scene, assets are easier to manage if the scale is adjusted in the imported assets.

3. Select the AnimationObjects in the Project view.

4. In the Inspector, near the top of the Model section, change the Scale Factor to **0.0032** (see Figure 7-8).

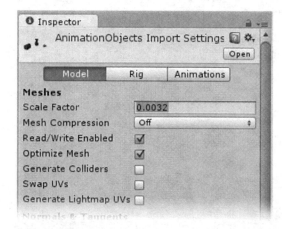

***Figure 7-8.** Changing the Scale Factor in the Model section*

5. Click Apply (the button is about halfway down the panel, on the right side).

6. Change the Scene view to an iso Right view (click the Right label to toggle perspective and iso), to see the results without the distortion of perspective (see Figure 7-9).

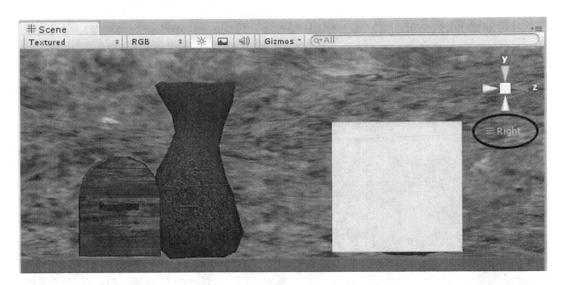

Figure 7-9. Scale comparison, as seen in an iso Right view

7. Rotate the view and click the label to turn it back to a Perspective view.

8. Delete the test cube.

With something more recognizable in the scene, the ground texture looks a bit large. Now is a good time to briefly revisit the Terrain editor and adjust the texture scales.

9. Select the Terrain GameObject, the Paint Terrain tool, and the ground textures.

From Edit Texture, edit the ground textures and reduce the Tiling size to about **8**, then Apply the change. Figure 7-10 shows the ground before and after editing.

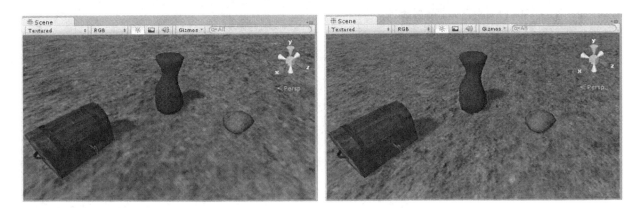

Figure 7-10. The ground with the default 15×15 scale (left) and the new 8×8 scale (right)

Tip In a fast-paced game, the large tiling would be less obvious, but in a classic point-and-click, the player is more likely to be focused on the immediate surroundings and will notice poorly scaled textures.

The final test of any adjustment is to go into Play mode and see how it looks "in game," as the player navigates the scene.

1. Toggle on Scene Lighting in the Scene view and move and rotate the group or the First Person Controller until the imported objects can be clearly seen in the Game view.

2. Click Play.

3. Drive up to the objects and look around them (Figure 7-11).

Figure 7-11. The view in the Scene view (left) and from the First Person Controller (right)

Either the objects have to be bigger, or you will have to adjust the camera's field of view.

In games, scale is not always exact. Often you'll have to increase the scale of an object to make it more playable. In our case, however, it turns out the camera field of view is more suited to a first-person shooter that requires more peripheral vision than for an adventure game where small objects need to be noticed.

1. Exit Play mode.

2. Open the First Person Controller.

3. Select the Main Camera.

4. In the Inspector, change the camera's Field of View to **32**.

5. Examine the objects again.

As Figure 7-12 shows, now you can get a good view of the objects when you are close.

Figure 7-12. *Reduced field of view on the First Person Controller's camera*

6. Stop Play mode.

7. Make the change to the camera permanent.

After you've finished with your test objects and have more of the scene completed, you'll probably want to adjust the camera's Field of View again, but while you are setting things up, you may as well make it easy to access the objects.

1. Select the Main Camera.

2. Set its X Rotation to about **12**, to get a better view of the objects for when they animate (Figure 7-13).

Figure 7-13. *The objects ready to view*

3. Adjust the AnimationObjects group and First Person Controller in the Scene view, so the objects are visible in the newly adjusted Game window. Do not move the individual objects.

4. Set the Game view back to Free Aspect.

Import Settings: Rig

With Unity's new Mecanim system, you have several choices to make for your animation. Eventually, the original animation system will be merged into Mecanim, but until then, you will have to wade through the lot. Mecanim was originally designed to control Humanoid characters. This precluded things such as tails, wings, and ponytails, so they added a Generic option. Then they discovered that there were cases that didn't lend themselves to Mecanim as it stands, so they re-exposed the Legacy option in the import settings.

If that sounds confusing, it's because Unity made a decision to release features throughout the point-release cycle. Instead of waiting for relatively finished features to be unveiled only during major releases, you can expect features to be altered, refined, and improved at any point release. Always be sure to check the Unity forum to learn how to deal with changes. This book has a thread on the Teaching forum using its title.

The next section of the Import Settings is the Rig section. As a default, imported objects are assigned the Generic Animation Type.

1. Select the AnimationObjects in the Project view and select the Rig section (Figure 7-14).

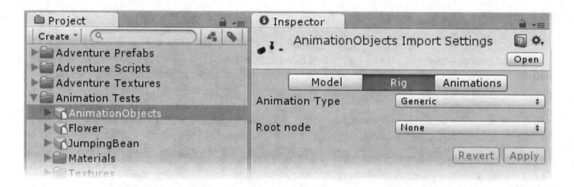

Figure 7-14. *The Rig section of the Import Settings*

2. Click the Animation Type drop-down (Figure 7-15).

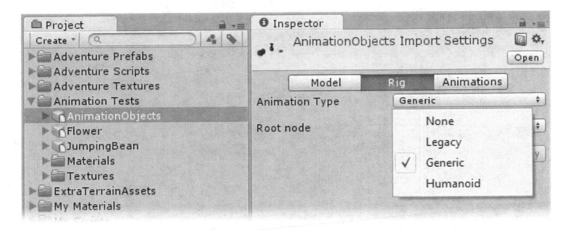

Figure 7-15. *The Animation Type choices*

The options are None, Legacy, Generic, and Humanoid. The objects, or at least some of them, have to animate, so None is not the right choice. The objects are obviously not Humanoid, so that one is out as well. So the two choices are Legacy and Generic.

Generic uses the Mecanim system and adds an Animator component.

1. Select the Animation objects in the Hierarchy view and check out the Animator component in the Inspector (Figure 7-16).

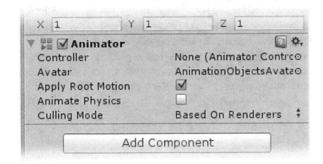

Figure 7-16. *The Animator component*

Half of the Animator component appears to be character-related. But the two important things to know about the Animator component/Mecanim system are that there is no way to test the animation in the scene when the objects are in place and that it has built-in blending. Blending moves an object from one animation smoothly into another. A typical example is a character in walk animation smoothly blending into a run animation. The animations, including the blends, are viewed in the Preview window.

Both issues, while advantageous when handling characters, will be detrimental to setting up the simple mechanical animations used on most of the action objects. To set up the action objects, you will want to observe the animations in the scene, to make sure they are correctly placed in respect to the animations they hold. The rock, for instance, needs to animate into a clear spot, without intersecting anything else on the way. The objects also have fully contained animations. Not only is blending unnecessary, most objects only have one animation. Blending also carries a lot of overhead, both in scripting and setup. Bottom line: Mecanim is not suited for the simple animation you need for most of the action objects.

2.   Select the AnimationObjects asset in the Project view.

3.   Change the Animation Type to Legacy and click Apply.

4.   Open the Generation drop down to view the choices (Figure 7-17).

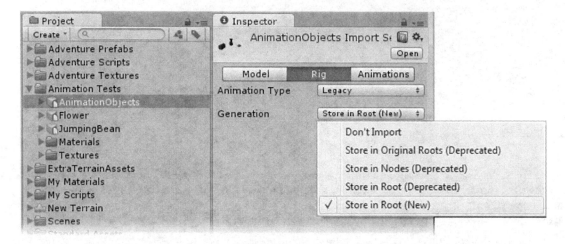

Figure 7-17. *The root Generation type*

As you can see, other than Don't Import, most of the options are deprecated. The default, Store in Root (New), is the preferred choice. This option puts the animation on the root object. For the current asset, this means the Animation component will be put only on the parent object, the AnimationObjects group. The Take 001 clip you saw earlier will be split up to define the animation clip for each individual object, but they will all be called on the parent object. One downside to this option is that you can only play one clip at a time. Triggering another while one is playing will cancel the clip currently playing. When setting up this type of animation, each behavior must have a unique place on the time line.

When you switched to the Legacy Animation Type, the Animator component was replaced by the Animation component. Let's take a look at it next.

1.   Select the AnimationObjects group in the Hierarchy view.

It now contains an Animation component (Figure 7-18).

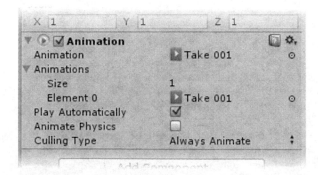

Figure 7-18. *The Animation component*

The Take 001 clip is the current default animation clip, because it is the only clip so far. The best part of this component is the Play Automatically option. This will allow you to see the animation in the scene, without setup or code, while you arrange the scene.

2. Click Play and watch the Game or Scene view to see the animation (Figure 7-19).

Figure 7-19. *The animations playing automatically at startup*

3. Stop Play mode.

Parenting

One of the most important concepts to understand in 3D animation is parenting. *Children inherit the transforms of their parent*. Transforms are translate (move), rotate, and scale. Inside the parent group, AnimationObjects, the individual objects have their own animations that are enacted relative to the parent group. No matter where you place the parent group, all the animations happen as expected.

Let's try a little experiment and see what happens if you move an object from inside the AnimationObjects group.

1. In the Hierarchy view, select the rock and move it back, away from the key (Figure 7-20).

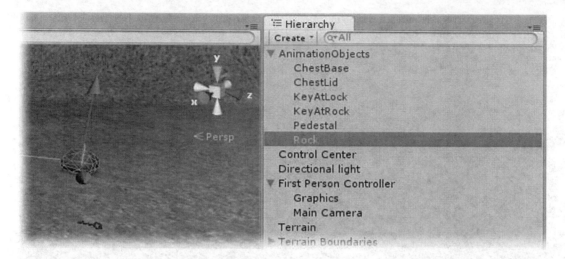

Figure 7-20. The rock moved away from the key

2. Click Play and watch what happens.

When it comes time for the rock to animate, it jumps back to animate from the original location relative to its parent, the AnimationObjects group.

You're probably wondering what would happen if you just removed it from the group.

3. Stop Play mode and do a couple of undo's to get it back to its original position.

4. In the Hierarchy view, drag the rock out of the parent group, and drop it below the other objects in the list.

5. Agree to the Losing Prefab warning.

6. Click Play.

Nothing happens, because it is no longer under the control of the group's Animation component. Even if you copy and paste the component onto the rock, the association has been lost. Looks like you'll need a different object for this test.

1. Select the JumpingBean from the Animation Tests folder in the Project view.

2. In the import settings, Rig, change the Animation Type to Legacy and click Apply.

Once you've switched from Generic to Legacy, the Take 001 will no longer show the animation in the Preview window. The message says you need to drag a model into the view. This means you need the whole asset, not just its mesh component (Figure 7-21).

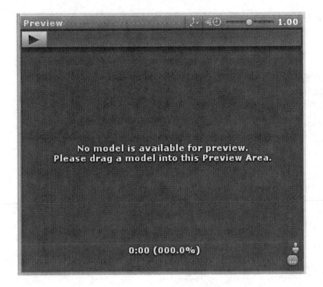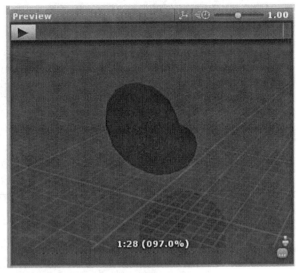

Figure 7-21. *Using the Preview with a Legacy animation clip*

■ **Tip**   The next time you want to preview an asset's animation, the bean will still be loaded, so you will have to drag the new asset into the window before its animation will show.

---

   3.   Drag the bean into the scene near the other objects.

In the Hierarchy view, you can see that it is a single object.

   4.   Click Play.

It completely disappears! If you double-click it in the Hierarchy view, you will find it below the terrain, somewhere close to 0,0,0, where it was originally animated in the original file. Without a parent, an imported object is automatically parented to the scene itself, so just like when you moved the rock, the bean jumped back to its original location to do its animation.

   1.   Delete the JumpingBean from the scene.

   2.   Drag a new one into the Hierarchy view, rather than directly into the Scene view.

   3.   Double-click it to find it in the Scene view.

Note that it is fairly close to 0,0,0.

   4.   Now create an Empty GameObject and name it **Bean Group**.

It is created at the focus spot—the same location as the bean.

   5.   In the Hierarchy view, drag the JumpingBean object onto the Bean Group.

   6.   Focus back on the AnimationObjects group, then use Move to View to move the Bean Group into place.

   7.   Click Play and watch the Bean Group.

This time the bean animates as expected. As long as you move the new parent object, not the object with the animation, everything will work correctly. So, the solution to an animated object that does not have a parent on import is to put it inside a group before you move it.

In this type of genre, it's not unusual to have several independently animating objects imported as a single grouped asset. With the AnimationObjects group, you can see that the key's position relative to the chest it unlocks is crucial. The rock, and key it covers, is a different case. While they should probably stay near the chest, you might find you have to make some minor adjustments to fit them into the scene just right. You now know you can't just move the rock around, so you need a solution that will let you separate animated objects from their parent group, without disrupting their animations. Turns out, it's easy. All you have to do is make a duplicated group and delete all the extra objects in it.

Let's start by getting the AnimationObjects group back to "stock."

1. Select the AnimationObjects group and, at the top of the Inspector, in the Model line, click Revert.

2. Delete the Rock that originally came out of the group.

3. Select the AnimationObjects group and use Ctrl+D to duplicate it.

4. Name the new group **Rock Group** and delete all but the Rock and KeyAtRock objects inside it.

5. Select the original group and delete the Rock and KeyAtRock.

6. Move the new Rock Group to a new location and click Play.

This time, the animation is still intact.

Prior to 4.0, Unity had an option to store imported animations on the object roots. This meant you could import a scene full of animated objects all together, yet have control of them as individuals. The option is still there, but it is one of the "deprecated" ones and is painful to set up. Hopefully, a new solution will eventually be developed to replace it. Until that time, you should now have a pretty good understanding of how to manage assets with multiple and distinct animating objects.

Import Settings: Animations

Now that you've got some objects in the scene and animating, you will need a way to both separate the animations for each object and to have them play on cue. The first step is to break the generic Take 001 into separate behaviors or animation clips. To begin, you will want a list of the frames used by each object's behaviors, so you can define the clips.

Table 7-1 shows the time segments for the various objects and the names you will use for the clips.

Table 7-1. *Object Behaviors in the Animation*

Clip Name	Start Frame	End Frame
rock move	0	30
key insert	31	60
chest open	61	90
chest close	91	110
key remove	121	150
chest rattle	151	163

■ **Tip** In scenes with multiple objects imported, name clips with the object name first and the behavior second, such as *chest open*, *chest close*, or *chest rattle*. This will make clips easier to locate in the browser. Another naming convention that you will be following is to use all lowercase for the legacy animation clips.

1. Select AnimationObjects in the Project view and expand it.

2. In the Inspector, click the Animations section of the Importer (Figure 7-22).

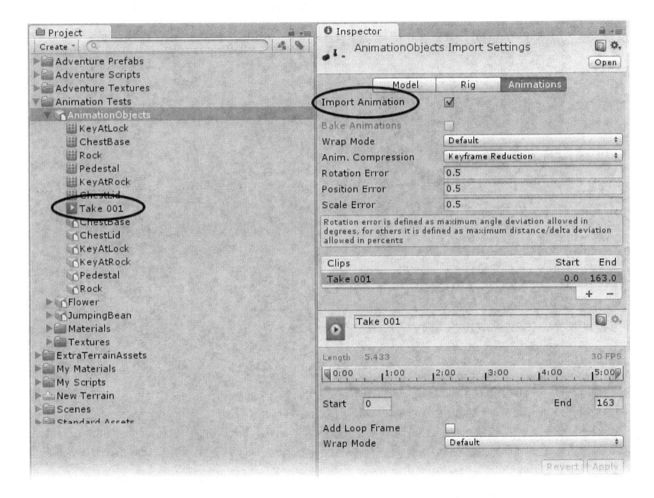

Figure 7-22. *The animation section and the default clip*

3. Note the location of Take 001, then, near the top of the Inspector, uncheck Import Animation.

4. Click Apply.

Take 001, which represented the animation, no longer appears in the Project view, and the Animation section is empty.

5. Click Play.

The AnimationObjects' animations no longer exist.

Just as it says, animation is not imported for the scene. Use this setting for things such as buildings, landscaping objects, and other static or non-animating objects.

6. Re-check Animation.

7. Click Apply, then click the Animations tab once, to load the clip information again.

The Take 001 clip is reinstated.

8. Select the AnimationObjects in the Hierarchy view and check out the Animation component (Figure 7-23).

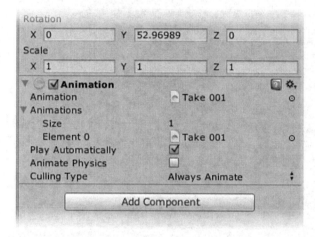

Figure 7-23. *The Animation Component showing the imported clip*

The Animation array has one element, and the default Animation is Take 001.

1. Select AnimationObjects in the Project view again.

2. In the Inspector, change Wrap Mode to Once (Figure 7-24).

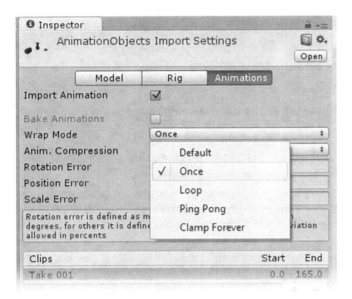

Figure 7-24. *The Wrap Mode setting that will be the default for all of this asset's clips*

3. In the Clips list, select the Take 001 clip and, next to the Play arrow, rename it **all** (Figure 7-25).

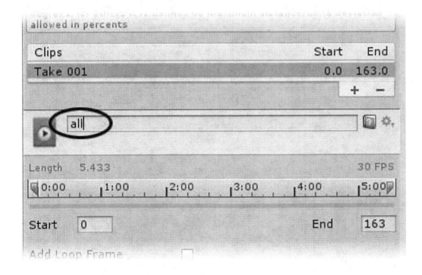

Figure 7-25. *Renaming a clip*

As soon as you press Enter, the Take 001 name will update. There are a few things happening here that bear explaining. By keeping the clip of the entire animation intact, you keep any easy means of testing a complicated sequence of animations. Also, in case you were wondering, if you look above the time line, it shows the length of the clip, 5.433 seconds, and the frame rate used when creating it, 30 frames per second. Unity quite happily uses whatever frame rate was used in the creation of the imported animation.

4. In the Clips list, click the + to generate a new clip.

5. Name it **rock move**.

6. Below the blue time line, leave Start at 0 and change End from 163 to **30**.

7. Drag the AnimationObjects asset into the Preview window.

8. Right-click the Preview's title bar to float it, so you can make the window larger.

9. Click the Play arrow to see the animation for the clip play.

10. Adjust the time the clip takes to play out by changing the 1.00 to 2.00 (faster) and 0.1 (slower). Return it to 1.00 when you are finished.

The Preview doesn't have an option for a wrap Once, so you will have to drag the time indicator manually to see if the time segment of 0-30 is good. You can re-dock the Preview wind by clicking the × at the upper right.

With the first regular clip now defined, let's add the rest of the clips, according to Table 7-1.

1. In the Clips list, click the + to generate a new clip.

2. Name the new clip **key insert.**

3. Set its Start to **31** and its End to **60**.

4. Repeat the procedure for the remaining clips, according to Table 7-1.

5. When you have finished, click Apply (see Figure 7-26).

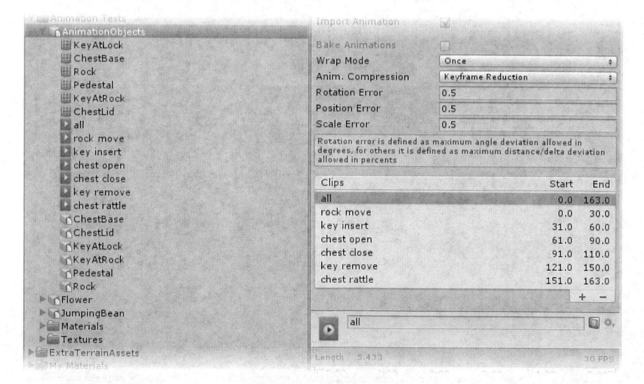

Figure 7-26. *The newly defined clips in the Project view and in the Inspector*

Having added several clips and renamed the original Take 001 for the AnimationObjects group, we ought to check back with the objects already in the current scene to see what, if any, changes were made in the Animation component.

1. Select the AnimationObjects in the Hierarchy view.

The Take 001 has been changed to *all*, but the new clips were not loaded because the prefab was broken.

2. Click Revert in the Inspector to load the new clips into the Animation component (Figure 7-27).

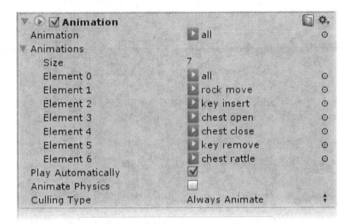

Figure 7-27. *The updated clips in the Animation component*

3. Load one of the new clips in as the default Animation through the browse icon.

Unfortunately, you can't just drag the one you want from the Animations list, hence the emphasis placed on naming and naming conventions for the clips. You can, however, click the existing clip. It will be briefly highlighted in the Project view, allowing you to quickly locate the one you really want and drag it into the field.

4. Click Play and watch your chosen animation.

5. Exit Play mode.

Now that the clips are safely added, you can delete the Rock and KeyAtRock from the group, once again breaking the prefab. The takeaway here is that you should usually set up the clips before doing much in the scenes. Since things tend to change, that won't always be possible, so you will get a chance to manually fix the Rock Group.

1. Delete the Rock and KeyAtRock from the AnimationObjects group.

2. Select the Rock Group.

3. Drag the rock move clip from the Project view onto the existing all clip in the Animations list.

Rather than replace the existing animation, the list Size is increased and the *all* clip is bumped down an element.

4. Set the default Animation to rock move.

5. Click Play.

You probably didn't notice anything different, because the rock move uses the first 30 frames of the whole animation. If it had started later in the original clip, you would now see it play immediately, instead of at its original position on the time line.

6.   Exit Play mode.

As a final cleanup, even though you are not going to use the JumpingBean in the game, you should probably rename its Take 001 clip to remove one more generic Take 001 from the project before you move on.

7.   Select the Jumping Bean in the Project view.

8.   In the Inspector, Animation section, rename Take 001 to bean jump and click Apply.

Importing Complex Hierarchies with Animations

So far you have seen fairly simple animations on an asset with several distinct members. The remaining import is the Flower. It has its own complicated bone system, as well as FK (forward kinematics) animation. Although the flower will not be hopping around the scene trying to eat unsuspecting players, it is controlled much as a character is, in that the Animation component is on the root or parent and clips animate all the children beneath the root.

1.   Select the Flower asset in the Project view.

2.   Change its Animation Type to Legacy in the Rig section of Import Settings.

3.   Add the clips shown in Table 7-2.

Table 7-2. New Flower Behaviors

Object, Behavior	Start Frame	End Frame
flower revive	0	124
flower idle	125	200

4.   Just above the Apply button, set the revive clip's Wrap Mode to Once and the idle clip's Wrap Mode to Loop.

5.   To ensure a smooth looping transition for the idle clip, check Add Loop Frame.

6.   Click Apply.

7.   Drag the Flower into the scene and move it so that it is visible in the Game view.

8.   Click Play to see its entire animation.

9.   Change its default animation to the idle clip and click Play.

The idle behavior loops. It turns out that the flower is just as ugly revived as wilted (Figure 7-28).

Figure 7-28. *The flower in its idle behavior*

Setting Up Materials

As mentioned earlier in the chapter, Unity imports materials only on a very limited basis, and most of the action objects, at least, deserve better than the default material. This means you'll definitely have to spend some time customizing and improving the defaults that are created on import. Unity uses shaders exclusively, so you'll be able to get a lot of rather nice effects once you understand how they can be manipulated.

Let's look, then, to see how the objects came in. Because the textures were brought in at the same time, most of the objects will have had a default material created from their Diffuse texture. The default material uses a simple Diffuse shader that has only a Base texture and a Main Color that can be used to tint the texture map. Naming is from the texture first, and the original material second, by default. If you wish, you can change the naming convention in the Model section of the Importer, under Materials, Material naming.

You will be going through the imported objects one at a time and will "doctor" them up a bit.

The Keys

The two keys, a couple of wrought iron types, originally had only a bump map. Because they had no diffuse, Unity named the material Key, after the original material (Figure 7-29).

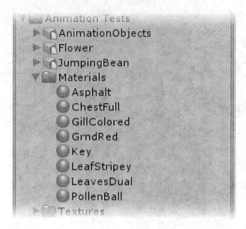

Figure 7-29. Materials generated for the imported objects

In 3ds Max, where the meshes were made, the bump uses a texture called Hammered.jpg. In Unity's shaders, you will use a Normal Map instead.

1. Select the Hammered texture from the Textures folder.

2. Check it out in the Preview window in the Inspector (Figure 7-30).

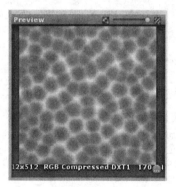

Figure 7-30. The Hammered texture in the Preview window

The texture has already been converted to a DXT1 texture format, and Mip Maps have been generated for it. Unity converts all non-dds formatted texture to dds on import.

Unity can automatically turn it into a normal map for you, so you will need to duplicate it first.

3. Use Ctrl+D (or Cmd+D on the Mac) to duplicate the Hammered texture.

4. Select Hammered 1.

5. In the Texture Importer, change the Texture Type to Normal map.

6. Change the Bumpiness to about 0.15 and the Filtering to Smooth.

7. Click Apply.

The map is now the distinctive Cyan/Magenta colors of a normal map (Figure 7-31).

Figure 7-31. *The Hammered texture converted to a normal map*

8. Rename the texture to reflect its new function: **HammeredBump**.

9. Select the Key material.

10. At the top of the Inspector, click the Shader drop-down and change it from Diffuse to Bumped Specular, the second option from the top.

11. Leave the Base map as None and drag and drop the HammeredBump onto its Normalmap thumbnail (Figure 7-32).

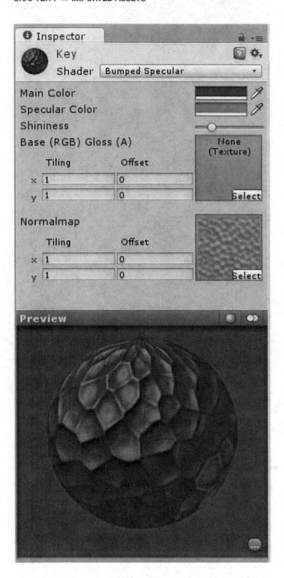

Figure 7-32. The HammeredBump material using the Bumped Specular shader

---

■ **Note** Normal maps are a means of creating virtual geometry for lighting calculations. When you start with actual geometry, the vertex normal for each vertex is recorded as a particular color on an image or texture. The texture map needs to be big enough to allocate at least 1 pixel for each vertex for full effect. In a game, the lighting calculations still take time to calculate, but the object itself has fewer vertices and takes up less overhead. As long as the normal map is not too big, the trade-off of polygons vs. texture memory is usually advantageous, providing the target platform has a graphics chip or card that can support it.

---

12. Next, select one of the keys in the Project view to check the end result in the Preview window, as in Figure 7-33.

Figure 7-33. *One of the keys with the doctored material*

The texture needs to be tiled more to fit the mesh better.

13.   For the Normalmap, change both the x and the y Tiling to **5**, as in Figure 7-34.

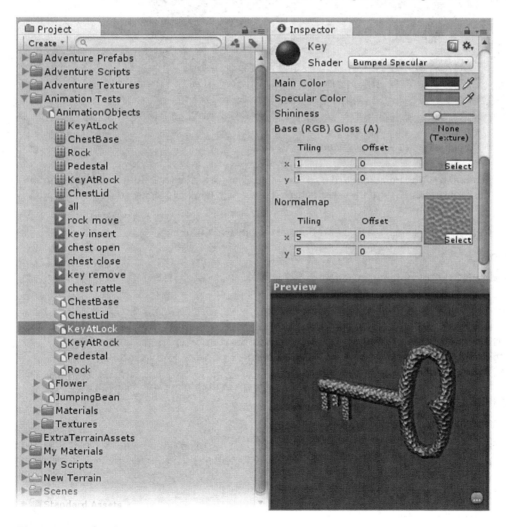

Figure 7-34. *The tiled Normalmap*

251

The material looks good in the preview, but you should check it in the scene.

14. Click Play and drive over to the key at the rock after it has been revealed (Figure 7-35).

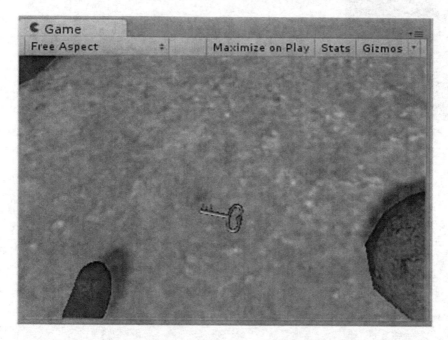

Figure 7-35. *One of the keys in the Game window at runtime*

The key doesn't stand out much. You may want to darken the Main Color or reduce the Shininess. It's important to test art assets in the game environment before they are finalized. For the key, you may decide gold or brass would be a better choice.

15. Experiment with the key material's settings until you are happy with the effect.

16. Exit Play mode.

Changes made to materials during runtime are retained.

The Chest

The chest base and lid share a texture map, ChestFull. However, because the texture represents three different "materials" (wood, leather, and metal), you will also want to use a glossiness map along with a normal map, to differentiate each beyond the diffuse color of the texture.

With shaders in Unity, it is not unusual to put other types of 8-bit maps in the alpha channel. Each shader will show what, if anything, the alpha channel is being used for.

1. Select the ChestFull material.

Even when the object's material comes in with a texture, you'll note that the Main Color defaults to mid-gray. This color gets added to the texture map, allowing you to tint it on an individual basis. If your texture looks too dark in the scene, you can change the Main Color to white.

Inspection of the default Diffuse shader shows the Base texture using RGB.

2. Load the Bumped Diffuse shader and look at its parameters.

The Base is again RGB. The Normalmap is also RGB. If you are used to using grayscale bump maps, this will remind you that in Unity, Shaders use RGB Normal maps. Using a grayscale bump map instead of a normal map will produce odd results.

▨ **Tip**   Wait to convert your grayscale bump maps to normal maps in Unity, so you can easily adjust their bumpiness strength.

---

3.   Select the next shader down, the Bumped Specular, for the ChestFull material.

This shader has a new parameter, Shininess, that will let you adjust the specular highlight of the material. More important, it uses the alpha channel of the Base texture as a specular mask.

4.   Set the Shininess about halfway along the slider, to tighten the highlight.

5.   Set the Specular Color to white.

6.   Now drag in the Preview window so you can see the difference in the "materials" as the view rotates around the sample sphere.

The straps are somewhat glossy, but the metal parts are more so.

7.   Select the ChestFull texture in the Project view.

8.   In the Inspector, toggle the diffuse/alpha button at the top of the Preview window to see the alpha channel of the texture.

This alpha channel was designed to be used as a bump and shininess map rather than an alpha mask. You may notice that there's a check box to Generate Alpha from Grayscale. That operation is permanent! If an alpha channel already exists (as with the ChestFull texture), it will be overwritten. If you want to experiment, make a duplicate of the texture first.

Figure 7-36 shows the superior contrast of the custom shininess map (center) compared with an automatically generated version. It will also be a better choice for generating a normal map.

Figure 7-36.   *The Diffuse texture (left), its custom alpha channel (middle), and an alpha channel generated in Unity, using its grayscale version (right)*

9. Select the ChestFullBump texture.

10. Change its Texture Type to Normal map and click Apply (Figure 7-36).

11. Set the Bumpiness to about **0.05** and click Apply.

1024×1024 is a bit of overkill for one small chest.

12. Set its Max Size to **512** and click Apply.

13. Select the ChestFull material again.

14. Drag and drop the newly generated normal map into its Normalmap thumbnail.

15. Click Play and navigate around the chest.

You may decide that the 1024×1024 diffuse/shininess map can be reduced as well. Once an asset is in the game environment, you'll have a better idea of how big of a texture map it rates. In this case, the 512 version is slightly blurrier on the wood section, but still provides good definition for the straps and hobnails, so it would be a worthwhile conservation of texture memory. On a mobile platform such as iPhone or Android, you'll need to keep texture sizes fairly small, to stay within their total texture limits.

The Flower

Let's look at another material. The flower is a bit different from the other objects in that it has multiple materials on one of its objects.

1. Open the Flower object in the Project view.

2. Select the Stem prefab.

In the Inspector, you will see that there are two materials listed for it: leafstripey and leavesdual.

3. Select the Stem from the Flower in the Hierarchy view and open the Materials array to view its contents.

The array has two elements, the two materials, as shown in Figure 7-37.

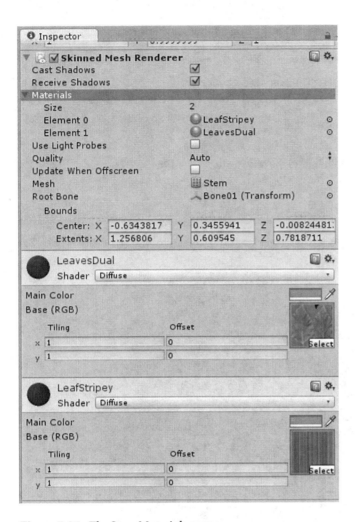

Figure 7-37. *The Stem Materials array*

▤ **Tip** Arrays always start counting their elements at 0. An array of 2 has element 0 and element 1.

If you wanted the flower to be an action object, that is, one you'd need to click, it would be better to use a single unwrap map to make the textures for the leaves and petals. Because you are only going to trigger its animation from a different object for now, you don't have to worry about it.

▤ **Tip** Assets with unwrap textures are generally easier to handle in games, but the trade-off is the possibility of using more texture memory to get the same resolution or settling for a reduction in quality.

The pollen ball in the center of the flower presents some nice texture possibilities. Because the pollen object is deep in the bone hierarchy, you will have to expand the Flower object to gain access to it.

Remember to hold down the Alt key when you open the group in the Hierarchy view.

4. Locate the pollen ball at the bottom of the Bone07 hierarchy and select it.

It is using a material called PollenBall.

5. Change the shader to Vertex Lit, set the Main and Emissive colors to mid-gray, the Specular Color to red, and the Shininess to the far left.

6. Drag the Pollen texture from the Textures folder onto the Base texture thumbnail.

7. Change the Tiling to 3×3.

8. Click Play to see the results when the flower opens up (see Figure 7-38).

Figure 7-38. *The pollen ball's new shader*

9. Try adjusting the Main Color down to black to see the full effect of the red specular.

Note that the changes to shaders are not lost when you stop Play mode.

The Rock uses the GrndRed texture.

1. Change the GrndRed's shader to Bumped Diffuse.

2. Use Ctrl+D to duplicate the Asphalt texture and turn the clone into a normal map.

3. Add the new normal map to the GrndRed shader.

Shadows

Now that you've used the materials to make the imported objects look much better, you are probably thinking some shadows would help to make them look like they belong in the scene and aren't just "Photoshopped" in. In Unity Pro, you can set the main light to cast soft shadows, and everything will look much nicer—at the cost of some frame rate, of course. If you are using Pro, you may already be using the soft shadows, and your scene may more closely resemble the screen shots.

Let's address shadows in Pro first, as it is more a matter of tweaking the shadow strength. Depending on where your light source is, you may need to adjust the shadow parameters.

1. If you are using Unity Pro, open the Lightmapping editor; change the Mode to Dual Lightmaps and Bake.

2. Select the Directional light.

In the Inspector, you can see the shadow parameters. Strength controls how dark or dense the shadow is.

3. Adjust the Strength until the dynamic shadows match the baked shadows.

Take a look at Figure 7-39. On the left, you see dual lightmaps with Lightmapping set to Auto for the directional light. In the Project's Quality settings, the Shadow Distance was set to 150. The real-time shadows blend into the lightmap shadows 45 meters out from the Main Camera. On the right, I turned off the Use Lightmaps parameter (open the Lightmapper and uncheck the option in the Scene view), to show where the real-time shadows blend with the lightmapped shadows.

Figure 7-39. *Shadows in Unity Pro (left), showing the end of the dynamic shadow zone (right)*

If you are using Unity Pro and have shadows, you may want to investigate Shadows further in the reference manual. You'll find some very nice examples of "Cascades" and see how they can improve the look of your shadows. You can find the Cascades setting in the Quality Settings.

Static Objects and Shadows

If you don't have Unity Pro, you have a couple of choices: no shadows or fake shadows. If the objects never move, they can be marked as Static, and shadows will be baked for them. But for animating objects, leaving a shadow behind as the object animates away from its original position is going to look pretty silly. In our example, some objects, such as the flower and chest lid, are probably fine with no shadows. Others, such as the rock, will need some help. Shadows, in any form, will cost. If they are baked in, they cost texture memory. If they are dynamic, they cost processor time. If we fake a few dynamic shadows with Unity's Blob Shadow preset—a light with a negative strength—they also cost processor time, but not as much.

Using shadows increases the quality of a scene, removes visual ambiguity, and, along with specular highlights, helps define a 3D shape. To put it bluntly, things just look better with shadows, but dealing with shadows in real time is vastly different than in DCC programs.

To generate baked secondary shadows in Unity, the object must be marked as Static.

1.   Select the ChestBase in the Hierarchy panel.

2.   In the Inspector, at the top right, check Static (Figure 7-40).

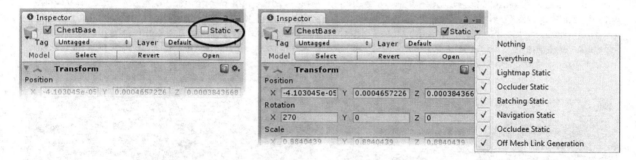

Figure 7-40. *Selecting the Static parameter in the Inspector, and the drop-down showing the default results*

The Pedestal does not animate either.

3.   Set the Pedestal to Static as well.

The next time you bake out the terrain lighting, the shadows will be added for the static objects.

Blob shadows are often used for generic character shadows when you're creating games for low-end platforms. Objects such as the rock are good candidates for a blob shadow.

If you don't see a Projectors folder in the Standard Assets folder (Figure 7-41), you'll need to import that package.

Figure 7-41. *The Projectors folder*

4. From the Assets menu, select Import Package ➤ Projectors.

5. Select all and Import.

6. If you are using Pro, set Shadow Type on the scene's Directional light to No Shadows.

7. From the Projectors folder, drag a Blob Shadow Projector into the Scene view.

8. Position it over the RockGroup and move it up or down until the "shadow" looks about the right size (Figure 7-42).

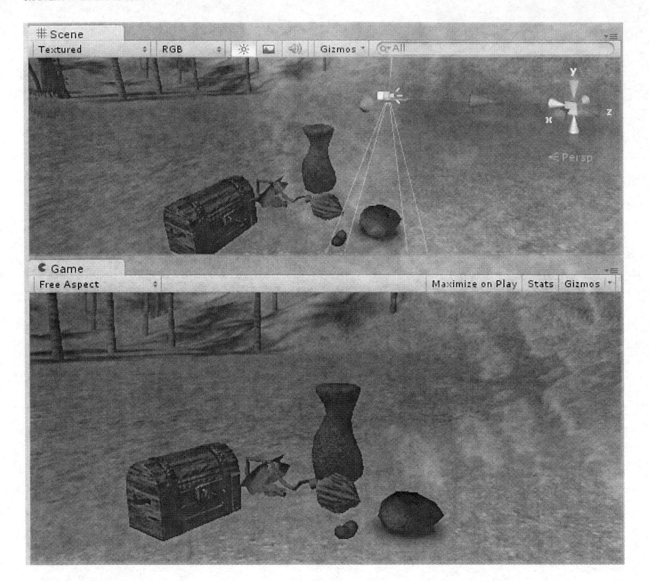

***Figure 7-42.** Positioning the blob shadow*

Right now, the projector light projects on the top of the rock group. With a character, you'd use layers to prevent the blob shadow from projecting on the character itself. You can use the same technique on the rock or any of the action objects. For the test subject, let's adjust the clipping plane until the shadow looks correct and then create a Layer, so we can exclude the rock itself from receiving the shadow. Layers provide a way to include and exclude objects and effects from mainly lights and cameras. The Blob Shadow is actually a kind of light with a negative value.

1. In the Inspector, change the Blob Shadow Projector's Projector component's Aspect Ratio to 1.4, to elongate it slightly.

2. Rotate the Blob Shadow Projector until it matches up to the rock better.

3. Change the Far Clip Plane to about 15—the rock won't be lifting very high.

Before you can use the Ignore Layers parameter, you will have to set up a layer for it to ignore. You will be doing more with layers later, so consider this a sneak peek. Layers and tags are a means of including or excluding objects. Layers are generally used with lights, and the Blob Shadow is a form of light.

4.　At the top of the Inspector, click the Layers drop-down and select Add or Edit Layer (Figure 7-43).

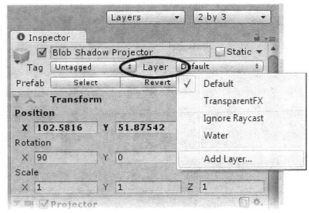

Figure 7-43.　Accessing Layers

5.　To the right of User Layer 8, click to locate and activate the text field and name the layer NoBlob.

6.　Select the Blob Shadow Projector again in the Hierarchy layer.

7.　Click the drop-down for Ignore Layers and select the new NoBlob layer.

8.　Select the Rock Group.

9.　At the top of the Inspector, click the Layer drop-down and select the NoBlob layer for the Rock Group and agree to Change Children.

The rock is now ignored by the Blob Shadow Projector, so only the ground receives the fake shadow, as shown in Figure 7-44 (left).

Figure 7-44.　Adjusting the Projector settings to fix the shadow(left), and the Rock Group in action (right)

10. Adjust the Blob Shadows parameters until it looks correct.

11. When it looks about right, drag the Blob Shadow Projector onto the Rock in the Hierarchy view.

12. Click Play and watch the Rock and its "shadow" (see preceding Figure 7-44 [right]).

Because of the falloff built into the shadow via the Gradient map, the "shadow" gets larger and paler as the rock, the projector's parent, moves up away from the ground.

13. Stop Play mode.

14. Deactivate the Rock Group.

15. If you are using Unity Pro, go ahead and turn shadows back on for the Directional Light.

16. Save the scene and save the project.

Summary

In this chapter, you imported assets for your scene and learned how to process them for animation and materials.

When importing animated assets, you learned how to correct scale. When the animated objects come in together, their animation component, either the newer Mecanim Animator or legacy Animation, was on the parent. Single animated objects, you found, need to be parented before you adjust their placement in a scene. You also learned how to split the Take 001 animation clip into individual behaviors.

On importing objects, you found that, as a default, Unity creates generic materials using the original material's Diffuse texture map as the name. If no texture map was used for the material, the Unity material was named for the file and appended with the original material name, unless a different option was chosen.

After importing, you discovered you could use different shaders to improve the look of the materials. One of the most important concepts was that of using the alpha channel component of a texture as something other than an alpha channel mask. You also found that you could have Unity generate normal maps, but that you needed to duplicate the original texture before doing so. Additionally, you found that Unity converts all texture maps to dds format internally.

CHAPTER 8

■ ■ ■

Action Objects

With a nice selection of imported assets processed and ready to go, you are probably itching to find out how to interact with them. Not only will you be triggering their animations, you will also be adding sound effects and getting a bit of insight into state management.

Colliders

Before delving into animations, let's do a quick scene check and navigate around our new objects. As you may remember, before you can interact with an object, it will need a collider. You will also need a collider to prevent the player from driving through larger objects. While Unity primitives come with their own colliders, imported assets will require some special handling.

1. Open the Animation Tests scene.

2. Click Play and try going over the chest.

If the chest is centered in the Scene view, you will see the First Person Controller's capsule drive right through it (Figure 8-1).

Figure 8-1. *The chest doesn't have a collider*

3. Open the Cursor Control scene by double-clicking it in the Project view.

4. Click Play.

5. Try going through the objects you created in Unity.

These objects cause the first person to either go around or go over.

6. Click each of the objects and look in the Inspector for colliders.

7. Stop Play mode.

You will see Box, Capsule, and Sphere colliders. When you create an object in Unity, the appropriate Collider component is automatically added. Colliders serve two main purposes. They provide a means of collision detection with the mesh in a physical manner, and they can also act just as a means to trigger an event or reaction.

Note the Is Trigger parameter present in each Collider component. As we saw briefly in the previous chapter, by using a trigger, you can define areas that turn lights off or on, activate enemies, load a new level, or start almost any other type of action that can occur in a given volume of space without stopping the First Person Controller.

Providing collision detection is, by far, though, the most common use for colliders.

In the Component menu, under the Physics submenu, you will see three more collider types. The Wheel and Raycast Colliders are mainly used for vehicles in physics simulations and are beyond the scope of this book. The Mesh Collider, however, is a mainstay for imported objects.

If the task of adding colliders to every object you import for your game seems daunting, don't panic. One of the import options is to create Mesh Colliders for every object on import automatically.

1. Open the Imported Animations scene again.

2. Select the AnimationObjects in the Project view.

In the Model section of the importer, a few lines below Scale Factor, you will see an option called Generate Colliders.

3. Check Generate Colliders and then click Apply.

4. Select the AnimationObjects in the Hierarchy view and click Revert to update the prefab.

5. Try driving into the chest now.

A quick look through the ChestGroup objects will show that a Mesh Collider has been added to each, as shown in Figure 8-2. To change any of the settings, you'll need to select the objects from the Hierarchy view.

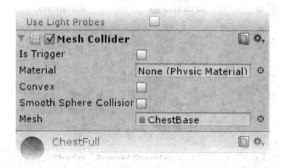

Figure 8-2. *The generated Mesh Collider*

6. Check Generate Colliders for the Flower.

If you forget to click Apply, you will receive a reminder as soon as you select another object.

Mesh Colliders are the most expensive of the shapes to use, as they calculate collision on a face basis from the actual geometry, rather than a simple primitive. Many imported meshes can have their colliders reassigned for better efficiency.

Let's go through our objects one at a time and assess their needs. The most important thing to note is that in a classic point-and-click adventure game, you will generally need prebaked animations to ensure the correct results from user interaction. With the exception of the occasional task that requires some sort of munitions, our main focus will be with object interaction that is not physics-based. In our test setup, at any rate, none of our objects will be controlled by physics, so their collider needs are fairly simple. The benefit is that you can conserve resources by making some intelligent choices.

Starting at the bottom of the list in the AnimationObjects group, the rock can easily use a sphere type of collider.

1. Select the Rock in the Hierarchy view.

2. Select the Rock and add a Sphere Collider from the Components ➤ Physics submenu.

You'll see a dialog that wants to know if it should Replace the existing collider, or Add, or Cancel.

3. Click Replace.

If you inspect the new collider in the Scene view, you may find it is a bit high (see Figure 8-3).

Figure 8-3. The Sphere Collider on the rock

4. From the Sphere Collider component, adjust its Z Center and Radius if necessary.

Next, look at the Pedestal object. The Mesh Collider follows the mesh exactly, including some concave areas. Concave mesh collision is the most expensive of the lot. Because we don't need that much accuracy for this static mesh, you could check the Convex Only check box. At this point, however, it looks suspiciously similar to the Capsule Collider, so you may as well use that instead.

5. Replace the Mesh Collider with a Capsule Collider.

6. Because the pedestal was imported with it z axis up, start by selecting Z Axis for the Direction parameter and then adjust the Radius and Height of the collider, if necessary.

■ **Tip** You may occasionally find that complex meshes fail to generate a viable collider at all. If this happens, and you can't use one of the standard colliders, consider creating and importing a low poly stand-in for the Mesh Collider to use. Simply remove or turn off its Mesh Renderer.

---

7. Next, select the KeyAtLock.

It is small enough not to even bother with a collider for the sake of collision, but we do need to be able to pick it. That's the other reason to use a collider: to be pickable with the cursor, an object must have a collider.

You are probably zoomed-in quite close at this point. If you zoom out a bit, you'll realize that the key mesh presents a pretty small target for a mouse pick. It would make much more sense to exchange its Mesh Collider for a Box Collider.

8. Replace the Mesh Collider with the Box Collider (Figure 8-4) and check Is Trigger.

Figure 8-4. *A Box Collider on the KeyAtLock*

9. You may also wish to increase the Box Collider's size to make picking easier.

10. Select the rock and temporarily turn off its Mesh Renderer, so you can see the key underneath it.

The KeyAtRock is a duplicate of the KeyAtLock, so you can repeat the previous steps for it. If you can't see it, raise it until it sits above the ground (it doesn't yet have an animation, so it's safe to do this). Remember to turn the rock's Mesh Renderer back on.

Let's deal with the Chest Lid next. A quick test with the automatically generated Mesh Collider shows that it is too high to "walk" over, so there's really no reason to use an expensive Mesh Collider.

11. Replace the Mesh Collider with a simple Box Collider (remember to stop Play mode before adding the collider).

12. Select the ChestBase.

You are probably thinking you'll use a Box Collider for the chest base. It certainly doesn't require the complexity of the handles or keyhole for a straight collision object. There is, however, another issue to factor in.

13. Temporarily turn off the ChestLid's Mesh Renderer.

14. Now look down inside the box.

If you use a Box Collider, it will intercept any picks aimed at objects placed within the box. Moreover, you can have only one of each kind of collider on each object, so you would need to create four GameObjects and parent them to the ChestBase, and then create and position a Box Collider for each to coincide with the ChestBase sides.

Given these issues, it's easier to simply use the generated Mesh Collider for the ChestBase.

If you wanted to make a complex lock sequence where the player had to insert and turn the key in two steps, you would want to create a collider that sits on the lock plate. The easiest way to do this complex positioning is to create a Cube, then delete its Mesh Renderer and Cube (Mesh Filter) components. You would also have to make sure the proxy collider protruded far enough from the ChestBase's collider to intercept the pick first.

Now all of the regular objects have colliders, as shown in Figure 8-5.

The Flower is a special case that you will handle later.

Figure 8-5. *The chest objects with their colliders*

Triggering Animation

Now that you've got some objects with animations that are set up with colliders for interaction, you will need a nice generic script to activate the clip of your choice.

So that you can see when you cause the animation to play, you'll call the script from an OnMouseDown function. You will have to turn off the Play Automatically setting on the objects you'll be testing. Because the Animation component may reside on a parent object or group, you may have to trigger the animation through the parents.

Testing will be easier if the camera is in the right place on startup.

1. Arrange the Scene window so you have easy access to the Chest, KeyAtChest, and Rock.

2. Select the First Person Controller in the Hierarchy view and use Align with View on the GameObject menu to move its starting position.

3. Make any other adjustments that are necessary, including the X Rotation of the Main Camera.

4. Select the AnimationObjects and JumpingBean in the Hierarchy view and uncheck Play Automatically in their Animation component.

You'll start by triggering an object's default animation by using animation.Play(). Then you will specify a clip by name. You will also need to specify the parent, if there is one.

1. Create a new JavaScript in the MyScripts folder and name it **AniTest**.

2. Open the script in the script editor.

3. Add the following variables to hold the clip and the parent:

```
var aniParent : GameObject;
var aniClip : AnimationClip;
```

You will use the OnMouseDown function, so you can see the animation when you pick the object.

4. Change the Update function to an OnMouseDown function.

5. Add the following code inside the function so it looks as follows:

```
function OnMouseDown () {
   print(name + " picked ");
   aniParent.animation.Play();
}
```

6. Save the script.

7. Drag and drop the script onto the Rock.

8. Drag the AnimationObjects into the Ani Parent parameter.

9. Click Play and pick the Rock.

Depending on what clip is set as the default Animation on the AnimationObjects, the object involved animates. After the Revert, it is probably the *all* clip. It is clear that you have to be able to specify the clip.

1. Make the following changes to the OnMouseDown function:

```
function OnMouseDown () {
    print(name + " picked using " + aniClip.name);
    aniParent.animation.Play(aniClip.name);
}
```

The Play() method is a bit odd. It takes an animation clip's name, hence aniClip.name. A little later you will discover that audio clips are just the opposite. They will need the clip, not its name.

2. Save the script.

3. Select the Rock and assign the rock move clip as its Ani Clip, so it won't throw an error when picked.

4. Add the AniTest script to the ChestLid object next.

5. Drag the AnimationObjects in as the Ani Parent.

6. Use the browser to load the chest open clip into the Ani Clip field.

7. Click Play and test by clicking the ChestLid and the Rock.

8. While still in Play mode, load the chest close clip and pick the lid again.

The lid closes. Now that you know that the clips can be triggered, you will eventually create a more robust script to handle the two-state animations of the key and chest lid.

Triggering Complex Hierarchies

Next, you will see how to deal with the complex hierarchy of the flower. The clips are easy to call, but the tricky part can be picking the object.

1. Select the Flower in the Project view.

2. In the Model section in the Inspector, check Generate Colliders and click Apply.

3. Hold the Alt key down and open the Flower hierarchy in the Hierarchy view.

4. Inspect the various components to see if any of them received a collider.

Close inspection will show that only the Pollen Ball and the Stem Base received a Mesh Collider. The stem base is too small to bother picking, and the Pollen Ball may as well have a Sphere Collider.

5. Select the Flower in the Project view.

6. Back in the Inspector, uncheck Generate Colliders and click Apply.

7. Select the Flower in the Hierarchy view and add a Box Collider to it.

8. Click Play and watch the green box representing the collider in the Scene view.

It doesn't move when the flower is animated. You could probably add a Box Collider to each bone, but it would be difficult to pick, so, instead, you will just adjust the Box Collider.

9. Size it to cover only the Flower's resting position, as per Figure 8-6, somewhere around 0, 0.18, 0.32 for Center, and 0.52, 0.5, 1.7 for Size.

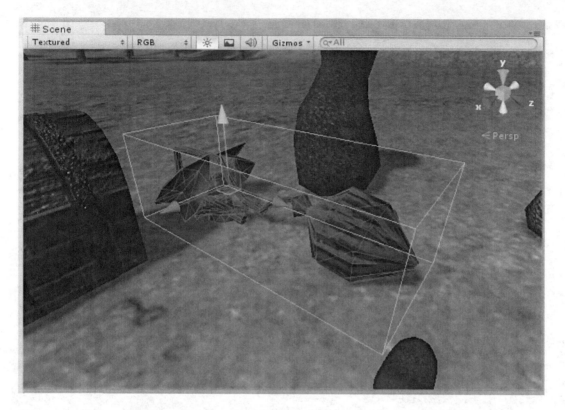

Figure 8-6. *The Box Collider on the Stem of the Flower*

10. In the Animation component, turn off Play Automatically.

11. Add the AniTest script to the Flower.

12. Set the Ani Parent variable to Flower.

13. Set the AniClip variable to flower revive.

14. Click Play and pick the Flower.

The flower slowly comes to life.

15. Stop Play mode.

Next you'll trigger the looping flower idle clip by picking the Pollen Ball. Rather than starting from scratch, you can copy and paste the script component.

1. Stop Play mode.

2. Expand the Flower in the Hierarchy until you can find the Pollen Ball.

3. Add a Sphere Collider to it and set its radius to **0.3**.

4. Click Play.

5. Pick the Flower and observe the Pollen Ball's collider in the Scene window to assure yourself that it will scale with the Pollen Ball (Figure 8-7).

Figure 8-7. *The Pollen Ball's scaled Sphere Collider on the revived Flower*

6.   Stop Play mode.

7.   Select the Flower.

8.   Right-click the AniTest script component's name in the Inspector.

9.   Choose Copy Component.

10.   Select the Pollen Ball.

11.   Right-click over any of the Pollen Ball's component labels.

12.   Select Paste Component as New.

13.   Set the Ani Clip parameter to flower idle.

14.   Leave the Ani Parent as Flower.

15.   Click Play, pick the Flower, then pick the Pollen Ball.

The flower happily goes into its looping idle animation when you pick the Pollen Ball.

Adding Sound F/X

Game play will almost always be more immersive with the addition of sound effects to go along with the animations. Okay, let's admit it—sound effects make almost any animation vastly more entertaining. Audio cues are also a way to give the player subtle (or not so subtle) hints. Traditionally, many adventure games even featured an entire world or level that was almost exclusively audio-based. There are a few sound files provided for this project, but you are encouraged to find more to use as you go along.

Unlike textures in Unity, sound-file conversion to a more efficient format is optional. After a sound file is added to the Asset folder, you can decide on compression, format, and load format.

1. Copy the TestSounds folder into the Asset folder from the Chapter 8 Assets folder.

Note that all of the sound clips have an extension of .ogg. Ogg Vorbis is an open-source format with compression similar to MPEGs. Unity can use other formats, such as .aif, .wav, and .mp3, but it's recommended that you convert longer sound files to .ogg, either in Unity or prior to importing. Free plug-ins are available for most sound-editing applications that don't already support Ogg Vorbis. Once you have the sound files, there are three things required to bring sound into your scene.

The first essential component is the Audio Listener. This may sound familiar, as you had a warning at the start of the navigation section about having too many of these. The Audio Listener acts as a master switch to enable sound in a scene. As there should only be one Audio Listener in a scene, Unity automatically adds the component to any camera that is created. Because a scene must have at least one camera, this ensures that there will always be a listener. Remember to delete extra Audio Listeners when you create additional cameras.

The second requirement for adding sound to your scene is the Audio Source component. This component is added to gameObjects throughout the scene when the sound needs to be emitted from specific locations. With 3D sound, the sound is sent to the speakers according to the player's position in relation to the Audio Source. For sounds that are ambient in nature, such as background music, or environmental, such as wind or bird songs, you may want to put the Audio Source component on the main camera or First Person Controller, or convert it to a 2D sound in the importer.

The third requirement is the sound file itself, which will usually be loaded into the Audio Source component. You will be adding a bit of code to the AniTest script to trigger the sound effect at the same time as the animation when the object is picked.

With the sound clips ready and waiting, it's time to add a few to the test scene. Let's start with the chest lid.

2. Select the ChestLid and, from the Add Component button at the bottom of the Inspector, choose Audio ➤ Audio Source.

3. Select the ChestOpen audio clip in the Test Sounds folder.

If the Audio icon (right side of the Preview window) is toggled on, the sound clip will play as soon as it is selected; otherwise, you can click the Play arrow to its left to preview it.

4. Select the ChestLid again.

5. Drag and drop the ChestOpen audio clip from the Test Sounds folder in the Project view or use the drop-down arrow and select it from the list (Figure 8-8).

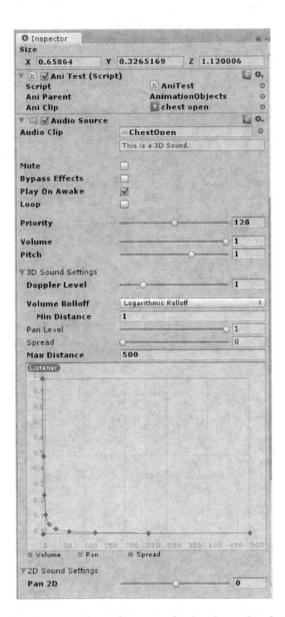

Figure 8-8. The Audio Source for the ChestLid in the Inspector

By letting the clip Play On Awake, you can make adjustments before hooking it up to a script.

6. Check Loop so you'll be able to test the various parameters.

The sound is very faint.

7. Change the Volume Rolloff to Linear Rolloff.

8. With Linear Rolloff, you will have to adjust the Max Distance to something more around **30**.

9. Click Play and use the arrow keys on the keyboard to look from side to side to get the effect of the 3D sound.

273

10. Now move back and forth to see if the Max Distance is acceptable.

11. Experiment with the Pitch, Volume, and other parameters.

12. Turn off Play mode and make your preferred changes permanent.

13. Turn off Play On Awake and Loop.

Because each action object's sound effects will be different, and may vary according to the animation clip being played, you will be adding to your AniTest script next.

1. Open the AniTest script.

2. Add the following to the `OnMouseDown` function, beneath the existing code:

```
audio.Play(); // play the default audio clip
```

3. Save the script and click Play.

4. Click the chest lid to test the sound effects.

5. Click the rock.

You get the usual MissingComponentException error shown in Figure 8-9.

MissingComponentException: There is no 'AudioSource' attached to the "Rock" game object, but a script is trying to access it.

Figure 8-9. *Missing Audio Source error message*

6. Stop Play mode and add an Audio Source component to the rock.

7. Click Play and pick the rock again.

The clip is not yet assigned, but at least you don't get an error message.

To avoid the missing component message, you can add a condition to make sure the component exists before trying to call its Play function.

8. Change the audio line as follows:

```
//check to make sure an Audio Source component exists before playing
if (GetComponent(AudioSource)) audio.Play();
```

9. Save the script.

10. Add the AniTest script to the KeyAtLock and load its parent, AnimationObjects, and clip, key insert.

11. Click Play and pick the KeyAtLock.

No error message is generated. Checking for things before calling functions that use them is one of the techniques that will help you create reusable generic scripts.

You've already seen how to copy and paste an entire component. You can also just paste values. You added an Audio Source to the Rock but have not yet set it up, so it is a perfect candidate for the paste feature.

1. Stop Play mode.

2. Select the Chest Lid and right-click over its Audio Source component.

3. Choose Copy Component from the drop-down list.

4. Select the Rock and right-click over its Audio Source component.

5. Choose Paste Component Values.

6. Change the Audio clip to plopsm.

Now that you have a couple of quick ways to copy and paste components, you can set up the KeyAtLock.

1. Use your favorite method to add the AniTest script and Audio Source components to the KeyAtLock.

2. Set up the AniTest to use the insert key animation clip.

3. Load the LoudClick sound clip into the KeyAtLock's Audio Clip.

4. Click Play and test the two new sound effects.

In both cases, the sound needs to play nearer the end of the animation, rather than at first pick. Once again, this is a factor that will be specific to each object, so you will have to add another public variable that can be overridden in the Inspector.

1. At the top of the script, add the following variable:

```
var audioDelay : float = 0.0;
```

By assigning the float value 0.0, you have a default delay for all objects.

In JavaScript, you can add a delay with the yield statement. A single yield pauses for one frame. For a specific time, say three seconds, the syntax is `yield WaitForSeconds(3.0)`, which would cause the script to wait for three seconds before processing the lines of code that follow. In your script, you'll use the variable named `audioDelay` to store the time.

2. Rearrange the audio line as follows:

```
if (GetComponent(AudioSource)) {
    yield new WaitForSeconds(audioDelay);
    audio.Play();
}
```

Note that you have to add the curly brackets, because more than one expression must be carried out when the condition is met.

CURLY BRACKETS

As you look at code from various sources, you will notice different ways to use curly brackets. In the simple conditional statements, as long as there is only one instruction, you can leave them off, if you wish. Think of curly brackets as shopping bags. If one hand holds the if and the other holds the else, you can have only one of each. If each hand holds a shopping bag, you can use it to hold one or several commands. The following are all equivalent:

```
//sample 1, the strippy version, in line
if (someCondition)  DoThisNext();
else DoTheOtherThing();
```

```
//sample 2, some people prefer always seeing the curly brackets
if (someCondition)  {DoThisNext();}
else {DoTheOtherThing();}

//sample 3, some people prefer them on a second line
if (someCondition)
        {DoThisNext();}
else
        {DoTheOtherThing();}

//sample 4, we use this layout a lot when we plan on adding more instructions later
if (someCondition)  {
    DoThisNext();
}
else {
    DoTheOtherThing();
}

//sample 5, another layout for the curly brackets and indents
if (someCondition)
    {
    DoThisNext();
    }
else
    {
    DoTheOtherThing();
    }
```

3. Save the script.

4. In the Inspector, change the delay variable to about **0.75** for the rock and key.

5. Click Play and check the animations and their sound effects.

You can also add the delay directly to the audio call.

6. Comment out the yield and audio.Play lines.

7. Change the audio.Play line to the following:

```
audio.PlayDelayed (audioDelay); // delay before playing default clip
```

8. Click Play and test.

The results are the same.

For generic sounds that can be used through the game, adding the delay feature avoids having several time variations of the sound file taking up memory.

Setting Up a Two-State Animation

You've probably been wondering when you were going to get around to closing the chest lid. You already have the animation; you just have to work out the logic and the mechanics.

You've already seen a sample of state management with the SimpleRotate script you created in Chapter 3. In that script, a variable called rotState tracked whether the object should rotate or not. You'll use a similar flag or variable now to track whether the chest lid is open or closed, so you know which animation clip to call.

In shooter-type games, state more often than not takes care of itself, as objects are simply destroyed or put into a permanent disabled mode. In point-and-click adventure games, it's not unusual for objects to move between states repeatedly. While some states could possibly be set up to work on a physical basis, others can't. States required by locked doors, for example, have no physical manifestation and, so, require management.

To test the two-state samples, you'll use a Boolean variable to indicate which state the object is in. Booleans are very economical, as they only take up one bit of memory. You can think of them as true/false, on/off, or 0/1.

You'll also have to allow for the second state's animation and audio delay, as it will very likely be different. In the case of a door or lid, the audio clip may have to be different as well.

Let's start by changing the aniClip and audioDelay variables to internal and making two new exposed variables for each. You will also need internal variables to keep track of the state of the lid (or key) and to hold the correct audio clip for the current state. Because there will be lots of changes to the script, you will be cloning and renaming it first.

1. Use Ctrl+D to duplicate the AniTest script.

2. Rename it to **AniTwoState**.

3. Open it in the editor.

4. Change the variables to the following:

    ```
    var aniParent : GameObject;
    var aniClipA : AnimationClip;
    var aniClipB : AnimationClip;
    var audioClipA : AudioClip;
    var audioClipB : AudioClip;
    var audioDelayA : float = 0.0;
    var audioDelayB : float = 0.0;

    internal var aniClip : AnimationClip;
    internal var fXClip : AudioClip;
    internal var audioDelay : float;
    internal var objState : boolean = true;  // true is the beginning state, false is the
    second state
    ```

You may have noticed that some of the variables are now internal variables. Because you now have two audio and animation clips, and two delays, the version that actually gets used will be dynamically assigned in the script itself, so the original variables are no longer exposed to the Inspector.

■ **Tip** Always comment state variables so you (or someone else) can see what each state represents.

Because the original variable names have been left intact, you can handle the state in the OnMouseDown function before you actually call the animation and sound. This will allow you to perform any other checks only once, rather than having to duplicate them for the two-state conditions.

If the state is true, you assign all of the A versions. If the state is false, you assign all of the B versions. And you also change the state to reflect the state that the animations have put the object into.

5.   Add the following inside, at the top of the OnMouseDown function, above the existing code, so it will be handled first:

```
if (objState) {              // if objState is true/ use A
    aniClip = aniClipA;      // set the new animation clip
    fXClip = audioClipA;     // set the new audio clip
    audioDelay = audioDelayA; // set the new delay
    objState = false;        // change its state to false
}
 else {                      // the objState must be false / use B
    aniClip = aniClipB;      // set the new animation clip
    fXClip = audioClipB;     // set the new audio clip
    audioDelay = audioDelayB; // set the new delay
    objState = true;         // change its state to true
}
```

Because you are going to play different audio clips for the same Audio Source, you have to use something slightly different. This allows you to use the same Audio Source for any sounds you want associated with the object using the script. The animation clip code stays the same, but because the clip played is no longer the clip loaded in the audio component, you will have to switch back to the yield delay.

6.   Uncomment the yield and audio.Play lines.

7.   Comment out the audio.PlayDelayed line.

8.   Change the audio.Play() to:

```
audio.PlayOneShot(fXClip); // play the substitute sound file
```

PlayOneShot temporarily overrides the audio clip loaded in the Audio Source component.

9.   Save the newly remodeled script.

10.   Select the ChestLid.

11.   In the Inspector, swap out the AniTwoState script for the AniTest script in the AniTest component's Script parameter.

So far, so good. Just one little problem: you no longer have a generic animation script. Some objects, such as the rock, only have a single state. Not to worry. You just have to add a little logic and make a few changes to make it work for single- and two-state objects. While you could have the script check for the presence of a second animation or audio, it might provide false information if one was loaded for future use or for any other reason. Instead, you can simply make a check box for two-state objects. It needs to be set up manually for each object, but it doesn't require any logic-handling code.

When setting up a check box, you may want to initialize it to the safest state, in case you forget to set it up on an object. A single-state object would throw errors, if treated like a two-state object. But either type will be okay when run as a single state. On the other hand, an error message will quickly remind you to finish setting up the object involved. In this script, you will be using the safe default.

1. Add the following line to the top of the public variables:

    ```
    var twoStates : boolean = false; // default for single state objects
    ```

2. Add the following line *above* the conditional that checks for state:

    ```
    if (twoStates == false) objState = true; // if twoStates is false, set objectState to true
    ```

    Or, you could use the logical not, the exclamation point !:

```
if (!twoStates) objState = true;  // if twoStates is not true, set objectState to true
```

Either line sets the one-state object to a fictional state B, so it always animates "into" state A.

3. Save the script.

4. Select the ChestLid.

5. Assign the chest open, chest close animation clips and ChestOpen and DoorClose audio clips to the appropriate A & B parameters, and set **0.5** for the Audio Delay B.

6. In the Inspector, be sure to check Two States for the ChestLid.

7. Click Play and try it out.

Now you must see if it works for a single-state object.

1. Replace the original AniTest script with the more robust two-state version on the Rock, assigning the same values as in the original.

2. Click Play and try it out.

3. Check to make sure the chest lid still works and the rock does not throw an error.

■ **Tip**   When adding new functionality to a script, be sure to test the original to make sure it still works as well. If you wait until you have made multiple changes, problem-solving can become a nightmare.

---

4. Change the KeyAtLock to the new script as well, assigning the appropriate values as needed.

5. Be sure to check Two States for the KeyAtLock.

6. Click Play and test the various objects for both sound and animation.

7. Save your scene and save your project.

Using Unity's Animation View

Sometimes, you may find it easier to add simple keyframe animations in Unity directly. You've experimented with adding scripted animations in the Update function, but that's much more suited to continuous action. As soon as you want to do something where the speed of the animation slows down, speeds up, varies, or just slows to a stop, there's a lot of math involved.

A better solution may be to use Unity's built-in Animation editor to create your own keyframe animations. As an introduction, you will be using it to lift the key from under the rock. First, you must hide the rock while you are setting up the key's animation.

1. Select the rock and deactivate it from the top of the Inspector.

2. Next, select the KeyAtRock.

3. Change its Mesh Collider to Box Collider.

4. From the Component menu, under Miscellaneous, add an Animation component, as shown in Figure 8-10.

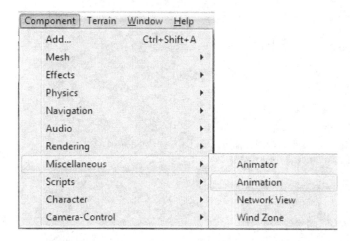

Figure 8-10. *Adding an Animation component*

In case you think it looks familiar, you're right—it's the same Animation component that's added on Legacy import.

5. From the Window menu, select Animation or use Ctrl+6 on your keyboard to bring up the Animation editor, shown in Figure 8-11.

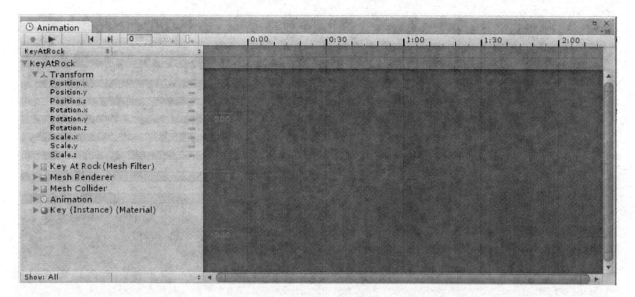

Figure 8-11. *The Animation editor*

Because it was selected, the Animation view comes up with the KeyAtRock featured. The key and all its components are listed, indicating that almost anything can be animated. This is important to note, because there are a lot of things you may wish to animate that will not export with the FBX format.

The components and materials are listed as in the Inspector and can also be expanded and contracted using the usual triangles or arrows.

Just as the imported animations came in as clips, a clip is what you'll create in the Animation view.

6. Click the empty selection box to the right of the one with the object's name.

7. Choose [Create New Clip]—your only choice at this point (see Figure 8-12).

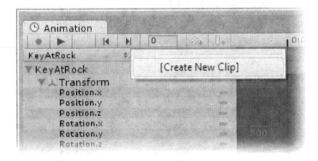

Figure 8-12. *Creating a new clip*

You will be prompted to name and save the clip in the Assets folder.

8. Create a new folder inside the Assets folder and name it **Animation Clips**.

9. Name the new clip **key up**.

Tip If you hadn't yet added an Animation component, one would now be added automatically.

10. Reselect the KeyAtRock, if need be.

The new clip shows up as Element 0 in its Animations array.

It also appears in what used to be the blank selection box in the Animation view, as shown in Figure 8-13.

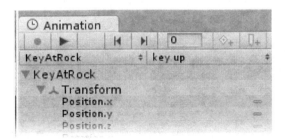

Figure 8-13. *The new clip in the Animation view*

11. Next, to begin animating, toggle on the Animation mode button—the red dot on the left, as shown in Figure 8-14.

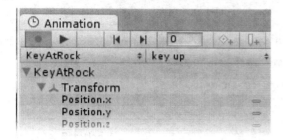

Figure 8-14. Animation mode

You now have an animation clip, and you are ready to animate the key object to move up in the Global y axis. There are several ways to approach this. You will begin by adding a new curve.

1. Before you go any further, at the top of the Editor, change the coordinate system from Local to Global.

2. Move the mouse over the small bar at the far right of the Position.y property.

The bar changes to show a drop-down (see Figure 8-15).

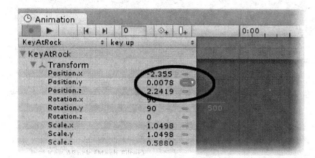

Figure 8-15. The icon after the mouseover

3. Click the icon to bring up the menu (see Figure 8-16).

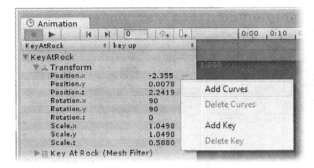

Figure 8-16. *The menu after clicking the icon*

4.   Select Add Curves.

Keyframes are created at frame 0 for Position.x, Position.y, and Position.z, establishing the key object's starting position in the animation (Figure 8-17).

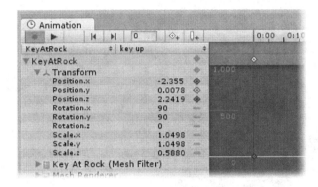

Figure 8-17. *The keys added via Add Curve*

The starting values of the object's transforms are now shown to the right of the parameter names, and color-coded markers are shown for the Position transform properties.

A vertical red line appears at frame 0 in the time line. The frame is also shown to the right of the play controls.

5.   Position your cursor over the red line on top of the time line.

6.   Click and drag to move it to time 1:00, watching the frame numbers change as you move the bar.

At 1:00, 1 second, you can see that Unity's Animation editor uses 60 frames per second for native animation (see Figure 8-18).

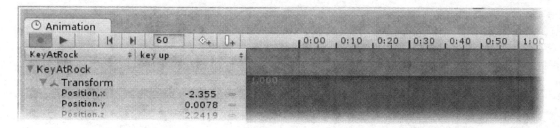

Figure 8-18. *60 frames at 1:00 (second)*

Let's go ahead and animate KeyAtRock by moving it in record mode. You should be at frame 60, and Animation mode should be on.

7. In the Scene view, move KeyAtRock up about a meter.

The new y position is reflected in both the Inspector and the value next to the Key Indicator.
The green (y) line generated appears flat, however, so let's check to make sure something happened.

8. Drag the time bar back to frame 0 and observe the key's position as you do so.

It animates, so you know you were successful.
You can also press the Play button in the Animation view to the right of the record button.
This has the additional benefit of zooming in on the animation's range as soon as you click the Animate mode button again to stop playback. You can now see the y position's curve (Figure 8-19).

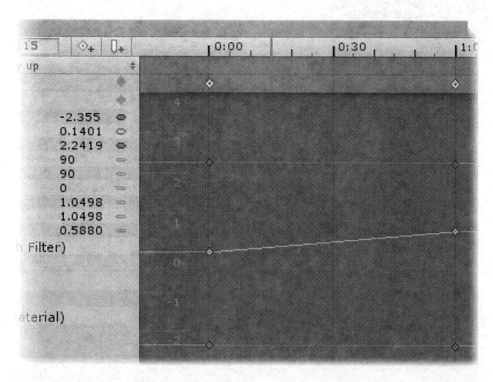

Figure 8-19. *A closer look at the new Position.y curve*

You can see by the straight line that the default animation curve for only two keys in Unity is constant; that is, the speed does not vary over the extent of the animation. While this is good for looping animations, it makes for very boring finite animation.

1. Right-click over the Position.y key at frame 0 to bring up the key tangent options, shown in Figure 8-20.

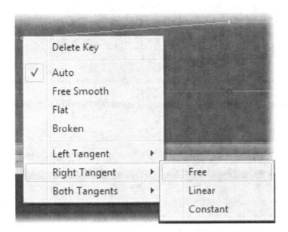

Figure 8-20. *The Key tangents in the right-click menu*

The first key goes only to the right, so, from Right Tangent, select Free, to get a Bezier handle to manipulate.

2. Click and drag down, so the right handle is horizontal.

3. Select the key at frame 60 and change its left tangent to Free.

4. Move its handle up until it is horizontal as well.

5. De-select the key and select the Position.y track.

6. Press the F key to zoom to the entire Position.y curve (Figure 8-21).

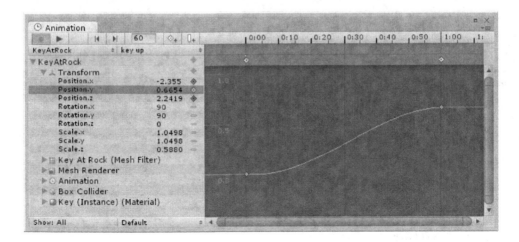

Figure 8-21. *The zoomed Position.y curve*

You now have a classic ease in/ease out animation: it starts slow, speeds up, and then slows down again.

7. Click the Animation view's Play button and observe the improved animation.

8. Press the F key to zoom to the entire Position.y curve.

To make sure the animation only plays once, you will want to set its wrap type.

9. At the bottom of the Animation editor, click the wrap type button (it currently shows "Default") and select Once in the drop-down.

You've just finished your first keyframe animation in Unity's Animation editor. If this was your first keyframe animation in any application, be sure to check out the Reading Animation Curves sidebar.

READING ANIMATION CURVES

If you find reading animation curves confusing, learning the rules will help—and there are really only a few rules to remember. Time is always on the horizontal, and the parameter that is being changed is on the vertical. Therefore, a line that is steep represents large change over a short amount of time. Because a flat line represents no change over time, a shallow curve is a slow change. If the curve is straight, the rate of change is constant. Finally, if the curve changes direction, the value of the animating parameter is reversed—whether direction, rotation, opacity, etc.

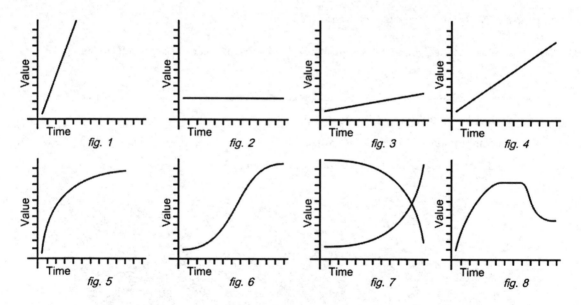

fig. 1

fig. 2

fig. 3

fig. 4

fig. 5

fig. 6

fig. 7

fig. 8

Some function curves:

fig. 1: Steep = Fast

fig. 2: Flat = Stopped or no change

fig. 3: Shallow = Slow

fig. 4: Straight = Constant rate

fig. 5: Fast at start, slow at end

fig. 6: Slow at start, then fast, then slow at end—classic ease in/ease out

fig. 7: Two slow at start, fast at end curves

fig. 8: Fast, then slow to dead stop, then fast back in the opposite direction (or value), then slow at end

Now that the key has its own animation, you will want to see it animating on cue.

1. Toggle off Animation mode in the Animation view and close the view for now.

2. In the Inspector, load the key up clip as the default animation and uncheck Play Automatically in the Animation component.

3. Drag the AniTwoState script onto the KeyAtRock.

4. Add the key-up clip to the AniClip A parameter.

Before you can test the key, there is one change you will want to make to the script. Because the animation is on the key itself, not its parent, like the imported animations, you will tell the script to use the object if no parent has been assigned. This is done in the Start function, so the value is assigned as soon as the game starts.

5. Open the AniTwoState script.

6. Add the Start function, or modify the existing one as follows:

```
function Start () {
        // if no parent was assigned, assume it is the object this script is on
        if (aniParent == null) aniParent = this.gameObject;
}
```

This translates as follows: If no gameObject was assigned as the aniParent, assign the gameObject that this component is on to that variable. If there should have been a parent assigned, you will get an error when no Animation component is found.

7. Save the script, click Play, and pick the key.

It animates as expected.

8. Stop Play mode and reactivate the rock.

9. Click Play and test again.

This time, you must move the rock to get to the key.

Eventually, the key will go into inventory, so you shouldn't just leave it hanging in midair. You could have it pop out of existence by scaling it down to almost nothing at the last part of its animation, but, instead, you will use the opportunity to experiment with something other than a transform. This time, you will have the key fade to transparent instead.

Unlike most DCC apps, where you can animate the visibility of an object as one of its properties, in Unity, you have to use its material to effect a fade-in or fade-out.

Before you fade out the key, you will want to think about timing. One second was pretty fast for the key to move. If you add a fade-out, it may happen too quickly to be visually effective. If you expand the y position animation to take place over two seconds, you can use the extra second to fade it out.

1. Stop Play mode and deactivate the rock again.

2. With KeyAtRock selected, open the Animation view.

3. Toggle on Animation mode (the red dot).

4. Select the y position key at frame 60 in the Keyframe Line (just below the time line) and move it to time 2:00, frame 120.

■ **Tip** To expose more frames before you move the key, use the arrows in the lower right corner of the Animation view or simply zoom out with the usual viewport controls.

---

5. Click the Play button in the Animation view to see the difference.

The animation time looks much more reasonable.

6. Stop Play mode.

Now, you need to make the key fade out via its material, so the next thing to do is get a better look at what you have to work with.

1. Expand the Key material track at the bottom of the list.

You might also need to widen the left-side panel.

2. Position the cursor over right-side edge where it meets the curves area and drag the edge over to expose the entire text for the material.

You will see that the material is shown as an instance. At this point, you may remember that KeyAtLock uses the same material. Fortunately, when we animate the opacity on the material for one key, it will not affect other objects using the same material. You will be using the alpha channel, the *a* in rgba (red, green, blue, alpha).

3. Select the KeyAtRock object.

4. At the bottom of the Inspector, select Material and click its Main Color swatch.

5. Make sure its Alpha value is set to **255**, fully opaque.

6. Open the Animation view and expand the material track again.

7. Select the Color.a parameter and right-click the Key Indicator marker and choose Add Curve.

A key is added at frame 0 with a value of 1, fully opaque. The values used for animating are normalized to use 1 for 100%.

The key should start fading at frame 60, 1 second, so you will have to add a key at that point.

8. Move the time bar to that position and click the Add Keyframes button next to the frame-indicator box (see Figure 8-22).

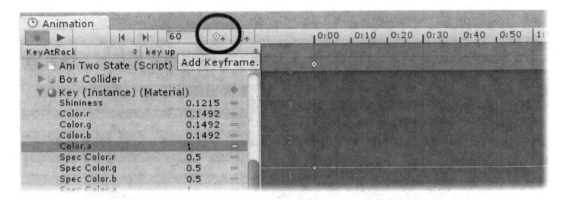

Figure 8-22. *Adding a Keyframe*

9. Repeat at frame 120, seconds 2:00.

10. While at frame 120, click to edit the value to the right of the Key Indicator, changing it from 1 (fully opaque) to 0 (fully transparent), as shown in Figure 8-23.

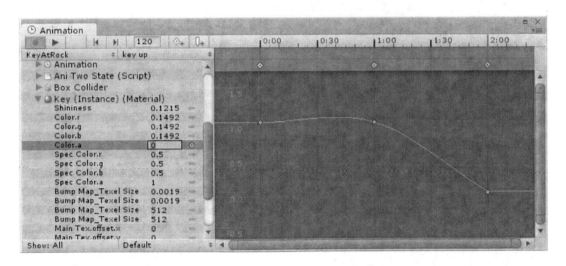

Figure 8-23. *A value of 0 at the last key*

Focusing on the Color.a curve shows that the addition of a second key changes the default curve to a Smooth curve; the keys' tangents are interpolated smoothly from one to the next. However, the material needs to retain the value 1 until it reaches frame 60. In Unity, you don't have to set a key at frame 0. Each clip will start at 0 and end at the last key of the longest track.

11. In the curve area, select the key at frame 0.

12. Right-click and choose Delete Key.

The curve straightens out nicely.

13. Adjust the rest of the curve with free tangents, as you did with the previous animation, to get an ease in/ease out curve (Figure 8-24).

289

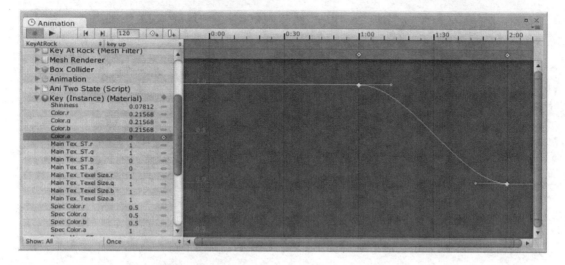

Figure 8-24. The adjusted alpha channel curve

14. Drag the time bar to see the results in the Scene view.

Nothing seems to be happening. The numbers are correct: 1 is fully opaque and 0 is fully transparent. There's one more thing you have to know about animating transparency in Unity.

It turns out that even though you're animating the alpha parameter, you actually have to use a shader that is able to animate it as well.

1. Select the Key material at the bottom of the Inspector.

2. Change its shader to the Bumped Specular from the Transparent section.

3. Zoom in closely in the Scene view so you will be able to see if it fades out.

4. Turn on the record button and scrub the time indicator again.

This time the key fades out as expected, leaving only its edges showing in the Scene view.

5. Activate the Rock again.

6. Click Play and test the sequence—pick rock, pick key.

This time, the key fades away as it lifts from the ground.

Changing Imported Animations

Now that you've added the fade-out to the KeyAtRock, it has probably occurred to you that you should take a look at KeyAtLock next. It came in with imported animations, but the animations can also be viewed in the Animation view. Turns out they can't be edited, though. You just reactivated the rock, so you will be taking a look at it first in the Animation editor.

1. With the Rock selected, open the Animation view.

2. Click the Transform track to see all of the transform curves, as shown in Figure 8-25.

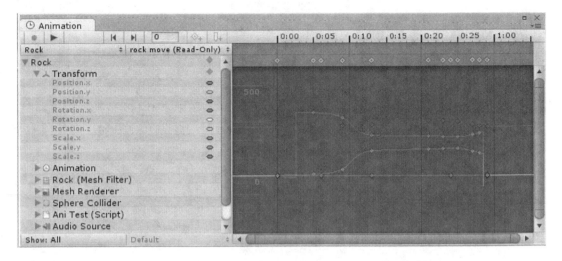

Figure 8-25. *The Rock's imported animation*

3. Try moving one of the keys.

Not only does nothing move, you can't even select a key in the first place.

If you click the clips list, you'll see that all of the clips are set to Read-Only.

To add animation to or edit an existing animation, you must make a copy of the Animation clip. While that sounds like a lot of extra work, it makes sense when you remember that the original clip belongs to the imported asset. The copy will be a duplicate but will not destroy the original.

4. Select the KeyAtLock in the Hierarchy view.

5. Locate its key insert clip in the Project view.

6. Use Ctrl+D to duplicate it.

The duplicate will be created in the root of the Animation Tests folder.

7. Locate the copy and append its name with "**_copy**."

8. Move the copy into the Animation Clips folder.

9. Select the AnimationObjects group.

10. Replace the original key insert clip with the copy in the Animation component.

11. Select the KeyAtLock and replace the original with the copy in the AniTwoState script.

12. In the Animation view, select the key insert_copy clip (Figure 8-26).

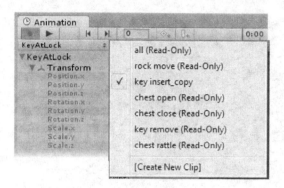

Figure 8-26. Selecting the key insert_copy clip

13. Use the F key in the curve area to view the existing animation tracks.

14. Toggle on Animation mode.

15. Scrub the time bar to see when the key gets inserted into the lock.

It appears to be all the way in by frame 15, half a second in.
It would be much nicer if it had a full second to fade in before it was inserted.

■ **Tip** The imported animation was created using 30 frames per second, so the duplicated animation clip continues to use the same number of frames per second, rather than Unity's native 60 frames per second.

---

1. Expand the Key material and select the Color.a parameter

With the KeyAtRock, you used Add Keyframe to add a key to an existing curve. You can also use it to create a new curve on a selected track or tracks.

2. Move the time bar to frame 0 and click the Add Keyframe button to set the first key.

3. At the bottom left of the view, toggle Show All to Show: Animated.

Once you have a curve, you can use the filter Show: Animated to make things simpler to find.

4. Select all of the animated parameters in both Transform and Material.

5. Use F to make sure you see all the keys.

6. In the Keyframe line (just below the time line), click and drag to select all of the keys—they will turn blue, as shown in Figure 8-27.

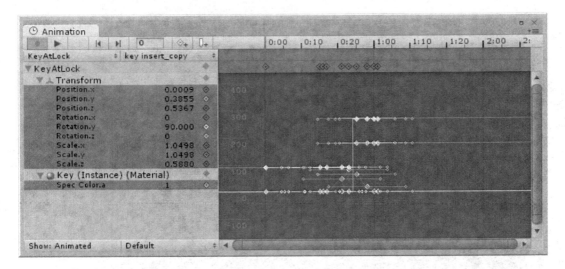

Figure 8-27. *Keys filtered for animated only*

7. Position the cursor over the key at frame 0 and move them to the right 30 frames/1 second.

8. Move the time indicator back to frame 0.

9. Select only the Color.a track.

10. Click Add Key to set a new key at frame 0.

11. Select the key at 0 and change its value from 1 to 0.

12. Use F to frame the new curve.

13. Change the tangents to Free and adjust the curve to an ease in/ease out if you wish.

14. Expand the horizontal slider at the bottom of the Animation view to see the full time line for the key.

15. Scrub the time indicator to see the results (Figure 8-28).

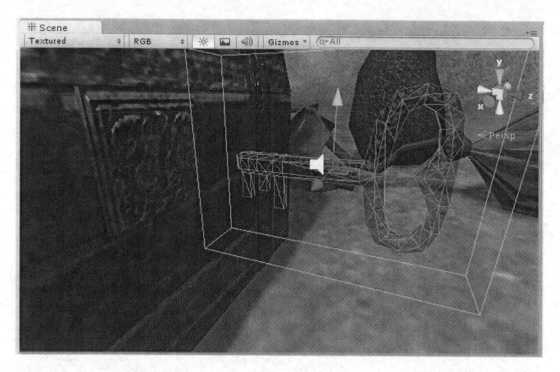

Figure 8-28. *The KeyAtLock fading in before starting to insert itself*

There seems to be a long gap between fade and move in. Animations tend to look more fluid when they overlap.

1. Select the Position.z transform and focus on it.

2. Select the first key on the left in the KeyFrame line and move it to the left, so that the move starts at frame 15 (Figure 8-29).

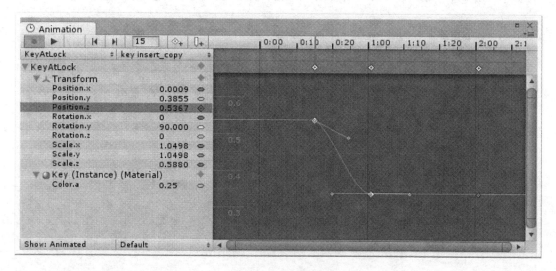

Figure 8-29. *Overlapping transform and fade by shifting transform keys left*

3.   Click Play in the Animation editor and watch the result.

Feel free to make further time adjustments.

4.   Close the editor.

5.   In the AniTwoState script component, you will have to add the extra second to the audio delay A.

6.   Click Play and pick the Key.

Unless you deliberately design it, you probably don't want to have a key floating in midair waiting to be picked. Furthermore, even if an object's Mesh Render is turned off, it is still pickable, so it stands to reason that even when its material is transparent, it can still be picked. Add to that the fact that you wouldn't know where to pick if it was invisible, and you'll quickly realize that the only logical way to activate the animation is to trigger it by picking another object.

The problem that raises is that all of your code is currently in the `OnMouseDown` function for the object it animates. Before you tackle a nice generic animation script, let's find out how to manually trigger another object's animation, so you can handle those intriguing multi-object sequences.

7.   Stop Play mode.

Triggering Another Object's Animations

Until now, you've clicked directly on the object you want to animate. At some point, you'll have to be able to trigger one object's animation or change its state by clicking on another. As mentioned before, the most typical example of this is a light switch. Pick the switch, and light goes on; the switch itself toggles up; and maybe even the material changes to illuminate a lightbulb and even a lampshade. In a classic point-and-click adventure, anything could be triggered by interacting with any action object.

It turns out, though, that because the imported animations are all on the parent group, you have already got the functionality for triggering from a second object!

As a test case, you will be triggering the flower's animation by picking on the pedestal. The pedestal already has a collider to prevent you from going through it, so it should also be good to go for picking.

1.   Drag the AniTwoState script onto the Pedestal object.

Before filling out the parameters, you may as well rename aniParent to aniObject, because it could be either the parent with the animation, or an entirely different object.

2.   Open the AniTwoState script.

3.   Rename the aniParent variable to **aniObject** throughout the script by using the Replace tool from the Search menu of the script editor.

4.   Click All to make the replacements.

5.   Save the script.

You will have to reassign the parents in the objects currently using the AniTwoState script, with the exception of the KeyAtRock, because it has its own Animation component.

Select the Flower gameObject in the Hierarchy view and check that it has the animation clips on its Animation component.

6.   Reselect the Pedestal and drag the Flower onto the AniObject parameter.

7.   Choose the flower revive clip for the Ani Clip A parameter.

8.   Click Play and test the triggering by picking the Pedestal.

9.   Stop Play mode.

10. Add the SynthUp sound clip for Audio Clip A and copy and paste an Audio Source onto the Pedestal to play it.

11. Set the Audio Delay A to about 1.

12. Click Play and pick the Pedestal.

To finish it off, you will add a looping clip that plays after the first animation is finished. This introduces the concept of setting a pause to match the length of a clip.

13. Open the AniTwoState script again.

14. Add another variable to hold the Flower's idle animation:

```
var aniLoopClip : AnimationClip; // if not null, this will be called after the first clip is finished
```

15. At the bottom of the OnMouseDown function, add the following:

```
if (aniLoopClip) {
        // wait the length of the first animation before you play the second
        yield new WaitForSeconds (aniClipA.length);
        aniObject.animation.Play(aniLoopClip.name); // this one needs to be set to loop
}
```

16. Save the script.

17. Stop Play mode.

18. Load the flower idle clip into the Ani Loop Clip parameter on the Pedestal.

19. Click Play and pick the Pedestal again.

The flower animates through its revive clip, pauses, then loops its idle clip. If you were surprised by the pause, take a look at the audio delay conditional. Because there was a delay, that delay caused the loop animation to be delayed the length of the first animation *plus* the audio delay length. To solve the dilemma, you could do a little math, aniClipA.length - audioDelay, or, instead of using PlayOneShot, you can *change* the audio component's sound clip directly and call it with PlayDelayed.

1.   Open the AniTwoState script again.

2.   Change the contents of the if (GetComponent(AudioSource)) section to:

```
audio.clip = fXClip; // change the audio component's assigned sound file
audio.PlayDelayed (audioDelay); // delay before playing it
```

3.   Click Play and test.

This time, the looping animation starts as soon as the original animation finishes.

4.   Double-check the new code by setting the audio delay to 0 and clicking the pedestal.

The looping animation should still loop immediately after the first animation is finished.

5.   Exit Play mode.

6.   Save the scene and save the project.

Now that your little scene is starting to act like an adventure game, you can see how much thought has to go into each object's animation sequence and how complicated things can get when you create complex sequences. By solving desired functionality a little bit at a time, you can arrive at a complex end result without getting overwhelmed.

Limitations

While your nice generic script now works under several different conditions, it is still somewhat limited. At present, it has at least the following shortcomings:

Handles only two states: The chest lid currently has two states, but with the lock, it needs at least three: closed and locked, closed and unlocked, and open. If you added a latch that sticks up when the chest is locked when the lid is open, it could prevent the lid from closing properly, adding an open and locked and a partially closed state, for a grand total of five states.

Triggers only one object's animation/audio: The hypothetical light switch illustrates this one most clearly. The switch needs to animate. The light needs to be activated. And the materials on the bulb and the lampshade need to be animated to change their appropriate parameters.

Doesn't manage visibility for objects that fade: This is really a couple of separate issues. Setting the material's opacity to 0 prevents you from seeing an object, but it is still being rendered, costing frame rate. This is negligible on a one-to-one basis, but still worth considering. You could disable the Mesh Renderer, but that would require specific code, as it is not an animation clip. The other problem is that even if an object is not rendered, its collider is still active, allowing the possibility of running into invisible walls. Its collider would also need to be disabled. You could handle it automatically—if the opacity is 0, disable the GameObject—but that will fail in cases where the GameObject exists for the sole purpose of providing something with which to interact. Ideally, you'll want to be able to enable or disable the entire GameObject.

Isn't able to call other scripts or functions for special events: This is what you need to ensure maximum flexibility and functionality in your generic animation script. You need to be able to instantiate things, such as particle systems and other non-keyframable events, by having access to bits of code as either scripts or functions.

Clearly, there are a lot of things yet to think about as you start to create a master script for handling your action objects (the objects that drive the game and story). The trick is going to be keeping it generic enough to use on all of the different types of objects, without giving up the flexibility to reuse the code throughout the game and in future games. Besides triggering animations and sound effects, you will need a means of keeping track of the state the objects are in before and after they have been triggered. You have to manage the state objects go into when they are picked, especially when it varies according to which object is picking it. This, and the mechanics of how you design it, is what is known as state management, the next chapter's topic.

Summary

In this chapter, you delved deeper into animation, learning how to trigger the legacy Animations and how to create your own clips using Unity's Animation editor.

You examined colliders, learning to replace resource-heavy Mesh Colliders with their more efficient primitive counterparts. With the addition of OnMouseDown(), you found that to pick an object in the scene, the object needs a collider. For mouse picks, using the Is Trigger option on objects that were too small to worry about collision was a good choice.

With the introduction of animation.Play(), you found out how to call the default animations but soon learned that you could call specific animation clips by name, using the same function. On adding an Audio Source component, you could call sound effects with audio.Play() in the same manner, though calling the clip with audio.PlayOneShot() made your script more flexible. With the addition of yield WaitForSeconds(), you found that it delayed everything following it, so it was better to change the audio component's audio clip directly and use PlayDelayed() instead.

As the AniTwoState script got more robust, you learned you could check for a component's existence with GetComponent() before trying to use it and thus avoid Null Reference Object errors. By the time you dealt with identifying parents with the Animation component, you found it was easy to adapt the script to call an object's animations by picking a different object, a key concept for interactive games.

Using Unity's Animation editor, you learned how to create and add animation clips after import for non-animated objects. You also found you could add or edit imported animation clips, but only after making copies of them first.

Finally, you saw the shortcomings in the AniTwoState script's functionality with respect to future needs for the book's adventure game project and found it somewhat lacking, even after all of the modifications made to it.

CHAPTER 9

■ ■ ■

Managing State

In classic point-and-click adventure games, one of the most entertaining and challenging goals is to collect anything and everything that is not nailed down and then try to figure out where it needs to be used. To make things even more interesting, many games require you to combine inventory items before they will be able to perform the necessary task. It may be as mechanically logical as combining a hammerhead with a wooden handle to make a usable tool, or as challenging as adding the correct ingredients to a brew. In the former, you might consider the combination object a totally new object that needs to be activated in the scene. In the latter, however, you might need to change its virtual state each time an ingredient is added. Even something as simple as a door can have two states: open and closed. While some states, such as with the door, physically prevent access to a location or crucial object, others, such as a lock on the same door, have no physical manifestation. If the door's state is *locked*, interaction with it might produce a rattle, but if its state is *unlocked*, it will open when picked, putting it into a third state, *open*. Once you consider adding save and restore functionality to the game, the need for a means to track state becomes even more important.

Thus far in your journey into the realm of developing the mechanisms for interaction for your game, you have used only a default pointer when clicking on your action objects. While changing the cursor to represent a particular object will be a simple reassigning of the texture, the manner in which the *picked* object responds may be vastly different. This sets you up for a dizzying amount of interaction possibilities when you stop to consider that *each* possibility must be considered. Besides tracking the state of objects, you must also have a list of objects with which they can interact, as well as the expected response from that interaction. Neglecting to check every possible interaction is one of the most common mistakes made by neophyte game developers. For that matter, even seasoned professionals are likely to miss a few, as the game develops and undergoes the inevitable design changes. Even when you *think* you have every possibility covered, you will find that people will do the most unlikely (to your way of thinking, anyway) things in your game, or, worse, *to* your game.

BETA TESTERS

Beta testers are invaluable when developing adventure-type games. Besides providing strong feedback on the logic, difficulty, and entertainment value of the puzzles or tasks in your game, they are masters at trying improbable actions and combinations of actions. When dealing with volunteer beta testers, there are a few important things to remember. Don't tell them any more about the game than what's available in the game's introduction. Don't stand over their shoulders prompting them to the correct paths or actions. If you must watch, keep your mouth closed (yes, that will be difficult) and your hands tightly clasped behind your back. Remember, their first run-through will be the most valuable. After they have played through as far as the game allows, you can ask for feedback. What may seem totally obvious to you may need more clues and vice versa.

Identifying the Action Objects

With the possibly daunting number of options for interactivity with your objects, cursors, and inventory in mind, you can now see the need to be able to keep track of each and every one as they are activated, retired, combined, or taken by the player. Tracking and managing each object's state is crucial to this type of genre, not only during game play, but also to enable the player to save and load the game at any time.

Let's begin by defining what constitutes an "action object." For the adventure game you will be creating, it will be any object that requires its state to be tracked, is responsible for changing another object's state, or imparts information to the player. It will store information about its description, animations, sound effects, and other properties associated with the transitions into its various states, as well as how it will affect other objects while the transitions are carried out. So, each action object will contain the metadata needed to manage its states and the code to make the state changes happen.

State management is a means or system used to handle conditionals on a large scale and in a fully generic manner. Before you delve into actually managing state, you will have to find a way of identifying and defining states and their associated actions (animations, audio and special effects, etc.) that you can apply to any and all of your action objects.

Before you can list the requirements for your action objects, you'll have to create a storyline involving the objects and then generate a walk-through. To begin, you will be using the objects you've already brought into the scene.

Introducing the Test Plot

In your first little scenario, the player will find that the chest is locked. Looking nearby, he spots a rock that looks suspiciously out of place. Picking it up, he finds a key. He inserts the key into the lock, turns it, and unlocks the chest, which he can now open. Inspecting the chest, he finds nothing inside.

While this mini-plot may seem simple, it requires several decisions to be made. With an inventory system, you have to know which items can be taken for later use. The key, because it is nearby, could become a cursor, as soon as it is picked, ready to use on the lock, or it could go automatically into inventory. The rock could either be moved aside, and no longer be pickable or go into inventory. Or, if you allow the key to be put back in its hiding place, the rock would have to be able to be put back into its original position. When the key is in the lock, and the chest is open, can it be turned? If so, what happens if the lid is closed? Does it automatically lock, or does it not shut all the way?

Walk-through

To help you decide exactly how everything will work, a walk-through, or critical path to start breaking the requirements into bite-sized pieces, can be helpful. Obviously, the game need not be totally linear, but there will be sections that require objectives to be met, in order to gain access to the next solution, so it helps to define them from the start. The test scenario could map out as follows:

1. Pick the rock so it moves aside to reveal a key.

2. The rock is no longer active in the scene.

3. The key (at rock) goes directly into inventory when picked.

4. Use the key (from inventory) with the lock plate on the chest to unlock the lid.

5. Open the lid.

6. Try to take the key with the lid open—it doesn't respond.

7. Inspect the contents of the chest.

8. Close the lid (optional).

9. Lock the chest (optional).

10. Take the key (optional).

Action Objects

Having the basic story and walk-through, you have to identify the action objects. As with any adventure game, not all action objects can be put into inventory. In this list, an asterisk indicates objects that can be put into inventory. In this scenario, the player picks the lock plate to insert the key. Because the lock plate is part of the chest base mesh, you will eventually have to make a collider to represent it.

Rock

*KeyAtRock

*KeyAtLock

Key Icon

LockPlate

ChestLid

With your list of action objects in hand, you have to start thinking about how you are going to manage their states. For example, what about the lock plate of the chest? Its states are strictly virtual, but it changes the states of the key and chest lid, as you interact with it. There are also two keys. How are they handled as inventory objects?

Stunt Doubles

Let's look into the concept of *stunt doubles*. Just as in the movies, where a stuntman performs the dangerous or skilled actions, you can use stunt doubles to reduce the complexity of many of your interactions. This allows you to swap out entirely different meshes, use UI textures for inventory or cursor objects, or avoid having to reposition and reorient keyframed objects. Obviously, there's some overhead involved in duplicating meshes, but until you're comfortable handling complex state management, it will simplify the process, by reducing the number of states an individual object can have.

The most obvious example of a stunt double in your test cases is the key that is used to unlock the chest. You have a Key at Rock and a Key at Lock. Using stand-in objects allows you to keep objects whose animations are dependent on the location and orientation of other objects from getting moved out of alignment by mistake.

Another extremely useful reason for stunt doubles is to allow you to use texture images of the objects as cursors or in inventory. By treating them as separate objects instead of a particular state of a single object, you are free to pick and choose how you handle each. In the case of the key, you can easily go between the two mesh objects and a texture for inventory and cursor.

Developing a State Machine

Once you've got the scenario blocked out, you have to take off your game *designer* hat and put on a game *developer* hat. Essentially, you have to break down the components of the interactions in preparation for handling the mechanics of making all the right things happen. In other words, you must develop a state machine. A state machine is simply a behavior that specifies the sequence of states an object occupies during its lifetime in response to events, along with any actions it triggers in response to those events.

Components of a State Machine

Let's take a moment to look at the components that make up a state machine. In an adventure game, the most notable component of the state machine is the *transition* from one state to the next.

To process a state change, you will have to know the object's *current state,* the *event* that will trigger the transition into the *resulting state,* and the *actions* that will be performed during the transition.

■ **Tip**   The most important concept to remember is that the actions corresponding to a state are the actions that happen to put the object *into* that state.

In the book's project, the *event* that triggers the state change will be one of three types. The first will be a pick with the default cursor; the second will be a pick from a specific cursor; and the third will be a trigger from some outside event. That event could be as mundane as clicking a doorbell to cue a butler-type character to appear, or a more shooter-type approach, where breaking a streetlamp with a projectile causes a policeman to appear.

The *action* during the transition may be an animation on the object itself, special effects, sound effects, text descriptions of the action onscreen, suspension of user input during the transition, animating or state changing of auxiliary objects, or just about anything else you might need to do.

Having a formal way to block out the objects, responses, and conditions that drive your state machine will be essential to developing your game. Because there are several ways to represent the data, you will be looking at several methods of representation, as you identify the states, actions, and events that trigger them.

The Pick Event

The pick event will be the most common means of transitioning the objects into their new state. The most familiar vehicle for tracking the possibilities of interaction is the flowchart. Let's start with the current action objects. Not necessarily all interaction will be user-picked, but some type of interaction will be needed to get things started. The interaction that starts the state change is traditionally called the *event.*

■ **Tip**   For those who have avoided flowcharts whenever possible, the symbols are simple: an ellipse represents the event that begins the action; a diamond queries the state of the objects involved for a yes-or-no response to clarify; and a box contains the resulting action.

For each action object, you have to chart the result of the possible action or event. If the resulting response varies according to a particular state or condition, the chart is branched accordingly.

Your first run at the objects' flowcharts with simple interaction/event possibilities might look something like Figure 9-1. You won't be developing the inventory functionality until Chapter 13, but at the design stage, it should definitely be included.

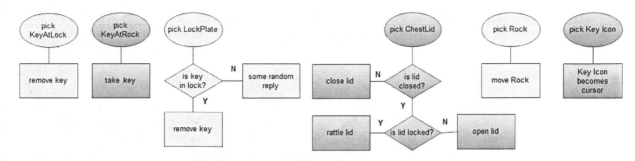

Figure 9-1. *Simple flowcharts for the test objects*

When you add more states and possible cursors into the mix (Figure 9-2), the possibilities increase exponentially. Adding the locked or unlocked state to the LockPlate and the ChestLid open and closed states now becomes 2×2,×3 key possibilities, if you plan on having the player put the key in the lock plate and turn it as two separate actions. Three of the objects, the Rock, KeyAtRock, KeyAtLock, and Key Icon, also have a state where they are either out of scene (the three key objects), or in scene but no longer pickable (the Rock). So, starting with 12 possibilities and discarding the impossible ones, you end up with 3 possible scenarios. There are obviously several different scenarios you could have just using these few objects. So, your first decision is how involved you want the interaction to be. Charting the possibilities will help you decide how complex you want to make the interaction.

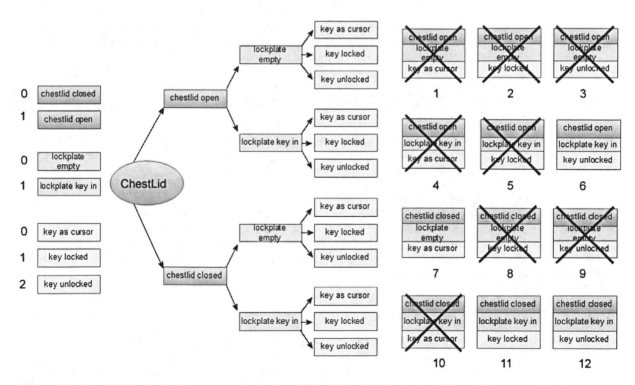

Figure 9-2. *Possibilities, including state, expanded, and filtered, to check for impossible combinations. This chart doesn't show how the states are changed on the objects after the interaction*

Even after discarding the impossible scenarios, adding more states and possible cursors starts to complicate the flowcharts. This time, possible cursors have been added to the events. In the next flowchart, the chest-lid sequence has been simplified by having the key automatically unlock the lock when in and lock it when removed (Figure 9-3).

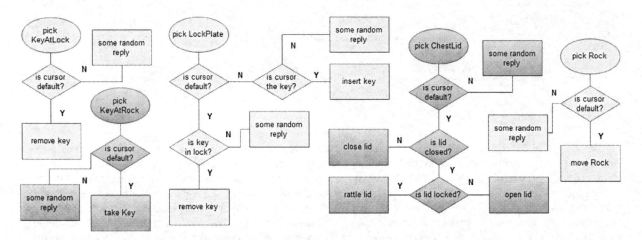

Figure 9-3. *Adding more cursors to the flowcharts*

The preceding flowchart does not show the actions associated with the transitions that put the objects into the states shown, nor does it show how some objects affect the states of the others. Let's continue to look for a better means of mapping out interactions and reactions for the action.

Separating State Metadata and Transition Action

With the previous charts, you tracked the event that triggered the state change. In reality, you will also have to factor in the actions initiated with the state change during the *transition*. This means you need to know the objects' states and how they transition from one state to another. For example, when you pick the LockPlate with the Key Icon cursor, the KeyAtLock appears and animates into its "inserted" state; the LockPlate changes to its "unlocked state" with a click sound effect; and the ChestLid changes to its "unlocked" state. So there are a variety of actions types that can be associated with an object's transition into a new state.

In the state machine that you will be developing, the objects themselves will eventually contain the metadata (information) for all of the *actions* associated with transitioning the object into its various states.

For now, you will use a simple description for each state while you work out the interactions. Eventually, the state will be represented only by a number, and the description of the state will be part of the metadata for that state, which the player will be able to read on mouseover.

Defining State and Transition

With the flowcharts, you were checking events to see what state they put the objects into. In the media rich environment of the game, the transitions take center stage, so this time, you will be trying a different means of visually depicting the various scenarios. Let's begin by looking at the rock. It has two states: in place and moved aside and no longer pickable (Figure 9-4, left). When picked in place, it goes into its second state: moved aside. It has only one transition animation: moving aside. Once in that state, the player can no longer interact with it. In a simple UML (universal markup language) diagram, the event that triggered the state change is not shown, only the arrow showing the transition. The chest lid (with no lock involved), is also simple. It has two states: open and closed. It has two transition animations: chest open and chest closed. Graphically represented, they form a loop (Figure 9-4, left). While the simple version is useful for virtual state changes, such as the LockPlate's locked/unlocked state, it doesn't provide enough information when there are actions such as animations or sound effects involved. With UML, the actions are often placed alongside the transition arrows (Figure 9-4, right).

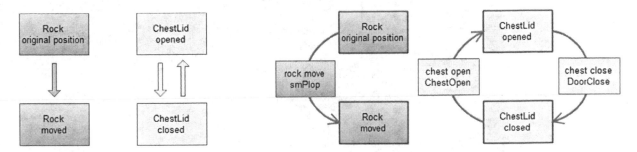

Figure 9-4. *Simple UML-style state diagrams for the rock and chest lid (left), and showing the actions (animation and audio clips) associated with the transitions (right). This type of diagram does not show the events required to trigger the transitions into the new states*

Visualizing Transitions

So far, the UML diagram holds up well. For the ChestLid, there is only one possible transition and outcome for each state. If it's in its open state, then put it into its closed state; otherwise, put it into its open state (because it must have been in its closed state). But as soon as you add a third possibility, locked/unlocked, you will need a way to determine which state the object *should* go into, as well as which transition to take to get to that state. Figure 9-5 shows the chest scenario with the addition of a locked state. Adding the actions triggered during the transitions as boxes on the arrows will get messy.

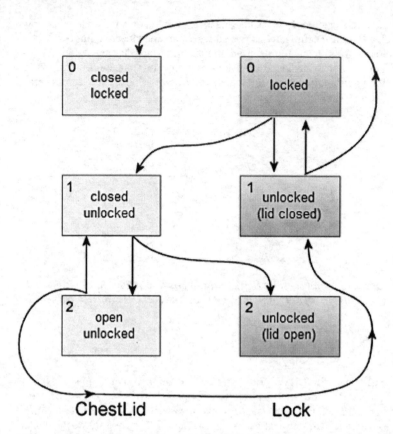

Figure 9-5. *Chest lid with a locked/unlocked state added to control its opened/closed states (left) and with a new state, 0, representing a deactivated or unavailable state (right). This type of diagram shows the states with their interdependencies but does not yet show what happens during the transitions*

With an adventure-style game, where most of the interaction is based on logic, rather than physics, transitions take center stage. That being the case, a variation on the traditional UML state diagram will be more useful. To keep things tidier, the next change to the state diagram will be to list the actions associated with the transition directly below the state.

Before making that change, it's a good time to discuss a convention that you will be using from this point onward. In a typical adventure game, many of the objects the player will interact with will either be deactivated or removed from the environment after use.

The inventory icons will all have the same behavior. They are not being used, 0, are in inventory, 1, or are used as cursor, 2. As the state-management system becomes more refined, you will be using only numbers to identify state. At that point, it will become massively easier to read the information if 0 represents out-of-scene for all objects. For objects that are always in scene, it adds the overhead of an extra state that is never used. It will make the diagramming a bit more complicated now, but will be well worth the trouble later on, when you have to read the state instructions in the Inspector.

■ **Convention** State 0 for all action objects represents out-of-scene. The object will be deactivated.

Now let's see what the chest lid and key look like when you list the actions that happen when the object is transitioned into each state (Figure 9-6, left). The current state is at the top of each block, followed by the state it transitions into and then the actions involved in the transition. In a few cases, the last box shows the other objects that must be triggered and the states they go into.

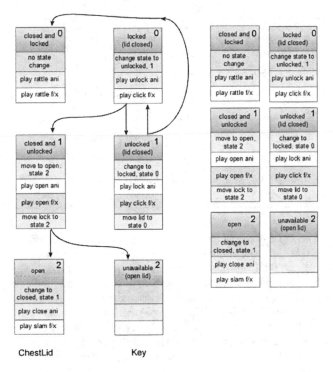

ChestLid   Key

Figure 9-6. *The modified state diagram for the chest lid and key. These diagrams show the interdependencies and the actions associated with the states, but not the events that trigger the state changes*

At some point, you may have realized that the addition of state numbers makes the transition arrows unnecessary and can simplify it even more (preceding Figure 9-6, right).

None of the visuals representations quite cover all the information and functionality you will be dealing with, but they do help to break it down into understandable components parts. At this point, you will probably be relieved to put the state information into a straight text format.

Organizing the Information

Having broken down the interaction to states, their corresponding actions, and the events that triggered the transitions, the next step is to put the information into an easy-to-access table or spreadsheet. One deviation from the traditional state data table you will make is to separate the actions performed on the picked objects from the actions performed on auxiliary objects. Picking a light switch animates the switch, the primary object, but it also affects secondary or auxiliary objects. The auxiliary object could perform a simple animation, or it also may have to transition into a new state. In this example, a light could be turned on, and a material on a lamp shade changed, to appear illuminated. Since each object will contain the information required for its various state transitions, the only thing your table will need to show is the state the auxiliary object has to transition into.

In the following table (Table 9-1), the event that transitions the object into the new state is inferred as the cursor pick. The actions for the transition are broken down into actions on the object and state changes on any affected auxiliary objects. (NA, not applicable, is used for objects that are never transitioned out of scene state 0.) See the State Management PDF for the full table of the test objects. The State Management PDF is one of the files included in the book's downloadable asset from the Apress web site (www.apress.com).

Table 9-1. *A Few Simple State Information Tables*

Object	Cursor	State	Transition Action	Description	Aux. Object / Action ➤ State
Chest Lid	default	0	NA	out of scene	NA
	default	1	[rattle lid]	closed and locked	none
	default	2	lid open	opened	move LockPlate to state 3
	default	3	lid close	closed and unlocked	move LockPlate to state 2
LockPlate	default	0	none	out of scene	move ChestLid to state 1
	default	1	none	closed and locked	[move KeyAtLock to state 0]
	Key Icon	2	none	unlocked, key in lock, unavailable	move KeyAtLock to state 1

You may have already spotted a flaw in this table. If the chest lid is closed and locked and anything interacts with it, it rattles and goes (back) into state 0. The problem comes when the Key at Lock is removed, and it puts the chest lid from state 1 back into state 0. In that case, it shouldn't rattle. Rather than creating a separate state for *every* possible scenario, you will be cheating a bit, by creating a means to process the state without triggering its associated actions.

Another important convention you will be following: objects only contain metadata/information about their own transition actions. To trigger both the action object and the auxiliary objects into the specified state, you will be creating a lookup table. The information, or metadata, for the states and their associated actions will be similar to that in Table 9-2. Eventually, it will hold all of the information associated with the state, including short and long descriptions to be displayed on mouseover and anything else required by the game. The only thing you will have to save for each action object is its current state, a simple integer.

Table 9-2. *ChestLid Metadata*

State	State Description	Animation Clip	Audio Clip
0	out of scene	NA	NA
1	closed and locked	rattle lid	Rattle
2	unlocked and opened	chest open	OpenChest
3	unlocked and closed	chest close	DoorClose

You will be setting up the Lookup table in the next section, but for now, you may want to keep a picture in your mind about what the object metadata will contain. Table 9-2 shows some metadata for the chest lid.

As you can see, the metadata does not have to know the event that will trigger the transition into the state, nor does it need to know what other objects need to be processed. It does, however, split up the actions, so they will be able to be triggered properly in your code, depending on type. See the State Management PDF, available from the Download area of the Apress web site (www.apress.com), for the rest of the test object's metadata.

Lookup Table

Unlike some scenarios, where there is only one possible way into and out of a state, your state machine will need to be more flexible. Objects, when picked, will have to be able to trigger the appropriate actions, depending on the current cursor. These actions will, of course, also vary according to the current state of the object.

So once you know what the possible states will be, you can put the state transitions information into its own table, a lookup table. The actions required to transition into a state will be fully contained within *each object's* own lookup table, so you need only refer to the state by number in the table. The metadata will be processed after the correct case/condition is found.

For each action object, the table will list its states, the cursor objects that can trigger a transition, the new states the various trigger objects will put the object into, and any other objects that have to be put into a different state (see Table 9-3). Note that for the auxiliary objects, you can assume that the trigger is the default cursor.

Table 9-3. Object Lookup Table for the ChestLid, LockPlate, and Key Icon

Object	Current State	Trigger Object	New State	Aux. Object	New State	Aux. Object	New State
ChestLid	1	default	1		0		
	2	default	3	KeyAtLock	1		
	3	default	2	KeyAtLock	2		
LockPlate	1	Key Icon	2	KeyAtLock	1	Key Icon	0
KeyAtLock	1	default	0	LockPlate	1	Key Icon	1

Without the descriptions, the tables are pretty cryptic; let's go through it from the top.

- ChestLid is in state 1, closed and locked. It "goes back" into state 1. Here you want its actions to be triggered.

- ChestLid is in state 2, opened. It goes into state 3, closed. The KeyAtLock reverts to state 1, available, but the animation should not play.

- ChestLid is in state 3, closed and unlocked. It goes into state 2, opened. The KeyAtLock goes to state 2, unavailable.

- LockPlate is in state 1, locked and empty. When picked by the Key Icon, it goes into state 2, unavailable, but it triggers the KeyAtLock into its state 1, inserted into lock and turned. It also tells the Key Icon to go into its state 0, out of scene.

Note there is no case for the LockPlate's state 2 for interaction. The only way it can get back to its state 1, locked and empty, is if the KeyAtLock is removed, e.g., KeyAtLock is in its state 1 and is picked.

- KeyAtLock is inserted and turned. It goes to state 0, out of scene. When the key is removed, the LockPlate goes to its locked and empty state, and the Key Icon goes to its state 1, in inventory.

Note there is no case for its state 2, unavailable, because, well, it's unavailable.
Now that you've got the data into a table, let's look at how it will be evaluated in the code.
The object is what holds the information in the first place. It has been picked.
The first check will be for the object's current state. It will be matched with column one. That tells you where to start looking.

Because the default cursor will usually be the correct event trigger, you will check for it first. In your table and in your code, you will identify it as "default." There aren't any examples in the test setup, but you would also list any cursors that would trigger a customized reply. An example would be if you tried to pick the locked chest lid with a Rock Icon. The lid would do nothing, but you might get a snappy reply, like "Chest bashing will get you nowhere."

The third column will be the state that the object is moved into as a result of the interaction. In some cases, there will be no state change, but there will be a transition back into the original.

Following the first two columns, the remainder will be evaluated in pairs. They will allow you to trigger any other objects that may need animating, instantiating, a state change, or any other special cases. The auxiliary object/new state pairs are optional, but you may add as many as necessary.

You will have to fill out a table for each action object's possible states, once you have determined and defined those states. See the State Management PDF, available from the Download area of the Apress web site (www.apress.com), for the full Lookup table information.

This Lookup table is what you will use to find out what each object should do when triggered by any other object. This, along with the metadata arrays you will create, will allow you to specify everything that needs to be done when a specific condition is met or identified. For more ambitious projects, you may wish to manage the lookup tables in the database of your choice.

Evaluating the Results

At this point, you now have the information you need to set things in motion. The order of evaluation is as follows:

1. To start, you have to know *which* object was picked.

2. You will then have to determine the object's present state.

3. And you will have to know what the current cursor object was that picked it.

4. Next, using that information, you have to see what state the object goes into.

Once you have *that* information, you can do the following:

5. Find and perform all of the actions (animations, sound effects, custom scripts, etc.) associated with the transition into its new state.

6. Check to see if there are any other objects affected and, if so, the states they will go into, so you can do all the associated actions for them as well.

The first is easy. You have access to that; it was the object that got picked.

The second is also easy. You will check the object's metadata (the fancy name for its variables that store its pertinent information) to find its current state.

The third is a little trickier. You only have one game pointer, but you will be swapping out the textures to create the illusion of different cursors. For now, assume that you can readily retrieve the cursor's texture information.

The fourth is also easy. Having identified the object that triggered the event, you will have the state the object is to go into.

The fifth is easy. With the new state, you will be able to trigger the animation, audio clip, and custom scripts that are associated with it.

And, finally, the sixth, is similar to the fifth. Any auxiliary objects listed are then put into the state specified for each and are, in effect, processed exactly like the original object, as if it had been picked by the default cursor.

Parsing a String

With the data organized, and the theory out of the way, it's time to start scripting the state "machine." But first, you will have to make a design decision that has to do with the way Unity exposes arrays in the Inspector. Your lookup table is essentially a multidimensional array. Unfortunately, you can't gain access to that kind of array directly through the Inspector with JavaScript.

▪ **Tip**　Unity's unique implementation of JavaScript has a special kind of array that can be visible in the Inspector. Because it must have its type declared, it is very fast. It also must have its number of elements declared. When the array is public and showing inside the Inspector, this is automatically done for you.

You do, however, have a means of parsing a string (such as this sentence) and breaking it into component parts, according to a specified character. This allows you to store data in one large string, as a single element of the array, and then evaluate it on need. While this is not a method you would want to use in a shooter-type game where response speed is crucial, it will not cause any problems in a slower-paced point-and-click-type game.

Parsing takes a string of characters and goes through them one at time (or however many you stipulate), to check for specific cases. In this case, you will be looking for commas. Additionally, you have a means to break the contents of the strings between the commas into elements of an internal array, for identification and processing.

With the parsing technique in mind, the table data for a few of the test objects will eventually be written into your array, as follows:

- ChestLid:
  - State 0: default,0
  - State 1: default,2,KeyAtLock,1
  - State 2: default,1,KeyAtLock,2
- KeyAtLock:
  - State 0: default,0,ChestLid,1
  - State 1: default,2,ChestLid,0
- Rock:
  - State 0: default,1
  - State 1: default,2
- LockPlate:
  - State 0: default,0
  - State 0: Key Icon,1,KeyAtLock,1,Key Icon,0
  - State 1: default,0,KeyAtLock,0,Key Icon,2

▪ **Note**　Make sure there is no space after the commas!

The states where the object is not available for interaction, such as state 0 (out of scene), are not listed for processing. You will create a variable for each of three possible states an object could be in (1,2,3). Later, you can increase the number, but for now, let's keep it simple. You will call your variables `lookupState_1`, `lookupState_2`, and `lookupState_3`.

Game Notes

About now, you are probably starting to get worried about remembering the rules and conventions you are setting up to make your game both powerful and extensible. It's time to introduce a handy method to store and access this information.

Besides adding comments in your scripts, you will find it crucial to have a brief document for notes on your game that is attached to the game itself. Unity's script editor is capable of reading and writing to several different file types, including a simple text file. You will create a file whose sole purpose is an easy-access repository for anything related to your rules and conventions. This will allow you to concentrate on the interactivity without constantly trying to remember where all the bits and pieces were introduced.

1. If it's not already open, open the Imported Animations scene.

2. Open the Interactor script to open the script editor.

3. From File, click New ➤ File.

4. Select Misc ➤ Empty Text File (Figure 9-7).

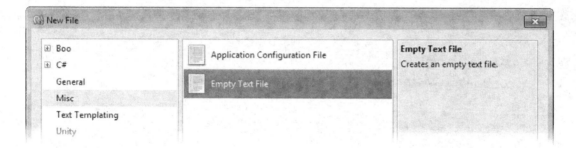

Figure 9-7. *Creating a text asset*

5. Make sure you are saving the new file to the Adventure Scripts folder and name it **GameNotes.txt**.

6. Add the definitions for *Object Lookup:*

Game Notes
ObjectLookup script:
For each Action Object and each of its states, the Lookup data will be in the following format:
cursor,new state,auxiliary object1, its new state, auxiliary object2, its new state, etc.
Auxiliary objects are optional.

7. Save the text asset. (Agree to converting endings, if the warning message appears.)

8. Note the icon for the text asset (Figure 9-8).

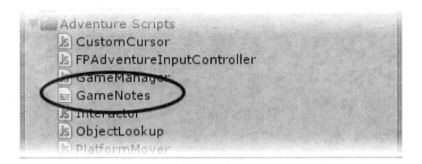

Figure 9-8. *The GameNotes text asset*

■ **Tip**   You will be adding lots of information to your GameNotes text asset as you work through the project. If you find yourself having to go back and look something else up, feel free to include it in the notes.

The Object Lookup Script

Just as with the Interactor script you started building in the cursor control chapter, you will be adding functionality throughout the development of your game to this next script. Inside it, you will store the instructions that will tell your game what to do when an object is picked or triggered.

Let's begin by creating a new script in the Adventure Scripts folder.

1. Create a new JavaScript in the Adventure Scripts folder.

2. Name it **ObjectLookup**.

3. Open it in the script editor.

4. Delete the Update function for now.

5. At the top of the new script, add the three variables and declare their types as Unity built-in arrays of type String:

```
// make a Unity array for the three possible states of the object, each will have:
// picking cursor, new state, other object, its state, another object, its state, etc...
// use 'default' for the default cursor name
var lookupState1 : String[];          //declare an array of string type content
var lookupState2 : String[];          //declare an array of string type content
var lookupState3 : String[];          //declare an array of string type content

var state : int = 1;                  // a variable to hold the state to process
internal var currentStateArray : String[]; // var to hold the current array to process
```

The brackets tell you that the variables are arrays, and String tells you what type of variables are in the arrays. With the Unity arrays, because they can be exposed in the Inspector, the engine must know what type of input to expect. You do not have to tell it how many elements to expect, as that can be changed in the Inspector and is found internally at runtime.

313

6. Save the script and ignore the warning in the console.

7. Add the new script to the LockPlate object (Figure 9-9).

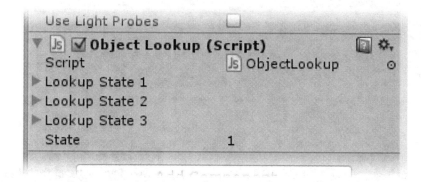

Figure 9-9. The new array parameters in the Inspector on the LockPlate object

For now, the LockPlate will have four states: out of scene (state 0—never used), locked and empty (state 1), key inserted and unavailable (state 2, when the lid is closed), and key inserted, but not available (state 3, when the lid is opened).

At state 1 (no key in the lock), if you click it with the Key Icon as cursor, the KeyAtLock divulges and inserts itself into the lock (it goes into its state 1), and the LockPlate goes to state 1. If you click it with anything else, you will eventually create a generic message about not being able to use the cursor object with the lock.

At state 2 (with the key in the lock, having been turned/unlocked, but the lid closed), the LockPlate is unavailable and does not change state. Once set up, the KeyAtLock, if picked, would be removed and *that* action would put the LockPlate back into state 1.

At state 3 (with the key in the lock, with the chest lid open), the LockPlate is unavailable and does not change state.

1. Select the LockPlate.

2. Open each of the three Lookup State parameters.

Because they are arrays, the first thing you will see is a parameter called Size. It is created automatically for the array and shows up in the Inspector.

You can fill out arrays two different ways. If you fill in the Size first, you will get that number of elements. Arrays always start with Element 0 as their first element.

The other way to fill them out is to set the Size to 1, fill in the information, then change the size. When this method is used, the contents are copied into the added elements. This will be quite useful when you start adding text to go along with states.

To begin, let's use the first method. This way, you'll know at the outset how many possibilities you need to account for.

3. In the Inspector, set the Size for Lookup State 1 to **3** and press Enter.

4. Three elements are generated (Figure 9-10).

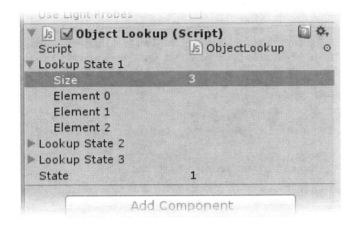

Figure 9-10. *Lookup State 1's three new elements*

Nothing is immediately obvious about where to enter the data.

1. Click below the Size's 3 to force the field into edit mode to Element 0's information (Figure 9-11).

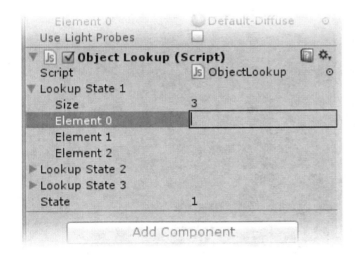

Figure 9-11. *Ready to enter data*

2. In Element 0, add the cursor, *default*, and the state it stays in, *1*, as follows:default,1

3. In Element 1, add the cursor, *Key Icon*, and the state it goes into, *2*, separated by a comma, the auxiliary object, *KeyAtLock*, and the state it needs to go into, *1*, as follows:

    Key Icon,2,KeyAtLock,1

315

The only interaction to produce results right now with the LockPlate is when it is being picked by the default cursor or the Key Icon, so there is no reason to have a third element, unless you wanted another cursor to produce a custom reply. The Rock Icon, for example, might produce: "Bashing the lock plate with the Rock is likely to dislocate your shoulder." The Vial of Elixir Icon could produce: "The vial of elixir is a life-giving fluid, not some common machine oil."

    4.   Change Lookup State 1's Size to **2** and press Enter.

The extra Element field goes away.

The LockPlate only responds when it is in state 1, but you can set it up for a reply and no state change for the other two states.

    5.   Set the other two arrays to Size **1** and fill in their data, as follows (your results should look like Figure 9-12):

- Lookup State 1:
    - Element 0: default,1
    - Element 1: Key Icon,2, KeyAtLock,1
- Lookup State 2:
    - Element 0: default,2
- Lookup State 3:
    - Element 0: default,3

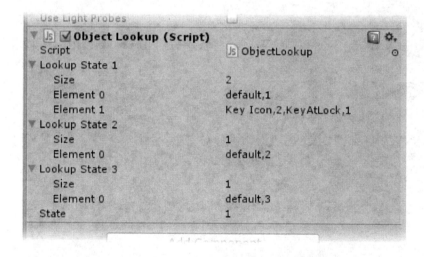

Figure 9-12. *The LockPlate's state transition information loaded*

■ **Tip**   Be sure there are no spaces after your commas. Should you leave a space after a comma, the parsing code will never find a match, because it would be looking for a name beginning with a space.

Let's read through it. If the LockPlate is in state 1 (empty), and is picked by the default cursor, it stays in state 1. If it is in state 1 and is picked by the cursor with the Key Icon texture on it, the LockPlate goes into state 2 (key in lock), and the KeyAtLock object goes into its state 1 (inserted and turned). Eventually, you will also have Key Icon go into state 0 (not in scene), but this is just a test run, so it is left out for now.

If the LockPlate is in state 2 (key inserted and turned, lid closed) and is picked by the default cursor, it remains in state 2.

If the LockPlate is in state 3 (key inserted and turned, lid open) and is picked by the default cursor, it remains in state 3.

For the first test, you will manually tell it which array to parse, via the state variable. Then, you will go through that string, chopping it up at each comma and putting the results into yet another array for final processing.

1. Open the ObjectLookup script.

2. Start an OnMouseDown function:

```
function OnMouseDown (){
```

Next, you will need a way to use the state number to load the correct lookupState array in as currentState. Using JavaScript arrays, you could have easily made an array of arrays and called up the element number with the state variable. The problem is that mobile platforms can't use JavaScript arrays, and Unity arrays cannot be of type Array (a generic, I'll-fill-in-the-real-type-later sort of thing). Unity has opted to add #pragma strict to the top of each new script, and that will cause an error to be thrown when a JavaScript array is used. You *could* remove the #pragma strict to avoid the error, because this game is designed for desktop deployment, but sticking to Unity arrays will give you an opportunity to learn how to use a switch statement, as well as being mobile-compliant.

■ **Tip** For more information on JavaScript arrays versus Unity built-in arrays, consult the Scripting Reference for *array*.

Switch avoids the need to nest multiple if conditions by setting a case for each value of the specified variable.

3. Add the following code inside the OnMouseDown function:

```
switch (state) { // use the state to assign the corresponding array

    case 1:
        currentStateArray = lookupState1;
    break;

    case 2:
        currentStateArray = lookupState2;
    break;

    case 3:
        currentStateArray = lookupState3;
    break;
}
```

Because state is an int, the cases must use integers. The line after each case statement assigns the correct LookupState array to the currentStateArray variable. Break prevents the remainder of the cases from being evaluated, once a condition that evaluates as true has been found. It "breaks" out of the switch block.

Once you have the array, you can read through it with a for/in loop. This variation of a for/to loop automatically gets the length (number of elements) in the array and iterates through the elements. It assigns each element to the variable named contents, of type String.

Then, when you have the element, contents, you parse, or go through it, one character at a time. Every time you encounter a comma, you put the characters since the previous comma into a new array named readString.

4. Add the following beneath the switch block:

```
print ("Results for state " + state );
// go through the array by element
for (var contents : String in currentStateArray) {
//view the contents of the current element in currentStateArray
print ("contents: " + contents);
//split the contents of the current element into a temporary string array
var readString : String[] = contents.Split(",".Chars[0]);
//} this will get uncommented later
// now read the first two split out pieces (elements) back out
print ("elements in array for state " + state + " = " + readString.length);
print ("Cursor = " + readString[0]);
print ("New state = " + readString[1]);
```

USING STRINGS IN ARRAYS TO STORE MULTIPLE TYPES OF INFORMATION

Still confused? Perhaps a less abstract example using your format would be a primary school. Your initial array will be a string containing the teacher's name, the number of years they have taught, then each child in the class, followed by his or her gender. You would have an array for each grade, containing an element for each teacher that teaches that grade. It would look something like the following:

Kindergarten:

- Element 0   Miss Smith,2,Eric,M,Alice,F,Leroy,M,Ryan,M,Sandy,F

- Element 1   Miss Phillips,3,Tommy,M,Jill,F,Mary Alice,F,Alex F.,M,Alex S.,M

First Grade:

- Element 0   Mrs. Whitney,30,Tiffany,F,Joey,M,Timmy,M,Terry,F,Greg,M

- Element 1   Mr. Garcia,5,Fred,M,Brittany,F,Garret,M,Louise,F

Second Grade:

- Element 0   Mr. Johnston,Abby,F,Kai,M,Henry,M,Jeremy,M,Lucrecia,F,Sumy,F

Let's process Kindergarten, Element 1, or kindergarten[1], into the readString array. The contents of kindergarten[1], a string of "Miss Phillips,3,Tommy,M,Jill,F,Mary Alice,F,Alex F.,M,Alex S.,M", become new elements of readString each time you encounter a comma.

The contents of the readString array are represented as ("Miss Phillips", "3","Tommy","M","Jill","F","Mar y Alice","F","Alex F.", "M","Alex S.","M"). Because each element is a string, it must be enclosed by quotation marks. Elements in an array are separated by commas. In your original string, you could just as easily use an asterisk for the split character, but an array must use commas.

Now that you have an array, you can quickly get the data you need. Element 0 contains the teacher's name. Element 1 contains the number of years the teacher has taught, and, starting at Element 2, the even-numbered elements are the names of the children in the class, and the element number + 1 will tell you their gender.

In code, it would look as follows:

```
kindergarten[1] = ("Miss Phillips","3","Tommy","M","Jill","F","Mary Alice","F",↵
"Alex F.",:M","Alex S.","M")
readString = ("Miss Phillips","3","Tommy","M","Jill","F","Mary Alice","F",↵
"Alex F.", "M","Alex S.","M")
readString[0] = "Miss Phillips"
readString[1] = "3"
readString[2] = "Tommy"
readString[3] = "M"
readString[4] = "Jill"
readString[5] = "F"
readString[6] = "Mary Alice"
readString[7] = "F"
readString[8] = "Alex F."
readString[9] = "M"
readString[8] = "Alex S."
readString[9] = "M"
```

Let's continue with your ObjectLookup script's OnMouseDown function.

5. Add the following beneath the previous code:

```
//now read through the remainder in pairs
//iterate through the array starting at element 2 and incrementing by 2
//as long as the counting variable i is less than the length of the array
for (var i = 2; i < readString.length; i= i + 2) {
    print ("auxiliary object = " + readString[i]);
    print (readString[i]  +  "'s new state = " + readString[i+1]);
}
} // close the for/in block

} // close the OnMouseDown function
```

6. Save the script.

To test, you will start with the one of the simpler states, 2, and work your way backward.

1. Click Play.

2. Select the LockPlate in the Hierarchy view.

3. In the Inspector, set the state variable to **2**.

4. Pick the LockPlate in the Game window.

5. Look at the results in the Console, Figure 9-13.

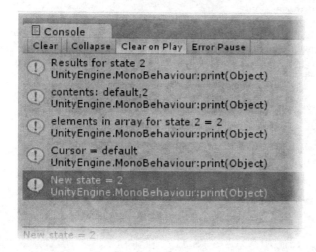

Figure 9-13. *Results of state 2*

6. Change the State to **1**.

7. Click the Clear button at the top of the console.

8. Pick the LockPlate again.

The auxiliary data for the KeyAtLock is neatly parsed, showing that it should go into state 1.

For state 1, you see both the contents of the first and second elements as they are processed (see preceding Figure 9-14). When you start using this code for the actual game functionality, you will search for a match for the cursor (its texture name), and, once found, process its data and then *look no further*.

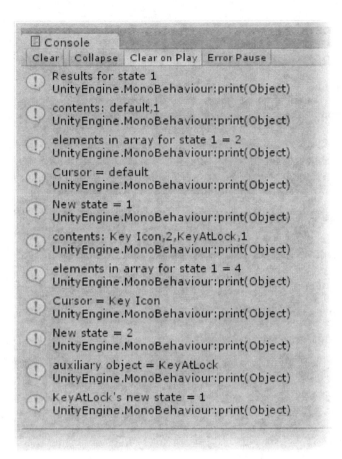

Figure 9-14. Results of state 1

Thus, you now have a means of storing and retrieving the event trigger data. You can add it directly into the Inspector for each action object. This is by no means the only way to manage and access the metadata, but, rather, a compromise between "easy to enter" and "easy to read." Ideally, one would want to create a custom GUI element for easier handling of the data, but that is beyond the scope of this book.

Besides triggering animations and audio on the picked object, you will also have to trigger actions on other objects. They may be as simple as state changes, or as complex as instantiating particle system events. You will eventually be adding a system for handling anything out of the ordinary.

■ **Tip**   As some of your data entries will be rather long, you may wish to use a text editor to type your data, then copy and paste it into Unity. This will make it easier to check for errors.

Action-Related Messages

Besides calling animations and sound files for the action object, you will want to display a message describing the action. In the old days of pure text games, these messages were necessary to describe what had just happened in a non-visual world. Additionally, they could also be quite entertaining. You will make use of the text message both to entertain and to make sure the player hasn't missed some key factor of the action that was just played out.

Because you will want to display messages corresponding to a specific object/trigger-object interaction, which, in most cases, will be the cursor and may or may not invoke a state change, these interaction messages will be handled separately from the object's regular metadata (the actions required by each transition). Because the messages are related to the event-triggering object, you will keep them in the ObjectLookUp script with the rest of the instructions for the state transitions.

■ **Rule**   The Reply arrays must be identical in size to the corresponding Lookup arrays. If the instructions say Element 2, the reply that goes with them must also be in Element 2.

---

1. Stop Play mode and open the ObjectLookUp script.

2. Add the message array variables following the lookupState variable declarations:

    ```
    // arrays of replies for each state and corresponding element
    var repliesState1 : String[];
    var repliesState2 : String[];
    var repliesState3 : String[];
    // generic reply in case a match for the cursor was not found
    var genericReplies : String[]; // Add one reply for each state
    ```

Note that you've also added an array for more generic replies. Because it's also tied in with the states, it must have one reply for each state only.

Just as with the currentStateArray to hold the currently selected lookupState array, you will need to have an array to store the current replies. It will be assigned in the case statements right below the currentStateArray assignments.

3. Add the following line below the internal var currentStateArray line:

    ```
    internal var currentReplyArray : String[]; // var to hold the current reply to process
    ```

4. And, finally, add the corresponding Reply array assignments to *each* of the case statements. Case 1 should look as follows:

    ```
    case 1:
       currentStateArray = lookupState1;
       currentReplyArray = repliesState1;
    break;
    ```

5. Save the script.

6. In the Inspector, for the LockPlate, set the Size of the new Replies State arrays to match the Lookup State arrays (Figure 9-15).

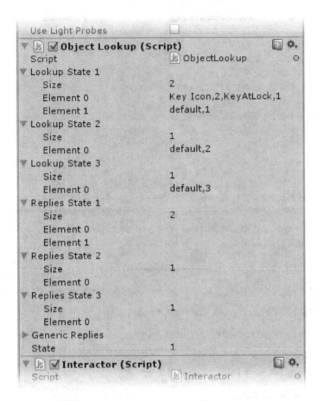

Figure 9-15. *The Replies arrays partially set up*

7. Save the scene and save the project.

You will start filling in messages as you get the other action objects up and running.

Object Metadata

In the previous section, you set up the beginnings of your state-management system. The ObjectLookup script, using the object's current state and the cursor or other object that interacted with it, will tell you what state the object goes into and the states that any auxiliary objects go into as well. The bulk of the information about the actions required by the state transitions will be stored on the individual object as metadata in the Interactor script. Each action object will have to know all of the information required to move into each of its states.

The most important variable you will add to your object is for its *current state*. The current state, because it will change throughout the object's lifetime, will have to be initialized. This will also give you an easy way to test interactions without having to go through all of the steps (state changes) to get to the one you want. By creating an additional variable, an *initial state* variable, you will have the flexibility to start objects at whichever state you wish. This is the starting point for processing object transitions.

1. Open the Interactor script.

2. Add the following above the `// Pick and Mouseover Info` section:

```
//state dependent variables
var initialState : int = 1; // this is the state the object starts in
```

You have initialized the state to 1, because that will usually be the object's initial state in your game.

State-Related Metadata

Besides the animations, delays, and sound effects, the individual states will require descriptive names, short and long descriptions (a *verbose* option) for mouseovers, and action text associated with each. The metadata will be kept in corresponding arrays with the states as the element numbers.

As with the ObjectLookup script's arrays, the arrays will be exposed to the Inspector, so you can load in each object's unique information. You will be storing the following information:

1. *Name*: A state descriptive name, such as "Open Chest Lid"

2. *Location*: The state of being of the object (visible, pickable, etc.)

3. *Visibility Type*: How to handle visibility for this state (fade in, pop in, fade out, etc.)

4. *Description (verbose)*: For example, "It is a beautifully constructed chest lid laying open for all to see."

5. *Animation*: The animation that will play when the object goes *into* this state

6. *Animation Delay*: The time delay associated with the animation

7. *Audio*: The sound effect associated with the animation

8. *Audio Delay*: The time before the sound clip is played

9. *Loop Animation*: The animation, if any, that will play after the initial animation

10. *Loop Audio*: The sound effect associated with the looping animation

With the default array handling in the Inspector, the array elements become the elements (see Table 9-4).

Table 9-4. *The Metadata, Arranged by State*

Location
State 0
State 1
State 2
Name
State 0
State 1
State 2
Description
State 0
State 1
State 2
Animation
State 0
State 1
State 2

Let's go ahead and create the variables for the object metadata.

1.   Open the Interactor script.

2.   Add the following public variables at the top of the script, just below the `initialState` variable:

```
//Object metadata
var location : int[];                        // see notes
var visibility : int[];                      // see notes
var objectName : String[];                   // name/label of the object in this state
var description : String[];                   // description of the object in this state
var animationClip : AnimationClip[];          // the animation that will play when picked
var animationDelay : float[];                 // the time delay before the animation plays
var soundClip : AudioClip[];                  // the sound that gets played when picked
var audioDelay : float[];                     // the time delay before the audio plays
var loopAnimation : AnimationClip[];          //animation that loops after main animation
var loopSoundFX : AudioClip[];                // sound that goes with it
var postLoop : boolean = false;               // flag to know if it has a looping animation to follow
var animates : boolean = true;                // var to know if it animates at all
var aniObject : GameObject;                   // object that holds the animation component for this object
```

3.   Save the script.

By keeping all of an object's critical information on the object itself, it is generally easier to maintain. In other words, it's easier to modify, easier to understand, and easier to make modular.

Let's look at a few of the variables to find out what they represent and how they are being stored. Most are pretty self-explanatory, but a few are definitely abstract.

State of Being/Location

You added a variable called location along with the other state-related variables. It will tell you the abstract state of the object in the scene—whether it can be picked, if it's in inventory or being used as a cursor, if it's currently visible, and other esoteric information not necessarily related to its physical state. For want of a better term (as you are already using the term *state*), it's called *location*. You will be assigning a number to represent each of the possibilities.

Location:

3D Objects

>> 0: Object is not in scene.

>> 1: Object is in scene and pickable.

>> 2: Object is not pickable (in scene).

2D Objects

>> 0: Object is not in scene.

>> 1: Object is in Inventory.

>> 2: Object is Cursor.

Add these definitions to your GameNotes.txt file.

Visibility Type

Another parameter that is assigned numbers to represent its options is visibility. When an object's location state changes, you have to know how and when to handle the change in visibility, if one is needed. Rather than going to the trouble of duplicating animations and keyframing them for, say, fade-ins or fade-outs, you can set up the action once in code, so any object with a transparency shader can be handled automatically. Once faded out, the object will eventually have to be deactivated.

If you remember what you learned when adding the fade-out to the KeyAtRock, you will realize that you can reduce the possibilities by checking for a transparent shader that will tell you when to use fades with the visibility changes. If it uses a Transparent shader, it fades in or out of its visibility type. The visibility type becomes simply:

Visibility:

>> 0: N/A (no transparency shader or don't fade)

>> 1: Show at start (fade in)

>> 2: Show at start, hide at end (fade in, fade out)

>> 3: Hide at end (fade out)

Add these definitions to your GameNotes.txt file.

■ **Tip** Other shaders can use the alpha channel through their textures, but only with the Transparency shaders can you change or animate it with the Color's alpha parameter.

Current State

Having added the state information arrays to the Interactor script, you will have to add variables to let the object keep track of the values using the current state.

1. Open the Interactor script.

2. At the top of the script, in the //state dependent variables section, add the following:

```
var currentState : int = 1;                          // this will get updated in Start
internal var currentLocation : int;                  // see notes
internal var currentVisibility : int;                //see notes
internal var currentObjectName : String;             // short description
internal var currentObjectDescription : String;      // full description
internal var currentSound : AudioClip;
internal var currentAudioDelay : float = 0.0;
internal var currentAnimationClip : AnimationClip;
internal var currentAnimationDelay : float = 0.0;
```

Several of the current values will have to be assigned on startup. Until you fill out the metadata on the objects, you will get an index-out-of-range error when the engine tries to assign nonexistent values, so they will be commented out to start.

3. Add the following to the Start function:

```
// load the initial values
currentState = initialState; // this allows override of starting state only
//currentObjectName = objectName[currentState];
//currentObjectDescription = description[currentState];
//currentLocation = location[currentState];
//currentVisibility = visibility[currentState];
```

4. Save the script.

Note that there is no delay on the loop sound and animation. You will be adding the animation delay to the animation length to calculate when to start the loop animation (and sound), if it exists.

Processing the Pick Event

To use the objects' metadata, you will need to process the mouseover and pick events. The current state is used with the mouseovers to show test descriptions and names, but the pick event requires a bit of processing. It will be queried for the current cursor texture. Armed with that information, it will find the picked object's current state and then find the object's new state. Once it knows that, it can go through the metadata and perform the various actions associated with the new state. Along the way, you will also be making decisions about how the cursor itself will behave.

As you may recall when you were experimenting with animations, you created a series of scripts. You will now start incorporating some of their features into your Interactor script, as well as a few other variables that will make your scripting more efficient and solve issues that may crop up.

Let's start by switching your test objects over to the script you are developing for the actual game.

1. Save the current scene as **Interaction** in the Scenes folder.

2. Delete Bean Group and Rock Group from the Hierarchy view (Figure 9-16).

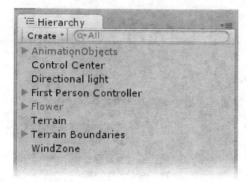

Figure 9-16. *The remaining objects in the newly renamed scene*

3. Remove the AniTest and AniTwoState components from the objects in the scene.

4. Add the Interactor script to the Rock, the Pedestal, and the KeyAtRock.

You will have to factor in mouse-pick logic before you worry about the actual animations, so you need not rush to fill out all of the new metadata arrays just yet. You have OnMouseEnter and OnMouseExit; now you need to add the OnMouseDown for your pick events.

1. Open the Interactor script.

2. Add an OnMouseDown function beneath the OnMouseExit function.

```
function OnMouseDown () {
    print   ("we have mouse down on " + this.name);
}
```

3. Back up at the top, under the //Pick and Mouseover Info section, add the following variables:

```
internal var picked : boolean = false;  // so you can temporarily prevent mouseover
action
internal var mousedown : boolean; // so you know when this is true
internal var processing : boolean = false; //so you can suspend mouseover actions, etc.
```

4. Save the script.

As per the comments, these variables will help you refine the existing functionality as you go forward.

5. Click Play and mouse over, then click either the Rock or Pedestal objects.

If you got a response from the pick but saw no mouseover response, you will have to increase the Trigger Distance or move the First Person Controller closer to the objects in the scene.

You have probably realized that the color changes are likely to interfere with the visual experience once the transition actions are hooked up. So, it makes sense to turn it off as soon as you have a mouse pick. You've already got the turn-off code in the OnMouseExit function, so you can just copy and paste it from there.

6. Add the following to the OnMouseDown function to turn off the cursor color change:

```
// *** send a message turn the cursor color back to original
controlCenter.SendMessage("CursorColorChange", false); // turn the pointer white;
```

7. Save the script.

8. Click Play and pick an object again.

The functionality is much nicer, but you need to try something else before you can move on.

9. Use the Clear button in the console to clear the existing messages.

10. Back away—far away—from the objects and mouse over, then mouse down/pick the object.

While the mouseover functionality was bypassed, the pick wasn't.

You can also copy and paste the distance-checking line from the `OnMouseEnter` into the `OnMouseDown` function. Make sure you add it before the print function, so you know if it worked.

11. Add the following at the top of the `OnMouseDown` function:

```
// exit if you are not within range
if (DistanceFromCamera() > triggerDistance) return;
```

12. Save the script.

13. Click play and back out of mouseover range, and then pick the object.

Nothing happens.

14. Move within range again and pick to make sure it still works.

■ **Tip** When adding functionality, it is always a good idea to make sure the original functionality still works before you no longer remember the changes you made.

After experimenting with picking the objects, you may have come to the conclusion that your Trigger Distance is really too far for picking. If you decrease it, the mouseover distance may be too close. The solution is to make two checks. By adding an offset distance, you can still get mouseover, but without messing up Trigger Distance. As an additional benefit, you can control just which prompts will be activated when you implement the text message.

Because you can override the Trigger Distance for an object in the Inspector, it makes sense to add the offset rather than hardcode a separate value for the total distance. This way, when you adjust the Trigger Distance, the offset will still be the same distance from it, wherever that may be.

1. Add the following variable beneath the `//Object metadata` section:

```
var moOffset : float = 8.0;  // additional distance to allow mouse over to be seen
```

2. Change the `if (DistanceFromCamera` line in the `OnMouseEnter` function to include the offset:

```
// exit if you are not within range
if (DistanceFromCamera() > triggerDistance + moOffset) return;
```

3. Save the script.

Be sure to test the distance and the offset thoroughly before you put the `Interactor` script on other objects. If you forget and have to change all of the defaults, you can change the variable to internal, save the script, and then change the variable back to public again.

4.   Click Play and test the distance checking (Figure 9-17).

Figure 9-17. *Mouseover, but no mouse pick, between range and range + offset*

You may have noticed the viewport jump when you first move forward in the scene. At one point, you changed the Main Camera's x rotation to 12, so you had a starting view looking down on the action objects. If you wish to set it back to 0, feel free to do so, after stopping Play mode.

5.   Stop Play mode.

Adding the Metadata

Now would be a good time to start filling in the metadata on a couple of your objects. Let's go with the simpler state objects, the Rock and the KeyAtRock. You will have the rock move aside, then become unpickable ("location" 2). The key only has two states: on the ground and out of the scene ("location" 0). It fades out as it goes out of scene (Visibility type 2).

1.   In the Inspector, locate the Rock's Interactor component.

2.   With the exception of the two Loop arrays, set the size of each array to **3**.

The Loop functionality has a check box telling you when to use it, so you don't have to worry about error messages about elements in those two arrays, if they don't exist.

3.   Fill in the metadata for the Rock and the KeyAtRock, as per Table 9-5.

Table 9-5. *Metadata for the Rock and the KeyAtRock*

Rock		KeyAtRock	
Initial State	1	Initial State	1
Location		Location	
Size	3	Size	2
Element 0	0	Element 0	0
Element 1	1	Element 1	1
Element 2	2		
Visibility		Visibility	
Size	3	Size	2
Element 0	0	Element 0	3
Element 1	0	Element 1	0
Element 2	0		
Object Name		Object Name	
Size	3	Size	2
Element 0	NA	Element 0	NA
Element 1	Large Rock	Element 1	Old Key
Element 2	Displaced Rock		
Description		Description	
Size	3	Size	2
Element 0	NA	Element 0	NA
Element 1	It is a large rock on the ground	Element 1	It is an old iron key on the ground
Element 2	It is a large rock that's been moved		
Animation Clip		Animation Clip	
Size	3	Size	2
Element 0	none	Element 0	key up
Element 1	none	Element 1	none
Element 2	rock move		
Animation Delay		Animation Delay	
Size	3	Size	2
Element 0	0	Element 0	0
Element 1	0	Element 1	0
Element 2	0		
Sound Clip		Sound FX	
Size	3	Size	2
Element 0	none	Element 0	none
Element 1	none	Element 1	none
Element 2	plopsm		
Audio Delay		Audio Delay	
Size	3	Size	2
Element 0	0	Element 0	0
Element 1	0	Element 1	0
Element 2	0.75		

(*continued*)

Table 9-5. (*continued*)

Rock		KeyAtRock	
Loop Animation		Loop Animation	
Size	0	Size	0
Loop Sound FX		Loop Sound FX	
Size	0	Size	0
Post Loop	false	Post Loop	false
Animates	true	Animates	true
Ani Object	AnimationObjects	Ani Object	AnimationObjects
Mo Offset	8	Mo Offset	8

4. Remove the Interactor component from the Pedestal object for now.

Next, you will need to assign the values to the "current" variables in the Interactor script.

5. Open the Interactor script.

6. Add the following lines to the Start function:

```
currentObjectName = objectName[currentState];
currentObjectDescription = description[currentState];
currentLocation = location[currentState];
currentVisibility = visibility[currentState];
```

7. Save the scene.

Review the location and visibility definitions in the GameNotes text asset for a reminder about the number assignments for location and visibility.

The important thing to remember about your metadata is that it contains the actions needed to put an object *into* its target state. Therefore, if the key is in state 1 (on the ground) when you pick it, the animation to lift it is in the state it goes *into*, state 0.

Activating the State Engine

At this point, you've got the beginnings of the two main scripts needed for your action objects' state engine. The Interactor stores the data associated with each state and will eventually be in charge of carrying out the actions for the transitions into the new states. The ObjectLookup script processes the pick to find out what the new state is and also any other objects included in the picked object's state change. So now you're probably anxious to see how the two scripts will come together to form your state engine. While there are still a lot of pieces missing from the final version, you can at least get a glimpse of things to come.

The first thing that will have to be changed is to let the Interactor handle all of the OnMouseDown functionality, because it's already got the distance checking and mouse handling. In the ObjectLookup script, the OnMouseDown function will have to be renamed, so that the Interactor script can call it from its OnMouseDown function.

Another requirement is that it will have to know which object to process, what that object's current state is, and what cursor triggered the state engine event. Those three variables will be passed into the function as arguments. Because SendMessage can only send one argument, you will have to call the function directly. Let's take care of those changes first.

1. Open the ObjectLookup script.

2. Rename and change the OnMouseDown function, as follows:

```
//look up the state of the object to see what needs to happen
function LookUpState (object : GameObject, currentState: int, picker : String) {
```

3. Change the closing bracket from } // close the OnMouseDown function, to:

```
} // close the LookUpState function
```

4. Save the script.

5. Open the Interactor script.

6. At the bottom of the OnMouseDown function, add

```
//send the picked object, its current state, and the cursor [its texture name]
//that picked it directly to the LookUpState function for processing
GetComponent(ObjectLookup).LookUpState(this.gameObject,currentState,cursor);
```

Because cursor change has not yet been implemented, you will need a temporary variable to hold the name of the real or, at this point, fictitious cursor texture name, a String type. Because most picks will be from the default cursor, you may as well initialize it to that. Leaving this variable exposed to the Inspector will also allow you to feed in non-default "cursors" during testing.

7. Add the following variable up near the top of the script:

```
var cursor : String = "default"; // temporary cursor for testing LookupState
```

8. Save the script.

Before you go any further, you ought to check to make sure the changes work. To do that, you will have to ensure that the test objects have both an ObjectLookup and an Interactor script. Only a few of the objects have an animation, so you will test those first.

1. Add the ObjectLookup script to the Rock and the KeyAtRock.

Both objects are unavailable after the first pick, so they only require a state 1 entry in the ObjectLookup. Additionally, they will only respond to the default cursor, so they only need an Element 0 for the state 1.

2. Set the Lookup State 1 Size to **1** for both of the objects.

3. Set the KeyAtRock to: default,0

4. And set the Rock to: default,2

5. Set the Replies State 1 Size to **1** for both of the objects.

You needn't fill out the replies until you add the functionality that prints the text to screen, but feel free to consult the StateManagement PDF, available from the Download area of the Apress web site (www.apress.com), if you wish to have it ready to go for later (Figure 9-18).

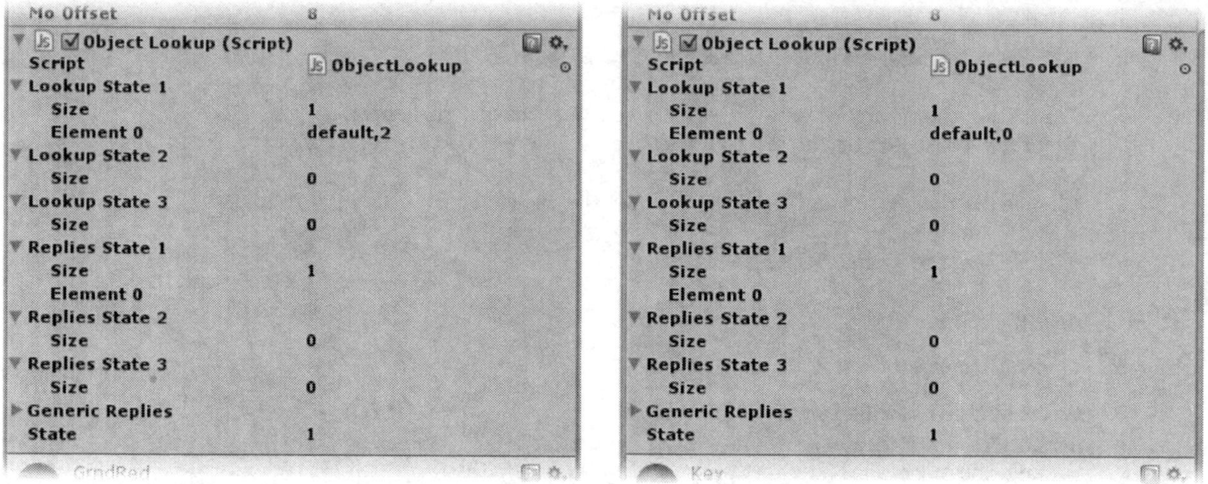

No Offset	8
▼ Js ☑ Object Lookup (Script)	🔲 ⚙,
Script	Js ObjectLookup ⊙
▼ Lookup State 1	
Size	1
Element 0	default,2
▼ Lookup State 2	
Size	0
▼ Lookup State 3	
Size	0
▼ Replies State 1	
Size	1
Element 0	
▼ Replies State 2	
Size	0
▼ Replies State 3	
Size	0
▶ Generic Replies	
State	1

No Offset	8
▼ Js ☑ Object Lookup (Script)	🔲 ⚙,
Script	Js ObjectLookup ⊙
▼ Lookup State 1	
Size	1
Element 0	default,0
▼ Lookup State 2	
Size	0
▼ Lookup State 3	
Size	0
▼ Replies State 1	
Size	1
Element 0	
▼ Replies State 2	
Size	0
▼ Replies State 3	
Size	0
▶ Generic Replies	
State	1

Figure 9-18. *Object Lookup data for the Rock (left) and KeyAtRock (right)*

6. Click Play and pick the Rock to make sure the code works as it did when you were checking the LockPlate, by checking the output in the console.

It should report the cursor as default and the new state to 2.

Now that you have a means to load the real current state in the LookupState function, you will have to either change the state variable to match the argument that is passed in, currentState, or just reassign it. Because the latter will keep the script easier to read, you will go with that method.

7. In the ObjectLookup script, add the following at the top of the LookupState function:

```
state = currentState; //assign current state to the state variable
```

You will eventually have to process the cursor to find its texture name, a string, before you can check for a match, so the next code is only temporary.

8. Add the following just below the state assignment:

```
// handle temp cursor texture name
var matchCursor : String = picker;
```

And now, you will have to see if the first element, 0, of the split array matches the passed-in cursor texture name. That check gets added after the current element is split up.

9. Add the following above the //now read through the remainder in pairs line:

```
// check for a cursor match with element 0 of the split
if (readString[0] == matchCursor) { // if there is a match...
```

If the match is found, you will have to get the next element of the split, the new state. The only problem is that it is in string form, so it will need to be converted to an integer using parseInt() before you can use it. Note that parseInt() is one of the exceptions to the capitalization rule in Unity's version of JavaScript.

10. Add the following below the line you just added:

```
//get the new state, element 1 of the split, then convert the string to an int
 var nextState : int = parseInt(readString [1]);
```

Now you've got everything you need to transition the object into its new state … the new state! Because most of the information for the actions associated with the object states lives on the Interactor script, you will send the number back to that script to process the object into its new state. Because there is only one argument to send, you can use SendMessage.

11. Add the following:

```
//transition the object into the new state over in the Interactor script
SendMessage("ProcessObject",nextState);
```

Now you have to close the match cursor block. By including the code that processes the auxiliary objects in the match cursor block, you ensure that it is only processed if there is a match.

12. Select the remainder of the lines down to the closing bracket for the for (var i = 2; line and indent them.

13. Immediately after that closing bracket, add the following:

```
} // close the matchCursor block
```

The Document Outline pane should be happy again (no longer be blank).

Eventually, you will set up the code to process the auxiliary objects pretty much the same as the picked object. It will need to loop through the remaining pairs from the split array until there are no more, so you will save that until later.

14. Save the script.

Finally, you will have to create the function that uses the metadata, to transition the object into the new state. As mentioned earlier, it will be in the Interactor script.

1. Open the Interactor script.

2. Add the new function:

```
function ProcessObject (newState : int) {

}
```

The first thing you need to do in it is to update the current state to the new state that was just passed in as an argument.

3. Add the following to the top of the function:

```
currentState = newState; // update the object's current state
```

Once you have the new current state, you can update several of the other current variables for use.

4. Add the following:

```
// update more of the data with the new state
currentObjectName = objectName[currentState];
currentObjectDescription = description[currentState];
currentLocation = location[currentState];
currentVisibility = visibility[currentState];
```

Next you will update the current audio and animation.

5. Add the following:

```
// assign the current clip and delay and audio for the new state
if (animates) currentAnimationClip = animationClip[currentState];
if (animates) currentAnimationDelay = animationDelay[currentState];
currentSound = soundClip[currentState];
currentAudioDelay = audioDelay[currentState];
```

Because the looping clip and sound will not be used much, you don't need to bother with a current variable for them. Note that the animations need to check to see if the object animates (using the animates variable you created earlier) before assigning the clips and delays.

Before you can play them, you will need to make sure they exist so you don't get an error. To coordinate the animation and the sound effects, you'll end up needing to call the audio in about three different places, so the most logical step is to create a little function to do the work for you. Occasionally, you might need to use it for the looping animation's audio, so to keep it flexible, you will be passing in the clip it needs to play. You will probably recognize some of the code from the AniTwoState script you created a while back. It replaces the audio clip on the object's Audio Source component so you can make use of PlayDelayed(). And, since not all transitions will include a sound clip, that will be the first thing to check for.

6. Create the following function somewhere below the ProcessObject function:

```
function ProcessAudio (theClip : AudioClip) {
   if(theClip)  { // if there is a sound clip
      //check to make sure an Audio Source component exists before playing
      if (GetComponent(AudioSource)) {
         audio.clip = theClip; // change the audio component's assigned sound file
         audio.PlayDelayed (currentAudioDelay); // delay before playing it
      }
   }
}
```

7. Back in the ProcessObject function, add the line to process the audio after the current assignments:

```
ProcessAudio (currentSound); // send audio clip off for processing
```

8. Save the script.

9. Click Play and pick the Rock.

You should hear the plopsm sound clip. Until the rock animates aside, you might want something else to test the sound effect on.

You've added the code to check for an Audio Component, but since most action objects will need one, it would be nice to be able to automatically have it added. It turns out you can do just that. It's an odd bit of code, but extremely useful. And as long as you are adding one for the Audio Source, you may as well tell it to add one for the ObjectLookup script as well.

1. At the top of the Interactor script, below #pragma strict, add:

```
@script RequireComponent(AudioSource)
@script RequireComponent(ObjectLookup)
```

2. Save the script.

Note that it does not require a semicolon. This will add the specified component, if one is not already present when the script is first added to an object. The lockplate doesn't have an Interactor script yet or an Audio Source, so you can see what happens when you add it.

3. Add the Interactor script to the LockPlate.

The Audio Source component is added to the LockPlate. If you try to remove the Audio component now, you won't be able to. Note that the component only gets added when the script is first added to an object. Also, it will have to be set up like the other object's Audio Source components.

4. Select the Rock, right-click over its Audio Source component and Copy Component.

5. Select the LockPlate, right-click over its new Audio Source and choose Paste Component Values.

The LockPlate will have three states, but it doesn't animate. Because you already have a variable that checks for that, animates, you can skip those arrays when you set up the LockPlate. See the State Management PDF, available from the Download area of the Apress web site (www.apress.com), for the full setup. Feel free to copy the values from the Rock's Interactor and Paste Component Values, to speed up the setup process.

6. Set all but its looping and animation array Sizes to 3.

7. For testing, select a different sound for each of the Sound clip elements.

8. Uncheck Animates.

The animation code will check for both the animates value and a valid clip, where the current audio clip is not null. In an earlier test, you used pause to add a delay before playing some audio clips. The problem with pause is that it holds up all the code that follows it. Because the audio will have the same delay as the animation, this time it works in your favor, so you will add the animation above the call to the audio function.

9. In the Interactor script, add the code for the animation *above* the ProcessAudio line:

```
if(animates && animationClip[currentState] != null) {
```

Before you call the animation, you will have to determine what object holds the Animation component. One of the variables you added, aniObject, lets you manually assign the object that holds the Animation component. If that variable has not been assigned, the code will assume the object itself holds its own animations.

10. Add the following code:

```
// find out if a alternate animation object was assigned, if not, assign the object itself
if (aniObject == null) aniObject = gameObject;
```

And now, add the code for the delay and the animation clip. Remember: You call animation clips by name. Because the delay was initialized as 0, there will be no effect, unless you overrode the value in the Inspector.

11. Add the following:

```
//pause before playing the animation yield new WaitForSeconds(currentAnimationDelay);
// play the animation aniObject.animation.Play(currentAnimationClip.name);
```

12. And, finally, add the closing bracket for the animation block *below* the `ProcessAudio` line.

There's only one little issue left to tackle before you can test the new code. In order for the audio clip to have the same delay as the animation clip, you left it inside the `if(animates` code block. Some objects, such as the LockPlate, don't animate at all, and some objects don't have an animation associated with all of their states. The solution is easy. You can copy the call to `ProcessAudio` and add it to an `else` statement.

1. Copy the `ProcessAudio` line.

2. Directly below the `if(animates` block's closing bracket, add:

```
else {
    ProcessAudio (currentSound); // send loop audio clip off for processing
}
```

3. Save the script.

Now you will be able to see your state machine in action. You should hear the audio, see the animation, and, if the object is selected, see its Current State change in the Inspector.

1. Select the Rock.

2. Click Play, pick the Rock, and watch its Current State change in the Interactor as it animates.

3. Select the KeyAtRock, pick it, and watch its Current State change as it animates.

4. Now select the LockPlate and pick it.

Unlike with the other two objects, its state doesn't change. A quick look at its ObjectLookup data will show that a pick with the default cursor keeps it in state 1. To see it change, you will have to feed it a different cursor texture name.

5. In the LockPlate's Interactor component, change the Cursor parameter to "Key Icon" (without the quotation marks) and pick it again.

This time, the Current State changes to 2. In the LookupState component, you will see that in order to put the LockPlate back to state 1, you will have to change the Lookup State 2 and set Cursor back to "default" (again, without the quotation marks).

6. Change Lookup State 2, Element 0 to: default,1

7. Change the Cursor back to "default" and pick it again.

The state goes back to 1. When you stop Play mode, the parameters will return to their previous values, but you can see how you can manually change values during runtime for testing purposes.

Now that you've got the primary animation handled, you can hook up the optional looping animation. Just as with the AniTwoState script, you will get the length of the animation before triggering the looping animation. By adding the code after the first animation, its delay will already have finished. This part is pretty straightforward, especially as you have already added a Boolean variable to tell you if there is a looping animation, `postLoop`. The clip itself must be marked to loop (when importing or creating in Unity's Animation editor), so all you have to do is trigger it.

1. Back in the Interactor script, in the `ProcessObject` function, below the `ProcessAudio` line, add the following:

```
// check for a looping animation to follow the primary animation
if(postLoop) { // if postLoop is checked/ true, there is a looping animation to trigger
    // wait the length of primary animation clip
    yield new WaitForSeconds(currentAnimationClip.length);
    aniObject.animation.Play(loopAnimation[currentState].name); // play the looping animation
}
```

You have a variable to hold an audio clip for the looping animation. It has to be called the same time as the animation and passes the loop audio clip to the little audio-processing function.

2. Add the following line below the line that plays the looping animation:

```
ProcessAudio (loopSoundFX[currentState]); // send loop audio clip off for processing
```

3. Save the script.

4. Click Play and pick the Rock and the LockPlate to make sure the sounds play, whether or not the object has an animation.

To check on the looping functionality, you will have to set up the Flower. It has three states: out-of-scene, 0, wilted, 1, and revived, 2. You added the collider to the Flower parent object to register mouse picks, so that is where you will add the two scripts.

1. Add an Interactor script to the Flower.

The Audio Source and ObjectLookup components are automatically added.

2. Select the Rock and copy its Interactor component in the Inspector.

3. Select the Flower, place the cursor over the Transform component label, and choose Paste Component Values from the right-click menu.

4. Repeat for the Audio Source.

5. Fill out the Interactor for the Flower, as per the State Management PDF. Especially make sure to load the flower revive animation in its Element 2 animation; check Post Loop; and load the flower idle animation into the Loop Animation, Element 1. The AniObject must be set to None or Flower.

6. Load SynthUp as the Loop Sound FX in Element 1.

7. In the Object Lookup component, set Lookup State 1 to Size 1. Set it as follows:

Lookup State 1:
Element 0: default,2

You don't need to have a Lookup State 2, because the flower is no longer pickable in that state.

8. Make sure you set the Size of the Replies arrays to match the Object Lookup arrays.

9. Click Play and pick the flower.

The regular animation plays, reviving the flower, then it immediately goes into its loop animation, and the loop sound effect plays. The sound clip doesn't loop, because Loop is turned off in the Audio Source component. If you wanted to have it loop, you could add `audio.loop = true;` right below the `ProcessAudio (loopSoundFX[currentState]);` line.

As usual, after adding to your code, you will have to check the other objects, to make sure you haven't broken the original functionality.

10. Pick the Rock, KeyAtRock, and LockPlate to make sure they still work.

Refining the Pick

Now that you've got the metadata actions working for the primary object, it's time to revisit the cursor behavior. When you pick the objects, there are a couple of things that ought to happen. First, you should prevent the player from picking anything while the animation plays out. While you're at it, it would also be nice to hide the cursor completely while the action is in play.

Let's begin by making use of the `processing` variable you added earlier in the chapter. If there are no matches to the pick, nothing will happen, so it will make more sense to block picks and turn off the cursor as soon as the `ProcessObject` function is called. Let's start with the picks.

1. Open the Interactor script.

2. Add the following line at the top of the `ProcessObject` function:

```
processing = true; // turn on flag to block picks
```

With the flag set, you will have to bypass both the mouse pick *and* the mouseover.

3. Add the following line to the `OnMouseDown` and `OnMouseEnter` functions, below the distance checks and at the top of the `OnMouseExit` function:

```
if (processing) return; // object is being processed, leave the function
```

Next, you will have to decide when to turn the flag back off. If there is an animation, it should be turned off after that. You've already got a pause the length of the animation in the `if postLoop` section, but if it doesn't have a loop animation, you'd have to add one as an `else` afterwards. If you are going to do that, you may as well move the one you've already got up above the `if postLoop` section.

4. Move the `yield new WaitForSeconds(currentAnimationClip.length)` line and its comment up out of the `if(postLoop)` line, just above its comment.

5. Below the `if(postLoop)` closing bracket, add the following:

```
processing = false; // turn off flag to block picks
```

If there was no animation, you will have to wait a token amount of time after playing the audio before turning off the flag. A second or so should do the job.

6. Inside the final `else` clause, under the `ProcessAudio (currentSound)`, add the following:

```
yield new WaitForSeconds(1.0);// give a short pause if there was no animation
processing = false;           // turn off flag to block picks
```

7. Save the script.

8. Click Play and test by clicking the flower several times, watching the console report.

When the cursor once again changes color, you will know that your pick will go through. The flower doesn't animate again, because it was set to state 2, unpickable, but the pick had to be processed to know that.

If you test the Rock, then the KeyAtRock, you will find that you can pick the KeyAtRock right away. The reason for the picking discrepancy is that the processing flag is not global; each instance of it belongs only to the object its script is on. This lets you block re-picks on the same object, but not picks on other objects. While this may at first sound undesirable, preventing the player from picking the newly revealed object immediately can prove frustrating.

You also may have noticed a real problem with the Rock. A drawback of the Store In Root (New) animation import type is that starting a new clip from the same Animation component stops the currently playing animation wherever it happens to be on the time line. Until the Legacy Animation is fully integrated into Mecanim, the easiest workaround is to duplicate the AnimationObjects group, deactivate or delete the Rock from the first group, and the rest of the objects from the second.

1. Duplicate the AnimationObjects group.

2. Name it **Rock Group**.

3. Delete all but the Rock inside it.

4. Agree to losing the prefab.

5. In the original AnimationObjects group, deactivate the Rock.

Deactivate retains the prefab in case it has to be updated at some point.

Hiding the Cursor

With re-picks managed, it's time to think about hiding the cursor after a valid pick. At first, you might think the answer will be to hook up the cursor hide/show to the processing flag. Testing on the flower, with its rather long animation, would soon make you realize that hiding the cursor for the duration of the picked object's animation will be frustrating. Even with the rock, the player will want to be able to pick the key as soon as she sees it.

Not hiding the cursor at all after a valid pick visually interferes with the "reward" of seeing a reaction, so that is not the answer either. Ideally, you will want to hide it for an amount of time independent of the animations. To do that, you can set up a timer.

1. Open the GameManager script.

2. Add the following variable:

    ```
    internal var suppressPointer : boolean = false; // flag to suppress cursor after pick
    ```

3. In the OnGUI function, change the if(!navigating) line to:

    ```
    if (!navigating && !suppressPointer) { //if not navigating or suppressing the pointer, draw it
    ```

4. Save the script.

5. Open the Interactor script.

6. In the ProcessObject function, beneath the processing = true line, add the line that turns on the suppressPointer flag:

    ```
    // tell the GameManager to suppress the cursor
    controlCenter.GetComponent(GameManager).suppressPointer = true;
    ```

7. Save the script.

8. Click Play and pick any of the action objects.

The cursor is turned off as soon as you pick an object. And stays off...

Now you will have to turn it on, after a given amount of time. The problem is where and when. If you wait until after the animation has finished, the player may become frustrated during the wait, if she wants to pick another object. If you add it in earlier with a pause, it will delay all of the rest of the actions. A better solution is to create a timer.

Creating a Timer

Timers have a couple of big advantages over the yield statements. They will not delay code like a yield and they can be canceled. A yield cannot be stopped once the line has been read. The downside of a timer is that, unlike the single yield line, a timer takes a bit of coding. Using time to control events is used in all different kinds of genres, so it will be well worth the effort.

To start, you will need a couple of variables. The first will tell the engine if it even needs to check the time. A simple Boolean check for true or false will use fewer resources than fetching the time and comparing it with another float value. The check goes in the Update function, so it checked every frame.

1. Open the Interactor script. Add a couple of variables for the timer:

```
//Misc vars
internal var pickTimer : boolean;    // flag to check timer
internal var pickTimerTime : float; // new time to check for
```

You will start the timer right after you turn off the cursor. To start a timer, you have to get Time.time—the amount of time elapsed since the application started. To that value, you will add the amount of time for the timer to run. When the current elapsed time is greater than your target time, the code inside its conditional is read.

2. Near the top of the ProcessObject function, after the controlCenter.GetComponent(GameManager) line, add the timer code:

```
// start timer
pickTimerTime = Time.time + 0.5; // set the timer to go for 0.5 seconds
pickTimer = true; // turn on the flag to check the timer
```

3. In the Update function (make a new one, if you deleted the original one), fill it out as follows:

```
function Update () {

    if (pickTimer && Time.time > pickTimerTime) { // if time is up and flag is on...
        pickTimer = false; // turn off the flag
        // turn off the flag to suppress the cursor
        controlCenter.GetComponent(GameManager).suppressPointer = false;
    }
}
```

4. Save the script.

5. Click Play and pick any of the action objects.

The cursor disappears when the objects are picked, then appears 0.5 seconds later, allowing you to pick another object.

If you want to use a different time, depending on the object, you could create a variable to hold the delay time, instead of hard-coding the 0.5 value.

The basics of the state engine are functional at this point. The object goes from its current state to a new state when the trigger event, a mouse pick, occurs. Depending on which cursor (simulated, at this point) picks it, it will transition the object into its new state, triggering the actions (sound effects and animations) associated with the new state. Processing the auxiliary objects has not yet been set up, nor have the replies that will give the player extra feedback for her efforts.

Obviously, there are still many refinements and extra functionality to be added to the two main scripts, but you may consider yourself well under way.

Summary

In this chapter, you started looking deeper into object state and how to manage it. By introducing a mini-plot for your game and a list of action objects, you were able to see the need for mapping out the actions and reactions of object/player interaction. You explored several different means of visualizing what states objects would need, which objects could interact with others, and what actions would be initialized upon interaction.

You found that flowcharts could be valuable to map out simple interaction and state, but once you allowed objects to influence or change each other's states, those models quickly became unwieldy. You got familiar with the common terms used in state machines. To move an object from one state to another, you found that you needed its current **state**, an **event** to trigger a **transition**, all the **actions** involved in that transition, and, finally, the new state the object would be put into. Actions, you found, are always associated with the state the object is going into.

Simple state diagrams provided a means of listing state, associated actions, and animations, as well as how objects transitioned from one state to the next. By the time you tested state diagrams against multiple interacting objects, they were also starting to get complicated.

The next step was to take the state diagram information and populate a table with it. At that point, you were getting a clearer idea of the data you had to work with and the critical path needed to process it. To simplify, you handled the state transitions independent of their associated actions.

You then defined the possible states available to an object, listed the possible triggering objects (usually a cursor, default or otherwise), and any auxiliary objects and the states they would be put into as a result of the primary interaction.

To store, manipulate, and manage the transitions, you created the first version of your ObjectLookup script. You found you could enter your pertinent data as a string into the built-in arrays available to the Inspector and later *parse* the string and separate the contents of the string into individual elements of a new array.

Next, you started fleshing out your Interactor script to be able to hold all of the object's transition action information, its metadata. By storing everything you need to know about the object in whatever state it is in, you are, in effect, creating a *smart object*. Using arrays, you can now store the object's short and long descriptions, location, animation, audio, and other properties you wish to access by state.

You also learned that you can keep the definitions and logic behind the setup stored in a text asset for quick access in the scene.

Finally, you were able to test the basic implementation of your state machine, using a few of the test objects. The event, mouse pick, transitioned the objects to their specified states, playing sounds and animations that were stored on the objects themselves

In the next chapter, you will get more creative with a few of the action objects' transitions.

CHAPTER 10

■ ■ ■

Exploring Transitions

In the previous chapter, you got the first part of the state engine working. The ObjectLookup script is now able to change the state of an object and process the actions that are identified with the transitions into its new state. It does so by using the first two pieces of data in the correct element in the correct Lookup State array. While the first two are essentially a lookup table for the *picked* object, the rest are instructions for handling the optional auxiliary objects that are also a part of the same transition.

As a reminder, the auxiliary objects are processed in pairs. The first piece of data is the action object's name, and the second is the state it will transition into. The simplest are processed directly into their new state through their own ObjectLookup and Interactor scripts. While that may seem straightforward, you will have to devise a way to activate objects that are currently in state 0, out of scene, before their scripts can be accessed. As you expand the functionality of the system, you will also allow for some objects to be processed without the animations, some to call specialized scripts, and others to fire off special effects.

As the code becomes more robust, you will add the functionality to have specific objects fade out of the scene, using transparency, without the need to create custom keyframe animations.

Finally, after building the framework that will let you handle any nonstandard actions required by the transitions, you will create a couple of scripts that will force the First Person Controller into the optimal position and orientation to watch the crucial action play out.

Processing the Auxiliary Objects

Let's start by handling the simplest auxiliary object cases first—those that are processed into the specified state and need only their regular animations and audio effects triggered.

In the existing code, you are already *reading* each of the pairs. Now you will send them off for processing.

1. If it's not already open, open the Interaction scene.

2. Open the ObjectLookup script and locate the ProcessObject function.

Take a minute to look near the bottom of the function for the loop that iterates through the rest of the data. Element 0 was the cursor used for the pick event, and Element 1 was the state to transition the picked object into. The for loop starts at Element 2, the first of the auxiliary objects. It iterates through the readString array by twos, i+2, so the data can easily be handled in pairs.

Both pieces of data are still string type. To process them, the first will have to be used to find the object of that name, and the second will have to be converted to an integer.

3. Below the two print statements in the section that reads through the rest of the data, add the following:

```
//assign the first piece of data in the pair to a temp var for processing
var tempS : String = readString[i];
```

4. Add a line as a place marker for handling special cases:

```
//check for special cases here- fill this out later
```

The next step can be a bit tricky. You will have to find the gameObject using its name. You've done that before, using gameObject. Find, but this time, there will be a possibility that the object is not active, out of scene. A prime example of this is the KeyAtLock. It starts out not in scene—deactivated. An object that is not active cannot be found with Find. But here's the catch, to activate it, the engine has to know it exists. Let's block in the basic code now, and then solve the problem after you have implemented activation functionality.

5. Send the auxiliary object name to a function to get the corresponding object:

```
// find and activate the object using its name
var auxObject : GameObject = CheckForActive(tempS);
```

In this line, you create a local variable and assign the results of the (not yet created) CheckForActive function directly to it.

After that, you will have to get the state the object will be going into.

6. Assign the second element to a temp var after converting it from a string to an int:

```
// convert the new state from a string value to an integer for use
var newState : int = parseInt(readString[i+1]);
```

7. Using the two temp variables, process the auxiliary object into its new state in its own ProcessObject function:

```
// process the axiliary object into the new state
auxObject.SendMessage( "ProcessObject",newState, SendMessageOptions.DontRequireReceiver);
```

And now, you can create the beginnings of the CheckForActive function, where the object is found and activated (if necessary).

8. Create a new function below the ProcessObject function:

```
function CheckForActive (name : String) {

    // check to see if the object is active before assigning it to auxObject
    if(gameObject.Find(name)) var auxObject = gameObject.Find(name);

    return auxObject; // return the gameObject to where the function was called

}
```

4. Save the script.

5. Click Play and try to pick the Pedestal.

The only results printed in the console are the contents of the state 1 lookup data.
Now, let's force the pedestal into state 1, when the player picks the rock.

1. Exit Play mode.

2. Select the Rock.

3. Change its Lookup State 1, Element 0 to:

    default,2,Pedestal,2

4. Select the Pedestal in the Hierarchy, so you can monitor its Current State, and click Play.

5. Click on the Pedestal.

Nothing happens.

6. Click on the Rock.

The Rock moves, and the Pedestal transitions into its state 2.

7. Now, pick the Pedestal.

Being in state 2 when you pick it, it goes to state 1.
Let's force it into state 1, when you pick the flower. While you're there, you can add a second auxiliary object to process to make sure the code will handle multiple auxiliary objects.

8. Exit Play mode.

9. Select the Flower.

10. Change its Lookup State 1, Element 0 to:

    default,2,Pedestal,2,Rock,2

11. Select the Pedestal in the Hierarchy view and click Play.

12. Pick the Flower.

The Rock moves, and the Pedestal goes into its state 2.

13. Test various combinations of picking.

The code processing auxiliary objects is working nicely.

14. Change the Flower's Lookup State 1, Element 0 back to:

    default,2

Handling Object Visibility

As with your small collection of test-case objects, you will have to manage visibility, as some of them go in and out of the scene. There are a few different ways to manage visibility. You could disable the object's renderer component, or you could deactivate the entire object.

If you turn off the renderer, you will also have to turn off the collider, so the player doesn't get stopped by an invisible object. While this seems like a reasonable solution at first glance, it can get quite complicated. Whereas you can refer to any type of collider with object.collider, for renderers, you must refer to each type specifically.

In this function, you first see if an object of the name you passed in can be found. If it can, you assign the object of that name to an internal variable. Just as you did with the DistanceFromCamera function in the Interactor, you will use return to send the value of its internal variable, auxObject, back to be assigned directly to the ProcessObject's own internal variable, auxObject.

9. Save the script.

Right now, the only object that has data for an auxiliary object is the LockPlate. Because the locked chest is the most complicated of all of the sequences, you will save it for later.

To test the auxiliary object handling, and to make sure you understand how it forces the object into the specified state, regardless of its current state, you will practice on the pedestal. It doesn't do anything, but you will be able to see its current state being changed by the other objects.

1. Select the Pedestal and add an Interactor script to it.

2. Copy and paste the values from the LockPlate onto it, if you wish, and then fill it out according to the State Management PDF.

3. Keep the assigned sound effects from the LockPlate.

4. For the Location, set Element 1 to 2, in scene but not pickable. Set Element 2 to 1, pickable.

5. Add an ObjectLookup script to it and set it up as follows:

Object State 1

   Element 0: na,1

Object State 2

   Element 0: default, 1

6. Set the Size in the Replies arrays to match.

So, as it stands, the object is not pickable at state 1, its initial state. Unless an outside object forces a state ⊄ on it, you will never be able to pick it. At this point, the pick will still be processed, but not finding a matching ⊂ nothing will happen.

Let's take a minute to add a bit of code to the OnMouseDown function to prevent it from even processing a when the object is not pickable. A quick check of the GameNotes text asset tells you that Location = 2 is in sc⌐ not pickable.

1. Open the Interactor script.

2. In the OnMouseDown function, at the top, above the distance check, add the following:

```
if(location[currentState] == 2) return; // object is not pickable in scene
```

Because the three print statements occur before an actual state change, they are misleading and no⌐ longer necessary.

3. Comment out the three print statements:

```
//print ("elements in array for state " + state + " = " + readString.length)
//print ("Cursor = " + readString[0]);
//print ("New state = " + readString[1]);
```

H

Ev
of
yo₁

invi
you

Regular objects have a MeshRenderer; skinned meshes (on characters) have a SkinnedMeshRenderer; cloth has a ClothRenderer; and so on. You could write code for each case, but that will mean a lot of conditions, if you are using different types of objects in your scene. The other downside is, if the object had children, such as a particle system or even several different objects in its hierarchy, they would all have to be turned off individually.

The alternative to dealing with renderers and colliders is to simply deactivate the whole object when it is "not in scene." Deactivating an object also deactivates all of its children. The only drawback to this method is that when an object is deactivated, it can't be "found" to be activated again. Fortunately, there is a way to get around this.

To solve this conundrum, you will have to create an array of gameObjects at the start of the game in an Awake function. All action objects will be put into their initial states in the Start function, which is always called after the Awake function. Because the array will also be useful later on when saving the game, it won't cost any extra overhead.

Using Tags

In order to be able to identify the action objects, you will make use of Unity **Tags**. In Unity, you can "tag" objects for easier, more efficient processing. A Tag is a keyword that you link to one or more GameObjects and is generally used when scripting conditionals.

Let's start by creating a tag for all of the action objects.

1. Click the Layers drop-down at the top right corner of the editor.

2. Select Edit Layers (Figure 10-1).

Figure 10-1. Adding a Tag in Edit Layers

Layers always show. Tags will automatically have an empty element, so you never have to change its size.

3. Click the expand arrow next to Tags at the top of the Inspector.

4. Add **ActionObject** to Element 0.

5. Make sure you don't have a trailing space after the name.

6. Select the Rock in the Hierarchy view.

7. At the top of the Inspector, click the Tag drop-down and change the object from Untagged to Action Object.

8. Select the other action objects in the scene and assign the ActionObject tag to them. This should be the ChestLid, KeyAtLock, KeyAtRock, Pedestal, Flower, Pollen Ball, and LockPlate.

Next, you will have to store them in an array. Because it will have to be accessed regularly, it makes sense to put it on the GameManager script, where you will be controlling several general game settings and functionality.

1. Open the GameManager script.

2. Add the following:

```
// array to hold the action objects for processing
internal var actionObjects = new GameObject[0];
```

Now you will need a way to find the action objects. Using the tag you assigned, you can use FindGameObjectsWithTag() to locate all of the action objects in the scene. It creates a *list* (similar to arrays) that you can use to populate a Unity array for faster handling.

3. Inside the Awake function add the following:

```
//get a list of the gameObjects with the ActionObject tag
var aObjects = GameObject.FindGameObjectsWithTag("ActionObject");
```

Now that you have a list, you can redefine the array with the list's length.

4. Add the following:

```
// redefine the ActionObject array with the number of elements in the list
actionObjects = new GameObject[aObjects.length];
```

And then iterate through the list assigning the list elements to the array elements.

5. Add the following:

```
//save the action objects into the array for easy access when deactivated
for (var i : int = 0;i < aObjects.length;i++) {
        actionObjects[i] = aObjects[i];
        print (actionObjects[i].name);
}
```

6. Save the script.

7. Click Play and check the console for the names of the ActionObjects (Figure 10-2).

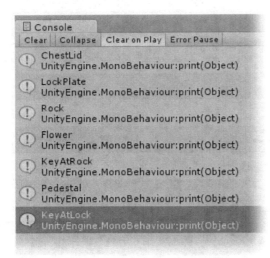

Figure 10-2. The scene's new ActionObjects

8.   When you are satisfied that the objects are all there, comment out the print line.

Now that the objects have all been identified and saved, you will be able to finish the CheckForActive function in the ObjectLookup script. If the object can't be found by name, it will iterate through the array of action objects, and when it finds a match, activate it and assign it to the auxObject var.

1.   Open the ObjectLookup script.

Let's start by introducing the Control Center object, so it won't have to be found each time.

2.   Add the following var to the script:

```
var controlCenter : GameObject; // where the actionObject array lives
```

3.   Find it in the Start function:

```
function Start () {

        controlCenter = GameObject.Find("Control Center");
}
```

4.   In the CheckForActive function, below the if statement, add an else clause:

```
else { // if no match was found, it must need to be activated


} // close the else
```

The first thing you will have to do is gain access to the actionObject array on the Control Center object's GameManager script. Then you will create a local variable to hold it, while you iterate through it.

5. Add the following inside the else clause:

```
//load the actionObject array from the GameManager script
var actionObjects : GameObject[] = controlCenter.GetComponent(GameManager).actionObjects;
```

And now iterate through the array with a for loop.

6. Add the following:

```
for (var y : int = 0; y < actionObjects.length; y++) { // iterate through the array

} // close the for loop
```

7. Inside the for loop, check for the condition that finds a match:

```
if (actionObjects[y].gameObject.name == name) {     // if there is a match for the name
        actionObjects[y].gameObject.SetActive(true);    // activate the matched object from
                                                        the array
        auxObject = gameObject.Find(name);              // assign the newly activated object
} // close the if
```

Because you passed a string, "name," into the CheckForActive function, you are checking it against the array member's name parameter. When you find a match, you activate the object with SetActive (true). Then, it being active in the scene, you Find and then assign the gameObject as the auxObject. At the bottom of the function, that gets sent back up to the LookupState function for processing with the return command.

8. Save the script.

To test the functionality, you will have to deactivate an object that will get processed as an auxiliary object, the Pedestal. It will have to be active at the start of the game to be included in the actionObject array. Once started, you can deactivate it, then try picking the rock. Since the rock is changing the state on the Pedestal, the new code activates it before it is processed.

9. Click Play, then deactivate the Pedestal in the Inspector.

The Pedestal disappears as you deactivate it.

10. Pick the Rock.

The Pedestal appears and is transitioned into its state 2, as per the instructions in the Rock's ObjectLookup data.
Now you will be able to process the action objects into their proper active state on startup, after the GameManager's Awake function has got them in its array.

1. Open the Interactor script.

2. Inside the Start function, *after* the current assignments, add the following:

```
// if the object's current location is not in scene, 0, deactivate it
if (initialState == 0) {
        gameObject.SetActive (false); // deactivate the object
}
```

3. Save the script.

The Pedestal starts out in state 1, unpickable, so let's change its Initial State to 0, not in scene, to see if the new code works.

4. Exit Play mode, if you haven't already.

5. Select the Pedestal.

6. Change its Initial State to 0.

7. Click Play

The Pedestal disappears on its own.

8. Pick the Rock.

It appears again.

If you pick it into state 2, then pick it again, it goes into state 0 again, where its location *should* return to 0, out of scene. The numbers are there, but the problem is that it doesn't have any code in its ProcessObject function to deal with visibility yet.

If you consult the GameNotes text file, you will see that the Visibility conventions are as follows:

0: N/A-no fading required.

1: Show at start.

2: Hide at start.

3: Show at start, hide at end.

4: Hide at end.

With this many possibilities, you will want to create a function to do the work.

Visibility

Let's go ahead and create the function to do the visibility processing. You will start by blocking it in, and then fill out each condition one at a time. The easiest is case 0, where the object disappears as soon as it is picked with no fading. There is a catch, though. When picked, the timer for the cursor is started to turn it on after the required amount of time. The problem is that the object is deactivated before the time is up.

1. Open the Interactor script.

2. Block in the HandleVisibility function:

```
function HandleVisibility () {

}
```

3. Add the following content to the new function:

```
switch (currentVisibility) {

    case 0 : // deactivate immediately, no fades
        if(currentLocation == 0 ) {
            // turn off the timer for the cursor before deactivating the object
            pickTimerTime = Time.time; // set timer to now to force it to finish
            yield;                     // give timer a chance to stop
```

```
            gameObject.SetActive(false); // deactivate the object
        }
        break;
    case 1 : // activate at start

        break;

    case 2 : // deactivate at start

        break;

    case 3 : // activate at start, deactivate at end

        break;

    case 4 : // deactivate at end

        break;
}
```

Visibility case 0 is for any object that should immediately go in or out of the scene and doesn't require an opacity change. The Pedestal fits that requirement, so you should be able to test the code on it. If the current location is 0, it means the object is taken out of scene as soon as the current values are updated. You will have to call the HandleVisibility function right after the updates.

4. Inside the ProcessObject function, below the currentAudioDelay = audioDelay[currentState]; line, add the following:

    ```
    // send it off for handling in case it has a visibility state that is
    processed at the start
    HandleVisibility();
    ```

5. Save the script.

6. Click Play and check to see that the Pedestal goes out of the scene.

It goes out of scene before any animation or audio can be played, because the script's parent object is deactivated.

You might want a brief sound to play as the object winks out of the scene. Theoretically, that would be handled in the case 3, hide at end (of transition), but for a simple audio clip, you can sneak in a few extra lines of code. You will have to call the ProcessAudio function before deactivating the object, and you will have to pause long enough for the clip to play.

7. Above the gameObject.SetActive(false) line in case 0, add:

    ```
    if(currentSound != null) {
        ProcessAudio (currentSound);                    // send audio clip off for processing first
        yield new WaitForSeconds(currentSound.length); // allow time to play the sound clip
    }
    ```

8. Save the script and test again.

This would be a good time to set up the Pollen Ball, as it, too, leaves the scene when picked.

1. Exit Play mode.

2. Select the Flower and remove the Loop Sound FX for Element 2.

3. Open the Flower hierarchy and select the Pollen Ball.

4. Remove the AniTwoState script and add the Interactor script to it.

The Pollen Ball can't be picked until the flower revives, because it is inside the Flower's collider, so it only requires two states. It also doesn't have to animate when transitioning, because its animation is controlled by the flower. You may want to copy and paste the KeyAtRock's Interactor to start.

5. Set the array sizes to 2 and uncheck Animates.

6. Fill in the metadata, as per the State Management PDF.

7. Make sure the Location Element 0 is 0, out of scene, and Element 1 is 1, pickable.

8. Both Visibility Elements will be 0—no opacity changes.

9. Assign the plopsm audio clip to its Element 0.

10. Click Play and pick first the Flower and then the Pollen Ball.

The Pollen Ball goes out of scene to a small plop sound when picked.

Handling Opacity Changes

To look into non-keyframed opacity changes during state transitions, you will need a new test subject. The KeyAtRock has its opacity adjusted as part of its regular animation. The KeyAtLock, however, only has the fade-in on its copied insert clip. It will look nice fading out of the scene, as well as fading in. And you may as well use it as a test subject for both fade-in and fade-out.

Table 10-1. *Location and Visibility for the KeyAtLock*

State- Description	Location	Code	Visibility	Code
State 0—Not in scene	Not in scene	0	Fade-out at End	3
State 1—Inserted into lock	In scene	1	Fade-in at Start	1 0
State 2—Unavailable	In scene	1	N/A	

With this information, the object knows what its final location will be and what the visibility is at the start and end of the animation (see Figure 10-1).

While you could probably keyframe visibility, it will be less work to script it once, rather than duplicate animation clips and keyframe it for each object. In doing so, you will have to make the assumption that *all action objects with transparency shaders will fade in and out of their visibility states.* Because you may occasionally have objects that are never fully opaque, you will also have to store their material's original alpha value at the start. If you are worried about objects that use transparency but do not fade in and out, you will create a variable to check whether the object should use the fades.

▓ **Rule** All action objects with transparency shaders will fade in and out of their visibility states. This will require any action object with a transparency shader to have its own unique material.

Let's set a flag to use to fade the material in and out, if the shader is a transparency shader. By keeping the variable public, you will be able to disable the fade manually, should the need ever arise. By initializing it to true, you can then go ahead and check internally to see if the material can be faded or not. The material is a parameter of the object's renderer; for most of the objects, it will be a MeshRenderer.

1. Select the KeyAtLock and add the Interactor (with Audio Source and Object Lookup) script.

2. Fill it out, as per the State Management PDF. It is a three element object.

3. Change its Lookup State 1, Element 0 to:

   default,0

4. Set the corresponding Replies array to match.

5. Open the Interactor script.

6. Add the following variable:

   ```
   //fade variables
   var useAlpha : boolean = true;  // flag to fade material during visibility change
   ```

7. In the Misc vars section, add a variable to store the object's material and the material's alpha value:

   ```
   var originalMaterial : Material;// store the object's material
   var originalColor : Color;       // store the object's material's color
   var alphaColor : Color;          // store color's transparent version
   ```

The Color type is a vector4; it uses R,G,B,A, the red, green, blue, and alpha values, to store a color.

The limitation here is that you are only storing a single material, so objects that require opacity changes can only use a single material. You will get and assign the material in the Start function.

8. Add the following in the Start function, below the controlCenter line:

   ```
   // Material and fades section
   if(GetComponent(MeshRenderer)) {// if the object has a MeshRenderer, get its material
           originalMaterial = GetComponent(MeshRenderer).material;
   }
   ```

As you discovered in a previous chapter, the material must be using a Transparency shader before you can animate its alpha value.

9. Under the originalMaterial line, temporarily add the following lines, so you can see what shader and what its color's alpha value gets returned:

```
print (this + "  " + "Shader: " + renderer.material.shader.name + "  " + renderer.material.color.a);
```

10. Save the script.

11. Click Play and then look at the results in the console (see Figure 10-3).

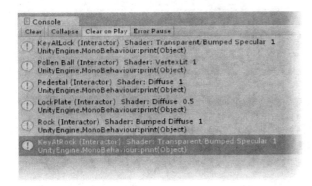

Figure 10-3. *The shader types and alpha values for the active action objects' materials*

With the exception of the KeyAtRock and KeyAtLock, which already have a transparency shader, the rest use a regular shader. The LockPlate has its MeshRenderer turned off, but its alpha value shows 0.5. The Flower doesn't have a Mesh Renderer, so it isn't included in the list.

Let's test your code by changing the Rock's Main Color's alpha value to 50%.

1. Stop Play mode.

2. Delete the Mesh Renderer component from the LockPlate, if you didn't earlier in the chapter.

3. Select the Rock.

4. At the bottom of the Inspector, open the Color dialog and set the alpha to about 128 (half of 256).

5. Click Play.

Although the Rock is still solid in the viewport, the console reports the new alpha value (see Figure 10-4). Let's change the shader this time.

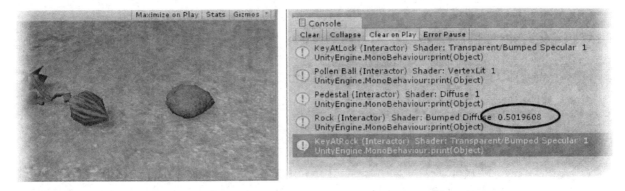

Figure 10-4. *Rock with alpha value not showing opacity*

6. Stop Play mode.

7. Change the Rock's shader to Transparent/Bumped Diffuse.

The alpha value is now apparent on the Rock in the Game view.

8. Click Play.

The console now reports the shader's name as "Transparent/BumpedDiffuse." This means you can use *SubString* to check for "Transparent" as the first 11 characters. The syntax is stringName.SubString (start character, length).

If you have a match, you set the usesAlpha flag to true. You also have to make sure the shader name is long enough to check for 11 characters. "Diffuse," for example, would throw an error, if you tried to access its (nonexistent) 11th character.

1. Stop Play mode.

2. Comment out the print statement.

3. Add the following code below them and read through the comments to see what is happening:

```
// prep for auto fade by checking shader, unless specified as false
if (useAlpha) { // if it isn't set to false by the author
    useAlpha = false; // set it to false, there will be only one condition to make it true
    var tempShadername : String = renderer.material.shader.name; //get the shader name,a String
    if (tempShadername.length > 11) { //check for short names- they aren't transparent shaders
        // check to see if the material's shader is a Transparency shader
        if(tempShadername.Substring (0,11) == "Transparent") {
            // set the flag to use alpha for changing opacity during a transitions
            useAlpha = true;
        }
    }
}
```

If you find that the shader is a transparency shader, you will go ahead and save the material's color, then use it to create a color that is the same, except that it will have an alpha value of 0, to make it transparent.

4. Under the use Alpha = true line, add the two color assignments:

```
// get fade colors
originalColor = renderer.material.color; // the material's original color
alphaColor = Color(originalColor.r,originalColor.g,originalColor.b,0);// alpha valued color
```

5. Save the script.

6. Click Play.

7. Check the action object's Interactor scripts to see the Original and Alpha Colors.

Only the two keys and the rock will have their materials processed. Both colors, originalColor and alphaColor, will be the same for their RGB values, but the alpha for the second will be 0. The alpha for the first will be its original material's alpha value. The keys are both 1, but the rock is currently ~0.5.

Now let's check the useAlpha logic. By setting it as true as the default, you can ignore it. If it is set to true, it goes through the code that checks to see if it has a Transparent shader, but is set to false at the start of the conditional. Now, the only way for it to be set to true is if it *does* have a Transparent shader. If the useAlpha flag is set to false, it never is checked in the code, allowing you to use transparent shaders on action objects that don't need to fade in or out.

Obviously, you could have just set each object individually and saved yourself two lines of code, but if you had a lot of objects to set up, with this system, you'd only have to set the value to the rare object that uses a Transparent shader but doesn't fade in or out.

1. Stop Play mode.

2. Select the Rock.

3. Uncheck its Use Alpha parameter.

4. Click Play and check the Inspector to see if it was processed through the alpha code.

Because it wasn't, both color parameters will be the original unassigned black, with 0 for alpha, (0,0,0,0), but because the flag is set to false, the code that changes the material's alpha is never used.

This should give you a good start toward automating the opacity fades on objects with Transparency shaders. With the conditions all set up, it's time to script the opacity changes.

Developing Non-Keyframed Fades

You now know whether an object needs to fade, and whether in or out, by the type of shader on its material. The next step is to think about implementing the functionality. Just like your very early experiments in the introduction to scripting, your auto-fade will be managed in the function. Given that most of the important events are handled in the Interactor script, this is where you will continue to work.

The fades will work on the material's Main Color alpha component and will go from the original value down to near 0 and back up again over time. If an object animates over one second (a typical animate time), the fade should probably be no longer than half a second.

You will have to set a flag to start the fade-in or fade-out and then turn it off when the function has finished. You will set the fade time to **2.0** for now, so you will be able to access the functionality easily during setup.

1. Open the Interactor script.

2. Add the following internal vars below the var useAlpha: boolean = true variable declaration:

```
var fadeIn : boolean = false;     // flags to assign end & out colors
var fadeOut : boolean = false;    //
var fadeTime : float = 2.0;       //default time over which the fades happen
internal var startColor : Color;  // variables for color/opacity transition
internal var endColor : Color;
var ent : float = 1;              // elapsed normalized time for fade, 1 = 100% or finished
```

The first two variables are temporary. They will allow you to test the fades. You will be using Color.Lerp to transition the material colors, so you will need the start color and the end color. For now, you will assign them according to whether fadeIn or fadeOut is true. Lerp stands for *linear interpretation* (between two values).

The last variable, ent, is what drives the Color.Lerp function. The arguments it takes are: start color, end color, and a float value between 0 and 1. To get that value, you will have to use Time.deltaTime, divide it by the fadeTime to get the rate or amount to add each update cycle, then add that to the ent value each cycle.

Time.deltaTme is the time in seconds it took to complete the last frame. The number you divide it by creates your rate.

Let's add the fade code to the Update function and test it out.

3. Inside the Update function, below the timer code, add:

```
if(!useAlpha) return; // skip the fade code if it is not being used
```

4. And add an else clause, if it is true:

```
else {
```

5. Then add the temporary code to set the start and end colors:

```
if(fadeIn) {
    startColor = alphaColor;
    endColor = originalColor;
}

if(fadeOut) {
    endColor = alphaColor;
    startColor = originalColor;
}
```

The color assignments will eventually go into the HandleVisibility function, but having them inside the Update function for now will let you to test the functionality from the Inspector.

And now you will be adding the code to do the transition. First, it should only run if the ent value has not reached 1. That would mean that it was already finished, or, it can also signify that it has not yet started. After that line, you will assign the current value from the Lerp function directly to the object's material's color. After updating the color, you will have to increase the ent value.

6. Add the following, also inside the else:

```
    if (ent < 1) {
        // calculate the current color using linear interpolation between start & end
while it is less than 1
            renderer.material.color = Color.Lerp(startColor, endColor, ent);
        // increase the ent value using the rate
        ent = ent + Time.deltaTime/fadeTime;
    } //end the if/ent
} // end the else
```

7. Save the script.

The Rock is currently semitransparent and will make a good first test subject.

1. Make sure the Use Alpha is on, so the alpha values will be recorded.

2. Click Play.

3. Select the Rock.

4. In the Inspector, in the Interactor component, toggle the Fade Out parameter on and the Fade In off.

5. Now set the ent value to **0** to start the fade.

The Rock fades out completely, and the ent value runs up past 1.0 and stops.

6. This time, turn FadeIn on and FadeOut off.

7. Set the ent value to **0** again.

The Rock fades back in to its semitransparent state.

8. Turn off Play mode and make the Rock fully opaque by changing its material's Main Color's alpha color to **white**.

9. Click Play and repeat the previous steps.

The Rock opacity behaves no matter how transparent it starts out. At this point, another concern may have occurred to you. What happens if two or more objects share the same material? Will they all share the fade? Let's find out by checking the two keys.

1. Click Play and pick the Rock, so you can see the KeyAtRock.

2. Select either of the keys, turn Fade Out on and Fade In off.

3. Set the ent parameter to **0** and watch both keys.

Changing the opacity on one object's material does not affect the other object, even though they share the same material. That means you can safely animate material properties on a per-object basis during runtime. Note that during runtime, the material's name changes from Key to Key (Instance).

4. Open the Interactor script.

5. Add Internal to all of the fade variables except the useAlpha variable.

6. Save the script.

By using a variable for the fade time, you will be able to have it adjust itself according to the length of the animation.

Completing Visibility Changes

Now that you have the mechanics of the visibility change in place, you can fill out the rest of the cases.

1. Open the Interactor script.

2. Fill in the case 1 block:

```
case 1: // currentVisibility is 1, Show at start
    if (useAlpha) {
        startColor = alphaColor;  // assign the start color
        endColor = originalColor; // assign the end color
        ent = 0;                  // start the fade
        }
    break;
```

3. Save the script.

To test show at start for the fade, you can change the pedestal's shader to a Transparent shader. It starts out of scene and appears when you pick the rock.

4. Stop Play mode.

5. Select the Pedestal and change its shader to Transparent/Diffuse.

6. Set its Visibility for Element 2 to 1.

7. Click Play and pick the rock to activate the Pedestal.

The pedestal now fades gently into the scene.

8. Exit Play mode.

In preparation for the chest sequence, you can also bring the KeyAtLock into the scene. Its shader is already set to Transparent, so it just needs to be triggered into its state transition. Until the inventory system is up and running, let's just trigger it on when you pick the KeyAtRock.

9. Select the KeyAtRock.

10. Change its Lookup State 1, Element 0 to:

    default,1,KeyAtLock,1.

11. Set the KeyAtLock's Initial State to 0.

Now, when you pick the KeyAtRock with the default cursor, it goes into state 1 as before, then it tells KeyAtLock to go into its state 1.

12. Click Play.

13. Pick the Rock, then pick the key.

The KeyAtLock flickers before it fades in. If you look at the code in the ObjectLookup script's Lookup State function, you will see that it is activated in the CheckForActive function *before* it is processed. This means that there is a small lag time when it is visible before it goes transparent and fades in. The solution is to set the transparency before the object is deactivated in the Interactor's Start function.

1. Open the Interactor script.

2. In the Start function, in the if (currentLocation == 0) conditional, above the gameObject.SetActive (false) line, add the following:

```
// if it is set to use fades, make it transparent before deactivating it
if(useAlpha) renderer.material.color = alphaColor; //assign the alpha version as its color
```

3. Save the script.

4. Click Play and pick the Rock and KeyAtRock again.

This time, the KeyAtRock fades smoothly into the scene.

The next visibility type, case 3, is when the object needs to fade in, do its animation, and then fade out from the scene. For the first part, the code will be the same as the previous case, fade-in. But for the fade-out, you will need to set a timer before activating the fade. As you have probably figured out, it will have to be the delay time plus the animation time.

1. In the Interactor script, add the variables for a fade timer in the //fade variables section:

```
internal var fadeTimer : boolean;    // flag to check timer
internal var fadeTimerTime : float; // new time to check for
```

2. In the Misc vars section, add:

```
internal var aniLength : float;       // temp var for animation clip length
```

This one will be useful in several places. You will go ahead and calculate it in the ProcessObject function, as long as there is a clip.

3. In the ProcessObject function, below the if (animates) currentAnimationDelay = line, add:

```
// if there is a clip, add its length and delay together
if(currentAnimationClip) aniLength = currentAnimationClip.length + currentAnimationDelay;
else aniLength = 0.0; // there is no animation for this state
```

4. Next, copy and paste the HandleVisibility function's case 1 and change it as follows for case 2:

```
case 2: // currentVisibility is 2, Show at start, hide at end
    if (useAlpha) {
        startColor = alphaColor;   // assign the start color
        endColor = originalColor;  // assign the end color
        ent = 0;                   // start the fade
    }
    // set up for fade out

break;
```

5. Below the // setup for fade-out line, add the following:

```
if (aniLength == 0.0) aniLength = 2.0; // at least let it show a couple of seconds
before the fade
fadeTimerTime = Time.time + aniLength;
fadeTimer = true;                       // turn on the flag to check the timer
```

The first line creates a temporary variable to hold the length of the animation clip. The next line checks to make sure a clip exists, then assigns its length to the variable. On the off chance that there was no clip, the else line assigns a time to let the object show. You could have just assumed the object would have an animation clip, if it was assigned case 2, but this way, if it didn't, you won't get errors.

Armed with an "animation" time, the next line gets Time.time, the current time since the application started, and adds the delay and animation time to it to create the target time to stop the timer. The next line sets the timer flag to start the timer.

Now, you will need to head up to the Update function, where you will add the code to start the fade-out as soon as the timer is up, if it uses fades, useAlpha, or to deactivate the object if it doesn't.

6. Inside the Update function, under the if(pickTimer block, add the following:

```
// timer for visibility fades
if (fadeTimer && Time.time > fadeTimerTime) {       // if time is up and flag is on...
        fadeTimer = false;                          // turn off the flag
        if(!useAlpha) gameObject.SetActive (false); // deactivate the object
        // set up for the fade out

}
```

The code starts out pretty much the same as the pick timer. First it checks to see if the timer is running, then it checks to see if Time.time has gone past the target time. If so, the flag for the timer is turned off. Then, if it doesn't have to fade, useAlpha is not true, you deactivate the object. If it does, you will have to set the start and end colors and set the fade code to running.

7. Under the // set up for fade line, add the following to set up the start and end colors for the fade-out:

```
endColor = alphaColor;
startColor = originalColor;
ent = 0; // start the fade
```

The last line sets the elapsed normalized time variable, ent, to 0, causing the fade to start.

8. Save the script.

Since nothing in the scene is really set up to fade in, animate, and then fade out, you will have to change one of the existing objects to see it in action. The Pedestal will do nicely, because it isn't part of the final game. Right now, if you pick the rock, the pedestal fades into its state 2. If you pick the pedestal, it then goes into its state 0. Let's set its state 0 visibility type to 2 to test. It is already visible, but you will still get to see it fade in, wait the 2 seconds, and then fade out.

9. Select the Pedestal.

10. In the Inspector, change its Visibility Element 0 to 2.

11. Click Play and test by picking the rock, then the Pedestal.

The pedestal, when picked, goes invisible, then fades in, stays visible a couple of seconds, then fades out.

There's just one problem. If the object fades out, its renderer and collider are still active. The renderer will probably just waste CPU cycles, but the collider could block player navigation, so you will also need to deactivate the object after the fade. In the code that handles the fade transition, you can add a check to see if the ent value is greater than or equal to 0 and also if it has just faded out, not faded in. If that condition is met, you will deactivate the object. You can tell if it was fading in or out by checking the endColor to see if it was the alphaColor or the originalColor. If it was alphaColor, you know it was fading out.

12. In the Update function, after the ent = ent + Time.deltaTime/fadeTime line, add the following:

```
//deactivate the object if it is finished fading out
if (ent >= 1 && endColor == alphaColor) gameObject.SetActive (false);
```

13. Save the script.

14. Click Play, pick the rock, then pick the Pedestal.

This time, after it has faded out, you should see it go gray in the Hierarchy view, as it has been deactivated.

Finally, you will have to set up case 3, a fade-out in the HandleVisibility function. Because you've already written the functionality for case 2, this one will be easy—it is case 3 with the first three lines removed. Note that aniLength has already been declared, so you don't have to declare it this time.

1. In the HandleVisibility function, add case 3:

```
case 3: // currentVisibility is 3, hide at end
        // set up for fade out
        if (aniLength == 0.0) aniLength = 2.0; // at least let it show a couple of
seconds before the fade
        fadeTimerTime = Time.time + aniLength;
        fadeTimer = true;                          // turn on the flag to check the timer
        break;
```

To test this case, let's change the Pedestal's visibility type once again.

2. Select the Pedestal.

3. Change its Visibility Element 0 to **3**.

4. Click Play, pick the rock, then pick the Pedestal.

This time, the pedestal fades out a couple of seconds after it was picked, allowing the SynthUp audioClip to play out. So now the code basically emulates the behavior of the original animation you added for the KeyAtRock—it plays the animation and then fades the object out of the scene. If you wanted a nice overlap of the animation and the fade, like the keyed fade-out as it moves up, you could shorten the timer's target time by a second or even the length of the fade, fadeTime. It might look like the following:

```
fadeTimerTime = Time.time + currentAnimationDelay + aniLength - 1.0;
```

or

```
fadeTimerTime = Time.time + currentAnimationDelay + aniLength - fadeTime;
```

In case you are thinking that that was a lot of code just to avoid duplicating an animation and manually keyframing a fade-in or -out, it makes sense when you have a lot of objects to handle. In the case of a maintenance trainer, a serious games application that uses pretty much the same functionality as a point-and-click adventure game, you might have hundreds of objects that all have to fade away after a short animation.

■ **Tip** When trying to decide how an object should leave the scene, a rule of thumb could be if the object goes directly into inventory, have it fade out. If it becomes a cursor, have it go out of scene immediately.

Handling Special Cases

As a segue into the special cases section that processes auxiliary objects, you will have to set up the ChestLid. It has four states: out of scene (never used), 0; closed and locked, 1; closed and unlocked, 2; and open, 3. When the key is inserted and turned, it transitions the lid to state 2 without animation. When the key is removed, it transitions the lid into state 1 without animation. When the player picks the lid in state 2, it animates open, transitioning to state 3. Good, so far. The problem comes when the player picks it again, transitioning it to state 2, closed and unlocked, because this time, it needs to animate closed. Last time it was transitioned to state 2, from state 0, it had no animation played. So this is one of the times the transition into a state acts differently, depending on what object initiated the transition.

If you are quite clever, you could define the states to get around this problem, but that will mean filling out all the extra ObjectLookup data. Another alternative is to write conditions for the state, depending on which object picked it. The downside of this is losing the generic functionality of the two main scripts.

The third alternative is to handle exceptions to the rules when they come up. In the chest scenario, you saw when the state transition was triggered by another object, rather than a direct pick, you would want to skip the regular animation. Because the primary picked object is handled in a different part of the code than the auxiliary objects, this will be relatively easy to engineer.

Let's set up the ChestLid.

1. Select the ChestLid and add an Interactor script to it.

2. Set it up for four states for all but the post-loop arrays.

3. Set its Location Elements to 1 and Visibility Elements to 0.

4. Add chest close and chest open to its Animation Clip Elements 2 and 3.

5. Add DoorClose and ChestOpen to its Sound Clip Elements 2 and 3.

6. Check Animates.

7. See the State Management PDF to fill out the rest of the data.

Next, you'll have to fill out the ObjectLookat.

1. Set its three Lookup State and Replies State array Sizes to **1**.

2. Add the following data:

Lookup State 1:

> *Element 0*: default,1

Lookup State 2:

> *Element 0*: default,3,KeyAtLock,2

Lookup State 3:

> *Element 0*: default,2,KeyAtLock,1

So, allowing for only user picks at this point, picking the lid at state 1, it stays in state 1, rattling. Picking it when it is in state 2, unlocked and closed, puts it in state 3, opened. It also has to tell the KeyAtLock to go into its state 2, unavailable. When the opened lid is picked, it goes from state 3, opened, to state 2, closed and unlocked. The KeyAtLock also has to be put back to its state 2.

If you click Play and pick the ChestLid, it will remain in state 1. To get it into state 2, you will have to add the instructions to the KeyAtRock, right after you tell it to put the KeyAtLock into its state 2.

1. Select the KeyAtRock.

2. Change its Lookup State 1, Element 2 to:

   default,0,KeyAtLock,1,ChestLid,2

3. Click Play, pick the Rock, then the KeyAtRock.

The chest lid flies open, then animates closed to get to its state 2. The KeyAtLock pops in immediately, and the KeyAtLock refuses to animate up. The ChestLid behaves as expected, because of the issue with two different ways to get into the same state. The two keys, however, are victims of the Store In Root animation type. As soon as any of the animations on the same parent play, the others either stop or go to the end of their present clip. The Rock was already cloned out to allow it to be moved independent of the rest of the AnimationObjects and, in doing so, already avoids animation conflicts.

1. Make two duplicates of the AnimationObjects group.

2. Name one of them KeyAtRock Group and delete all but the KeyAtRock.

3. Name one of them KeyAtLock Group and delete all but the KeyAtLock.

4. In the original AnimationObjects group, delete the KeyAtLock and the KeyAtRock.

5. Click Play and test again.

This time, the only objects not behaving are those with the state/transition conflicts.

Let's start the code that will allow for exceptions. You will use a coding system to tell the ObjectLookup function how to handle these special cases:

- Trigger an animation on a nonaction object.

- Change state only on the object.

- Send a message to call a function called "DoCameraMatch" on any script on the specified object.

- Send a message to call a function called "DoTheJob" on any script on the specified object.

- Instantiate a prefab.

■ **Tip** Instantiation is used for things such as particle systems and projectiles that are created from a prefab (template) during the game and have a limited lifespan (they are destroyed as soon as they have served their purpose).

So, how do you tell it to use a particular case? It turns out there is another benefit of being able to parse a string—it allows you to use naming conventions to increase functionality. You can preface the object name with characters that will allow you to handle special cases. You will start by allowing for four special cases, for now. You will be using the following naming conventions for the special cases:

- **a0_** will trigger an animation on a nonaction object.

- **b0_** will change state only on the object.

- **c0_** will send a message to call a function called "DoCameraMatch" on any script on the specified object.

- **s0_** will send a message to call a function called "DoTheJob" on any script on the specified object.

- **p0_** will instantiate a prefab.

The underscore means that you are dealing with a special case. The first character, a letter, tells you which case, and the number allows you to specify specific cases within a case. By putting the underscore third, it makes the code easier to read, even though you will be checking it first.

The syntax might look as follows:

- Flower:

- Lookup State 1:

- Element 0: default,1,s0_Sparkles

First, you will check for the *third* character, the underscore, to ascertain that it is a special case. If found, it means that you have set aside the first three characters as reserved. With this convention defined, you won't be able to use the underscore as the third character in *any* regular object names.

The b0_ flag will be useful for objects such as the chest lid. By using the b0_ flag, you can tell it to bypass the animation and just change the state. Using the KeyAtRock scenario, where you are currently transitioning the ChestLid to state 1, it will look as follows:

- KeyAtRock:

- Lookup State 1:

- Element 0:

    default,2,KeyAtLock,2,b0_ChestLid,2

You will start by blocking in the code for the four cases.

1. Open the ObjectLookup script.

2. In the LookupState function, below the //check for special cases here- line, add the following:

```
if (tempS.Substring(2,1) == "_") {                          // if there is a
special case
    var s : String = tempS.Substring(0,1);
    var s2 : int = parseInt(tempS.Substring(1,1));          // convert the second
character to an integer
    var auxObject : GameObject = CheckForActive(tempS.Substring(3)); // find the object by
name & activate
    var bypass : boolean = false; //set a flag if the object shouldn't be transitioned into its
new state
```

Let's see what's happening here. You're inside the for loop that parses the data for the match, so it will take the characters between each comma, assign them to a temporary string named tempS, and process them.

The first thing it does with tempS is check its third character to see if it is dealing with a special case. If it discovers an underscore, that condition is true.

Now it creates variables to hold the important parts of the string. Using Substring (0,1), it assigns the first character, Element 0 of the string the single character, to the variable s, of type String. The second single character of the string, Element 1, it assigns to a variable of type int, after converting it to an integer using parseInt(). ParseInt, you may remember, is one of those exceptions that doesn't follow the capitalization conventions used in Unity's JavaScript. S2 will allow you to differentiate between variations of the same case.

Next, starting at Element 3, and because there is no argument for the number of character to use, it takes all the remaining characters and sends them down to the CheckForActive function to find the object by name and activate it, if it wasn't already active. Because the auxObject was defined in the function already, it is good to use as is.

The last variable is a flag that you will use to decide whether to process the object with a state transition. This will be useful for nonaction objects as well as action objects, where you want to change the state without any associated actions. It is set as false, so the objects will be processed, unless told otherwise.

Next, you will set up the switch clause to look for a matching case.

3. Add the following below the var bypass line:

```
// look for the matching case

switch (s) {
    case "a":  // trigger animation only on the auxiliary object
            // add guts here
            bypass = true; // skip the regular processing
            break;
```

```
    case "b": // change the state on the object only- no animations
        auxObject.GetComponent(Interactor).currentState= parseInt(readString[i+1]);
        bypass = true;            // skip the regular processing
        break;
    case "c": // send a message to "DoCameraMatch" function a script on the auxiliary
object
        auxObject.SendMessage("DoCameraMatch");
        bypass = true;            // skip the regular processing
        break;
    case "s": // send a message to the "DoTheJob" function on a script on the auxiliary
object
        auxObject.SendMessage("DoTheJob");
        if (s2 == 1) bypass = true; // skip the regular processing
        break;
    case "p": // instantiate a prefab
        // add guts here
        break;
```

The first case, the string "a" (for *animation*), will be finished later, but as it only triggers an animation, it sets the bypass variable to true.

The second case, "b" (for *bypass*), manually goes into the auxiliary object's Interactor script and manually sets its current state to the second value in the auxiliary object pair, after converting it to and int. It, of course, sets the bypass flag to true.

The third case, "c" (for *camera match*), sends a message to a function named DoCameraMatch on any script on the object. This essentially does the same thing as the "s" case, but because the camera match uses the same code for any object, giving it its own case will make the data more readable in the ObjectLookup in the Inspector. Because it doesn't affect the state, the second element of the pair is never used.

The fourth case, "s" (for *script*), will send a message to any object to call a function named DoTheJob on any of its scripts. Because you will want to make sure there is a function of that name somewhere on the object (or you wouldn't be calling it), there is no optional don't require receiver flag, such as you would normally have added. In this case, it will throw an error if it can't find a function of that name. This case makes use of the second character of the system to tell it whether to process the object as usual or to bypass the processing. This allows you to call specialty functions on both action objects and nonaction objects.

The last case, "p" (for *prefab*), will allow you to instantiate a prefab, such as a particle system or other special effect, that only comes into the scene at that time and possibly leaves the scene shortly thereafter. An example might be the special effects from adding two ingredients together.

4. Now, add the closing brackets for the switch and the special cases:

```
    } // end switch
} // end special case
```

The first instruction after the switch block is to find and activate the auxiliary object. Because that was already done if it was a special case, you can add an else in front of the line, so it will only be checked if it wasn't. It wouldn't hurt to process it twice, but it's an easy condition to add.

5. Change the var auxObject : GameObject line that follows the switch block as follows:

```
else auxObject = CheckForActive(tempS);
```

The declaration for auxObject was added to the if part of the special effects block, so it needed to be removed in the else.

Finally, you have to add the condition that checks the state of the bypass flag before sending the object off to be processed. Imediately after, you will clear the flag for the next data pair.

6. Below the `//process the object into the specified state` line, change the existing code to:

```
if(!bypass) {
    auxObject.SendMessage( "ProcessObject",newState, SendMessageOptions.DontRequireReceiver);
}
// reset bypass
bypass = false;
```

7. Save the script.

Because the special cases are represented by letters, you will want to add their meaning to the GameNotes text file.

1. Open the GameNotes text file from the Adventure Scripts folder.

2. Add the following:

pecial case assignments:

```
"a" trigger animation only on the auxiliary object
"b" change the state on the object only- no animations
"c" send a message to "DoCameraMatch" function a script on the auxiliary object
"s" send a message to the "DoTheJob" function on a script on the auxiliary object
"p" instantiate a prefab
```

3. Save the text file and close it.

Now comes the moment of truth—at least for the chest sequence. Let's update the first of the problem children and see if the code will work.

1. Select the KeyAtRock and change its Lookup State 0, Element 0 data as follows:

default,0,KeyAtLock,1,b0_ChestLid,2

2. Select the ChestLid, so you can monitor its Current State during runtime.

3. Click Play and pick the rock and the key.

This time, the chest lid goes quietly into its state 2, closed and unlocked.
Before you pick the lid, you will have to add the same bypass to the key states on the ChestLid.

4. Exit Play mode.

5. Select the ChestLid.

6. Change its data as follows:

Lookup State 1:

   Element 0: default,3,b0_KeyAtLock,2

Lookup State 2:

   Element 0: default,2,b0_KeyAtLock,1

7. Click Play and pick the objects in the following order:

ChestLid (rattles), Rock, KeyAtRock, ChestLid (opens), KeyAtLock (no response), ChestLid (closes), KeyAtLock (removes)

Until you start creating the inventory system, once you pick the KeyAtLock when it is in state 1, you won't be able to get it back, but it is worth checking.

8. Stop Play mode, then start it again.

9. Pick the rock, the KeyAtRock, the KeyAtLock, and then the ChestLid.

The key is removed from the lock (and scene), but the ChestLid rattles into its locked state.

1. Select the KeyAtLock.

2. Change its data as follows:

Lookup State 1:

> *Element 0*: default,0,b0_ChestLid,1

3. Click Play and pick the objects in the same order as before.

This time everything behaves as expected.

If you wanted to get fancy with the chest sequence, you could break the two KeyAtLock animations into insert, unlock-turn, lock-turn, and remove. This would set up a key-pick conflict between picking to unlock and picking to remove. By assigning remove to a pick on the lockplate, you could solve the problem.

Ensuring Player Focus

At this point, you've got picking and triggering working nicely for your action objects. In traditional point-and-click-type games, where the game was played out in a series of still shots, player focus during an important state transition was never an issue. But with the shift to realtime 3D environments, there is little to guarantee that the player will be in position to watch the response after picking something important.

There are two things involved here. First, you will have to stop player input for navigation. Right now, the player can pick and wander off during an object's state transition. The second requirement is to actually take control of the First Person Controller and animate it into position and orientation, while a sequence plays out.

Blocking Player Input

This functionality is crucial but easy to implement. This will be useful for preventing the player from leaving during key actions, and it will also be useful with in-game menus and character conversations.

1. Open the FPAdventurerInputController script from the Adventure Scripts folder.

2. Add the following variable near the top:

```
internal var blockInput : boolean = true; // flag to prevent user navigation
```

3. At the top of the Update function, add:

```
// block navigation input
if(blockInput) Input.ResetInputAxes();
```

ResetInputAxes basically cancels input from Unity's Input Manager system. The player will still have the use of keyboard commands for anything that isn't set up through the Input system and have full use of the mouse for cursor position and picking.

4. Save the script.

5. Click Play and try moving and looking around the scene using mouse and keyboard. Be sure to try the arrow keys as well.

Because there was a slight response from the turn arrows, if you were being tenacious, you will have to add the two lines of code to the FixedUpdate function as well.

6. Add the same two lines at the top of the FixedUpdate function:

```
// block navigation input
if(blockInput) Input.ResetInputAxes();
```

7. Save the script and test the arrow keys again.

This time there is no movement.

Now that movement is suppressed, you will have to make sure the pick functionality has not been affected.

8. Try mousing over and picking on the various objects.

The cursor functionality remains unaffected.

Now you must decide how to use the new functionality with the actions. You've allowed the player to pick additional objects before the previous ones have finished animating, but that is really only reasonable if they are in the same immediate location. They are also handled on the individual object's scripts.

Because navigation suppression should be a global function, its timer code should be on the FPAdventurerInputController script. That way, if one object starts the timer, then another gets picked, its time can overwrite the first, if it is longer, or be ignored, if it is not. You can do the checks in a function that also will receive the timer target time from the picked objects

1. Change the blockInput variable to false:

```
internal var blockInput : boolean = false; // flag to prevent user navigation
```

2. Add a couple of variables for a timer:

```
internal var blockerTimer : boolean;       // flag to check timer
internal var blockerTimerTime : float;     // new time to check for
```

3. Create a new function to handle input blocking:

```
function ManageInput (aniTime: float) {
    // add the aniTime to the current time
    aniTime = Time.time + aniTime;
    // check to see if it is greater than the current time
    // if it is, update the timer target time
    if (aniTime > blockerTimerTime) blockerTimerTime = aniTime;
    if (blockerTimerTime > Time.time) {
        // turn on the flag to block user input
        blockInput = true; // turn on the blocker if it isn't already on
        blockerTimer = true; // turn on timer if it isn't already on
    }
}
```

Next, you'll need to add the timer checking code to the Update function. Theoretically, it ought to go above the block navigation line, but realistically, it won't make much difference time-wise.

4. Below the if(blockInput) line in the Update function, add the timer code:

```
// timer for blocking navigation
if (blockerTimer && Time.time > blockerTimerTime) { // if time is up and flag is on...
        blockerTimer = false; // turn off the flag
        // turn off the flag to block user input
        blockInput = false;    // turn off the blocker
}
```

Once again, you are using a flag to turn the timer check off and on. Because the first thing to be checked will be the Boolean, blockerTimer, the engine won't need to waste time making a comparison of float values, unless the timer is on.

5. Save the script.

Now, you will have to decide how long the timer should run before sending the target time off to the FPAdventurerInputController script. Because you already have the aniLength calculated, the clip time plus the delay, you may as well use it. If it is 0, there is no point in sending it off, so you will check for that condition first. You can also save calculations by checking after the call to VisibilityHandler, because there is a possibility the object will go immediately out of scene.

1. Open the Interactor script.

2. In the ProcessObject function, below the HandleVisibility() line, add the following:

```
// block player input while action plays out
if (aniLength != 0.0) {
    gameObject.Find("First Person Controller").SendMessage("ManageInput",aniLength);
}
```

3. Save the script.

To test the functionality, you will have to pick something with a longer animation. The flower will be perfect.

4. Click Play and pick the flower.

5. Try to move or look around while it plays out.

Navigation is restored as soon as the flower revives.

You may want to add in the length of the looping clip, or maybe just an extra second, before allowing the player to move. Or, you may decide the player can move halfway through the animation. Either way, you will just have to do a bit of math.

6. In the FPAdventurerInputController script's ManageInput function, change the aniTime = Time.time + aniTime line to:

```
aniTime = Time.time + aniTime/2; // prevent player from moving intil half way through the animation
```

7. Save the script.

8. Click Play and test the flower again.

The timing is better, but unless you are a decent distance from the flower before picking, you will miss the animation that goes out of frame as the flower rises up and opens.

Directing Player Focus

Now that the player can no longer wander off in the midst of an important sequence, you will occasionally have times when you will have to make sure he or she is in the optimal position to view the action. This may mean a location change, an orientation change, or both.

You will need several pieces of information. You will need the target location of the First Person Controller and the target orientation of the camera. Then you will need the duration of the transition. Because only a few of the sequences will require a forced camera match, you will be making a new script.

Exploring Lerp

You've encountered Lerp before with the fade-in/fade-out code. You lerped, linear interpolated, between two color variables, Vector4 type. This time you only need three, x, y, and z, so you will be using a Vector3. Just as with Color. Lerp(), you will need a start and end number and also that normalized segment of the rate.

1. Create a new script in the Adventure Scripts folder.

2. Name it **CameraMatch**.

3. Open it in the editor.

4. Add the following variables to the script:

```
var targetPos : Transform ;        // destination position
internal var source : Transform ;  // the position of the object the script is on, start pos
var duration : float = 1.0 ;       // seconds duration of the camera match
```

Next you will need a function to do the work.

5. Create the new function:

```
function MatchTransforms () {

}
```

Just as with Color.Lerp, you will derive the elapsed normalized time slice from the duration and current time, Time.deltaTime. The ent variable is of type float.

6. Add the following line inside, at the top of the function:

```
var ent : float = 0.0;// normalized chunk of time
```

Next, you will separate the position and rotation for processing.

7. Add the following below that:

```
var startPos : Vector3 = transform.position;   // this object's position
var startRot : Quaternion = transform.rotation;// this object's rotation
```

Instead of running the code through the Update function, you will be using a while loop. While the condition remains true, the contents are run through. Because the duration is normalized to fit between 0 and 1, the while loop runs until the ent value is 1 or greater.

8. Add the following to move the object to the current location:

```
while (ent <= 1.0) {
        ent = ent + Time.deltaTime/duration; // get the latest time slice
        // set the new position
        transform.position = Vector3.Lerp(startPos, targetPos.position, ent);
        yield; // make sure the last line gets processed before looping to the next time
slice
} // end while
```

Next, you will need a way to trigger the match. While you are experimenting, you can use a key down in the Update function to test.

9. In the Update function, add the following:

```
if (Input.GetKeyDown("p")){
        // trigger the match
        MatchTransforms ();
}
```

10. Save the script.

It's time to test the match. The pedestal doesn't have an animation, so it will be a good test subject. Its pivot point is at its base. The First Person Controller's pivot point is midway up, and the match uses the location of the pivot point.

1. Add the CameraMatch script to the Pedestal and set the Pedestal's Initial state to **1** (so it will be visible at the start).

2. Disable the Pedestal's collider.

3. Drag the First Person Controller onto its Target Pos parameter.

4. Click Play and press the P key, watching the action in the Scene view.

The pedestal moves to the First Person Controller's position at a steady rate.

5. Drive the First Person Controller to a different location and press P again.

The Pedestal again moves at a steady, but boring, rate to the First Person Controller.

A better match animation would be if the object moved with a classic ease-in/ease-out speed. To make that happen, you can use one of the Mathf functions, Mathf.SmoothStep(), to rearrange the time slices. Here's the catch—you aren't replacing the Lerp function, you're going to replace the ent variable, then feed it back into the Mathf.SmoothStep function.

1. Replace ent in the transform.position = Vector3.Lerp(startPos, targetPos. position, ent) line with Mathf.SmoothStep(0.0,1.0,ent):

```
transform.position = Vector3.Lerp(startPos, targetPos.position,
Mathf.SmoothStep(0.0,1.0,ent));
```

2. Save the script, click Play and press the P key again.

This time the rate is not quite as constant.

3. Replace the new ent variable with the same `Mathf.SmoothStep(0.0,1.0,ent)` function:

```
transform.position = Vector3.Lerp(startPos, targetPos.position,
Mathf.SmoothStep(0.0,1.0, Mathf.SmoothStep(0.0,1.0,ent)));
```

4. Save the script, click Play and press the P key again.

This time, the pedestal definitely exhibits a nice ease-in, ease-out behavior.
With the position lerp working, it's time to do the same for the rotation. The variable type for rotation is Quaternion.

5. Add the line to update the rotation below the `transform.position = Vector3.Lerp` line:

```
transform.rotation = Quaternion.Lerp(startRot, targetPos.rotation,
Mathf.SmoothStep(0.0,1.0,Mathf.SmoothStep(0.0,1.0,ent)));
```

6. Save the script

Let's see how the rotation match works next.

1. Change the coordinate system to Local and Pivot, instead of Global and Center, so you will be able to compare the local rotations.

2. Click Play.

3. Select the Pedestal and note which direction it is currently pointing.

4. Press the P key and watch the pedestal move and rotate to match the First Person Controller.

5. Select the First Person Controller.

The Pedestal's pivot point is the same as that of the First Person Controller.
For the real functionality, the camera match script will be on the First Person Controller. A second Rotation match will be needed to match the Main Camera's rotation. For that, you will need another variable for a target, and you will need one for access to the camera.

1. Add the following variables at the top of the script, above the `duration` var:

```
var targetLook : Transform;        // camera's target for lookAt
internal var fPCamera : GameObject;   // main camera
```

2. Add the `startCam` variable inside the `MatchTransforms` function, below `var startRot`:

```
var startCamRot : Quaternion = fPCamera.transform.rotation;// the main camera's rotation
```

3. In the Start function, find the camera:

```
fPCamera = GameObject.Find("Main Camera");
```

To make setup easier, you will add the camera matching code in an `if` statement that checks for the existence of a targetLook object before doing the match. This will allow you to create the position target first, load it in, and then create the camera target from the correct location.

4. Add the following beneath the current transform.rotation line to update the camera's rotation:

```
//match camera if targetLook exists
if (targetLook) {
    var endCamRot : Quaternion = targetLook.rotation;// get the rotation from the cam target
    fPCamera.transform.rotation = Quaternion.Lerp(startCamRot, endCamRot, Mathf.
SmoothStep(0.0,1.0,Mathf.SmoothStep(0.0,1.0,ent)));
}
```

Before testing the updated camera match, you will have to create a couple of target locations. It's easier to find the correct position in Play mode, because you can also use the mouse look to help with the positioning. In the scripts, you'll match the First Person Controller's *position* to the target gameObject's position, and the Main Camera's rotation to another target object.

Of the current test objects, the inside of the chest and the flower are the two most in need of a camera match. You will eventually have to look inside the chest as it opens, so you can create a target for it first.

1. Remove the CameraMatch script from the Pedestal and enable its collider.

2. Zero any rotations you may have put on the First Person Controller (except the Y Rotation) and Main Camera.

3. Disable the chest lid, so you can see inside the chest.

4. If you were using Free Aspect in the Game window, change it to Standalone, so you get a true view of where the target needs to be.

5. Click Play.

6. Navigate to the chest and look down until you have a nice view of the contents, as shown in Figure 10-5.

Figure 10-5. *A good view of the inside of the chest*

7. Select the First Person Controller in the Hierarchy view.

8. From the GameObject menu, choose Align View to Selected.

The view moves to where the First Person Controller is in the scene.

1. Stop Play mode.

2. Create a new Empty GameObject.

3. Name it **Target Chest**.

4. From the GameObject menu, choose Align With View.

The new target object jumps to the First Person Controller's position, where it was during runtime.

5. Select the First Person Controller and add the CameraMatch script to it.

6. Drag the TargetChest onto its Target Pos parameter.

7. Click Play and press P to move the First Person Controller to the target position.

Now, you will set up the lookAt target just like the position target, but using the Main Camera.

1. Use Mouse look to look down at the chest's interior again.

2. Select the Main Camera from the First Person Controller hierarchy.

3. From the GameObject menu, choose Align View to Selected.

4. Stop Play mode.

5. Create a new Empty GameObject.

6. Name it **Target Chest Look**.

7. From the GameObject menu, choose Align With View.

8. Select the First Person Controller.

9. Drag the Target Chest Look onto its new Target Look parameter.

10. Set the Duration to **3.**

11. Click Play and drive the First Person Controller away from the chest.

12. Press P.

The First Person Controller glides into position in front of the chest, and the main camera looks down inside it.

1. Stop Play mode.

2. Activate the ChestLid again.

You'll also want a good view of the plant reviving. The setup is the same for the Flower as for the chest.

1. Click Play.

2. Pick the plant to revive it.

3. Navigate to a good vantage point (see Figure 10-6).

Figure 10-6. *A good view for the plant revival*

4. Select the First Person Controller again.

5. From the GameObject menu, choose Align View to Selected.

6. Stop Play mode.

7. Create a new Empty GameObject.

8. Name it **Target Pollen Ball**.

9. From the GameObject menu, choose Align With View.

10. Select the First Person Controller.

11. Drag the Target Pollen Ball onto its Target Pos parameter.

12. Click Play and press P to move the First Person Controller to the target position.

13. Pick the flower to get it to transition into its revived state.

Now set up the lookAt target using the Main Camera.

1. Use Mouse look to look up at the open flower.

2. Select the Main Camera from the First Person Controller hierarchy.

3. From the GameObject menu, choose Align View to Selected.

4. Stop Play mode.

5. Create a new Empty GameObject.

6. Name it **Target Pollen Ball Look.**

7. From the GameObject menu, choose Align With View.

8. Select the First Person Controller.

9. Drag the Target Pollen Ball Look onto its Target Look parameter.

10. Click Play and pick the flower.

11. Drive the First Person Controller away from the flower.

12. Press P.

The First Person Controller glides into position in front of the flower, and the main camera looks up to watch the animation. You probably noticed a glitch when starting the mouse look after a camera match. You will eventually send the new rotation values to the appropriate navigation scripts to update them.

13. Stop Play mode.

Having invested a bit of time in setting up the two targets, it is a good time to save.

14. Save the scene and save the project.

■ **Tip** Because the camera match can happen from any direction, you may want to provide natural barriers to prevent awkward position matches.

Camera Match Metadata

While setting up the targets, you loaded the targets directly into the First Person Controller and triggered the match with the P key. For the game, the match will be triggered when the player clicks the action object. When that happens, the object will send the target information to the First Person Controller. You will need a new script to house the data that will get sent to the First Person Controller.

1. Create a new script in the Adventure Scripts folder.

2. Name it **CameraMatchData**.

3. Open it in the script editor.

4. Add the following variables:

```
// camera match metadata - resides on action objects
var targetPos : Transform;  // where the First Person Controller needs to ends up
var targetLook : Transform; // where the main camera needs to end up looking
var matchDelay = 0.0;       // any delay time needed before the match
var duration = 1.0 ;        //  the time the camera match animates over
var addTime = 0.0;          // additional time after the match before control is
returned to the player
```

5. You will need access to the Control Center to turn navigation and mouse functionality off and on, so add the following:

```
internal var controlCenter : GameObject;
```

And you'll need to put the mechanism for the camera match on the Main Camera itself, so you'll need to "find" it as well.

6. Add the following:

```
internal var fPCamera: GameObject;      // first person's camera, Main Camera
```

And because the script that does the actual animation for the match will be on the First Person Controller object, you will need access to it.

7. Add the following:

```
internal var fPController: GameObject; // the first person controller
```

And, as usual, you will load the objects in the Start function.

8. In the Start function, assign the internal variables' values:

```
function Start () {

    // gain access to these objects
    controlCenter = GameObject.Find("Control Center");
    fPCamera = GameObject.Find("Main Camera");
    fPController = GameObject.Find("First Person Controller");
}
```

Because you have to trigger everything involved with the camera match from one place, create a function called DoCameraMatch, as specified by the c special case section you added earlier in the ObjectLookUp script.

9. Block in the following function:

```
function DoCameraMatch () {

// disable cursor visibility and mouse functionality
controlCenter.GetComponent(GameManager).camMatch = true;//disable mouse functions

//send off position and look-at values to First Person Controller

// Wait for the delay if any

// trigger the camera match

}
```

Let's start by sending all of this object's variable values to the First Person Controller's CameraMatch script, so they can be used to perform the camera match.

10. In the // send off section, add the following:

```
fPController.GetComponent(CameraMatch).targetPos = targetPos;    // the position target
fPController.GetComponent(CameraMatch).targetLook = targetLook;  // the lookAt target
fPController.GetComponent(CameraMatch).duration = duration;      // the match time
//fPController.GetComponent(CameraMatch).addTime = addTime;      // extra observation time
```

Before you actually trigger the camera match to start, you may want to wait. This is the matchDelay. As a default, it is set to 0.0, in case there is no delay.

11. Add the following in the // wait for delay section:

```
yield new WaitForSeconds(matchDelay);
```

And after the values are in place and the delay served, you will trigger the match with a call to the function in the CameraMatch script that will start the match.

12. Add the following in the // trigger the camera match section:

```
fPController.SendMessage("MatchTransforms"); // start the match
```

13. Save the script.

You should receive an error message for a missing camMatch variable in the GameManager script. That's an easy fix. You can add it now and finish the functionality later, to suppress the cursor and suspend player input during the match.

14. Open the GameManager script.

15. Add the following under the internal var supressPointer line:

```
internal var camMatch : boolean = false; // flag to suspend all during camera match
```

16. Save the script.

With the data script completed, you will have to add it to the objects that trigger the match—the ChestLid and the Flower.

1. Add the CameraMarchData script to the ChestLid.

2. Drag the TargetChest onto its Target Pos parameter.

3. Drag the Target Chest Look onto its Target Look parameter.

4. In the Inspector, change the ChestLid object's LookupState 2, Element 0 to read as follows:

default,3,b0_KeyAtLock,2,c0_ChestLid,3.

The 3 at the end is not processed in the special cases code, but it is probably less confusing to have it match the state the chest is going into.

Next, let's set up the Flower.

5. Add the CameraMarchData script to the Flower.

6. Drag the TargetFlower onto its Target Pos parameter.

7. Drag the Target Flower Look onto its Target Look parameter.

8. In the Inspector, change the Flower object's LookupState 1, Element 0 to read as follows:

   default,2,c0_Flower,2

9. Open the CameraMatch script.

10. Add internal to all of the top variables:

```
internal var targetPos : Transform ;  // destination position
internal var source : Transform ; // the position of the object the script is on, start pos
internal var targetLook : Transform;  // camera's target for lookAt
internal var fPCamera : GameObject;   // main camera
internal var duration : float = 1.0 ; // seconds duration of the camera match
```

11. Save the script.

You should now be ready to test the camera match by picking the action objects!

12. Click Play and test both the ChestLid sequence and the Flower.

Both objects bring the player smoothly into position and correct orientation to watch the actions play out.

There are still a few things to take care of, though. As soon as you turned to interact with the other object, you may have noticed the view snapped back to what it was before the camera match started. You also might want to have a quick camera match for a longer animation.

Refining the Camera Match

The first thing to fix is the problem with the main Camera orientation when you start looking around after a camera match. You've probably forgotten by now, but when you allowed the player to use the arrow keys to turn the First Person Controller, you needed to be able to update both the First Person Controller's orientation and the Main Camera's orientation in the MouseLookRestricted script. This is because for the y axis mouse look, it is being calculated with a variable that is local to the script.

Now that you've got a bit of coding under your belt, let's take another look at the MouseLookRestricted script. Remember that it is C#, not JavaScript. It is found in the Standard Assets, Character Controllers, Sources, Scripts folder.

1. Open the MouseLookRestricted.cs script.

Let's start by clearing out extra code. In this game, the first option, MouseXAndY, is never used, so let's start by clearing away the code for it in the Update function

2. Delete the following section from the Update function:

```
if (axes == RotationAxes.MouseXAndY)
{
    float rotationX = transform.localEulerAngles.y + Input.GetAxis("Mouse X") * sensitivityX;

    rotationY += Input.GetAxis("Mouse Y") * sensitivityY;
    rotationY = Mathf.Clamp (rotationY, minimumY, maximumY);

    transform.localEulerAngles = new Vector3(-rotationY, rotationX, 0);
}
```

3. Remove the `else` from the `else if` line right below the code you just removed:

```
if (axes == RotationAxes.MouseX) // horizontal mouse for FPC y axis rotation
```

Before clicking Save, let's see what enum is about.

4. Select the First Person Controller and inspect its Axes parameter.

5. Click the drop-down.

You can see three options: MouseXandY, MouseX, and MouseY.
Enum lets you define a new type and assign values that will show up as options in the Inspector. Having removed the code, let's clear it out of the enum as well and renumber the others.

6. Change the public enum RotationAxes { MouseXAndY = 0, MouseX = 1, MouseY = 2 } line to :

```
public enum RotationAxes { MouseX = 0, MouseY = 1 }
```

7. And instead of initializing the enum variable axes, of type RotationAxes, to RotationAxes. MouseXAndY, initialize it to:

```
public RotationAxes axes = RotationAxes.MouseX;
```

8. Save the script.

    a. Select the First Person Controller and check the newly tweaked Axes parameter in the Inspector by clicking its down arrow.

Because you changed the order, you will have to reassign MouseX to the First Person Controller's Axes parameter in the MouseLookRestricted component. Because the second enum is now MouseY, it is incorrect.

1. Assign **MouseX** to the Axes parameter from the drop-down.

For the Main Camera, there is no longer a third element, so it has become blank.

2. Select the Main Camera from the First Person Controller hierarchy.

3. Open the drop-down and assign **MouseY** to its Axes parameter.

4. Just for fun, add your own enum value so it becomes:

```
public enum RotationAxes { MouseX = 0, MouseY = 1, PinkElephant = 2 }
```

5. Save the script and open one of the axes drop-downs in the Inspector.

Your new value, PinkElephant appears as the third option.

6. Remove your addition so the code returns to:

```
public enum RotationAxes { MouseX = 0, MouseY = 1 }
```

7. Save the script.

Now that the script has been cleared out, let's look at the two options available, if the conditions you added originally are met. As a refresher, with Input Axes, MouseX means you are moving the mouse from side to side. MouseY means you are moving the mouse forward and backward. Do not confuse this X and Y with the x and y axis of any of the scene objects.

Now might be a good time to add a couple of comments to remind you which object uses which. The First Person Controller uses MouseX (side to side) to turn left and right on its y axis.

1. Add the comment to the `if` condition line:

```
if (axes == RotationAxes.MouseX) // horizontal mouse for First Person Controller y axis turns
```

2. Change the `else` line to:

```
else // vertical mouse for main camera x axis rotation
```

Now comes the interesting part. The rotation for the First Person Controller y axis needs only one line of code, `transform.Rotate(0, Input.GetAxis("Mouse X") * sensitivityX, 0)`. And if you think back on the camera match, the direction the First Person Controller was facing at the end of the match hadn't changed when you clicked the right mouse button or pressed a navigation key. That is because it builds the orientation from scratch each time the code is run. The x and z axes are always set to 0, and the y orientation is constructed from the mouseX movement times the sensitivity. If you tried adjusting the sensitivity, you would have found the rotation got very sluggish if the sensitivityX was small. Another thing going on here is that, because the First Person Controller is always oriented up, the y rotation will always be world coordinate system.

Now take a look at the else clause for the MouseY. This is the vertical mouse movement that makes the main Camera rotate up and down on its local x axis. The other problem here is that you needed to restrict the camera from being able to rotate freely 360 degrees, like the First Person Controller's y axis counterpart. So now, a variable has been introduced to process the rotation, `rotationY`.

The minimumX and MaximumX are never used or tested.

3. Remove the following variables:

```
public float minimumX = -360F;
public float maximumX = 360F;
```

Back in the else clause, the `rotationY` variable gets processed, and the result is *clamped*. `Mathf.Clamp()` clamps or restricts the values between the min and max values, -60 degrees and +60 degrees. That means if it is greater than 60, it gets set back to 60, and if it is less than -60, it gets set back to -60.

When the clamping has adjusted the `rotationY` value, it is fed back into the object by using localEulerAngles. The MouseX uses `transform.Rotate()`, which puts the x, y, and z values in as a Quaternion rotation/orientation. Because the MouseY needs to use local orientation numbers, it uses `transform.localEulerAngles()` to update the camera's orientation.

To determine where the camera match goes wrong, let's add a print variable to see what the `rotationY` variable is.

4. Above the `transform.localEulerAngles` line, add a print statement:

```
print(rotationY);
```

5. Save the script.

6. Click Play and watch the value, as you look up and down in the scene.

As expected, it stays between -60 and +60.

Now, think about the camera-match problem—when you start to look after a camera match (you can right-click, just to initialize a look). The main Camera pops back to its last rotationY orientation before the camera match.

So it looks like you need to update the `rotationY` as soon as the match is finished. For that, you can send a message from the RestrictedMouseLook script.

1. Open the CameraMatch script.

Let's send a message to the MouseLookRestricted script when the match is finished (the while loop is finished).

2. Add the following lines at the bottom of the `MatchTransforms` function:

```
//tell the MouseLookRestricted script the match is finished via the ResetRotationY
function fPCamera.SendMessage("ResetRotationY",SendMessageOptions.DontRequireReceiver);
```

3. Save the script

4. Open the MouseLookRestricted.cs script.

5. Add the following function above the final closing bracket:

```
public void ResetRotationY()
{
        // get the current rotation for the x axis
        print(transform.rotation.eulerAngles.x);
}
```

6. Save the script.

7. Click Play and approach the flower, looking down at the ground, so that the value reported is about -50.

8. Pick the Flower.

9. Check the status bar at the end of the camera match.

The value reported is about 7 degrees.

10. Right-click to initialize navigation again, without actually moving.

The console reports the same value it had before the Camera Match, about -50.

11. Now compare the x rotation in the Main Camera's Transform component with the rotateY value reported in the console as you look up and down.

12. Click Play and look up and down, watching the values reported.

The values appear to be the same, so it would seem logical that you could just send the new value to the RestrictedMouseLook script. Let's see what happens.

1. In the MouseLookRestricted.cs script, add the following beneath the `print(transform.rotation.eulerAngles.x)` line in the `ResetRotationY()` function:

```
rotationY = transform.rotation.eulerAngles.x;
```

2. Save the script.

3. Click Play and try the Flower pick again.

4. When the animation has finished, right-click to go into navigation mode and "load" the new value.

Now the value reported is about 353 degrees, which sounds suspiciously like 360-7. Clearly, there is something fishy going on.

5. Try looking up and down to see if you can figure out what is happening to the value.

The rotationY values are 60 looking up, 0 straight ahead, and minus, to -60, looking down.

The x transform shows 300 looking up, 360/0 looking straight ahead, and 60 looking down.

So it looks like the two are using different counting systems. A little math will help you update the rotationY to the current x axis value.

6. Replace the rotationY = transform.rotation.eulerAngles.x line with:

```
float tempY =  transform.rotation.eulerAngles.x ;
if (tempY <= 360 && tempY >= 300) rotationY = 360 - tempY;
else rotationY = - tempY;
```

7. Comment out the print line.

8. Comment out the print(rotationY) line in the Update function.

9. Save the script.

10. Click Play and try the Flower pick again.

11. Now try the chest sequence.

Both camera matches transition seamlessly back to the player's control.

With the camera match performing well, you will want to prevent user navigation and mouse functionality, starting with the visibility.

The cursor is active through most of the match. To fix that, you will have to finish the code that hides the cursor and disables the mouse functionality during the camera match.

In the GameManager script, you added the camMatch variable to store the current state of any ongoing camera matching, but it is the Interactor script that will have to access it before allowing mouseovers and mouse picks.

1. Open the GameManager script.

2. At the top of the OnGUI function, add the camMatch to the conditional that draws the cursor:

```
if (!navigating && !suppressPointer && !camMatch) {
```

3. Save the script.

Even with the cursor hidden, mouseover and mouse pick functionality is still possible. Adding another condition to the Interactor is fairly easy and will prevent mishaps.

4. Open the Interactor script.

5. In the OnMouseEnter function, above the if(DistanceFromCamera line, add the following:

```
// if there is an active camera match in process, exit the function now
if (controlCenter.GetComponent(GameManager).camMatch) return;
```

6. In the OnMouseDown function, above the if(DistanceFromCamera line, add the same:

```
// if there is an active camera match in process, exit the function now
if (controlCenter.GetComponent(GameManager).camMatch) return;
```

7. Save the script.

■ **Tip** When deciding where to add new conditionals that will exit the function when evaluated to true, try to order them to cause the least amount of evaluation time. If the condition is common and uses a variable local to the script, check it near the top of the list. If it is less likely to evaluate as true and requires calculation time (as with the distance checks), put it near the bottom of the list.

---

8. Click Play and test the sequences.

Now the cursor stays hidden while the camera match plays out...and doesnt come back.

The issue here is the time allotted for the matches. Sometimes you want the matches to end earlier than the animation, so the player can watch more of it once there. You've already got a variable, addTime, in the CameraMatchData script. Let's start by uncommenting it, so it will send the value to the CameraMatch script.

1. Open the CameraMatchData script.

2. In the DoCameraMatch function, uncomment the addTime line:

```
fPController.GetComponent(CameraMatch).addTime = addTime; // extra observation time
```

3. Save the script.

4. Open the CameraMatch script.

5. Add the addTime variable near the top of the script:

```
var addTime = 0.0; // additional time after the match before control is returned to the player
```

6. In the MatchTransforms function, above the fPCamera.SendMessage("ResetRotationY" line, add:

```
yield new WaitForSeconds(addTime); // pause before returning control to player
```

7. Under the fPCamera.SendMessage("ResetRotationY" line, add:

```
// enable cursor visibility and mouse functionality
gameObject.Find("Control Center").GetComponent(GameManager).camMatch = false;
//enable mouse functions
```

8. Save the script.

9. Click Play and test the flower.

Now you can add a little "freeze" time to the cursor, blocking it past the camera match for the Flower sequence.

1. Stop Play mode and restart.

2. In the Inspector, set the Flower's Add Time to **4**.

3. Click Play and test the flower.

This time, the cursor and mouse-pick functionality stay away long after the match is finished.

4. Stop Play mode.

The final problem is that navigation is active again as soon as the match has finished, even if the addTime is still running. In the FPAdventureInputController script, you already have a blockInput variable that will block navigation, but it is tied in to a timer. To help solve this last little issue, you will send a message to extend the timer to include the addTime value.

1. Open the CameraMatchData script.

2. In the DoCameraMatch function, change the yield new WaitForSeconds(addTime) line as follows:

```
// block navigation during addTime (extend blockInput time)
gameObject.Find("First Person Controller").GetComponent
(FPAdventureInputController).ManageInput(addTime);
```

3. Save the script.

4. In the Inspector, change the Flower's Add Time parameter to about **10**, so you can make sure navigation input is being blocked.

5. Click Play and test the Flower for navigation blocking after camera match has finished.

This time, the player is blocked from moving *or* looking around until the Add Time has expired.

6. Exit Play mode and set the Add Time back to **5**.

7. Save the scene and save the project.

Summary

In this chapter, you added sophistication and flexibility to your state engine. You finished the auxiliary object parsing code by having it call the state processing code on the auxiliary object itself. In doing so, you made it possible to transition any number of action objects into their own unique states with a single pick event.

By adding a special cases section to the object lookup, you provided a means of dealing with typical issues, such as two ways to get into or return to the same state, and any specialty cases that may crop up.

You also implemented a code-based means of fading action objects in and out of the scene. It made use of the Lerp function, which provided you with a means of smoothly going between a start and end value over a duration that you could also define.

With the state transitions working smoothly, you turned your attention to improving the mechanics of the interactions, by refining the cursor functionality. This helped to prevent the player from missing important transitions. Then you took it one step further by repurposing the Lerp functionality and introducing a camera match. This allowed you to make sure the player was in the perfect spot to watch the action play out and also prevent him or her from leaving or looking elsewhere during the action.

■ ■ ■

CHAPTER 11

Physics and Special Effects

In the traditional first-person point-and-click adventure game, backgrounds were prerendered, and action took place as sprites replacing a small portion of screen to show a 2D animation. Even after 3D-rendered backgrounds took the place of hand-painted backdrops, sprites were still the most typical means of showing the action.

Today, however, with real-time 3D technology getting close enough to prerender quality, the whole game can be produced within the 3D environment. This opens up the possibility of using physics, particle systems, and other physical-based effects to enhance or even replace keyframed animation sequences.

You've already got the framework to stray from point and click, in that you can trigger action remotely. In this chapter, after an introduction and a bit of the usual experimentation, you will start incorporating physics, particle systems, and other Unity functionality into your action sequences.

The great part about taking advantage of the physically based features is that they are useful across all genres. What may seem like a typical first-person shooter element may work perfectly in an adventure game, and vice versa. Don't be afraid to look beyond your favorite game for ideas.

Adding New Assets

Before delving into the new topics, you'll need a few more assets. While you can certainly do a lot of testing with Unity's primitive objects, you may as well start creating prefabs that can be used in the game.

1. Drag the Action Objects folder from the Chapter 11 Assets directly into the Project view.

It contains several non-animating objects in one FBX file, an animated vial in the other, and some new textures.

2. Open the new Action Objects folder and select the ActionsObjects asset.

In the Inspector, Preview window, you will see a handwritten message or note, a plugged vial, a crystal, a sleeve for the crystal, and a combination sleeve and crystal. In the Model section, the Animation Type should be None. None of these objects will animate, so to prevent the automatic generation of an Animation component, you will have to change the settings.

3. In the Rig section, select None for the Animation Type and click Apply (Figure 11-1).

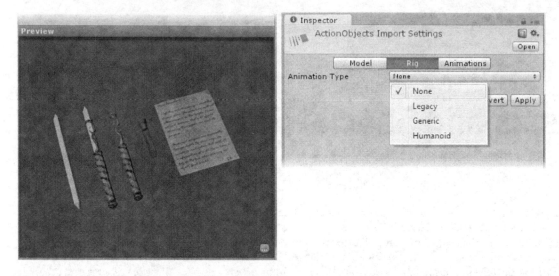

Figure 11-1. *Setting Animation Type to None for the new ActionObjects*

4. In the Model section, adjust the import Scale Factor to **0.0025**.

5. In the Animations section, uncheck Import Animation and click Apply.

6. In the Interaction scene, drag the ActionObjects into the scene near the existing items (Figure 11-2).

Figure 11-2. *The new additions*

The materials will need a bit of adjustment. Although it isn't necessary at this stage, it's a good habit to take care of it right after import.

For the Golden Sleeve and Crystal with Sleeve, do the following:

1. Select the SleeveGold texture in the Action Textures subfolder.

2. Duplicate it and append its name with Bmp, so you can recognize it easily.

3. Turn the copy's Texture Type into a Normal map in the Inspector.

4. Set its bumpiness to about **0.05** and click Apply.

5. Select the Sleeve Gold material in the Materials folder.

6. Change the shader to Bumped Specular and add the normal map.

7. Click the Main Color swatch and make sure it is showing RGBA instead of HSVA. (You may have to toggle the icon just below the color bar on the right side.)

8. Set the Main Color to a yellowish color, about 255,220,125.

9. Set the Specular Color to a stronger yellowish gold, about 255,195,60.

10. Adjust the Shininess slider, so it is almost to the far left and the Specular Color is fairly bright.

For the Vial of Elixir:

1. Select the Vial of Elixir in the Hierarchy view.

2. Lighten the Cork material's Main Color.

3. For the GlassRef material, choose the Reflective ➤ Specular shader.

4. Set the Main Color to a strong turquoise, 0,130,225.

5. Set the Specular Color to a mid-pink, 250,105,255.

6. Adjust the Shininess slider to about 25 percent.

You should see a pink highlight on the bluish vial.

7. Leave the Reflection Cubemap empty.

For the Message:

1. Change the shader to a Specular shader.

2. Lighten both the Main and Specular colors by about half.

The crystal will require a special shader that uses refraction and reflection. You will have to get that shader from the Unity Asset Store.

■ **Note** The Diamond shader and the light reflection cubemap and refractions textures are from the Unity Gem Shader, a free asset package available from the Asset Store. You can access the Asset Store through the Window menu or by pressing Ctrl+9.

To download it via the Asset Store:

1. Select Asset Store from the Window Menu.

2. From Catagories, select Textures and Materials ➤ Shaders.

3. Select the Gem Shader from Unity Technologies.

4. Click Download, sign in with your Unity account (you may have to create one), then click Import.

When the download finishes, you will get the Import Packages dialog. For this project, you will need the shader, diamond shader, the light reflection cubemap, and the refractions cubemap. Feel free to Import All, if you wish.

5. Select the items you wish to import and click Import.

6. Take a look through the Gem Shader folder and make sure you can locate the required three assets.

For the Crystal:

7. Select the Crystal material.

8. Assign the FX/Diamond shader to it.

9. Drag the light reflection cubemap into its Reflection Texture.

10. Drag the refractions texture into its Refraction Texture (see Figure 11-3).

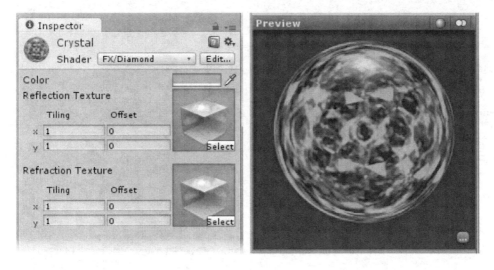

Figure 11-3. *The Crystal material*

11. Orbit the Scene view to see the Diamond shader in action.

Before you can use the objects in the scene, they will each need a collider.

1. In the Hierarchy view, add a Box collider to the Message.

2. Add a Capsule collider to the Crystal with Sleeve object.

3. Set its Direction to Z-Axis, Radius to **0.08** and its Height to **1.3.**

4. Right-click over the component name and Copy Component.

5. Select the Crystal, right-click over an existing component and select Paste Component as New.

6. Repeat for the Golden Sleeve and Vial objects.

7. Adjust the parameters as needed.

Leave the Radius large for now—it will make picking easier.

Your collection of action objects should now look similar to Figure 11-4.

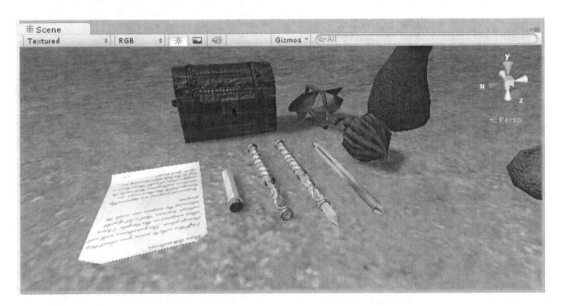

Figure 11-4. The newly revamped materials

With the imports squared away, it's time to have some fun with physics.

Physics

The first thing to be aware of with game-engine physics is that they are not real physics. To calculate physics using accurate equations would take far too long. So, game physics are simulations that can be computed quickly enough to produce a believable result.

If you need a specific result every time, you will want to stick with keyframed animation. If you are looking for randomness that adds to the impact of effects, then physics may be just the thing. Physics come in many useful forms. In first-person shooters, the player is required to disable enemies with projectiles of various types. In other genres, you may use them only for physically transforming objects to help move the story along, or, if the game is physics-based, such as marble madness–type games, they may be the star attraction.

Because any of these scenarios can enhance your games, you will be trying a little of each.

Physics Basics

Let's start by creating a new little scene for the preliminary tests. This will allow you to retain and revisit the basics whenever you wish.

1. Save the current scene.

2. Create a New Scene in the Scenes folder and name it **Physics Tests**.

3. Create a Plane object in the Scene view.

4. Set its y position to 0 and focus in on it.

5. Now create a cube in the middle of the plane and raise it a few meters.

6. Click Play and watch the cube.

Nothing happens. It turns out, the key ingredient for physics is a Rigidbody component. It is responsible for the object's reactions to other objects in the scene. The other objects must at least have a collider.

1. Stop Play mode and, from the Physics submenu, add a Rigidbody component to the cube.

2. Click Play and watch the cube.

This time, the cube falls to the plane.

3. Raise the cube higher and click Play again.

The cube falls again, but nothing more happens. You might think it should bounce a little when it is dropped from a greater height, but it doesn't. To change its behavior, you will have to add a Physics material. To access the physics materials, you will have to import the package if you haven't already done so.

1. From Assets, Import Package, select Physic Materials.

2. Import All.

Five premade Physic Materials are brought into the project. You can find them in the Standard Assets folder. You can also create your own from the Project view's right-click menu, Create, Physic Material. The Physic Material is added through Material parameter in the Collider component.

3. Stop Play mode and open the Box Collider component.

4. Click the browse icon to the right of the Material parameter.

5. Select the Bouncy material.

6. Click Play and watch the difference.

The cube looks like it may keep bouncing forever...
Let's test some of the Rigidbody's parameters.

7. While still in Play mode, set the Drag to about 5 when the cube is at its zenith.

This time, the cube slows as it falls and no longer bounces when it hits.

8. Restart Play mode and, this time, uncheck Gravity just before the cube hits the ground.

Gravity uses the value set in the PhysicsManager. The Physics Manager can be found in Edit ➤ Project Settings ▨ Physics. Of interest in the PhysicsManager are the sleep settings. When an object reaches the set values, it is put in sleep mode to conserve resources.

With no gravity, the cube continues up out of the scene.

1. Stop Play mode.

2. Change the collider's Material to Wood.

3. Set the Mass to 100 and click Play.

4. Stop Play mode.

5. Set the mass to 0.01 and click Play again.

The Mass does not affect the speed the object drops (just as Galileo predicted). To differentiate between a feather and a lump of lead, you will need to add Drag. It will, however, make a difference if the object is hit by another.

6. Stop Play mode and set the Mass back to 1 again.

7. Duplicate the cube and name it **Cube2.**

8. Move it down to the plane, then move it aside, so the first cube will hit it on the way down.

9. Try setting the grounded cube's Mass to 0.01, 1 and 100, to see how the two cubes react when you click Play for each setting.

10. Set the Mass back to 1.

You can restrict transforms through the Rigidbody. This can be useful for creating 2D platform jumpers where toppled obstacles should only tumble along one axis.

11. Try checking various axis constraints in the original cube's Constraints parameters.

So far, you've seen gravity, mass, friction (drag), and physics material in action. Next, you will try adding some forces and see what happens.

Forces

To move an object with physics, you can apply a Constant Force component. This component applies a constant force to the object it resides on.

1. Deactivate Cube for now.

2. Duplicate Cube2 and name it **Cube3**.

3. Move it away from Cube2 on the positive x direction (the direction the x axis points on the transform gizmo) about 2 or 3 meters.

4. From the Physics submenu, add a Constant Force component to Cube3.

5. Set the X Relative Force to **-20** to send it back toward Cube2.

6. Click Play.

The cube rolls over, then stops, because the force is pointing down as soon as it rolls over.

7. Change the collider's Material to Ice, so it won't get stuck and tip over.

8. Click Play.

This time, it pushes Cube2 off the plane. You can also keep it moving in the original direction using Force.

9. Set the collider's Material back to Wood.

10. Set Relative Force X back to **0** and Force X to **-20**.

11. Click Play.

The Force continues to push the cube in the X global direction, regardless of collision.

12. Set the Force to **-2** and click Play.

13. Under Constraints, check Z to prevent the cube from rolling over.

14. Increase the Force until it goes forward and gets stopped at Cube2.

15. Adjust the amount of Force to a positive number to reverse the direction.

The cube can now spin, but no longer rolls in its z axis.

To simulate wind in the scene, you will want to use Force for predictable results. If you need to add force to a projectile, you will use Relative Force, so the object goes forward from the direction it, or its parent, is pointing.

Torque is rotation. Let's do a couple of tests with it next.

1. Reactivate Cube and add a Constant Force component to it.

2. Set the Torque Y to **2,** and set the Mass to **100** again.

3. In the Rigidbody component, uncheck Use Gravity.

4. Click Play.

The cube starts slowly, then ramps up to spin nicely, without falling.

5. Set its Mass to **1**.

6. Slowly add Angular Drag to slow it down.

7. Stop Play mode and set the Torque Y back to **0**.

Joints

There are several joint components. Let's try a simple Hinge.

1. Duplicate Cube and name it **Board**.

2. Move it down and scale it thinner, so it looks like a board hanging from the lower edge on the positive X side.

3. Remove the Constant Force component.

4. Add a Hinge Joint component.

5. Drag Cube in as its Connecting Body.

6. In the Board's Rigidbody component, check Use Gravity.

7. Click Play.

The Cube, not using gravity, is affected by the weight of the board.

1. Select the Cube and check all the Constraints, except Y Rotation in the Rigidbody component.

2. Select the Board and, under Axis, change its X axis to **0** and its Z axis to **1**.

3. Under Anchor, adjust the Y value until the little orange marker in the Scene view is even with the bottom of Cube, about **0.5.**

4. Click Play.

Now the "hinge" is in the correct place and alignment.

5. Select the Cube and increase the Constant Force's Y Torque until the board starts moving out/up (Figure 11-5).

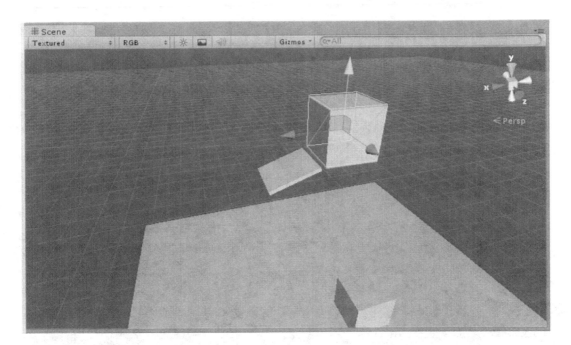

Figure 11-5. *The board flying out as the Cube spins*

6. Stop Play mode.

7. Select the Board and under Break Torque, set it to **3** and click Play again.

8. Select the Cube and increase the Constant Force's Y Torque until the board flies off.

9. Select the Board again.

The Hinge Joint component is removed when the joint breaks.

10. Stop Play mode and set the Break Torque back to Infinity by typing the word back in to the field.

Combining Physics and Keyframe Animation

If you spent any time experimenting to get the rotation of the box just right, you will have realized that using Physics to animate the Cube was painful. It also uses more overhead than is necessary. Sometimes you may be better off using keyframed or scripted animation. Either way, you should also use a Rigidbody, but set to Is Kinematic. Without the Rigidbody, animated objects are checked more often for interactions with physics operations.

1. Select Cube and in its Physics component, set it to Is Kinematic.

2. Disable the Constant Force component.

3. Drag the SimpleRotate script from the MyScripts folder onto the Cube.

4. Click Play.

The cube rotates at a predictable rate, and the board hinges just as before.

Cloth

One of the very cool features in Unity is Cloth. It is extremely easy to set up and use, so it is worth a quick look. You will be using it later in the game.

1. Exit Play mode.

2. From the GameObject menu, Create Other, select Cloth.

It comes in parallel to the ground.

3. Scale it so it is about 0.22×0.22×0.22 and drag it slightly above the Cube.

4. Click Play, speed up the rotation, and watch the result (Figure 11-6).

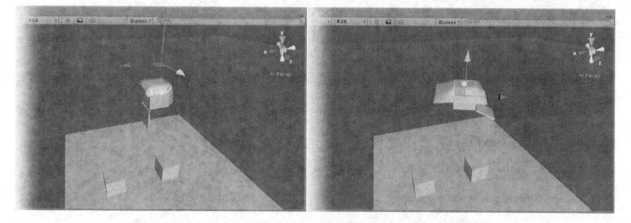

Figure 11-6. *The cloth dropping onto the cube and then sliding off as the cube spins*

The cloth eventually flies off.

1. Stop Play mode.

2. Rotate the cloth, so it is vertical.

3. Scale it in and move it, so the top edge intersects with the Cube's lower edge on the opposite side as the Board.

4. Open Attached Colliders and set the Size to **1**.

5. Open the new Element 0 and drag Cube into the Collider field.

6. Click Play and watch the cube spin the cloth around (Figure 11-7).

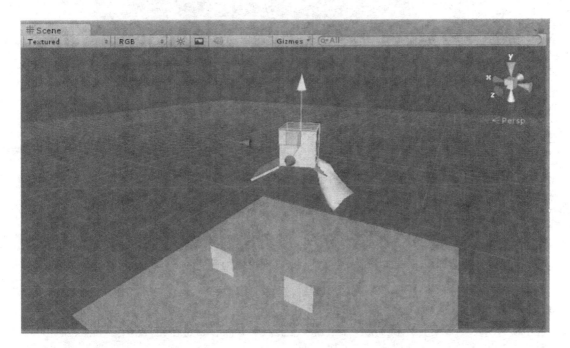

Figure 11-7. *The cloth attached to the Cube, flaring out as the cube spins*

7. Select the Cube and increase the rotation speed until the cloth flies out just like the board.

You've probably noticed that the cloth is single-sided. To use it in a real scene, you might need to use a double-sided shader, if it is not against another surface.

To have the cloth affected by wind, you will have to use the Interactive Cloth component's External Acceleration.

1. Set External Acceleration X to about **-6**.

2. Select the Cube and disable the SimpleRotate script.

3. Click Play.

4. Once the cloth settles down, try adding some Random Acceleration to it.

Let's see what happens if all of the top vertices do not intersect the Cube.

5. Stop Play mode.

6. Drag the cloth sideways (Z direction), so it is halfway off the Cube (Figure 11-8).

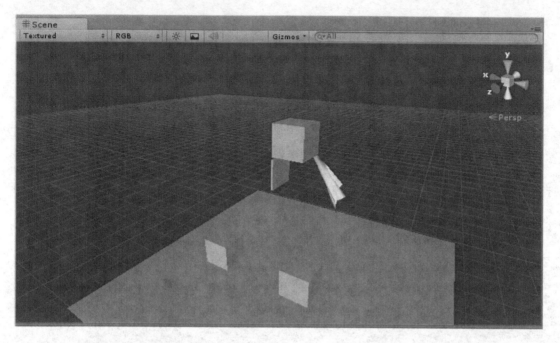

Figure 11-8. *The cloth attached to the Cube with a single collider*

7. Click Play.

The loose end folds over and drops. If you added a second Attached Collider to hold that end up, the cloth would sag slightly between the two.

Just like the Hinge Joint, the Interactive Cloth can also be torn. Feel free to experiment with some of the other parameters.

Projectiles

Now that you've had a look at some of the basics of physics, it's time to try some typical uses that require scripting. Gravity may be free with rigid bodies, but pretty much everything else needs to be scripted.

In addition to projectiles, you will be introduced to the concept of instantiation. Instantiation is more than just creating an object on the fly. With the action objects, you activated and deactivated the objects, as needed, throughout the game play. With instantiation, the objects are not in the Hierarchy view or scene until needed and, typically, are destroyed and taken back out of the scene and Hierarchy view when you are finished with them.

To perform the instantiation, a prefab must exist in the Project view first. The prefab, being a GameObject, could be as simple as a mesh object or as complex as a character with scripts, child objects, specials effects, and anything else it needs to be spawned into the scene and ready to go.

You will start with a simple projectile. Even if your goal is not to make first-person shooters, a lot of adventure games include an entertaining segment where the player needs to use projectiles to move the game forward. As a game designer, your job will be to keep the task easy enough that even the least dexterous player will have success with it.

Let's head back to the Interactionscene.

1. Save the Physics Tests scene and save the project, if you haven't done so recently.

2. Open the Interaction scene.

3. Create a new script in the Adventure Scripts folder and name it **Projectile**.

4. Add the following variable:

```
var projectile : GameObject; // the object to instantiate
```

The variable is of type GameObject, because you'll eventually need access to more than just its transforms.

5. In the Update function, add the following:

```
if (Input.GetButton ("Fire1")) { // if the Fire1 button (default is ctrl) is pressed
    Activate(); // do whatever the fire button controls
}
```

The code starts in the Update function, because the engine needs to constantly check to see if the player has pressed the fire button. You've used several virtual buttons for navigating already. If you check the Input Manager (Edit ➤ Project Settings ➤ Input), you will see that the left Ctrl key and mouse button 0 (the left button) are mapped to "fire1." Because you are using the left mouse button for picking, you will need to remove the left mouse option from the Input manager.

6. From the Edit menu, select Project Settings and choose Input.

7. Open Fire1 and delete mouse 0.

8. Create a function to handle the action:

```
function Activate () {
    // create a clone of the projectile at the location & orientation of the script's parent
    var clone : GameObject = Instantiate (projectile, transform.position, transform.rotation);
}
```

This line creates a variable named clone, of type GameObject, and Instantiates, or creates a new copy of the object you will load into the projectile variable. And it does it at the location and orientation of the object this script is sitting on, transform.position and transform.rotation. It won't go anywhere yet, but the specified gameObject will be created.

You are probably wondering why you don't just put the Instantiate code directly into the if clause in the Update function. At this early stage, you certainly could. But later on, you will discover that you will require more control. A ray gun might need to be active as long as the fire button or key is pressed, but a large projectile such as the cannonball should be forced to never fire more than a certain number per second. The player will just mash the key or button down, so you will have to do the checking. Another scenario is a flashlight, where the light is toggled on and off the first time the button or key down happens.

9. Save the script.

Next, you have to decide where to put the new script. You could put it directly on the First Person Controller, but that would make it hard to position, so, instead, you will create a parent object to hold any gear your player may need to handle. Because the aim is a requirement, the holder object will have to be parented to the Main Camera.

1. Select the main camera and Focus in on it.

2. Create an empty gameObject and name it **Gear Handler**.

3. Drag it onto the main camera.

4. Now create a proxy weapon from a cube to give the projectile a place to be instantiated from.

5. Name it **Proxy Weapon** and scale it to about **0.15×0.15×1**.

6. Disable its Box Collider.

You will have to rotate it to match the direction of the First Person Controller. In Unity, since Y is up, Z is considered to be pointing "forward."

7. Select the First Person Controller and use Align View to Selected.

8. Select the Proxy Weapon and use Align With View.

9. Move the Proxy Weapon up and forward until you can see it in the scene (Figure 11-9).

Figure 11-9. *The Proxy Weapon, as seen from the First Person Controller*

10. Put the Projectile script on the Proxy Weapon object.

11. Drop the Proxy Weapon object onto the Gear Handler in the Hierarchy.

Now you'll need a projectile.

1. Create a Sphere.

Because the Instantiate code tells it where to be created, it doesn't matter where you create it. To create a prefab, you first have to build it in the scene. Once it is finished and assigned to a new prefab, it is generally deleted from the scene.

2. Scale it down to about **0.25** and name it **Cannonball**.

3. Add a Rigidbody component to it.

Now you will turn it into a prefab.

4. Select the Adventure Prefabs folder in the Project view.

5. From the right-click menu, Create, select Prefab.

6. Name the new prefab **Cannonball** also.

Note that the icon is currently a white cube.

7. Drag the Cannonball object from the Hierarchy view onto the empty Prefab.

The icon turns light blue to indicate it is no longer empty.

Now that you have created the prefab, you can delete it from the scene. It is part of the project and, unlike an object that only exists in a single level, the prefab can be instantiated anytime, anywhere. If you ever have to edit it, you can easily drag the prefab back into the scene.

8. Delete the Cannonball from the Hierarchy view.

Now that you've got a prefab, you can assign it to the projectile parameter in the Projectile component.

1. Select the Proxy Weapon.

2. Drag the Cannonball prefab onto its Projectile parameter from the Project view.

Now you are ready to test the instantiation.

3. Save the scene and save the project.

4. Focus in on the First Person Controller in the Scene view.

5. Click Play and press either the left Ctrl key or the left mouse button a few times (Figure 11-10).

Figure 11-10. Lots of "cannonballs" instantiated in the scene

The spheres are instantiated in the middle of the Proxy Weapon—right at its pivot point. So far, gravity and collision with each other are the only things at work on the cannonballs, but if you watch the Hierarchy you can see there are lots of cannonball clones being created. Because they are not leaving the scene, you may quickly kill the frame rate or even freeze the game.

Another thing that is probably happening is that the First Person Controller is being moved around. From your earlier experiments, you know that an object must have a Rigidbody attached to it to be affected by other rigid bodies. But if you inspect the First Person Controller, you will find it doesn't have a rigid body.

It turns out, the Rigidbody code is already embedded in the Character Controller component. Knowing that, you can now understand how the First Person Controller is able to react to the shape of the terrain, be stopped by objects with colliders and other physical-based events. Taking it one step further, you know the First Person Controller always remains upright, no matter the slope of the terrain. This indicates that the equivalent of Freeze Rotation for x and y is probably active on the Character Controller.

Getting back to the projectiles, you've probably figured out that the cannonballs are going to require a physics Force to get them under way.

In the Constant Force components, you adjusted the force to affect the speed of the rigid body. The next logical step is to create a variable, so you can easily adjust the speed in the script.

1. Open the Projectile script.

2. Add the following variable:

    ```
    var speed : float = 10.0; // default speed
    ```

3. Inside the Activate function, below the Instantiate line, add:

    ```
    // add some force to send the projectile off in its forward direction
    clone.rigidbody.velocity = transform.TransformDirection(Vector3 (0,0,speed));
    ```

Because the Z direction is considered "forward" in Unity space, you could also use:

```
clone.rigibody.velocity = transform.forward * speed;
```

The TransformDirection function or method sets the clone's velocity, through its rigid body, to speed, sending it off in the forward or Z direction. If speed were put in the middle of the Vector3 value, it would send it upward on its Y direction.

4. Save the script.

5. Click Play and give the firing mechanism a quick try.

Now the projectiles go shooting out in the forward direction, unless they've collided with something else, which right now is most of the time.

Another useful bit of script is instructions that tell the projectile to ignore the collider of its parent. In this case, you deactivated the Proxy Weapon's collider, but if you wanted to prevent it from going through a wall before the First Person Controller was stopped, you would have to keep it active.

6. Select the Proxy Weapon and activate its collider.

7. Click Play and fire the projectile a few times.

The scene quickly bogs down.

8. In the Projectile script, add the following below the velocity line:

    ```
    // ignore the collider on the object the script is on
    Physics.IgnoreCollision(clone.collider, transform. collider);
    ```

9. Save the script.

Collision with the Proxy Weapon is no longer calculated, and the collider is still active. Before you test, let's fix one more issue by fine-tuning the firing mechanism. To control the fire rate, you will once again have to create a timer. You will also need a variable for the firing rate.

1. In the Projectile script, create a couple of new variables as follows:

```
var activateRate : float = 0.5;        // how often to trigger the action
internal var nextActivationTime : float; // target time
```

2. In the Update function's if clause, add the time condition, so it is as follows:

```
// if the Fire1 button (default is left ctrl) is pressed and the alloted time has passed
if (Input.GetButton ("Fire1") && Time.time > nextActivationTime) {
```

As soon as the condition is met, you will have to reset the timer. As usual, the time you want for the suppression, activateRate, is added to the elapsed time, Time.time, since the game was started.

3. Above the Activate() line, add the following:

```
nextActivationTime = Time.time + activateRate; // reset the timer
```

4. Save the script

5. Click Play and test the firing mechanism by holding down the left Ctrl key.

Without the sphere-to-sphere collision, the speed looks rather paltry. The gravity pulling the projectile down is also more apparent. If you are shooting rockets, you might want to consider turning off Use Gravity.

6. Stop Play mode.

7. Increase the speed in both the script and the component to about **20**.

8. Save the script, click Play, and try shooting again.

The speed is better.

9. Select the Cannonball prefab in the Hierarchy view and uncheck Use Gravity.

10. Try a few shots.

The spheres continue on into the scene and head off into the hills (Figure 11-11).

Figure 11-11. *The cannonballs with no gravity*

11. Recheck Use Gravity.

Because the prefab is in the Project view, the change in settings won't be carried over after you stop Play mode, so it must be done manually.

Let's look at another issue you may have discovered.

1. Try shooting at the test objects in the scene, specifically the ChestBase.

Occasionally, you may see the projectile go through the chest. What happens is the object passes completely through the thin walls of the chest base's Mesh Collider between one frame and the next when collision is tested. The default Collision Detection for Rigidbodies is Discreet. To get it to check more often for just the projectile, you can use Continuous.

2. Select the Cannonball in the Project view.

3. Change its Collision Detection to Continuous.

4. Click Play and shoot the chest.

This time the cannonballs all hit and bounce.

As you probably guessed, Continuous uses a lot more resources than the default Discreet, but because the weapon is only fired intermittently, it shouldn't pose a problem. For more on physics and how it is calculated in game, be sure to check the documentation.

Finally, let's take a look at Instantiate's counterpart, Destroy. If you are to trigger an explosion when and where the cannonball hit something (more like a grenade behavior), you would want the projectile to go out of the scene shortly after the hit. To kill off an object permanently, you would use Destroy on collision.

Because the cannonball is not exploding, you can set a timer in the Start function to destroy it after a set amount of time.

1.   Create a new script in the Adventure Scripts folder.

2.   Name it **Terminator**.

3.   Add a variable for life:

```
var life : float = 5.0; // time before destroying the object
```

4.   In the Start function, add the following:

```
// wait for life seconds before destroying the object the script is on
yield new WaitForSeconds(life);
Destroy(this.gameObject);
```

5.   Save the script.

6.   Drag the script onto the Cannonball prefab in the Project view.

Because the timer only starts when the object is instantiated, you can use simple pause created by the yield's WaitForSeconds function.

7.   Click Play and shoot off a few rounds.

Now the cannonballs wink out of existence in both the scene and the Hierarchy view after the required 5 seconds. Many projectiles, when accompanied by an explosion, are destroyed on their first collision, but that takes a bit more code.

With some very basic projectile functionality covered, let's turn off the Proxy Weapon for now and create something that you will be using later in the game.

8.   Select the Proxy Weapon and Deactivate it.

RockFall

You've already created a simple prefab, the cannonball. Let's take a minute to look up Instantiate in the Scripting reference. For the cannonball, you used the first variation. It is instantiated at the transform of the object the script calling it is on.

If you wanted to do something like instantiate a Genie in a puff of smoke in a fixed position, you'd leave off the position and rotation arguments, and the instance would be created using the prefab's original transforms—from when it was set up in the scene. In this case, the last form of instantiate would be the one you will want to use. Let's try that with something more down to earth, like a rock.

Because the code is already written for you in the scripting reference, you may as well trigger the instantiation with OnTriggerEnter.

1.   Create a Cube near the test objects.

2.   Check Is Trigger on its Collider component.

3.   Name it **Rock Zone**.

4.   Scale the cube to about **2×2×3**.

5.   Disable the Mesh Renderer.

6.   Create a new script in the Adventure Scripts folder.

7. Name it **Rocks**.

8. Open it in the script editor and copy and paste the sample code from the docs.

```
// Instantiates prefab when any rigid body enters the trigger.
// It preserves the prefab's original position and rotation.
var prefab : Transform;

function OnTriggerEnter () {

        Instantiate (prefab);

}
```

9. Save the script.

10. Drag it onto the **Rock Zone** GameObject.

Next, you'll need a rock. There's one in the animation test objects, but it already has an animation on it. Let's use the rock that came in with the ExtraTerrain Objects instead.

As you saw earlier, the usual procedure for creating a prefab is the following:

- Create an object in the scene.

- Create a new prefab in the Project view.

- Drag the object from the Hierarchy view onto the prefab.

- Delete the original from the scene.

Let's put it into practice.

1. Locate the rock in the ExtraTerrainAssets folder.

2. Position it near the First Person Controller and scale it to about **0.25**.

3. Create a new prefab in the Project view in the Adventure Prefabs folder and drag the rock into it.

The prefab icon turns blue.

In case you noticed, the object's name in the Hierarchy view was already blue, because it is an instance of an asset already in the Project view.

4. To avoid confusion, let's name this one **Rock Prefab**.

Your prefab is ready to use.

5. In the Hierarchy view, delete the rock from the scene.

6. Next, assign the Rock Prefab to the prefab parameter of the Rock Zone.

7. Click Play and move the First Person Controller into the Rock Zone.

The rock appears right where you placed it in the scene (Figure 11-12).

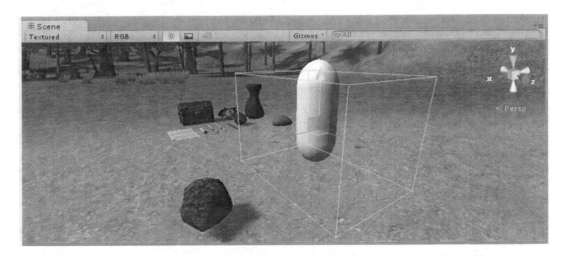

Figure 11-12. *The Rock instantiated when the First Person Controller intersects the Rock Zone*

But what if you wanted the prefab to be instantiated in a different position? Simple, move it and update the prefab.

8. Drag the rock prefab into the Hierarchy view.

It appears in the scene, right where you originally put it.

9. In the Scene view, move it off to the side a bit.

Now you will need to update the prefab to register the transform change.

1. At the top of the Inspector, on the prefab line, click Apply.

2. Delete the moved rock from the scene.

3. Click Play and drive the rock into the zone.

4. It is instantiated in the new position.

5. Exit Play mode.

If you wanted to include several rocks in the prefab, you could put them all in an empty GameObject and drag that back onto the prefab; using that method gives a warning about overwriting but allows you to make more serious changes to an existing prefab.

As an added benefit, once an object or group of objects has been turned into a prefab, you can export the prefab as a Unity Package.

Let's make a Unity Package from the Rock Prefab after making a few improvements.

1. Select the rock prefab in the Project view.

2. Add a Mesh Collider.

3. Check Convex.

This won't be as accurate as the full Mesh Collider, but it will use less resources to calculate while giving better results than a simple sphere collider.

4. Select Wood for the Physics Material.

5. Next, add a Rigidbody component.

411

From the right-click menu, select Export Package and Export (Figure 11-13).

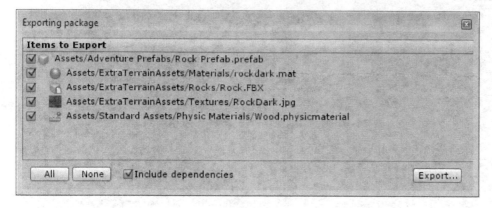

Figure 11-13. *The Rock's various associated assets also being exported*

6. Give it a name, **SingleRock**, and save it somewhere outside of the project folder.

You've just made your first Unity package, SingleRock.unitypackage. Unity packages retain relationships, preserve materials and shaders, scripts, and various other non-project-based elements. To test it, you can change your original rock prefab.

1. Select the Rock Prefab.

2. Drag it into the Hierarchy view.

3. In Scene view, change its orientation and one of its scale dimensions.

4. Move it up above the ground a couple of meters in the Scene view. Make sure it is not above the Rock Zone.

5. Create a new Prefab and name it and the scene rock **Rock1**.

6. Drag the new configuration of the rock onto the new prefab.

7. Click Play and watch it drop and settle.

8. Delete the original Rock Prefab from the Project view.

Now let's import the package you just saved out.

9. From the Assets menu, Import Package, select Custom Package.

10. Locate your SingleRock package and import it.

The Import dialog shows only the name of the prefab; if you had imported it to an empty scene, all of the meshes, textures, scripts, etc., would have appeared as well.

If you had altered the original Rock Prefab and left it in the scene, importing would have caused it to revert to the imported version.

11. Drag the Rock Prefab into the Hierarchy view, to assure yourself it is the same as when you exported it.

Introducing Randomness

One of the great things about games is never knowing what to expect. Out of a number of possibilities, only one will be chosen to occur at any given time. In the next part of creating the rockfall, you will use the Random function, to determine which of four different rocks to drop into the scene.

For that, you will need a few more rocks.

1. Create two more new rock prefabs, **Rock2** and **Rock3**, using scale and rotation to make them different from the first two.

2. Rename the Rock Prefab to **Rock0** in the Project view.

3. Move all of the rocks up to about the same spot as Rock1 and Update all of the prefabs.

4. Delete all of the new rocks from the scene.

5. Close the Rocks script.

6. Rename it in the Project view to **Rockfall**.

And, yes, you could also rename it in the script editor, but then the original would still be around.

1. Open it again.

2. Replace `var prefab : Transform` with the following to hold the various Rocks:

```
var rocks : GameObject[];  // create an array to hold the rocks
```

Because the array will be loaded in the Inspector, and you may decide you want to create more than four different rocks, you will want another variable to keep track of the number of elements in the array.

3. Create another variable to hold the length of the array:

```
internal var arrayLength : int; // var to hold number of elements in the array
```

4. Create a Start function and assign the number of elements:

```
function Start () {
    arrayLength = rocks.length; // number of elements in the array
}
```

5. Change the Instantiate line to:

```
Instantiate (rocks[0]);
```

You will start by testing just the Element 0 rock.

6. Save the script.

7. Select the Rock Zone object in the Hierarchy view and set the Rock array Size to **4**.

8. Load each of the rock prefabs into the elements.

9. Click Play and drive the First Person Controller back and forth to drop the rock over and over.

The basics are working, so it's time to add randomness.

1. Change the Instantiate line to:

```
// get a random number between 0 and the length of the array
var num = Random.Range(0, arrayLength);
//instanciate that element
Instantiate (rocks[num]);
```

Random.Range is interesting. With integers, it is exclusive of the second number. So a range of 0 to 4 means it could be 0,1,2 and 3. This works out well, considering arrays always start at Element 0.

With floats, 0.0–4.0 means it could be anything between and including the two range numbers.

2. Save the script.

3. Click Play and drive the First Person Controller back and forth to watch the randomly selected rocks fall.

4. Better yet, temporarily enable the Proxy Weapon and shoot the cannonballs into the Rock Zone.

Since the cannonballs have rigid bodies, they also can trigger the rockfall.

Even shooting to trigger is tedious. Let's try a self-perpetuating trigger. You may need to drag one of the rocks into the Hierarchy view to see the instantiation point.

5. Move the Rock Zone beneath the instantiation point for the rocks.

6. Click Play and trigger the first rock.

After one outside hit or collision, the falling rocks will become the triggers. Eventually, the ensuing rock pile should totally block the zone. Unfortunately, the collision calculations will bring your machine to a crawl, so a clever addition to the rock prefabs will be a script that removes the Rigidbody component after a certain amount of time. You can easily repurpose the Terminator script for that usage.

1. Exit Play mode.

2. Select the Terminator script.

3. Duplicate it and name the clone **KillPhysics**.

4. Change Destroy(this.gameObject) to:

```
Destroy(this.rigidbody);
```

5. Change the comments to match.

6. Save the script.

7. Add it to each of the four rock prefabs.

8. Click Play and initialize the rockfall.

9. This time, select clones in the Hierarchy view and watch as their Rigidbody component is removed.

Not only does the frame rate stay reasonable this time, the rock pile also shuts itself off … eventually (Figure 11-14).

Figure 11-14. *The self-perpetuating rockfall*

For the game, you'll need a better way to switch off the rocks, to enable you to drop the crystal on top of the pile, so it tumbles down at the feet of the player. In the Rockfall script, you can start a yield timer that will destroy the RockZone and turn on the crystal by telling it to transition to its state 1 (state 0 being out of scene).

Finding the Crystal

Before setting up the action scripts, let's get the functionality working.

1. Select the Crystal.

2. Add a Rigidbody component to it.

3. Position it above the rocks starting position (drag one of the prefabs temporarily into the scene, if necessary).

4. Click Play and make sure it drops.

5. Exit Play mode and deactivate it.

Unlike the projectiles, where you could start the timer as soon as they got instantiated from the Start function, you will have to start this timer after the first rock has been dropped. To prevent the timer from being started each time a new rock is dropped, you will have to add a flag that tracks the state of the timer.

1. Open the RockFall script.

2. Add the following variables:

```
var prize : GameObject;              // the crystal
var pileTime : float = 10.0;         // time to let rocks drop
var startTimer : boolean = false;    // flag for timer after first rock drop
```

3. In the OnTriggerEnter function, add the following after the Instantiate line:

```
if(!startTimer) DropPrize ();        // start the timer function
```

4. Create the function to handle the end scenario:

```
function DropPrize () {

}
```

5. In it, clear the flag and start the timer:

```
startTimer = true;                           // timer running
yield new WaitForSeconds(pileTime + 0.5);    // allow extra to let rocks settle
```

6. Then cue the prize:

```
//activate prize
prize.SetActive(true);
```

You can activate the object, because it has already been identified before the game starts.

7. And, finally, destroy the Rock Zone after a pause:

```
yield;                          // wait a frame
Destroy(this.gameObject);       // terminate the Rock Zone object
```

8. Save the script.

9. Assign the Crystal as the Prize to the Rock Zone object.

10. Deactivate the Crystal.

11. Click Play, wait a bit, and then trigger the rockfall.

After 10 seconds, the rocks stop, and the crystal falls among them (Figure 11-15).

Figure 11-15. *The Crystal in its final resting place on the rockpile*

Now let's set up the crystal's action object scripts and data.

1. Add an Interactor script.

The crystal has two states, 0, not in scene, and 1, in scene. Like the Pollen Ball, the Crystal doesn't have a keyframe animation.

2. Copy the Interactor component from the Pollen ball and paste its values onto the Crystal.

3. Change the text as per the State Management PDF.

4. Change the Location to **0** for Element 0 and **1** for Element 1.

5. Set the Initial state to **0**.

6. Set the Size of Lookup State 1 to **1**.

7. Fill them out as follows:

Lookup State 1, Element 0: default,0
At state 0, out of scene, the rockfall will tell the Crystal to transition to state 1, in scene. It will do so manually (it's not processed through the ProcessObject), because that's the only thing that transition does, but it may help to see it in the Object Lookup component, even if the data is never used. When the Player picks it from state 1, in scene, it will go out of scene, state 0.

8. And, at the top of the Inspector, tag the Crystal as an ActionObject.

9. Because the two action scripts are now controlling its visibility, reactivate it in the Inspector.

And make a last change to the Rockfall script, by manually changing the Crystal's state to 1, in scene.

10.　Below the `prize.SetActive(true)` line, add the following:

```
prize.GetComponent(Interactor).currentState = 1; // manually change its state
```

11.　Save the script.

12.　Click Play, trigger the rocks, then pick up the crystal.

The crystal goes out of scene with the player pick (if it is in picking range).

13.　Save the scene and save the project.

Particle Systems

A big part of interactive games, regardless of genre, is particle systems. Particle systems make up most of the eye candy in a game and enhance the impact of animations and other events.

One of the unique things about particle systems is that they usually can't be imported from regular 3D authoring applications such as Max or Maya. They generally have to be developed almost exclusively in the game engine.

Unity has a complex and powerful system for creating and combining particles to give you all sorts of special effects. You will become more familiar with them as you set up a few useful ones for the game and perform the usual experiments.

Even though you will be creating particles with the newer Shuriken particle system, there are plenty of useful ready-made particle prefabs to be found in the legacy particles package. Importing it also brings lots of useful textures. If you don't see the Particles folder in the Standard Assets folder, you will have to import the package.

1.　From Assets, Import Assets, select Particles.

2.　Import.

The particle system prefabs can be found in the Standard Assets folder.

Let's create a new scene for a few particle system experiments. If you aren't familiar with particle systems, now is a good time to see a few of the possibilities.

1.　Create a New Scene and save it as **Particle Tests**.

2.　From the Standard Assets folder, open the Particles folder and the Dust folder.

3.　Drag Dust Storm into the Scene view and position the view so you have a good view of the particles.

While the particles are selected, they animate in both the Scene view and the Game view. The legacy particles, unfortunately, show their geometry—generally, a flat, two triangle plane—in the Scene view while active, so you will have to position the camera to watch them in the Game view.

4.　Use Align with View to position the Main Camera, so you can see the particles in the Game view.

The dust particles could be useful while the rocks are falling…
Let's look at Flame from the Fire folder.

5.　Drag Flame into the scene and adjust the camera for a good view of it in the Game view.

6.　Now open the Flame group in the Hierarchy view.

It contains three particle systems and a light source.

Create a cube and drag it near the flame, so that you can see the light affecting it (Figure 11-16).

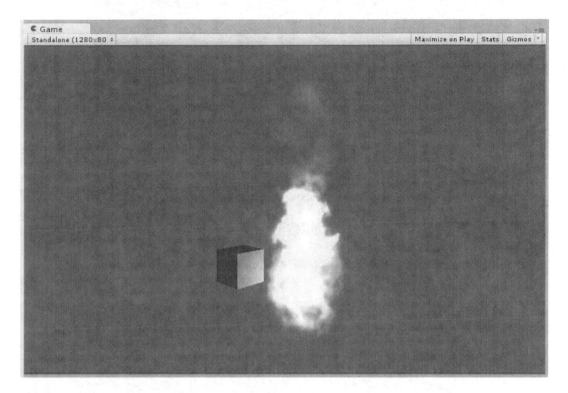

Figure 11-16. *The Flame group's light source enhancing the particle systems*

You will be building your own version of the flame in Shuriken a little later on.

1. From legacy particles, drag Sparks into the scene.

2. Position them so you can see them in the Game view.

3. While the others were continuous, the sparks come in bursts and are useful for times when a projectile hits something.

4. Another version of sparks can be found in the Misc. folder—try those as well.

5. And, finally, try the Soap Bubbles—also found in the Misc folder.

If you haven't already, go ahead and try Light Snow, Fireworks, and anything else that sounds interesting (Figure 11-17).

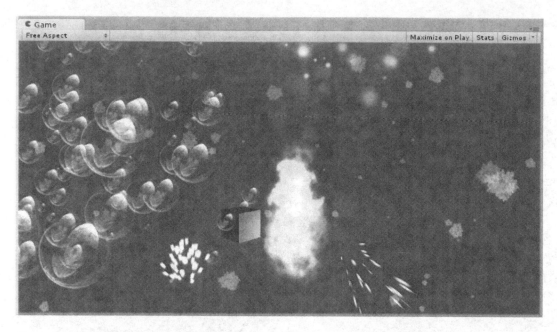

Figure 11-17. Several Legacy particle systems

In looking at the various prefabs, you can see several things at work (aside from the obvious texture map differences). Particles can be affected by gravity, have different velocities and life spans, and be emitted from a single spot or across a large area. They can vary in size throughout their lives, or they can start one size and grow or shrink during their lifetimes. Their opacities can vary, and they can be made additive to produce bright fire-like effects. And these are just a few of their parameters!

Obviously, one could easily write an entire book on particle systems, so you will only be touching on the more commonly used features. Hopefully, that will give you a good basis for hours of experimenting on your own. Let's get started.

Shuriken Basics

1. Deactivate all of the particle systems and the cube you added to the new scene.

2. From GameObjects, Create Other, select Particle System.

Just as with the legacy particles, it plays while it is selected. Unlike the legacy particles, the geometry's edges are not shown. You also get a small dialog in the Scene view.

It happily spews particles at a casual speed.

1. Deselect the particle system in the Hierarchy view.

The particles are no longer active.

Because you won't need the Game window for a while, you can switch to Wide layout.

2. From 2×3, Layout, above the Inspector, switch to the Wide layout.

3. Focus back in to the particle system by double-clicking it in the Hierarchy view.

4. Select them again.

The particles start flowing again, and the dialog shows up again.
You can scrub through the time line in the dialog.

5. Click to the left of the Playback Time and try dragging back and forth.

The animation can be made to go forward or backward.

6. Set the Playback speed to **0.5**.

The particles slow to half speed. It is worth noting that this is just an editor playback feature; it doesn't change any of the actual parameters.

7. Click Stop in the Particle Effect dialog, then deselect the particles.

The particles are no longer showing in the Scene view.

Particle Types

There are basically two types of particles in a scene: those that are happening throughout, such as a fountain, and those that are instantiated during runtime and have a short life span, such as an explosion or the sparks you saw.

To see how the finite life span ones behave, you can use Stop and Simulate. It's time to delve into the Inspector and see what some of the parameters do.

1. Select the particle system again, and, in the Inspector, uncheck **Looping**.

If the Playback time is greater than the **Duration** (5 seconds, the default), the particles stop emitting immediately. If not, they continue until the Duration is reached.

2. Click Stop, then Simulate.

This time, the particles stop after the duration time is met.

3. Click Stop.

Let's look at a few more of the basic parameters.
Prewarm starts the particles fully into the cycle, so things such as waterfalls and chimney smoke are already going when the scene starts.

4. Check Looping again and Prewarm, then, in the Scene view dialog, Simulate.

The particles are already fully under way.

5. Click Stop.

Start Delay is a built-in pause before the particles start up. This is useful when you are combining several particle systems to make complex Particle Effects—Unity's term for several particles that are used together, such as the Flame prefab. In an explosion, for example, you wouldn't want the smoke to start until the pyrotechnics were nearly finished.
Start Lifetime is the default life of each individual particle.

6. Click Simulate and try to change the Start Lifetime to see what happens.

Start Lifetime, in addition to the next four parameters, lets you add variation through the little right-hand drop-downs.

7. Click the small down arrow to the far right of Start Lifetime.

You get a choice of four options (Figure 11-18).

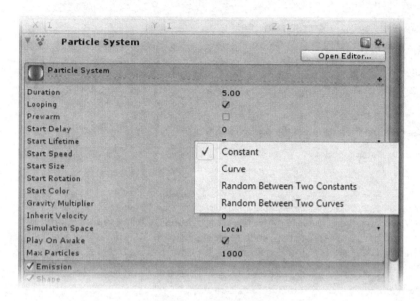

Figure 11-18. *Control options for the Start Lifetime*

8.   Select Random Between Two Constants.

9.   Set the numbers to **3** and **3,** to get a feel for where they die/disappear.

10.   Now set the first number to **0** and watch some of them pop out sooner.

Start Color offers a few different choices.

1.   Click its drop-down arrow and select Gradient.

Nothing happens.

2.   Double-click the white color swatch to open the Gradient Editor.

The top markers control the opacity, and the bottom markers control the color.

3.   Select the top right marker.

4.   Set the Alpha slider to **0**.

The effect may be difficult to figure out.

5.   Uncheck Looping, then click Stop, then Simulate in the Scene view.

This time it is obvious that the opacity fade occurs over the Duration of the particle system (Figure 11-19).

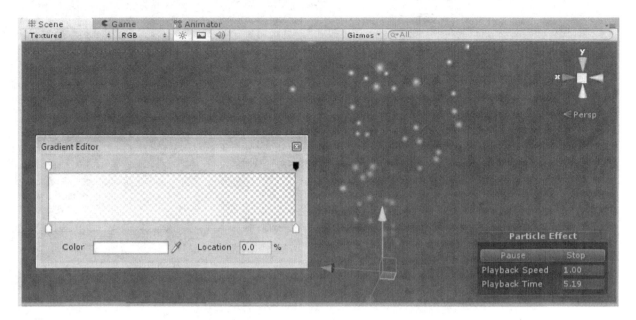

Figure 11-19. *Start Color gradient with Alpha adjusted*

6. Open the color Gradient Editor again and set the top right marker back to **255**.

7. Select the lower left marker and click the smaller color swatch to open the regular Color dialog.

8. Change the color to **red**.

9. Select the lower right marker and change it to **green**.

10. Right-click midway between the two, below the color swatch, to create a new marker.

11. Set it to **yellow**.

12. Click Simulate and watch the results.

As expected, the particles start out red, become yellow, and finish green (Figure 11-20).

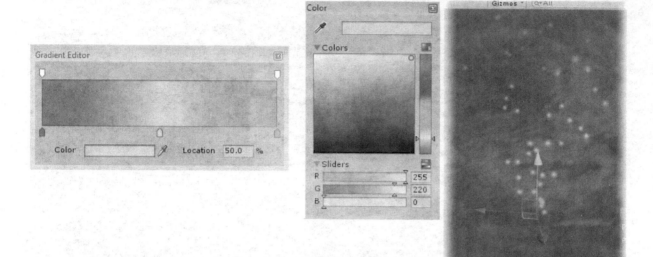

Figure 11-20. *Start Color gradient with Color adjusted*

1. Turn Looping back on and set the color back to Color (constant).

2. While the particles are being Simulated, adjust the **Gravity Multiplier** between -5 and 5.

The particles go up quicker with the negative numbers and head downward with the positive numbers.

Inherit Velocity will determine what happens when the emitter is transformed. At 0, the particles ignore the transform. To see this one work, you would have to add a script to transform it and observe it during Play mode. Make sure to use the local coordinate system.

Simulation Space determines whether the particles are emitted in local space or world space. For something that moves around like a fire hose, you'd want to use local space.

3. Set the Gravity Multiplier back to **0** and set Simulation Space to **Local**.

4. Rotate the Particle system in the Scene view and observe the particle direction as you turn it.

5. Put the particles upright again.

Play On Awake is just like the audio component—the particles start up as soon as the scene starts, or, if they are on a prefab, as soon as the object is instantiated.

Max Particles limits the number of live particles that will be on screen at any given time. When reached, the particle system will quit emitting until the old ones start dying off.

6. Set the Max Particles to **2**.

A new replacement for each of the particles is only made when one of the existing ones dies.

7. Set the Max Particles to **1000**.

8. Save the scene.

Shuriken Modules

Below the regular parameters are several modules where you can do all sorts of things to customize the particles even more.

You may as well create a few of the particle systems you will need for the game as you explore the modules.

Pouring Particles

With the change from the 2×3 layout, the Project view was changed to the Two Columns Layout. You can use the slider at the lower right to change the icon size.

1. Select the Scenes folder in the left column.

2. Choose the Interaction scene from the second column and load it.

The Scene view remains focused on its previous target.
Let's switch back to 2×3, so that you will have instant access to both Scene and Game views.

3. From the layout drop-down, currently showing Wide, select 2×3.

4. Change back to the single column layout by right clicking the Project tab label and selecting One Column Layout if you wish.

Feel free to use the layout of your choice. The images and instruction in this book will assume the One Column Layout for the most part, the differences will be minor.

5. Focus back in on the Flower in the Scene view.

In the game, the ugly flower will be installed in its own little shrine, so you will need to reduce its size before you introduce the vial of restorative elixir.

1. Select the Flower from the Animations test folder in the Project view.

2. In the Model section of the Inspector, change its Scale Factor to **0.0075** and click Apply.

3. Reduce the scene Flower's collider to fit.

4. From the Action Objects folder, select the AnimatedVial.

5. Set its Scale Factor to **0.0025**.

6. In the Animations section, select Take001 and rename it to **pour elixir**.

7. Next to the warning message, let it Clamp Range.

8. Drag the time indicator in the Preview window to see the animation.

9. Click Apply.

10. Drag the AnimatedVial from the Project view into the Hierarchy view.

11. Position it over the flower base, about 1 and 1/2 times its height above the ground.

As a Generic rig, it automatically gets an Animator component. You won't be using that one.

12. Select the Animated Vial in the Project view and change its Animation Type to Legacy.

13. Click Apply.

The Animator component is replaced with an Animation component, and the clip is ready to play. Click Play and watch the animation (Figure 11-21).

Figure 11-21. *The animated Vial, at the end of its animation*

Next, you will be using a particle system to make the elixir.

1. Stop Play mode.

2. Focus in on the Cork.

3. From the GameObject menu, Create Other, create a new Particle System.

4. Name it **Elixir**.

5. Drag it onto the Vial in the Animated Vial's hierarchy, so it will move with the vial during the animation.

6. Set its x, y, and z Scale back to 1,1, and 1.

It will need its timing to coincide with the animation as well.

7. Set Duration to **2.00**.

8. Give it a Start Delay of **0.5** to allow the vial to tip first.

9. Click the down arrow to the right of Start Lifetime and change it to Random Between Two Constants, then set them to **1** and **1.2**.

This adds a little variation, so they won't all disappear at the same distance from the emitter.

10. Click the down arrow to the right of Start Speed and change it to Random Between Two Constants, then set them to **0** and **0.1**.

This adds more variation, so they move at slightly different speeds.
Next, they need just a little gravity to start falling to the ground, instead of floating off like fluff.

11. Set the Gravity Multiplier to **0.2**.

12. Set Simulation Space to World, so they will drop straight down as the vial animates.

The rate is controlled from the first module, Emission. It is already checked as active.

1. Click in an empty section of the module's title bar to open it.

2. Set Rate to **80**, using Time.

Next, you'll want to constrain them to the vial. For that, you will have to change the emitter size in the Emission module. You must also control the rate the particles are emitted.

3. Open the Shape module, select Cone for the Shape, and set its Angle to **20**.

4. And, finally, to round up all the wayward particles, set its Radius to **0.01**, and Emit from: Base.

Now that they are all in one spot, you can adjust the size back in the upper part of the component.

5. Click the down arrow to the right of Start Size and change it to Random Between Two Constants, then set them to **0.08** and **0.11**.

For Color over Lifetime, you will first have to enable the module.

6. Click the check box to the left of the Color over Lifetime label and open the module.

7. Click on the color bar to open the gradient editor.

8. Right-click to create a new alpha marker on the top side of the color preview.

9. Select the far-right marker and set the Alpha slider to **0**.

10. On the bottom side, create a gradient from magenta, 0, to blue, 25%, to cyan, 50%, to green, 75%, and yellow at 100% (Figure 11-22).

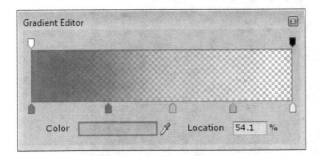

Figure 11-22. *Color over Time's gradient settings*

You can improve on the size by using Size over Lifetime. Now you can make the particles start small, get larger, then taper off to nothing, before they pop out of existence.

1. Check the Size over Lifetime module and open it.

Its default type is a curve.

2. Click the mini-curve to see it in the Preview window, then right-click the Preview title bar to float the window.

3. Over 0.1 (10%) time, right-click over the curve and Add Key.

4. Do the same at about 0.7.

5. Drag the keys at 0 and 1.0 down to 0.

6. Click the X on the right side to dock the preview window.

The particle flow tapers nicely at the end. The other enabled Module is the Renderer module. The defaults should be okay for this particle system.

Billboard turns the default planer shaped particles to always face the viewport. Normal direction makes sure they are rendered on the correct side of the plane. Sort Mode is valuable when solving alpha draw issues. Max Particle Size restricts the size as the player gets closer and closer to the particles.

Now that you've got the particles working, it's a good idea to go back to Max Emission and turn the number down to the most economical amount you can get away with, so you can conserve resources.

7. Set the Max Particles to somewhere between **80** and **100**.

8. Uncheck Looping.

9. Finally, click Play and watch the particles as they pour from the animated vial (Figure 11-23).

Figure 11-23. *The magic elixir pouring from the vial*

With so many settings to fiddle with, it would be a good idea to go ahead and create a prefab for the vial.

1.   Stop Play mode.

2.   In the Adventure Prefabs folder, create a new Prefab and name it **Vial Animated**.

3.   Drag the AnimatedVial object onto it from the Hierarchy view.

4.   Test it by dragging the prefab into the Scene view and clicking Play.

5.   Delete the one you just added to the scene.

Now that you've had a look at several of the particle system features, there are a couple of useful buttons to try.

1.   Click the tiny ! icon to the left of the + icon.

This toggles the general parameters off and on in the component.

2.   Now Click the + icon.

This allows you to show only the modules you want.

Particle Groups

One of the great things about the Shuriken system is the ability to edit multiple particle systems at the same time. If you think back, earlier in this chapter you saw the Flame prefab that was created with the Legacy particle systems. Re-creating it in Shuriken will give you a good, up-to-date prefab for future use. Feel free to bring the original into the scene temporarily for comparison. This time, you will set up the parameters to affect the end result, rather than just going down the panel in order, filling out numbers.

Let's start with the inner core. It will need to have flames that lick upward and taper to a point.
Inner core:

1.   Create a new particle system near the other objects and name it **Flame Inner**.

Because it can be difficult to set up a particle system with "cotton balls," let's jump to the last module and assign the material first. When you imported the legacy particles, they came in with several nice textures and materials that you can make use of. As the particle system takes shape, you will have a chance to look into the shaders used by the particle system.

2.   In the Renderer module, select FlameB as the material.

The texture uses an alpha channel with a jagged arc shape.
It also helps to take care of the Emission and Shape early on.

3.   In the Shape module, use Cone, set Angle to **0.05** and Radius to **0.01**.

By keeping the system contained, you will be able to shape the overall effect using Size.

4.   Back in the regular parameters, keep the Duration at **5**.

5.   Set Looping to true and Prewarm (starts fully formed) to true.

6.   Using the far-right arrow to open the choices, change Start Lifetime to Random Between Two Constants, **1** and **1.5**.

7.   Start Speed to **1.75**.

8.   Set the Start Size to **0.5**.

9. In the Emission module, temporarily set the Rate to **5**.

10. Change Start Rotation to Random Between Two Constants, **-180** and **180**.

This gives the particles a random starting rotation.

11. Having seen the effect of Rotation, bump the emission rate up to **20** and set Max Particles to **100**.

The rest of the adjustments will be made in the modules. Be sure to turn them on before you try to adjust their parameters.

Let's get size sorted out first. This is a good time to introduce the Particle Effect editor.

1. Turn on the Size over Lifetime module.

It defaults to a curve type. If you click on it, you can see and adjust the curve in the Preview window, but if you detach it to make it larger, it may not update as you make adjustments. This is where the Editor comes in handy. You can keep it open and edit any of the regular parameters, because the entire component is also shown there.

2. At the top of the Particle System component, on the right, pick the Open Editor button.

3. Set the left/start value to **2.0**.

4. Move the left key down to **1.0** and move the right/end key to **0.5**.

5. Right-click over the curve at about .25 (25%) and Add Key, drag it up to **2.0**.

This causes the particles to start small, then ramp up quickly, then shrink back down over time (Figure 11-24).

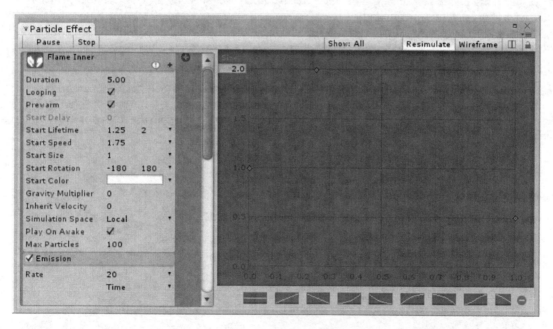

Figure 11-24. *The Particle Effect editor with the parameters and modules now off to the left*

Time (on the horizontal) in the curves shows percent of the actual duration, so 1.0 on the far right is 100% of that. Also important to understand is that the curves affect, not overwrite, the original parameters. Let's tweak the Start Size to see this in action.

6. Try different Start Sizes to see the affect.

The particles retain the size scaling set in the curve.

7. Set the Start Size to **0.8**.

Let's add the color and opacity next.

8. In the Color over Lifetime module, set the color markers to red, orange, gold, orange, and black (Figure 11-25).

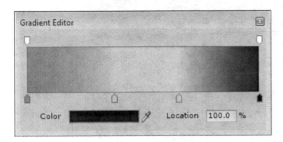

Figure 11-25. *The Flame gradient for Color over Lifetime*

9. Set the alpha to **0, 150, 175, 50,** and **0**.

By setting the start alpha to 0, the large particles will fade rather than pop into existence. Also showing an effect is the additive shader. You set the colors as gold and orange near the start and end, but when several particles overlap, the color is blown out, using an additive scheme, to yellow or even white, if the base color is light enough. As you reduced the opacity, the outer edges, where less particles overlap, show more of their original color.

10. At the bottom of the Inspector, try testing some of the other Particles shaders for the FlameB material, then set it back to Particles/Additive.

So, the flame is looking better, but it still is not quite as dynamic as it could be. For that, you have to get the particles rotating as they go upward.

1. Turn on the Rotation over Lifetime module.

Its default is set to a constant, 45, so not much rotation is happening.

2. Set the value to about **125** to get the fire roiling.

Let's try using a curve to control the rotation, so it won't be so constant.

3. Click the arrow to the right of the value and choose Curve.

4. Open the Editor again if you have closed it.

A new curve appears with its name in the upper left corner. Because there was only one constant used previously, there is only one key with that value.

5. Set the start number to **150**, then move the key down to **125**, so your end key can be higher.

6. Right-click, double-click, over the curve and add a key for and end value of **150**.

7. Use the Bezier handles on the two keys to give the curve a dip in the middle, slowing the rotation in the middle of the particle's lives (Figure 11-26).

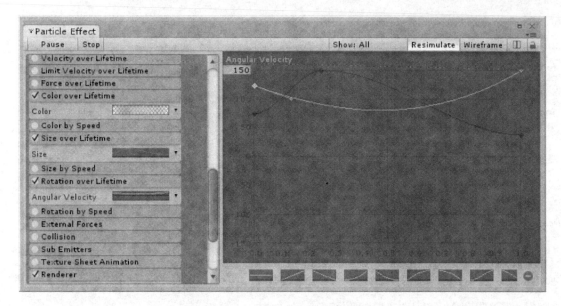

Figure 11-26. *The Rotation over Lifetime curve, green, with the Color over Lifetime curve darkened (not selected)*

8. In the Velocity over Lifetime module, set the z velocity to **-0.5** to slow the speed over time.

The fire looks a little rolly-polly. Let's use a curve instead. Also note that Z is the local up direction for the Shuriken system.

9. Change to Curve and select the Z curve (by color).

10. Add a key at its right side, then drag the left-side key up to 0.

11. Adjust the handles to get a nice Slow out, fast in curve.

The 0 value at the start means the Start Speed value you set earlier is in full effect. At the end, it is only using 0.5 of that value.

A great improvement over the legacy particles is that Shuriken will react to Wind Zones. To enable the wind effect, you will have to turn on the External Forces module. You won't need it for the final game, but it is worth a try.

1. Turn on the External Forces module.

2. Orbit the Scene view until you can see the effect (Figure 11-27).

Figure 11-27. External Forces turned on

    3.   Try setting the Multiplier to **2**.

    4.   Turn off the External Forces module.

Outer Core:
The outer core particles are slower and denser with a shorter life, but you can still start by duplicating Flame Inner.

    1.   Duplicate Flame Inner and name it **Flame Base**.

    2.   Deactivate Flame Inner and select Flame Base.

    3.   Change the material to FlameC.

    4.   Start Speed to **0.5**.

    5.   Set the Start Size to **1.25**.

You won't be needing a couple of the modules, because this guy is more of a fire-ball.

    6.   Turn off Size over Lifetime.

    7.   Open Velocity over Time.

    8.   Click to turn off the X and Z curves.

They will go gray and no longer appear in the graph area.

    9.   Set the right-side key to **0.2**, then set the left key to **-0.5**.

This will keep the particles balled up at the bottom and then let a few (the ones with longer lives) escape upward. The fireball is denser than it needs to be, because it will be added to the inner core flame's effects.

    10.   Open the Color over Time and set the middle opacity markers to about **50**, **60**, and **5**.

And, finally, let's look at the two particle systems together. As mentioned earlier, you can view and edit more than one particle system at the same time, by creating a Particle Effect. Basically, you just parent the ones you want to an existing particle system.

1. Activate Flame Inner and drop it onto Flame Base in the Hierarchy view.

Both particle systems are now animating together.

2. Select the Flame Base and click the Open Editor button.

Here's the tricky part: you may have to reveal the Flame Inner to see it.

3. Position the cursor over the divider between the component and the graph area.

4. Drag it right to reveal the Flame Inner.

5. Adjust the curve area wider, as needed.

6. Now you can work on either of the particle systems with both active in the viewport (Figure 11-28).

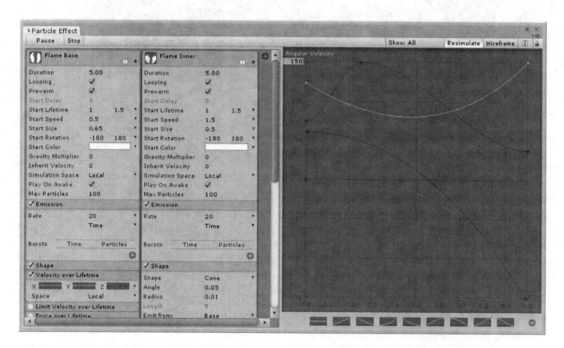

Figure 11-28. *The new Flame "effect" in the Editor with both particle systems showing*

To finish the new fire effect, you will need a few more goodies. The Smoke part is similar to the ones you've already set up, so you can import a prefab for it.

1. Import the Smoke package from this chapter's assets in the Download area of the Apress web site (www.apress.com).

2. Move the Smoke Prefab to the Adventure Prefabs folder.

3. Drag it into the scene and position it at the Flame Base particle system.

4. Now drag it onto the Flame Base group.

5. Set its Start Time to **1.0** and **2.0** and its Start Size to **1.2**.

The particles happily work together.
Some sparks would be a nice addition.
Fire Sparks:

1. Create a new particle System and name it **Fire Sparks**.

2. Position it next to the fire.

3. In the Renderer module, set its material to Spark.

4. Turn on Prewarm.

5. Set Start Lifetime to **0.5** and **1.5**.

6. Set Start Speed to **0.1** and **2**.

7. Set Start Size to **0.01** and **0.08**.

8. Make sure Simulation Space is set to Local.

9. For Emission, set the Rate to **50**.

10. Set Max Particles to **100**.

11. For Shape, use Cone set to **0** Angle and **0.7** Radius or whatever you need to restrict it to the radius of the fire.

12. Turn on Velocity over Time and change it to Random between Two Constants.

13. Set their second x, y, z values to **0.5**.

Take a look at the particle system's X Rotation in the Transform component. As a default, it is set to -90, indicating the Shuriken system originally used Z as up in the world. The random velocities look a bit skewed, so let's just adjust the rotation of the entire system to get the sparks going up better.

14. Adjust the Rotation in the Transform component until the sparks are not straying too far from the fire in any one direction.

15. Now drag the Fire Sparks onto the Flame Base parent to see the full effect.

If you think back to the legacy prefab, you should remember that it had one more thing—a light source. As it's just a simple Point light, it will be a quick addition.

1. Create a Point Light, and center it on the particle systems.

2. Name it **Fire Light**.

3. Set its Range to **6** and its Color to **orange**.

4. Leave its Intensity at **0.5** and don't turn on Shadows.

5. Set its height to about a 1/4 meter up from the bottom of the particle system.

6. Drag the light into the particle system group (Figure 11-29).

Figure 11-29. *The fire with smoke, sparks, and light*

Having spent a good amount of time creating the fire effect, now would be a really good time to make a prefab of it.

1. Create a new Prefab in the Adventure Prefabs folder.

2. Name it **Fire Effect**.

3. Drag the Flame Base group onto it in the Project view.

If you make any changes to the particle systems, be sure to update the prefab by clicking Apply at the top of the Inspector in the Prefab line.

Welding Sparks:

In the next section, you will be making a laser beam. When it hits action objects, it will instantiate a particle system of a short burst of sparks. Let's go ahead and create it now. Be sure to click Simulate in the Particle Effect dialog in the Scene view as you fill in the values, so you can see the immediate result.

1. Create a new particle system and name it **Sparks**.

Because the particles are a response to a Z direction projectile of sorts, you will be creating it with the z axis, its primary direction.

2. In the Transform component, set x rotation to **0**.

3. Lift it about half a meter up from the ground.

4. Assign the Spark material to it.

5. Set Duration to **0.1**.

6. Set Start Lifetime to **0.1** and **1.25**.

7. For Start Speed, change type to Curve, open the Editor, and set the curve limit to **4**.

8. Set the left key to **1.5**, add a middle key at about **3,** and an end key at about **1** (Figure 11-30).

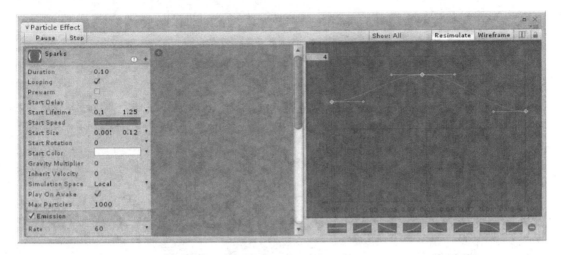

Figure 11-30. The Speed curve in the Particle Effect Editor

9. Set Start Size to **0.005** and **0.12**.

10. In Emission, set Rate to **60**.

And here's the important part for this particle system. The particles need to come out as a burst.

1. Click the Bursts + to create a new Burst.

2. Set it to burst at 0.00 time with **60** particles.

3. Now uncheck Looping and click Simulate to see the results.

4. Set Gravity Multiplier to **0.5** so they'll drop.

5. Next, set the Shape Cone to **70** Angle and **0.001** Radius.

■ **Tip** You can drag the single light blue square to increase or decrease the emitter gizmo in the Scene view. The other markers will change the Angle and Base Size.

---

6. Turn on Velocity over Lifetime and change it to Random Between Two Constants.

7. Set the top line to **0** and the bottom line to **0.1**, **0.1**, and **5**.

In Color over Lifetime, you will adjust only the opacity, because the texture already has color. By holding the 0 alpha to a third of the way along, you will avoid a lot of the particle overlap at the start.

8. In Color over Lifetime, set the alphas to **0, 0, 255, 255, 85** (Figure 11-31).

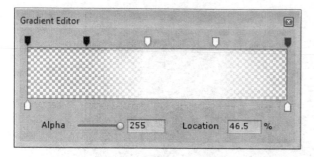

Figure 11-31. *The Color over Lifetime alpha markers*

9. In Size over Lifetime, use a preset Curve to get a slow out and a delayed fast in for full-sized, 1, and no size, 0 (Figure 11-32).

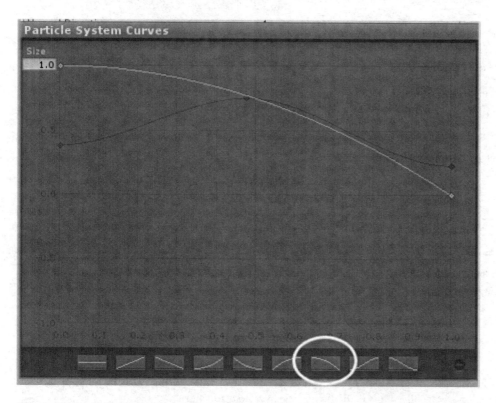

Figure 11-32. *Using a curve preset*

And, finally, in the Renderer module, you will set the particles to stretch.

10. In the Renderer module, set Render Mode to Stretched Billboard from the drop-down arrow on the right side.

11. Set the Speed Scale to **0.15** and the Length Scale to **1.5**.

12. Give the particle system a final test in the Scene view and create a prefab out of it named **Sparks**.

13. Delete the particle system from the Hierarchy view.

Now you're all set for creating a laser.

Other Special Effects

For the last section of this chapter, you will be creating a laser effect. When the player combines the fabulous crystal with the golden sleeve, the crystal is activated to produce a laser beam. This will be needed to access one of the structures you will be importing.

Creating the Laser Beam

For the beam, you will be using a Line Renderer component. The Line Renderer creates a simple surface using a minimum of two faces and has built-in billboarding functionality. You will base it at the Crystal with Sleeve, and script its ending location. While you could add the component to the Crystal with Sleeve, it's better to put it on its own gameObject. This will allow you to do such things as animate its texture later on.

1. Change the Scene view to a Top/Ortho view.

2. Focus in on the Crystal with Sleeve.

3. Create a new Empty gameObject and move it near the end of the crystal.

4. Switch to a side view and adjust the position so that it is just behind the end facets of the crystal.

5. In Local coordinate system, make sure the new object's orientation matches the Crystal with Sleeve (Figure 11-33).

***Figure 11-33.** Laser at the end of the Golden Sleeve with Crystal*

Both should point Z forward.

6. Name it **Laser** and drop it onto the Crystal with Sleeve object in the Hierarchy view.

7. Add a Line Renderer component to it from the Component ➤ Effects submenu.

8. Uncheck Cast and Receive Shadows, and uncheck Use World Space.

This part is important: when left checked, the plane is left at 0,0,0 in world space. You should now see a large magenta plane stuck on the Crystal with Sleeve.

9. Under Parameters, set the Start Width and End Width to **0.03**, and set the Positions Element 1, Z to **0.01**.

10. Set its Start and End Colors to blue-green.

This last value is the line's default length, until it knows how far out to go. Element 0 is the starting point that is always calculated at the Laser's location.

The Laser material uses a simple Particles/Additive shader and a texture that masks the edges along the top and bottom of the image. Let's create it now.

1. Select the Materials folder on the Action Objects folder.

2. From the right-click menu or the Assets menu, Create ➤ Material.

3. Name it **Laser**.

4. Assign the Particles/Additive shader to it and set the Tint Color to mystic blue-green.

5. Drag the SoftEdges texture from the Action Textures folder in as its Particle Texture.

6. Select the Laser object and assign the new material to its Material, Element 0.

Building the Laser Device

1. Select the First Person Controller and give it a Y Rotation of **0**.

2. Focus to the First Person Controller in the Scene view.

3. Select the Crystal with Sleeve object and remove it from the ActionObjects group.

4. Agree to losing the prefab.

5. Use Move to View to bring it to the First Person Controller.

6. Adjust the position and its local z rotation until you can see it in the Game view, as if the player were holding it out in front of him- or herself (Figure 11-34).

Figure 11-34. The Crystal with Sleeve object in position

To aim the device, the player will use the mouse-look functionality, so the object needs to be parented to the First Person Controller's camera via the Gear Handler, just like the Proxy Weapon.

7. Drag the Crystal with Sleeve object and drop it onto the Gear Handler.

Currently, the Sleeve with Crystal has a capsule collider. If you had a nearby wall to test with, you could set the collider to Is Trigger and drive close enough so that it would go through the wall until the First Person Controller was stopped. Because it has a collider, it will probably stop the First Person Controller too soon. A trick often used in first-person shooters is to create a camera specifically for the handheld weapons. The weapon then goes on its own layer, and the collider can be set to Is Trigger. By parenting the weapon camera with the Main camera, they always go together, but the weapon is drawn last, or on top of other scene objects. You will be introduced to Camera layers in the Inventory chapter 13. Until there are objects with walls in the scene, you needn't worry about it.

Activating the Laser

To control the laser beam, you will be using Physics.Raycast. The version you will be using starts with a location, uses a direction, then checks for an intersection with anything with a collider within the specified range.

1. Create a new script in the Adventure Scripts folder and name it **Laser**.

2. Open the new script and add the following:

```
var laser : Transform;        // the object with the Line Renderer component
var range : int = 30;         // the distance to check within

internal var hit : RaycastHit; // holds some of the properties of the object that is
detected with the raycast

function Update () {

        // Did we hit anything?
        if (Physics.Raycast (transform.position, transform.forward, hit, range)) {
                laser.GetComponent(LineRenderer).SetPosition (1, Vector3(0, 0,hit.distance));
//update end position
        }
        else {
                //print ("There's nothing directly ahead");
        }
}
```

Take a minute to read the comments, then look up RaycastHit in the scripting reference. You can see that it stores several useful bits of information about the intersection. The first one you will need is distance, so you can tell the Line Renderer where to set its Element 1 x, y, and z location in a Vector3 format.

3. Save the script and add it to Crystal with Sleeve object.

4. Drag the Laser object into its laser parameter.

5. Click Play and look around the scene.

When the laser beam hits an object with a collider, such as the action objects, it goes only a little farther. The extra distance is because the distance is calculated from the Sleeve with Crystal's transform, which is at its center.

6. Change Vector3(0, 0,hit.distance) to:

```
Vector3(0, 0,hit.distance -0.45)
```

7. Save the script.

Now the laser no longer goes through the Action Objects when it intersects them (Figure 11-35).

Figure 11-35. *The laser stopped at a collider*

Rather than have it remain active, you will be setting a condition on the raycast. For this project, you will have it active only when the virtual button, "ML Enable," is being pressed. You could easily assign a different key to the preset "Fire1" virtual input, if you wish, but in this case, the player has one less input to deal with, if it is hooked up with the mouse-look.

1. Add the following lines above the `Physics.Raycast` line:

```
// is right mouse button down?
if(Input.GetButton("ML Enable") ) { // if player is looking around
```

2. Add the closing curly bracket above the else line and indent the original contents.

And next, you will have to set the Line Renderer's length back to 0 when the laser is not in use. When you set it up originally, you assigned 0.01 as the length, or offset from Element 0.

3. In the `else` clause (which now belongs to the mouse-down conditional), under the print statement, add:

```
laser.GetComponent(LineRenderer).SetPosition (1,Vector3(0, 0, 0)); // shorten the laser
```

4. Save the script.

5. Click Play and test.

The laser now "shuts off" when you let up on the right mouse button.

There are a couple of fun things you can add to make it more interesting. The first is an animated texture, or, more precisely, animated mapping, or UVs.

6. Stop Play mode.

This little script comes in handy for lots of things, so as long as you are adding code to animate the regular texture, you will include the means to animate the bump as well. Because you may not want to use both all the time, you will make them both optional.

Texture offsets work on a 0-to-1 basis, where 1 is a full loop.

Creating the UV Animator Script

1. Create a new script in the Adventure scripts folder.

2. Name it **UVAnimator**.

3. Open it in the script editor.

4. Add the following variables:

```
// Script to scroll main texture and bump based on time
var materialIndex : int = 0; // in case the objects has more than one material

var animateUV = true;          // flag for option to scroll texture
var scrollSpeedU1 = 0.0;       // variables to scroll texture
var scrollSpeedV1 = 0.0;

var animateBump = false;       // flag for option to scroll bump texture
var scrollSpeedU2 = 0.0;       // variables to scroll bump texture
var scrollSpeedV2 = 0.0;
```

To animate the Offset for the main texture and bump maps, you can use Time.deltaTime and the speed to control the Offset.

5. Change the Update function to a FixedUpdate function.

6. Add the following in the FixedUpdate function:

```
// texture offset variables
var offsetU1 = Time.time  * -scrollSpeedU1;
var offsetV1 = Time.time * -scrollSpeedV1;
// bump texture offset variables
var offsetU2 = Time.time * -scrollSpeedU2;
var offsetV2 = Time.time * -scrollSpeedV2;
```

7. Add the following to change the texture offset value:

```
if (animateUV) { // if the flag to animate the texture is true...
        renderer.materials[materialIndex].SetTextureOffset
("_MainTex",Vector2(offsetU1,offsetV1));
}
```

You can access the material through the Renderer component with renderer.material if there is only one material, or renderer.materials(index number), if there might be more than one. Setting the index number to 0 will use the first material, unless otherwise specified.

The trickiest part about this script is discovering what the internal name of the shader parameter is in the script, so you can feed it into the SetTextureOffset method.

8. Add the version of it to animate the bump.

```
if (animateBump) { // if the flag to animate the bump texture is true...
    renderer.materials[materialIndex].SetTextureOffset ("_BumpMap", Vector2(offsetU2,offsetV2));
}
```

9. To experiment with accessing other shader properties, you may want to include the following:

```
function Start () {

    //print ("shininess " + renderer.materials[materialIndex].HasProperty("_Shininess"));
    //print ("parallax " + renderer.materials[materialIndex].HasProperty("_Parallax"));

}
```

10. Save the script.

Applying the UV Animator Script

1. Select the Laser object in the Hierarchy view.

2. Add the UVAnimator script to it.

3. Set Scroll Speed U1 to **5**.

4. Click Play and watch the laser beam.

Nothing much appears to be happening. The problem is that the texture stretches the entire length of the beam. Let's increase the tiling in the material.

5. Locate the Laser material.

6. Try changing its x Tiling parameter to **10**.

The tiling is spread out along the current length of the beam. If you wanted to be fancy, you could adjust the tiling according to the length of the beam, but there are more things you will add that will spice it up just fine. The next will be a light that will use the hit position for its location.

1. Create a new Point Light and name it **Laser Light**.

2. Set its Range to **1**, its Color to match the laser beam, and its Intensity to **0**.

3. In the Laser script, add the following variable:

```
var hitLight : Light; // light at the end of the laser
```

4. Inside the Raycast conditional, add:

```
hitLight.intensity = 5.0;                    // turn the intensity up
hitLight.transform.position = hit.point; // move the light to the hit point
```

5. And in the else clause, add:

```
hitLight.intensity = 0.0; // turn the intensity off if there was no hit
```

6. Save the script.

7. Assign the Laser Light object to the Hit Light parameter on the Crystal with Sleeve object's Laser script component.

8. Click Play and test by running the laser over the action objects.

The last special effect you will add is some sparks, to let the player know when he or she has hit the correct object. You will be using the Sparks prefab from the previous section.

1. In the Laser script, add the following variable:

```
var hitParticles : GameObject;// the sparks prefab
```

2. In the Raycast conditional, above the hitLight lines, add:

```
if (hitParticles) { // if particles were assigned, instantiate them at the hit point
        var temp : GameObject = Instantiate(hitParticles,
hit.point,Quaternion.FromToRotation(Vector3.up, hit.normal));
        Destroy(temp, 0.3);
}
```

If hitParticles have been assigned, they are instantiated at the hit point, but they are oriented to the face normal of hit surface, so they spray back toward the player. Then the prefabs are allowed to live for 0.3 seconds before being destroyed.

3. Save the script.

4. Assign the Sparks prefab from Adventure Prefabs folder to the new Hit Particles parameter.

5. Click Play and test.

With a real target for the particles and the realization that the prefab is instantiated over and over as the player aims at an action object, you will want to make a few adjustments.

1. Stop Play mode.

2. Select the Sparks prefab in the Project view.

3. In the Emissive module, reduce the number to **20** for rate and burst.

4. Set Max Particles to **20** as well.

5. In the Renderer module, reduce the Speed Scale to **0.05**.

6. Test with the new settings and make any necessary adjustments.

The sparks definitely add interest, but until you limit their use, the player will not have a clue about the correct target. Once you have the final target, you can change the script. For now, you can keep it from reacting to anything that is not an action object. To do that, you can make good use of tags.

1. Open the laser script.

2. Change the if (hitParticles) conditional to:

```
if (hitParticles && hit.collider.tag == "ActionObject")
```

3. Save the script.

4. Click Play and try lasering the objects around the scene (Figure 11-36).

Figure 11-36. *The laser with light and sparks hitting an object tagged as an ActionObject*

This time, only the objects already set up and tagged as ActionObjects get sparks.

With the laser functionality well under way, you will deactivate the Sleeve with Crystal until the inventory functionality allows you to combine its two base objects.

5. Select the Sleeve with Crystal.

6. Deactivate it in the Inspector.

7. Click Play and make sure the laser is deactivated as well.

A Few Loose Ends

In order to stay on track with the particle systems, you left the Vial of Elixir literally hanging in midair after delivering its contents. Now you must decide what to do with it. It's not an action object, it's just an extra bit of animation that gets played when the flower gets revived. You've animated material transparencies, so let's try something different this time. To make the Vial disappear, let's scale it down to almost nothing. As before, you will have to make a copy of the imported animation before you can edit it.

1. Select the pour elixir clip and duplicate it.

2. Name the new clip **pour elixir copy** and move it to the Animation clips folder.

3. Select the AnimatedVial group and drop the Pour Elixir Copy clip onto it.

The animation array is increased, and the new clip is in at Element 1.

4. Uncheck Play Automatically.

5. Make sure you are not in Play mode.

6. Select only the Vial and open the Animation editor from the Window menu.

447

The newly duplicated clip should be selected.

The Elixir particle system has a delay of 0.5 seconds and plays out over 2 seconds, so you will want to allow 2.5 seconds before getting rid of the vial. If you select the transform tracks, you can see that the last frame of vial animation is at 47, 1:17 on the time line. The first thing you'll have to do is shift the view over, so you can add more keys.

7. Hold the mouse roller down and pan the Animation view over until you can see 3:00.

8. Turn the Record button on.

9. Move the time indicator to 2:20 and select the Scale transform tracks.

10. Click the Add Keyframe button to create the start keys.

11. Move the indicator to 2:24 and set the vial's x, y, and z Scales to 0, either in the Inspector or the Animation editor.

12. Repeat the steps for the Cork.

13. Stretch the window view slider at the bottom of the Animation view to include 0.

14. Click the Play button and watch the vial and cork wink out of the scene.

So now, the particles have finished, and the vial and cork are no longer visible, but none of them is actually out of the scene. Before you update the VialAnimated prefab, you will want to add the Terminator script to take care of that. It defaults to 5 seconds, so you shouldn't need to change the Life.

1. Add the Terminator script to the Animated Vial in the Hierarchy view.

2. Click Play and watch it go out of the scene and Hierarchy.

3. Stop Play mode.

4. Select the Animated Vial and click Apply at the top of the Inspector to update the prefab.

5. Delete the Animated Vial from the Hierarchy view.

Next you will instantiate the prefab when the flower is picked. Your ObjectLookup script is already set up to allow for instantiating prefabs. Let's finish setting that up and test with the updated prefab.

1. Open the ObjectLookup script.

2. Add the following variable to hold an array of prefabs:

```
var prefabs : GameObject[]; // holder array for prefab objects
```

3. In the special cases section for case "p," replace //add guts here with:

```
// use the s2 number to specify which element of the prefabs array to instantiate
Instantiate (prefabs[s2]);
bypass = true; // skip the regular processing
```

This time, because most action objects won't have any prefabs to instantiate, you will tell the game engine which prefab to use by setting the second character of the three character special cases to the element you want to instantiate.

4. Save the script.

5. Select the Flower.

6. Near the bottom of the ObjectLookup component, set the Size of the Prefab array to **1**.

7. Drag the Vial Animated into Element 0.

8. Add the p0_Flower,0 to the Lookup State 0, Element 0 to read as follows:
   default,2,c0_Flower,0,p0_Flower,0

In this case, p0 is really all that gets evaluated, but it still needs the rest, so that it doesn't throw an error when it parses the instructions. To "read" through it now, when picked by the default cursor when it (the flower) is in state 1, it transitions into state 2 (doing all the animations and sound effects associated with state 1), does the camera match, and instantiates the prefab at Element 0 of the Prefab array.

1. Click Play and pick the Flower.

The vial appears on cue, but now the flower revives and camera match may have to be delayed.

2. In the Interactor component, set the Animation Delay for Element 2 to **2**.

3. In the Camera Match Data component, set the Duration to **4**.

The look target will probably have to be adjusted, but you can do that when the flower is in its final location.

4. Save the Scene and save the Project.

Summary

In this chapter, you imported several new Action objects that you will eventually use in the game. While setting up the materials for the new objects, you took a trip to Unity's asset store and took advantage of a free asset package, the GemPack. It contained a shader that uses a couple of cube maps for reflection and refraction.

Next, you were introduced to physics, starting with the Rigidbody component. Along with it, you experimented with physic Materials that you assigned to the colliders, hinges, and forces. You had a first look at cloth and were able to see how it could interact with other objects, both animated and static. After a few tests, you used the Rigidbody's Velocity parameter to create a very simple projectile. You learned to limit the number and frequency of projectiles available to the player by scripting a little timer.

To incorporate physics into the game, you created a rockfall that instantiated random rocks from an array. After adding a collider, a rigid body, and some scripts to control them, you used a rock to make your first UnityPackage. At a specified time, you then instantiated an action object, the Crystal, so that it could drop on top of the randomly generated rock pile.

You then took advantage of Unity's legacy particle system to take a quick look at several useful prefabs. Delving into Unity's Shuriken particle system, you took advantage of several of the imported textures to set up a few different particle systems that will come in handy later on in the game. With the fire effect, you learned how you could use multiple Shuriken particle systems together as a Particle Effect. You also found that a simple point light could enhance particle effects.

Finally, you made a laser beam with the help of the Line Renderer and Physics.Raycast. With the information returned by Raycast.hit, you were able to control the length of the laser beam and instantiate particles and a light at its hit point. You created a useful little script that animates a material's U and V Offset and applied it to the laser beam to give it a more dynamic look.

CHAPTER 12

■ ■ ■

Message Text

One of the most common features of a classic point-and-click adventure game is the text prompt, or message, that identifies an action object as you mouse over. In your game, you will display the name and description of the object on mouseover when a player is within range, as well as a message informing him if he tries to pick the object and isn't close enough.

UnityGUI text design is patterned after the concept of cascading style sheets (CSS). You define colors and fonts for a particular style, and all of the GUI elements inherit those properties with GUISkin. This makes for a consistent look and feel throughout. It also means the GUI elements involved are treated quite differently from 3D objects.

In Unity, there are currently two types of GUI elements. Of the objects that can be created through the GameObject menu, you have already used the GUI Texture. The GameObject varieties of text and texture objects are handled individually and exist in the game hierarchy. They are not affected by the GUI Skin specifications.

The second type of GUI elements, Unity GUI, *must be scripted to exist*. You've used it to create your cursor using a texture, but now that you are a bit more comfortable with scripting, you'll be using the Unity GUI to create and handle text for the game.

The Unity GUI consists of a GUI Skin and GUI Styles. The "skin" is where you define the defaults of the GUI, and the "style" is what you will use to override the skin.

GUI Skin

The first step in getting text on screen is to create a GUI Skin. This gives us the default look and feel for the various types of GUI elements.

1. Open the book project and load the Interaction scene.

2. Deactivate the Gear handler object on the First Person Controller's main Camera.

3. Right-click in the Project view and choose GUI Skin from the bottom of the Create submenu.

4. Rename it **Game GUISkin**.

Take a few minutes to look through the parameters for the various elements in the Inspector. The GUISkin is a collection of predefined GUIStyles or templates that dictate the look and much of the behavior (by way of its name) of each element.

To see what the various control elements look like, see the Reference Manual ➤ GUI Scripting Guide ➤ GUI Basics. For this game, you'll be using only a simple Label element for the onscreen text.

5. Open the Label element.

6. Under Normal, adjust the Text Color to something that will show up in your scene (see Figure 12-1).

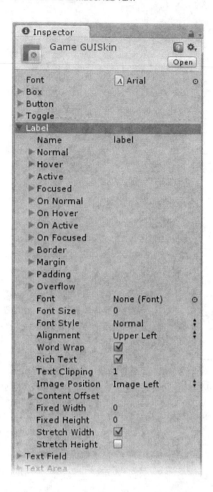

Figure 12-1. GUISkin with Label selected in the Inspector

At the top of the Inspector, you'll probably see that the default font is Arial. We will leave it as is for now. The font indicated here is the default font used by your operating system.

As previously mentioned, the GUI elements exist only in scripts, which means you'll need a GameObject to put the script on. There are a couple of choices at this point. You could create a new empty GameObject to hold the script, giving it a name that would remind you where you put it. The downside of this is that you'd need to add it to the list of objects that have to be accessed by each action object.

An alternative is to put the script on an object that is already being accessed by the action objects. This cuts down a bit on the overhead and clutter. The important thing is to give the script a nice descriptive name, so you can locate it quickly. As it happens, you have an ideal candidate—the Control Center object. It already holds the GameManager script, which is a pretty good place to manage the text.

1. Select the Control Center object.

2. Open its GameManager script.

3. Inside the OnGUI function, above the cursor code, add the following:

```
GUI.Label (Rect (0,0,100,50), "This is the text string for a Label Control");
```

452

The OnGUI function is the GUI equivalent of the Update function. It is called at least once every frame and is another of the system functions.

4.   Save the script.

Nothing shows in the Game window. GUI elements show only during runtime. Because the function is continually being called, you can make changes inside the OnGUI function, save the script, then return focus to the Game window to see the results without restarting the scene.

5.   Click Play.

6.   Look up toward the sky if it is hard to see in your environment.

The text appears in the upper left corner of the Game window (Figure 12-2).

Figure 12-2. *The Label's text in the upper left corner of the viewport*

The code (Rect (0,0,100,50) defines the pixel location and boundary the text must fit into. The Rect type uses a four-element array that defines the x and y screen location and the width and height, Rect (x_pos, y_pos, width, height).

7.   Change the line to read:

```
GUI.Label (Rect (10,10,500,20), "This is the text string for a Label Control");
```

8.   Save the file then click in the Game window to change focus and see the result.

The text no longer needs to wrap, as shown in Figure 12-3.

Figure 12-3. The new location and bounds for the text

     9.   Stop Play mode and click the Maximize on Play toggle on the Game view.

   10.   Click Play.

The text is still the same size. As with the GUI Texture object, it is a constant pixel size that does not scale with the window.

   11.   Stop Play mode.

OS Font Support

Unity will use the operating system's default font, Arial, until you provide something else. Using the OS default font makes the file size smaller but carries a small risk that the text could appear different on different systems. For this game, let's start with Arial.

To change the size of the text, you have to access the font assigned to the GUI Skin. Because you haven't yet introduced a font, you can't yet change the font size.

     1.   Stop Play mode.

     2.   From the book's Assets folder, drag the Fonts folder into the project's Assets folder.

     3.   From the newly added Fonts folder, select the font, Arial (Figure 12-4).

Figure 12-4. *The Arial font in the Inspector*

The most important thing to understand about fonts in Unity is that they can have only *one* size, unless they are set to *Dynamic* (see preceding Figure 12-4). If the font isn't dynamic, for *each* font size, you will have to make a duplicate font and use either a duplicate GUISkin or a custom GUIStyle. Dynamic fonts allow you to override the size for separate templates or GUI styles.

4. Use Ctrl+D (Cmd+D on a Mac) to duplicate the Arial font.

5. Name it **arial2**.

6. Change its Font Size to **25**.

7. Keep its Character set to Dynamic and click Apply.

When using a font in most 3D engines for 2D text, a bitmap of the full alphabet and characters is generated for *each* font *and* size specified. When you specify Dynamic in Unity, the bitmap generated by the operating system is used, saving download time and texture memory during runtime. The downside is that if you specify a font that is not present on the operating system, a fallback font will be used in its place. Even when using generic fonts such as Arial, there may be slight differences among systems. You will investigate this further when you experiment with different fonts later on in the project. Dynamic fonts are currently supported only on desktop platforms (i.e., Mac and Windows).

8. Open the arial2 font in the Project view and look at its font material and font texture in the Preview window.

You won't see anything there right now, because the alphabet is being generated by the operating system.

9. Change the Character to ASCII default set and click Apply.

Both a texture and a material are generated for the font, as shown in Figure 12-5. It's worth noting that you can also choose all uppercase or all lowercase to reduce the size of the texture map.

Figure 12-5. *Font material and texture generated for non-dynamic character type*

10. Select the Game GUISkin and load the duplicate font, arial2, at the top of the Inspector.

11. Check the Game view where you are still in Play mode.

The font doesn't change because, until you tell Unity otherwise, you are still using the default styles. You'll do that in the script that draws the GUI elements in its OnGUI function.

1. Open the GameManager script.

2. At the top of the script, below the existing variables, add the following:

```
var customSkin : GUISkin;
```

3. Then, in the OnGUI function, above the GUI.Label line, add:

```
GUI.skin = customSkin;
```

4. Save the script.

5. Stop Play mode and select the Control Center object.

6. Drag the Game GUISkin into the new Custom Skin parameter.

7. Click Play and observe the result (Figure 12-6).

Figure 12-6. *The GUISkin in use, showing the larger default font*

The changes you made to the font and GUISkin now appear, but at Font Size 25, the font gets cropped.

8. Change the GUI.Label line as follows:

```
GUI.Label (Rect (10,10,500,40), "This is the text string for a Label Control");
```

9. Save the script.

10. Click in the Game window to return focus to it and observe the change (Figure 12-7).

Figure 12-7. *The rectangle resized to fit the text*

The text color may get lost against the background. Let's use a Box element instead, to make the text easier to read.

1. Comment out the GUI.Label line

2. Add the following beneath the GUI.Label line:

```
GUI.Box (Rect (0,40,500,50), " This is the text string for a Box Control ");
```

3. Save the script and observe the changes (see Figure 12-8).

Figure 12-8. *The Box control*

4.   Change the rectangle's parameters to fit your text.

The box itself uses an internal image for its background, which is scaled, keeping its outline intact. You can no longer see only the box, because Unity now uses a PSD file with all of the control images on various layers, but it is just 12×12 pixels (Figure 12-9). Note also that the text in the Box control is centered, as opposed to the Label's default—left-justified.

Figure 12-9.   The Alpha channel of the box texture used on the Box GUI control

The tiny 12×12 pixel texture shows a mostly rounded-corner box. The corners are set not to stretch in the Box template's settings, so the box image appears correct at any size.

■ **Warning**   Before you experiment with different textures in the GUISkin, you should know that if the texture does not show up in the asset browser, you won't be able to get it back without creating a new GUISkin.

In the Fonts folder, you will see a texture called MyBox. It is a variation on the default box, but it has the advantage of remaining a PSD file, so you can alter it. Let's load it into the skin.

1.   Select the Game GUISkin again.

2.   Click the down arrow to browse the texture assets for the Background field again for the Box element.

3.   Choose MyBox.

4.   Click Play, if you are not already in play mode, to see the changes (Figure 12-10).

Figure 12-10.   Experimenting with the Box control's settings

5.   Experiment with the Text Color and other parameters until you are happy with the result.

Note that the box transparency is a function of the MyBox texture's alpha channel.

Now that we have gained a bit of control over the visual aspects of the text, let's look into alignment of the box itself.

If you are not planning on limiting the screen resolution, the user will be able to choose a resolution at runtime. If you remember that GUI elements retain their pixel size regardless of screen resolution, it becomes clear that you need access to the screen size in order to center the text messages. Fortunately, you can use Screen.width, Screen.height, and a bit of math inside the command to get what you want. Let's go ahead and move the Box control to the bottom center of the screen.

6.   Change the two GUI control lines as follows:

```
GUI.Label (Rect (Screen.width/2 - 250, 10, 500,35), " This is the text string for a Label
Control");

GUI.Box (Rect (Screen.width/2 - 250, Screen.height - 37, 500,35), " This is the text
string for a Box Control ");
```

7.   Save the script.

8.   Turn on Maximize on Play in the Game window.

9.   Click Play and observe the changes.

The Box control text centers no matter what the screen size is, but the Label control text looks to be left-justified.

10.   Select the Game GUISkin and change the Label's Alignment to Upper Center (Figure 12-11).

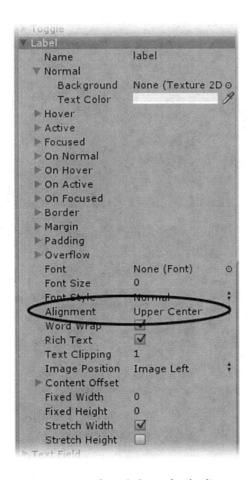

Figure 12-11.   *The Label template's Alignment property*

You will be displaying three types of text messages. The first is the short description of the object that will be called currentObjectName in the metadata. You may decide that the text for the short description label should be different. Instead of duplicating the GUISkin and changing it inside the OnGUI function at runtime, you can create a GUI Style that can override the regular skin's version of *any* control.

Unlike the previous changes you've made, because this is a variable in a script, you will have to make sure you are not in Play mode when changing it.

1. Add the following line near the top of the GameManager script:

    ```
    var customGUIStyle : GUIStyle; // override the skin
    ```

2. Save the script and stop Play mode.

3. Select the Control Center object and look for the new Custom GUIStyle variable in the Inspector.

4. Expand the new variable as shown in Figure 12-12.

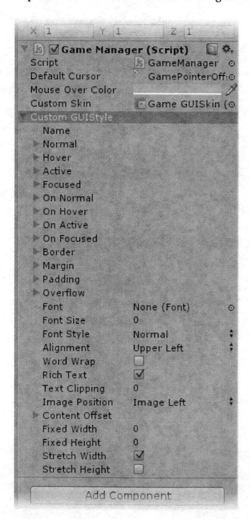

Figure 12-12. *The new Custom GUIStyle in the GameManager script*

Because the variable is of GUIStyle type, it automatically generates all of the parameters needed to create a new *style* or template of GUI control.

5. Change the Text Color in the Normal section to a paler shade of your regular label text.

6. Set the Alignment to Upper Center.

7. Duplicate the Label line and make the following changes:

```
GUI.Label (Rect (Screen.width/2 - 250, Screen.height - 65, 500,35), "Short Name",
customGUIStyle);
```

Note the new GUIStyle variable is added as the *last* argument inside the parentheses. This is how the GUIStyle overrides the GUISkin specified at the top of the OnGUI function.

8. Save the script and click Play.

The new override version of the label behaves nicely, as shown in Figure 12-13.

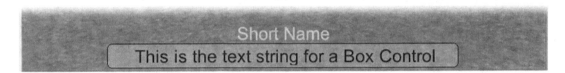

Figure 12-13. *The new custom version of the Label control*

For those with no experience in web design and 2D text layout, the concept of CSS may be a bit nebulous. A GUISkin is a collection of styles. Each has the same list of parameters, but depending on the control it is named for, it may not use all of them. The Label, for example, never uses Hover, Active, Focused, or Normal, or many of the several other settings listed under it.

When you use GUI.Label, the defined preset for a Label control knows what kind of behavior is associated with the control and makes use only of the style's parameters that are applicable to a label. A custom GUIStyle, as you probably noticed, has the same settings as the rest of the prefabs, but it is not associated with any particular control *until it is added as an override*. At that time, only the applicable settings are used. You could, then, use the same GUIStyle for several different control types. If you set it up to look like a button and override a Label control, the label would look like a button but still have the behavior of a label. If you override a Box control with it, it will look like a button and act like a box. If you override a Horizontal Slider with it, it will *not* look like a button, because a Horizontal Slider does not use the same settings from the list as a button. This allows you to make custom GUIStyles for any control you need, but it comes with some overhead, because a good portion of the settings are never used.

Next, you need a means of turning the text off and on.

1. While in Play mode, try turning the Main Camera's GUILayer off.

Nothing happens. Apparently, UnityGUI is not affected by the GUI layer, as are the GUIText and GUITexture components of GameObjects. You'll have to devise another means of turning them off and on.

2. Stop Play mode.

Text Visibility

If you remember, the OnGUI function is similar to the Update function in that it is called at least every frame, and that's where your code must be to create the GUI controls. Much as you did with the first scripting tests, you have to set a *flag* to tell the engine whether or not to draw the text. Let's start with a simple test to make sure we're on the right track.

1.   Open the GameManager script.

2.   Add the following variable with the other GUI variables:

```
var useText : boolean = true; // flag to suppress or allow all text
```

3.   Then add the conditional to check for it, so it wraps the labels and box lines:

```
if (useText){
  GUI.Label (Rect (Screen.width/2 - 250, 10, 500,35), " This is the text string for a
Label Control");
  GUI.Label (Rect (Screen.width/2 - 250, Screen.height - 65, 500,35), "Short Name",
customGUIStyle);
  GUI.Box (Rect (Screen.width/2 - 250, Screen.height - 37, 500,35), " This is the text
string for a Box Control ");
  }
```

4.   Save the script.

5.   Click Play.

6.   Select the Control Center object and try turning the useText parameter off and on.

The controls now turn *all* GUI text off and on. This gives you a means of turning *all text* off and on for the game when you allow players to customize their game experience.

Because the text needs to show and hide with mouseovers, you need two types of flags. The *show* flag will be used for turning the text off and on during regular game play, and the *use* flag will globally control whether the text is being used at all. Show flags will be handled by the script, so they will always be internal variables.

As the variable name useText indicates, you'll use this flag to tell whether to show any text at all. But you also need a variable to let you know when the text should actually be seen during the course of the game. This means that when the object the cursor is over sends a message to the pointer object to change color, it should *also* tell the GameManager script to change a showText variable there as well. You should assign a false to this variable, because the text should only show when the cursor is over an action object.

1.   Add the showText variable beneath the useText variable declaration:

```
var showText : boolean= false; // flag to toggle text during play
```

And now you can embed the showText conditional within the useText conditional.

Add the showText conditional so the GUI elements look as follows:

```
if (useText){     //global toggle
   if (showText){ //local toggle
   GUI.Label (Rect (Screen.width/2 - 250, 10, 500,35), " This is the text string for a
Label Control");
```

```
    GUI.Box (Rect (Screen.width/2 - 250, Screen.height - 37, 500,35), " This is the text string for a
Box Control ");
    GUI.Label (Rect (Screen.width/2 - 250, Screen.height - 65, 500,35), "Short name",
customGUIStyle);
    }
}
```

2. Save the script.

3. Click Play

The text no longer appears in the Game window.

4. Try checking and un-checking the two new text parameters at the bottom of the GameManager component to see the text turned off and on.

5. Stop Play mode.

Next let's hook up the cursor visibility and the text visibility.

You've seen how to send messages (i.e., call functions) from other objects with the GamePointer color change in the Interactor. Now let's try something different. You can set the value of a variable directly, if you have access to the object it's on and know the script name. To control text visibility, you change the showText variable's value. With dot notation, you can access it as soon as you locate the object and the script. Because the mouseover check is done on the object, you have to look at the Interactor script.

1. Add a comment to the top of the cursor section:

    ```
    // Cursor control
    ```

2. Open the Interactor script.

In the Start function, you can see that the Control Center object has already been introduced, so you are good to go.

3. Inside the OnMouseEnter function, above the controlCenter.SendMessage("CursorColorChange", true) line, add the following:

    ```
    //activate the text visibility on mouseover
    controlCenter.GetComponent(GameManager).showText = true;
    ```

4. Inside the OnMouseExit function, above the controlCenter.SendMessage("CursorColorChange", false) line, add the following:

    ```
    //deactivate the text visibility on mouseover
    controlCenter.GetComponent(GameManager).showText = false;
    ```

5. Save the script.

6. Click Play and test the functionality.

7. Be sure to move out of range and check it as well.

So far things look pretty good, but you need to do more thorough testing.

1. Move close enough so that the text box is over part of the action objects.

2. Try to mouse over them.

The text flickers badly (Figure 12-14).

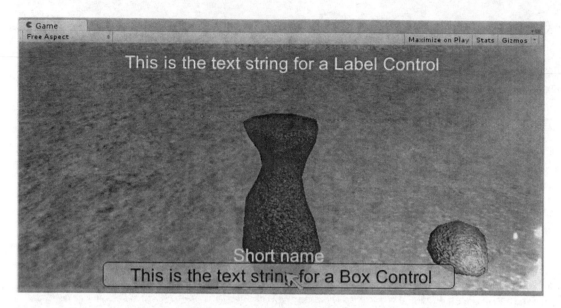

Figure 12-14. The Box control, behaving as a Box control, blocks mouseovers

Let's take a moment to figure out what is happening. On mouseover, the text is displayed. The problem comes with the Box control, because it blocks mouseover activity behind it. That triggers a mouse off, which turns off the control, which in turn unblocks it and causes another mouseover … and so on. Fortunately, it is not the graphic of the box that is the problem; it is the internal functionality of a Box GUI control.

3. Open the GameManager script.

4. Add another variable for a custom GUIStyle above the text variables:

   ```
   var boxStyleLabel : GUIStyle; // make a label that looks like a box
   ```

5. Save the script.

6. Stop Play mode.

7. Select the Control Center object.

8. In the Normal section of the new custom GUIStyle parameter, load the MyBox texture into the Background field.

9. Set Alignment to Upper Center.

10. Change the GUI.Box line as follows:

    ```
    GUI.Label (Rect (Screen.width/2 - 250, Screen.height - 37, 500,35), "This is the text
    string for a fake Box Control", boxStyleLabel);
    ```

11. Save the script.

12. Click Play and mouse over the action objects.

The entire box texture is stretched to fit the specified rectangle (Figure 12-15).

Figure 12-15. The MyBox texture, stretched to fit the rectangle's dimensions

1. From the Project view, select the Game GUISkin.

2. Compare its Box control's parameters with your Box Style Label's parameters.

Close inspection shows that the Box control uses a value of 6 in the Border parameters to avoid stretching the whole texture (the texture happens to be 12×12 pixels) and 4 in the Padding, to prevent the text from getting too close to the edge of the texture.

3. Stop Play mode.

4. Change the Box Style Label's Border, Left, Right, Top, and Center, to **6** each (see Figure 12-16).

Figure 12-16. Setting the Label's Border to match the Box control's Border

5. Save your scene and project.

It is time to think about feeding the object metadata into the text. You may want to add the Interactor script to the rest of the action objects at this time and fill out the object name and description arrays. Consult the State Management PDF for the set up and values.

Using the Object Metadata

Before accessing the action object's metadata, there are a few more things to do. In keeping with the rest of the optional functionality, you'll want to include the short and long descriptions. At this time, you also have to make an executive decision on what exactly the user will be able to turn off and on. Presently, the user can toggle mouseover cursor color, mouseover object color (material), and GUI text. The next options to consider are long and short descriptions of the object the mouse is over and the message that will appear when the object is activated, the *action* message.

If useText is on, let's assume the player wants to see the short description and the action text. If useLongDesc is on, let's include the long description as well.

1. Open the GameManager script from the Control Center and add the following variables near the top:

```
var useLongDesc : boolean = true;           // flag to suppress or allow long description
internal var showShortDesc : boolean = true; // flag to toggle short description during play
internal var showLongDesc : boolean = true; // flag to toggle long description during play
internal var showActionMsg : boolean = true;
```

As this will be feeding new text into the GUI controls every time the player mouse overs and mouse offs objects, you should also clear the text, in case some objects don't yet have their data filled in.

2. Add the following to clear the values:

```
internal var shortDesc : String = "";
internal var longDesc : String = "";
internal var actionMsg : String = "";
```

Now, you can make changes to the OnGUI function to add the individual conditions and also use the variables instead of static text.

3. Change the text part of the OnGUI functions as follows:

```
if (useText){      //global toggle
   if (showText){ //local toggle
      if (showActionMsg) GUI.Label (Rect (Screen.width/2 - 250, 10, 500,35), actionMsg);
         if (useLongDesc) {
            if (showLongDesc) GUI.Label (Rect (Screen.width/2 - 250, Screen.height - 37,
500,35), longDesc, boxStyleLabel);
            }
         if (showShortDesc) GUI.Label (Rect (Screen.width/2 - 250, Screen.height - 65,
500,35), shortDesc, customGUIStyle);
      }
}
```

4. Save the script.

If you test the functionality now, you should see nothing but the box texture on mouseover, because the current values for the text are all "", empty strings. Let's head back to the Interactor script and have it send out the information we need.

1. Open the Interactor script.

2. In the OnMouseEnter function, under the
controlCenter.GetComponent(GameManager).showText = true line, add:

```
//send the correct text to the GameManager for display
controlCenter.GetComponent(GameManager). shortDesc = objectName[1];
controlCenter.GetComponent(GameManager).longDesc = description[1];
```

Until you have your code loading the current state's metadata values, you can just use Element 1's values. Element 0 is out of scene, so the names and descriptions aren't needed.

The actionMsg, in case you are wondering, resides in the ObjectLookUp script. You will finish it when you hook up the state management results.

3. Click Play and hover over each of the objects you've filled out Interactors for.

4. Remembering the text showing is for Element 1 names and descriptions, make any necessary repairs left over from the cut and paste.

If you received an "Array index is out of range." error message, it probably means the array size for the object name and object description is still 0. If you disable the Interactor script on an object, you'll still get mouseover events happening and errors generated.

It might be nice if the long message were shown only when within the pick distance. It's just a few more lines of code, but aesthetically worth the trouble.

5. In the Interactor script, in the OnMouseEnter function, beneath the lines you just added to send the correct text to the GameManager for display, add the following:

```
// automatic bypass flag
if(DistanceFromCamera() <= triggerDistance) {
        controlCenter.GetComponent(GameManager).inRange =true;}
else   controlCenter.GetComponent(GameManager).inRange =false;
```

These lines set a flag you will call, inRange, in the GameManager that will bypass the long description, if the inRange variable is false.

6. Save the Interactor script.

7. Open the GameManager script.

8. Add the following internal variable near the top:

```
internal var inRange : boolean; // distance flag for long desc
```

9. In the OnGUI function, in the showLongDesc conditional, add the "and", &&, so *both* conditions must be met in order for the long description to be shown:

```
if (showLongDesc && inRange)
    GUI.Label (Rect (Screen.width/2 - 250, Screen.height - 37, 500,35), longDesc);
```

10. Save the script.

11. Click Play and test the functionality (see Figure 12-17).

Figure 12-17. The ChestLid in range (left) and outside of picking distance (right)

Now, when the player is beyond pick range, the long description will not show.

The next step is to use the correct text for the current state. Instead of using Element 1, you will use currentState, the variable that holds the current state.

1. Open the Interactor script.

2. In the OnMouseEnter function, under the controlCenter.GetComponent(GameManager). showText = true line, change the Element 1 to currentState:

```
//send the correct text to the GameManager for display
controlCenter.GetComponent(GameManager). shortDesc = objectName[1];
controlCenter.GetComponent(GameManager).longDesc = description[1];
```

3. Save the script.

4. Click Play and test by clicking the various objects into their next state.

The states change, and as long as you mouse over a new object, then return, the mouseover text reports the correct name and state. The problem is that the text persists after the pick. So, in addition to hiding the cursor, you will have to turn off the short and long descriptions on a valid mousedown.

5. In the Interactor script, in the ProcessObject function, above the // start timer line, add:

```
//deactivate the text messages
controlCenter.GetComponent(GameManager).showText = false;
```

6. Save the script.

7. Click Play and test by clicking the various objects into their next state.

Now you have a clear view of the objects animating. The showText variable is turned on as soon as the cursor moves over the next action object, as long as the cursor is on and the object is not being processed. If you wanted the cursor to re-trigger the text without having to mouse off then back over, you could use an OnMouseOver instead of the current OnMouseEnter. Before testing that, you should get the replies text going.

Currently, you bump out of the OnMouseDown function when the Player tries to pick an object that is in the scene but not pickable, location state 2. Now that you've got the mouseover text up and running, you'll want to prevent those messages from showing up on the non-pickable objects as well.

1. In the Interactor script, at the top of the OnMouseOver function, add the following:

```
if(location[currentState] == 2) return; // object is not pickable in scene
```

2. Save the script.

3. Click Play and pick the rock, so that it moves into its non-pickable state, then try mouse overing it.

Now the rock no longer registers as an action object.

4. Exit Play mode.

Tweaking the Text

You are probably thinking it would be easier to test the text if there were something to read after a pick. This is where you can have some fun. You might, for example, add something like this for the rock: "You grunt with effort as you move the rock aside, barely missing your foot as it thuds into place."

1. Fill out the Replies according to the State Management PDF for this chapter.

The pedestal ought to be updated before you go any further.

2.   Change the Pedestal's Interactor data while you're there.

▓ **Tip** The Inspector is not an ideal place to type a lot of text into your arrays. It makes more sense to keep a text file with the information from which you can copy and paste. You can also undock the Inspector view by clicking and dragging on the tab at its top. The quickest way to put it back is to set the layout back to one of the presets.

Let's finish adjusting the action text in the GameManager. You can have it display in the same spot as the description text, but you may have to make some changes in order to fit a nice, chatty account of the events.

3.   Open the GameManager script.

The action message line is already there, but it is inside the if(showText) block, as well as in its own showActionMsg conditional. While you are working out how you want it to look, let's use a text string in a duplicate GUI element, instead of the actual message.

4.   Add the following test line inside the OnGUI function, just below the GUI.skin line:

```
GUI.Label (Rect (Screen.width/2 - 300, Screen.height - 47, 600, 32), "This is a really
long and complicated bit of text, so we can test the text on screen size.");
```

5.   Remove the boxStyleLabel from the showLongDesc line, so it uses the regular Game GUISkin again:

```
if (showLongDesc && inRange) GUI.Label (Rect (Screen.width/2 - 250, Screen.height - 37,
500,35), longDesc);
```

6.   Save the script.

7.   Click Play.

8.   Select the Game GUISkin in the Project view and open the Label preset.

▓ **Tip** Font and Style overrides are only supported for dynamic fonts.

---

9.   Try adjusting the Font Size.

Nothing happens, because arial2 is not set to Dynamic (Figure 12-18).

Figure 12-18. Arial2 is not dynamic, so the font size doesn't change

10.   Change the Overflow Font to **Arial** and adjust the Font Size to **16.**

This time, the font size changes, as shown in Figure 12-19.

Figure 12-19. *With Arial, the font size changes*

11. Adjust the size, so that all of the text shows.

12. Now mouse over one of the action objects.

The long description text has *also* been scaled (Figure 12-20). The short description text uses a custom GUIStyle and is not affected.

Figure 12-20. *All Game GUISkin font sizes are affected*

13. Back in the Inspector, increase the Font Size to **24**.

The text is once again clipped at the end of the line.

14. Experiment with the Font Style.

Arial has versions for italic, bold, and bold italic included.

15. Set the Font Style back to Normal.

16. Uncheck Word Wrap.

The text is centered but clipped at both ends of the line (Figure 12-21).

Figure 12-21. *The text is now clipped at both ends of the line*

17. Change Text Clipping to **0**.

The text extends over both sides of its rectangular (the Rect dimensions) bounds (Figure 12-22).

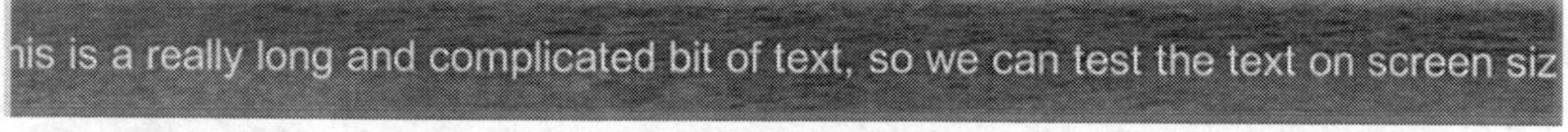

Figure 12-22. *The text extending beyond its bounds*

18. Check Word Wrap, set Alignment to Middle Center and adjust the Font Size to **22**.

The text reverts to its originally specified size and wraps to a second line, instead of being clipped or overflowing the rectangle (Figure 12-23).

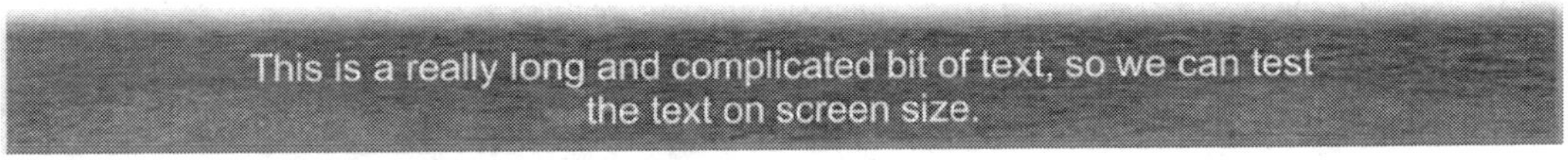

Figure 12-23. *The text wrapping to a second line*

Next, you will experiment with a different font.

1.   Load the *WIZZARD* font into the Overflow Font.

Figure 12-24 shows the result.

Figure 12-24. *The WIZZARD font*

2.   Try adjusting the Font Style.

The *WIZZARD* font changes accordingly.
Note that changes to the GUISkin during runtime are retained.

3.   Drag and drop a TrueType font of your own choosing into the Fonts folder if you wish.

4.   In the GameManager script, adjust the Rect size and placement to suit the font you chose,

5.   Copy these Rect settings into the actionMsg line:

```
if(showActionMsg)
    GUI.Label (Rect (Screen.width/2 - 300, Screen.height - 75, 600, 32),actionMsg);
```

6.   Delete the test line.

7.   Save the script.

At some point, you may have seen the warning message shown in Figure 12-25 in the status line.

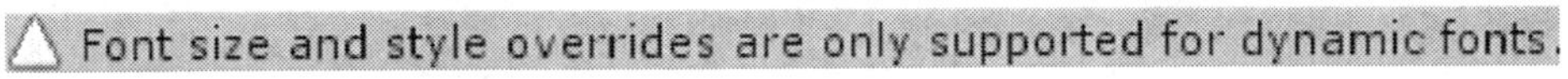

Figure 12-25. *The warning message*

8.   Check to make sure the fonts you are using are all set to Dynamic.

9.   Stop Play mode.

Activating the Action Message

Now that you've learned a bit more about fonts, you can see about activating the action message and the other tasks that go with that. First, though, you may want to either move the Flame Base object aside or simply deactivate it for now.

1. Deactivate, or move, the Flame Base away from the rest of the action objects.

2. Open the ObjectLookup script.

If you look at the for(var contents, etc.... block of code in the LookUpState function, you'll remember that it loops through each of the elements of the state you sent it, looking for a match for the cursor in each element. The problem with that type of for loop is that it doesn't have an obvious way to know where it is in the process. You can easily add a local (to the LookUpState function) variable to keep track.

3. Inside the LookUpState function, below the switch block, add the following:

```
var element : int = 0; // variable to track the element number for a match
```

In the switch code, you may recall, you loaded the Unity built-in repliesState arrays into a single string-type array named currentReplyArray, according to which state was passed in. The element where the match was found is used to find the corresponding element in the replies. Take a few moments to digest the logic behind what is happening if you need to.

4. Underneath the if (readString[0] == matchCursor) line, add the following:

```
print (currentReplyArray[element]);//print reply that corresponds to the matched
stateArray
```

5. Above the for loop's closing curly bracket, } // close the for/in block, increment the counter:

```
element ++; //increment the element counter by 1
```

6. Save the script.

You've got a lot of messages still printing from the ObjectLookup, so now would be a good time to comment out or delete the old ones.

7. Comment out or delete all but the print statement you just added from the LookupState function.

8. Click Play and try picking the rock and the chest lid (see Figure 12-26).

> ⓘ You grunt with effort as you move the heavy rock aside.

Figure 12-26. The reply from picking the rock in the console

The correct action text appears in the console (preceding Figure 12-26), so now you can send it off to the other scripts for processing and tell GameManager to show the action text.

9. Replace your print statement so it sends the data to the GameManager, instead of printing to the console:

```
//send the correct text message off to the GameManager
controlCenter.GetComponent(GameManager).actionMsg = currentReplyArray[element];
```

10. Save the script.

11. Open the Interactor script.

12. In the ProcessObject function, under the //deactivate the text messages section, add the following:

```
//tell the GameManager to show the action text
controlCenter.GetComponent(GameManager).showActionMsg=true;
```

13. Save the script.

14. Click Play and test the pick, then mouse over a different object.

At this point, you can see that there's a problem. The OnMouseDown function has a line that tells the showText flag to be false, so the text is hidden as soon as the player picks an object.

1. Open the GameManager script and inspect the OnGUI function.

The problem is that the actionMsg line is inside the showText conditional and is turned off, in addition to the short and long mouseover description text. Fortunately, this is an easy problem to fix. Keeping in mind that it still needs to be under the control of the global useText flag, you can move it below the useText line and above the showText line. In this case, it might have been better to name showText to showMoText (for mouseover).

2. Move the actionMsg text line above the showText conditional so the if(useText) section looks like this:

```
if (useText){  //global toggle
    if (showActionMsg)
        GUI.Label (Rect (Screen.width/2 - 300, Screen.height - 47, 600, 35), actionMsg);
    if (showText){ //local toggle
        if (useLongDesc) {
            if (showLongDesc && inRange) GUI.Label (Rect (Screen.width/2 - 250,
Screen.height - 37, 500,35), longDesc);
        }
        if (showShortDesc) GUI.Label (Rect (Screen.width/2 - 250, Screen.height - 65, 500,35),
shortDesc, customGUIStyle);
    }
}
//reset mouseover s
if (resetMO) GUI.Box (Rect (0, 0, Screen.width,Screen.height),"",customGUIStyle);
}
```

3. Save the script.

4. Click Play and test.

Now, the action message appears when the object is picked, and the mouseover text disappears. But, as Figure 12-27 shows, if you are still hovering over an action object when the time is up, the mouseover text is drawn on top of it.

Figure 12-27. The action message and mouseover text showing at the same time

So, finally, you need to tell GameManager when to turn the action text off. You've already created a timer to turn the cursor back on after a pick, but it's too quick to allow the player to read the reply. Let's increase the time to about two and a half seconds and see what it looks like.

1. Open the Interactor script.

2. In the `// start timer` section of the `ProcessObject` function, change the 0.5 to **2.5**:

    ```
    pickTimerTime = Time.time + 2.5; // set the timer to go for 2.5 seconds
    ```

3. In the `Update` function, just below the timer code that tells the `GameManager` to quit suppressing the pointer, add:

    ```
    //tell the GameManager to hide the action text
    controlCenter.GetComponent(GameManager).showActionMsg = false;
    ```

4. Save the script.

5. Click Play and test the action objects.

■ **Tip**   If you get an ArgumentOutOfRangeException, it probably means you have not yet correctly defined the size of the Reply Arrays for that object.

Because the objects are still clustered rather close together, you may have discovered that mouseover text from another object could be drawn on top of the action text before it finishes displaying. You can easily add another condition to the GameManager to prevent this from happening.

1. Open the GameManager.

2. Change the `if(showText)` conditional to read:

    ```
    if(showText && !showActionMsg) {
    ```

Now the two descriptions will not show if the action text is still showing.

3. Save the script and test.

Now you have a new problem. The mouseovers don't show up until the object has been picked in the scene. This suggests that the showActionMsg flag is initialized as true, thereby blocking the mouseover text display. It's an easy fix.

4. Open the GameManager script.

5. Change the showActionMsg flag to false:

```
internal var showActionMsg = false;
```

6. Save the script and test again.

This time all behaves as expected.

The messages behave well except for one minor issue. If you pick an object, then move quickly over to another and pick it, its action message disappears too quickly. While it seems unlikely at this point that you'd have two action objects this close together, it is important to work out how to solve this little problem. The first step is to figure out what's happening.

When Object 1 is picked, a timer is started in its Interactor script's Update function to allow processing time. When Object 2 is picked, its action message text replaces Object 1's text, and another timer is started in *its* Interactor script's Update function. The problem is that they are *both* going to tell the GameManager to turn off the action message text. Object 1 will finish sooner and will tell the GameManager to turn the text off before Object 2's timer is finished, thus shortening player reading time. The challenge is to devise a means of knowing if another object is already using the action message text.

To do that, you have to tell GameManager which object has activated the actionMsg text and, more important, which object is trying to deactivate it. If the two are not one and the same, the message should not be deactivated. Let's start by creating a variable in GameManager to hold the name of the currently active actionMsg.

1. Open the GameManager script.

2. Add the following variable below the rest of the text vars:

```
internal var actionObject : String; // the name of the last action object to turn
on the actionMsg
```

The script will update the variable each time something turns on the actionMsg and will consult it before turning the actionMsg off.

3. Save the script.

4. Open the Interactor script.

5. In the ProcessObject function, add the following line beneath the // start timer section:

```
//tell the GameManager which object just started the pickTimer
controlCenter.GetComponent(GameManager).actionObject = this.name;
```

6. Inside the Update function, change the pickTimer section as follows:

```
if (controlCenter.GetComponent(GameManager).actionObject == this.name) {
    //tell the GameManager to hide the action text
    controlCenter.GetComponent(GameManager).showActionMsg = false;
}
```

7. Save the script.

8. Click Play and test.

The messages are now working smoothly, but now the cursor timing is too long. Instead of making yet another timer, you can add an offset that will turn the cursor on sooner than it turns on the text.

1. Remove the suppressPointer line and put it into its own if clause:

```
if (pickTimer && Time.time > pickTimerTime -1.5) { // if time is up and flag is on...
    // turn off the flag to suppress the cursor
    controlCenter.GetComponent(GameManager).suppressPointer = false;
}
```

This time, you are checking the timer 1.5 seconds earlier than it's set to be turned off. Feel free to adjust the offset.

2. The text and the timer are turned off in the remaining code:

```
if (pickTimer && Time.time > pickTimerTime) { // if time is up and flag is on...
    pickTimer = false;                         // turn off the flag
    if (controlCenter.GetComponent(GameManager).actionObject  == this.name) {
        //tell the GameManager to hide the action text
        controlCenter.GetComponent(GameManager).showActionMsg = false;
    }
}
```

3. Save the script.

4. Click Play and test.

The cursor appears sooner than the text disappears, allowing the player to continue reading or go find another object to interact with. The only problem is with objects that go out of scene right after picking.

5. Click Play and test by picking the Flower, then the Pollen Ball.

As soon as the Pollen Ball is picked, the visibility state 0, deactivate at start, turns off the timer, so the action message text goes off before the player can even see it, and the cursor goes back on. Then it waits for the sound to play and then deactivates the object.

If you comment out the line that kills the timer, the action message won't go away, nor the cursor reappear until you mouse over something else. If you try setting the time to the offset time, the object will probably be deactivated before the message text can be turned off.

So the solution will be to create a little function on the GameManager script that can do an emergency reset of the suppress cursor and hide message text. Let's start by copying the timer code.

1. In the Interactor script's Update function, copy the timer code for the suppress pointer and turn off action message sections.

2. Paste them at the top of the GameManager's Update function and remove the control center part (you're already in the correct script now):

```
if (pickTimer && Time.time > pickTimerTime -1.5) { // if time is up and flag is on...
    // turn off the flag to suppress the cursor
    suppressPointer = false;
}
```

In the second clause you'll check the name of the (soon-to-be) deactivated object against the last picked object before turning off the action message.

```
if (pickTimer && Time.time > pickTimerTime) { // if time is up and flag is on...
   pickTimer = false; // turn off the flag
   if (actionObject  == tempActionObject) {    // make sure another object hasn't started its timer
       // hide the action text
       showActionMsg = false;
   }
}
```

You'll need timer variables and the new variable to hold the object's name.

3. Add the following variables to the GameManager, just under the internal var actionObject : String declaration:

```
internal var pickTimer : boolean;        // flag to check timer
internal var pickTimerTime : float;      // new time to check for
internal var tempActionObject : String; // var to holdth e emergency reset object name
```

And now you will need the little function that the (soon-to-be) deactivated object calls with its dying breath...

4. Add the following function to the GameManager:

```
function EmergencyTimer (dyingObject : String) {

    tempActionObject = dyingObject;   // assign the name of the dying object to the temp var
    // start the pickTimer
    pickTimerTime = Time.time + 2.5; // set the timer to go for 2.5 seconds
    pickTimer = true;                // turn on the flag to check the timer
}
```

5. Save the script.

And, finally, you will have to swap out the line that originally turned the timer off for the one that will trigger the emergency timer.

6. In the Interactor script, in the HandleVisibility function's case 0, replace:

```
// turn off the timer for the cursor before deactivating the object
pickTimerTime = Time.time; // set timer to now to force it to finish
yield; // make sure the timer has been stopped
```

with:

```
// turn on the emergency timer to finish handling the pointer and action message
controlCenter.GetComponent(GameManager).EmergencyTimer(this.name);
yield; // make sure the action is carried out
```

7. Save the script.

8. Click Play and test the Flower/Pollen ball sequence.

This time, the action message shows long after the Pollen Ball has been removed from the scene.

Tracking Cursor Movement

The timing seems reasonable for reading a short action message but may be too rushed for something longer or for players with a different native language. One of the traps that it is easy to fall into while authoring interactivity is to make the response times too short. After seeing a particular sequence so many times, it's all too easy to start thinking it is too slow. Whatever the reason, if you allow the player to turn off the message himself with his own cursor movement, you're covered. The assumption is that if the player is busy reading the message, he won't be moving the cursor off to look at something else.

So now, instead of turning the cursor off at the end of the timer, you will set a flag to look for cursor movement. This way, the player still gets the original read time, but if he doesn't shift the cursor from that point on, the text will now remain until he does.

1. Open the GameManager script.

2. Add a variable for watching the player mouse position in the // Pick and mouseover info section:

```
internal var watchForInput : boolean = false; // flag to watch for mouse movement after
action message
internal var lastMousePos : Vector3;          // last mouse position
```

3. In the Update function, add the code that watches and monitors the position:

```
if (watchForInput) {                            // if the flag is on,
   if (Input.mousePosition.x != lastMousePos.x) { // if the cursor has moved,
        //player has moved the mouse, so hide the action text
        showActionMsg = false;
        //turn off the flag
        watchForInput = false;
   }
}
```

In case you're wondering why you are only checking the cursor's x position for change, logically, it's pretty unlikely the player will be able to move the mouse on only one axis. You could just as easily have used the y axis.

The Interactor, when its timer is up for the action message, will have to tell the GameManager to start watching for cursor movement. It will also have to report the current cursor position. If the EmergencyTimer in the GameManager is running, it will also need to set the flag and the current cursor position, so you may as well make a little function for the tasks.

4. In the GameManager script, add the following function:

```
function StartWatching () {

    watchForInput = true;                 // turn on the watching flag
    lastMousePos = Input.mousePosition;   // record the latest cursor position
}
```

Now you can replace the instructions to turn off the text with the call to the new function. A side benefit of the new functionality is that you no longer need to prevent the message from turning off, if the player picks a new action object right away. This time, the player is in control of when it turns off.

5. In the Update function, in the pickTimer conditional that turns off the action message, change:

```
if (actionObject  == tempActionObject) {
   //hide the action text
   showActionMsg = false;
}
```

To:

```
// start watching for player mouse movement
StartWatching ();
```

6. Delete both lines that track the action object:

```
internal var actionObject : String; // the name of the last action object to turn on
the actionMsg
```

and:

```
internal var tempActionObject : String; // var to hold the emergency reset object name
```

7. And delete the assignment of that variable from the EmergencyTimer function:

```
tempActionObject = dyingObject; // assign the name of the dying object to the temp var
```

8. Save the script.

The pickTimer code in the Interactor script needs the change as well.

9. Open the Interactor script.

10. In the Update function, in the pickTimer conditional that tells the GameManager to turn off the action message, change:

```
if (controlCenter.GetComponent(GameManager).actionObject  == this.name) {
   //tell the GameManager to hide the action text
   controlCenter.GetComponent(GameManager).showActionMsg = false;
}
```

to:

```
//tell the GameManager to start watching for player mouse movement
controlCenter.GetComponent(GameManager).StartWatching ();
```

11. In the ProcessObject function, just below the pickTimer = true line, delete the following:

```
//tell the GameManager which object just started the pickTimer
controlCenter.GetComponent(GameManager).actionObject  = this.name;
```

12. Save the script.

With the improved player functionality in place, you're ready to test.

13. Click Play and try picking the various objects, changing your response speed between them.

A Final Refinement

With the mechanics in place for all of the messaging, you now have the opportunity to add a nice touch with little extra trouble. When a player is close enough to an object to get the short description but not yet close enough to pick the object, it would be nice to tell him that he is not close enough to interact with the object. You need only slip a bit of code into the OnMouseDown function.

The logic is as follows: if the pick is made between the triggerDistance and the triggerDistance + moOffset, the script will display a message using the actionMsg text for a couple of seconds, and then turn off the message and exit the OnMouseDown function.

1. Open the *Interactor* script.

2. Inside the OnMouseDown function, change the if (DistanceFromCamera() > triggerDistance) return line to include the offset distance:

    ```
    // exit if we are not within the range plus offset
    if (DistanceFromCamera() > triggerDistance + moOffset) return;
    ```

3. Comment out or delete the print line while you are there.

4. Directly beneath that line, add the following:

    ```
    // if the player is within mouseover but not picking distance...
    if (DistanceFromCamera()  > triggerDistance ) {
       var tempMsg : String = "You are too far from the " + objectName[currentState].
    ToLower() + " to interact with it";
       //send the GameManager the action text
       controlCenter.GetComponent(GameManager).actionMsg = tempMsg;
       //tell the GameManager to show the action text
       controlCenter.GetComponent(GameManager).showActionMsg = true;
       //wait two seconds then turn off the action text and then leave the function
       yield new WaitForSeconds(2.0);
       controlCenter.GetComponent(GameManager).showActionMsg = false;
       return;
    }
    ```

The script already knows you are within triggerDistance + moOffset (or you would have exited the function in the first distance check), so you need only check to see if you are farther than the trigger distance. If the condition is met, the code creates a string using the object's current state short description, sends it to the GameManager as an actionMsg text, and turns the actionMsg on. Next, the function uses a simple yield command to wait a couple of seconds and then tells the GameManager to turn the actionMsg text off. You then exit the function, so nothing further is done with the pick. Note the use of the ToLower() function to convert the object's current short description name to lowercase, for use inside a sentence.

5. Save the script.

6. Click Play.

7. Back away from the action objects just far enough to stop the mouseover description and pick an object (Figure 12-28).

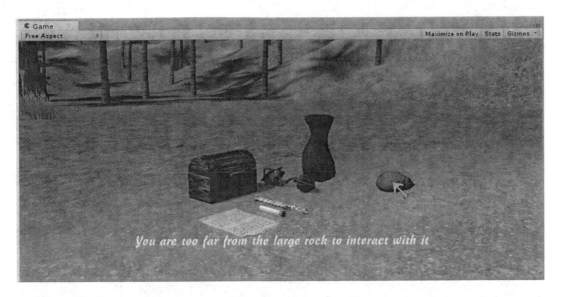

Figure 12-28. Telling a player he is too far to pick

The new message tells you you're not close enough for a pick.

8. Save the scene and save the project.

You've now got the basics of a simple, interactive adventure game blocked in. Inventory, of course, would make it a *lot* more interesting, so you'll tackle that next.

Summary

In this chapter, you were introduced to the Unity GUI as a means of adding 2D text on screen to display mouseover and message text. You discovered the GUISkin, which provides a way of creating GUI elements with a consistent look and feel, and, later, the GUIStyle, which is a means of overriding the skin in particular places. You experimented with the parameters for the GUI controls and found you could make label controls look like box controls while still acting like labels. After you learned that the GUI elements exist only through scripting, you found that Rect parameters define the position and region a control will occupy.

You learned that dynamic fonts from the OS use less texture memory, but include the risk of dropping back to a default, if the font you specify doesn't exist on the player's system. When using the alternative to dynamic fonts, the ASCII default sets, you discovered that a duplicate font must be created for each font for each size you need, and that a texture containing the entire set of characters is created for each.

Being able to draw text onscreen led to the next logical step—tapping the action object's metadata for the correct messages for both mouseover and action message. It seemed best to break the distance to the object into two zones. The outer zone provided the mouseover short description and didn't allow for picked objects. The inner zone provided long descriptions and allowed the action objects to be picked.

Once the correct messages were working, you started hooking the animations and audio clips to the pick, using the Lookup information to determine which state the objects needed to go into and then using the object's metadata to handle the appropriate actions.

And, finally, you allowed the player control over the time the action message was shown on screen.

In the next chapter, you will start to develop an inventory system and allow for different cursors, as the player collects various action objects for use through the game.

CHAPTER 13

■ ■ ■

Inventory Logic

In shooter-type games where the cursor is hidden during game play, when the user has to access and interact with menus or other option information, it's usually handled by stopping game play and loading in an entirely different level for that express purpose. This bypasses the need to suspend navigation, reinstate the cursor, and a number of other issues, many of which you have already solved in previous chapters.

In a classic point-and-click adventure, interacting with the inventory is one of the most important features. That being the case, the inventory mode will be a layer that lives over the regular scene and can be brought up with a minimum of interference. Although you'll briefly look into a technique for creating an off-screen collection of 3D objects, you will be using 2D textures for the cursors and inventory representations for your game. To get started

1. Open the Interaction scene in the project.

2. Use Save Scene As to save it as **Inventory** in the Scenes folder.

3. Save the project.

Using Layers

In order to manage the inventory without resorting to a different level, you will have to make use of Unity's Layers. Layers are mostly used by cameras and lights to define which objects get rendered or lit. They give you a way to define a collection of objects for processing. For cameras, you can think of the layers as you would compositing. Each layer can be turned off and on, but just as important, you can easily control the layering order. When you were experimenting with the rock, you used a layer to prevent a blob shadow from being drawn on the rock it was "being cast by." This time, you will be handing the entire inventory system through them.

Let's go ahead and create a few layers, so you can start organizing things in preparation for the inventory.

1. At the top of the Inspector, click the Layer drop-down and choose Add Layer.

2. Click User Layer 9 and click in the field area to the right of it to put it into edit mode.

3. Name the layer **Inventory**, as shown in Figure 13-1.

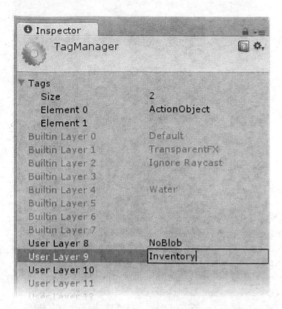

Figure 13-1. *The new Pointer layer*

You will have to refer to these layers by number in specific instances, so you may want to note the numbers that correspond to the names you have assigned to each.

Next, you will be adding a new camera to the scene.

1. From the GameObject menu, choose Create Other and create a new Camera.

2. Name it **Camera Inventory** and remove its Audio Listener component.

3. In its Camera component, click the Clear Flags drop-down and select Depth Only.

4. Under Culling Mask, click Nothing.

5. Open Culling Mask again and choose the Inventory layer, as shown in Figure 13-2.

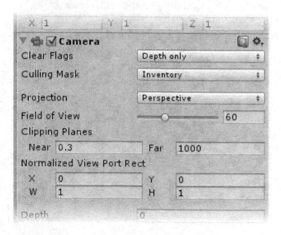

Figure 13-2. *Camera settings for Camera Inventory*

As of yet, you have nothing assigned to this layer, so you once again see the main camera's view in the Game view window.

1. Select the original Main Camera (on the First Person Controller).

2. In its Camera component, make note of its Depth setting, 0.

3. Select the Camera Inventory again.

4. Because it will be drawn after (in front of) the main camera's view, set the Depth to **1**.

The Depth parameter orders the draw order of the camera layers. The layers get drawn from lowest number to highest number. The main camera has a Depth of 0 so it is drawn first. The next item drawn is the Inventory camera with a Depth number of 1.

While you will be using 2D images for the inventory objects, let's see how you *could* use 3D objects in inventory, instead of 2D texture objects. With layers, you could place a duplicate set of 3D objects in a nice, clear spot in the scene for the inventory. It doesn't necessarily need to be in a clear area, because of layers, but that would make it easier to edit.

Now it's time to give your new layers a test run.

1. Select the Camera Inventory in the Hierarchy view.

2. In the Scene view, switch to the Z iso view by using the Scene Gizmo.

3. Move the camera well below the lowest point of the terrain (Figure 13-3).

Figure 13-3. Camera Inventory placed below the terrain (camera icons turned on in Gizmos)

4. From GameObjects menu, choose Align View to Selected, to see what the camera sees.

5. Create a new Cube and rename it to **CubeInv**.

6. In the Inspector, change its layer to Inventory (Figure 13-4).

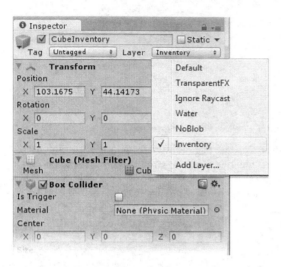

Figure 13-4. *Adding the CubeInventory to the Inventory layer*

7. Change the Scene view to the X view and move the cube away from the camera until it appears in the Game window.

It should appear in the Game view in front of the regular scene objects, as shown in Figure 13-5.

Figure 13-5. *The cube in the Inventory layer seen by the Camera Inventory (Overlay and Scene Lights toggles off)*

8. Add the SimpleRotateToggle script from the MyScripts folder to the Cube.

9. Click Play and pick the cube.

The functionality remains the same even with different layers.

10. Try navigating the scene.

The cube remains in the same place in relation to the 2D screen space, as shown in Figure 13-6.

Figure 13-6. *The cube happily rotating in front of everything, wherever you go in the scene*

11. Stop Play mode.

12. Delete the cube.

If you were tempted to drag the Interactor script onto the cube, you probably realized at some point that the distance to camera is checking with the main camera, not the inventory camera, so you could never be close enough to pick the cube.

Now that layers have provided you with a good way to organize the inventory, let's start building its framework.

Creating the Inventory Screen

At this point, you need to make an executive decision. You have used the UnityGUI to create and handle your text and pointer. While it makes continuity of style throughout the game easier, it has the major drawback that there is nothing tangible to work within the Hierarchy view. As this book is written more for those of you with an art background than a programming background, you will be using the object-based GUI Texture option for the inventory's construction, so it will not be so abstract. This also allows you to continue using metadata and state lookups as with the 3D objects. Let's get building.

Rather than take up the entire screen, the inventory will allow the regular scene to show in the background to keep the feeling of "game" going. For this, you will need a texture upon which you can arrange the icons representing your collection of loot, tools, and objects of questionable purpose.

1. Copy the Inventory Assets folder from the BookAssets folder into the project's Assets folder.

2. Open the folder and examine its contents (Figure 13-7).

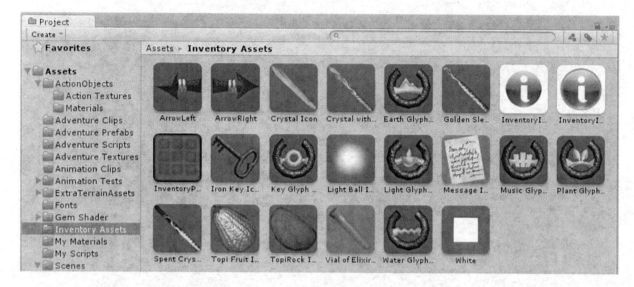

Figure 13-7. The contents of the Inventory Assets folder in the two-column Project view

3. Select the InventoryPanel texture in the Project view.

4. In the Inspector, set the Texture Type to GUI.

5. Click Apply.

6. Repeat the procedure for each of the textures in the folder.

This automatically removes things such as MIP Mapping and other high-resource, unneeded options.

7. From the GameObject menu ➤ Create Other, select GUI Texture.

A new semitransparent 2D object appears in the scene and in the Hierarchy view, but not in the Scene or Game views.

8. In the Inspector, change its Layer to Inventory.

9. The GUI Texture object now shows in the Game view (Figure 13-8).

Figure 13-8. *The InventoryPanel GUI texture object in the Game view*

10. Select the First Person Controller's Main Camera.

11. In its Culling Mask drop-down, uncheck Inventory (Figure 13-9).

Figure 13-9. *The Main Camera's Culling Mask with Inventory removed*

The mask now says Mixed...instead of Everything.

12. Select the Camera Inventory.

13. Try toggling its GUI layer off and on.

The panel disappears and reappears.

Theoretically, you could control the inventory without the use of other cameras and layers, because you are using GUI Textures for it. However, taking into consideration that you may opt to experiment with 3D inventory objects at some point, you will make use of the camera layer as planned. You'll also be disabling the entire Camera component, because there's no other reason to leave it on when the inventory is not showing.

14. Select the InventoryPanel in the Hierarchy view.

15. Try rescaling the Game window to observe the placement and centering the panel has by default.

16. Click Play and see how it affects your current game functionality.

At present, there is no effect. Mouseovers and picks are still recognized. You may be thinking that this would have been a logical time to use the Box UnityGUI control that blocks interaction with the 3D objects underneath it. On the other hand, if you had Maximize on Play toggled on, you would realize that objects outside the panel would act as usual.

The first thing you will need to do, then, is come up with a means of knowing when the inventory is showing or, more expressly, when you are in Inventory mode. As usual, you can create a variable to hold that information. At this point, however, you need to decide where to put your variable. Let's start by adding it to the GameManager script, because that is where you are storing most of the other variables that have to be accessed by other scripts.

1. Open the GameManager script.

2. Add the following internal variable:

```
internal var iMode = false; // flag for whether inventory mode is off or on
```

3. Save the script.

Because you will have to add a lot of functionality to manage the inventory, let's go ahead and create a script for it.

4. Create a new JavaScript in the Adventure Scripts folder and name it **InventoryManager**.

5. Open the new script.

First off, it will need to use the iMode variable. You can expose this one to the Inspector, so you can test it easier.

6. Add the following to the top of the script:

```
var iMode = false;          // local flag for whether inventory mode is off or on
internal var controlCenter : GameObject;
```

7. Next, create a Start function and add it as follows:

```
function Start () {
   camera.enabled = false;
   controlCenter = GameObject.Find("Control Center"); // access the control center
   iMode = controlCenter.GetComponent(GameManager).iMode;
}
```

To start testing the inventory mode, you will use the Ikey to toggle it off and on, because this is a fairly standard key to use, regardless of genre. Key presses are checked for constantly, so this code will go into the Update function. Unlike the virtual keys used by Unity's Input manager, the player won't be able to remap this one, unless you write code for it. Because there will be several things to take care of, you can make the key press call a function that you can add to as you go.

1. In the Update function, add the following code:

```
if (Input.GetKeyDown("i")) ToggleMode(); // call the function if i key is pressed
```

Because you are using layers, all you have to do is disable the camera to turn the visual part of the inventory off. You also need to inform the GameManager script of state changes in iMode.

2. Create the ToggleMode function as follows:

```
// toggle inventory visibility
function ToggleMode () {

   if (iMode) {                    // if you are in inventory mode, turn it off
      camera.enabled = false;// turn off the camera

      iMode = false;            // change the flag
      controlCenter.GetComponent(GameManager).iMode = false; // inform the manager
      return;                     // make sure the function is exited
   }
   else {                          // else it was off so turn it on
      camera.enabled = true; // turn on the camera

      iMode = true;             // change the flag
      controlCenter.GetComponent(GameManager).iMode = true; // inform the manager
      return;                     // make sure the function is exited  }

}
```

3. Save the script.

If you don't specify a particular camera, the camera component must be on the gameObject that contains the script, in this case, the Camera Inventory.

4. Add the InventoryManager script to the Camera Inventory object.

5. Turn the Camera component of the Camera Inventory object off (the panel will disappear from the Game window).

6. Click Play and press the I key on the keyboard a few times to check the functionality.

A bit further along, you will also give the player an icon on screen to get in and out of Inventory mode, but for now, let's concentrate on the additional requirements for the functionality.

1. Try navigating the scene with the inventory panel showing, picking and mousing over the action objects.

As you can see, there are several things you have to prevent while in inventory. Let's start with the most obvious: scene navigation.

2. While in Play mode, try turning off various navigation components on the First Person Controller gameObject to see what will be required.

3. Stop Play mode.

After a bit of experimentation, you will have found that you must disable the First Person Controller but not its children, as you still need the main camera to render the 3D scene. But you also need to turn off the MouseLookRestricted script on the camera. If you are wondering whether the Input.ResetInputAxes() code could do the job, it won't. A quick test will show you that the I key is also considered input—even though it doesn't have a virtual key in the Input Manager.

To do both restrictions, you will have to introduce the First Person Controller object to the script. Because it need only be once, you can just drag and drop it into a variable, rather than script it to be found at startup. You may as well do the same for the camera, while you're at it.

1. Open the InventoryManager script.

2. Add the following variables:

```
var fPController : GameObject;
var fPCamera : GameObject;
```

3. Save the script.

4. Select the Camera Inventory object.

5. Drag the First Person Controller and the Main Camera onto the appropriate variables in the Inspector.

6. Back in the InventoryManager script, in the ToggleMode function, add the following lines inside the if clause, just below the camera.enabled=false line:

```
// unblock navigation
fPController.GetComponent(CharacterMotor).enabled = true;                // turn on navigation
fPController.GetComponent(FPAdventurerInputController).enabled = true; // turn on navigation
fPController.GetComponent(MouseLookRestricted).enabled = true;          // turn on navigation
fPCamera.GetComponent(MouseLookRestricted).enabled = true;
```

7. And in the else clause, under its camera.enabled=true line, add:

```
// block navigation
fPController.GetComponent(CharacterMotor).enabled = false;                // turn off navigation
fPController.GetComponent(FPAdventurerInputController).enabled = false; // turn off navigation
fPController.GetComponent(MouseLookRestricted).enabled = false;          // turn off navigation
fPCamera.GetComponent(MouseLookRestricted).enabled = false;
```

8. Save the script.

9. Click Play, toggle the inventory panel on, and test the navigation functionality.

Next, you have to block mouseovers and picks on anything that is not part of the inventory layer. In the Interactor script, when the OnMouseEnter and OnMouseDown functions are called, you must find out whether you are in inventory mode, by checking with the GameManager and then checking on the layer that the parent object is in.

1. Open the Interactor script.

2. Add the following internal var in the //Misc vars section:

    ```
    internal var iMode : boolean; // inventory mode flag
    ```

3. In the OnMouseOver function, below the if(processing) return line, add the following:

    ```
    iMode = controlCenter.GetComponent(GameManager).iMode; // get current iMode
    if (iMode && gameObject.layer != 9) return;          // return if the mouse was not
    over and inventory object and you are in inventory mode
    ```

Remember that layers are referred to in the code by their layer number and that the Inventory layer is using number 9. GameObject.layer gets the layer assignment for the object that this script is on. If it returns layer 9 and you are in inventory mode, you exit the OnMouseOver function.

For the mouse pick, OnMouseDown, you already got the updated iMode during the mouseover, so you only need the conditional.

4. In the OnMouseDown function, below the if(processing) return line, add the following:

    ```
    if (iMode && gameObject.layer != 9) return; // currently in inventory mode
    ```

5. Save the script.

6. Click Play and test the inventory mode, trying to interact with the action objects.

Nothing is processed from the 3D scene layer.

Let's add an icon on screen as an alternative means of toggling inventory. It has to be accessible, whether the Inventory layer is invisible or the scene interaction is blocked. Because you are filtering out interaction from both layers at one time or other, your icon either has to go on a different layer or be a UnityGUI control.

The UnityGUI Button control has a lot of functionality built in, so let's look at it first. Buttons, by their very nature, are conditionals: *if* the button is picked, *do* something. The UnityGUI Button is no exception. The nice thing about having made your ToggleMode function is that it makes testing different modes of access easy.

1. Open the GameManager script.

2. Add the following in the OnGUI function, above the pointer section:

    ```
    if (GUI.Button (Rect(5,Screen.height - 35,32,32),"i")) {
        // call the Toggle Mode function when this button is picked
        GameObject.Find("Camera Inventory").SendMessage("ToggleMode");
    }
    ```

3. Save the script.

4. Click Play and test the button, as shown in Figure 13-10.

Figure 13-10. *The Unity GUI Button control to access Inventory mode*

    5.   Test a combination of button and keyboard to toggle the inventory screen.

The problem with the UnityGUI Button control is that it really doesn't work well as a button, visually. You could change the Button style in your GUISkin, but then when you have to make regular buttons, they would all look like the inventory button. A better solution would be to add another Custom Style variable to create a style just for the inventory icon, using custom textures and behaviors. Fortunately, there just happens to be one sitting around that is no longer being used, the Box Style Label in the GameManager. As long as you use it with a GUIButton, it will act like a button.

    1.   Change the (GUI.Button line you just added to the GameManager as follows:

```
if (GUI.Button (Rect(5,Screen.height - 35,32,32), "", boxStyleLabel)) {
```

    2.   Save the script.

    3.   Stop Play mode.

    4.   Select the Control Panel object and load the InventoryIconA texture into its Normal Background (Figure 13-11, left).

    5.   Load the InventoryIcon texture into its Hover Background (Figure 13-11, left).

    6.   Set the Border values to **0**.

    7.   Click Play and check out the newly textured button in the Game view (Figure 13-11, right).

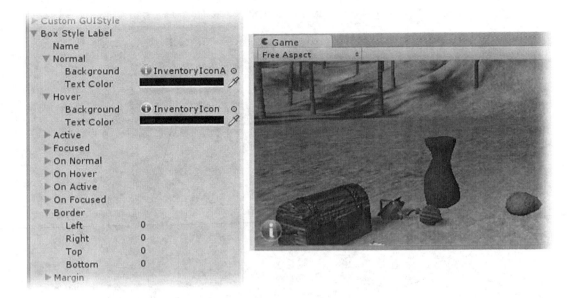

Figure 13-11. *The newly repurposed Box Style Label*

The Inventory Icon now works well, visually and functionally.

8. Turn off Play mode.

Adding Inventory Icons

As with the inventory panel, the 2D icons for your game will be GUI Texture objects, so you will have something tangible to access in the Hierarchy view. Because they need mouseover events and pick events, just like their 3D counterparts, they will need the same metadata and lookup handling as well.

The problem you will run into is that these do not have a Mesh Renderer and will throw an error when you add the Interactor script to them as it tries to handle a mouseover color change. Rather than create an Interactor script just for the 2D objects, you can reuse the color-change code from the CustomCursor script for color change and write in a condition for which type of color change to use.

Let's add an inventory object, so you will have something to test with.

1. In the Project view, open the Inventory Assets folder and select the Crystal Icon texture.

2. From the Create Object menu, create a new GUI Texture with the Crystal texture.

3. Set its Width and Height to **64**.

4. Set the X and Y Pixel Insets to **−32**.

5. In the Inspector, set its X location to **0.25**, so it won't be over any of the 3D action objects, as shown in Figure 13-12.

Figure 13-12. The Crystal icon in the scene

6. Add the Interactor script to it.

Inventory objects always have the same states. State 0 is not in scene (location 0); state 1 is object is in inventory (location 1); and state 2 is object is cursor (location 2). If an inventory object is combined with another, it becomes a different object, so there are no other states. Inventory objects are always shown or hidden immediately.

7. Open the GameNotes text asset from the Adventure Scripts folder.

8. Add the following to it:

    Cursor States:

    > 0: not in scene

    > 1: is in Inventory

    > 2: is Cursor

9. Save the text asset.

10. Select the Crystal Icon object.

11. Fill out the Interactor metadata for the icon, unchecking Animates, and giving it three elements for each array, including the sound arrays, but not the animation arrays, as per the State Manager PDF for this chapter.

12. Fill out the name and description for the elements. Use the same name and description for each array's three elements for now, as shown in Figure 13-13.

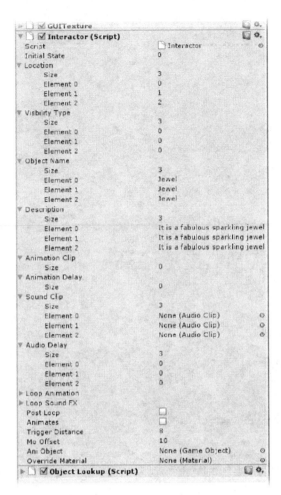
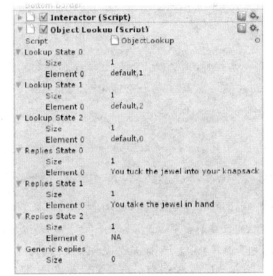

Figure 13-13. *The Crystal Icon's metadata and lookup information*

Next, you will need to adjust the code to skip the 2d objects when appropriate.

1. Open the Interactor script.

2. Then add the following variable somewhere near the top of the //ObjectMetadata section, so you will only have to check its type once:

```
var objectIs3D = true; //flag to identify GUI Texture objects
```

3. Save the script.

4. Select the Crystal icon.

5. Uncheck the new Object Is 3d variable.

6. Set the Crystal's Initial State to **1**, so you can test it in the scene.

7. Click Play and mouse over the Crystal.

When the icons are on screen in the inventory panel, they should display their metadata messages, just as the regular 3D objects. The problem here is that they don't exist in 3D space, so you can't get a proper distance value.

8. Comment out the `if (DistanceFromCamera())` line.

9. Save the script.

10. Click Play and test.

To get around this little issue, you can add the check for `objectIs3D`.

1. Uncomment the distance check line and add the `objectIs3D` condition to it:

```
// exit if you are not within range and it is a 3d object
if (objectIs3D && DistanceFromCamera() > triggerDistance + moOffset) return;
```

By checking whether the object is 3D first, the engine won't have to make the distance calculation for the second condition, if the object is not 3D.

Now you get the mouseover cursor color change. In the inventory panel, you may want to have the icons change as you mouse over them. Because GUI Textures in Unity default to having gray added to them, you will see nice results if you change the color to white. It will give a nice brightening affect.

2. In the `OnMouseEnter` function, add the following:

```
if (!objectIs3D) guiTexture.color = Color.white;
```

3. Add its counterpart in the `OnMouseExit` function, below the `if (processing)` line:

```
if (!objectIs3D) guiTexture.color = Color.grey;
```

Note the use of the British spelling of *gray*. It will take it spelled either way.

4. Click Play and test the mouseover.

White is probably too much. The default texture color is `Color.grey`, or `Color(0.5,0.5,0.5,1)`, so if you go halfway between, the color brightens just a bit, to indicate the mouseover.

5. Change the line in the `OnMouseOver` function to the following:

```
if (!objectIs3D)  guiTexture.color = Color(0.75, 0.75, 0.75,1); // brighten the 2D icon a little
```

6. Click Play and test.

The effect is more subtle.

And you will also have to restore the icon's original color after being picked.

7. In the `OnMouseExit` function, below the `if(processing)` line:

```
// restore the 2D object color
if (!objectIs3D)  guiTexture.color = Color.grey;
```

8. Save the script.

To get the rest of the mouseover text to appear, you will have to deal with the other distance checks.

1. In the OnMouseOver function, in the // automatic bypass section, add the !objectIs3D condition:

```
// automatic bypass flag
if(!objectIs3D || DistanceFromCamera() <= triggerDistance) {
```

This time, the operator is the or operator, so if the object is not 3D or it is within range, show the description. The OnMouseDown also needs the distance checks updated.

2. In the OnMouseDown function, in the // exit, if you are not within range section, change the conditional as follows:

```
// exit if you are not within range and it is a 3D object
if (objectIs3D && DistanceFromCamera() > triggerDistance + moOffset) return;
```

3. Change the if(DistanceFromCamera() > triggerDistance) line to:

```
if (objectIs3D && DistanceFromCamera() > triggerDistance ) {
```

4. Save the script.

5. Click Play and test by picking the crystal.

The action message shows nicely, and the object pops out of the scene.

With the action object functionality working for the 2D object, now you will have to put the icon into the Inventory layer, so it only appears during inventory mode.

1. Stop Play mode.

2. Assign the Crystal icon to the Inventory layer.

3. Turn off Maximize on Play if it was on, so the crystal will be within the panel object.

4. Click Play and go into inventory mode and test the mouseover on the crystal.

The first thing you notice is the Crystal icon is behind the InventoryPanel, but at least the mouseover is working (Figure 13-14).

Figure 13-14. *The Crystal icon, drawn before the inventory panel*

For GUI Texture objects, you can adjust their Z position in the scene. Essentially, it adjusts their "distance" from the camera. A lower number is "closer" to the camera.

5. Select the Inventory Panel.

6. Decrease its Z Position until it is behind the icon; it has to be less than 0.

7. Stop Play mode and set the InventoryPanel's Z Position to **–1**.

▪ **Tip**　GUI Texture and GUI Text objects can be draw-ordered, using their Z Position in the Inspector.

2D Object Handling

Let's forge ahead and handle the visibility of the 2D objects. Unlike the 3D objects, the 2D GUI objects all have the same three states: not in scene, is in inventory, and is cursor. As such, the functionality is fairly predictable and should be handled separately from the 3D objects. When an object is picked from inventory, it becomes the cursor. When it is used on a 3D action object, it may have to go back into inventory, or it may be removed altogether. If it is being used as a cursor and picks an object in inventory, it has to be exchanged for the picked object or, possibly, "combined" to make a new object.

As you can see, the functionality is fairly complex. The key to icon functionality handling is knowing the icon's previous state. This will let you deal with icons in inventory and as cursors at the same time.

The six possible combinations where the states have changed are shown in Table 13-1.

Table 13-1. *State Change Combinations*

States, Previous ➤ Current	Required Action
Not in Scene ➤ Is Cursor	Put to Cursor
Not in Scene ➤ Is in Inventory	Add to Inventory Enable GUITexture
Is Cursor ➤ Not in Scene	Reset Cursor
Is Cursor ➤ Is in Inventory	Reset Cursor Add to Inventory Enable GUITexture
Is in Inventory ➤ Not in Scene	Remove from Inventory Disable GUITexture
Is in Inventory ➤ Is Cursor	Remove from Inventory Disable GUITexture Put to Cursor

To begin with, you have to store the previous state before you update it with the new location. You will also want a variable to store the object's element number when it is in the inventory array, so you will know which one to remove when it is taken out of inventory.

1. Open the Interactor script.

2. In the //State dependent variables section, add the following internal variables:

```
internal var previousState :int; // need for 2D objects
```

3. Inside the ProcessObject function, above the currentState = newState line, add the following:

```
previousState = currentState;    // store the previous state before updating
```

You will be making a function called Handle2D to process the 2D objects' functionality.

4. In the if animates conditional's else clause, above the ProcessAudio() line, add the following:

```
if(!objectIs3D) Handle2D();     // send 2D objects off for processing
```

Because visibility will be handled with the rest of the processing, the 2D objects don't have to be run through the HandleVisibility function.

5. Change the HandleVisibility() line to:

```
if (objectIs3D) HandleVisibility();
```

Besides the Handle2D function, you will be making some other new functions to add and remove objects from inventory and manage the cursor. Because the cursor is handled in the GameManager script, you will either call a ResetCursor function or change the default cursor's value directly, by assigning the 2D action object's texture to it. Because the action object doesn't know what the default cursor on the GameManager is, it will have to send a message to a function, ResetCursor, to reset the cursor.

1. At the bottom of the Interactor script, start the new function and fill in the combinations of previous and current states as conditionals with your future functions to do the work:

```
//handle 2D objects
function Handle2D () {

  // Not in scene -> Is Cursor
  if (previousState == 0 && currentState == 2) {
    controlCenter.GetComponent(GameManager).currentCursor = guiTexture.texture;
    gameObject.guiTexture.enabled = false;
  }

  // Not in scene -> In Inventory
  if (previousState == 0 && currentState == 1) {
    controlCenter.SendMessage("AddToInventory", gameObject);
    gameObject.guiTexture.enabled = true;
  }

  // Is Cursor -> Not in scene
  if (previousState == 2 && currentState == 0) {
    controlCenter.SendMessage("ResetCursor");
    yield;
    gameObject.SetActive(false); // deactivate the object immediately
  }
  // Is Cursor -> In Inventory
  if (previousState == 2 && currentState == 1) {
    controlCenter.SendMessage("AddToInventory", gameObject);
    gameObject.guiTexture.enabled = true;
    controlCenter.SendMessage("ResetCursor");
  }
  // In Inventory -> Not in scene
  if (previousState == 1 && currentState == 0) {
    gameObject.guiTexture.enabled = false;
    controlCenter.SendMessage("RemoveFromInventory", gameObject);
    yield;
    gameObject.SetActive(false); // deactivate the object immediately
  }
  // In Inventory -> Is Cursor
  if (previousState == 1 && currentState == 2) {
    gameObject.guiTexture.enabled = false;
    controlCenter.SendMessage("RemoveFromInventory", gameObject);
    controlCenter.GetComponent(GameManager).currentCursor = guiTexture.texture;
  }
}
```

2. Save the script.

3. Open the GameManager script.

4. Add the following function at the bottom of the script to reset the cursor to the default:

```
function ResetCursor() {
    currentCursor = defaultCursor; // reset the cursor to the default
}
```

This might be a good time to block in the AddToInventory and RemoveFromInventory functions. Because they need to know what object to remove or add, they will be receiving an argument inside their parentheses.

5. Continuing with the GameManager script, block in the following functions:

```
function AddToInventory (object : GameObject) {

    print ("adding " + object.name + " to inventory");

}

function RemoveFromInventory (object : GameObject) {

    print ("removing" + object.name + "  from inventory");

}
```

6. Save the script.

Although you have hooked up a lot of functionality, you still have more to do. You can, however, test a small bit. The Crystal is currently in state 1 and showing in the inventory. If you pick it, it will get processed from case 1 to case 2. The cursor will become the Crystal, and the icon in inventory disappears, thanks to your Handle2D function.

7. Click Play and test the Crystal icon.

Before you can test picks with the crystal, you will have to update the code that sends everything off to the LookupState function. In the Interactor script, for testing purposes, you created a variable named cursor to pass the name of the cursor texture to the LookupState function. As of now, it is only passing the value "default" that was assigned when the variable was declared. So next, you will get the current cursor's real texture name from the GameManager.

1. Open the Interactor script.

2. Above the //send the picked object, its current state, and the cursor line, add the following:

```
// get and assign the current cursor from the GameManager
cursor = controlCenter.GetComponent(GameManager).currentCursor.name;
```

If you were to test the code now, you'd soon discover the default cursor's texture name is not "default," it's "GamePointerOffset." Rather than hard-code the cursor's name, let's go and get the texture that is assigned to the defaultCursor. This will give you the ability to change the cursor during runtime, or just whenever you want to use a different one.

3. Add the code that substitutes "default" for the defaultCursor's true texture name:

```
if (cursor == controlCenter.GetComponent(GameManager).defaultCursor.name) cursor = "default";
```

4. Save the script.

5. Click Play and make sure the default cursor still works as expected.

6. Now test with the Crystal cursor.

If you pick the regular action objects with the new Crystal cursor, they will no longer react, because interaction with your current 3D objects requires the default cursor. In the LookupState function, the cursor's texture name is passed in as the picker and reassigned as the matchCursor.

```
// check for a cursor match with element 0 of the split
if (readString[0] == matchCursor) { // if there is a match...
```

It will be nice to have a semi-generic message telling the player that a particular cursor has no effect on the picked object. Because you have already handled the "You are too far from the…" message in a similar manner, you can borrow its code and adapt it for the "no match" message.

First you'll need to create an internal variable to look for matches, match. It needs to start out as false near the top of the LookupState function and get turned to true, if there is a match. After the metadata has been fully parsed, if there was no match, you can send it off for a customized reply.

1. Open the ObjectLookup script.

2. In the LookupState function, below the var element: int = 0 line, add:

```
var match : boolean = false;                    // flag to check for cursor match
```

3. Just under the if (readString[0] == matchCursor) line, add:

```
match = true;                                   // there is a match
```

4. Below the } // close the for/in block line, and above the closing curly bracket for the LookUpState function, add the following:

```
// The current cursor, passed in as "picker", was not a match, so did not provoke
any reaction- show a reply
if (!match) HandleNoMatchReplies (picker);
```

You can create the HandleNoMatchReplies function next.

5. Start the new function:

```
function HandleNoMatchReplies (picker : String) {
```

6. Inside the new function add:

```
picker = picker.ToLower();                      // make the string all lower case
picker = picker.Substring(0,picker.length - 5); // strip off the ' Icon' part of the name
var tempObjectName = this.GetComponent(Interactor).currentObjectName.ToLower();
```

The first thing you do inside the function is reuse the picker variable; it is the name of the current cursor passed into the LookUpState function. Next, convert the name to lowercase. Then you use Substring to strip off the "Icon" part of the name. Then you get the currentObjectName from the Interactor component of the object, instead of using its object name from the Hierarchy view. Now you are ready to construct a reply and then activate the action message to display it for a couple of seconds.

7. Add the following:

```
var tempMsg = "The " + picker + " does not seem to affect the " + tempObjectName ;
//send the GameManager the action text
controlCenter.GetComponent(GameManager).actionMsg=tempMsg;
//tell the GameManager to show the action text
controlCenter.GetComponent(GameManager).showActionMsg = true;
//wait two seconds then turn off the action text and leave the function
yield new WaitForSeconds(2.0);
controlCenter.GetComponent(GameManager).showActionMsg = false;
return;
}
```

8. Save the script.

9. Click Play.

10. Pick the Crystal from inventory, leave inventory, and pick the ChestLid.

You get a nice message telling you that it doesn't do anything, as shown in Figure 13-15.

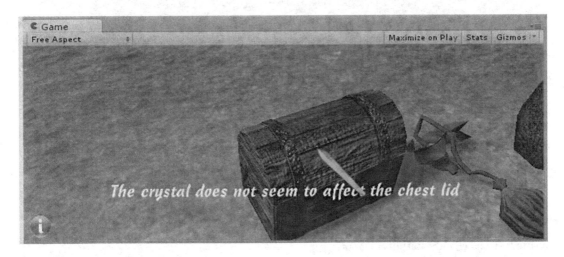

Figure 13-15. *Crystal icon picking the ChestLid*

11. Save the scene and save the project.

Cursor-Based Responses

Now that you can test different cursors against the action objects, it would be a good time to check on those objects that have different replies, depending on the cursor. Because the only thing we've got right now is the Crystal, we can set up a test case using it.

1. Select the Pedestal and change its Object Lookup data, as per Figure 13-16.

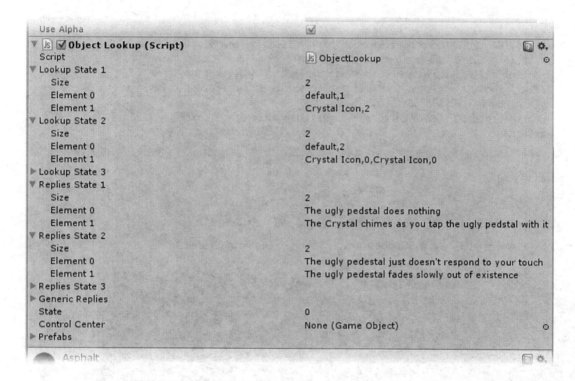

Figure 13-16. *Pedestal Object Lookup data to respond to different cursors*

In the new scenario, picking the Pedestal will get you a response but not change its state. Picking it with the Crystal as cursor will push it into state 2. Picking it again with the Crystal will put it into state 0 and will also take the Crystal out of scene with it.

2. Click Play.

3. Pick the Pedestal with the default cursor first.

You get the response for the default cursor.

4. Get the Crystal from Inventory.

5. Pick the Pedestal with it to put it into state 2.

6. Now pick it again with the Crystal.

The Crystal goes into its state 0, and the default cursor replaces it.

Dropping Cursors in the 3D Scene

Eventually, when you click the Inventory Panel with a non-default cursor, the cursor will go into inventory. If you click outside the Inventory Panel, the inventory will close, and you will have the object as cursor in the 3D scene. You may be wondering what happens if you decide you no longer want the object as cursor. To have to open the inventory and drop it in is a lot of trouble for something so minor.

You have made a start to have the cursor handled if it picks an action object, but so far, it does nothing if the object is not an action object. This would be the perfect opportunity to put the cursor back into inventory. The only problem is that unless the object has a collider, it will not even register a pick—the sky being one big example. You would also rather not have to put a script on every other object in the scene just to register a pick. The answer lies in casting a ray into the scene whenever the left mouse button is used.

Ray-casting is used regularly when shooting projectiles. The hit object is queried for type or tag, and if matched, a message is sent to set off a series of events. You will have to check to see if the hit object is an ActionObject, and, if not, send the cursor back to inventory. Because the ray is associated with a camera's GUILayer, you get the added benefit that other camera layers, such as inventory, will be ignored.

1. Open the GameManager script.

The first thing you have to add is a means of knowing when the mouse button is pressed. Because it has nothing to do with an object, where you have been using OnMouseDown, you will have always to be checking the input for that event, so you add it to the Update function.

2. Add the following inside the Update function:

```
// handle dropped cursors
if (Input.GetMouseButtonDown(0)) { // if the left button, 0, is pressed

} // close handle dropped cursors
```

Next, you will have to make a few local variables with some new variable types, so you can use the raycast.

3. Add the following inside the Input.GetMouseButtonDown block:

```
var ray : Ray = Camera.main.ScreenPointToRay(Input.mousePosition);
var hit : RaycastHit;
var didHit : boolean = Physics.Raycast(ray,hit); // did it hit anything?

if (didHit) { // you did hit something
    if (hit.transform.tag == "ActionObject") print ("Action Object : " + hit.transform.name);
    else {
    print ("nothing of note... " + hit.transform.name);
    // drop cursor here
    }
}
else  { // you hit nothing
    print ("air...");
    // drop cursor here
}
```

You do not yet have it resetting the cursor, but you will now be able to see what the cursor was over when you pressed the left mouse button.

4. Save the script.

5. Click Play and get the Crystal from Inventory.

6. Test picking around the scene and in inventory.

The console reports what you have hit (see Figure 13-17).

Figure 13-17. *Results of the raycast from a mouse pick in the scene*

Because you are in the GameManager script, where the cursor is controlled, it will be easy to change the code to add the desired functionality. The cursor and icons are identified by the textures they use, so you will have to use the texture's name to locate the icon object it represents.

7. Add another local variable below the var didHit : boolean line:

```
var cursor : GameObject = gameObject.Find(currentCursor.name);// find the inventory object from its name
```

8. Remove the print statements and rewrite the if(didHit) block as follows:

```
if (didHit) { // you did hit something
    if (hit.transform.tag == "ActionObject")  return;     // do nothing
    else {
        AddToInventory(cursor); //add the current cursor
        ResetCursor();  // reset to default
        cursor.GetComponent(Interactor).currentState = 1; // update current state
    }
}
```

Because both terrain, nonaction objects, and "nothing" will get the drop cursor functionality, you can get rid of the last else clause.

9. Remove the "air" else statement:

```
else  { // you hit nothing
   print ("air...");
   // drop cursor here
}
```

If you tested the code now, you would discover that it would put the Crystal straight into inventory when you picked it from Inventory. You'll have to check for iMode and also the default cursor. Either case being true will mean you shouldn't go any further.

10. Add the two conditions to the if (Input.GetMouseButtonDown line:

```
// if the left button, 0, is pressed and cursor is not default and not in inventory mode...
if (Input.GetMouseButtonDown(0) && currentCursor != defaultCursor && !iMode)
```

11. Save the script.

12. Click Play and test.

You haven't finished the code for the AddToInventory and RemoveFromInventory functions, but if you watch the Crystal Icon's Interactor component, you can see its states change.

You may wish to add a noninvasive sound effect to the code that handles the dropped cursor, to give the player an audio clue that it went into inventory. Because the GameManager script is on the Control Center object, that's where you'll start.

1. Stop Play mode.

2. Select the Control Center object in the Hierarchy view.

3. From the Component menu, add an Audio Source.

4. Load a sound such as plopsm into the Audio Clip.

5. Uncheck Play On Awake.

Play On Awake is useful for objects that are instantiated or created during runtime, such as explosions or other ordnance. This sound, however, is needed throughout the game.

6. Back in the GameManager script's Update function, add the following line below the cursor.GetComponent(Interactor).currentState line:

```
audio.Play();
```

7. Save the script.

8. Click Play and test.

9. Stop Play mode.

Depending on where in the scene the Control Center object is, you may or may not hear the sound. As a default in Unity, sounds are imported as 3D. Because you still might need the sound you chose as a 3D sound, let's go ahead and duplicate it, and then convert the new sound to a 2D sound.

1. Select the Ding sound asset in the Test Sounds folder.

2. Duplicate it and rename it **Drop2D**.

3. In the Inspector, uncheck 3D Sound.

4. Click Apply.

5. Select the Control Center object and assign the new object to its Audio Source.

6. Click Play and test.

7. Adjust the volume as necessary, then make the changes permanent.

8. Save the scene and save the project.

With a little bit of logic and some extra functionality, you've got the start of your inventory system. You'll be working out the mechanics of it in the next chapter.

Summary

In this chapter, you got your first look at using Layers to be able to composite multiple camera views together. Armed with this new knowledge, you created a camera and layer to house the Inventory screen as an overlay of the regular scene. Adding a new flag, iMode, you devised a means of toggling your new Inventory mode off and on with both a keyboard and onscreen icon. You also repurposed the test GUI Style, Box Style Label, to use for the inventory toggle button.

In electing to keep your scene running in the background while accessing inventory, you discovered that you needed to disable navigation and disable mouseover functionality and picks from your 3D action objects yet allow interaction with your 2D inventory and keyboard.

With the introduction of a 2D inventory object, you discovered that by adding a new flag to your action objects, objectIs3D, you could make a few changes to your Interactor script and use it for both types of objects. You specified that icon objects would only have three possible states and that enabled you to streamline their processing. For that processing, you blocked in a few new functions, AddToInventory and RemoveFromInventory.

With the addition of the fledgling cursor code, you finished the code that passes the correct cursor texture name off to the LookupState function. With that in place, you were able to check the processing with multiple cursors. If no match was found at all, you generated a semi-custom message using the cursor name and the name of the object it picked.

Finally, you found that to monitor picks on objects without OnMouseDown functions, you needed to use a raycast when the left mouse button was picked, to find out what object was under the cursor. Once found, you could get its information though a local variable of type RaycastHit. Armed with the new knowledge, you added the functionality to drop a cursor back into its inventory state from a non–Action Object pick.

In the next chapter, you will add the functionality that will manage the inventory's visual representation on screen and allow for as many objects as you need in your game.

■ ■ ■

CHAPTER 14

Managing the Inventory

Having taken care of most of the preliminary setup for your inventory system, in this chapter, you will be adding the code that handles its onscreen presentation and layout. Because an array of all the objects currently in inventory is key to the task, you will be adding most of the inventory-related code to the GameManager script, so it can be easily accessed.

Organizing the Inventory Objects

To start, let's add an internal array to hold the objects. Because it will be constantly growing and shrinking, it would be nice to be able to use a JavaScript type array. But because JavaScript arrays are dynamically typed, you wouldn't be able to use it on a mobile device. It will be a bit more work, but it will be more portable using a Unity built-in array.

1. Open the Inventory scene from the book project.

2. Open the GameManager script.

3. Below the existing variables, add the following:

```
// array of objects currently in inventory
internal var currentInventoryObjects = new GameObject[0]; // nothing in it yet
```

Next, you will have to define the layout grid for placing the icons. This will fit the panel texture supplied. If you wish to create your own texture, you may have to adjust some of the numbers, if you change the size or aspect ratio.

4. Add the following:

```
// inventory layout
internal var startPos = 140;
internal var iconSize = 90;
```

5. Save the script.

Your inventory grid will show nine items at once and scroll as needed, offering navigation arrows to access overflow. To be able to shift the inventory left and right, you will have to put all inventory objects into a parent gameObject and move it left or right, showing columns of icons as they fall within range of the inventory panel and hiding them when they do not.

1. Make sure you are not in Play mode.

2. Create an empty gameObject, and name it **Inventory Items**.

3. Drag the Crystal Icon onto the new gameObject.

4. Create another empty gameObject and name it **Inventory Group**.

5. Drag the Inventory Items group and the Inventory Panel object into it.

6. Set the X and Y Positions for the Inventory Panel object to **0.5** and **0.5**.

7. Set its Z Position to **-0.5**.

8. Select the Crystal Icon and set its X and Y Positions to **0.5** and its Z Position to **0.**

To test the functionality as you go, you will require several items to go into inventory. While developing the inventory system, you will need 11 active icons. If you wish to set up all 16 from the Inventory Assets folder, simply deactivate the extra 5.

1. Open the Inventory Assets folder in the Project view and check out the textures with names that end in "Icon."

Because you will have to keep track of the inventory objects, it will be useful to create a tag for them.

2. Click the drop-down next to Tags and select Add New... .

3. Create a new Tag and name it **InventoryObject** (Figure 14-1).

Figure 14-1. *The new tag, InventoryObject*

4. Select the Crystal Icon object.

5. Assign the InventoryObject tag to it.

6. In the Object Lookup, set its Lookup State 1, Element 0 to :

   default, 1

7. Duplicate the Crystal Icon object 15 times.

8. Copy and paste the texture names from the Inventory Assets folder into the new objects.

The objects must have the exact same names as the textures they represent, so copy/paste is the safest way to rename the new icon objects.

9. Drag the matching icon texture into each object's Texture field.

10. Save the scene and save the project.

You won't need the data updated for a while, but if you want to set it up now, consult the StateManager PDF for each object's data values for this chapter.

11. Select the Inventory Group object.

12. Assign it to the Inventory layer and agree to changing its children as well (Figure 14-2).

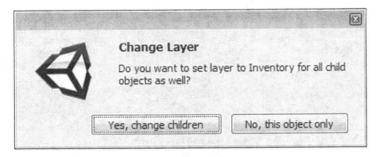

Figure 14-2. *The query dialog for changing a parent's layer*

The contents of the Inventory Group are shown in Figure 14-3.

Figure 14-3. *The inventory objects in the Hierarchy view*

You do not have to fill out the action replies at this point.

You will eventually want some objects to go directly into inventory for future use. Others, especially when their use is obvious and in the same location as the objects with which they interact, will be better off as cursors immediately. An example of this would be a rock that is launched via physics as ammunition. In this case, with a rock pile nearby, and a limitless supply of rocks, game play is much smoother, avoiding inventory, unless expressly entered.

In the test phase of setting up the inventory, you'll have all of the current icons start in inventory, go straight to cursors from state 1, and go back to inventory from state 2, cursors.

Before you start arranging the inventory, let's add a bit more functionality to the inventory mode. So far, to get in and out of inventory mode, you can either pick the icon or use the keyboard to toggle the mode. It would be nice to be able to pick outside the inventory panel to exit inventory mode, especially after selecting an inventory item as a cursor. Conversely, if you pick the panel in an empty area, it should "drop" the cursor object back into inventory.

For the latter, you will have to make a script just for the inventory panel. Because you have only one panel, it is perfectly okay to make a script solely for its use.

1. Create a new script in the Adventure Scripts folder.

2. Name it **InventoryPanel**.

3. Add it to the InventoryPanel object in the Hierarchy view.

4. Open the new script.

5. Change the Update function to OnMouseDown and add the following temporary print statement:

```
function OnMouseDown () {

    print ("I've been hit!");

}
```

6. Save the script.

7. Click Play, go into inventory mode, and pick the panel.

The message appears on the console's status line.

As long as you have an object to receive a pick, it is fairly easy to add instructions to it. Your challenge, then, is to make an object *behind* the inventory panel that covers the whole screen. It can, of course, be easily met by creating another GUI Texture object.

1. Stop Play mode.

2. Select the White texture from the Inventory Assets folder.

3. Create a new GUI Texture object.

4. Rename it **Inventory Screen**.

5. Add it to the Inventory Group object.

6. Assign it to the Inventory layer.

7. Set its size to something large, like **2048** Width by **2048** Height.

8. Select the White texture in the Project view; increase its Max Size to **2048**; and click Apply.

Theoretically, you ought to make the GUI Texture object size itself to the screen size dynamically. Realistically, unless you plan to use an image as a texture, an overly large size will probably work just as well.

1. Select the Inventory Screen object.

2. Set the Pixel Inset to **0** and **0**.

3. Set its X and Y Positions to **0**.

4. Set its Z Position to **-2,** to put it back behind the InventoryPanel.

5. Make sure the InventoryPanel's Z Position is set to **-0**.

The icons should all be at 0.5,0.5,0.

6. Click Play and decide on any changes it needs visually.

7. Stop Play mode and finalize the changes.

At this point, you have to make some executive decisions. You could set the texture's alpha to **0,** to make it totally transparent, or you could change its Color and bring down the alpha amount until it is just noticeable enough to remind users that they cannot interact with the 3D scene. Let's choose the latter for now, but feel free to change it if you wish.

1. Turn on the Camera Inventory's Camera component to see the Inventory layer in the Game view.

2. Select the Inventory Screen object.

3. Adjust the opacity and color of the Inventory Screen's GUI Texture component until you are happy with the effect (see Figure 14-4).

Figure 14-4. *The Inventory Screen, with color and opacity adjusted*

4. Turn off the Camera Inventory's Camera component.

5. Create a new script in the Adventure Scripts folder.

6. Name it **Inventory Screen**.

7. Add it to the Inventory Screen object.

8. Open it in the script editor.

9. In the Start function, add the following, to get the screen size, and then set the GUI Texture size:

```
function Start () {

    // set the GUI Texture  to match the screen size on startup
    guiTexture.pixelInset = Rect (0, 0, Screen.width, Screen.height);

}
```

Note that setting the Pixel Inset parameters works just like the UnityGUI controls.

To toggle inventory mode off when clicking the screen, you will have to access the ToggleMode function over in the InventoryIcon script.

1. In the new InventoryScreen script, create an OnMouseDown function below the Start function, as follows:

```
function OnMouseDown () {

    GameObject.Find("Camera Inventory").SendMessage("ToggleMode");

}
```

2. Save the script.

3. Turn on Maximize on Play in the Game window.

4. Click Play and go into inventory mode.

5. Click the Inventory Screen (outside the panel) to exit inventory mode.

You've got a small problem. When the inventory is toggled off, the code you added in the last chapter to put the cursor away on an empty pick is triggered. To solve that, you can delay the toggle slightly, to allow the mode switch to be evaluated after the pick.

1. At the top of the OnMouseDown function, add

```
yield new WaitForSeconds(0.25); // allow time for mouse down evaluation before toggling mode
```

2. Save the script.

3. Click Play, select the Crystal, and then pick outside the panel.

Now there is a slight pause, inventory mode is exited, and the cursor does not revert to the default cursor until you click again in the scene.

If you did not test the screen in Maximize on Play, you will notice the screen is still the size of the original Game window after resizing. In this case, the window is resized after the Start function was called, so the Inventory Screen is not updated.

■ **Speed vs. Memory**   You may have noticed that in the foregoing script, you are not defining a variable to hold the camera—finding the camera in the Start function and accessing its scripts elsewhere in this script. Instead, the script is finding the camera every time it needs to access it. Because it is accessed only once in this script, it shouldn't be a problem. While this method is slower, it doesn't use memory to store the camera. In a classic point-and-click adventure, speed is less of an issue, whereas you might wish to spend memory on nice art assets instead.

Let's continue and finish the InventoryPanel's script. As specified, when you click the panel, the current icon, if it is not the default pointer, should go into inventory. So, really, all you need to do is check which texture is on the pointer and then call the AddToInventory function from the GameManager.

1.   Open the InventoryPanel script.

Because you will have to identify the cursor prior to and while processing the pick, you should use the faster method to "introduce" the Control Center. You have to get the default cursor (texture) only once, so it makes sense to get it in the Start function as well.

2.   Add the following to the top of the script:

```
internal var controlCenter : GameObject;
internal var defaultCursor : Texture;
internal var currentCursor : Texture;

function Start () {

    controlCenter = GameObject.Find("Control Center");
    defaultCursor = controlCenter.GetComponent(GameManager). defaultCursor;

}
```

3.   And now inside the OnMouseDown function, delete the print statement and add the following:

```
// check the current cursor against the default cursor

currentCursor = controlCenter.GetComponent(GameManager). currentCursor;

if (currentCursor == defaultCursor) return; // take no action—it was the default cursor

else { // there is an action icon as cursor, so process it

    // use the cursor texture's name to find the GUI Texture object of the same name
    var addObject = GameObject.Find(currentCursor.name);

    // update the icon's current state to in inventory, 1, in the Interactor script
    addObject.GetComponent(Interactor).currentState = 1;

    //after you store the cursor's texture, reset the cursor to default
     controlCenter.SendMessage("ResetCursor");
```

```
        // and add the new object to inventory
        controlCenter.SendMessage("AddToInventory", addObject);

    }
```

Because the texture on the current cursor is also the name of the GUI Texture object, you can use its name to locate the object, update its current state, and pass it into the AddToInventory function on the GameManager script.

You should now be able to do a bit more testing. You should be able to go into inventory, click the pile of icons, "drop" the selected one by clicking an empty spot, and then select another. Other than the Pedestal and Crystal interaction, you should not yet be able to pick any object, 2D or 3D, with anything other than the default cursor.

1. Click Play.

2. Pick and drop each of the icons in inventory.

3. Check the console message for each pick.

The console reports the objects going back into inventory, but you have not written the code for it, so they are not yet visible after being dropped.

■ **Note** If you have errors, make sure the object names are exactly the same as the texture names (capitalization, spaces, and spelling).

---

1. Open the GameManager script.

Inside the Start function, you have to add a local variable to hold the inventory objects as it finds them and then go through it and assign them to the currentInventoryObjects array. This is pretty much the same code as you used to load the actionObjects array in the Awake function, but this time you are only checking for active objects. GameObject.FindGameObjectsWithTag makes a list of all the objects it finds, then you create a new built-in (as opposed to a JavaScript) array, then load the contents of the list into the array.

2. In the Start function, add the following code:

```
//get a list of the gameObjects with the InventoryObject tag
var iObjects = GameObject.FindGameObjectsWithTag("InventoryObject");

// redefine the currentInventoryObjects array with the number of elements in the list
currentInventoryObjects = new GameObject[iObjects.length];

//save the inventory objects into the array for processing in iMode
for (var i : int = 0;i < iObjects.length;i++) {
        currentInventoryObjects[i] = iObjects[i];
        print (currentInventoryObjects[i].name);
}
```

3. Save the script.

4. Click Play.

5. Inspect the console to see the list of objects (Figure 14-5, left).

6. Stop Play mode.

7. Deactivate any three icons.

8. Click Play and inspect the console again (Figure 14-5, right).

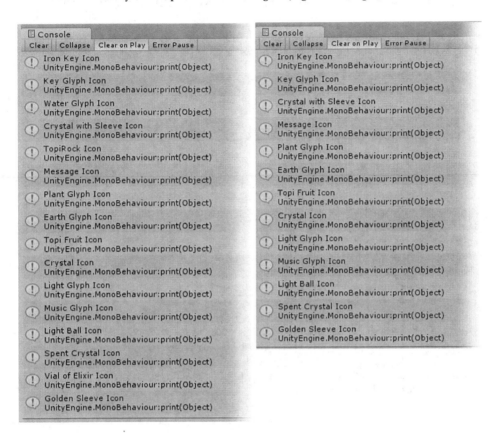

Figure 14-5. *The tagged inventory objects—all active (left) and with three deactivated (right)*

9. Stop Play mode.

When you set up all sixteen icons and disabled three, you found that the three disabled objects were not included. Now that you can generate a list, you have to take it one step further. The initial state 0 objects have already been deactivated in their own start functions—at least they should be, because the GameManager was added to the project after the Interactor script.

■ **Tip** On the off chance you ever have to control the order scripts is evaluated, you can do so through the top right button in the Inspector, Execution Order, when a script is selected.

So now you need a means of evaluating their order in inventory. Each object will have to keep track of its own position in the array. Objects that are not in the array, having a state 0 or 2, will be assigned a bogus array element number of 100, so they can easily be filtered out when updating the array.

Because the currentInventoryObjects array has been initialized to the number of active objects, and you will only be adding state 1 objects, the array could have null elements, if any of the objects is currently a cursor, state 2.

Because you will have to update the array regularly, let's break the assignment process into two parts. The first run through the inventory objects in the Start function will be to assign currentInventoryObjects element positions. It will also allow you to find out how many objects will be in the current inventory, before you create the currentInventoryObjects array.

1. Create a new variable to keep the number of elements in the current inventory array under the // array of objects currently in inventory section, as follows:

```
internal var iLength : int; // var to store the current inventory array's length
```

2. Change the inventory array code in the Start function, as follows:

```
//get a list of the gameObjects with the InventoryObject tag
var iObjects = GameObject.FindGameObjectsWithTag("InventoryObject");

var element = 0;              // initialize a counter for ordering active inventory objects

//assign objects a position number for the current inventory array
for (var i : int = 0;i < iObjects.length;i++) {
//only if its current state is 1 ( in inventory)
   if(iObjects[i].GetComponent(Interactor).initialState == 1) {
   // assign the element number to the current object
   iObjects[i].GetComponent(Interactor).iElement = element;
   element ++;              //increment the element
   }
   //else it's initial state was 2, as cursor, assign 100, state 0 is already inactive
   else iObjects[i].GetComponent(Interactor).iElement = 100;

   print (iObjects[i].GetComponent(Interactor).name + "  " + iObjects[i].
   GetComponent(Interactor).iElement);
}
iLength = element;          // save the number of elements, the number of state 1 objects
```

Next, you will have to populate the currentInventoryObjects array with all of the objects that have an initial state 1, an iElement value less than 100. They also have to be in the correct order. The first time the iElement was assigned, they were automatically in order, but once the player starts adding and removing objects from inventory, the numbers will become scrambled. Because the currentInventoryObjects array will have to be regenerated every time a change is made, it will make sense to create a function for that task.

You already know the length it will be, iLength, so you will initialize the "new" currentInventoryObjects array, then iterate through the Inventory objects, looking for a match for the current element, as you fill the new array. As you find a match, you will bump out of that for loop, by telling it you've reached the end.

3. Create a new function to order and load the array.

```
function OrderInventoryArray () {

}
```

4. Inside it, re-initialize the currentInventoryObjects array.

```
// re-initialize array for new length
currentInventoryObjects = new GameObject[iLength];
```

5. Get the Inventory objects list.

```
//get a list of the gameObjects with the InventoryObject tag
var iObjects = GameObject.FindGameObjectsWithTag("InventoryObject");
```

6. Create the nested for loops to assign the elements.

```
// load the new array with the state 1 objects, according to their iElement numbers/order
for (var e : int = 0; e < iLength; e++) { // currentInventoryObjects elements
        for (var i : int = 0; i < iObjects.length; i++) {
                // if there is a match
                if (iObjects[i].GetComponent(Interactor).iElement == e) {
                        // add that object to the new array
                        currentInventoryObjects[e] = iObjects[i];
                        // tell it you're finished looking for that element number
                        i = iObjects.length; // reached the end
                }
        }
        print (currentInventoryObjects[e] + " * " + e); // print the new entry
} // loop back to look for next element, e
```

Now, you can call the new function from the Start function, after the element numbers have been assigned.

7. In the Start function, below the iLength = element line, add the call to the new function.

```
OrderInventoryArray (); // load the currentInventoryObjects array
```

8. Save the script.

Before you can test the code, you will have to create an iElement var in the Interactor, so each object can store its current position in inventory.

9. Open the Interactor script.

10. Add the following var under the var currentState : int = 1 declaration:

```
var iElement = 100; // holds the object's element in inventory number, 100 = not state 1
```

11. Save the script.

Now you can check to see if it all works!

12. Select the Crystal with Sleeve Icon in the Hierarchy view.

13. Set its Initial State to **2**.

14. Repeat for a couple of other icon objects of your choice.

15. Click Play and inspect the console, to make sure the Crystal with Sleeve Icon is no longer included (Figure 14-6).

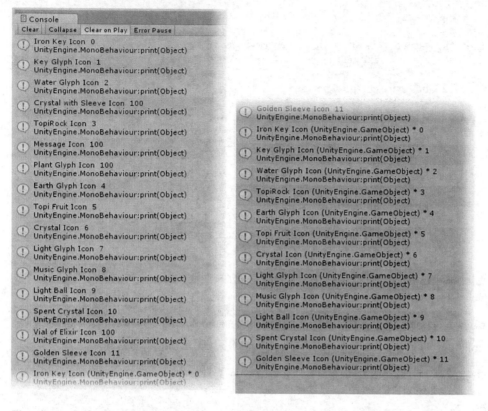

Figure 14-6. *The tagged inventory objects and their newly assigned element numbers (left), and the contents of the newly generated currentInventoryObjects array (right)*

The first group of printouts contains all of the active Inventory objects. The second group shows all of the objects in the new currentInventoryObjects array—only objects with a valid iElement value.

You should do one last check before moving on.

16. Stop Play mode.

17. Deactivate a couple of the icons and click Play.

The deactivated icons should not show in either printout.

18. Stop Play mode and reactivate the objects.

19. Comment out the print statements in the Awake and OrderInventoryObjects functions.

20. Save the script.

21. Set all inventory objects back to the Initial State of **1**.

Inventory Layout

With the groundwork taken care of, it's time to arrange the icons. You are going to be arranging them in columns of three, using the layout variables you defined earlier. Because you will need to rearrange them each time one is added or removed, let's create a function you can call when needed.

1. Open the GameManager script.

2. Create the function for the grid arrangement.

```
// arrange icons in inventory
function InventoryGrid () {

} // close the function
```

You have the starting offset for the icons from the startPos variable. It starts the first icon at the center of the slot, but the icons are actually positioned from their upper left, as they are also used as pointer textures. In screen space, 0,0 is at the lower left of the viewport, so the x offset will be a negative direction adjustment of the start position, and the y offset will be a positive.

Both x and y start positions are also dependent on the icon size, as is the space between the rows and columns. The first thing to do is adjust those values to fit the icon size.

3. Add the following local variables inside the InventoryGrid function:

```
var xPos = -startPos - iconSize/2; // adjust column offset start position according to icon
var spacer = startPos - iconSize; // calculate the spacer size
```

When iterating through an array, you always have to know how long it is, so you can stop before it throws an *index out of range* error. Because the length may change every time you rearrange the grid, you will have to define its variable also, as local inside the function.

4. Add the following line to get the inventory array's length:

```
var iLength = currentInventoryObjects.length; // length of the array
```

And then you will have to set up the for loop, to iterate through the array. As mentioned earlier, you will process the elements in threes, as the position of the rows will always be the same. In this script, you will use k as the counter, starting it at element 0, and continuing to increment it by three, while the k value is less than the array length.

5. Add the for loop.

```
for (var k = 0; k < iLength; k = k + 3) {
```

Because the y position has to be reset for each new column, it gets adjusted and set inside the for loop.

6. Add the first row's icon's position PixelInset information.

```
//row 1
var yPos = startPos - iconSize/2;
currentInventoryObjects[k].guiTexture.pixelInset = Rect(xPos, yPos, iconSize,iconSize);
```

Because you are incrementing the counter by three, you could conceivably go beyond the array length for the k+1 and k+2 elements; therefore, they have to be checked before the code tries to position a nonexistent element and throws an error.

7. Add the following, with its length-checking conditional.

```
//row 2
yPos = yPos - iconSize - spacer + 3;
if (k + 1 < iLength)
    currentInventoryObjects[k+1].guiTexture.pixelInset = Rect(xPos, yPos, iconSize,iconSize);
```

8. Add the code for the third row.

```
//row 3
yPos = yPos - iconSize - spacer + 6;
if (k + 2 < iLength)
    currentInventoryObjects[k+2].guiTexture.pixelInset = Rect(xPos, yPos, iconSize,iconSize);
```

And, finally, you will increment the column position for the next group of three icons and then add a curly bracket to close the for loop.

9. Add the following code:

```
    xPos = xPos + iconSize + spacer;  // update column position for the next group

    } // close for loop
```

Before you can test the function, you must call it from somewhere. The first place will be as soon as the objects have gone into the inventory array in the GameManager's Start function.

10. Near the bottom of the GameManager's Start function, add the following, to call your new function:

```
InventoryGrid();// arrange the inventory icons
```

11. Save the script.

12. Set the Crystal with Sleeve Icon's Initial State back to **1,** if you haven't already done so.

13. Deactivate enough icons, so that you are left with 11 active.

14. Click Play, and check the inventory to see how the code worked.

Note the overflow of two of the objects.

■ **Tip**   If you have more than one object in the center position, check to make sure the Initial state is 1. You have not yet handled visibility for state 0 on start.

The inventory panel is not symmetrical, so the icons are a bit low. Rather than fuss with the arranging script, you can easily adjust the position of their parent, the Inventory Items ameObject.

1. While still in Play mode, with the inventory showing, change the Inventory Items Y Position to about **0.01**.

2. Stop Play mode and enter it again, to make it permanent (see Figure 14-7).

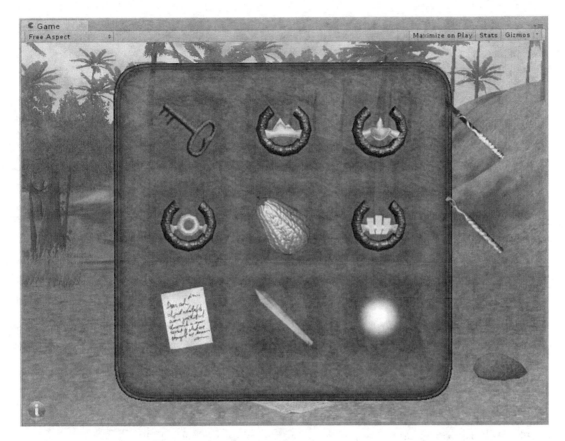

Figure 14-7. *Preliminary inventory layout*

3. Click Play and test the inventory.

The spacing isn't quite right for the rows, so you will have to add a little offset up to rows 2 and 3.

4. Add **3** to row 2.

```
//row 2
yPos = yPos - iconSize - spacer + 3;
```

5. Add **6** to row 3.

```
yPos = yPos - iconSize - spacer + 6;
```

6. Save the script.

7. Click Play and check the alignment.

If you couldn't resist picking up a cursor and picking other objects, remember that you have not yet hooked up functionality for non-default cursors picking 2D or 3D objects.

■ **Tip** If you wish to create your own inventory panel and adjust the spacing of the inventory grid, you can change the icon textures to normal maps, to see their true size, or load solid textures and then take a screenshot of the layout into your favorite paint program. If you prefer, you could just do the math and count pixels.

Inventory Overflow

So far, the inventory works well for a maximum of nine objects in inventory at any one time. It fails visibly when the number exceeds that, as the fourth column of items falls to the right of the panel, just as you would expect. Concurrent with shifting the Inventory Items GameObject left and right, you will also have to control the visibility of the overflow columns.

Before you tackle visibility, you can go ahead and get the shifting working.

1. Turn on the Camera Inventory's Camera component, if it is not already on.

2. Create a LeftArrow and RightArrow GUI Texture object from the images of the same name in the Inventory Assets folder.

3. Change their Texture Type to GUI and click Apply.

4. Change their Height and Width to **64**.

5. Assign the arrows to the Inventory layer.

6. Move them into the Inventory Group gameObject.

7. Set their Y Pixel Inset to **-245**.

8. Set the left arrow's X Pixel Inset to **-235**.

9. Set the right arrow's X Pixel Inset to **166**.

10. Click Play and go into inventory mode to observe their placement (see Figure 14-8).

Figure 14-8. *Inventory arrows added*

Feel free to adjust their position further.

You will have to make a behavior for mouseover and the functionality for picking. Let's keep it simple and merely increase the Color to a light gray. Remember the default for textures is a middle gray.

1. Create a new script in the Adventure Scripts folder.

2. Name it **ClickArrows**.

3. Change the `Update` function to an `OnMouseEnter`.

4. Add the following line, so the function looks as follows:

```
function OnMouseEnter () {

guiTexture .color = Color(0.75,0.75,0.75,1);          // brighten the texture

}
```

5. And for its `OnMouseExit` counterpart, add the following:

```
function OnMouseExit () {

guiTexture .color = Color.gray;          // return the texture to normal

}
```

6. Save the script.

7. Add it to the ArrowLeft and ArrowRight objects.

8. Click Play and test the mouseover.

Next, you have to tell the Inventory Items group to move left on mousedown. You will have to add conditions later, but for now, let's just get it started. First, you have to introduce the Inventory Items object and the Control Center object into the ClickArrows script.

1. Add the following internal variables at the top of the script:

```
internal var inventoryItems : GameObject;
internal var controlCenter : GameObject;
internal var gridOffset : int; // gridoffset
```

2. In the `Start` function, add the following, to get access to the grid offset variable and be able to move the grid:

```
inventoryItems = GameObject.Find("Inventory Items");
controlCenter = GameObject.Find("Control Center");
gridOffset = controlCenter.GetComponent(GameManager).startPos;
```

As it stands, you are positioning the icons in *pixels*, but you must shift the parent ameObject in *percent of screen*. Fortunately, because you have access to screen width and height, you can do a little math to get the answer in percent. After getting the width of the screen, you can use it to divide the grid offset or start position, startPos, from the GameManager script and arrive at the percent of the screen that the Inventory Items group requires to move left or right.

3. Add the following function:

```
function OnMouseDown () {

// convert screen width from percent to pixels for shift amount
    var amount : float = 1.0 * gridOffset/Screen.width; // divide screen width by the startPos
```

```
        if (this.name == "ArrowLeft")  { // decide on direction to shift
            amount = -amount;

        }
        inventoryItems.transform.position.x  =  inventoryItems.transform.position.x + amount;

    }
```

4. Save the script.

5. Click Play and test the arrows (see Figure 14-9).

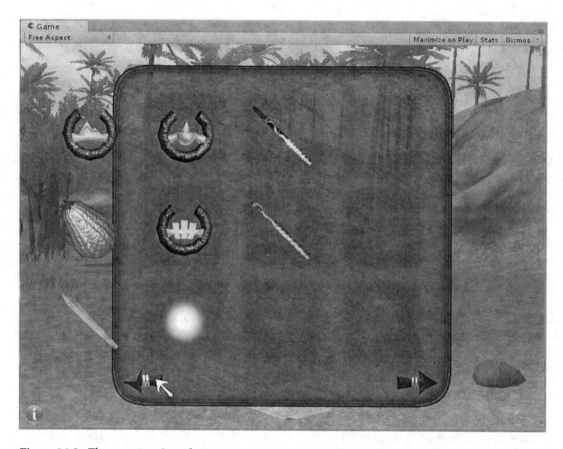

Figure 14-9. *The arrows activated*

Note where you decide which way to move the panel, by checking to see what object was picked. Remember that both arrows use the same script.

Now that the icon grid shifting is working, you need a way to determine which icons are shown. If you consider the default position to be position 0, a left-click -1, and a right-click +1, you can figure out which columns to hide. Any number less than 0 multiplied by 3 will be the number of elements from the start of the array that have to be hidden. The next nine will be visible, and any after that will be hidden.

Therefore, you will require a click-counter variable that represents the grid's position and sends itself off to the GameManager script, where the layout is being handled. The catch is that it needs to be stored and accessed from *only one* location, and you have *two* buttons that use the same script. To solve this, you will put it in the GameManager, as that script has to have access to it anyway.

1. Open the ClickArrows script.

2. Add the following variable to the top of the script, to store the updated variable when you get it:

```
internal var gridPosition : int;
```

Next, you have to get the latest value from the GameManager.

3. At the top of the OnMouseDown function, add the following:

```
gridPosition = controlCenter.GetComponent(GameManager).gridPosition; // get latest
 gridPosition
```

4. Inside the if (this.name == "ArrowLeft") clause, add the following below amount = - amount:

```
gridPosition ++; // increment the gridPosition counter by 1
```

5. And, immediately below the if block, add an else for right arrow picks, as follows:

```
// else it was the right arrow
else {

    gridPosition --; // decrement the gridPosition counter by 1

}
```

6. And, finally, send the updated gridPosition off to the GameManager, by adding the following at the bottom of the OnMouseDown function:

```
controlCenter.GetComponent(GameManager).gridPosition = gridPosition; // send it off
```

7. Save the script.

Before you can test, you have to add the gridPosition variable to the GameManager.

1. Open the GameManager script.

2. Add the following variable to the main group of variables at the top of the script:

```
var gridPosition = 0; // the default position of the inventory grid
```

3. Save the script.

4. Select the ControlCenter object.

5. Click Play and test, watching the value of the Grid Position variable in the Inspector (see Figure 14-10).

Figure 14-10. *The Inspector reporting the grid position, -1*

The counter works nicely; however, you should also consider what will happen when a new object is added to the inventory. If the object in question's element number is divisible by three, it is at the top of a *new* column. If it is greater than element 8 (remember arrays start at element 0), its new column will be off the grid. This means that when a new object is added, you should probably move the grid over, to make its column visible—especially if the user drops the object in from a cursor, rather than when it goes straight into inventory from a pick event.

The result of this logic is that, besides having the grid position sending its updates to the GameManager script, the InventoryGrid function may have to update the position on its own. The conclusion here is that instead of putting the grid shifting functionality in the OnMouseDown function, it should have its own function, which is called from the OnMouseDown function. Let's take care of that before you get any further.

1. Continuing with the ClickArrows script, change the OnMouseDown function name to ShiftGrid; it will also require a direction argument passed to it.

```
function ShiftGrid (shiftDirection: String) {
```

2. Change:

```
if(this.name == "ArrowLeft") {
```

to the following so it will use the argument that will be passed to it:

```
if (shiftDirection == "left")  {
```

■ **Note** You *could* use a Boolean, true o`r false, for the variable type, to represent left or right, because it uses fewer resources, but using a string keeps it more readable. For this script, you will use the more readable option.

---

3. To call the new function, you will make a replacement OnMouseDown function, as follows:

```
function OnMouseDown () {

    if (this.name == "ArrowLeft")  var shiftDirection = "left";
    else shiftDirection = "right";

    ShiftGrid (shiftDirection);

}
```

4. Save the script.

5. Click Play and test to make sure everything still works.

6. Save the scene and save the project.

Setting the Limits

Our inventory grid shifts nicely from left to right with the arrows, using your new ShiftArrows function. The next logical step is to limit the use of the arrows, according to the number of objects in inventory and the grid's current position. This will have to be done both when the arrows are picked and any time the inventory grid is updated.

To visually indicate an unavailable arrow, you can change its opacity, so that it appears grayed out. It should also, at that point, no longer react to mouseovers. Let's start by creating a flag to track its state. Chances are the inventory will have fewer than ten items on startup, so you can initialize the active state for either arrow to false.

1. Open the ClickArrows script.

2. Add the following internal variable near the top of the script, as follows:

```
internal var isActive : boolean = false; // keeps track of state
```

3. Inside the OnMouseEnter function, above the guiTexture.color line, add the following:

```
if (!isActive) return; // skip the mouse-over functionality if the arrow is not active
```

And, to prevent a pick registering, you will have to add the same to the OnMouseDown function.

4. Inside the OnMouseDown function, at the top, add the following:

```
if (!isActive) return; // skip the mouse-down functionality if the arrow is not active
```

Because you will have to check the limits when updating the grid *and* picking the arrows, it would be nice to have a function that can be called from either script. You will pass in the new state of the arrow as an argument.

5. Add the following function:

```
function ArrowState (newState : boolean) {

    isActive = newState;
    if (isActive) guiTexture.color  = Color(0.5,0.5,0.5,1.0); // full opacity
    else guiTexture.color = Color(0.5,0.5,0.5,0.2);           // half opacity

}
```

If you were to save the script and click play, you would notice that the arrows are not yet grayed out, even though you set the starting isActive value to false. The reason is that you have not yet called the function that adjusts the opacity. One logical place to call it will be the Start function, so it can be initialized on startup.

6. Add the following line inside the Start function:

```
ArrowState (isActive); // update the arrow opacity
```

7. Save the script.

8. Click Play and test.

Everything works fine, until you mouse off the arrows, at which point their opacity reverts to the default color—*including* the alpha value. Take a moment to look at the OnMouseExit function, to see why the arrow's transparency gets lost. The last value in the Color variable is 1.0. Because you are *not* using the default color when inactive, you cannot ignore the OnMouseExit function, as you have been able to in other scripts. Fortunately, this is easily remedied.

1. Copy and paste the same line you added to the OnMouseEnter function to the OnMouseExit function, as follows:

```
if (!isActive) return; // skip the mouse exit functionality if the arrow is not active
```

2. Save the script.

3. Test the mouseoff functionality again.

Everything works as expected. There is no activity with the arrows.

4. Change the isActive variable to true and retest, to make sure the arrows still work when active.

You will work out the logic for isActive next, as what state each arrow is in is dependent on the position of the inventory grid, as much as on the number of objects in inventory.

Inventory Grid Limits

You have to do a few calculations to manage the inventory items' visibility. Let's start with the InventoryGrid function, where the items are first laid out. There are only three possibilities for the items. They are either to the left of the grid, on the grid, or to the right of the grid.

To calculate where an item is, you have to know the current grid position. If you multiply the grid position by three (the number of icons in each column), you can get the array element number at the top row of the grid position. Now, you can check whether the item is less than the top element, gridPosition * 3, or greater than the top element plus eight, gridPosition * 3 + 8, which puts it off the grid, to the right. You have to deal with only top elements, e.g., row 1, because the rest of the rows, 2 and 3, inherit the same visibility as row 1.

1. Try the calculations on some random top elements in the following figures (see Figure 14-11).

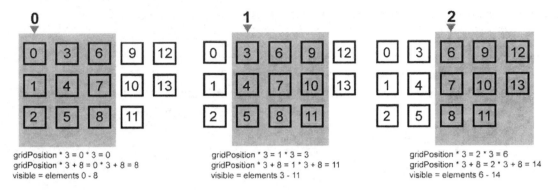

Figure 14-11. *Possible scenarios for inventory grid's current position*

The script for the visibility checking will only be a couple of lines, but it makes more sense to hide the ones that will be hidden *before* they are placed outside the grid and show the ones that are on the grid *after* they are in place. It will also keep the code cleaner to use functions to handle the actual hiding and showing of the icons. For those reasons, you will use a variable, local to the InventoryGrid function, to represent visibility. You will add the new variable and then set up the conditional that determines whether it will be true or false for each column of elements. To help check the possibilities quicker, you will also be creating a variable called iLength to keep track of the length of the inventory array.

2. Open the GameManager script.

3. In the //inventory layout section, add the following variable:

```
internal var iLength : int; // length of the array of inventory objects
```

As soon as you fill the array in the Start function, you can get the length.

4. Above the InventoryGrid() line in the Start function, add the following:

```
iLength = currentInventoryObjects.length;
```

5. Near the top of the InventoryGrid function, add the following local variable:

```
var visibility: boolean;     // variable for column visibility
```

6. Beneath the for (k = 0; k < iLength; k = k + 3)... statement, add the following visibility checker:

```
//calculate the column visibility for the top element, k, using the or, ||
if (k < gridPosition * 3 || k > gridPosition * 3 + 8) visibility = false;
else visibility = true;     // else it was on the grid
```

To do the actual hiding and showing of the objects, you will make a couple of functions—one to show and one to hide. You could make a single function for both, but then you would have to pass in both the top element for the column *and* whether the column will have to be shown or hidden.

While that is not an issue when calling the function inside the *same* script, it will prevent you from using the SendMessage command from other scripts, as it can take only one argument.

Let's add the show function first. The GameManager script already "knows" all the objects in its currentInventoryObjects array, so you will be enabling their GUI Textures.

■ **Tip** If you wanted to use 3D objects from another camera view, you would have to enable and disable the object's MeshRenderer. You could adapt this script by checking the objects' objectIs3D state and having code for both.

---

7. Add the following function to the GameManager script:

```
function ShowColumn ( topElement : int) {

    // show the elements in the 3 rows for the top element's column
    currentInventoryObjects[topElement].guiTexture.enabled = true; // row 1 element
    if (topElement + 1 < iLength)
        currentInventoryObjects[topElement + 1].guiTexture.enabled = true; // row 2
    if (topElement + 2 < iLength)
        currentInventoryObjects[topElement + 2].guiTexture.enabled = true; // row 3
}
```

Note that you have to check if the second- and third-row elements exist, before you set their visibility.

8. Next, add the ShowColumn's counterpart, the HideColumn function:

```
function HideColumn ( topElement : int) {

    // hide the elements in the 3 rows for the top element's column
    currentInventoryObjects[topElement].guiTexture.enabled = false; // row 1 element
    if (topElement + 1 < iLength)
        currentInventoryObjects[topElement + 1].guiTexture.enabled = false; // row 2
    if (topElement + 2 < iLength)
        currentInventoryObjects[topElement + 2].guiTexture.enabled = false; // row 3
}
```

Now you can call the functions within the InventoryGrid function.

9. Below the visibility check conditional you just added and above the //row 1 positioning line, add the following:

```
// if elements need to be hidden, do so before positioning
if (!visibility) HideColumn(k); // send the top row element for processing
```

Below the //row 3 positioning and above the xPos incrementing line, add the following show function:

```
// if elements need to be shown, do so after positioning
if (visibility) ShowColumn(k); // send the top row element for processing
```

10. Save the script.

11. Click Play and bring up the inventory.

The arrows have not yet been processed, but you should no longer see the overflow icons on startup (see Figure 14-12).

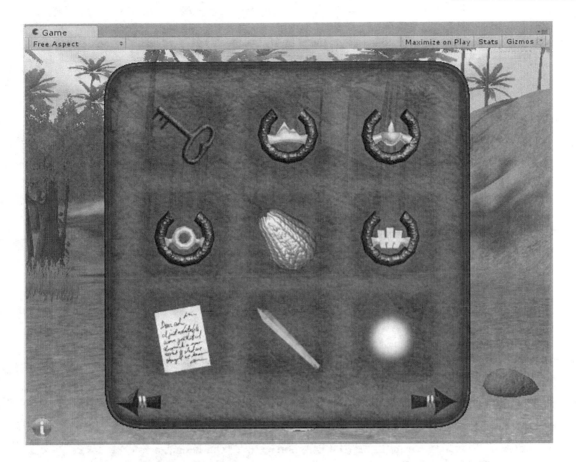

Figure 14-12. *No overflow icons on startup*

To handle the arrow states, you have to check only the grid position and the length of the array. If the grid position is greater than 0, you know there are icons to the left, so you have to activate the right arrow to access them. If there are more elements than grid positions (grid position times three plus eight; those on the grid), you have to activate the left arrow to access them. In both cases, if the condition is not met, that arrow will be deactivated.

Because there is no reason to calculate the arrows after each array element, you will process them once the item positioning is completed.

1. Add the following lines to check for items left of the grid just above the closing curly bracket of the InventoryGrid function:

```
//if there are icons to the left of the grid, activate the right arrow
if (gridPosition > 0) GameObject.Find("ArrowRight").SendMessage("ArrowState", true);
else GameObject.Find("ArrowRight").SendMessage("ArrowState", false);
```

2. And, to check the right side overflow, add the following:

```
//if there are icons to the right of the grid, activate the left arrow
if (iLength > gridPosition * 3 + 9)
  GameObject.Find("ArrowLeft").SendMessage("ArrowState", true);
else GameObject.Find("ArrowLeft").SendMessage("ArrowState", false);
```

■ **Tip** Remember :Arrays start at element 0, so the length might be 10, but the last element number would be 9.

---

3. Save the script.

4. Click Play and open the inventory.

The arrow states are correct, as long as you don't shift the grid with them.

5. Stop Play mode.

6. Disable several of the icons, so you have less than ten enabled.

7. Click Play and check that both arrows are disabled.

8. Enable all of the test icons this time.

Arrow Limits

Now that the inventory grid works on update, you will have to get the arrow state and item visibility working when the grid position is changed—in other words, when the player clicks the arrows.

Whereas you iterated through the entire inventory array in the `InventoryGrid` function, for the arrows, you only have to worry about the columns to the left and to the right of the grid, for visibility.

When you click the left arrow, the current grid-position column will move right and must be hidden. In the last section, you created a function, `HideColumn`, to do just that. It wants the top element number to be able to process the elements column. As the column is currently the grid-position column, you can multiply it by three and send the resulting top element number off to the hide function. You must do that before you update the grid position.

1. Open the ClickArrows script.

2. Inside the `ShiftGrid` function, inside the (shiftDirection == "left") conditional, below the `amount = -amount` line, add the following:

```
// hide the column on the left, send its top element
controlCenter.SendMessage("HideColumn", gridPosition *3);
```

3. At the bottom of the left conditional, beneath the `gridPosition ++` line, you can now tell it to show the new column on the right, as follows:

```
// show the new column on the right, send its top element
controlCenter.SendMessage("ShowColumn", gridPosition *3 + 6);
```

And now, the arrows can be managed. By definition, because the left arrow just moved a column to the left of the grid, the right arrow must be activated. However, it is the left arrow whose instance of the script you are processing, so the right arrow must be "found" before it can be activated by calling its `ArrowState` function and passing it a true argument.

4. Add the following line below the ShowColumn line you just added:

```
//activate the right arrow
GameObject.Find("ArrowRight").SendMessage("ArrowState", true);
```

The left arrow moves the grid to the left, so it has to know how long the inventory array is, in case there are no more columns to the right of the grid and it has to be deactivated. You have to access the number of inventory items only once in the ClickArrows script, but the line will get rather long, so you will create a local variable for it to make it easier to read.

5. Add the following beneath the lines you just added:

```
// if there are no more columns to the right, disable the left arrow
var iLength = controlCenter.GetComponent(GameManager).currentInventoryObjects.length;
 if(gridPosition *  3 + 9 >= iLength) ArrowState(false); // deactivate the left arrow
```

6. Save the script.

7. Click Play and test the left arrow.

It should stay active until the end of the inventory array and then become inactive.
The right arrow will be slightly easier to process. First, you will deal with the visibility.

1. In the else clause for the right arrow, add the following above the gridPosition -- line, to hide the far-right column, as it is shifted right:

```
//hide the column on the right, send its top element
controlCenter.SendMessage("HideColumn", gridPosition *3 +6);
```

2. At the bottom of the else clause, below the gridPosition -- line, add the following, to show the new grid-position column from the left:

```
//show the column on the left, send its top element
controlCenter.SendMessage("ShowColumn", gridPosition *3);
```

Because you just shifted a row to the right, by definition, the left arrow must be activated. Because you are in the right arrow's instance of the script, if you are in the else clause, it has to be "found" before activating.

3. Add the following below the lines you just added:

```
//activate the left arrow
GameObject.Find("ArrowLeft").SendMessage("ArrowState", true);
```

For the right arrow, you have to check only for the grid position. If it is 0, the right arrow has to be deactivated.

4. Add the following beneath the last line you added:

```
if(gridPosition == 0) ArrowState(false);// deactivate the right arrow
```

5. Save the script.

6. Click Play and test the inventory arrows (see Figure 14-13).

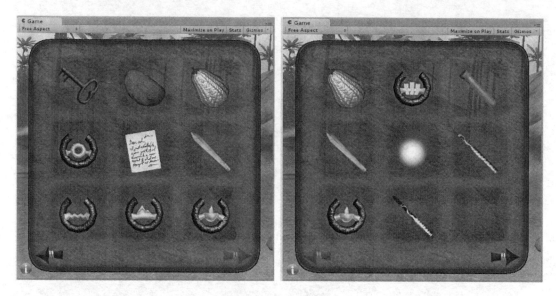

Figure 14-13. *The grid shifted right (left) and shifted left (right)*

This time, visibility and arrow states should all be up and running correctly.

7. Reactivate all of the Inventory objects.

8. Click Play and test with the larger number.

Adding and Removing Objects from Inventory

Now that you've got the mechanics of the extensible inventory working, you can go back and see about adding and removing the icons from inventory. The scripts already hide, show, and change the states on the icons. Now, you just have to fill out the blocked-in functions.

Let's think about the functionality for a moment. When you remove an object, e.g., pick it with the default cursor, you will have to remove it from the array and then call the InventoryGrid function to update the grid. That is probably the most straightforward action.

When you add an object, either by picking a scene object, or picking an empty area of the inventory panel, the object will be added to the end of the array. At its simplest, the grid will be updated, but if the inventory is open, one would expect the grid position to be shifted to the end, to show the object. This will take a bit more work, as it involves shifting the grid, changing arrow states, and other things.

The final scenario is when an object is dropped on another object. Right now, the cursor is dropped as an addition to inventory. Eventually, you have to check if the objects can combine to make a new object. In that case, both objects have to be removed from inventory and scene, and then a new object set in its position in inventory. While this scenario avoids a grid shifting, it will require a bit of work to get everything in the right place. The results, however, will be worth the extra work.

Let's start with what appears to be the simplest—removing an object from inventory.

Removing Objects from Inventory

Next, you will finish the RemoveFromInventory function where it has been waiting patiently in the GameManager. With JavaScript arrays, you could use RemoveAt() to remove an item from its current position in an array. But with the Unity built-in array, you will have to rebuild the inventory array, without disrupting the order of the contents. You'll start by getting the object's iElement number, then going through the Inventory objects and updating (shifting) their iElement values, then updating the removed object's iElement, and then updating the currentInventoryObjects array.

1. Open the GameManager script.

2. Inside the RemoveFromInventory function, below the print statement, assign the object's iElement value as the one to remove, as follows:

```
// retrieve the picked icon/object's inventory element number
var iRemove = object.GetComponent(Interactor).iElement;
```

3. Once again, add the following to access the Inventory:objects:

```
//get the list of the active gameObjects with the InventoryObject tag
var iObjects = GameObject.FindGameObjectsWithTag("InventoryObject");
```

4. Iterate through the Inventory objects and shift the iElement value back one, if the value is more than the iRemove number.

```
// go through the list and decrement the iElement
// numbers for all objects past the iRemove number
for (var i : int = 0;i < iObjects.length;i++) {
    //only if its current state is 1 (in inventory)
    if(iObjects[i].GetComponent(Interactor).iElement > iRemove) {
        // decrement if the value is greater than the iRemove value
        iObjects[i].GetComponent(Interactor).iElement --;
    }
}
```

5. Next, reduce the iLength var by one.

```
iLength = iLength -1; // decrement the length of the current Inventory objects
```

6. And update the removed object's iElement value.

```
//update the iRemove object's element to be out of the array
object.GetComponent(Interactor).iElement = 100;
```

7. Now update the array.

```
//update the currentInventoryObject array
OrderInventoryArray ();
```

8. And, finally, update the inventory display on screen.

```
// update the grid
InventoryGrid();
```

9. Save the script.

10. Click Play.

11. Pick one of the inventory objects.

12. Stop Play mode.

The object becomes the cursor, as before, but this time, the inventory closes the gap and updates itself. There are a few more things you have to do.

If you start removing objects, you will get an out-of-range error at some point.

1. Adjust the amount of active inventory items you have, until they number 13 or 15.

2. Click Play and open the inventory.

3. Click the left arrow until you are at the end of the grid.

You should see one icon at the top of the last column.

4. Pick and drop several of the icons.

You should now have at least one empty column.
The console will eventually report an out-of-range error.

5. Open the console and double-click the error line, to see where the problem is.

One possible error is in the HideColumn function. Earlier on, you made the assumption that whenever the grid was shifted, there would at least be an icon at the top of the column. Now that you are removing elements, the assumption is no longer valid. Fortunately, it is an easy fix. You *could* copy the syntax from the rows 2 and 3 lines, using if (topElement < iLength) to bypass the error, but there is really no reason to check the other two when failing the first condition tells you that you are dealing with an empty column. The better solution is to check for the opposite and return if *it* evaluates as true.

6. Add the following at the top of the HideColumn function:

```
if (topElement >= iLength) return; // there are no icons in the column, return
```

7. Add the same line to the top of the ShowColumn function.

8. Save the script.

9. Click Play and remove only the last icon each time.

This time, there is no error, but you still have the empty column to address. You already have a function that will shift the grid. Right now it is being used solely by the arrows, but because you were clever enough to turn it into a function, you can now call it from anywhere you wish. You will, however, have to set the condition to evaluate to true when the top element of the third column doesn't exist, e.g., its number is greater than or equal to (remember elements start at 0) the number of items in inventory.

1. Inside the RemoveFromInventory function, above the InventoryGrid() line, add the following:

```
//if the third column is empty, shift the grid to the right
if(gridPosition * 3 + 6 >= iLength  && iLength>= 9)
GameObject.Find("ArrowRight").SendMessage("ShiftGrid", "right");
```

2. Save the script.

3. Click Play and test.

4. Delete or comment out the print statement from the `RemoveFromInventory` function.

The grid behaves, regardless of where you remove an object, closing the gap and managing the required grid shifting.

Adding Objects to Inventory

Let's move on to the `AddToInventory` function. You will handle it much the same as the remove. To start, you will just get it adding the object to the end of the array and leaving the grid position as is. You are passing the picked object into the function, so all you have to do is update its iElement number, increment the iLength, then update the currentInventoryObject array.

1. Open the GameManager script.

2. Delete or comment out the print statement from the `AddToInventory` function.

3. Add the following to the `AddToInventory` function to store the object's new element number :

   ```
   //update the object's element to be the new last element
   object.GetComponent(Interactor).iElement = iLength;.
   ```

The length of the array is always one more than the last element's number, because arrays start at 0, so it's easy to update the object to add.

4. Next, update the `iLength` variable to reflect the addition to the array:

   ```
   iLength = iLength +1; // increment the length of the current Inventory objects
   ```

5. Now update the array.

   ```
   //update the currentInventoryObject array
   OrderInventoryArray ();
   ```

6. And, finally, update the inventory display on screen.

   ```
   // update the grid
   InventoryGrid();
   ```

7. Save the script.

8. Deactivate an object so that you have an empty slot at the end of the inventory panel and can see new additions without having to scroll the panel.

9. Click Play and try removing and adding objects to the inventory.

So far, so good. The dropped item is returned to the end of the inventory. Let's tackle the grid page next. As usual, you first have to consider the desired functionality and then work out the details and dependencies. When you manually add an item to inventory, that is, take the cursor object into inventory and drop it, you would like the grid to go to the last page, so that you can see it.

Because you will be using the `AddToInventory` function to add 3D objects from the scene directly into inventory, you must first check whether the inventory is open, by looking at the `iMode` variable.

10. Add the following conditional below the `InventoryGrid()` line:

```
if (iMode && iLength > 9) {

}
```

If you are in inventory mode, and there are more than nine items, you have to call the `ShiftGrid` function until you are at the end. This introduces new functionality in the form of the `While` function. As long as the expression being evaluated returns true, the instructions will be carried out.

11. Add the following inside the `if(iMode...` block:

```
// shift the grid to the right until you get to the end where the new object was added
while (gridPosition * 3 + 9 < iLength)
GameObject.Find("ArrowLeft").SendMessage("ShiftGrid", "left");
```

12. Save the script.

13. Click Play and test the functionality.

The grid jumps nicely to the end to reveal the recently added object.

Combining Items

The next case is what happens when a non-default cursor is used to pick an inventory object. If the two objects can be combined, both the cursor and the inventory object go out of scene, and the combination object goes into inventory.

Before you can test, you will have to add to the Object Look Up table information for the Crystal Icon and fill out the Golden Sleeve Icon's Element 1. See the StateManagement PDF for the full metadata.

1. Select the Crystal Icon.

2. In the Interactor component in the Inspector, add an Element 1 to Look Up State 1 by changing the Size to **2**.

3. Fill out Element 1 as follows:

   Golden Sleeve Icon,0,Golden Sleeve Icon,0,Crystal with Sleeve Icon,1

This tells it the Crystal Icon was picked by the Golden Sleeve Icon, so move it out of scene, then move the Golden Sleeve Icon out of scene, and move the Crystal with Sleeve Icon into Inventory.

4. Increase Replies State 1 to **2** elements to match.

5. Fill out Replies State 1, Element 1, as follows:

   You slip the Crystal neatly onto the golden sleeve

6. Select the Golden Sleeve Icon.

7. In the Interactor component in the Inspector, add an Element 1 to Look Up State 1, by changing the Size to **2**.

8. Fill out Element 1 as follows:

   Crystal Icon,0,Crystal Icon,0,Crystal with Sleeve Icon,1

9. Add a matching element to Replies State 1, and fill it in as follows:

   The Golden Sleeve slides smoothly over the fabulous Crystal

The Golden Sleeve Icon, when picked by the Crystal Icon, goes out of scene, 0, the Crystal Icon also goes out of scene, and then the combo icon, Crystal with Sleeve Icon, goes into Inventory, 1.

■ **Tip**   Type the entries into a text editor, then copy and paste, to put them into the Inspector. Make sure spelling, capitalization, and spaces are correct.

---

10. Select the Crystal with Sleeve Icon in the Hierarchy view.

11. Change its initial state to 0.

12. Click Play.

13. Open the Inventory and pick the Crystal.

14. Once the Crystal is the cursor, pick the Golden Sleeve with it.

The cursor disappears, and the message about the crystal slipping easily into the golden sleeve plays, but you get an error message from the console about a null reference.

While you've been adding and removing icons from inventory, they've remained active, so their states can switch between cursor and in inventory. This time, however, you are trying to access an object that is inactive in the scene. If you check the code for the ObjectLookup script that activates objects, the `CheckForActive` function, you will see that it only checks objects with the ActionObject tag. Because the inventory objects use the Inventory tag, you will have to check through those objects as well.

You discovered earlier that once the game has started, only the active objects with tags can be found, so you will have create an array to hold all of the Inventory objects, just as you did with the ActionObjects.

1. Open the GameManager script.

2. Under the `internal var actionObjects = new GameObject[0]` line, add the following:

```
// array to hold the Inventory objects for processing
internal var inventoryObjects = new GameObject[0];
```

3. Copy the code in the Awake function that loads the ActionObjects into an array.

4. Paste it below the existing code, and change it over, to work for the Inventory objects, as follows:

```
//get a list of the gameObjects with the Inventory tag
var iObjects = GameObject.FindGameObjectsWithTag("InventoryObject");
// redefine the inventoryObject array with the number of elements in the list
inventoryObjects = new GameObject[iObjects.length];
//save the inventory objects into the array for easy access when deactivated
for (var k : int = 0;k < iObjects.length; k++) {
    inventoryObjects[k] = iObjects[k];
    print (inventoryObjects[k].name);
}
```

5. Save the script.

6. Deactivate a few of the inventory icon objects.

7. Click Play and check the console to make sure that they are listed in the console.

8. Stop Play mode and reactive the icons.

9. Delete or comment out the print line and save the script.

Now that you have an array from before the objects are deactivated, you can have the `CheckForActive` function look for a match in it, when it processes the picks in the ObjectLookup script.

1. Open the ObjectLookup script.

2. In the `CheckForActive` function, copy the code for checking the ActionObjects.

3. Paste it above the } // close the else line and convert it to use for the Inventory objects, as follows:

```
//load the inventoryObject array from the GameManager script
var inventoryObjects : GameObject[] = controlCenter.GetComponent(GameManager).inventoryObjects;
for (var x : int = 0; x < inventoryObjects.length; x++) { // iterate through the array
print (inventoryObjects[x].gameObject.name + "  " + name);
        if (inventoryObjects[x].gameObject.name == name)   { // if there is a match for the name
            inventoryObjects[x].gameObject.SetActive(true); // activate the matched
            object from the array
            auxObject = gameObject.Find(name);           // assign the newly activated object
        } // close the if

} // close the for loop
```

4. Click Play.

5. Open the Inventory, and pick the Crystal.

6. Once the Crystal is the cursor, pick the Golden Sleeve with it.

The Crystal is replaced by the Crystal with Sleeve.

7. Restart the scene, and go into inventory.

8. This time, start with the Golden Sleeve, and use it to pick the Crystal.

The cursor disappears, and the Golden Sleeve becomes the Crystal with sleeve.
If you want the Crystal with Sleeve to become a cursor directly, change the 1 to a 2.

1. Stop Play mode.

2. In the Golden Sleeve Icon's Object Lookup's Lookup State1, Element 1, change the 1 to a **2**.

    `Crystal Icon,0,Crystal Icon,0,Crystal with Sleeve Icon,1`

3. In the Crystal Icon's Object Lookup's Lookup State1, Element 1, change the 1 to a **2**.

    `Golden Sleeve Icon,0,Golden Sleeve Icon,0,Crystal with Sleeve Icon,2`

4. Click Play and test.

This time, the Crystal with Sleeve becomes the cursor as soon as the two objects are "combined."

5. Pick a different inventory object, so it becomes the pointer.

6. Click any of the other inventory objects.

While the generic reply works well with the objects in the 3D scene, in inventory, you would probably expect the picked object to become the new cursor and the old cursor to be put back into inventory, in anticipation of using the new one.

Wrong Picks

The only thing you have not yet dealt with in the inventory is what happens when the player picks an object in inventory with the wrong cursor. In the Object Look Up, when there is no match and the for loop has finished looking through the options, you will have to put the cursor back into inventory, because it was a wrong pick. If it was the default cursor, or the correct cursor, or a cursor with a special message, it was handled and returned, so only "no match found" will get to this next code.

1. Open the ObjectLookUp script.

2. At the bottom of the LookUpState function, change the HandleNoMatchReplies(picker) line as follows:

    ```
    // if the picked object is not an inventory object, build a no match reply for it
    if (gameObject.tag != "InventoryObject" && !match) HandleNoMatchReplies(picker);
    ```

3. Below it, just above the closing curly bracket for the LookUpState function, add the following:

    ```
    // if the cursor was not a match and the picked object has the Inventory tag
    else if (matchCursor != "default" && !match){  //swap out the cursor with the object it picked

        //put the old cursor in inventory
        GameObject.Find(picker).SendMessage("ProcessObject",1);

        //pick up the new cursor
        SendMessage("ProcessObject",2);

    }
    ```

4. Save the script.

5. Click Play.

6. Select the Crystal Icon.

7. Pick the Vial of Elixir Icon with it.

The Vial of Elixir Icon becomes the cursor, and the Crystal Icon goes into the inventory as the last item.

While this functionality works, it would be nicer if the two would swap places, so that the cursor took the place in inventory of the object it picked. By doing a bit of creative state management, you can get the results you want. Once you know you are swapping the two, e.g., you are in the else clause, you can assign new states before you process them into their correct states. This will allow you to create a couple of new clauses in the Handle2D function you created earlier. The high number states act as a flag to tell the code it's handling special cases, and you will need a new variable, replaceElement, to store the picked object's location.

8. Inside the else clause, above the //put the old cursor in inventory line, add the
    following:

```
//change the picked object's state to 10,special handling
GetComponent(Interactor).currentState = 10;
//change the cursor object's state to 11, special handling
GameObject.Find(picker).GetComponent(Interactor).currentState = 11;
//store the picked object's current inventory element number on the GameManager
controlCenter.GetComponent(GameManager).replaceElement = GetComponent(Interactor).
iElement;
```

9. Save the script.

Now, you need to store the picked object's inventory element number somewhere it can be found, while the cursor is being processed. Because you are storing the rest of the generic variables on the GameManager script, it makes sense to use that for your replaceElement as well.

1. Open the GameManager script.

2. Add the following in the //inventory layout section:

```
internal var replaceElement : int; // var to store the current inventory object's element
```

3. Save the script.

And, finally, you will add the special-case conditionals to the Handle2D function in the Interactor.

1. Open the Interactor script.

At the top of the ProcessObject function, you have to turn your temporary states into the previous states and assign the actual new states.

2. Near the top of the ProcessObject function, just beneath the processing = true line, add
    the following:

```
//handle replace
if(newState == 10) {
    newState = 1;
    currentState = 10;
}
 if (newState == 11) {
    newState = 2;
    currentState = 11;
}
```

And now, you can add the conditions that fit your doctored previousState.

3. Add the following conditional to the Handle2D function to handle the picked object:

```
// In Inventory, will be replaced
if (previousState == 10) {
    //turn off the object
    gameObject.guiTexture.enabled = false;
```

```
      //turn it into the cursor
      controlCenter.GetComponent(GameManager).currentCursor = guiTexture.texture;
      //update its iElement to not state 1
      iElement = 100;
    }
```

4.   Add the following conditional to handle the cursor that goes into the picked object's place:

```
    //the new object that takes the picked object's position
    if (previousState == 11) {
      controlCenter.SendMessage("ResetCursor");
      //set its state to inventory
      currentState = 1;
      gameObject.guiTexture.enabled = true;
      //get the element number in inventory that it replaces
      iElement = controlCenter.GetComponent(GameManager).replaceElement;
      yield; // make sure the value has time to update
      //update the currentInventoryObjects array
      controlCenter.GetComponent(GameManager).OrderInventoryArray();
      //update the inventory grid
      controlCenter.GetComponent(GameManager).InventoryGrid();
    }
```

5.   Save the script.

6.   Click Play and test.

The cursor and inventory object swap out nicely.

The only thing missing is a message text. With a few changes, you can reuse the HandleNoMatchReplies function you are using for the non-inventory replies.

1.   Open the ObjectLookup script.

2.   Clone the entire HandleNoMatchReplies function.

3.   Name it **HandleCursorSwapReplies**.

4.   Change its var tempMsg line to the following:

```
    var tempMsg = "You exchange the " + picker + " for the " + tempObjectName ;
```

And add the line that calls the function.

5.   In the ObjectLookupState function, inside the else if (matchCursor != "default")
      conditional block, just above its closing curly bracket, add the following:

```
    HandleCursorSwapReplies (picker); // build a reply for the swapped cursor
```

6.   Save the script.

7.   Click Play and test the new message (Figure 14-14).

Figure 14-14. Cursor exchange in inventory

8. Test the Crystal/Golden Sleeve combination to make sure it still works.

As a final tweak on the inventory functionality, you may want to shorten the time that the cursor takes to reappear. In the Interactor, you set a timer on pick for 2.5 seconds to read the message. In the Update function, you turned the cursor back on 1.5 seconds, before that time was up. If you set it to 2 seconds before the time is up, you will still get a short pause, but it will make the inventory picks seem more responsive.

1. Open the Interactor script.

2. In the Update function, change if (pickTimer && Time.time > pickTimerTime -1.5) to the following:

```
if (pickTimer && Time.time > pickTimerTime -2.0)
```

3. Save the script.

4. Click Play and test the improved timing.

5. Save the Scene and save the project.

If you still prefer a longer pause for 3D objects, you can easily create variables to hold both the message read time and the cursor return time. By keeping the read time exposed to the Inspector, you also have the benefit of being able to customize the read time for longer action messages.

6. Add the following variables:

```
var messageRead : float = 2.5;        // time allowed for reading action message
internal var cursorReturn : float;    // time before cursor returns after pick
```

7. In the `ProcessObject` function, replace the 2.5 with the new variable.

```
pickTimerTime = Time.time + messageRead;
```

8. Above that, assign the cursor return time values.

```
if (objectIs3D) cursorReturn = 1.5;   // longer pause for in 3d scene
else cursorReturn = 2.0;              // shorter pause for in inventory
```

9. In the timer section, replace the `if (pickTimer && Time.time > pickTimerTime -2.0)` line with the following:

```
if (pickTimer && Time.time > pickTimerTime -cursorReturn ) { // if time is up and flag is on...
```

10. Save the script.

11. Click Play and test both in-scene and in-inventory interaction.

With the inventory working smoothly, it's time to hook up cursor/Action Object interactions and disable unused inventory icons.

Revisiting the Action Objects

As a final task in this chapter, you will incorporate the non-default cursor requirements into the object's Object Lookup data. The requirements are as follows:

> Key At Rock goes into inventory [as Key At Rock Icon], when picked.
>
> The LockPlate must be picked with the Key Icon.
>
> The Flower must be picked with the Vial of Elixir Icon.
>
> The Pollen Ball goes into inventory [as Light Ball Icon], when picked.

1. Consult the StateManagement PDF for Chapter 14 for the new data.

2. Update the Key At Rock, the LockPlate, the Flower, and the Pollen Ball.

The three remaining Action Objects can also be set up now.

3. Set up the Message, Vial of Elixir, and Golden Sleeve, as per the State Management PDF.

Summary

In this chapter, you implemented the functionality for the inventory system. Starting with a grid system for the layout, you used GUI Texture objects for the inventory icons. With the use of tags, you were able to access all of the objects tagged as InventoryObjects and iterate through them to load the active objects into an array.

Using a bit of math, you were able to design an extensible system to allow any number of inventory items past the visible nine displayed on the panel texture. Using arrows to navigate the inventory grid, you were able to determine visibility, according to the grid's position and the current number of items in inventory.

After you got the grid working, you considered the possibilities for interaction with non-default cursors. You were able to see how the metadata system allows you to combine two cursors in inventory to create a new combination object. Continuing with non-default cursors, you decided to have a pick using a "wrong" cursor pick up the inventory object and drop the current cursor object into inventory in its place.

Being able to dynamically add and remove objects from inventory, you then implemented "custom" generic replies for wrong picks in inventory that differed from the reply for wrong picks in the 3D scene. By stretching a small semitransparent texture across the screen, you gave the player a view of the 3D world in action, while accessing inventory that also provided a means of intercepting picks outside the inventory panel.

And, finally, you adjusted the cursor size to give a better view of the inventory items when they were used as the current cursor.

In the next chapter, you will deal with object visibility using tags, refine object interaction, and experiment with random replies.

CHAPTER 15

■ ■ ■

Dialogue Trees

A mainstay of classic adventure games, as well as of many other genres, is dialogue between the player and other characters. NPCs, nonplayer characters, help to move the game forward, by dispensing clues, advice, snappy rejoinders, or witty observations. In the days of the text adventure, the player was able to construct sentences at will and try them out in various situations. In today's graphic games, the most common type of conversation limits the player's choices, by presenting only a handful of topics at a time. Both methods are based on the concept of a dialogue tree.

At its simplest, the player selects a topic from a list, and the reply for that topic is then presented. The two biggest drawbacks are getting the same exact replies each time and the fact that many topics should not be revealed until the player has gained sufficient information even to know what to ask.

Managing the conditions and retrieving the data from the dialogue tree can be handled in many different ways, but as with much of the other functionality in the game, you will start simple and add features along the way. As with any new feature, a list of requirements, preferably in order of importance, is the best way to get started.

Dialogue Tree Feature List:

1. Be able to reveal new topics.

2. Be able to randomly choose an appropriate reply from a list.

3. Be able to give out more information each time a topic is chosen.

4. Be able to "branch" a topic.

5. Make the system work for more than one NPC.

The Scenario

When the player has gained access to the temple you will be importing, he will find a large golden fruit in the niche on the balcony. When he tries to take it, he will be transported into a large maze. There, he will meet a character who will be able to tell him what happened and why. The dialogue will provide him with sufficient information to be able to get the golden object. Once he's got the prize, however, he will have to find out what he must do with it. A dialogue with a second character will provide clues.

You can find the full dialogue tree in the StateManagement PDF under Chapter 15. (See the Source Code/ Downloads tab of the book's Apress product page [www.apress.com/9781430248996].)

■ **Note** You may be tempted to make things more entertaining by changing the topics and replies, as you work through this chapter. If you do, you will have to change them back, so they will correspond to the audio clips and, more important, the prefab that the clips have been loaded into.

Setting Up the New GUI Skin

The dialogue GUI has several special needs. You will be setting the Buttons and Toggles to deviate from the norm.

1. In the Assets folder, create a new folder and name it **GUI Skins**.

2. Drag the Game GUISkin into it.

3. Right-click and, from Create, create a new GUI Skin.

4. Name it **Dialogue GUISkin.**

5. With the new skin selected, change the font to Wizzard.

6. Now, open Box and load AlphaGradient into its Background field.

7. In Button, set all the backgrounds to none (top of the textures list in the browser).

8. In Toggle, set all the backgrounds to none, *except for Hover.*

9. Set the Content Offset X to **10**, so there is space before the text.

Starting a Conversation

To make things easier, the framework for this feature can easily be started in a separate scene. Rather than enter each reply and topic in the Inspector, you will be adding everything to one master script. In this case, the large script is a small price to pay for being able to see everything at the same time.

1. Start by creating a New Scene.

2. Save it as **Test Dialogue**.

3. Create a new folder in the Project view and name it **NPC Assets**.

4. Create a new script in the NPC Assets folder named **DialogueManager**.

5. In the scene, create an empty gameObject and name it **Dialogue Manager**.

6. Add the new script to the gameObject, and open it in the script editor.

7. Above the Start function, create a variable for an array of topics, named topics_1, with six elements.

```
// Player conversation topics with npc_1
internal var topics_1 = new String[6];
```

8. Beneath it, fill them out as follows:

```
topics_1[0] = "null";
topics_1[1] = "Hi";
topics_1[2] = "Where am I?";
topics_1[3] = "How do I get out of the maze?";
topics_1[4] = "What happened to me?";
topics_1[5] = "Gotta go";
```

Because arrays always start numbering at 0 and that can get confusing, you will set element 0 to null, and use it only as a placeholder.

Next, you will have to create a variable to hold the topic text that will be displayed onscreen. In this game, the limit will be seven topics, so you won't have to worry about a topic-scrolling mechanism. You will also create a new GUI skin, just for use with the dialogues.

9. At the top of the s script, define an array named UI_Text, with six elements, and create a variable for a new GUI Skin.

```
var dialogueSkin : GUISkin;
internal var toggleBool = false; // variable for GUI toggles

internal var uiText = new String[6]; // store the topic text for the display
```

10. Create an OnGUI function beneath the Update function and add the new skin.

```
function OnGUI () {
   GUI.skin = dialogueSkin;

}
```

11. Inside it, below the GUI skin line, create a GUI Group and a GUI Box box.

```
// Make a group on the center of the screen
GUI.BeginGroup (Rect (0, Screen.height / 2 , 650, 500));
var y = 35; // this will increment the y position for each topic

//text panel
GUI.Box(Rect (0, 20 , 400, 230),"");
```

For each of the six topics, you will need a conditional, to prevent it from being displayed if the text assigned to it is empty, or "". When picked, the topic's GUI Button will call a function to process the reply. Eventually, you will not use a texture for the button's background. You will leave the function call commented out for now. The GUI Toggles are used for their hover functionality and to display the topic text. The "uiText[1]" string is only to give you something to look at before you load the actual text.

12. Add the first topic code.

```
//Topic 1
if (uiText[1] != "") {
   if (GUI.Button (Rect (0, y, 500, 35), "")) {
      //ProcessReply(uiReply[1]);
   }
   toggleBool = GUI.Toggle (Rect (25, y, 600, 35), false, "uiText[1]" );
   y += 35; // increment the next GUI position by 35
}
```

13. Add the closing group line.

```
GUI.EndGroup ();
```

14. Save the script.

15. Load the new Dialogue GUISkin into the Dialogue Skin parameter.

16. Click Play and check out the start of the GUI in the Game view (Figure 15-1).

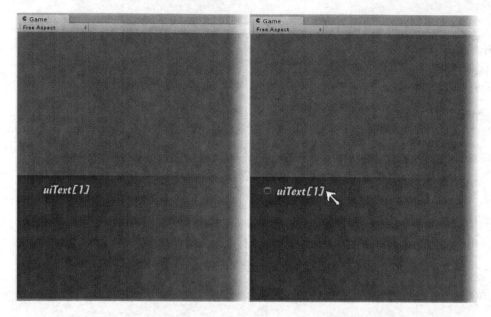

Figure 15-1. *The first topic text, showing in the GUI (left) and on hover (right)*

The dialogueSkin, found in the GUI Skins folder, uses an alpha gradient, AlphaG, as the Box Background texture. The GUI Button uses no Background and has no text but will catch the pick. The GUI Toggle has mouseover text color change and will hold the text for the topic.

Next, you will need a function to load the topic text into the uiText array. It will iterate through the array of topics and assign each to a GUI.

1. Remove the quotation marks from "uiText[1]".

    ```
    toggleBool = GUI.Toggle (Rect (25, y, 600, 35), false, uiText[1] );
    ```

2. Add the topic code for the second topic.

    ```
    //Topic 2
    if (uiText[2] != "") {
       if (GUI.Button (Rect (0, y, 500, 35), "")) {
          //ProcessReply(uiReply[2]);
       }
       toggleBool = GUI.Toggle (Rect (25, y, 600, 35), false, uiText[2]);
       y += 35; // increment the next GUI position by 35
    }
    ```

3. Duplicate the code for topics 3, 4, 5, and 6, changing the four topic numbers in each.

Now, you can create the function that loads the topics into the GUI.

4. Beneath the Update function, create the function called LoadTopics, as follows:

    ```
    // load topics into GUI
    function LoadTopic () { // start at 1 since 0 is null
       for (var i : int = 1; i < 6; i++){ // only allow 5 topics to be displayed *******
    ```

```
            uiText[i] = " "; // clear the current text in case there is no new text
            //assign the topic text
            uiText[i] = topics_1[i];
        }
    }
```

5. Call the function in the Start function, for the time being.

```
function Start () {

    LoadTopic ();

}
```

6. Save the script.

7. Click Play and view the topics (Figure 15-2).

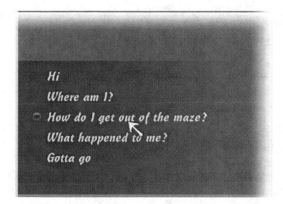

Figure 15-2. *The first five topics showing in the GUI*

Filtering Topics

To begin implementing the system that will manage the dialogue tree, you'll add a three-character code to the front of each topic string. The first character will tell you if the topic is active or not. The second and third will eventually hold the element number of the audio clip that goes with the topic. Because the system is totally arbitrary, you will be making notes in the GameNotes text file as you develop it.

1. Open the GameNotes text file.

2. Add the following to start the notes on the dialogue tree:

    Dialogue Tree Conventions-

    Topic format = 000 000 The text for the topic here

    1- topic's active state, 1 is active, 0 is not, 9 will mean exit the conversation

    2 & 3 - element number of audio clip for the topic

3. Save the GameNotes text file.

Now, you will have to add the code to the front of each of the topic strings.

1. Open the DialogueManager script.

2. Add 100 to the front of all the topic strings, followed by a space.

```
topics_1[0] = "100 null";
topics_1[1] = "100 Hi";
topics_1[2] = "100 Where am I?";
topics_1[3] = "100 How do I get out of the maze?";
topics_1[4] = "100 What happened to me?";
topics_1[5] = "100 Gotta go";
```

3. Change element 3 to the following:

```
topics_1[3] = "000 How do I get out of the maze?"; // not active yet
```

With the code in place, the LoadTopic function has to be adjusted. First, you will use Substring to determine if the topic is active, then you will use Substring again, to assign the noncode part of the string to the topic UI.

As long as you're making changes to the LoadTopic function, it will be a good time to set it up to use different topic arrays, without resorting to JavaScript arrays. JavaScript arrays can hold arrays of arrays, but Unity arrays can't, so you will eventually make use of Switch, to tell the function which character the player is talking with.

4. Near the top of the script, add the following variable declaration beneath the uiText declaration:

```
internal var topics = new String[20]; // store the current topic strings here for processing
```

5. At the top of the LoadTopic function, add the following local variables:

```
topics = new String [topics_1.length]; // re-initialize the array
topics = topics_1; // assign the existing array to it for now
```

When you re-declare the topics variable, you can reset its length to the correct length, to match the array you are assigning to it.

Now, instead of a 1 to 1, you will be assigning the element numbers of the topics array—but only if they are active. The *i* is the variable used for the uiText iteration, so for the topics iteration, you will be using *j*. To avoid getting an index-out-of-range error if you run out of topics before you run out of uiText, you will also need a check, to make sure there *are* more topics, before trying to assign them. The existing text for the uiText element is always cleared first, regardless.

6. Modify the rest of the LoadTopic function, as follows:

```
// generate the next topic list from the current reply
var j : int = 1; // initialize the topics array to start at the first real reply
for (var i : int = 1; i < 6; i++){ // only allow 5 topics to be displayed
    uiText[i] = ""; // clear the current text
    if (j < topics.length) { // check to seeif there are more topics
        // if first char is not zero/naught, topic is active, so process the string
        if (topics[j].Substring(0,1) != "0") {
            //use the string from the 4th character onwards
            uiText[i] = topics[j].Substring(4);
            }
```

```
         else i--;  // else it wasn't active, so adjust the topic list number so you
         don't have a blank spot
         j++; // increment the topics element number
      }
   }// end the for loop
```

Note that the i value is decremented, if the current topic string isn't active. This prevents gaps in the GUI, as well as allowing the full amount of topics to be displayed. Note also that the string is chopped up using Substring, to check the first character to see if the topic is active and also to assign the correct remaining part of the string for the ui topic.

7. Save the script.

8. Click Play.

Topic 3 is skipped this time, but the text should appear the same as before.

Getting Answers

Now that the topics are behaving themselves, it's time to show the replies. They will correspond exactly to the topics.

1. Under the topics_1 array, make a variable for a new array, replies_1, also of six elements.

```
// replies_1 character reply text
internal var replies_1 = new String[6];
```

2. Fill out the elements by adding the following:

```
replies_1[0] = "You shouldn't see this";
replies_1[1] = "I've been expecting you";
replies_1[2] = "You are in the Maze";
replies_1[3] = "No idea, I've been stuck here for ages";
replies_1[4] = "You were transported here";
replies_1[5] = "Good luck";
```

3. In the OnGUI function, uncomment the ProcessReply lines for each of the topics. Make sure the element numbers match the topics.

With the call to ProcessReply, you will be sending an argument, uiReply. It will be the element number of the uiText, the string that displays the topic. Because the topics and replies match, that element number will also be used to get the reply. You will have to store that number when you are laying out the topics for the GUI.

4. In the LoadTopic function, beneath the uiText[i] = topics[j]... line, add the following:

```
uiReply[i] = j; // save the topic number to get its reply later on
```

And it will need a variable declared for it.

5. At the top of the script, beneath the uiText declaration, add the following:

```
internal var uiReply = new int[6]; // store the reply element number for future processing
```

557

6. To process the replies, create a function called ProcessReplies, which will receive an argument with the reply element number.

```
// process the reply by its element number
function ProcessReply (replyElement : int) {

}
```

7. Near the top of the script, under the topics variable, create the replies variable:

```
internal var replies = new String[20]; // store the reply strings here for processing
```

You will also need two variables to store the reply: one for the full text string and one for just the reply section of it, because it, too, will eventually get codes to tell the script how to handle it. And just in case it's needed again, you'll also need a variable to store the current reply's element number.

1. Create three new variables beneath the replies declaration at the top of the script.

```
internal var fullReply : String; // stores the current full reply string (including codes)
internal var textReply : String; // stores the current reply text part of the fullReply string
internal var currentReplyNum : int; // stores the element number of the current reply
```

Just as with the topic array, it makes sense to plan ahead for when you will have more than one NPC. So, instead of getting the element of the reply, you will assign the whole reply array to a new array, replies.

2. Back in the ProcessReply function, add the following local variables:

```
replies = new String [replies_1.length]; // re-initialize the array
replies = replies_1; // assign the existing array to it for now
```

3. And below those, add the line that assigns the current reply and its element number, as follows:

```
currentReplyNum = replyElement; // assign the newly found element number to the var
fullReply = replies[currentReplyNum]; // get the full reply for that element
textReply = fullReply; // temporary assignment
```

4. Next, in the OnGUI function, just below the EndGroup() line, create a GUI label to show the replies at the top left.

```
GUI.Label (Rect (25, 25, 500, 35), textReply);
```

5. Save the script.

6. Click Play and test by picking the topics. The reply should change as you select new topics (Figure 15-3).

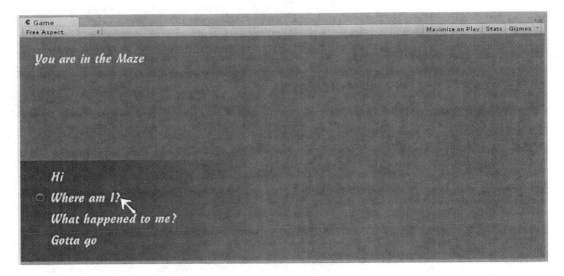

Figure 15-3. The reply, showing after picking a topic

Timing the Text

Now that you've got something that actually looks like a dialogue going on, it's time to stop and think about timing, e.g., what is showing, how long it should show, and even when it should be updated. Assuming the topics will be showing, the player first selects one, to begin the conversation. When the audio clips are added, you will have to let the topic audio play before presenting the reply.

The easiest way to make a timed pause is with yield new WaitForSeconds(someNumberHere). But the problem with yields is that they can't be canceled, so if you don't want to wait for the topic audio to finish, you're out of luck. Setting up timers in the Update function is more work, but well worth the flexibility of being able to cancel.

The first order of business is to wrap the OnGUI topics section and reply lines with a conditional, to know when they can be shown. For that, you'll need a couple of flags—playerTalking and npcResponding. You'll also need a few more to work the timers—two for timer flags, and two to hold the time limit of each, because they will vary with the length of the audio.

1. Add the following variables to the script:

```
// timers and dialogue control
internal var playerTalking : boolean = false; // topic list visibility flag, player can talk/choose topic
internal var npcResponding : boolean = false; // character reply visibility flag, npc is talking
internal var pauseForReply : boolean = false; // flag to check pause timer before replying
internal var pauseForReplyLimit : float; // var to hold the target system time for the timer
internal var timerR : boolean = false; // flag to check the timer
internal var timeLimitR : float; //
internal var pauseForTopic : boolean = false;// flag to check the timer before showing topics
internal var pauseForTopicLimit : float; // var to hold the target system time for the timer
```

2. In the OnGUI function, just below the Gui.skin line, add the following:

```
if (playerTalking) {  // player can select topic
```

3. Below the EndGroup, add the closing } and then indent the contents, to make it more readable.

4. Below that, add the condition for the reply.

```
if (npcResponding) {  // npc is talking
```

5. Close the condition, so it looks as follows:

```
if (npcResponding) {  // npc is talking
   GUI.Label (Rect (25, 25, 500, 35), textReply);
}
```

6. In the Start function, set the two GUI flags.

```
playerTalking = true; // topic list visible
npcResponding = false; // reply hidden
```

7. Save the script.

8. Click Play and test.

The topic shows, but now the reply has to be cued. When the reply is chosen, the timer for the topic has to be started. For now, a pause of 0.5 will do the job.

1. At the top of the ProcessReply function, start the reply timer.

```
// start timer before showing reply
pauseForReplyLimit = Time.time  + 0.5;
pauseForReply = true; // start the timer
```

2. In the Update function, add the code to show the reply, then start the timer for the topics to show again.

```
//timer for the reply
if(pauseForReply && Time.time > pauseForReplyLimit) {
   pauseForReply = false; // turn off the timer

   //show the reply
   playerTalking = false; // turn off player topics
   npcResponding = true; // turn on reply text

   // start the timer for when to show the topics again
   pauseForTopicLimit =  Time.time + 2.0; // give player time to read reply
   pauseForTopic = true;

   //load the next list of topics in preparation for showing them
   LoadTopic ();
}
```

3. Beneath that, add the timer code, to handle showing the topics again.

```
    //timer to start the topics again
    if(pauseForTopic && Time.time > pauseForTopicLimit) {
        npcResponding = false; // hide the reply
        playerTalking = true; // show the topics
        pauseForTopic = false; // turn off the timer
    }
```

4. Save the script.

5. Click Play and test.

The hide and show for topics and replies is in place.

Revealing More Info

Now that you've got the dialogue working smoothly, it's time to make it more fun. The most logical place to start is with that topic that isn't active yet.

By working out a system for various types of replies and managing topics, you will be able to make a fairly sophisticated mechanism to control the dialogue tree.

To start, you'll be adding a four-character code to the front of each *reply* string. The first character will state what to do with the current topic. 0 is no change; 1 is turn off the topic; 2 is turn it off and turn on another topic; 3 is turn on a different topic. The second and third characters hold the number of a different topic to be turned off or on. The fourth character will be used in the next section, to control replies. Once again, you will add the conventions to the GameNote text file first.

1. Open the GameNotes text file.

2. Add the following to continue the notes on the dialogue tree:

    Reply Conventions-

    Reply format = 0000 The text for the reply here

    1- how to process the reply:

    0 is no change

    1 is turn off the topic

    2 is turn it off and turn on another topic

    3 is turn on a different topic

    2 & 3 - element number of the topic to turn on or off

    4- Reply Types

3. Save the GameNotes text file.

With the notes on the dialogue tree conventions safely recorded, you can start implementing the new enhancements.

1. In the DialogueManager script, add 0000 plus a space, at the start of each reply string.

2. For replies_1[2], "You are in the maze," use 3030 (3, turn on a different topic, topic 03).

    ```
    replies_1[2] = "3030 You are in the Maze";
    ```

3. In the ProcessReply function, before the textReply line, add the following:

    ```
    //check to see if any topics need to change their state, first character
    var stateInstructions : String = fullReply.Substring(0,1); // read the first character
    if (stateInstructions != "0") ActivationHandler(stateInstructions);// special handling
    ```

If the first code character is not 0, you will be activating or deactivating *topics* in a new function, ActivationHandler. In other words, as soon as the character asks the right question, the reply contains the code to reveal more topics.

4. Create the function to handle activation, ActivationHandler.

```
function ActivationHandler (instructions : String) {

}
```

To process the topics, you will be changing their codes and changing their string values. The deactivated element 3, "000 How do I get out of the maze?", for example, becomes "100 How do I get out of the maze?", so the next time the topics are listed, it will appear.

You will be rebuilding the strings using the Substring function. Remember that even though you are using "numbers" in the strings, they are still considered characters and will have to be converted with parseInt, if they have to be treated as numbers. In the conditionals, the numbers are simply treated as strings, by using quotation marks.

Also, remember that the code to modify the topics is embedded in the reply strings. That's why you will have to get the topic numbers from the reply strings and convert them to numbers that will be used as element numbers.

5. Inside the new function, create and clear the variables for updating the topics.

```
// clear the variables used to change the states
var newState : String = "null"; // the new State for the current topic
var auxNewState : String = "null"; // the new state for the auxillary topic
var auxTopicNum : int ; // auxillary topic number
```

If you look at the four scenarios, you will see that several modify the current topic *and* another topic, an auxiliary topic, while some don't change the current topic but activate or deactivate another. This should give you plenty of control over the dialogue tree topics.

6. Add the condition for the first case.

```
if (instructions == "1" ) { // deactivate the current topic and activate a new topic
   newState = "0"; // the current topic gets a state change
   auxTopicNum =  parseInt(fullReply.Substring(1,2));
   auxNewState = "1";
}
```

7. Add the condition for the second case.

```
if (instructions == "2" ) { // don't change the current topic, but activate a new topic
   auxTopicNum =  parseInt(fullReply.Substring(1,2));
   auxNewState = "1";
}
```

8. Add the condition for the third case.

```
if (instructions == "3" ) { //   deactivate the current topic and deactivate a different topic
   newState = "0";// the current topic gets a state change
   auxTopicNum =  parseInt(fullReply.Substring(1,2));
   auxNewState = "1";
}
```

9. Add the condition for the fourth case.

```
if (instructions == "4" ) { // don't change the current topic, but deactivate a different topic
    auxTopicNum = parseInt(fullReply.Substring(1,2));
    auxNewState = "1";
}
```

10. Rebuild the topic strings and update.

```
// update the active/inactive topic state - hardcode topics_1 for now
// update the current topic
if (newState != "null") topics_1[currentReplyNum] =  newState +
topics_1[currentReplyNum].Substring(1);
// update the auxiliary topic
if (auxNewState != "null") topics_1[auxTopicNum] =  auxNewState + topics_1[auxTopicNum].Substring(1);
```

Before testing the new functionality, you will have to remove the code part of the string from the full reply.

1. In the ProcessReply function, change the textReply line as follows:

```
textReply = fullReply.Substring(5); // use just the reply part of the string
```

2. Save the script.

3. Click Play and test.

Now, after you find out where you are, you can ask how to get out of the maze! And because you now know you are in the maze, that topic is no longer displayed.

Introducing Random Replies

With the first phase of topic control set up, you can start making the replies more interesting. The fourth character of the reply string will hold the code for what type of reply to get from the string.

Type 0 will mean a regular reply. The next part gets tricky—the code number for a random reply type will be 9. A type between 1 and 8 will mean a reply from a sequence. Here's the cool part: each time the topic is accessed, the type number is incremented, so the reply keeps track of which one it's at.

Both types will have strings that have multiple replies contained within them, so they will have to be parsed and split. For the split, you will be using a special character, the ^.

If the reply type is not 0, the string will be sent off for extra processing. The simplest case is type 9, a random reply for the same topic. Element 3, the reply to "How do I get out of the maze?", will be a good test case.

1. Open the GameNotes text file.

2. Add the following to add to the reply types:

    4- Reply Types

    0, a simple reply, no processing required

    1-8, a sequential reply, the current position in the sequence, a reply of "reset" causes it to loop

    9, a random reply

3. Save the GameNotes text file.

Random Replies to the Same Question

If the reply type is number 9, a random reply, the reply string will have to be parsed and split, and one of the newly accessed "sub" replies chosen. As with any random selection, there is nothing to prevent the same one from being chosen twice in a row. If you wanted to prevent that from happening, you would have to save the element number of the previous reply and choose until the new number did not match the old number.

1. In the DialogueManager script, change the element 3, replies_1, to the following:

```
replies_1[3] = "0009^Trial and error?^Sorry, can't help you with that^It is ever
changing, there is no map^No idea, I've been stuck here for ages^I wish I knew";
```

Next, you'll parse the string, using the ^ as the separator, and put the results into a temporary array of its own. This time, you will use parseInt, so that the conditionals use numbers rather than strings.

2. Create a new function, ProcessReplyString.

```
function ProcessReplyString () {

}
```

3. Inside the function, create a local variable to hold the reply type and assign it the fourth code character.

```
// get the type and convert to an int to be able to do some math on it
var type : int = parseInt(fullReply.Substring(3,1));
```

4. Add the condition for normal handling.

```
// normal, single reply, 4th character (element 3) = 0
if (type == 0) {
   textReply = fullReply.Substring(5);
   return;
}
```

5. Create a new var to hold the split up string.

```
// the rest need to be split up into a temporary array
var readString : String[] = fullReply.Split("^".Chars[0]);
```

6. Process the random reply type.

```
// if 4th char = 9, choose a random sub string
if (type == 9) {
   var randNum : int = Random.Range(1, readString.length);
   textReply = readString[randNum];
   audioOffset = randNum;// offset for random & sequential reply audio clips
   return;
}
```

As soon as you introduce multiple replies to the same topic, the audio clip element numbers will no longer be able to match up with the topic element numbers. When you eventually add audio, the audio clips for the random number type will use the random number as an *offset,* to get the correct clip. The audioOffset variable will store that number.

7. Replace the textReply line at the bottom of the ProcessReply function to call the new function.

   ```
   ProcessReplyString (); // process the reply string
   ```

8. Create a new variable near the top of the script.

   ```
   internal var audioOffset: int; // offset for random & sequential replies
   ```

9. Save the script.

10. Click Play and test by clicking the "How do I get out of the maze?" question several times after it has been revealed.

Sequential Replies

For the last reply type, the replies will be delivered in order. This gives you a great way to impart a little bit more information each time the player chooses the topic. Alternatively, it gives you a means of having a unique reply, the first time the player chooses it. A few extra lines of code will allow you to stop at the last reply—or loop back through it.

For the test run, you will be changing reply 1, the NPC's reply to the player's greeting.

1. Change replies_1[1] to the following:

   ```
   replies_1[1] = "0001^I've been expecting you^You have questions, perhaps?^Hello again";
   ```

2. In the ProcessReplyString function, beneath the existing code, add the following:

   ```
   // else 4th code charactor is less than 9 and greater than 0 (they've already been processed)
   // the type/number tells you where in the sequence the current reply is at
   textReply = readString[type]; // this is the current reply in the sequence
   audioOffset = type; // it is also the audio offset
   ```

3. Add the next condition to handle incrementing the type/counter, as follows:

   ```
   // increment the type number if you haven't reached the last reply yet
   if (type < readString.length -1) {
      type +=1; //increment type
      //check to see if the replies need to reset/loop, "reset"
      // as the last reply will be ignored and cause the type to reset to 1
      if (readString[type] == "reset") type = 1;
   }
   ```

4. And then update the code characters in the replies array.

   ```
   // increment or reset the 4th code char (element 3) for the next time, update the
   original string with the correct number
   replies_1[currentReplyNum] = replies_1[currentReplyNum].Substring(0,3) + type.ToString() +
   replies_1[currentReplyNum].Substring(4);
   ```

5. Save the script.

6. Click Play and test by picking the "Hi" topic several times.

The replies stop at the last one.

7. Add "^reset" to the string.

```
replies_1[1] = "0001^I've been expecting you^You have questions, perhaps?^Hello again^reset";
```

8. Save the script.

9. Click Play and test again by picking the "Hi" topic several times.

This time, the replies loop back to the first one again.

10. Remove ^reset and save the script.

You can find the DialogueManager script thus far as DialogueManager[1].js, in this chapter's scripts folder. (See the Source Code/Downloads tab of the book's Apress product page [www.apress.com/9781430248996].)

Branching the Conversation

Up until now, the code has iterated through all of the topics, to see which ones are active. To get the dialogue to branch, our system will track a list of available topics. Each reply will contain the code number of the topic list that goes with it. For the book's project, you will only use a root list and a single "branch" for each NPC, but you could add more if needed.

1. Add/modify the remainder of the topics and replies for the first NPC.

```
topics_1[3] = "000 How do  I get out of the maze?";
topics_1[4] = "100 What happened to me?";
topics_1[5] = "000 Why was I transported here?";
topics_1[6] = "000 Is there a way to acquire the topi fruit?";
topics_1[7] = "000 Can you help me with a replacement?";
topics_1[8] = "100 Gotta go";
topics_1[9] = "100 OK, thanks";

replies_1[2] = "3030 You are in the Maze";
replies_1[3] = "0009^Trial and error?^Sorry, can't help you with that^It is ever
changing, there is no map^No idea, I've been stuck here for ages^I wish I knew";
replies_1[4] = "2050 You were transported here";
replies_1[5] = "2060 You tried to steal the golden Topi fruit";
replies_1[6] = "2070 Yes, you must replace it with something of similar size and weight";
replies_1[7] = "0001^Try using this rock^You haven't tried the rock?^Sorry, you're on your own now";
replies_1[8] = "0000 Good luck";
replies_1[9] = "0000 No problem";
```

2. Update the two arrays sizes to match the new contents.

```
internal var topics_1 = new String[10];

internal var replies_1 = new String[10];
```

The next function, SetNPC, will tell the script which NPC the player is conversing with. This is a good time to start accounting for multiple NPCs using switch.

3. Add the following variables:

```
// NPC control
internal var rootTopicList = new int[2];
internal var branchTopicList = new int[2];
internal var currentTopicsList = new int[20]; // this holds the currently available topics
internal var currentNpc : int = 0; // holds the current npc's id #
```

4. Create a new function called SetNPC.

```
// set the conversation npc character as current
// this info is sent when the player clicks on the npc via ObjectLookup, special cases
function SetNPC (npcID : int) {

    // need to hard code these in
    switch (npcID) {
        case 1 :
        var rootTopics : String = "1,2,3,4,8";
        var branchTopics : String = "5,6,7,9";
        rootTopicList = ConvertToArray (rootTopics); // convert the string to an array
        branchTopicList = ConvertToArray (branchTopics); // convert the string to an array
        currentTopicsList = rootTopicList;
        break;

    } // end switch
} // end SetNPC
```

The rootTopic variable is a string that holds the topics available to the main topics list. This means that if the topic is in the list, and it is also active, it will be shown.

For topic 4, "What happened to me?", there is a string of replies that reveals more topics in turn. If you look at the rootTopics string in the code you just added, you can see by the topics numbers that, once selected, topic 4 branches into its own conversation, that is, 5, 6, 7, and 9 are not included in the rootTopic list; they are in the branchTopic list. To return to the original, the number 9 will point back to the rootTopics. Once you've added the new code, you will be modifying the LoadTopic function to read in the new information. Topic 8 is also a special case, as it will allow the player to leave the conversation.

The list of topics for the root and the branch are introduced as strings, so they will be easier to read. If they were left that way, you would have to parse and split them when you needed to update the topics after every reply. To get the best of both, the strings get parsed and put into arrays right away, with the help of a new function, ConvertToArray, and are immediately assigned to the new variables. This function splits the string at the commas.

5. Add the following function to split up the strings:

```
function ConvertToArray (theString : String) {

    var tempTopics : String[] = theString.Split(",".Chars[0]);
    var tempTopicsList   = new int[tempTopics.length];
    for (var i : int = 0; i < tempTopics.length; i++) {
        tempTopicsList[i] = parseInt(tempTopics[i]);
    }
    return tempTopicsList; // return the new array
}
```

The SetNPC function will be called when the player clicks on an NPC. The NPC will send its ID off to the DialogueManager script, and the conversation is started. Until the characters are set up, you can modify the Start function to simulate the action.

6. Move the current contents of the Start function beneath the switch case closing bracket in the SetNPC function, changing the NPC assignment to take the passed-in number.

```
currentNpc = npcID; // assign the npc that was passed into the function
playerTalking = true; // the player is now able to "talk" to the npc - topics will display
npcResponding = false; // reply hidden
LoadTopic(); // load the topics that can be discussed with the current npc into the GUI
```

7. For now, set the NPC's "ID" from the Start function with the following:

```
SetNPC(1); // set the current NPC's ID number by calling the SetNPC function
```

8. Save the script, click Play, and test, by picking the "What happened to me?" topic.

The new topic for "What happened to me?" is revealed, but following it through bumps later topics off the limited number of topics shown by the GUI. Some of the more conversation-heavy games implement a "scrolling" feature, to allow the player access to more topics. The book project will use the branch system to limit the number of topics, but adding your own scrolling mechanism would be fairly simple.

So now, the LoadTopics function has to be changed from reading sequential numbers to reading elements in an array. The variable *j* is now used to keep track of the element in the currentTopicsList array—j becomes currentTopicsList[j].

9. In the LoadTopics function, beneath the two topics lines, change the topic-generating code to the following:

```
// generate the next topic list from the current reply
var j : int = 0; // this will go through the currentTopicsList array
for (var i : int = 1; i < 6; i++){ // only allow 5 topics to be displayed, i is for GUI
    uiText[i] = ""; // clear the current text
    //check for a valid topic
    if (i <= currentTopicsList.length && j < currentTopicsList.length) {//new
        // if first char is not 0, topic is active, so process
        if (topics[currentTopicsList[j]].Substring(0,1) != "0") {
            //use the string from the 4th character onward as the currentReply
            uiText[i] = topics[currentTopicsList[j]].Substring(4);// new
            // store the element number of the topic for later use
            uiReply[i] = currentTopicsList[j];// new
        }
        else i--; // else it wasn't active, so adjust the topic list number so you don't have a blank spot
        j++; // increment the topics element number
    }
} // end the for loop
```

And, finally, you have to add the code to the replies, to tell the system which topics list to use. As long as you are making changes there, it will be a good time to block in the last two sets of character code numbers as well. You will have one character for the topic list, two characters to handle special cases, and two characters to hold the audio clip number for the reply. Because the length of the code string is starting to look suspiciously like a bar code, you'll be breaking it up by putting a space on either side of the topic list character/number. The result will look something like the following:

```
replies_1[0] = "0000 0 0000 You shouldn't see this";
```

1. Open the GameNotes text file.

2. Change the replies format to the following:

Repliles Format= 0000 0 0000 The text for the reply here

3. Under 4, add the following:

5- blank

6-which topic tree to use- 0 is root, 1 is branch

7- blank

8 & 9 - for special cases

10 & 11- audio clip element number for the reply

4. Save the GameNotes text file.

Now, you will have to update the replies with the new conventions.

1. Open the DialogueManager script.

2. Add the new " 0 0000" characters to the 0, 1, 2, 3, 8, 9 replies.

3. Add " 1 0000" to the 4, 5, 6, 7 replies, to bring up the branch topics (Figure 15-4).

```
replies_1[0] = "0000 0 0000 You shouldn't see this";
replies_1[1] = "0001 0 0000^I've been expecting you^You have questions, perhaps?^Hello again";
replies_1[2] = "3030 0 0000  You are in the Maze";
replies_1[3] = "0009 0 0000^Trial and error?^Sorry, can't help you with that^It is ever changing,
replies_1[4] = "2050 1 0000  You were transported here";
replies_1[5] = "2060 1 0000  You tried to steal the golden Topi fruit";
replies_1[6] = "2070 1 0000  Yes, you must replace it with something of similar size and weight";
replies_1[7] = "0001 1 0100^Try using this rock^You haven't tried the rock?^Sorry, you're on your
replies_1[8] = "0000 0 0000  Good luck";
replies_1[9] = "0000 0 0000  No problem";
```

Figure 15-4. *The replies, with new character codes (cropped on right side)*

With this change, you'll have to shift the Substring number for the full reply over in a few places. Instead of character 5, the reply now starts at character 12.

4. In ProcessReplyString, make the following change:

```
// normal, single reply, 4th character (element 3) = 0
if (type == 0) {
    textReply = fullReply.Substring(12);
    return;
}
```

If you look at the root and branch topic lists, you will see that each must contain one reply that gets you to the other topic list. In the root, topic 4 points to the branch, and in the branch, topic 9 points back to the root. The code to load the correct topic list array gets added after the reply is processed.

5. Add the following to the ProcessReply function, right after the call to ProcessReplyString():

```
//get the topics list for this reply
var useList : String = replies[currentReplyNum].Substring(5,1);

if (useList == "0") {
   currentTopicsList = new int[rootTopicList.length];
   currentTopicsList = rootTopicList;
}
if (useList == "1") {
   currentTopicsList = new int[branchTopicList.length];
   currentTopicsList = branchTopicList;
}
```

6. Save the script.

7. Click Play and test.

The conversation now goes smoothly between root and branch, with new topics introduced as information is revealed!

You've probably noticed the reply topic rect is too short.

8. In the OnGUI function, change the rect width to **700**.

```
if (npcResponding) {  // npc is talking
    GUI.Label (Rect (25, 25, 700, 35), textReply);
}
```

Your dialogue tree now handles branching of subtopics.

You can find the DialogueManager script thus far as DialogueManager[2].js, in this chapter's scripts folder. (See the Source Code/Downloads tab of the book's Apress product page [www.apress.com/9781430248996].)

Special Instructions

There are a few more scenarios you will want to allow for. The first is special cases. Basically, this is a wild card that lets you handle just about anything that isn't covered by the system. It can be as mundane as activating an extra topic or as complex as triggering any kind of event, animation, or special effect.

The mechanism is simple—the special case is assigned a number. That number, in string form, is passed as an argument to the function, and a switch is used to find the correct instructions.

Eventually, the first NPC character will offer the player a rock, and the second will perform a bit of magic to help the player along. For now, you will only have some text, indicating the action, print out to the console. In some cases, the special instructions can only be used once, so the character code must be modified to allow that.

1. Create the SpecialInstructions function.

```
//this lets you do extra stuff, trigger animations, special effects, just about anything
function SpecialInstructions (code : String) {
  if(code == "00") return;

  switch (code) {
    case "01" : // offers rock- this is a one off
        print ("npc offers player a rock");
```

```
                 //clear the special instructions flag by rebuilding the string
                 replies_1[7] =  replies_1[7].Substring(0,7) + "00" + replies_1[7].Substring(9);
                 break;

          case "02" : //
              // to be filled in later
              break;

       }// end switch
    } // end SpecialInstructions
```

All replies will be processed by sending their eighth and ninth characters into this function for processing, or more accurately, the seventh and eighth, because Substring also counts from 0. If the characters are "00", there are no special instructions, so you are returned. You will be calling the SpecialInstructions function from the ProcessReplyString function.

2. At the top of the ProcessReplyString function, add the code to process special cases.

```
//Process special instructions, the 7th and 8th char
SpecialInstructions(fullReply.Substring(7,2));
```

3. Now, change the code in the number 7 reply to the following:

```
"0001 1 0100^Try using this rock^You haven't tried the rock?^Sorry, you're on your own now";
```

4. Save the script.

5. Click Play and test. Watch the console for the message. When you see it, clear the console and select the "Can you help me with a replacement?" topic again.

This time, the special case is no longer called. You could also remove the internal from the replies_1 array and watch the special cases characters being cleared in the inspector.

Exiting the Conversation

The final bit of functionality you need to set a code for is to know when the conversation should end, so the topic text will disappear, and the player is free to wander off.

Rather than add yet another character to the code string, however, you will repurpose one of the existing ones. The first character (element 0) processes instructions for changing the state of the current topic or reply. Because the exit topic shouldn't ever have to change state, and the code only checks for four scenarios, you can safely highjack number 9 to use as the exit code.

1. Add the following at the very top of the ActivationHandler function:

```
// leaving the conversation
if (instructions == "9" ) {
   exitConv = true; // set the flag to suppress GUI
   //currentGO.SendMessage("Conversation", false, SendMessageOptions.DontRequireReceiver);
   return;
}
```

The second line in the condition reports back to the NPC that the conversation has ended; it is commented out for now. The first line sets a flag to suppress the topics from being listed, so that flag must be added to a few other places.

2. Add the declaration for the exitConv variable, a Boolean type, to the script.

```
internal var exitConv : boolean = false; // flag to end conversation
```

3. Near the bottom of the Update function, make the following change:

```
playerTalking = true; // show the topics
```

to:

```
if (!exitConv) playerTalking = true;// show the topics if the conversation has not finished
```

4. Reply 8 should end the conversation, so change its code to the following:

```
replies_1[8] = "9000 0 0000 Good luck";
```

5. Save the script.

6. Click Play and test the exit topic.

The conversation ends gracefully when you select the "Gotta go" topic.

You can find the DialogueManager script thus far as DialogueManager[3].js, in this chapter's scripts folder. (See the Source Code/Downloads tab of the book's Apress product page [www.apress.com/9781430248996].)

Adding the Second NPC Conversation

So far, you have been creating a framework that will allow for multiple NPC conversations. As mentioned earlier, because Unity arrays have to be typed, they can't contain other arrays, so to keep your code working with additional characters, you will be making a few more changes.

You'll have to add a switch to any other function where the Replies_1 and topics_1 arrays have been directly assigned.

1. Add Switch to the ProcessReply function—replace

```
replies = new String [replies_1.length];
replies = replies_1;
```

with

```
switch (currentNpc) {

   case 1 :
      replies = new String [replies_1.length];
      replies = replies_1;
      break;

   case 2 :
      replies = new String [replies_2.length];
      replies = replies_2;
      break;
} // end switch
```

2. Add switch to the LoadTopic function—replace

```
topics = new String [topics_1.length];
topics = topics_1;
```

with

```
switch (currentNpc) {

    case 1 :
        topics = new String [topics_1.length];// re-initialize array
        topics = topics_1; // load it
        break;

    case 2 :
        topics = new String [topics_2.length]; // re-initialize array
        topics = topics_2; // load it
        break;

} // end switch
```

3. In the SetNPC function, add case 2 to the switch.

```
case 2 :
    rootTopics = "1,2,3,7,9";
    branchTopics  = "3,4,5,6,10";
    rootTopicList = ConvertToArray (rootTopics);
    branchTopicList = ConvertToArray (branchTopics);
    currentTopicsList = rootTopicList;
    break;
```

4. At the bottom of the ActivationHandler function, replace

```
// update the active/inactive states
if (newState != "null") topics_1[currentReplyNum] =  newState +
topics_1[currentReplyNum].Substring(1);
if (auxNewState != "null") topics_1[auxTopicNum] =  auxNewState +
topics_1[auxTopicNum].Substring(1);
```

with

```
//update the topic states as needed
switch (currentNpc) {
    case 1 :
        if (newState != "null") topics_1[currentReplyNum] =  newState +
        topics_1[currentReplyNum].Substring(1);
        if (auxNewState != "null") topics_1[auxTopicNum] =  auxNewState +
        topics_1[auxTopicNum].Substring(1);
        break;
```

```
case 2 :
    if (newState != "null") topics_2[currentReplyNum] = newState +
    topics_2[currentReplyNum].Substring(1);
    if (auxNewState != "null") topics_2[auxTopicNum] = auxNewState +
    topics_2[auxTopicNum].Substring(1);
    break;

} // end switch
```

5. At the bottom of the ProcessReplyString function, replace

```
// increment or reset the 4th char (element 3) for the next time, update [rebuild]
original string with the correct number
replies_1[currentReplyNum] = replies_1[currentReplyNum].Substring(0,3) + type.ToString()
+ replies_1[currentReplyNum].Substring(4);
```

with

```
// increment or reset the 5th char (element 4)for the next time,
// update [rebuild] original string with the correct number
switch (currentNpc) {

    case 1 :
        replies_1[currentReplyNum] = replies_1[currentReplyNum].Substring(0,3)
        + type.ToString() + replies_1[currentReplyNum].Substring(4);
        break;

    case 2 :
        replies_2[currentReplyNum] = replies_2[currentReplyNum].Substring(0,3)
        + type.ToString() + replies_2[currentReplyNum].Substring(4);
        break;
} // end switch
```

Once the hardcoded bits have been converted to switch statements, it's time to add the topics and replies for the second NPC. Feel free to copy and paste this from the e-book or the DialogueManager[4] script.

1. Add the new topic and reply arrays for the second conversation.

```
// Player conversation topics  with npc 2
internal var topics_2 = new String[11];
topics_2[0] = "000 null";
topics_2[1] = "100 Hi";
topics_2[2] = "100 What happened to the other guy?";
topics_2[3] = "100 I got the topi fruit, what am I supposed to do with it?";
topics_2[4] = "000 Where do I find the Tree of Life?";
topics_2[5] = "000 How do I find the tunnels?";
topics_2[6] = "000 Can you help me?";
topics_2[7] = "100 I keep blacking out in the tunnels, any idea where I can find a lantern?";
topics_2[8] = "100 The maze looks different, how do I get out of it?";
topics_2[9] = "100 See you around";
topics_2[10] = "100 Thanks for your help";
```

```
// replies_2 character reply text
internal var replies_2 = new String[11];
replies_2[0] = "0000 0 0000 You shouldn't see this";
replies_2[1] = "0000 0 0000 Greetings, adventurer";
replies_2[2] = "0000 0 0000 He's on break";
replies_2[3] = "2040 1 0000 You must replace the dying Tree of Life by planting the new fruit";
replies_2[4] = "2050 1 0000 You will find a way to it in the tunnels";
replies_2[5] = "2060 1 0000 The tunnels are in the rock dome, there used to be a map of
them in the temple";
replies_2[6] = "0001 1 0200^I have marked a trail to the top for you and cleared the
entrance^There's nothing more I can do for you";
replies_2[7] = "0000 0 0000 The flower of a local, but rare plant is said to be quite
illuminating";
replies_2[8] = "0009 0 0000^Trial and error^I cannot help you with that^It is ever
changing, there is no map^No idea, I've been stuck here for ages";
replies_2[9] = "9009 0 0000^I wish you success^See you around^Good luck^May your quest
bear fruit";
replies_2[10] = "0000 0 0000 Any time";
```

Topic 6 has a similar need for a special case, so you will have to add the code for the specified case 02.

2.   Add the special case for reply 6 in the SpecialInstructions function, as follows:

```
case "02" : // activates path
   print ("activates path markers");
   //clear the special instructions flag by rebuilding the string
   replies_2[6] = replies_2[6].Substring(0,7) + "00" + replies_2[6].Substring(9);
   break;
```

3.   In the Start function, replace 1 with 2, to be able to test the second conversation.

```
SetNPC(2); // set the current NPC's ID number
```

4.   Save the script.

5.   Click Play and test.

The second dialogue plays out with its own branch.

You can find the DialogueManager script thus far as DialogueManager[4].js, in this chapter's scripts folder. See the Source Code/Downloads tab of the book's Apress product page (www.apress.com/9781430248996).

Adding Audio Clips

The conversation is pretty solid now, so it's time to add the audio. You'll have to locate an audio clip when the player selects a topic *and* after the reply for that topic is processed. Next, you'll have to adjust the timers to allow for the length of the clip being played. And, of course, you will have to add the clip numbers to topic and reply codes.

If you were creating the game from scratch, you'd probably want to create the array for the audio clip in the DialogueManager script, for easy access. To save you the monotony of dragging audio clips into a long array, I've created a prefab, with the sounds already loaded for you.

The only rule for the audio clip array is that topics that have sequential or random replies *must* be grouped together—and in order. The random number or current position in the sequence acts as an offset from the first reply's element number in the audio clip array. The number of the first reply is not important; it just acts as a pointer to the rest.

1. Import DialogueAudio.unitypackage into the project.

The package imports a script, DialogueAudioClips, into the NPC Assets folder; a prefab, DialogueAudioClips, which has all of the clips loaded and ready to use; and an Audio Dialogue folder, containing all of the audio clips for the two conversations. The Audio Dialogue folder also contains the assignment list for the audio clips.

2. Locate the Dialogue Audio Clips *prefab,* and drag it into the the NPC Assets folder.

3. From the NPC Assets folder, drag the Dialogue Audio Clips *prefab* into the scene.

4. Save the scene.

5. Assign the numbers to the appropriate replies and topics' last two code characters. They should be as follows:

```
topics_1  =  00,01,02,03,04,05,06,07,08,09
replies_1 =  00,01,04,05,10,11,12,13,16,17
topics_2  =  00,01,02,03,04,05,06,07,08,09,10
replies_2 =  00,01,02,03,04,05,06,08,09,13,17
```

So, the final topics and replies arrays should be as follows:

```
// Player conversation topics with npc_1
internal var topics_1 = new String[10];
topics_1[0] = "100 null";
topics_1[1] = "101 Hi";
topics_1[2] = "102 Where am I?";
topics_1[3] = "003 How do I get out of the maze?";
topics_1[4] = "104 What happened to me?";
topics_1[5] = "005 Why was I transported here?";
topics_1[6] = "006 Is there a way to acquire the topi fruit?";
topics_1[7] = "007 Can you help me with a replacement?";
topics_1[8] = "108 Gotta go";
topics_1[9] = "109 OK, thanks";

// replies_1 character reply text
internal var replies_1 = new String[10];
replies_1[0] = "0000 0 0000 You shouldn't see this";
replies_1[1] = "0001 0 0001^I've been expecting you^You have questions, perhaps?^Hello
again^reset";
replies_1[2] = "3030 0 0004 You are in the Maze";
replies_1[3] = "0009 0 0005^Trial and error?^Sorry, can't help you with that^It is ever
changing, there is no map^No idea, I've been stuck here for ages^I wish I knew";
replies_1[4] = "2050 1 0010 You were transported here";
replies_1[5] = "2060 1 0011 You tried to steal the golden Topi fruit";
replies_1[6] = "2070 1 0012 Yes, you must replace it with something of similar size and weight";
replies_1[7] = "0001 1 0113^Try using this rock^You haven't tried the rock?^Sorry, you're
on your own now";
replies_1[8] = "9000 0 0016 Good luck";
replies_1[9] = "0000 0 0017 No problem";
```

```
// Player conversation topics  with npc 2
internal var topics_2 = new String[11];
topics_2[0] = "000 null";
topics_2[1] = "101 Hi";
topics_2[2] = "102 What happened to the other guy?";
topics_2[3] = "103 I got the topi fruit, what am I supposed to do with it?";
topics_2[4] = "004 Where do I find the Tree of Life?";
topics_2[5] = "005 How do I find the tunnels?";
topics_2[6] = "006 Can you help me?";
topics_2[7] = "107 I keep blacking out in the tunnels, any idea where I can find a lantern?";
topics_2[8] = "108 The maze looks different, how do I get out of it?";
topics_2[9] = "109 See you around";
topics_2[10] = "110 Thanks for your help";

// replies_2 character reply text
internal var replies_2 = new String[11];
replies_2[0] = "0000 0 0000 You shouldn't see this";
replies_2[1] = "0000 0 0001 Greetings, adventurer";
replies_2[2] = "0000 0 0002 He's on break";
replies_2[3] = "2040 1 0003 You must replace the dying Tree of Life by planting the new fruit";
replies_2[4] = "2050 1 0004 You will find a way to it in the tunnels";
replies_2[5] = "2060 1 0005 The tunnels are in the rock dome, there used to be a map of
them in the temple";
replies_2[6] = "0001 1 0206^I have marked a trail to the top for you and cleared the
entrance^There's nothing more I can do for you";
replies_2[7] = "0000 0 0008 The flower of a local, but rare plant is said to be quite
illuminating";
replies_2[8] = "0009 0 0009^Trial and error^I cannot help you with that^It is ever
changing, there is no map^No idea, I've been stuck here for ages";
replies_2[9] = "9009 0 0013^I wish you success^See you around^Good luck^May your quest
bear fruit";
replies_2[10] = "0000 0 0017 Any time";
```

6. Save the script.

Adding the Audio Source

Unity offers two types of audio: 2D and 3D. With 2D, the sound plays regardless of where the object that contains the script and audio source is in the scene. With 3D sound, the Rolloff determines how close the player has to be before it can be heard.

In the type of onscreen dialogue you have just developed, 2D audio would seem like the most logical choice. But unlike the traditional point-and-click adventures, where the environment consists of a static image per location, this game exists in a 3D world. If the player comes upon a character who is off to his right, it makes sense to be able to hear the NPC's dialogue more from the right speaker or earphone.

The downside of 2D sound is that audio clips come in as 3D by default and have to be changed manually to 2D. The downside of 3D clips is that they have to be played from a nearby object's audio source to be able to be heard.

Until you move back into the actual game, it will be easiest to move the Dialogue Manager object to the location of the scene cameras. That way, you will be able to hear the conversation, without making any major changes in the code or setup.

1. Select and focus in on the Main Camera.

2. Select the Dialogue Manager object.

3. From the GameObject menu, use Move to View.

The dialogue clips will be audible during the rest of the testing.

Scripting for the Audio Clips

Next, the DialogueManager script will require access to the script with the audio clips.

1. Open the DialogueManager script.

2. Near the top, add the following variables:

```
//audio variables
var clipSource : DialogueAudioClips; // the script with the audio clip arrays

internal var currentTopicAudio = new AudioClip[2]; // array for current topics audio
internal var currentReplyAudio = new AudioClip[2]; // array for current replies audio
internal var uiAudio : int; // element number for current topic audio
internal var currentAudioReply : AudioClip; // holds the reply audio until the topic
audio is finished
internal var audioElement : int; // audio clip element number for the current reply
```

3. In the Start function, "find" and assign the audio script.

```
clipSource  = gameObject.Find("DialogueAudioClips").GetComponent(DialogueAudioClips);
```

4. Load the audio arrays for the current NPC in the SetNPC function switch blocks, above the break line in the appropriate cases.

For case 1,

```
currentTopicAudio = new AudioClip[clipSource.audioTopics1.length];
currentTopicAudio = clipSource.audioTopics1;
currentReplyAudio = new AudioClip[clipSource.audioReplies1.length];
currentReplyAudio = clipSource.audioReplies1;
```

And case 2,

```
currentTopicAudio = new AudioClip[clipSource.audioTopics2.length];
currentTopicAudio = clipSource.audioTopics2;
currentReplyAudio = new AudioClip[clipSource.audioReplies2.length];
currentReplyAudio = clipSource.audioReplies2;
```

5. Load and play the topic audio at the top of the ProcessReply function.

```
// locate and load the topic audio clip for the topic/reply element
var tempAudioElement : int = parseInt(topics[replyElement].Substring(1,2));
audio.clip = currentTopicAudio[tempAudioElement];
audio.Play(); // play the topic audio
```

6. Then add the length of the clip to the timer in the next section down, so it becomes the following:

```
// start timer before showing reply
pauseForReplyLimit = Time.time + audio.clip.length + 0.5;
pauseForReply = true; // start the timer
```

7. At the top of the ProcessReplyString function, get the base element number for the reply.

```
// locate the reply audio element
audioElement = parseInt(fullReply.Substring(9,2));
```

8. In ProcessReplyString, if (type == 0), above the return, assign the base audio clip.

```
currentAudioReply = currentReplyAudio[audioElement];
```

9. In the if (type == 9) block, above its return, add the following to account for the offset:

```
currentAudioReply = currentReplyAudio[audioElement + audioOffset -1];
```

10. In the last section, below the audioOffset = type line, add the same line as before.

```
currentAudioReply = currentReplyAudio[audioElement + audioOffset -1];
```

Now you'll have to nip back up to the Update function to trigger the reply audio, and then add the clip length to the reply timer.

11. In the Update function, in the timer for the reply section, beneath the npcResponding line, add the following:

```
// reply audio
audio.clip = currentAudioReply; // load the processed reply
audio.Play(); // play the reply audio
```

12. Then add the length of the clip to the pauseForTopicLimit.

```
pauseForTopicLimit =  Time.time + currentAudioReply.length + 0.5; // give player time to read reply
```

Before you can test your handiwork, you'll have to add an Audio Source component to the Dialogue Manager object, so that you will hear the audio. By putting it on the gameObject, you will be able to hear it anywhere.

1. Save the script.

2. Select the Dialogue Manager object.

3. Drag the DialogueAudioClips object into its Clip Source parameter.

4. Add an Audio Source component to the **Dialogue Manager**.

5. Set its Rolloff to Linear and uncheck Play On Awake.

6. Click Play and test the current NPC.

7. Stop Playback and change the NPC ID in the Start function.

8. Save the script.

9.   Click Play and test the other NPC ID.

10. Save the scene and save the project.

With the audio working nicely, the next step will be to hook it up to a couple of characters. You will do that in the next chapter. But first, having done all the hard work, it makes sense to make a prefab before leaving this scene.

1.   Select the NPC Assets folder.

2.   Create a new Prefab and name it **Dialogue Manager**.

3.   Select the Dialogue Manager in the Hierarchy view and drag it onto the new prefab.

4.   Save the scene and save the project.

Next, you will introduce the characters into the test scene.

You can find the DialogueManager script thus far as DialogueManager[5].js in this chapter's scripts folder. (See the Source Code/Downloads tab of the book's Apress product page [`www.apress.com/9781430248996`].)

Summary

In this chapter, you began with a list of requirements for a dialogue tree that you could use with a couple of NPCs, nonplayer characters.

You started the master script, by creating a Unity array for a list of topics, then used the Unity GUI elements to display them onscreen.

With the topics displaying, you added another array of replies and then added a timing mechanism to hide and show the appropriate text.

Next, you started implementing a system that allowed you to control visibility of topics, so that the player could be given new topics only after accessing the correct predecessor.

Making use of the new system, you then added a way to process multiple replies to the same topic. Using the same position in the system character code, you were able to pull random replies from the parsed optional replies or sequential replies. Just as with the revealed or single-access topics, you also adjusted the reply codes to control subsequent accessing of the replies.

With the five-topic limit onscreen, you refined the system to allow branched topic lists. Once again, the code was designed to allow the conversation to return to the root topics and, finally, to be able to exit gracefully out of the conversation. The addition of a specialty function provided a means of scripting any "wild card" functionality beyond simple conversation.

With the basics covered, you extended the code, to be able to handle multiple-character conversations. Without the luxury of JavaScript arrays that can be nested to produces multidimensional arrays, you made good use of the switch case, to set up for the different conversations.

Finally, you imported a Unity package containing the audio clips that go with each of the topics and replies. On inspecting the assets, you found how they, too, fit in with the system and were called along with the text. A bit of adjusting, and the timing of both topics and replies was refined to take the clips' lengths into account.

In the next chapter, you will introduce two characters into the conversations.

■ ■ ■

CHAPTER 16

Mecanim and Characters

Before you can hook up the dialogue you created in the previous chapter, you will have to set up a couple of characters. New to Unity 4.0 was the character animation system, Mecanim. With Mecanim, you can use animation clips from one humanoid character on most any other similar characters.

It also comes with a nice state machine that takes a lot of the painful scripting out of triggering different clips or behaviors. More important, it handles masking and blending with ease. *Masking* allows you to override parts of characters, while the rest of the character's body continues to use the original animation clip. For example, you can have a character walking along, and then have an arm wave override only the arm. The animation is blended as the character continues walking, but now he waves as he walks. *Blending* smoothly handles the transition from one animation to the next, matching the foot placement as it goes.

Mecanim is a complex and powerful system for controlling characters. There is easily enough material to fill a book on its own, so you will be getting to test out a few of the main features and then set it up to control the two characters your player will come across in the game.

Adding Characters

Because Mecanim allows for the control of characters through their animations, you will start by writing a very simple character controller, to move a character around a scene. Although the game uses first-person navigation, you can still make excellent use of Mecanim's functionality when controlling the two characters in the conversation scenarios. Before returning to the conversations, you will be running the usual experiments, to get familiar with the basics of Mecanim, and then you will incorporate the characters into the conversations.

You will start by importing a few characters. Two of the files contain the animations you will be using, and the other two are the rigged characters you will be using in the game. The animations are simple proxies done with 3ds Max's Character Animation Toolkit (CAT). This system provides a quick way to rough-in character animations for prototyping your game. There are also several nice motion capture animations available from Unity's Asset Store in the free Mecanim Tutorial scene. Feel free to give them a try, instead of the generic idle and walk provided with the book.

Importing the Characters

Let's get started.

1. Create a new scene and save it as **Character Tests**.

2. Import the four characters, Gimbok, Kahmi, Sitter, and Walking Man, by dragging the *contents* of the Mecanim Assets folder, from the chapter's Assets folder to the project's NPC Assets folder.

3. Create a plane for the ground, and scale it up to about 10×10×10.

4. Drop the Ground texture from the NPC Assets folder on it and set the tiling to about 10×10.

Unlike the legacy Animation system, you can't just drag the new assets into the scene and click Play to see the animations. But there are a few benefits to dropping them in right away, one of which is to check their scale. With Mecanim, changing scale will mean having to re-set up the bone targeting, so it's best to take care of scale first.

5. Drag the four characters into the scene and move them apart a bit, then add a light, so you can see them.

If you inspect the four characters, you will see that one, Sitter, contains only a bone system but has no mesh. You can delete it from the Hierarchy view. The Kahmi and Gimbok characters are rigged but not animated. This means they have a full bone system, with weights applied to tell each vertex how much influence the various bones have over them.

6. From the Edit menu, open Quality Settings, and under Other, open the Blend Weights drop-down.

You can see that Unity allows one, two, or four bones to affect each vertex. As you may have guessed, more bones to blend the weights take more resources. Bone-weight assignments are automatically recalculated on import, when there are more than four bones per vertex. This is one of the reasons why rigging may not act as it did in the application the character was rigged in.

The WalkingMan character doesn't have a skinned mesh, but when exported as an FBX, Convert Deforming Dummies to Bones was left unchecked, so the boxes that made up the bone system come in as meshes. This means that characters do not have to be made with skinned meshes. Any objects can form the skeleton hierarchy.

7. To get a feel for scale, drag a new First Person Controller, from the Standard Assets folder, into the scene next to the characters.

8. Set its Main Camera's Field of View to **30,** to match the First Person Controller you set up in the regular scenes.

The three remaining characters are dwarfed by the First Person Controller (Figure 16-1).

Figure 16-1. *The tiny characters*

The two game characters will need their scale changed. Theoretically, the WalkingMan shouldn't have to be adjusted, because only the animations will be used. You can leave him as is for now and then see what happens when the scale is changed later on.

9. Select Kahmi in the Project view, and in the Model section of the Inspector, change her Scale Factor to **0.027** and click Apply.

10. Select Gimbok, set his Scale Factor to **0.028,** and click Apply.

11. Delete the First Person Controller from the scene.

12. Change the two character's shaders to Bumped Specular and set the Main Color to white.

13. Add the matching normal maps.

Setting Up the Avatars

Unless you are using Legacy or None for the Animation Type, Unity creates an avatar to store information on the imported objects. For Humanoid characters, you may have to complete the configuration process, to allow the mapping that is needed for retargeting with different animations and different characters. If a check mark appears to the left of the Configure button after you have applied the Humanoid Animation Type, it means that Mecanim thinks it has made a successful mapping.

1. Select Gimbok in the Project view.

2. In the Inspector, Rig section, change Animation Type to Humanoid and click Apply (Figure 16-2).

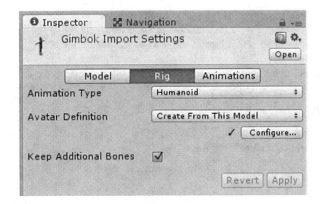

Figure 16-2. *The Rig section*

3. When it is finished, click the newly revealed Configure button.

When configuring an avatar, Unity takes over the Scene view. You will be asked if you want to save the scene. Agree to this. The Avatar Mapping comes up first, as shown in Figure 16-3.

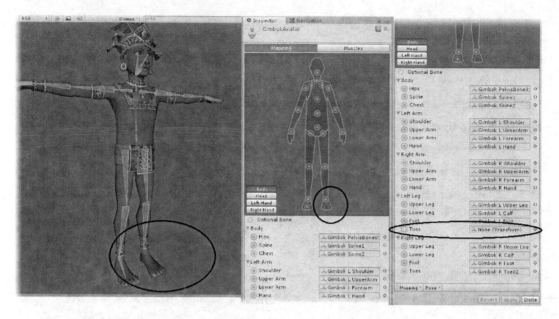

Figure 16-3. *The Avatar Mapping panel and missing toe*

The figure should be fully green, indicating that all of its body parts were recognized. If there were any red areas on the body map, you would have to manually select the missing parts. In this figure, the left toe was not found, but because the toe is optional, no error was shown. Note the naming differences. Mecanim is usually pretty good at assigning the correct humanoid body parts. It does so by looking for a variety of key words, as well as the object's position in the hierarchy.

4.   Check to make sure the Left Leg Toes are assigned; if not, assign the missing part, Gimbok L Toe02, by dragging the toe from the Hierarchy view into the mapping list.

Because the character has a jaw bone for talking, you should check the head next.

5.   Click the Head button at the lower left of the figure and make sure the jaw was found.

6.   Check the Hands to make sure the finger bones were found.

7.   Click Apply.

■ **Tip**   To qualify as Humanoid, your character must have at least 15 bones. In the assignment list, you can see which bones are mandatory and which are optional (Figure 16-3). The mandatory bones are marked by solid circles around the body parts in the list. Optional bones have dashed circles. The last bone is the Head bone and is found in the head section.

Next let's open the Muscles tab next to the Mapping tab.

The Muscles tab is where you can adjust the targeting to account for character physique differences. Mapping a skinny bone system to a pudgy character, for example, would require the arms to be offset outward from the body, to prevent them from intersecting the body during various behaviors.

The top section is where you can contort the poor character to check the extremes of the bone positions. Don't panic if the rigging doesn't hold up to a pose that the character will never get into. The middle section is where you can set the ranges for the various body parts. And the lower section contains a few more specialty adjustments. If the animations you will be using never put the character beyond its logical ranges, you won't need to set them.

Fortunately, the Gimbok character shouldn't need adjusting. You will, however, have to adjust the Kahmi character shortly.

1. Click Done to return to the regular editor.

2. Select the WalkingMan in the Project view and set its Animation Type to Humanoid.

3. Repeat the steps to configure the WalkingMan.

The WalkingMan starts with his arms near his sides, but is automatically put into T-pose. If a character is not able to go into T-pose, he or she may need bone reassignments. If any of the bones show red in the Scene view, you may have to click the Pose button, select Reset, and then select Enforce T-Pose (Figure 16-4). If a character cannot be corrected with the Mapping or Pose options, it may have to be reexamined in its native format.

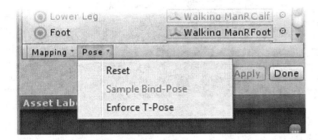

Figure 16-4. *T-pose options at the bottom of the Mapping view*

4. Click Done and select the Kahmi character from the Project view.

5. Repeat the steps to configure the Kahmi character.

The Kahmi character will require ranges set for her right arm for the wave test you will be performing. Her hand will go through her headdress, so you will have to set its range limits.

1. In Configure, go to the Muscles section.

2. Open the Right Arm drop-down by clicking open its arrow.

3. Select the Arm Down-Up and open its arrow.

4. To the left, try moving the preview slider all the way to the left—this is the down range and should be okay.

5. Now move the preview slider all the way to the right, to see the upper range—the hand intersects the headdress.

6. Now move the Range slider's right end to the left, to lower the arm and adjust the other arm preview sliders to put the upper arm into the wave position.

7. Adjust the right end of the range slider to about 64.87 (Figure 16-5).

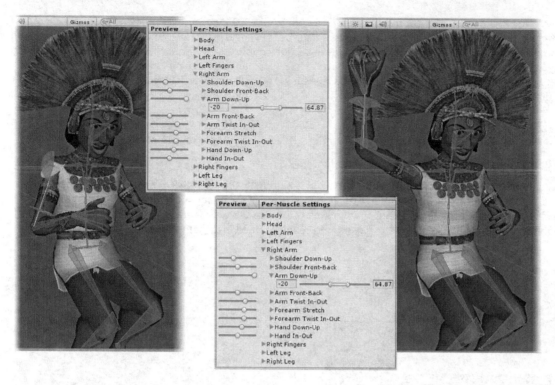

Figure 16-5. *Muscle setup*

8.   Click Apply to make the changes permanent.

Finally, you will have to set up the Sitter.

9.   Repeat for the Sitter.

When the Sitter is configured, you will see that there are only bones and no mesh (see Figure 16-6). Note the extra "bone" for the root node, Sitter. Unused bones are grayed out. In this character, you may decide that Sitter Spine4 would be a better assignment as the chest than Sitter Spine2. Mecanim usually does a pretty good job on the assignments, so wait until you see how the other characters move with Sitter's animation clips before reassigning the spine bones.

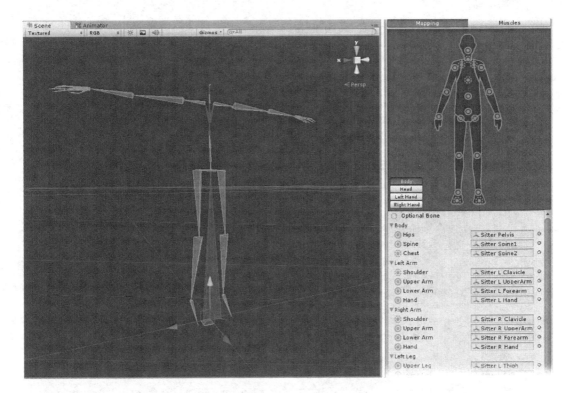

Figure 16-6. The Sitter configured—just bones

You may have noticed that Kahmi has a ponytail. In the Rig section, before you clicked Configure, you may have noticed a check box for Keep Additional Bones. The ponytail bones will not be affected by any other humanoid animation clips, because there are no ponytail bones on the humanoid, but if they *had* been animated, the animation would have been included for their character only. To control non-humanoids with a mask, you would use an Avatar Skeleton Mask instead of an Avatar Body Mask.

Defining the Animation Clips

The WalkingMan and Sitter characters have animations, so you will have to set up a few of the clips next. For the full clip assignments, see the accompanying StateManagement PDF for this chapter. (See the Source Code/Downloads tab of the book's Apress product page www.apress.com/9781430248996.)

1. Select the WalkingMan in the Project view.

2. In the Importer/Inspector, switch to the Animations section.

3. Under Clips, select Take 001.

As soon as you select the clip, you will see all of the setup options for the clip (Figure 16-7, left).

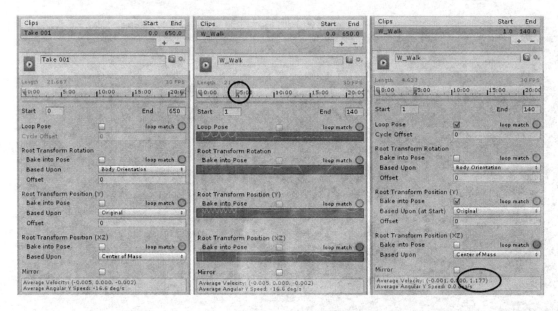

Figure 16-7. *The clip options for a humanoid (left), for adjusting the end-time marker (middle), and for noting Z—forward velocity—for the W_Walk clip (right)*

4. Click Play in the Preview window to see the animation.

The character starts out in a reference pose for frame 0. He then walks several strides, idles for a while, executes a couple of turn-in-place animations, and, finally, a wave animation. You'll start by setting up just a few of the possible clips. Because you may wish to bring in more animations with their own versions of the behaviors, naming will be important.

5. In the naming section, rename the clip to **W_Walk**.

Under the Start and End fields, you will see a check box for Loop Pose. Because the character starts and ends the total animation in the neutral pose, the loop match indicator is green. Watch it as you change the start and end frames, as it shows mismatch, red, then match again.

6. Set Start to **1** and End to **140** and check Loop Pose.

Because the walk *should* loop, check Loop Pose to define it as the clip's default wrap type.

This behavior already loops correctly, but if it was a little off, the Loop Pose would tweak the entire animation to make sure everything looped seamlessly. If you start the clip at 0, where the character is in reference pose, you can see the effect.

You can also set the Start and End frames, by moving their markers in the time line. As soon as you do so, a small curve pops up under the transform parameters, to help you see where the animations loop (Figure 16-7, middle). This workflow is especially valuable if you don't have the frame numbers for the behaviors or if you have to create new clips from existing animations.

1. Under Root Transform Position (Y), check Bake into Pose.

This cryptic setting is only left unchecked when the animation is something like a jump or roll, where the up axis requires radical height adjustment set by physics or some other outside controls. If left unchecked, a character whose hips drop near the ground for a crawl behavior would instead be "crawling" in midair at pelvis height.

2. With Bake into Pose checked, click the Play button in the Preview window, to see the animation.

The character strolls nonchalantly along, while the grid moves underneath him.

3. Stop the preview and click the Plus button at the bottom of the clip list to create another clip (the Minus button will remove the selected clip).

4. Name it **W_Idle**.

5. Set Start to **145** and End to **240**.

6. Check Loop Pose and, under Root Transform Position (Y), check Bake into Pose.

7. Click Play in the Preview window to observe the animation.

Before you set up the next two animations, take a look at the section near the bottom of the panel that shows Average Velocity. The Z value for the Idle is 0.000.

8. Select the W_Walk clip again.

Its Z (forward) velocity is 1.177 (Figure 16-7, right). This shows you that the walk cycle was not a "walk in place" animation. This will be important when you create the simple character controller in a little while, because you will let Mecanim move the character according to the clip's velocity.

Let's go ahead and add the next clip.

1. Create another clip and name it **W_Talk**.

2. Set its Start to **541** and its End to **600**.

3. Check Loop Pose and under Root Transform Position (Y), check Bake into Pose.

4. Play the preview.

To see this one, you'll need a better view. You can spin the Preview window but not zoom in or out. If you want a bigger view, you can right-click its title bar to undock it. Clicking the X on the right-hand side re-docks it. Now you should be able to see his jaw moving. It's a boring animation, but you will only be using the head by using a mask. The rest of the body will be cycling through its current behavior.

This is all you need for this guy for now.

5. Go ahead and click Apply.

The rest of the animation is on the Sitter. It contains the cross-legged pose Gimbok will use, as well as a clapping behavior that both characters will use to perform feats of magic to help the player with his quest. There is also a listening behavior that both characters will make use of.

6. Select the Sitter from the Project view.

7. In the Inspector, switch to the Animations section.

8. Select Take 001.

Because there is no mesh associated with the Sitter's bones, "Dude," the default Mecanim character, is used in the Preview window.

9. Click Play to watch the entire clip in the Preview window.

10. Rename the Take 001 clip to **Sitter Idle**.

11. Set Start to **21** and End to **60**.

12. Check Loop Pose and check Root Transform Position (Y); check Bake into Pose.

13. Add another clip and name it **Listening**.

14. Set Start to **61** and End to **150**.

15. Check Loop Pose and, under Root Transform Position (Y), check Bake into Pose.

16. Click Play.

The character inclines his head and politely nods while listening to the player's questions. He also moves forward and backward from his base pose. Because Mecanim will handle the transition for you, it will be better to start and end the pose already forward.

1. Set the Start to **75** and the End to **120**.

Note the Average Angular Y speed just below the regular velocity. If it were any greater, you would probably see the character slowly turning. Because he shouldn't turn, you can lock in the Y Rotation.

2. Check Root Transform Rotation, Bake into Pose.

Finally, you will need a clap hands behavior. This one is a one-off, so you don't need Loop Pose.

3. Click Add clip again; name the new one **Clap Hands**.

4. Set Start to **181** and End to **280**.

5. Under Root Transform Position (Y), check Bake into Pose.

If you look closely, you can see that Dude's hands overlap at the clap. If you wanted to use him in the scene, you would have to adjust his arm ranges to prevent that. Because you will be using Gimbok and Kahmi, you should see what they look like with the clap hands behavior.

6. Drag the Gimbok character into the Preview window, to see how his body works with the Clap Hands.

7. Repeat for the Kahmi character.

8. Click Apply.

Having set up the characters and animation clips, now would be a good time to save the scene and save the project.

Controlling the Characters

Along with the avatar created for each of the imports, Unity also added an Animator component to each, as you will see if you check out the characters in the Hierarchy view. As a default, it adds the avatar that matches the character. There are two things it still needs to get the character up and running in the scene. It will need an Animator Controller, to define the states, transitions, and associated animation clips, and it will need a script, to drive the transitions.

The Animator Controller

The Animator Controller is Mecanim's powerful state engine. This is where you will set up transitions and blend trees, layers, and other features that let you get the most from your characters. One thing to remember is that some changes to the Animator Controller made during runtime will not be lost when you exit Play mode.

1. Select the NPC Assets folder in the Project view.

2. From the right-click menu ➤ Create, near the bottom of the list, select Animator Controller.

3. Name it **Test Controller**.

The Inspector remains blank. That's because this feature requires its own window in conjunction with the Inspector.

4. Double-click to open it in the Animator view (Figure 16-8).

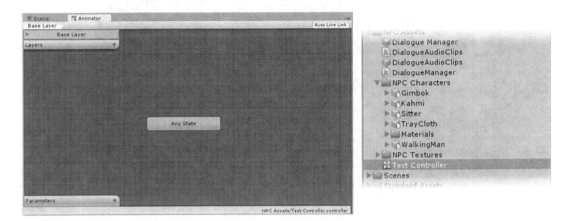

Figure 16-8. The Animator view for the new controller

The Animator view opens, showing the Base Layer in the upper left and the name of the controller in the lower right.

To start, you will have to drag a clip into the view. The first, or default, State is usually an idle clip. Ignore the Any State for the time being. You can use the usual viewport controls to pan it off to the left for now, if you wish.

5. Locate the Sitter Idle clip in the NPC Assets folder, under the Sitter asset, and drag it into the Animator view.

It becomes the default State and is color-coded orange.

6. Add the new Test Controller to each of the three characters by dragging it from the Project view and dropping it onto each one in the Hierarchy view.

The controller is added to the Animator component automatically.

7. Click Play.

All three characters immediately drop to the cross-legged pose (Figure 16-9). Kahmi's skirt suffers, but she won't be sitting in the game, so you needn't worry about it. Gimbok will eventually have a tray in his lap (in case you were wondering what was going on with the hands in the sitting poses).

Figure 16-9. *The three characters displaying the default Sitter Idle state*

Let's swap out the animation for something more fun.

1. With the Sitter Idle State selected, in the Inspector, change the State's name to **Idle**.

2. A few lines below the name field, click the Browse button and select the Clap Hands clip from the Assets for the Motion field and click Play again.

The three characters go through the motions, then freeze, because the Clap Hands clip was not set to loop.

3. This time, substitute the W_Walk clip, switch to the Scene view tab, and zoom out a way.

4. Click Play and watch the characters walk away.

The WalkingMan, because he is quite small, gets quickly left behind. Mecanim not only adjusts the clip to the skeleton size, it adjusts the clip's velocity to match.

Making Changes

Let's see what happens if you want to change a character's scale.

1. With the WalkingMan selected in the Project view, open the Model section and change the Scale Factor to **0.03**.

2. Click Apply.

The character pops up to match the other characters' scale.

3. Click Play.

The two other characters are now walking straight-legged aboveground, and the WalkingMan's body parts have been adjusted down to the original locations. To fix these problems, you will have to reset the WalkingMan's pose, because you are using his walk cycle.

4. With the WalkingMan still selected, open the Rig section and click Configure.

5. Agree to saving the scene.

6. At the bottom left of the window, open the Pose drop-down and select Reset.

The bones sort themselves out, but the character has lost his T-pose (Figure 16-10).

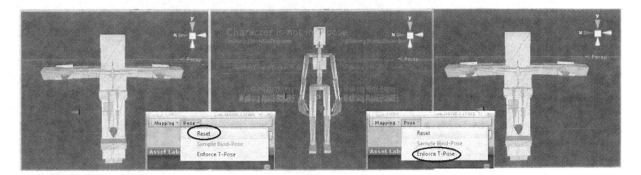

Figure 16-10. *The results of the new Scale Factor, the lost T-Pose, and the T-Pose recovered*

7. Click the drop-down again and choose Enforce T-Pose.

Everything is green and happy again.

8. Click Apply and then Done.

9. Click Play and watch the characters march off together.

Everything is back to normal.

Transitions

Although the game won't be using player-controlled characters, you will still get a chance to set one up in the test scene. To do this, you will have to make your first transition into another state. Let's put an idle clip back into the idle state first.

1. Click on the Animator tab.

2. Select the Idle state in the view.

3. In the Inspector, drag the W_Idle clip into the Motion field from the WalkingMan's folder, or chose it from the Browse dialog.

4. Next, drag the W_Walk into the Animator view, to create a new state.

A new state is created, inheriting its name from the W_Clip. This time it is gray, indicating that it is not the default clip for the Base Layer.

5. Select the new state and rename it **Walk,** at the top of the Inspector.

There are three parameters at the top of the Transition panel. The first, Speed, is the playback speed of the animation clip. Motion is the animation clip. The foot IK checkbox tells the engine to use the feet as the targets, during a blend from one state to the other. An example would be a character in a walk state. If the left foot was forward when the transition was called for a run, the run would be started at the point in its clip where the left foot was also forward. All of these parameters, by the way, can be changed through scripting.

6. Right-click the Idle state in the view and choose Make Transition.

The cursor now has a stretchy line with an arrow attached to it.

7. Move the cursor up to the new Walk state and click to finalize the transition's end state.

8. Select the Idle state.

In the Inspector, the Idle state now lists the new transition (see Figure 16-11).

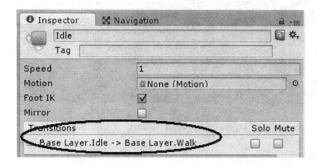

Figure 16-11. *The newly created transition for the Idle state*

9. Right-click the Walk state and select Make Transition again.

10. Drag this one back and click to attach it to the Idle state.

Now, Transitions lists the transitions set up for that state as well. The two check boxes, Solo and Mute, allow you more control when testing transitions. In edit mode, you can turn a transition off with Mute or make a transition the only active one, with Solo. Mute will turn the transition arrow red, while Solo will turn it green.

With Mecanim, creating a transition automatically defines its end state. But just like the transitions you defined for the action objects, the transition will have to know what condition *triggers* the state change. For that, you will have to add parameters to the Animator Controller, so they can be monitored in scripts.

For the Walk clip, you will create a parameter that you will name V Input. It will be checking the player's input for navigation from the virtual keys handled by the Input Manager. When the keys are pressed for "Vertical," the value returned is between -1, backward, and +1, forward. When it is not being pressed, 0 is returned.

1. In the Animation Controller window, click the plus next to Parameters at the lower left.

2. Select Float as the type for the variable or parameter.

3. Name it **V Input** and leave its initial value as 0.0 (Figure 16-12).

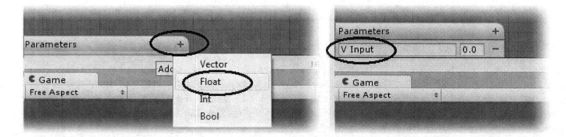

Figure 16-12. *The newly created parameter, V Input*

Now you have to set up the transition, to be able to use the V Input parameter.

    4.   Select the transition from the Idle state to the Walk state.

The line goes blue, and the transition appears in the Inspector (Figure 16-13, left). Near the top, you can give the transition a better name (Figure 16-13, A). It's not really necessary, but it's nice, if you like to keep things tidy.

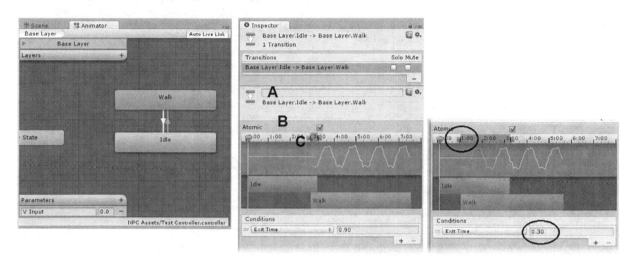

Figure 16-13. *The selected transition in the Animator view (left), and in the Inspector (right)*

The next section down shows the transition between the two clips. Checking Atomic ensures that the transition can't be interrupted once it has started (Figure 16-13, B).

You can navigate the transition time line using the usual middle mouse-roller methods to pan and zoom. Zoom in to see a closer view of the transition—the overlap. You can scrub the time line with the blue marker or the indicator in the Preview window. If you click the Preview's play arrow, only the part of the clips that is visible will be played. You can adjust the overlap to make the transition time longer or shorter.

    5.   Select the transition marker on the left side of the transition, and move it left to **1:00**, to make the transition longer.

The Walk clip is shifted over to meet the new transition overlap. Exit Time is the default condition that causes the state to go into the walk state, but rather than wait until the Idle clip is finished, the transition starts at about 0.30 into the Idle clip and blends it into the Walk clip (Figure 16-13, C).

    6.   Click play in the Preview window to see the transition.

Now, the character takes a few small steps before going into the full walk cycle.

    7.   Set the left marker to **3:00**.

This time, the clip is not moved back to line up with the transition. If you scrub the time indicator now, you will see that the part of the Walk clip to the left of the transition markers is ignored. With Foot IK checked, the transition will start in the correct part of the clip, regardless.

    8.   Move the transition back to the original overlap, at about 2:25.

    9.   Move the Walk clip to match—it will snap into place.

You can watch where in the clip the transition or state is in the Animator Controller window.

10. Select one of the characters in the Hierarchy view.

11. Click Play for the scene and watch the two states in the Animator Controller view.

A blue progress bar moves across the bottom of the Idle state (Figure 16-14). When it gets to the end, the Walk state's progress bar starts up, and you will see just the overlap amount of the idle in its progress bar, before the walk takes over completely. At the end, because its transition also contains a default, Exit Time, the Walk state transitions back to the Idle state. Let's try one more adjustment.

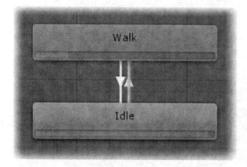

Figure 16-14. The transition shows the location in each of the clip's time lines as it blends them

12. While the scene is still playing, switch to the Scene view and locate the characters.

The characters walk and pause their way across the area.

13. Stop Play mode.

If you watch the characters, they walk and pause their way across the scene. While the Exit Time condition is useful for non-looping clips, you will generally want to use something else as a condition. The V Input doesn't yet have any scripting to control it, but you will be able to test it by typing values directly into it in the Animator. Let's change the conditions for both transitions to use it.

1. In the Animator view, click the transition arrow for Idle to Walk.

2. In the Inspector, under Conditions, click the drop-down and change Exit Time to V Input (Figure 16-15, left).

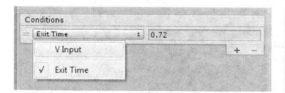 

Figure 16-15. The Conditions drop-down, showing the V Input parameter(left) and the final setting (right)

3. Leave the Conditions to Greater, and set the value to **0.1** (Figure 16-15, right).

You will also have to change the transition from the Walk state to the Idle state.

4. Select the transition arrow from the Walk back to the Idle.

5. Change its condition to V Input, Less than **0.1**.

Because there is no Equal option, you have to use a value slightly higher than 0, no key pressed, to catch the changes.

6. Click Play.

The characters no longer walk off after the short idle clip, but they are not yet responding to the user input.

7. Select one of the characters in the Hierarchy view.

8. Click Play and then change the V Input value to **1**.

The chosen character shows just below the parameters and walks off when you type in the new value (Figure 16-16). This value change is not retained after exiting Play mode and is only applied to the selected character.

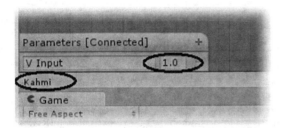

Figure 16-16. *A character selected in the Hierarchy view, and the value manually set during runtime*

Scripting the Action

Animation clips or behaviors do not necessarily control the character's location or speed. They can, however, be controlled by scripting. Because the walk animation is not a walk in place, the character moves when it is triggered. If it wasn't triggered, you would have to script the forward motion.

Earlier, you set up a parameter called V Input that will be used to tell the Animator Controller when the user is pressing the forward or backward input keys. To check for input, you will have to create a new script, to communicate with the Animator Controller through the Animator component.

1. In the NPC Assets folder, create a new script and name it **NavControl**.

The first thing it will need is a variable to hold the Animator component.

2. Add the following variable declaration:

```
internal var animator : Animator; // var to store the animator component
```

3. In the Start function, assign it the following:

```
animator = GetComponent(Animator); // assign the Animator component
```

Next, you will need a couple of variables to hold the current values for the input from both horizontal (for turning) and vertical. Controlling the character occurs in a FixedUpdate function, and input is handled in the regular Update, so this will let you reuse the values. Let's not make them internal, so you can watch the values change during runtime.

4. Add the following variables near the top of the script:

```
var h : float; // variable to hold user horizontal input, turns
var v : float; // variable to hold user vertical input, forward/backward
```

5. Assign the input values in the Update function, as follows:

```
// Get Input each frame and assign it to the variables
h = Input.GetAxis("Horizontal");
v = Input.GetAxis("Vertical");
```

6. Save the script.

7. Assign it to each of the three characters.

8. Click Play and select one of the characters, so you can watch the h and v values in the Inspector.

9. Try pressing the W/Up and S/Down keys.

You can see the v value go between -1 and +1. When neither key is pressed, the value is 0.

10. Try pressing the A and D keys.

Remembering that you removed the Left and Right arrow keys from the Horizontal input earlier in the book, you can see the h value go between -1 and +1. When neither key is pressed, the value is 0. Because you set up a "Turn" virtual input key, you could easily use "Turn" instead of "Horizontal," if you find yourself trying to use the left and right arrows instead of A and D.

As long as you're in the Animator Controller, now is a good time to set up a parameter for direction. It doesn't need a clip, state, or transition yet, but it will let you control the characters' orientation.

1. In the Animator Controller view, click the + on the Parameters widget, to create a new Float parameter.

2. Name it **Direction**.

The next step is to send the input values to the Animator Controller, where they are assigned to the V Input and Direction parameters.

The syntax for this is a little bit like the SendMessage command. You will use SetFloat with the parameter name as a string, and then, after a comma, put the value you are assigning.

3. Create the FixedUpdate function with the new instructions.

```
function FixedUpdate () {

    // Set V Input and Direction Parameters to H and V axes
    animator.SetFloat ("V Input", v);
    animator.SetFloat("Direction", h);
}
```

4. Save the script and click Play.

5. Use the input keys to test the character controls.

Now, the characters walk and idle on cue, but the transition back to idle looks a bit abrupt.

6. Select the Walk to Idle transition and drag the right transition marker arrow to the right to double the length of the transition.

7. Click Play and test the new timing.

The transition back to Idle is much better, but you may have noticed that the characters are not yet turning. If you think back, you may remember that the walk animation included position change—it was not just a walk-in-place animation. In the Animator component, Apply Root Motion is set as default, so along with the character animation, you get the root transform, as well as the position change. Because there is no turn animation yet, let alone one with root motion, the character doesn't turn. To make that happen without a turn clip, you just need a bit of code. First, you'll need a variable to set the speed of the rotation.

1. Add the following:

```
var rotVSpeed : float  = 90.0; //rotation speed
```

2. In the FixedUpdate function, below the existing code, add the following:

```
// rotate the character according to input and rotation speed
transform.Rotate (new Vector3(0,h*Time.deltaTime*rotVSpeed,0));
```

3. Save the script and test the rotation. Remember to use only the A and D keys, unless you are using "Turn" instead of "Horizontal" for the h GetAxis.

The characters now walk, turn, and idle on cue. The problem now, of course, is that there is no turn-in-place animation to go with the turns when the character is in the Idle state. For a turn in place, the character ought to turn its head either left or right, and, depending on how fancy the animation is, maybe even turn the feet as well. The problem comes with the head turning. In real life, we stop turning our head and let the body catch up, as we locate our target orientation. In the game, we have no way to predict when the player will stop pressing the turn key, so the character's head turn will always overshoot, then come back as Mecanim blends back to the new state. For this reason, you'll start with a simple walk-in-place animation for the turns. It has the added advantage of only needing one clip for both directions.

4. Select the WalkingMan in the Project view.

5. In the Animations section in the Inspector, add a new clip.

6. Name it **W_Walk In Place**.

7. Set its Start frame to **316** and its end frame to **388**.

8. Check Loop Pose and, under Root Transform Position (Y), check Bake into Pose.

9. Click Apply.

Now you'll need a Turning state to play the new clip.

10. This time, right-click in the Animator view and select Create State ➤ Empty.

11. Name it **Turning** and load the W_Walk In Place clip into it.

12. Create the transitions in and out of the new state to the Idle state.

13. For the transition in, set the Conditions to Direction Greater than 0.1.

14. For the transition out, set the Conditions to Direction Less than 0.1.

15. Click Apply.

You're probably wondering how the character will be able to turn both ways. Back in the NavControl script, you can tell the script to send the absolute value of the h variable. That will remove a negative sign, if there was one

16. Duplicate the animator.SetFloat("Direction" line and comment out the original, then change the copy as follows:

```
//animator.SetFloat("Direction", h);
animator.SetFloat("Direction", Mathf.Abs(h)); // scripted single input turn
```

17. Save the script.

18. Click Play and test the turn.

It works okay and will be useful for the game, but we really ought to investigate one of Mecanim's major features—the Blend tree. For that, we'll need the Turn in Place animation, so let's set it up now.

1. Select the WalkingMan in the Project view and add a new clip.

2. Name it W_Turn In Place.

3. Set its Start frame to **401** and its end frame to **539**.

4. Check Loop Pose and, under Root Transform Position (Y), check Bake into Pose.

5. Click Apply.

The Turn in Place is a little bouncy, but that will help you to see when it is in action.

Blend Trees

Blend trees help you to keep the Animator Controller tidier, by allowing similar states to be handled and blended together. One of the Unity Mecanim sample projects has a nice example of a run-straight, run-turn-left, and run-turn-right blend tree, where the foot placement stays correct, as the player switches seamlessly between the three forward-motion options.

With the Run/Turn example, "Vertical" input transitions the state machine from an idle to a blend/run. Once in the blend tree, the addition of "Horizontal" dictates whether the animation used is left, 1, straight, 0, or right, -1.

With a turn in place, there is no input for the idle, because it is already the default. The turns will take -1 and 1 from "Horizontal" axis, and Idle will be the value of -1 to 0.1.

Let's start by duplicating the Animator Controller, so you will have a separate version for the blend tree.

1. Select the Test Controller in the NPC Assets folder.

2. Duplicate it, and name it **Blend Controller**.

3. Double-click to open it in the Animator view.

4. Drag it onto the three characters in the Hierarchy view.

5. Delete the Turning state in the Animator view.

Next, you'll have to change the Idle state into a blend tree.

6. Select the Idle state node.

7. Right-click and choose Create New Blend Tree from State.

The state's Motion field now has Blend Tree in it, instead of the W_Idle clip. To get to the blend tree part of the state, you must double-click the Idle Blend's node in the Animator view.

8. Double-click the new Blend Tree node.

The Blend Tree is the only node now shown in the Animator view. If you look at the top, you will see the indicator showing that it is derived from the Base Layer (Figure 16-17, A).

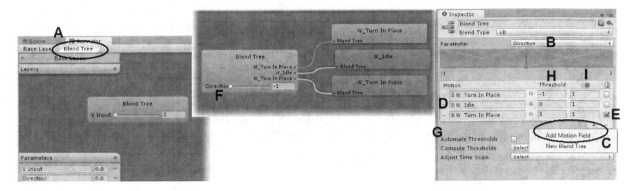

Figure 16-17. *The Blend Tree*

If you look in the Inspector, you can see an empty Motion list, complete with plus mark, to let you add clips to the list.

9. At the top of the Inspector, change the Parameter to Direction (Figure 16-17, B).

10. Click the + and add three new Motion fields (Figure 16-17, C).

11. Load the W_Turn In Place clip into the top slot, the W_Idle into the middle slot, and the W_Turn In Place into the bottom slot (Figure 16-17, D).

12. Check the Mirror clip button at the far right (Figure 16-17, E).

■ **Tip** If you have to rearrange the Motion list, you can drag the items up and down, by grabbing the "=" icons at their left sides.

---

13. Click Play in the Preview.

The top clip plays.

14. In the Animator view, drag the Direction slider (Figure 16-17, F) to the far left.

Now the other clip plays.

15. Drag the slider back and forth, to see the smooth blend between the three clips.

If you stop it halfway, the character goes into the idle behavior.

16. Click Play in the editor and test the turn-in-place animations, along with the walk animation.

Something is definitely wrong. The top animation is playing as a default. The clips are dealing with rotation, or angular movement, so the threshold values are all wrong. They have to match the Direction values, -1 to 1.

17. Uncheck Automate Thresholds (Figure 16-17, G).

18. Set the Threshold values as follows: unmirrored turn to **-1**, the idle to **0**, and the mirrored turn to **1** (Figure 16-17, H).

You will also have to switch the code back to send the actual h value.

19. Switch the commented lines in the NavControl script, as follows:

```
animator.SetFloat("Direction", h);
//animator.SetFloat("Direction", Mathf.Abs(h)); // scripted single input turn
```

20. Save the script.

21. Click Play and Test the turns in the Game view.

The Blend is behaving better, but the turns are way too fast, because both the script and the clips are turning them. The far-right column (Figure 16-17, I) is for the speed of the clips, so you could set the turn speeds to 0.75 to sync up the rotation and clips. Alternatively, you could just comment out the line in the script that turns them.

1. Comment out the rotation line in the script, as follows:

```
//transform.Rotate (new Vector3(0,h*Time.deltaTime*rotVSpeed,0));
```

2. Save the script and test the turns again, both from the idle and the walk.

This time, the turn in places look okay, but now you've lost the turn while walking. To get the best of both, you will have to see if the character is walking or idling, before using the transform.rotate. To do that, you use GetFloat, to check the parameter's current value.

3. Change the rotate line to the following:

```
if (animator.GetFloat("V Input") > 0.1)transform.Rotate(new Vector3 (0,h*Time.
deltaTime*rotVSpeed,0));
```

4. Save the script.

5. Click Play and test.

This time, if the character is walking, V Input is greater than 0.1, the rotation is added.
So you can now see how you can run the transforms from the clip, the script, *or* a combination of both.
If you wanted to control the turns using something like the mouse input, where the values are not -1 to 1, the blend tree is ideal. Instead of using the input axis values of -1 to 1, you would have to watch the input values and adjust the thresholds accordingly.
Let's have a bit more fun with the animation speed, before heading back to the original controller. You changed the turn clips' speed in the blend tree. To change a regular clip speed, you do it in the state node.

1. To get back to the Base Layer, double-click in a clear part of the Animator view or click the Base Layer marker above the Base Layer Rollout.

2. Select the Walk node.

3. In the Inspector, change the Speed to **3**.

4. Click Play and start the characters walking…fast!

You are probably thinking that it might be a good idea to create a speed parameter in the script, to allow you to adjust the speed on individual characters. This would allow you to have short-legged characters be able to keep up with their longer-legged companions. But because the controller is instanced among the characters, you would have to create a different controller for the shorter-legged characters.

Layers and Layer Masks

Next up with Mecanim are Layers and Masks. Masks allow you to isolate parts of the character's body and trigger animations that pertain to that part only, blending the base and specialty layer.

Let's start by making a couple of masks.

1.   Select the NPC Assets folder in the Project view.

2.   Right-click and Create ➤ Avatar Body Mask.

3.   Name it **Mask Arm Right**.

4.   Select and open the Body Mask at the top of the Inspector.

A familiar green humanoid body appears in the Inspector.

5.   Click within the body's bounding box, but outside the actual body, to toggle it red.

6.   Select the (character's) right arm and right hand to turn them green.

7.   Create another Avatar Body Mask and name it **Mask Head**.

8.   Toggle it red, then select the head to turn it green (Figure 16-18).

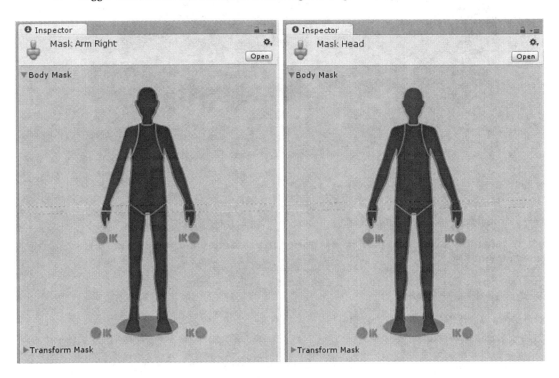

Figure 16-18. *The new masks: Mask Arm Right (left) and Mask Head (right)*

Next, you will need a wave animation clip. There just happens to be one on the WalkingMan.

9.   Create a new clip for the WalkingMan.

10. Name it **W_Wave**.

11. Set its Start frame to **601** and its End to **650**.

This wave will be a one-off, so you won't click Loop. If you wanted a looping wave, you would have to use only the frames for the wave, not the transitions in and out of it. Mecanim will do the transitions for you.

12.   Click Apply.

To trigger the transition into the wave, you will have to create a Boolean parameter.

1.   In the Parameters widget in the lower left of the Animator view, click the plus, to create a new Bool parameter.

2.   Name it **Wave** (Figure 16-19, A).

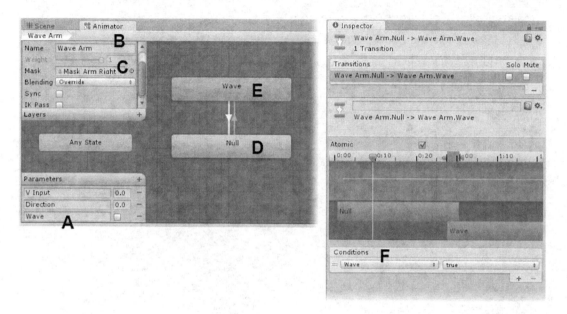

Figure 16-19. *The Wave layer, states, and transition from Null to Wave*

3.   Leave its initial state to false or unchecked.

Now that you've got a mask, a clip, and a parameter to use to trigger the transition, you will have to create a new layer in the Animator Controller.

4.   In the Layers widget, in the upper left of the Animator view, click the plus sign on the right side of the Layers drop-down.

5.   Name the new layer **Wave Arm** (Figure 16-19, B).

Next you will load the mask.

6.   Click Browse for Mask and select the Mask Arm Right mask (Figure 16-19, C).

7.   Leave Blending set to Override, so the entire arm will inherit the animation clip.

8.   Right-click in the view and create a new Empty state.

9.   Name it **Null** (Figure 16-19, D).

This empty state prevents the Wave Arm layer from overriding the arm when it is not in wave mode.

10. Drag the W_Wave clip into the Animator view, or create a new state and load it into it, and name it **Wave** (Figure 16-19, E).

11. Now create the transition from the Default node to the W_Wave state.

12. Select the transition and change Conditions to Wave and true (Figure 16-19, F).

13. Add a transition from the Wave back to Default.

You can leave the transition, using the default Exit Time Condition.

And now you'll have to add a bit of scripting to trigger the transition into the Wave state. You will be using the virtual "Fire1" button to change the Wave parameter's state to true. The "Fire1" button only has the left Ctrl key assigned to it, because, earlier in the book, you reserved the left mouse button for picking only.

Last time, you changed a float parameter with SetFloat(). This time, the parameter is a Boolean, so you will be using SetBool(). It's also a good idea to check for an Animator component before trying to change something in it.

14. In the Update function, to avoid errors, start by adding the condition to check for the existence of the Animator component.

```
if(animator) { // if there is an animator compomonent

}
```

15. Inside the condition, check for the "Fire1" key.

```
// if the fire button was pressed, set the Wave parameter to true
if(Input.GetButtonDown("Fire1")) animator.SetBool("Wave", true );
else animator.SetBool("Wave", false );
```

Because it uses Exit Time to transition back, the animation turns itself off, but if the parameter is left on true, the animation will trigger again, as soon as it is finished, so the else clause is necessary.

There's one more thing you will need to make this one work. If you look at the Wave Arm layer, you will see that there is a Weight parameter that is grayed out (Figure 16-19, F). It shows as 1, but as soon as you click Play, it goes to 0, and the wave doesn't trigger, even when the Wave parameter shows true.

The Weight dictates how much of the clip replaces the currently playing clip for the masked body part, and in this case, you will want 100%, or 1.

1. Add the following lines to the Start function after the Animator component has been assigned:

```
if(animator.layerCount > 1){
animator.SetLayerWeight(1,1.0); // set layer 1's weight to 1
}
```

2. Save the script.

3. Click Play and press the left Ctrl key, to test the wave in the Idle, turn, and Walk states.

The characters wave regardless of the current state—the Mask Wave overriding the arm animation and substituting it with the wave clip.

4. Exit Play mode.

Physics

So far, you've got the characters animating and changing state on demand. But there's one important thing you haven't tried yet. You haven't checked to see how the characters react to collision objects.

1. Create a low cube, Y scale to 0.2, in front of the characters, and try walking them over it.

They go through the box, and because the box is a Unity primitive, you know it has a collider. The characters don't have one yet.

2. Add a Capsule collider to each, and adjust the capsule size to about Height **2**, Radius **0.35,** and Y offset about **1**.

3. Add a Rigidbody component to each.

4. Click Play and drive them forward.

They all fall over onto their faces. You'll have to set some constraints on the Rigidbody component.

5. Exit Play mode.

6. Open Constraints at the bottom of the Rigidbody component.

7. Check Freeze Rotation X, Y, and Z on each of the characters.

8. Click Play and drive them forward again.

This time, they stay upright and react to the box (Figure 16-20).

Figure 16-20. *The characters, with colliders and rigidbodies, stepping smartly up onto the platform*

In case you've been wondering why you've been Baking into Pose for the Y Root Transform Position on all of the clips, the next experiment will show you.

1. Select the WalkingMan in the Project view.

2. Select the W_Idle clip in the Animations section and uncheck the Bake into Pose for Root Transform Position (Y).

3. Click Apply.

4. Click Play and watch as the characters float slowly upwards.

5. Drive them forward.

They drop back down, because the W_Walk clip is still set to Bake into Pose. The Bake into Pose will keep the characters grounded. That's okay for walks and idles, but if you wanted the character to respond to a physics push during a jump, that is, go higher than the animation, you would have to leave it unchecked. If you do that, you will have to check the Animate Physics parameter in the characters' Animator components.

6. Exit Play mode.

7. Check Animate Physics for each of the characters.

8. Click Play and drive them around, stopping and waiting to see if they float off.

This time, because Animate Physics is on, they no longer float away during idle, but, as you may have guessed, calculating physics adds overhead.

9. Exit Play mode and uncheck Animate Physics for each character.

10. Check Bake into Pose for the W_Idle's Root Transform Position (Y).

Now that the characters are hanging around, you may have noticed one more thing. In the Idle state, instead of shifting their weight slightly from side to side, they seem to be tipping from the pelvis with their *feet* moving from side to side. Before clicking Apply, let's fix that little issue.

11. Check Bake into Pose for the W_Idle's Root Transform Position (X, Z).

12. Click Apply.

Now, the feet stay put better, and the characters sway slightly from the pelvis.

13. Save the scene and save the project.

NPC Controller

Now that you've had an introduction to Mecanim, it's time to think about how the characters will have to be controlled in the game. As NPCs (nonplayer characters), the player will not be controlling them directly. This means that you will have to provide Parameters, of Boolean type, to trigger their various actions.

The first character the player will encounter is Gimbok. He will be floating cross-legged, with a tray in his lap. When the player clicks on him and selects a question from the dialog list, he will nod and listen attentively.

When the character is replying, you will set his mouth in motion. There's no fancy lip-syncing animation for each reply, but the generic mouth movement will eventually be controlled by the length of the audio clip.

When asked for help, he will go into a magical trance, and with the clap of his hands, make a useful object appear.

Kahmi will converse from a standing idle state. She'll also need the Listening, Talk, and Clap Hands states. Additionally, she will need the Walk state, to approach the player.

Other than the different Idle clips, the Animator Controllers will be the same.

The next task is to create a mask to use with the Clap Hands behavior. In order for Kahmi to use it, you will have to make a mask, so that only the upper body is used.

1. Create a new Avatar Mask and name it **Mask No Legs**.

2. In Body Mask, toggle off all the legs and all other lower parts.

To control the various behaviors needed for the game, you will need a new Animator Controller.

3. Create a new Animator Controller.

4. Name it **NPC Controller**.

5. Open it in the Animator view.

Because you will need them for the various transitions, let's do the Parameters first.

6. Create a Bool parameter named **Listen**.

7. Create a Bool parameter named **Talk**.

8. Create a Bool parameter named **Clap**.

9. Create a Bool parameter named **Walk**.

And now, you can add the states.

10. Drag the Sitter Idle state into the Animator view as the default state.

11. Drag the W_Walk clip into the view and rename the state **Walk**.

12. Make the transitions between it and the Idle state.

13. Open the transition leading into the Walk state and set its Condition to Walk and true.

14. Set the outgoing transition to Walk and false.

And now, you can set up the layers.

1. Create a new layer in the Layer widget and name it **Listening**.

2. Set the Human mask to Mask Head.

3. Repeat for a **Talking** layer

4. Create a new layer for Clap Hands, and name it **Clapping**.

5. Set its Human mask to NoLegs.

6. Create an Empty state and name it Null.

7. Right-click and copy, then paste it into the other layers (except the Base layer).

8. Now Add the matching animation clip to each layer.

9. Create the transitions to and from the clips.

10. Set each transition into the new state, to match its parameter and true.

11. Set Talking and Listening transitions out of the state to their parameter and false.

Tweaking for Game

The test scene will require more changes as you prepare the characters for their roles in the game. Now would be a good time to make a duplicate of the current scene.

1. Save the scene.

2. Select the Character Tests scene in the Scenes folder and duplicate it.

3. Name the new version **Character Dialogues** and open it.

4. Delete the WalkingMan from the scene.

5. Replace the Test Controller with the NPC Controller in both characters' Animator component.

6. Remove the NavController script component from both characters.

7. Click Play.

Both characters go into the sitter idle state. The easiest way to get Kahmi standing is to duplicate the Animator Controller and load a different clip.

8. Exit Play mode.

9. Select the NPC Controller in the Project view and duplicate it.

10. Name it.

11. Open it in the Animator view and substitute the W_Idle clip for the Sitter Idle clip, rename the state **Idle**.

12. Drag the new NPC Controller Kahmi animator controller into Kahmi's Animator component.

13. Click Play.

This time, Gimbok sits, and Kahmi remains standing. As mentioned earlier, however, Gimbok is going to be doing a mystic floating trick, so he still needs a few adjustments.

1. Exit Play mode and select Gimbok.

2. In the Scene view, move him up about 0.7 units.

3. Click Play.

Because he is set to use gravity, he falls immediately to the ground.

4. Exit Play mode.

5. In the Rigidbody component, uncheck Use Gravity.

6. Click Play.

This time Gimbok remains afloat.

Now, he just needs his floating tray. Open Gimbok's hierarchy and select the Tray Position object. You can see in the Inspector that it contains only a transform.

7. Exit Play mode.

8. Double-click it to focus the Scene view to it.

9. In the Project view, locate the TrayCloth object.

10. In the Inspector, Model section, set its scale factor to **0.028,** to match the rest of the characters and click Apply.

11. In the Rig section, select None for Animation Type and click Apply.

12. Drag the TrayCloth into the Hierarchy view, and drop it onto the Gimbok parent.

13. Click Play and zoom in on Gimbok and his tray (Figure 16-21).

Figure 16-21. *Gimbok and tray at runtime*

In the Scene view, you will be able to see that the tray moves back and forth with him. This motion is inherited from the parent root motion. In the original animation, the hands were stuck to the tray location with IK. With Mecanim in charge, the animation no longer holds. If you have Unity Pro, you could use IK targets for the hands, to stick them back onto the tray location. It is beyond the scope of this book to cover Mecanim IK, but there is an excellent example in the Mecanim sample scenes available from the Asset store.

Because most of the states are dialogue-driven, they will be controlled elsewhere. The generic script for the character control will be similar to the NavControl script.

1. Move the NavControl script to the My Scripts folder.

2. Create a new script and name it **NPC_BaseControl**.

3. Open it and add the following variables:

```
internal var animator : Animator; // var to store the animator component
var walk : boolean;               // flag to move character
var turn : boolean;               // flag to turn character
var h : float;                    // variable to hold directional input, turns
var v : float;                    // variable to hold directional input, forward/backward
var rotSpeed : float  = 90.0;     //rotation speed
var animSpeed: float  = 1.0;      // animation clip speed
```

4. In the Start function, add the following:

```
animator = GetComponent(Animator); // assign the Animator component
animator.speed = animSpeed;        // set the animation speed for this character
var layers : int = animator.layerCount;
if (layers >= 2) {
    for (var i : int = 1; i < layers; i++ ) {
        animator.SetLayerWeight(i, 1);
    }
}
```

Once the animator is identified, the script can find out how many layers it contains, then iterate through them, setting their weights to 1.

5. Create the FixedUpdate function, as follows:

```
function FixedUpdate () {
    // Set speed and Direction Parameters using the variables
    if (walk) animator.SetFloat("V Input", v);
    if (turn) {
        animator.SetFloat("Direction", h);
        // rotate the character according to input and rotation speed
            transform.Rotate (new Vector3(0,h*Time.deltaTime*rotSpeed,0));
    }
}
```

6. Save the script.

Now that you've had a chance to poke at Mecanim, you've probably figured out that all you have to do to sync up the animation with the conversation is to change the parameter conditions to true or false, at the same time you manage the timers for the topics and replies. A SetNPC function in the Dialogue Manager is where the character will pass its ID number. But it will also have to pass itself as a GameObject, so the Dialogue Manager can control the events in the Animator component.

Synchronizing Audio and Animation States

The characters will each require a script of their own, to hold their ID, and functions, to send the info around. They will also need a way to know when they should initiate a conversation when picked. For that, you will create a conversing variable, to track that in the Dialogue Manager. This script will check that variable before initializing a new conversation.

Before you continue, you may want to spend a few moments reviewing the DialogueManager script to remember what was going on.

This next script is simple, but important.

1. Create a new script in the NPC Assets folder and name it **CharacterID**.

2. Add a few variables.

```
var iD : int;                                  // character ID number for switch
internal var dialogueManager : GameObject; // so it can contact the  dialogueManager
internal var animator : Animator;            // the Animator component for controlling the
animation
```

3. Assign the Animator and find the Dialogue Manager in the Start function.

```
function Start () {
   animator = GetComponent(Animator);
   dialogueManager = gameObject.Find("Dialogue Manager");

   var layers : int = animator.layerCount;
   if (layers >= 2) {
      for (var i : int = 1; i < layers; i++ ) {
         animator.SetLayerWeight(i, 1);
```

```
            print(i);
        }
    }

}
```

4. Create a new function to transfer information.

```
function SendID () {

}
```

5. Inside it, check to see if the character is already talking.

```
// check with the DialogueManager to see if it is already in conversation
var conversing : boolean = dialogueManager.GetComponent(DialogueManager).conversing;
```

6. Add the following to the function, to pass information to the Dialogue Manager:

```
// if the npc is picked, and not already active in conversation, start the conversation
if (!conversing) {
    dialogueManager.SendMessage("SetNPC",iD, SendMessageOptions.DontRequireReceiver);
    dialogueManager.SendMessage("SetGO",this.gameObject,SendMessageOptions.DontRequireReceiver);
}
```

If the character is not already in a conversation, it will send its ID (that will be used in the switch statements) to the SetNPC function that you already have, and it will send itself, so its Animator component can be informed when the state changes have to happen.

7. Save the script.

In the Dialogue Manager, in addition to a flag for Conversing, you will have to add a variable to hold the current character, the gameObject. Before you do so, you will duplicate the script and save it to keep as a test script. That way, you will have an easy way to test further enhancements or functionality, without the overhead of needing a character tied to it.

1. In the Project View, select the DialogueManager script.

2. Use Ctrl+D to duplicate it.

3. Change the 1 to "Simple" and move it to the My Scripts folder.

You will have to substitute DialogueManagerSimple script for the original in the Dialogue Tests scene before it can be used again. You won't be doing that now, but you will have to, should you wish to revisit that scene.

Back in the regular DialogueManager script, you will have to start adapting it for the characters.

4. Open the DialogueManager script.

5. Start by adding the conversing variable just above the Start function:

```
internal var conversing : boolean = false; // need this to make sure not to interrupt an
ongoing conversation
```

6. Save the script.

7. Add the NPC_BaseControl script to each character.

8. Add the CharacterID script to each.

The switch cases in the Dialogue Manager use 1 and 2, so you will have to set the IDs on both characters.

9. Set Gimbok's ID to **1**.

10. Set Kahmi's ID to **2**.

Now you are ready to complete the DialogueManager script.

11. Back in the DialogueManager script, add the variable for the NPC gameObject, as follows:

```
internal var currentGO : GameObject; // the current npc
```

12. And add a variable for the GameObject's Animator component, as follows:

```
internal var animator : Animator; // the currentGO's animator component
```

Because the NPC will change throughout the game, the two new variables will be set up when the new ID is sent to the SetNPC.

13. The NPC will be sending its ID when picked, so comment out the following line in the Start function:

```
//SetNPC(1); // set the current NPC's ID number
```

14. Add the function to receive the GameObject and assign its Animator component.

```
function SetGO ( npcObj : GameObject) {

    currentGO = npcObj;                        // the newly active npc -
    animator = currentGO.GetComponent(Animator); // its animator component
}
```

This is the first function that receives the message sent by the CharacterID script when the character is picked. Once it has the character, it gets the character's Animator component.

To tell the NPC the conversation has ended (and he is pickable again), the Dialogue Manager has to send a message back to it as soon as the conversation has been flagged to end. If it was added in the ActivationHandler function, when the exitConv is first set to true, the player could pick the character again, while it was still saying good-bye. To allow time for it to fully end, you will add it to the Update function, where the timer is set to show the topics after a reply. There's already an if for exitConv, so all you need is the else.

1. In the Update function, in the //timer to start the topics again conditional, above the pauseForTopic = false line, add the following:

```
else conversing = false; // the conversation has finished
```

613

In the SetNPC function, when the NPC has been picked and sends its ID, you will have to turn on the new conversing flag and clear the exitCov variable:

2. In the SetNPC function, near the bottom, add the following:

```
exitConv = false;  // reset the flag
conversing = true; // turn this flag on
```

Because all of the events that control the NPC's animation are Booleans and do not depend on player input directly, as in the test scene, they will be handled at the same time you turn the topics and replies off and on. During topic audio, the NPC will nod. During his reply, he will talk—or at least flap his jaw to indicate talking. And, yes, this is a bit cheesy, but it allows you to substitute other languages, so it does have valid uses.

The easiest place to start is with the topic pick and the nod animation. The character will "listen" as the audio for the chosen topic plays.

3. In the ProccessReply function, near the top, add

```
animator.SetBool("Listen", true); // trigger the NPC's Listen state animation on
```

When the pauseForReply timer is finished, you will turn the Listen off and start the character's talking behavior.

4. In the Update function, in the //timer for the reply section under //show the reply, add

```
animator.SetBool("Listen", false); // trigger the Listen state/animation off
animator.SetBool("Talk", true);    // trigger the Talk state/animation on
```

The pauseForTopic timer uses the currentAudioReply.length + 0.5 as its time limit. This means that if you turned the Talk behavior off then, the character would still be moving his jaw 0.5 seconds after the audio clip finished. If you actually had lip-synced animations for each reply, the animation would automatically stop it at the correct time. To end the talk animation at the same time as the audio *and* leave the text on screen a little longer, you will have to check the timer limit minus the 0.5 second offset. You won't be turning the timer off, only the event/variable for the animation. The text and the rest will be handled at the regular time.

5. Above the //timer to start the topics again section, add

```
// stop the talk animation when the audio is finished
if(pauseForTopic && Time.time > pauseForTopicLimit - 0.5) {
    animator.SetBool("Talk", false); // trigger the Talk state/animation off
}
```

The last animation, the clap hands, gets triggered from the SpecialInstructions function. Both special cases use the same animation. In one, Gimbok will offer a rock; in the other, Kahmi will open the way to the game's end objective.

6. In the SpecialInstructions function, above both cases' break line, add the following:

```
animator.SetBool("Clap", true);  // turn the Clap parameter on to trigger its clip
yield new WaitForSeconds(0.5);   // reset the flag
animator.SetBool("Clap", false); // turn the Clap parameter back to false before the
animation finishes
```

7. Save the script.

Those were a lot of little additions to make before you had anything you could test, but it's time to reward yourself and try it out with the characters and dialogue together.

Combining Characters and Dialogue

To test the new additions, you will need a temporary bit of code in the CharacterID script to trigger the character. In the game, the Interactor and ObjectLookup scripts will handle the interaction for you. Because the characters already contain a collider, they are ready to be picked.

1. Open the CharacterID script.

2. Add the following function:

```
function OnMouseDown () {

        SendID(); // trigger the conversation
}
```

3. Save the script.

Now that you have modified the DialogueManager script, you will have to bring it and the audio clips into the same scene as the characters. Fortunately, you made a prefab of the DialogueManager object in the Test Dialogues scene.

Hooking Up the Dialogue to the Characters

With the characters already in their game configuration, you can bring in the dialogue prefabs and finally get to see how everything comes together.

1. From the NPC Assets folder, drag the Dialogue Audio Clips prefab into the scene.

2. Also from the NPC Assets folder, drag the DialogueManager prefab into the scene.

3. Select the Dialogue Manager in the Hierarchy view and from it drag the Dialogue Audio Clips object into the Clip Source parameter.

4. Go ahead and Click Play.

5. Pick a character and run through the dialogue tree.

6. Try the other character's dialogue tree.

Remember that you will have to choose the exit topic to "close" a conversation, before striking up a new conversation with the other character. The exit topic is in the root conversation.

As you can see, the generic talk animation works pretty well. If you are heavily into character animation and lip-syncing in particular, you could create animation clips to match each audio clip and trigger them at the same time.

With most of the setup taken care of, and the functionality working well, it's time to take it all into the main level and get it hooked up to the rest of the game.

The characters will only appear on cue, so they'll be inactive until needed. Because they will now be controlled through the action object scripts, you will have to comment out the mousedown event in the CharacterID script.

7. Open the CharacterID script.

8. Highlight the OnMouseDown function.

9. From the right-click menu, choose Toggle Line Comment(s).

10. Save the script.

Finalizing Gimbok

It may be possible to approach the characters from different directions. Because Gimbok will be in a mystic floating pose, he should always turn to face the First Person Controller's camera. To avoid interfering with the regular animation, you can parent him to an empty gameObject.

1. Double-click Gimbok in the Hierarchy view to focus in on him in the Scene view.

2. Create an empty gameObject.

3. Name it **Gimbok Group**.

4. Drag Gimbok into the newly made group.

5. In the Local coordinate system, select Gimbok and then the group, to make sure their Z axes are pointing in the same direction.

If you consult the docs, at first it would seem that Transform.LookAt is the answer to getting the characters rotating. But if you read further, you will realize that it may also cause the NPCs to tip. What is needed here is a classic billboard function, where the object spins on its up axis to face the target, rather than tips to face it.

If the target, the First Person Controller, was always at the same height as the NPC, transform.LookAt would work fine. Here's the fun part: instead of trying to write a mathematical equation to calculate the correct rotation for a restricted look-at, you are going to use a simple cheat. Because you have both the target's position and the NPC's position, you can combine them to get the spot below or above the target that is on the same level as the NPC. It doesn't even have to be an actual position, just a Vector3 number—the x, y and z numbers.

1. In the NPC Assets folder, create a new script and name it **BillboardLookAt**.

2. Add the following code:

```
var target : Transform;              // the target object
internal var tempTarget : Vector3;   // var to hold the target's position adjusted
for height

// Rotate the camera every frame so it keeps looking at the target,
// but rotates only on its Y, or up axis
function Update() {

    tempTarget.x = target.position.x;   // use target's x and z
    tempTarget.z = target.position.z;
    tempTarget.y = transform.position.y; // use this object's y value

    //face the target
    transform.LookAt(tempTarget);
}
```

3. Apply the new script to the Gimbok Group and drag the Main Camera into the Target field.

4. Click Play and test, by moving the camera around and up and down in the Scene view.

Gimbok spins to face the camera (Figure 16-22).

Figure 16-22. *Gimbok facing the camera*

Because the character should appear to mystically "float," you will have to add a bit of code to accomplish that. This script comes in handy for a lot of uses, so is well worth keeping around. It starts at the current Y position, so you will have variables for the up and down range. It uses a cosine curve to plot the smooth movement.

1. Create a new script in the Adventure Scripts folder and name it **V_PositionCycler**.

2. Add the following variables to it:

    ```
    var upRange : float =1.0;
    var downRange : float =1.0;
    var speed : float = 0.2;

    internal var yPos : float; // starting position
    internal var upPos : float;
    internal var downPos : float;
    ```

3. In the Start function, assign the current Y position.

    ```
    yPos = transform.position.y;
    ```

4. Create a FixedUpdate function to hold the calculations.

    ```
    function FixedUpdate () {

    }
    ```

5. Add the lines to calculate the target positions inside the FixedUpdate function.

    ```
    upPos = yPos + upRange;     // calculate the target up position
    downPos = yPos - downRange; // calculate the target down position
    ```

617

By adding these lines inside the FixedUpdate function, you will be able to adjust the ranges during runtime, until they look just right. It does cost a little overhead, so you might eventually want to move them to the Start function.

6. Next, add the lines that do the work.

```
// use cosine to get smooth ease in/ease out motion
var weight = Mathf.Cos((Time.time) * speed * 2 * Mathf.PI) * 0.5 + 0.5;
// apply the new y position
transform.position.y = upPos * weight  + downPos * (1-weight);
```

7. Save the script.

8. Add the new V_PositionCycler script to the Gimbok Group.

9. Set the Up Range to **0.1** and the Down Range to **0**.

10. Click Play and observe the results.

11. Adjust the amounts as necessary.

12. Exit Play mode and make the amounts permanent.

The next thing you will have to do with Gimbok is set his collider to a more appropriate size for his pose. With Unity Pro, you could use the Curves in the transitions to dynamically adjust the collider size to match the pose, but because this is the only pose you will use for Gimbok, the collider size never has to be changed.

1. With Gimbok selected, set the collider radius to **0.65**.

2. Set the collider's Y Center to **0.4**.

3. Set the collider Height to **1.5**.

Now there's one last little issue you will have to deal with.

4. Click Play.

5. Select Kahmi and move her in the Scene view, until she bumps into Gimbok.

Gimbok gets moved around the scene. To prevent him from being bumped by the player later on, you will have to adjust the Rigidbody a bit.

6. Select Gimbok from inside the Gimbok Group.

7. Check Is Kinematic in the Rigidbody component.

You can only use this setting if the Animator component is not set to Use Root Motion.

8. Click Play and bump the Gimbok group again with Kahmi.

This time, Gimbok stays put.

Activating Kahmi

While Gimbok will live in the game's maze, Kahmi will first appear in the temple when the player finally gets hold of the golden topi fruit. As he comes down from the upper level, she will approach and wait for him to initialize a conversation. Unity has a path-finding system, but it is only for Unity Pro. Because the requirements for this character are fairly simple, you will be creating a very basic means to accomplish the task of moving her to the player at the opportune moment.

To start, you will need a target, the First Person Controller. Then you will need to be checking the distance between Kahmi and the target. And you will also need a flag to tell her when to start moving. At a preset distance from the target, she will have to stop and wait for the player to initiate a conversation. If he doesn't, or he moves out of range, she should turn, after a set amount of time, and walk back to her starting point, and, finally, turn back to face the player again, to be ready to start again.

1. Create a new script in the NPC Assets folder and name it **SimpleAI**.

2. Add the following variables to it:

```
var fpc : Transform;                    // the First Person Controller's transform (Player tag)
var startCollider : Transform;          // place holder object for start location (Player tag)
internal var target : Transform;        // place holder for the target
internal var startDistance : float = 18.0; // the distance from the target to start walking at
internal var stopDistance : float = 3.0;  // the distance from the target to stop at
internal var distance : float;          // the current distance between the target and this object
internal var progress : int = 0;        // flag for character's progress, 0 = not started
```

The progress flag will keep track of the character as she progresses through the various states. They are as follows:

- 0 = not started
- 1 = walking toward the target (the First Person Controller)
- -1 = paused while walking toward the target
- 2 = at the target and waiting for player to initiate a conversation
- -2 = engaged in conversation
- 3 = starting to head back to base
- 4 = waiting back at base

3. Add the progress definitions to the GameNotes text file.

To keep track of where the start position is, you will need an object with a collider, so it can be processed the same as the First Person Controller. It will be assigned its position in the Start function, so you can create it anywhere in the scene.

4. Create a Capsule and name it **Start Collider**.

5. Set its Radius to **0.25**.

6. In the Inspector, right-click and Remove its Mesh Renderer and its Capsule (Mesh Filter).

7. Check Is Trigger in its Capsule Collider component.

8. Under Tags, assign the Player tag to it.

9. Back in the SimpleAI script, in the Start function, assign the starting position and assign the first target.

```
target = fpc; //assign the first  target
// the starting point/base
startCollider.position = Vector3(transform.position.x,transform.position.y,transform.position.z);
```

10. In the Update function, calculate the distance.

```
distance = Vector3.Distance(target.position, transform.position);
print (distance);
```

11. Save the script.

Before going any further, let's give the script a try.

1. Add the script to the Kahmi character.

2. Drag the Main Camera in as the Fpc for now.

3. Drag the Start Collider object into its field.

4. Click Play and drag the camera around in the Scene view and check the distances in the console line.

5. Exit Play mode and move the camera back away from the characters.

Now that you can see the distance, let's set Kahmi walking, by turning on the Mecanim Walk parameter. To do that, you will have to contact the Animator component.

6. Add the following variable:

```
var animator : Animator; // this object's animator component
```

7. And assign it in the Start function.

```
animator = GetComponent(Animator); // assign the animator component
```

And now let's add the bit that checks the distance and sets the flag that means the character is in motion.

8. In the Update function, after the print line, add the following:

```
if(distance <  startDistance && progress == 0) {
    progress = 1;                     // set the flag to walking toward the target
    animator.SetBool("Walk", true); // trigger the walk
}
```

The progress flag is set to 1 for walking toward, when she reaches the goal, it will be set to 2, and when she heads back, it will be set to 3.

9. Save the script.

10. Make sure the camera is at least 20 meters away from the character.

11. Click Play and move the camera slowly toward Kahmi in the Scene view.

When the camera is close enough, she starts walking straight ahead.
Now let's get her stopping.

1. Add the following below the first if clause :

```
if(distance <  stopDistance && progress == 1) {
    progress = 2;                     // set the flag to waiting
    animator.SetBool("Walk", false); // trigger the walk
}
```

2. Save the script.

3. Click Play and move the camera toward the character until she starts walking.

As long as the camera is somewhat in front of her, she will stop as soon as she gets within two meters of it.

If you have her look at the target, you can move it anywhere, and she will walk toward it. You will be using some of the code from the BillboardLookAt script.

4. Add the variable declaration from the BillboardLookAt script:

```
internal var tempTarget : Vector3;// var for calculating look at
```

5. And add the contents of its Update function at the bottom of this script's Update function:

```
// look at code
tempTarget.x = target.position.x;     // use target's x and z
tempTarget.z = target.position.z;
tempTarget.y = transform.position.y; // use this object's y value

transform.LookAt(tempTarget);
```

This is the same bit of code used in the billboard look at that makes sure the object stays upright.

6. Save the script.

7. Click Play and test by moving the camera slowly around the character.

Kahmi heads toward the camera and stops when she is within range. This behavior would be great if there were nothing else in the scene, but if there was a wall or other obstacle in the way, the character would get stuck. Because you are not using pathfinding, logically, she should only move toward him, if he is within line of sight and within range. Let's engage in a bit of ray tracing to make sure he's visible.

The first thing you need to know about the raycast is that it comes from the character's transform or pivot point. Let's see where that is on the character.

8. Select Kahmi and set the transform gizmo's location to Pivot, rather than Center (to the right of the coordinate system's button), Figure 16-23.

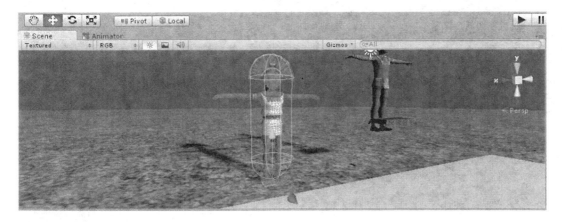

Figure 16-23. *The character's pivot point at its feet*

As you can see, the character's pivot point is at the bottom. To trace a ray, you will have to offset the ray's start location up almost two meters, to put it at eye level.

9. Comment out the direction's print statement.

10. Beneath it, add the following:

```
var hit : RaycastHit;                                    // holds information about the hit
var fwd : Vector3 = transform.TransformDirection (Vector3.forward); // forward direction
var offset : Vector3 = transform.position;               // var to hold offset position
offset.y += 1.5;                                         // add the offset to the y element
to get eye level
if (Physics.Raycast (offset, fwd, hit, 30)) {            // check for a hit within 30 meters
   Debug.DrawLine (offset, hit.point);                   // draw a line to check the
position in Scene view
   print ("There is a " + hit.collider.transform.name + " ahead");
}
```

You've used Physics.Raycast before in the Laser script. It needs an origin, a direction, a range, and can return information about the hit object, if you provide a variable of RaycastHit type. Debug.DrawLine draws a line in the Scene view, so you can both see where the raycast is pointing and, by using the hit.point, where it hits something with a collider.

1. Save the script.

2. Rescale the platform cube to make a wall between the camera and Kahmi.

3. Click Play and drag the camera around, so you can see what happens when the raycast hits and stops at Gimbok or the cube.

The status line reports the cube and Gimbok as hit by the raycast, so you know it is working. The camera, because it has no collider, is ignored. Let's make a stand-in for the First Person Controller, to make sure the script will be able to do its job.

4. Create a capsule in the scene.

5. Set its collider to Is Trigger.

6. Replace the camera with the new capsule in Kahmi's Fpc parameter.

7. Move it behind the wall, out of range.

8. Click Play and move the capsule around, watching as the ray detects it.

Now that you can find out which object was hit, you will be able to use it in conditionals to control the action. In the print statement, you used hit.collider.transform.name. By the time you check for the First Person Controller by name, things will get pretty long and complicated-looking. To keep things easier to read, you can assign the Player tag to the capsule and later to the First Person Controller. Better yet, you can create a variable for the tag. This has the advantage of being able to assign it a value, when there was no hit, and to the tag value, when there is no hit object—in other words, it was null.

1. In the Tag dropdown, assign "Player" to the capsule.

2. Below the print line in the Raycast section, add

```
var hitTag = hit.collider.tag; // shorten the tag to a variable
```

3. Just below the Raycast section, add

```
else hitTag = ""; // assign a value in case it was null
```

With something closer to the actual First Person Controller, you can finish the script. Let's get Kahmi to pause, if the First Person Controller goes out of sight, and resume, if he reappears.

4. Add the following conditional below the else line:

```
if (hitTag != "Player" && progress == 1) {
   progress = -1;                    // paused
   animator.SetBool("Walk", false); // pause the walk
}
```

The walk condition should also be updated to include the raycast results.

5. Add the new raycast condition, so that the walk = true conditional becomes

```
if(distance <  startDistance && progress <= 0 && hitTag == "Player") {
```

6. Save the script.

7. Click Play and test.

As long as the character hasn't reached the stop distance, she will continue to move toward the target.

So now you need to send the character back to the starting point. There are a couple of reasons to give it its own function. One is because it will need to be called when a conversation ends, so that a message will be sent to start the process. The other is to allow you to add a yield statement before changing to the last flag. Yield statements can't be used in Update functions, and a timer for this little bit of functionality would probably be overkill.

1. Create a new function and name it BackToStart.

```
function BackToStart () {

}
```

2. Inside it, add the following:

```
progress = 3;                       // heading back
target = startCollider;             // set the target back to the start object
yield new WaitForSeconds(1.1);      // give the lookat some turnaround time
animator.SetBool("Walk", true);     // trigger the walk
```

There are two conditions for which you will want to send the character back to the start. The first is when the character has reached the target, but only after she has been there a while and no conversation has been started. The second is when the player has gone out of view and not returned after a short amount of time. Because the wait times will be different for different conditions you will create a StartTimer function that will be passed a variable for the time. The main reason to use a timer over a yield statement is that timers can be canceled, and yield statements cannot. So if the player returns before the time is up, or initializes a conversation before the timer has gone off, the timer is canceled, and the character is not sent back. Let's start by creating the timer function and adding the code that calls it in the various conditionals.

3. Above the Start function, add the following variables for the timer:

```
internal var timer : float = 0;          // hold the timer's target time
internal var timerOn : boolean = false; // timer flag
```

4. Create the function.

```
function StartTimer (seconds : float) { // pass in the time for the timer
    timer = Time.time + seconds;
    timerOn = true;                      // start the timer
}
```

And now let's call the timer to start the return sequence.

5. In the if (hitTag != "Player" && progress == 1) section, add

```
StartTimer(3.0); // start timer in case player doesn't return to view
```

6. In the if(distance < stopDistance && progress == 1) section, add

```
StartTimer(5.0); // give the player a few seconds to initialize conversation
```

7. In the if(distance < startDistance && progress <= 0... line, add

```
timerOn = false; //cancel the timer in case it was running
```

And, of course, you'll need the timer code itself in the Update function.

8. In the Update function, at the top, add the code that handles the timer.

```
if (Time.time >= timer && timerOn) {
    timerOn = false;
    BackToStart (); // send the character back to the starting place
}
```

Now you can add the code to stop the character when she has reached the starting position. And then, add a bit more to turn the character back around. Let's start with the turnaround function. Basically, it works by reassigning the target.

9. Create the following function to turn the character around:

```
function TurnAbout() {
    animator.SetBool("Walk", false); // stop the walk
    target = fpc; // set the target back to the fpc
    yield new WaitForSeconds(2.1); // allow character to settle
}
```

Next, you have to create the Reset function. It calls the TurnAbout function to turn the character, sets the progress variable to 4 to prevent the character from heading off to the target right away, and then, using a Yield statement for the amount of downtime, resets the flag to 0, so the character will move again if the target is within range.

10. Add the Reset function:

```
function Reset() {
    TurnAbout();                    // do the turn
    progress = 4;                   // disabled
    yield new WaitForSeconds(10);   // wait before allowing it to start out again
    progress = 0;                   // ready to go again
}
```

11. In the Update function, add the conditional that triggers the reset just above the // look at code.

```
if(progress >= 3 &&  distance <= 0.1) {
    Reset(); // get the character back to the starting state
}
```

12. Save the script.

13. Click Play and test the walk back functionality.

Now the character walks up to the target if it is in range, waits a bit, then heads back. On reaching the original starting point, she turns around, waits a bit more, then heads out toward the target again, if it is within range.

At this point, you've probably recognized a big drawback to using the LookAt function. When you change the target, the character immediately snaps to face the new target. Chances are that the player may not be around to see some of the turnarounds, but if he is, it would be nicer to have a dampening effect on the turns.

1. Start by commenting out the transform.LookAt line for now.

2. And then add the following just above it:

```
// dampened lookAt
transform.rotation = Quaternion.Lerp(transform.rotation,
    Quaternion.LookRotation(tempTarget - transform.position), Time.deltaTime * 3.0);
```

The Quaternion.LookRotation calculates the target rotation from the current object and target object's location. Then, that value is fed into Quaternion.Lerp and the rotation is smoothly managed using Time.deltaTime, using a value for speed, in this case, 3.0.

3. Save the script.

4. Click Play and test by allowing the character to come up to the capsule, then return to the start position.

The character turns at a reasonable rate before completing the current behavior.

5. Now, try moving the capsule around while the character is coming toward it.

The problem now is that the dampening turn makes the character pause to find the capsule before continuing on toward it.

You are probably thinking it would be nice to have the best of both methods. Turns out, you can. You can query the Animator Controller to see if the character is walking or not. If she is, use the LookAt; if not, use the dampened version to rotate her. You used SetBool to set the "Walk" flag, and now you'll use GetBool to check it.

6. Wrap the dampened rotate code in an if statement, as follows:

```
if(animator.GetBool("Walk") == false){ // if the character is not walking...
   // dampened lookAt
   transform.rotation = Quaternion.Lerp(transform.rotation,
      Quaternion.LookRotation(tempTarget - transform.position), Time.deltaTime * 2.0);
}
```

7. Uncomment and add an else to the regular LookAt line

```
else transform.LookAt(tempTarget); // use regular LookAt when walking
```

8. Save the script.

9. Click Play and test both the turnaround from the idle state and the walk states.

There's a little glitch when the character heads back to the start, as it switches from the dampening code to the LookAt code. Because the start position will not move, you can use the dampening code for the trip back—when progress is 3.

10. Add the progress check to the dampening conditional

```
// if the character is not walking, or walking back, use dampening
if(animator.GetBool("Walk") == false || progress == 3){
```

11. Save the script and test.

Now you've got the best of both turning types.

Adding a Turn in Place

So now that the motion is smooth, it would be nice to add some animation. Unity's Mecanim starter scene, available through the Asset Store, has a nice sample of a turn in place, but it has a complicated Animator Controller and has to know the target rotation ahead of time. With your player able to influence the character's path, you will need something a little different. It won't be as accurate as the complicated version, but the player may not stick around to watch the turnarounds anyway.

The first task will be to get the direction of the turn. You will have to use the code whenever you switch the target, so let's start by adding the call to the function you will be creating.

1. In the BackToStart function, after the target = line, add the following:

```
TurnAni (); // trigger the turn state
```

2. In the TurnAbout function, after the target = line, add the same.

```
TurnAni (); // trigger the turn state
```

3. Now create the TurnAni function.

```
function TurnAni () {

}
```

The code to get the direction will have to check the difference in the direction when the character starts to turn. The problem comes when the direction is near 360 degrees. You will have to adjust the results to avoid getting values that make no sense. Since you need degrees, you will have to use transform.eulerAngles or transform.localEulerAngles. It doesn't matter which, because you are only getting the delta, or difference.

4. Inside the new function, add the following:

```
var oldTurn : float = transform.eulerAngles.y;           // get the current y rotation
yield;                                                    // allow time to have started turning
var deltaTurn : float = transform.eulerAngles.y - oldTurn; // get the difference
if (deltaTurn > 180) deltaTurn -= 360;                    // degree correction
if (deltaTurn < -180) deltaTurn += 360;                   // degree correction
print(deltaTurn);
```

5. Save the script.

6. Click Play and watch the printout as the character walks back and forth.

The number is negative as the character turns left and positive as it turns right. So now you have enough information to call the correct animation according to the direction the character turned. The turn will usually be about 180 degrees in total, so the animation clip will not be set to loop. If you use an integer, you can use -1 as turn left, +1 as turn right, and 0 as not turning.

Next, you will have to create the turn states in the Animator Controller. The character goes into the turn from the idle state, when in front of the character, but goes into the turn from the walk, when she reaches the start position. Theoretically, she reverts to idle before the turn, but the timing is so close that it's safer to put the turns into a layer. Because you will need three states, you will be using an integer-type parameter for -1, 0, and 1.

1. Open the NPC Controller Kahmi in the Animator view and add a new Int type parameter.

2. Name it **Turning** and set the initial value to **0**.

3. Create a new layer and name it **Turns**.

You don't need a mask, because you want the turns to override the entire body.

4. Create an Empty state in the new layer and name it **Null**.

5. Drag the W_Turn In Place clip into the Animator view.

6. Set the clip Speed to **1.2** in the Inspector.

7. Make transitions to and from the empty New State to the turn state.

8. For the transition into the Turn s state, set the Condition to Turning, Not Equal to 0.

9. For the transitions back, use Equal to 0.

Now, you will add the script to control the turn states.

10. In the SimpleAI script, Start function, set the weight for the new layer.

```
animator.SetLayerWeight(4, 1); // set layer 4's weight to 1
```

11. In the TurnAni function, beneath the print statement, add

```
if (deltaTurn > 0 ) animator.SetInteger("Turning", 1); // trigger the turn right
else animator.SetInteger("Turning", -1);               // trigger the turn left
yield new WaitForSeconds(0.75);                         // allow turn time
animator.SetInteger("Turning", 0);                     // reset the turn flag
```

627

12. Save the script.

13. Click Play and watch the results.

14. Adjust the transitions to be a bit longer, if you wish.

Now, she moves her feet as she turns but doesn't turn her head, because the turn animation is unidirectional. For the head turn, we'll use the head mask and a turn head animation, so she will blend into and out of the head turn, independent of the rest of the body. You'll need a new layer but can reuse the Turning parameter and head mask, so it will be a quick addition.

1. Select the Walking Man asset in the Project view.

2. Create a **W_Head Turn Left** clip from **246** to **299.**

3. Repeat for **W_Head Turn Right** and click the Mirror option just above the velocity section.

4. Click Apply.

The head turn is only to the left, so you will have to create the right turn in the layer.

5. In the NPC Controller Kahmi, add one more layer and name it **Head Turns**.

6. Set the Mask Head as its Mask.

7. Create the usual **Null** state and then create two head turn states with the new clips—Look Left and Look Right.

8. Create the transitions in and out of the new states and leave the exits to Exit Time.

9. For the transition to Look Left, Turning Greater than 0, and for Look Right, Turning Less than 0.

10. Adjust the transitions, so they are quick going in and longer going back out.

With the head turns in place, you may want to increase the transitions into the body turn states. Feel free to do so, if you wish.

11. Click Play and test the turns.

12. Try moving the capsule to trigger the turn in the opposite direction, if you haven't seen it yet.

13. Comment out the `print` statement in the `TurnAni` function.

Allowing for Conversation

And, finally, if the character *is* engaged in conversation, progress = -2, you must bypass the whole `Update` function by exiting it with a `return`.

1. Back in the SimpleAI script, at the top of the `Update` function, below the timer section, add

   ```
   if (progress == -2) return; // in conversation
   ```

2. Save the script.

3. Click Play and test.

Blocking the Character

Everything should be working smoothly at this point. But you may have found that you could leave the character walking against the wall, when she tries to make a beeline home. In the game, you will keep the character from leaving the area by using a few barriers to send her back.

1. Create a new script and name it **NPC_Barrier**.

2. Add the variables, then assign them in the Start function.

```
var target : GameObject;           // character to block
internal var simpleAI : SimpleAI; // script with the character AI

function Start () {
   simpleAI = target.GetComponent(SimpleAI);
}
```

3. Add an OnTriggerEnter function to stop the character, then send it back.

```
function OnTriggerEnter () {
   simpleAI.progress = 2;                      // set progress to waiting
   simpleAI.animator.SetBool("Walk", false); // stop the walk
   simpleAI.StartTimer(5.0);                   //start the timer in the SimpleAI script to
send the character back
}
```

4. Save the script and add it to the wall in the scene.

5. Select the wall and turn off its Mesh Renderer, then turn on Is Trigger.

6. Drag Kahmi into its Target field.

7. Position the wall in the scene, so that the character's ray is higher than the barrier (Figure 16-24).

Figure 16-24. Kahmi's raycast over the barrier

8. Move it between the character and the Capsule (the target).

9. Click Play and test.

The character tries to reach the First Person Controller, but is prevented from continuing by the invisible barrier, waits a bit, then heads back to the starting position. Because the raycast is higher than the barrier, the player gets stopped although still attempting to reach the target. Because the barrier uses Is Trigger, it won't stop the player.

Communicating with the Dialogue Manager

The engaged in conversation flag, progress = -2, will be sent from the Character ID script at the same time it sends the character's ID to the DialogueManager script. Because the SimpleAI script is not on both characters, you will have to make sure it exists before you send it instructions.

The script needs to tell the SimpleAI script how to handle the character, depending on when the character was picked. At the top is the conditional that brings the character back, if it was picked while heading back to the start position, or if it is already back, but in the time-out period. The yield statement allows the character time to return to the player before the dialogue text is displayed.

1. Open the CharacterID script.

2. At the top of the if (!conversing) section, add the following:

```
if (GetComponent(SimpleAI)) {                    // if there is a SimpleAI script...
    // get the NPC turned around if walking away or, start moving if picked from the time out
    if(GetComponent(SimpleAI).progress > 2) { // if walking away or waiting at start
        GetComponent(SimpleAI).TurnAbout();      // turn back if not facing the player already
        GetComponent(SimpleAI).progress = 0;     // set flag to start walking (already in range)
        yield new WaitForSeconds(3);             // allow the character to return to the player
    }
    // inform the SimpleAI script that the character is conversing
    GetComponent(SimpleAI).progress = -2;
    // cancel the timer in case it was running
    GetComponent(SimpleAI).timerOn = false;
    // turn off the walk in case she was picked before stopping
    GetComponent(Animator).SetBool("Walk", false);
}
```

This script is on the same object as the CharacterID script, so contacting it is easy. On Gimbok, who doesn't have a SimpleAI script, the instructions will be skipped.

3. Save the script.

From the Dialogue Manager, where the conversation gets ended, you will have to change the progress variable and a few other things as well. The problem is that the Dialogue Manager only has a number for the current character. It will make things easier if it knows which characters belong to which numbers. To do that, you'll make an array. That way, you can still use the numbers for the element numbers. The array will require three elements, because the characters don't use element 0.

1. Open the DialogueManager script.

2. At the top of the script, add the following:

```
var character : GameObject[]; // holds the npc characters
```

3. Save the script.

4. In the Inspector, set the array Size to **3**.

5. Add Gimbok (not Gimbok Group) to element 1 and Kahmi to element2 (Figure 16-25).

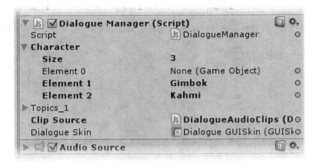

Figure 16-25. *The characters loaded into the Dialogue Manager*

6. In the `//timer to start the topics again` section of the `Update` function, change:

```
else conversing = false;
```

to:

```
else {                                      // the conversation is finished
    conversing = false;                     // the conversation has finished
    // if finished, start the timer to send the npc back to the start position
    if (character[currentNpc].GetComponent(SimpleAI)) { // if the character the script...
        character[currentNpc].GetComponent(SimpleAI).StartTimer(5.0);
    }
}
```

7. Save the script.

8. Update the DialogueManager prefab by clicking Apply at the top of the Inspector.

So you've just created a very simple bit of AI. Scripting AI pathfinding consists of a lot of logic, combined with ray-casting and quite a bit of recursive code. If you have Unity Pro, you may eventually wish to try your hand at using it to control the character. You will still have to give the agent instructions for what to do when the different distances and goals are reached, and surprisingly, you will still need to account for an agent occasionally getting stuck as well. That being said, it's loads of fun giving an agent a tricky target and watching it try to get there on its own.

Wrapping Up the Test Scene

Having set up the NPCs in a test scene, it's time to make prefabs of the characters, so you can reuse them without going through the setup process again.

1. In the NPC Assets folder, create a new folder and name it **NPC Prefabs**.

2. Create three new prefabs in it.

3. Name them **Kahmi Prefab**, **Gimbok Group**, and **Start Collider**.

4. Assign the two characters, Kahmi and Gimbok Group, and the Start Collider object to the corresponding prefabs.

5. Drag the rest of the NPC Assets folder's prefabs into the new prefab folder. (Their icons are the plain blue boxes.)

As long as you are tidying up, let's make a few more folders inside the NPC Assets folder.

6. Create another folder and name it **NPC Scripts**.

7. Drag the scripts into it.

8. Create another folder and name it **Mecanim**.

9. Put the masks and animator controllers into it.

10. Save the scene and save the project.

Preparing the ObjectLookup

Because picking the character needs to be part of the regular action-object system, you will have to modify the ObjectLookup script to be able to handle character dialogue. Fortunately, the code that processes interaction among the player and action objects already has an easy way to take care of nonstandard functionality.

1. Open the ObjectLookup script.

2. In the LookUpState function, switch section, add case "d" after case "c":

```
case "d":                                  // send a message to a script on the object/character
to the "SendID" function
    auxObject.SendMessage("SendID");       // start the conversation with the character/NPC
    GetComponent(Interactor).processing = true; // turn on flag to block picks;
    bypass = true;                         // skip the regular processing
    break;
```

The special case "d" calls the SetNPC function on the object, which in turn initiates the conversation. The bypass flag means that the object will not be processed into a new state, so you will have to manually set the processing flag to true, to block mouseovers and picks on the character while the conversation is going on.

3. Save the script.

The processing flag also has to be turned off when the conversation ends.

4. Open the DialogueManager script.

5. In the //timer to start the topics again section of the Update function, inside the else clause, below the conversing = false line, add the following:

```
// turn off flag to block picks;
character[currentNpc].GetComponent(Interactor).processing = false;
```

6. Save the script.

Adding the NPCs to the Game

While everything is still fresh in your mind, you will bring the dialogue and NPC assets into the main scene. In the next chapter, you will be importing the structures that will flesh out the game, so don't worry too much about location.

1. Open the Inventory scene.

2. Drag the Dialogue Manager and Dialogue Audio Clips prefabs into the scene.

3. Drag the three NPC prefabs into the scene.

4. Move the Gimbok Group's Y position up to about **51.8**.

5. Assign the First Person Controller to the two character's scripts (parameters: Target on the Gimbok Group and Fpc on the Kahmi Prefab).

6. Assign the Start Collider object to Kahmi Prefab's Simple AI component.

7. Assign the Dialogue Audio Clips to the DialogueManager object's Clips parameter.

8. Select the First Person Controller and assign the Player tag to it.

Now comes the part where you make the characters part of the action object system, by adding the two main scripts—the Interactor and the ObjectLookup. In the Interactor, fill out the arrays for just 2 elements, no animation. Location will be 0 for element 1, not in scene, and 1 for element 1, in scene and active. Start them as in scene for now, Initial State as 1. The names and descriptions are important, because they can show in the range message, but everything else will be bypassed.

1. Add the Interactor script to Gimbok, not the Gimbok Group (it doesn't have the collider).

2. Fill out the parameters in the Inspector, as per the StateManagement PDF.

3. Set the Name to "Odd Little Man."

4. Set the Description to "It is an odd little man floating a meter or so off the ground."

For the ObjectLookup, give Lookup State 1 one element and Reply State 1, one element.

5. Set the Lookup State 1, element 1 todefault,-1,d0_Gimbok,0

6. Copy the two scripts and paste them onto the Kahmi prefab.

7. Change the Name to "Diminutive Female."

8. Set the Description to "It is a diminutive female with a large feather headdress."

9. Set the Lookup State 1, element 1 todefault,-1,d0_Kahmi Prefab,0

10. Tag both characters as Action Objects.

11. Save the scene.

The d0 is the instruction to use the special case for the dialogue. You are probably scratching your head over the transition into state being -1 for both characters, because there is no such state. Let's see what's going on.

1. Open the Interactor script. From the Tools menu, select Find and type in `processing`.

At the bottom of the `ProcessObject` function, you will see where the `processing` flag is turned off. The problem is that you want it to stay off until the conversation is finished.

2. Open the ObjectLookup script and do a Find using `ProcessObject`, the call to the function that manages the `processing` flag.

You'll find it in a couple of places. The one near the bottom of the LookupState function you've already dealt with, by setting the bypass flag to true in the special cases section. But the one that processes the picked object calls the ProcessObject function on that object, regardless of the state it transitions into. So, you need a means of bypassing it for any action object that shouldn't go through the regular processing. To manage that, the solution is surprisingly simple. You can set a conditional before the call to the ProcessObject function using -1, a state that can't exist.

3. In the // check for a cursor match section, change the SendMessage("ProcessObject",nextState) line to

```
if (nextState >= 0) SendMessage("ProcessObject",nextState);//call if the new state # is valid
```

4. Save the script.

Since that's a pretty important convention, you will want to add it to the game notes file.

5. Open the GameNotes test file from the Adventure scripts folder.

6. Add the following below the special cases section:

"d" character dialogue is called for
In the LookUpState function, a transition into a state of -1 will keep the picked object from being processed.

7. Save the text file.

With that little detail taken care of, it's time to test the conversation in the scene.

8. Click Play, then, when you are close enough, click on one of the characters to initiate conversation.

The Object Lookup and Interactor scripts take care of all of the usual functionality, range checking, etc., but as soon as you click on the character, the dialogue scripts take over. Remember the "exit" topic is the last one on the primary dialogue.

Blocking In User Navigation

There are a few more things you have to do to tidy things up. First, you have to disable all player navigation during conversation. The only thing he should be able to do is click on the topics. You already have a flag to do that, blockInput. Along with that, you have to block the regular mouseover and action text.

1. Open the FPAdventureInputController script.

2. Below the Update function, add the function that will handle the state changes for the flag.

```
function ToggleInput (block : boolean) {

        blockInput = block;
}
```

3. Save the script.

The Game Manager will need a flag as well.

4. Open the Game Manager and add the following variable:

```
internal var conversing  : boolean = false; // flag to suppress text & cursor color change
```

5. In the OnGUI function, add the conversing flag to the global if (useText) conditional:

```
if (useText && !conversing){  //global toggle
```

6. In the // cursor control section, near the bottom of the OnGUI function, add the condition to the line that changes the cursor color on mouseover.

```
if (!conversing) GUI.color = currentCursorColor; // set the cursor color to current
```

7. Create a function to toggle the flag.

```
function ToggleConversing (talking : boolean) {

        conversing = talking;
}
```

8. Save the script.

To turn the input off and on for conversation, the Dialogue Manager will have to be able to contact the First Person Controller's scripts and the Game Manager.

1. Open the DialogueManager script.

2. Add the following variable near the top of the script:

```
var fpc : GameObject;        // need to control user navigation/input during conversation
var gameManager : GameObject; // need to suppress action object text & mouseover
```

3. In the SetNPC function, before the call to LoadTopic() line, add

```
fpc.SendMessage("ToggleInput",true, SendMessageOptions.DontRequireReceiver);
gameManager.SendMessage("ToggleConversing",true, SendMessageOptions.DontRequireReceiver);
```

4. In the //timer to start the topics again section of the Update function, inside the else clause, below the conversing = false line, add

```
fpc.SendMessage("ToggleInput",false, SendMessageOptions.DontRequireReceiver);
gameManager.SendMessage("ToggleConversing ",false, SendMessageOptions.DontRequireReceiver);
```

5. Save the script.

6. Assign the First Person Controller to the Dialogue Manager's new Fpc parameter in the Inspector.

7. Assign the Control Center (the object that holds the GameManager script) to the to the Dialogue Manager's new GameManager parameter.

8. Click Play and test.

Now the player is no longer able to walk away from the character, or interact with another action object, until he leaves the conversation and the regular text is cleared.

9. Update the Kahmi and Gimbok prefabs by dragging the newer objects onto them or by clicking Apply at the top of the Inspector.

10. Save the scene and save the project.

Summary

In this chapter, you've gotten a taste of using Mecanim to control characters in a scene. You started by setting their Animation Type to Humanoid, which, after configuring their muscles, allowed you to share the animation clips between them, whether or not they had animations of their own. For characters that did not quite fit the animations, you found you could refine the configuration by adjusting the range of the various body parts.

In setting up animation clips, you discovered that Humanoid characters offered some new options when setting the ranges for the clips, as well as several other options to help control the character during the clips. Mecanim, you discovered, can use the animation clip's velocity to move the character through the scene, or its angular velocity to turn it.

With the Animation Controller, Mecanim's powerful state engine, you then used your clips to create states. The addition of Parameters gave you variables to set the conditions that moved your character from one state to the next.

The introduction of Masking and Layers provided you with a means of overriding part of the character with a different animation. This allowed you to incorporate a talking-and-listening behavior into the characters, as they were hooked up to the conversations you created in the previous chapter.

Finally, you developed a simple AI script to allow one of the characters to approach the player and wait for an invitation to converse. After suspending the regular text and mouseovers, your player was ready for conversation with the NPCs.

CHAPTER 17

■ ■ ■

Game Environment

In this chapter, you will be putting the game project together in a ready-made environment. Besides finalizing several of the existing action objects' functionality, you will also be adding a few little touches that will improve the game with very little effort. Additionally, once the assets have been imported, you will be introducing one major feature: a dynamic maze.

Adding the Final Assets

To provide an environment in which to put all your hard-earned functionality into play, you will import most of the rest of the 3D art assets that are included with the book. (See the Source Code/Downloads tab of the book's Apress product page www.apress.com/9781430248996.) They include

- The Temple of Tizzleblat, with its attendant guardian beasts

- Six steles, or standing stones, representing the six natural elements of the Tizzleblat pantheon

- Six glyphs representing the elements that can act as keys to activate things

- Six shrines, each dedicated to one of the elements, scattered about the environment

- A small cave system with tunnels

You will be using only a small number of the assets to finish the book project, but they may come in handy, if you wish to continue to experiment and create more functionality to challenge the end player.

Most objects come with lightmaps, in case you are using Unity free and prefer a GI (Global Illumination) solution. The temple comes in as two parts. The inner temple has a lightmap that should not be rebaked, unless you want lots of practice with lighting and Beast in Unity Pro.

Preparing for the New Assets

The assets for the environment will be brought in as a Unity package, so you won't have to set up materials for every object. Feel free to inspect them closer whenever you wish. Because you already have a lot of functionality in the Inventory scene, it will make sense to clone and rename it before importing.

1. Open the Inventory scene.

2. Delete the Terrain and the Directional Light.

3. Make sure the prefabs have been updated, and then delete the Kahmi Prefab, Collider Start Prefab, and the Gimbok Group Prefab.

4. From File ➤ Save Scene As. . . save the scene as **MainLevel** in the Scenes folder.

5.   From the Assets menu, choose Import Package ➤ Custom Package.

6.   From the BookAssets folder for Chapter 17, select and import GameEnvironment.
     unitypackage. (See the Source Code/Downloads tab of the book's Apress product page
     www.apress.com/9781430248996.)

7.   In the dialog, choose Import and import all.

The package adds a Structures folder and a GameEnvironment prefab, among other bits and pieces.

8.   From the Adventure Prefabs folder, drag the new GameEnvironment prefab into the
     Hierarchy view.

9.   Turn on the Scene lighting toggle in the Scene view.

10. Adjust the Scene view to see what you've got (Figure 17-1).

Figure 17-1. *The newly imported game environment assets*

Because several of the main objects had lightmaps prepared in the modeling app, a new directional light was included with the package. At this point, you have to make a decision. If you have Unity Pro and want to bake your own maps with Beast, feel free to delete the Sun for Lightmaps directional light and rotate the individual objects at will.

The book will go ahead and use the provided lightmaps and light source.

1.   Open the GameEnvironment prefab in the Hierarchy view, but don't expand it all the way.

While you are setting up the last bits of functionality and special effects, you will want to keep the objects fairly close to each other in the scene. Move only the objects or groups at this level of the prefab's hierarchy (see Figure 17-2). The Temple Group and Group Water have had the terrain altered, so unless you plan on doing some excavation, they should not be moved.

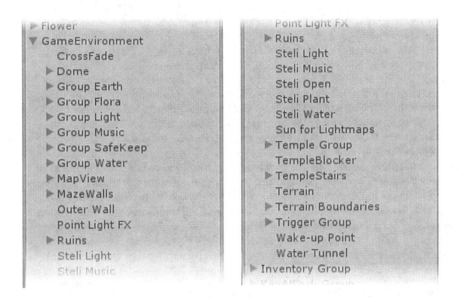

***Figure 17-2.** The partialy expanded GameEnvironment prefab in the Hierarchy view*

2.   Select all but the new GameEnvironment prefab, the Inventory Group, and the Terrain Boundaries in the Hierarchy view and move the existing objects somewhere near the temple and shrines. They should already be the correct height for the terrain in front of the temple.

3.   Click Play and investigate the new assets.

4.   Save the scene.

Revisiting Materials and Lightmapping

Before going inside the temple, let's take a moment to look at the material options included in the package. With the addition of Beast, the lightmapping solution in Unity 3.x the shaders that made use of the lightmaps took a hit. Though the shaders were still supposedly available for options such as Bumped Specular, the only apparent option was an additive combination of the regular diffuse texture plus the darker parts of the lightmap, where white was ignored. While that is as expected, the downside is a shader that is fully self-illuminated—it doesn't respond to scene lighting.

Typically, if you were using lightmaps on objects, you would create a layer called Lightmapped and exclude its objects from being lit by lights in the scene, to conserve resources. It is an efficient solution, but leaves a lot to be desired visually. The lack of highlights leaves things looking chalky and a little flat.

You had a brief look at Beast in an early chapter with the terrain editor. Now that you have several structural objects in the scene, it's time to revisit it. Beast is included in both the free and Pro versions of Unity. In Pro, you get all the bells and whistles to bake lightmaps with GI, global illumination, allowing you to fine-tune the lighting solution. In the free version, you get the ability to bake simple shadows and choose how dark they will be.

If that still leaves you scratching your head, think of the difference atmosphere makes in lighting. We've all seen pictures from the Moon. The shadows are dark and crisp, and there is a lot of contrast between light and dark areas. Deserts have similar lighting, because of the low moisture in the atmosphere. Moisture, tiny water droplets, bounce light, scattering it every which way, producing softer shadows and less contrast between light and dark. GI simulates the bounced light typical of moister climates or local weather patterns.

The game's environment is obviously more subtropical than desert, but not everyone will have Pro, so the main structures come with their own prebaked lightmaps and unique materials.

The current material assignments for the gray stone textures are built with a custom shader created with the Strumpy Shader Editor, a free visual shader editor that can be found on the Unity forum's Showcase area or downloaded from the Unity Asset Store. With the exception of the water shrine, which needed a glossy wet look, the shrines are built with a brown stone texture that looks okay with the legacy lightmap shaders.

If you *do* want to have a go at Beast, you can leave the current materials on the objects and change the shaders. Unity supports two mapping channels. The first is for the diffuse texture, and the second is for lightmaps. The main objects in the scene, the temple, shrines, and steles, all have a map channel 2, with the unwrapped geometry fully within the mapping boundary. Typically, when using diffuse plus lightmaps, the diffuse texture will be tiled many times. With lightmaps, on the other hand, every face must have a unique spot on the map to hold its own lighting information. Unity currently supports only two map channels.

Here's the advantage of using Beast to create the lighting solution: instead of having to create a unique material for each lightmapped object, Unity uses the object's regular material and then adds the generated lightmap internally. This means a lot less materials for you to set up. In the game's structures, there are really only two basic materials, a gray stone block material and a brown stone material. Providing you with prebaked lightmaps necessitated creating unique materials for each major object.

Now that you have a bit of background on Beast and lightmapping in Unity, let's do some research into the lightmapping and materials available. There are a few rules you will have to follow. Any object that will cast shadows and receive lightmaps must be marked as Static.

1. Select the Temple Outside object from the Scene view and arrange the Scene view to give yourself a good view of the temple.

■ **Tip** If there are too many icons for lights, cameras, windZones, or other specialty objects showing in the Scene view, you may toggle the icons off and on in Scene view's Gizmos drop-down.

Note the effect of the specular highlight as you adjust the view.

2. In the upper right corner of the Inspector, you will see that it is marked as Static.

3. Deactivate the Temple Outside and select the Temple of Tizzleblat, the temple's interior (see Figure 17-3).

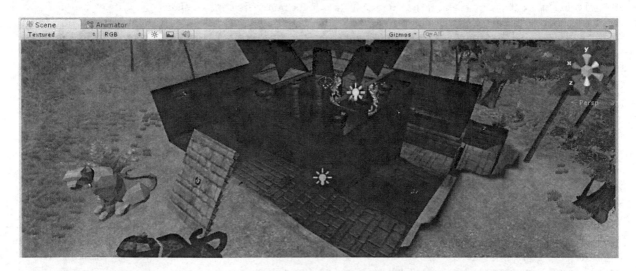

Figure 17-3. *The sparsely lit interior of the temple revealed*

The interior already has a lightmap that was created using the V-Ray renderer in the modeling app using carefully positioned lights. Having Beast create a lightmap for the interior would mean creating and adjusting several lights in the scene, not to mention the time necessary to tweak their properties to get the right look. Because the interior is covered by the exterior that will be casting shadows, it doesn't have to cast any shadows of its own. Unchecking Static will remove it from the light-baking solution.

4. Uncheck Static for the temple interior.

5. In its Mesh Renderer, note that it is not set to receive shadows.

6. Set the two temple guardians, Gertrude and Harvey, to Static, so they will cast baked shadows.

7. Activate the Temple Outside.

The Temple Outside object uses the Temple Outside 1 material with a custom shader that adds specular highlights from the scene lighting. While this helps remove the chalky look of a traditional fully emissive shader that ignores scene lights, it does use more resources when computing the lighting solution.

■ **Note** Because the Unity game engine is constantly evolving, and the Strumpy Shader Editor is a third-party add-on, there is a chance the custom shaders will occasionally require updating, to be compatible with the newer versions of Unity. If the structures appear a violent shade of magenta, you may have to use the standard shader versions of the materials. They are in the Legacy Shader Materials folder for this chapter's assets, under the same names and without being appended with a "1." Be sure to check this book's web page or forum thread for updated assets. (See the Source Code/Downloads tab of the book's Apress product page [www.apress.com/9781430248996].)

If you are using Unity Pro, you may be seeing dynamic shadows, so let's turn those off while you are experimenting with the lightmapping. The imported light, Sun for shadows, has already been set to no shadows, but in case you've left other light casting shadows on, you will temporarily disable the effect.

1. If you are using Pro, from Edit ➤ Project Settings ➤ Quality, Shadows, make note of the value, and then set Shadow Distance to **0**.

2. Also, if you are using Pro, from Edit ➤ Project Settings ➤ Player ➤ Other Settings, set the Rendering Path to Forward.

This will let you see the scene using only baked shadows. The distance is how far away dynamic shadows start calculating. Beyond that distance, baked shadows take over. The 0 distance should prevent dynamic shadows.

3. Select the Temple Outside.

4. In its Mesh Renderer component, click on its Element 0 material, to locate the Temple Outside 1 material quickly in the Project view.

5. Duplicate it and name the new material **Temple Outside**.

6. Drag it onto the temple in the Scene view or directly into the Element 0 slot.

7. Change its shader to Legacy Shaders/Lightmapped/Diffuse and set the Main Color to a mid-gray.

The shadowed areas are less apparent, because the legacy shader is providing most of the light for the material. To see what's going on, you can turn off the scene light.

8. Select the Sun for Lightmaps light object inside the GameEnvironment prefab, just above the Temple Group.

■ **Tip**   In this chapter, you will have to locate several of the imported objects by name. A handy way to do that is by using the Search function at the top of the Project view. Type in the name to locate the object, select it, then click the X next to it, to return to the regular view.

---

9. Disable the light.

Because you haven't yet baked light into your terrain, it will appear dark, as in Figure 17-4. If you had baked lighting into the terrain, it would appear self-illuminated, along with the temple.

Figure 17-4. *The scene light turned off*

10. Enable the Sun for Lightmaps light again.

11. Turn on Soft Shadows for its Shadow Type.

To see what baked light from Beast looks like without GI, you can test the Temple Outside object with the base stone material. It uses a Bumped Specular shader.

1. From the Structures ➤ Materials folder, select the stonetexture material.

2. Apply the material to the Temple Outside.

The temple outside's lightmap is not used in this base material, so, with the dynamic shadows effectively disabled, there is no longer a shadow from the ledge (Figure 17-5).

Figure 17-5. *The Bumped Specular texture with Pro's dynamic shadows set to 0 distance*

3. Select the Temple Outside object.

4. From the Window menu, open Lightmapping.

5. In the Bake section, select Low Quality and set it to Single Lightmaps.

6. If you are using Pro, set the Bounces to **0,** to disable GI.

7. In the Bake section, click Bake Scene.

When the baking is finished, you should see something like Figure 17-6.

Figure 17-6. *Lightmap baked in Unity, no GI, hard dark shadows on the structure*

The terrain is baked, and the new lightmaps added internally. With the use of Beast-generated lightmaps, you don't need to generate a material for each different object using the same texture. The downside is that the specular is no longer calculated for the object in the scene, so the bump map is not used either. The object also does not receive any of the bounced light and color it would with GI, so it never quite looks like it is part of the scene.

8. Select the stone texture material again.

9. Try adjusting the Specular Color and the Shininess.

10. Undo to return it to its original values.

643

The material changes on the wall between the entry, but the temple no longer responds, even though it currently uses the same material.

Of interest is what happens with the generated alpha channel. When you used the legacy Lightmap shader, you had to adjust the main color to a darkish mid-gray to get the right look. When a lightmap is generated in Unity, such a color adjustment is added to the copy of the map in its alpha channel. To view the generated lightmap, you can look in either the folder created to hold lightmaps for the scene or in the Lightmapping window.

11. From the Scenes folder in the Project view, open the newly added MainLevel folder.

12. Select LightmapFar-0 in the Project view.

13. In the Inspector, toggle the alpha/diffuse button to see the dark shade added to the alpha, as shown in Figure 17-7.

Figure 17-7. The lightmap and its alpha channel

Investigating Pro Lightmapping Features

To take advantage of Beast's GI feature in Unity Pro, you use Dual Lightmaps. The Far version contains both GI and regular shadows. The Near version contains only GI, and the real-time shadows are added inside the Shadow Distance.

1. In Unity Pro, in the Bake section of the Lightmapping window, set Mode to Dual Lightmaps.

To see the GI in action, you will have to turn up the Bounces.

2. Set the Bounces back to 1.

3. Click Bake Scene.

This time, after a much longer bake time, the temple shadow under the ledge is softer and shows variation from bounced light (Figure 17-8).

Figure 17-8. *The softer shadows produced by Beast's GI*

Now let's see what happens when the dynamic lighting is activated again. As long as the Lightmapping window is still open, you can temporarily adjust the Shadow Distance in the Lightmap Display inset in the Scene view.

4. Set the Shadow Distance to about **40** in the Lightmap Display.

Nothing happens. To use the dynamic lighting, you also have to use the Pro feature, Deferred Lighting.

5. From Edit ➤ Project Settings ➤ Player ➤ Other Settings, set the Rendering Path to Deferred Lighting.

The baked shadows are replaced with the real-time light as far out as the Shadow Distance, and the Material is once again showing its bumped and specular shader.

6. Try decreasing the distance, to see the baked shadows blend in as the distance gets closer.

As the Dynamic light takes over, the material in its original state takes over, and you once again see the specular highlight on the stones.
Once you've baked the lightmaps, you will need to match the dynamic shadows to it.

7. Select the Sun for Lightmaps object and adjust its shadow Strength, so the dynamic shadow looks about the same as the baked shadow as you move the Shadow Distance value back and forth (Figure 17-9).

Figure 17-9. *The baked shadow (left), the dynamic shadow (center), and the light's shadow Strength darkened for a better match with the baked shadow (right)*

8. From Edit ➤ Project Settings ➤ Quality, Shadows, set Shadow Distance to **60**.

Using Imported Lightmaps in Beast

A third lighting possibility is to use imported lightmaps directly in Beast. To do so, the lightmap must be of the .exr file type and contain the illumination data in its alpha channel. You can replace Beast-rendered lightmaps by dragging the replacements onto the existing maps in the Lightmapping window. If maps have not yet been baked, you will have to increase the array size in the Maps section and assign the correct map index to the corresponding object. If you are using a single map and not using dynamic lighting, be sure to set the Mode to Single Lightmaps. Examine existing lightmaps in the Inspector, to see how dark the alpha channel versions need to be. Unity uses a multiplier on the alpha channel maps to brighten the materials. No alpha channel is interpreted as white and will make the material look blown out in the scene.

Reinstating the Custom Shader

While the material looked good as soon as the temple was within the dynamic shadow range, it still lost a lot of quality when the lightmapped version was substituted. If you remember, the custom shader had both specular and bump, along with its shadow map. Not only that, it was correct in either Forward or Deferred Lighting.

With the inner temple, you turned off Static to prevent a lightmap from being generated. It didn't have to cast a shadow. For the Temple Outside and other structures that came in with pre-rendered lightmaps, you want the objects casting shadows, but you do not want new lightmaps calculated for them. To do that, you will have to change the Scale in Lightmap.

1. Open the Lightmapping window again.

2. Select the Temple Outside.

3. On the Object tab, set the Scale in Lightmap to **0.**

The scale tells Beast how much real estate the object can take up on the lightmap. Higher values mean more of the space is given to the object. At 0, none is allocated for the object, and it is not lightmapped.

4. Repeat the procedure for the shrines, steles, Outer Wall, Dome, Harvey, Gertrude, and RuinStones.

The Maze walls and temple stairs will animate, so they are not marked as Static. Most of the other objects are too small or the wrong kind of material to rate shadows.

5. Add the Temple Outside 1 material back to the temple.

6. Set the light's shadow Strength down to about **0.6**.

As you set the Lightmap Size to 0 on the objects, under Atlas, their Lightmap Index number is assigned to 255, indicating they will not be baked.

Before you rebake the scene, you may as well splurge a bit and increase the terrain shadow size. The terrain always gets its own lightmap, and its size can be set manually. The rest of the baked objects are "atlased," or combined on an array of lightmaps.

1. Open the Lightmapping window.

2. Select the Terrain and set its Map Size to **2048**, so the tree shadows will have more resolution.

3. Above the maps Preview, click Clear, to delete the existing lightmaps.

4. Bake the scene.

There are a couple of extra maps. They aren't named after the objects, because multiple objects are often "atlased," or combined on a single map. You can identify which objects are on each map by right-clicking the map in the Lightmapping dialog and clicking on Select Lightmap Users.

5. Set all of the remaining objects' Lightmap Size to **0**, leaving only the Terrain to be baked.

6. Make sure the Terrain object uses Lightmap Index 0, as it is the only one remaining.

7. In the Bake section, set the quality to High again.

8. Click Bake Scene.

9. Close the Lightmapping window.

10. Save the scene and save the project.

If you are using Pro, you should now have the best of both dynamic lighting and nice shader. If you don't have Pro, you will have a better looking baked material for the lightmaps.

Accessing the Lower Levels of the Temple

With the lightmaps under control, it's time to investigate the inside of the temple. As you will remember, there is a portion of it that is below ground. While the terrain contains a depression to account for most of it, there are two storage rooms that lie directly under the entry area. To allow access, you will have to deal with the terrain.

Currently, Unity's terrain-generation system doesn't allow you to cut holes in the terrain. You can turn off the Terrain component once you're inside a building, but because you can't easily disable the Terrain Collider and then enable it again, you can't get below the surface. The other problem is the time it takes to regenerate the terrain when you turn it back on. If you have very little vegetation, it will regenerate almost immediately; if you have a lot, there will be an annoying pause when the controls seem to lag. There are several workarounds—from using shaders and forcing draw order to stitching multiple terrain maps together and leaving the hole where they do not meet. If the building is large and important, you might even have a separate level or scene for it. For this project, the solution you will use will be to lower the ground out of the way when the player is in the temple.

Before you can look inside, you'll have to trigger the animation that drops the stairs into place. For now, you can set the animation to play on startup.

1. Select the TempleStairs object.

2. In the Animation component, turn on Play Automatically.

3. Click Play, wait for the stairs to drop, then go into the temple.

The stairs, unless you are coming at them at an angle, are difficult to climb, because they were designed on a scale to make humble pilgrims feel small and insignificant. To make game play better, you could try adjusting the Character Controller component's Step offset higher. If that doesn't work, you could set the Slope Limit to 90 degrees. The problem with that is that the player will be able to climb the sides of the temple. In this case, because the stairs are separate from the rest of the temple, you can simply set the Mesh Collider to Convex. You are essentially turning the collider into a box shape without the setup a box collider would require, using only a few more resources.

4. With the Stairs object still selected, in the Mesh Collider component, turn on Convex and try the stairs again.

This time, the First Person Controller goes smoothly up the stairs.

5. Stop Play mode and make the changes permanent.

If you have Pro and are still using Deferred Lighting, when you finally make it into the temple, it will be almost too dark to see anything. Even if you set the Temple of Tizzleblat's Mesh Renderer to not cast or receive shadows, there are shadows darkening the inside. To retain the advantage of the dynamic shadows, you will have to change the lighting, by changing which layers the lights affect. This is done with the light's Culling Mask.

1. Select the Sun for Lightmaps object.

2. In its Culling Mask, uncheck TransparentFX.

3. Duplicate the light and name it **Sun for Temple.**

4. Set Shadow Type to None.

5. Check Everything, then uncheck Default.

6. Set Lightmapping to RealtimeOnly.

7. Select the Temple of Tizzleblat and assign it to the TransparentFX layer.

8. Repeat for the Door Upper and Door Lower.

9. Click Play and explore the inside of the temple.

The inside of the temple no longer lies in added shadow. You could have made a new layer, but because the TransparentFX layer isn't being used, it's as good as any for the purpose of controlling the lights.

Inside the inner chamber of the temple, you will come up against the terrain where there should be another passage. Until you devise a permanent solution, you will start by creating a simple toggle to turn the terrain off and on.

1. Create a new script in the My Scripts folder.

2. Name it **Deactivate** and open it in the script editor.

3. Add the following:

```
var object : GameObject;

function OnMouseDown () {

        if (object. activeSelf == false) object.SetActive(true);
        else object.SetActive(false);
}
```

If you have used earlier versions of Unity, you will notice that the syntax for changing and querying an object's active state has changed.

4.   Save the script.

5.   Add the Deactivate script to Harvey, one of the temple guardians.

6.   Drag the Terrain object into the Object field.

7.   Click Play.

8.   Explore the inside of the temple.

You will be stopped by the terrain at the other side of the inner chamber.

9.   Head back to the temple steps and pick Harvey.

The terrain disappears.

10.   Explore the rest of the inside of the temple (see Figure 17-10).

Figure 17-10. *The temple's lower passageway is uncovered when the terrain is removed*

11.   Head out and click Harvey again, to reactivate the terrain.

12.   Stop Play mode.

13.   Remove the script from Harvey.

For the scene, you have to go in and out of the building at will, so you need a solution that is easy to script but effective. Let's move the terrain up and down, as it is the least problematic of the various options currently available in Unity.

Dropping the Terrain

To see how the triggering system works, you will have to turn off the outer temple. The temple model was originally a single model, but because there was going to be a lot going on inside it during the game, not to mention the light mapping options, it was split into two parts.

1. Select the Temple Outside and deactivate it.

2. Change the Scene view to Top/orthographic and zoom in on the temple inside (Temple of Tizzleblat object).

With the outer temple turned off, you will be able to see the logic behind the trigger objects..

3. Locate the Trigger Group in the Hierarchy view and select it.

4. Set the Scene view to Top and ortho, to get a good view (Figure 17-11).

Figure 17-11. *The terrain triggers' positions in the passageway*

You will want to minimize the possibility of the player seeing the terrain being turned off and on, yet have the triggers placed so that the action is only carried out when the player approaches the transition point. By having the triggers in the corner area, the terrain will be dropped shortly after the player enters the temple and replaced only when he gets close enough to leave it.

5. Select and identify each of the four terrain triggers to see their location in the temple.

The triggers are simple colliders set to Is Trigger. You might think a single collider using OnTriggerEnter and OnTriggerExit would do the job. If the player enters the trigger, however, then backs out of it, he could end up back outside with no terrain. By having a double trigger set up at each access, you will be able to prevent that from happening. It also allows you to have more control over placement.

If you are wondering about the layout of the triggers, think about the sequence of events. The first trigger usually tells the terrain to go into a state that it's already in, so the instruction is ignored. The second trigger changes state as the player is closer to needing the change. The logic holds for approaching in either direction.

The terrain-managing script will be implemented, so that it will raise and lower the terrain as needed. Because the script will be used for both the on and off triggers, you'll need a variable for using On or Off. You will also need to recognize the Terrain.

6.   Create a new script in the Adventure Scripts folder.

7.   Name it **TerrainManager**.

8.   Open it in the editor.

9.   Add the following variables to the new script:

```
var showTerrain = true; // true means show on enter, false means hide on enter

internal var terrain : GameObject;
internal var terrainPosY : float;
```

In the Start function, you will find the terrain and then assign its starting location.

10.   Add the following Start function:

```
function Start () {

    terrain = GameObject.Find("Terrain");
    terrainPosY = terrain.transform.position.y ; // get terrain y pos
}
```

Because you'll have to pass *through* the trigger object, you will trigger the event with an OnTriggerEnter function. Additionally, because you will, at some time, be required to toggle the state from elsewhere, the functionality will be in its own function.

11.   Add the following:

```
function ManageTerrain () {

    if (showTerrain) {
        terrain.transform.position.y = terrainPosY; // restore the terrain
    }
    else {
        terrain.transform.position.y = terrainPosY - 20; // drop the terrain
    }
}
```

12.   Add the call to manage the terrain.

```
function OnTriggerEnter () {

    ManageTerrain ();
}
```

13.   Save the script.

Now you can add the script to the triggers. Because they are prefabs, you will also have to update them.

1. Drag the new TerrainManager script onto each Terrain Trigger On and Off object.

2. With one of the objects selected, click Apply in the Inspector to update the prefab.

3. For the Terrain Trigger Off objects, in the Inspector, set their Show Terrain parameters to false.

4. For the Terrain Trigger On objects, in the Inspector, set their Show Terrain parameters to true.

Now you are ready to test the terrain-dropping functionality.

5. Turn on the Temple Outside and adjust the Scene view to be able to see the terrain drop.

6. Click Play and enter the temple.

7. Test the triggers and watch the Scene view as you go through them.

The terrain is raised and lowered, depending on your travels through the temple.

Dressing Up the Entryway

It now becomes a design problem to keep the player from seeing the terrain inside the temple before you hide it and not seeing it outside when he is in the temple. The floor plan of the temple is such that, with careful placement, you could probably get away with the temple as is. To make it more fun, let's help hide the deception, with the addition of a couple of hanging cloths at the opening.

1. Deactivate the TempleStairs.

2. Locate the Entry Hanger group and activate it.

The gameObject only has a Box collider component, but it has two children—a couple of Interactive Cloth objects.

3. Click Play.

The cloths crumple into heaps, because they don't have hangers assigned yet.

4. Stop Play mode.

5. Select one of the cloths and at the bottom of the Interactive Cloth component, set its Attached Colliders array Size to 1.

6. Assign the Entry Hanger object as its Element 0.

7. Repeat for the other cloth.

8. Click Play again.

This time, the cloths twitch a couple of times and then move gently on their own.

9. Turn off Play mode and reactivate the TempleStairs.

10. Click Play.

11. Drive up into the temple, through the cloths, and then turn and view the cloth from the back side.

They move nicely, as the First Person Controller moves through them, but as you turn, you will see that they have no faces on the back side. To fix that, you will require a two-sided shader.

A check of the standard Unity shaders shows that the only shaders that are two-sided are for particle systems and tree foliage, neither of which is appropriate for the temple entryway cloths.

Although the Unity shaders that ship with the editor have already been compiled, you can download the original source code from `www.Unity3d/support/resources/assets/built-in-shaders`. By comparing the two-sided shaders with the regular shaders and checking the shaderlab help, you can see that, in many cases, all you need to do is add two words to make your shader double-sided: "cull off."

1. Locate the DS BumpSpec shader in the Structures ➤ Custom Shaders folder.

2. Open the shader (it also uses the Mono Develop editor).

3. After the `Tags{ "RenderType"="Opaque" }` line, add the following:

   ```
   Cull Off
   ```

4. Save the shader (agree to Convert Endings, if you get an ending warning).

5. Click Play and test the cloth again.

This time, the cloth can be seen from the back side (see Figure 17-12).

Figure 17-12. *The double-sided cloth*

Creating a Simple Volumetric Light Effect

Inside the inner chamber of the temple, a central light source will be more believable with a nice bit of volumetric light. For a quick fake volumetric light effect, you can use another Line Renderer. Unlike the one that you used for the laser, this one will be stationary.

1. Select the Chandelier from the Temple Group and focus in on it.

2. Create a new Empty GameObject.

3. Name it **Volume Light Effect**.

4. Add a Line Renderer component from Component ➤ Effects.

5. Uncheck Use World Space.

6. In Positions, change its Element 1 Z to **0** and Y to **-10**.

7. Zoom back until you can see the full object.

8. In Parameters, set its Start Width and its End Width to **4**.

9. Add the Fairy Dust material to its Materials Element 0.

10. In the Start and End Colors, adjust its Alpha value to **255** and the colors to a light golden color.

The mapping looks better, but the texture could be better.

11. Select the Fairy Dust material in the Project view.

12. Duplicate the material and name it **VolumeRay**.

13. Move the new material to one of the game material folders.

14. Load the new material into the Line Renderer.

15. Change the material's Particle Texture to the Volumetric texture (Figure 17-13).

Figure 17-13. *The fake volume light using the Line Renderer*

The combination of the fake volumetric light and the simple Smoke particle system from the brazier below it add a nice feel to the inner chamber. Feel free to change the smoke in the brazier to something more mystic.

The Balcony

To access the balcony, you'll have to open one of the secret passageway doors for the player. Once up there, the player will find a large golden topi fruit.

1. Select Door Upper in the Hierarchy and double-click to focus in on it in the Scene view.

2. Set its Z Value to **78**.

■ **Note** The z axis is up for the door, because it was created in 3ds Max.

---

3. Click Play and make your way up to the balcony, via the secret passage (see Figure 17-14).

Figure 17-14. *The bowl, on the ledge of the balcony and with the golden topi fruit*

4. Stop Play mode.

In the Scene view, you will have to toggle on the FX button (next to Toggle Scene Lights) to see the glow effect from the Glow object.

Setting Up the Shrines

In addition to the temple, you imported six themed shrines: the Llight shrine, the water shrine, the earth shrine, the flora shrine, the music shrine, and the key shrine. Each is associated with its own particular glyph, which is also found on a matching stele. The player will have to make use of several of the shrines, either through the suggested functionality, their glyphs, or both, to move the game forward. You will be adding some new effects to some of the shrines and incorporating some of the objects and functionality you created in earlier chapters into others.

Hydrating the Water Shrine

Unity comes with two very useful legacy particle systems for creating waterfalls. Combining these with animating the UVs on the mesh objects, you can create quite respectable waterfalls in the free version of Unity.

1. Focus in on the Shrine Water object, as shown in Figure 17-15.

2. Click Play and inspect the various objects.

Figure 17-15. *Terrain prepared for water shrine group*

Take a moment to inspect the materials used for the rocky cliff, waterfalls, and water surfaces. The waterfalls use a variation of the water surface texture with an alpha edge.

While the water texture looks okay in a still shot, it will require some animation to bring it to life. For that, you will be using a modified version of the UVAnimator script that you built for the laser. The script, UV_AnimatorPlus, includes variables for specular and bump animation. It has already been applied to several of the objects in the waterfall group, but not the water itself. One trick used to make a water surface interesting without a reflection (if you are using the free version of Unity) is to animate the Diffuse, or main color, at a slightly different speed or direction from the bump and then repeat the process with a second layer of water beneath the first, using an offset direction.

3. Stop Play mode.

4. Select the lower water surface, Water Hole.

5. From the Adventure scripts folder, apply the UV_AnimatorPlus script to it.

6. Set the Scroll Speed U1 to -0.03, the Scroll Speed V1 to 0.05, the Scroll Speed U2 to 0.05, and the scroll Speed V2 to 0.03 (Figure 17-16, left).

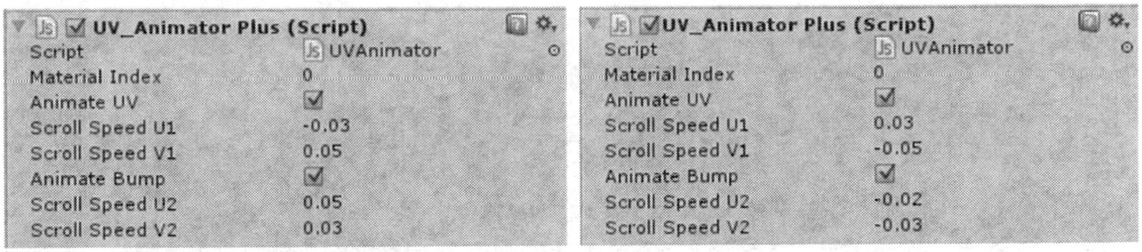

Figure 17-16. *The settings for the Water Hole (left) and Water Hole Radial (right)*

7. Click Play and watch the result.

The lower water animates showing a nice drift but doesn't appear to be affected by the waterfall. For that, you will need an object with radial mapping. The top level water, Water Hole Radial, has just that. In the modeling app, a cone was created with almost zero height and the bottom removed.

8. Stop Play mode.

9. Select the upper water surface, Water Hole Radial.

10. Apply the UV_AnimatorPlus script to it.

11. Set the Scroll Speed U1 to 0.03, the Scroll Speed V1 to -0.05, the Scroll Speed U2 to -0.02, and the Scroll Speed V2 to -0.03 (Figure 17-16, right).

12. Click Play and zoom in close to see the effect of the slightly different speeds and directions.

13. Stop Play mode.

■ **Tip**   You could adapt this script to animate a shininess or glossiness texture on a rock wall by having the UV 2 channel mapped to "flow" downhill. The rock is already using the UV 2 channel for the lightmap, but it is an interesting effect to consider.

Illuminating the Light Shrine

Remember the fire effect particle system you made? Although it doesn't play an active part in this version of the book project, it will be just the thing to put into the Light shrine.

1. Focus in on the Group Light's Small Bowl.

2. Select the Flame Base object and use Move to View to position it inside the Shrine Light object.

3. Adjust the positions of the children as necessary and click Simulate in the Scene view to see the results.

The fire should now fit nicely into the shrine (Figure 17-17).

657

Figure 17-17. The fire particle effect installed in the Light shrine

Setting Up the Maze

The maze has always been a mainstay of adventure games. In the early days of text adventures, as well as modern-day restricted camera-type navigation, the game was free to pop up exits or treasure-trove areas according to any criteria. In free-navigation-type games, however, the maze should be based on a physical reality. Moreover, at the very least, it should change every time the game runs or, better yet, change in-game when specific events occur.

With that in mind, when the player tries to steal the golden topi fruit from the temple, he will be transported to the maze, but not before it has been reset.

Examining the Maze Geometry

The walls that make up the interior of the maze are prefabs of seven slightly different walls. Each contains a collider and an empty script that will eventually rotate the wall on cue.

1. Zoom to get an ortho top view of the maze in the Scene view.

2. Open the MazeWalls group in the Hierarchy view.

There are 30 DropPoint objects and 42 MazeWall objects. The DropPoint objects are simple gameObjects that consist of their transforms and little else. They will be used as possible locations to drop whatever needs to go into the maze. To view the DropPoint objects in the Scene view, you'll have to turn on the Move button and select a DropPoint object. Each is centered between corresponding walls.

Managing the Maze Functionality

To manage the maze, you'll have to create a couple of scripts. The functionality is fairly simple. The script will turn each wall 0, 90, 180, or 270 degrees on its local z axis. The number of degrees rotated will be randomly selected from the available choices. To make the configuration slightly more interesting, let's decrease the odds of a zero rotation by doubling each of the others in the array you'll create to store the options.

1. From the Adventure Scripts folder, open the empty MazeWalls script.

2. At the top of the script, define and populate the array as follows:

```
internal var rotAngles = new int[7];
rotAngles[0] = 0;
rotAngles[1] = 90;
rotAngles[2] = 90;
rotAngles[3] = 180;
rotAngles[4] = 180;
rotAngles[5] = 270;
rotAngles[6] = 270;
```

Because you'll need to call this function periodically throughout the game, it makes sense to create a function to do the work for you.

3. Create a scramble function.

```
function Scramble () {
    // get a random element number in the array's range
    var element = Random.Range(0, 6); //remember arrays start at element 0
    //rotate the object on its local Z the number of degrees represented by that element
    transform.localEulerAngles.z = rotAngles[element];
}
```

The maze will always have to be set at scene start, so, for now, you'll have to call the new function from the Start function.

4. Add the following Start function to your script:

```
function Start () {
    Scramble();
}
```

5. Save the script.

The script already exists on the 42 walls, so all you have to do to test is click Play.

6. Click Play.

The walls rotate into a random configuration, creating a simple maze as shown in Figure 17-18.

Figure 17-18. *A few maze configurations on startup*

The maze now sets itself up as soon as you click the Play button, but at various times during the game, it will be reset to a new configuration. You'll need a new script to handle the event. This script will be in charge of contacting each wall object and triggering its Scramble function. As with many scripts, the trick is often deciding on which object the script should reside.

You will obviously want to use some sort of SendMessage to trigger the Scramble function, but the trouble with SendMessage is that it sends the message to all components of the GameObject on which it resides. The problem is how to contact the 42 GameObject walls that are *children*, not components of the MazeWalls object. If you search the scripting help for SendMessage, you will notice a related option, GameObject.BroadcastMessage. It "Calls the method named methodName on every MonoBehaviour in this game object or any of its children." This is the perfect solution. You can put a script with the broadcast message on the parent of all the maze walls, the MazeWalls group.

1. Stop Play mode.

2. Create a new script in the Adventure Scripts folder.

3. Name it **MazeManager**.

4. Open it in the script editor.

5. Change the Update function to the following:

    ```
    function ResetMaze () {
        // trigger the wall rotations on all of the children
        gameObject.BroadcastMessage("Scramble");
    }
    ```

6. Save the script.

7. Add the new script to the MazeWalls object in the Hierarchy view.

With the new script in place, there should be a simple way to test it without having to hook it up to an actual event at this time. One possible solution is to create a texture object and use it to trigger the event. Once you are satisfied with the maze and related functionality, you can deactivate or delete the texture object.

1. Make sure you are not in Play mode.

2. From the GameObject menu, create a GUI Texture object.

This object uses the UnityWatermark image as a default and is named after the image.

3. Change the X and Y Pixel Inset values in the Inspector to move the object off to the side of the Game window if you wish.

Now you will need a little script to trigger the maze reset.

4. Create a new script in the Adventure Scripts folder and name it **Transporter**.

5. Add the following variable:

```
internal var mazeManager : MazeManager; // var to hold MazeWalls' MazeManager component
```

6. In the Start function, locate the component.

```
mazeManager = GameObject.Find("MazeWalls").GetComponent(MazeManager);// find & assign it
```

7. Create an OnMouseDown function and call the MazeReset function.

```
function OnMouseDown () {
    mazeManager.ResetMaze(); // trigger the maze reset
}
```

8. Save the script.

9. Drag and drop the Transporter script onto the UnityWatermark-small object.

10. Click Play and try picking the GUI Texture object several times.

The maze resets nicely.

If you reset the maze enough times, you will notice an occasional closed block of four walls. If it were just a matter of traveling through the maze, you could safely ignore this, but in the next section, you will be dealing with positioning objects in the maze, and you'll need a way to make sure they are accessible from any drop point.

Checking for Drop Point Access

As you have seen, a drop point is nothing more than an empty gameObject with a transform and a name. Now that you have the maze working, you have to select a drop point for placing an object in the maze. Once the maze has been reset, a random number between 1 and 30 (the numbers of drop points) can be generated. That number is then cast to a character string and added to the base name, DropPoint. You will get the X and Z coordinates from DropPoint and use a previously stored Z position for the terrain height under the maze, then check to see if the position is accessible.

You'll be using a fairly simple method to check to see if the chosen position is trapped or not. This will provide you with a chance to revisit the raycast functionality.

You will be casting rays in the Cartesian directions to check for walls. If the distance to the wall that is being checked is less than half the cell size, and all four wall checks return that result, the position is trapped, and the maze must be reset.

Less likely is when three walls are close, but the next open direction is trapped as well.

And rare, but within reasonable probability, is when three cells in a row are closed, as shown in Figure 17-19.

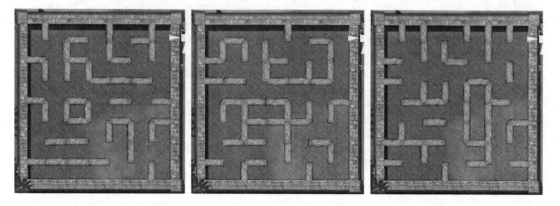

Figure 17-19. *Three configurations that will prevent player access to the relocated weapon: a common single, a double, and very rare triple trap*

So, the logic behind the checking could be as follows:

- If four walls are close, the position is inaccessible, so reset the maze and test again.

- If only one wall is close, it is safe, return.

- If two walls are close, test the position in each direction. If each direction is closed off in the three other directions, the cell is inaccessible, so reset the maze and test again; otherwise, if there was at least one other opening, it is probably safe.

- If three walls are close, move to the next position and test again. If only one new direction is open in the new position, move to it and test again. If there is at least one new open direction, let's assume it is accessible; otherwise, reset the maze and test again.

Let's start with the easy part of the script, generating a random position from the drop points.

Because the object drop point has to be checked every time the maze is reset, it makes sense to add the new code to the MazeManager script, where you reset the maze. Because the code is likely to get complex, you will want to create a couple of functions. One will choose a drop point, and the other will check to see if it is valid. If it's not valid, it will cause the maze to reset and be checked again. By breaking them up, you will be able to use both preset and randomly generated locations.

1. Open the Transporter script.

2. Add the following under the ResetMaze() line:

   ```
   mazeManager.FindDropPoint(); // find a drop point
   ```

3. Save the script.

4. Open the MazeManager script.

5. Add a variable for the dropPoint.

   ```
   internal var dropPoint : GameObject; // this gets built and found
   ```

6. Block in the `FindDropPoint` function.

```
function FindDropPoint() {
    //randomly generate the name of one of the 30 drop points
    var num : int = Random.Range(1,30);
    var name : String = "DropPoint"+ parseInt(num); // parseInt changes the integer to a string
    print (name);
}
```

7. Save the script.

8. Click Play.

9. Pick the GUI Texture object.

Nothing is reported in the console until you pick the GUI Texture object. If you remember, the MazeWalls script on each of the walls initializes in a `Start` function. In order to generate the drop point at the start of the scene, you must remove the `Start` function from that script and add one to the MazeManager script.

1. Open the MazeWalls script.

2. Comment out the `Start` function.

3. Save the script.

4. Open the MazeManager script.

5. Call the reset and drop point finder from inside the `Start` function.

```
ResetMaze ();
yield;            // make sure it is in place
FindDropPoint (); // find a random drop point
```

6. Save the script.

7. Click Play.

The maze walls all use the same number on startup! If you click the GUI Texture object, the maze behaves as expected. To make sure all of the walls have been processed, add a yield at the top of the `Start` function.

8. Add the following to the top of the MazeManager's `Start` function:

```
yield;// give the walls time to be processed
```

9. And to give the maze sufficient setup time, at the bottom of the `ResetMaze` function, add

```
yield new WaitForSeconds(0.05); // give maze time to reset
```

10. Save the script and click Play.

This time, it works as expected.

■ **Tip** Occasionally, code that looks okay will not run correctly when evaluation is too quick. Often, a simple yield statement will allow previous instructions time to finish, so that the code beneath evaluates as expected.

The console reports the randomly chosen drop point each time the maze is reset, after giving the walls enough time to reconfigure themselves.

Now that you have the name of the drop point, you can get its location and move an object to it. To do this, you can make a variable and drag and drop an object into it in the Inspector. Let's test using a sphere.

1. At the top of the MazeManager script, add the following variable:

    ```
    var dropObject : GameObject; // object to move to the drop point
    ```

2. Save the script.

3. Make sure you are not in Play mode.

4. Create a new Sphere object and name it **Drop Object**.

5. Scale it up to about 3 meters, so you will be able to see it in the top viewport.

6. Select the MazeWalls group.

7. In the Inspector, drag and drop the new sphere onto the Drop Object parameter.

Now you will retrieve the X and Z position from the drop point, so you can pass it on to the drop object.

8. Add the following to the MazeManager's FindDropPoint function:

    ```
    dropPoint = GameObject.Find(name); // local var to hold selected drop point
    print (dropPoint.transform.position.x);
    print (dropPoint.transform.position.z);
    ```

9. Save the script.

10. Click Play.

If the number generated was less than ten, you will get a Null Reference Exception message, because the object names/numbers contain zeros. You could rename the objects, but this is a typical problem when dealing with cloned objects, so let's adjust the script to account for it instead.

11. In the MazeManager's FindDropPoint function, change the var name = "DropPoint" + parseInt(num) line to the following:

    ```
    // parseInt changes the integer to a string
    if (num > 9) var name : String = "DropPoint" + parseInt(num);
    else   name = "DropPoint0" + parseInt(num);
    ```

12. Save the script.

13. Click Play again.

With the code behaving, you have to check to make sure the correct location is being reported.

1. Select the generated DropPoint in the Hierarchy view.

2. Compare the reported X and Z to the values in the Inspector.

You have probably noticed that they don't match. Remember, however, that the values in the Inspector show the *offset* from the parent's position. Let's go ahead and feed the numbers into the drop object's transform and see what happens.

3. Delete the two print statements at the bottom of the FindDropPoint function and add the following:

```
//move the drop object to the dropPoint's location
dropObject.transform.position.x = dropPoint.transform.position.x;
dropObject.transform.position.y = dropPoint.transform.position.y;
dropObject.transform.position.z = dropPoint.transform.position.z;
```

4. Save the script.

5. Click Play.

6. Pick the GUI Texture object and watch the sphere get positioned.

7. Locate the reported drop point in the Hierarchy view to assure yourself they are in the same place.

8. Reset the maze several times.

Eventually, the sphere will land in a trapped position. Next, you'll add a bit of code, to prevent the most common trap.

Checking for Traps

To check for a trapped drop object, you have to cast rays in four directions. If you look in the Script Reference for Physics.Raycast, you'll see that it requires several bits of information. The first is the position of the object you are casting from. In this case, it will be the DropPoint object.

The second piece of information is the direction, encoded as a Vector3 type. A search for Vector3 shows us that the forward direction for the object, Vector3(0,0,1), can also be written as Vector3.forward. The right direction can be written as Vector3(1,0,0) or Vector3.right. For the opposite directions, you add a minus in front of the direction. So, backward is -Vector3.forward, and left is -Vector3.right.

Third, you will create a variable of type RaycastHit to store the hit object. With that, you can then get the distance from the source object to the hit object.

To hit an object, it must have a collider. On the off chance that your raycast might escape out the entrance of the maze and manage to miss all colliders in the scene, you should put the entire operation inside a conditional statement.

And, last, because you will want to perform the same operation for each of the four directions, you may as well create a little function that returns the distance when you pass it the source object's position and the direction.

Let's get started.

1. Open the MazeManager script.

2. Create a new function to check the locations.

```
function CheckDropPoint (obj : GameObject) {

}
```

By feeding it an object directly, you will be able to call it, whether you are using preset or random locations. You will also be drawing a line in the editor, so each direction will have a different color.

3. Inside the new function, add the following to get the distances to the walls in each of the four directions:

```
// get distances to surrounding walls clockwise from 12 o'clock
var dForward : float = DistToWall(obj.transform .position, Vector3.forward , Color.blue);
var dRight : float = DistToWall(obj.transform .position, Vector3.right , Color.yellow);
var dBackward : float = DistToWall(obj.transform .position,-Vector3.forward , Color.red);
var dLeft : float = DistToWall(obj.transform .position,-Vector3.right , Color.green);
```

Each call to the DistToWall function returns the distance that is immediately assigned to the local variables. While you are setting this up, it is also useful to know which drop point was selected.

4. Add a local variable to store the total, and then print out the results.

```
var total : float = dForward + dRight +  dBackward +  dLeft;
print (dForward + "  " + dRight +  "  " +  dBackward +  "  " + dLeft + "  " + total);
```

Before you can test the code, you will have to create the DistToWall function. DistToWall will receive the arguments passed to it from the lines that call it for each direction. On the off chance there wasn't a hit in that direction, in the else, you can assign it a large number on the assumption that the ray went out one of the doorways in the outer wall.

5. Below the CheckDropPoint function, create the DistToWall function.

```
function DistToWall (origin: Vector3, direction : Vector3, lineColor : Color) {
    // pass the source/origin and direction in to be checked
    // do raycasting
    var hit : RaycastHit; // create a variable to hold the collider that was hit
    if (Physics.Raycast(origin, direction, hit)) {
        Debug.DrawLine (origin, hit.point, lineColor,1.0); // draw a line to check the
position
        return hit.distance; // send the distance back to the caller
    }
    else return 1000.0; // didn't hit anything, so assign a large number
}
```

While you are setting up the functionality, the DrawLine method will show you that the distance check is working correctly. After the Color argument is the time that the line will show, in this case, one second.

With the two new functions started, you will pass in a drop point to check.

6. In the FindDropPoint function, under the dropPoint = GameObject.Find(name) line, add

```
CheckDropPoint(dropPoint); // pass the object in to have its distance checked
```

7. Save the script.

8. Click Play and test the results, checking the totals when the sphere is trapped.

9. Comment out the print(name) statement in the FindDropPoint function.

10. Save the script.

To check the results of the ray-casting, you can check the total distances for the most common trap. The drop points are about 8.4 meters apart, with walls that are 3 meters thick. Halving the remaining distance, you will arrive at about 2.7 meters to the closest walls. At the average range of 2.7 meters, a total of 10.8 should tell you that there is a wall on each of the four sides. It follows, then, that if there were only three close walls, and the fourth is only a single square away, the next total should be 19.2. You can safely assume that anything less than a well-padded 14 or 15 means the drop point is trapped. For some cases, you may want to play it safe and check for less than 20. For that reason, you will be using a local variable for the check.

Having determined that any total less than 14 means the drop point is enclosed within a single square, you can tell the maze to reset. To prove this to yourself visually, you can create a template cube to test with.

1.   Create a cube in the Hierarchy.

2.   Set its scale to 7×7×7.

3.   Click Play.

4.   In the Scene view, Top, move the cube into one of the squares.

It should overlap the walls, assuring you that the number is good for a valid test.

5.   Delete the cube.

6.   In the FindDropPoint function, comment out the print (name + " " + dForward line.

```
//print (dForward + "   " + dRight + "   " +  dBackward +  "   " + dLeft + "   " + total);
```

7.   Below it, add the following to perform the single square check:

```
// check for single square trap
if (total < trapLimit) {
    print ("trapped");
}
```

Once you know it is trapped, you can reset the maze and check again.

8.   Beneath the print ("trapped") line, add the following:

```
ResetMaze (); // get a new maze configuration
CheckDropPoint(dropPoint, trapLimit); // and check the drop point again
```

9.   Add the new argument to the CheckDropPoint function.

```
function CheckDropPoint (obj : GameObject, trapLimit : float) {
```

10.   Back up in the FindDropPoint function, pass in the lower limit number.

```
CheckDropPoint(dropPoint, 12.0); // pass the object in to have its distance checked
```

11.   Save the script.

12.   Click Play.

13.   Test the maze several times, watching to see if the drop point is ever trapped.

If it is trapped, the reset is called recursively, until a valid point is returned. Now you should see the message, but not the trapped sphere, if you are tenacious enough to keep clicking the GUI Texture object long enough to get it trapped. When the player meets Gimbok in the maze, he will not have the opportunity to get out of a trap, so the check will be made for the higher number, 20.

Using the Drop Point

Now that you have a means of checking an object's location in the maze, you can go ahead and use it to transport outside objects to the random locations. One such object will be the Golden Sleeve that the player will need to complete the laser. It will be floating on a tray with no character in sight. The main code change will be to use a supplied Y value.

The easiest way to relocate an object is probably going to be to pass its target Y value into the FindDropPoint function as an argument and letting it get moved from there after the drop point location has been vetted.

1. Change the function FindDropPoint(){ line to the following:

   ```
   function FindDropPoint (obj : GameObject, yPos : float) {
   ```

2. At the top of the FindDropPoint function, assign obj to the dropObject.

   ```
   dropObject = obj; // assign the new drop object
   ```

3. In the FindDropPoint function, change the y position assignment as follows:

   ```
   dropObject.transform.position.y = yPos; // in case it is a different y location
   ```

And you will need to change the call to FindDropPoint in the Start function. For that you will pass in the DropObject and its current y location.

4. In the Start function, change the FindDropPoint line to match the following:

   ```
   FindDropPoint (dropObject,dropObject.transform.position.y); // find a random location for
   the drop point
   ```

5. Save the script.

And, finally, the Transporter script must be changed to match, but first, it will need a variable to hold the object to be transported.

1. Open the Transporter script.

2. Add the following variable:

   ```
   var object : GameObject; // object to be transported
   ```

3. Change the FindDropPoint line to

   ```
   mazeManager.FindDropPoint(object, object.transform.position.y); // find a drop point for
   the object
   ```

With this line, you can now see why you didn't use the SendMessage function to call the FindDropPoint function—it can only pass one argument.

4.   Save the script and drag the Drop Point object onto its new parameter.

5.   Click Play and test.

6.   Change the height of the Drop Point Object and keep testing.

If all went well, you should see pretty much the same functionality as before, except that now, the object's y position will not be affected. This will allow you to set different objects at different heights without worrying about the distance check.

With the y position covered, it's time to switch the Transporter over from the OnMouseDown, so it can be used in the rest of the game.

1.   Open the Transporter script.

2.   Create a variable to store a y position in case it is other than the current one.

```
var yPos : float; // the y position destination in the maze
```

3.   Also, add a variable to tell the object it is on if it should be transported immediately.

```
internal var transportAtStart : boolean = false;
```

4.   In the Start function, add

```
if (transportAtStart == true) BeamMeUpScotty();
```

5.   Create a new function.

```
function BeamMeUpScotty () {
    if (yPos == 0) yPos = this.transform.position.y; // use the object's current y if none assigned
    // send this object off to be moved to a random position in the maze
    mazeManager.FindDropPoint(this.gameObject,yPos);
}
```

With the new code using the object the script is on, you can comment out the older code.

6.   Comment out the OnMouseDown function and var object line.

7.   Save the script.

8.   Delete the UnityWaterMark-small object.

9.   Click Play and watch to see where the Sphere turns up.

10. Disable the Sphere's Mesh Renderer and Sphere Collider.

Playing the Odds

There is a small chance that the maze configuration will produce a closed two-square block and an even smaller chance that the drop point will be inside it. Therefore, at this point, you have to make an executive decision on the maze. The three most logical options are to perform more sophisticated trap-checking; reset for a single, single, double distance; increase the minimum trapped distance to 20; or allow the player to reset the maze himself, if he can't find what he's looking for.

Allowing Player Reset

The more intriguing option is to allow the player to reset the maze. Obviously, you shouldn't allow the player to stand at the entrance and click a button until a configuration appears with the object in clear sight. It follows that you'll need to place the button at some distance from the maze, to discourage that unsportsmanlike behavior.

But if the mechanism to reset the maze is not near the maze entrance, you will face the problem of association. A button on the trunk of a palm tree 100 meters away is not likely to provide much of a clue to its function. Therefore, you'll have to devise a way to provide a clue, subtle or blatant, to the operation of the maze-resetting mechanism. You can do this in several ways.

A very subtle way would be to trigger a tune or chord to play every time the player passes into the maze. You can associate the sound to the maze and Music shrine by having it play when the drawer in the Music shrine is activated.

Let's start by creating a collider for the entry passages into the maze, in order to help the player with some special effects as hints.

1. Change the Scene view to a top view and focus in on the entrance closest to the temple.

You can use the simplest collider, the Box Collider, to trigger an eerie musical chord.

2. Create a cube and name it **MazeFX**.

3. Set it to **6×6×6**.

4. Set the collider to Is Trigger.

5. Remove the Mesh Renderer and Mesh Filtercomponents (Figure 17-20).

Figure 17-20. *The MazeFX collider*

6. Change the view to Perspective and adjust the Y Position to make sure the collider will be at the right height for the First Person Controller to trigger it.

Now let's add some sound effects.

1. From the Components menu, add an Audio Source.

2. For the Audio Clip, choose MazeChord.

3. Check Loop.

4. Click Play and go into the maze.

The looping sound gives the maze an eerie feel, but you'll have to trigger the sound on and off when you enter and exit the collider.

5. Uncheck Play on Awake.

6. In the Adventure Scripts folder, create a new script.

7. Name it **MazeFX**.

8. Open it in the editor.

9. Remove the default functions and replace them with the following:

```
function OnTriggerEnter () {
    audio.Play(); // start the sound
}

function OnTriggerExit() {
    audio.Stop(); // stop the sound
}
```

10. Save the script.

11. Drag the script onto the MazeFX object.

12. Click Play and travel into the maze and out.

13. Stop Play mode.

The sound is nice, but not eerie enough. Let's add a reverb zone to improve it.

1. With the MazeFX object selected, add an Audio Reverb Zone component from the Audio section of the Component menu.

2. Click Play.

3. Test some of the presets and then choose Auditorium.

4. Stop Play mode and make the change permanent.

5. Duplicate the MazeFX object and put the clone at the other maze entrance.

Activating the Drawer

Whether or not you decide to make the music glyph an action object, the drawer will have to be set up as an action object. Let's start by getting everything organized to trigger on pick, then switch it over later.

1. From Group Music in the Structures prefab, select the DrawerMusic object.

You should see the MusicGlyph in DrawerMusic as its child (Figure 17-21).

Figure 17-21. The DrawerMusic and its child, the Music Glyph

The drawer already has an animation and audio source component that you will have to trigger.

2. Create a new script in the Adventure Scripts folder.

3. Name it **TriggerMusicDrawer**.

4. Open it in the editor and replace the existing functions with the following:

```
function OnMouseDown () {
    CloseDrawer();
}

function CloseDrawer() {
    animation.Play();
    yield new WaitForSeconds(1.75);
    audio.Play();
}
```

5. Save the script.

6. Add it to the DrawerMusic object.

7. Move the First Person Controller to the music shrine.

8. Click Play and pick the drawer.

9. Adjust the Volume if necessary.

10. Add an Audio Reverb and choose a nice preset.

The audio effect is nice, but it never hurts to add a visual effect to reinforce the association. Let's add a point light to spice up the effect. This one is already set up for you. It has an animation, to bring the intensity up and down.

1. Select the Point Light FX object, duplicate it, and name it **Point Light FX2**.

2. Set its Intensity to **3**, while you adjust the position.

3. Move it to the front of the Shrine Music object, then turn the Intensity back to **0**.

4. Open the TriggerMusicDrawer script.

5. Add the following line below the yield line:

```
GameObject.Find("Point Light FX2").animation.Play();
```

6. Save the script.

7. Click Play and test the drawer.

8. Stop Play mode (Figure 17-22).

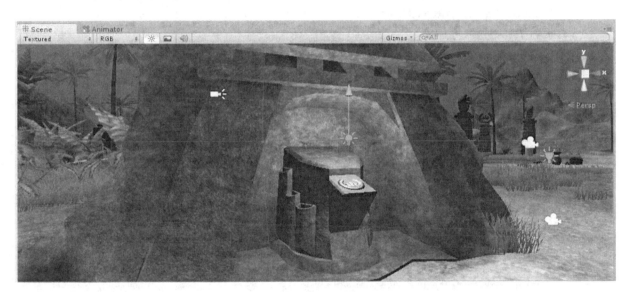

Figure 17-22. *The FX light at the Music shrine*

As long as you've got an animated light, it would be nice to be able to reuse it at the maze entrances, to ensure that the player makes the connection. In the case of the maze entrances, the player could miss the effect entirely, if he moves through too quickly, so rather than use a statically placed light for each position, let's parent the light to the First Person Controller. That way, it will be handy wherever you choose to use it.

1. Open the MazeFX script.

2. Add the following line to the OnTriggerEnter function:

```
GameObject.Find("Point Light FX2").animation.Play();
```

3. Save the script.

673

4. Focus in on the First Person Controller and move the new light to it.

5. Drag the light onto the First Person Controller in the Hierarchy view.

6. Position it in the middle of the Capsule mesh.

7. Click Play and travel into the maze.

8. Stop Play mode.

The light and sound effects work nicely to provide audio and visual clues to the maze. Now, you will need to have the drawer operation reset the maze configuration to tie it all together.

1. Open the TriggerMusicDrawer script again.

2. Add the following line after the `audio.Play()` line:

```
GameObject.Find("MazeWalls").SendMessage("ResetMaze");// reset the maze
```

3. Save the script.

4. Focus the Top viewport on the maze.

5. Click Play and test the drawer, watching the maze as you do so.

6. Stop Play mode.

To prevent the player from re-picking the drawer before the animation is finished, you could add a bit more code, `if(animation.IsPlaying("music drawer")) return;`. But the next step will be to set the drawer up as an action object, so it will automatically be taken care of.

So now, as you have trained the player to expect action objects to react to cursor mouseovers, you can go ahead and finish it up.

1. Add the Interactor script to the DrawerMusic (which will also add the ObjectLookup script automatically).

2. Tag it as an ActionObject.

Set it up as if the player needs to add the Music Glyph before it can be activated, but start it in the state that tells you the key is in place. You can use the script to call the rest of the media effects, but call the animation, music drawer, from the Interactor, so the pick blocking will work. The animation, music drawer, is on state 1 and state 2. The drawer has two states, empty and with the music glyph in place. State 1 is empty; state 2 has the glyph. It is always in scene, so location is always 1, and state 0 doesn't need to be filled out.

3. See the StateManagement PDF (see the Source Code/Downloads tab of the book's Apress product page www.apress.com/9781430248996) for the full data for the DrawerMusic.

4. For short descriptions, use "Stone Drawer," 1, and "Stone Drawer with Glyph," 2.

5. For the long ones, use "It is a stone drawer with an odd-shaped depression," 1, and "It is a stone drawer with a music glyph," 2.

6. For Lookup State 1, use

default,1
Music Glyph Icon,2

7. For Lookup State 2, use

default,2,s0_DrawerMusic,2

8. Corresponding Replies will be

Nothing happens
The Music Glyph fits snugly into the depression and:
The door closes and re-opens triggering an eerie light and sound.
Having rerouted the drawer's functionality to an action object, you must do a few things.

1. Open the TriggerMusicDrawer script.

2. Comment out the `OnMouseDown` function.

3. Rename the `CloseDrawer` function to `DoTheJob`.

4. Comment out `animation.Play()`.

5. Save the script.

6. Click Play and make sure the functionality still works.

7. Save the scene and save the project.

Creating an "Easter Egg"

With Unity Pro, you can render a camera view to a texture, which lets you create surveillance cameras that update the materials on monitors in your scene in real time. In your scene, however, it would be fun to add a bit of undocumented functionality (aka, an "Easter Egg") in the form of a "minimap" of the maze. Because you are not putting it on a mesh object in the scene, you can achieve this without using the Pro Render Texture feature. You will be creating a camera that will render to a portion of the screen when a secret keyboard key is toggled.

1. Create a new camera.

2. Name it **Camera MazeView** and delete its Audio Listener.

3. Position it so it is centered over the maze.

4. Set its Rotation to **90,300,300**.

5. Set Culling Mask to Nothing, then to Default.

6. Move the camera up in the Inspector until you can see the entire maze in the Camera Preview window (Figure 17-23).

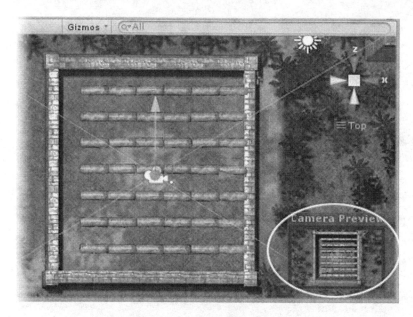

Figure 17-23. *The new camera with the maze in view*

7. Set Clear Flags to Depth Only.

8. Set the Projection to Orthographic.

9. Set its Near Clipping Plane to **10** and its Far Clipping plane to **25**.

10. Adjust the camera's Y Position until the maze and the terrain both show in the preview again.

11. Set the (orthographic) Size to about **34**, or until the maze fills the preview.

Unlike GUI Textures and Unity GUI scripted 2D screen-space objects, cameras use normalized screen space instead of pixel size. That is, the camera will use a percent of the screen size for both location and rectangle draw size. Normalized values are between 0 and 1.

1. Set the Game window to Standalone instead of Free Aspect.

2. For the camera, set the X and Y Normalized Rect Viewport values to **0.82** and **0.72**.

3. Set the W and H values to **0.15** and **0.24**.

Because you are specifying a screen size, the aspect ratio will be okay, but you could use Screen.Width and Screen.height in the Start function of the script, if you wanted more options.

4. Click Play.

The minimap disappears.

5. Try clicking the camera component off and on.

The maze reappears. Because you don't want it on at the start, it will probably be okay if you toggle it on later through a script. The real issue here, though, is Depth. With a value of 0, just like the main camera, it only gets precedence when it gets newly activated. Let's start by fixing the depth, then create a script to turn it off and on.

6. Set the camera's Depth to **5**.

7. Create a new script in the Adventure Scripts folder.

8. Name it **ToggleMiniMap**.

9. Open it in the editor.

10. Add the following code to change the Start and Update functions:

```
function Start () {
    //add adjustments to compensate for aspect ratio here
}

function Update () {
    if (Input.GetKeyDown("m")) { // check for m keyboard key press
        if(camera.enabled == false) camera.enabled = true;
        else camera.enabled = false;
    }
}
```

11. Save the script.

12. Add the script to the Camera MazeView and turn off the Camera component.

13. Click play and test by toggling the "M" key.

14. While the map is showing, reset the maze, by using the music drawer.

The cheat key toggles the maze minimap off and on, giving the player a nice little Easter Egg.

15. Save the scene and save the project.

Summary

In this chapter, you imported the environment for the main level of the game and had another look at lightmapping and some options that are available if you don't have Pro, or if you just prefer to bake imported objects' lightmaps in an outside application.

Next, you started setting up the functionality required to get the player into the temple and its lower level. By moving the terrain down once the player was safely inside the temple, you found an easy work-around for Unity's current lack of support for making holes in a terrain object. A couple of hanging interactive cloths, made double-sided with a couple of words added to their shader, masked the illusion.

You experimented with a few special effects to produce a billboarded glow and an inexpensive moving water effect, to improve the imported environmental assets.

And, finally, you were introduced to a classic adventure game element—the maze. In 3D form, you added the functionality to randomly reset its configuration. As the maze serves as a place to relocate both key objects and characters, you added the functionality, to find if a given location was in the most common of traps, a single cell. By recursively resetting the maze until the location was in the clear, you increased the odds that it was going to be available to the player.

On the off chance the player couldn't find an object at the randomly chosen location, you allowed him to reset the maze from the music shrine, providing audio and visual clues to help him make the connections. To make things more entertaining, you created an "Easter Egg" that allows the player to see a minimap of the maze onscreen, with a particular keypress.

CHAPTER 18

■ ■ ■

Setting Up the Game

With the major landmarks in place, it's time to put all the pieces together for game play. You will be starting the player somewhere near the chest, where he can find the first clue. Although his path through the game need not be linear, the next task will be to find the golden sleeve somewhere within the maze. A short raft ride will help him secure the vial of life-giving elixir. Examining the earth shrine will trigger the rockfall from which the player will gain access to the crystal. With both the crystal and golden sleeve, he will be able to construct the laser that is required to open the temple. Access to the temple will allow the player to discover a fabulous golden topi fruit. Unfortunately, when he tries to take it, he will be sent deep into the maze, where he will be able to talk to the first character. With a few clues and a large rock, he can head back into the temple and have better luck taking the golden fruit. Still somewhat clueless, he will then encounter the second character. She will provide him with the knowledge to finish the quest and give him some enlightening hints about how to get through the tunnels.

Finishing the Main Level

In the previous chapter, you imported the remainder of the game's environmental assets and began setting up their functionality. Now, you will finish the task by revisiting, refining, and combining many of the objects you have been working with throughout the book. You will also continue creating game play with several of the new environmental assets.

Reading Material

The rock/chest key functionality is already complete, so your first task will be to have the player retrieve the message from the chest, read it, and put it into inventory. And, of course, enable him to reread the message at any time.

A typical feature of the adventure genre is the existence of objects, such as books, notes, and letters, that provide the player with clues to the story or necessary game play. While giving written clues and other information may seem a bit too obvious, it does provide a nice variation from the other action objects. Clues, of course, can be blatant to obscure. In your game, you will use a bitmap with the writing already on it, but you could also use an empty page object and the Unity GUI to provide the actual text. That method would make changing languages or hint levels more economical.

You will require three objects for your text message: the message on the ground, Message; the Message Icon in inventory; and a message in front of the camera, MessageView. Let's start with the easy ones.

When picked from inventory, the Message Icon will go out of scene, and the MessageView will become active.

1. Select the Message Icon.

2. Change the Lookup State 1, as follows:

   default,0,MessageView,1

3. Change the Reply State 1 as follows:

You take the Message out for a closer look.

The (original) Message, when taken from the chest, will go directly into inventory. It doesn't have any animation and only has two states.

4. Select the Message from the ActionObjects group.

5. Add the Interactor script to it (which will also add the ObjectLookup script).

6. Fill them out as per the StateManagement PDF.

7. Tag the Message as an ActionObject.

8. Set the Lookup State 1 as follows:

default,0,Message Icon,1

9. Set the Reply State 1 as follows:

You tuck the Message carefully into your pack.

To allow your players to read the Message, you will create a copy and put it in front of the camera. The trick here is to remember that you will also have to read it from inventory, where you have turned off your Main Camera layer and are using the inventory camera. For the reading material, the message, and the map of the tunnels, you will create a new camera and new layer.

1. Duplicate the Message object and name it **MessageView**.

2. Locate the MapView object and focus in on it.

3. Move the new MessageView to it with Move to View.

4. Rotate it to match (Figure 18-1).

Figure 18-1. *The MessageView and MapView objects in the Scene view*

To make sure the Camera View will be seen on top, you will be creating a layer for it to render to.

5. From Layer, Add Layer, select User Layer 10, and name it **In View**.

6. Create a new camera and name it **Camera View**.

7. Remove its Audio Listener component.

8. Set its Clear Flags to Depth Only, Culling Mask to In View and Depth to **2**.

9. Use Align to View and adjust its position, for a good view of the message in the Game view.

10. Set Rendering Path for both the Camera Inventory and Camera View to Forward, to avoid depth-related issues.

11. Select the MessageView object and assign it to the new In View layer.

12. Click Play and test by picking the message on the ground and in inventory.

Everything works until you try to close the message to put it back in inventory. The pick is not processed, because you have a return, if you are in iMode and the layer is not 9—the inventory camera's layer. There are several possible solutions, but the most logical is simply to turn off inventory mode.

The script that toggles inventory mode is found on the Camera Inventory, so you must include it in the instructions for the Message Icon. The usual DoTheJob function is the best way to handle the extra functionality. While you're at it, you can enable the camera, so it doesn't have to be on during editing

1. Stop Play mode.

2. Select the Message Icon object.

3. Change its Lookup State 1, Element 0 to

   default,0,MessageView,1,s1_Camera Inventory,0

4. Open the InventoryManager script.

5. Add the following function to it:

```
function DoTheJob () {

    if(iMode) ToggleMode ();
    // activate Camera View if it wasn't already
    gameObject.Find("Camera View").camera.enabled= true;
}
```

6. Save the script.

7. Disable Camera View's Camera component.

The inventory is closed, to allow the player to read the message without distractions. Depending on where you have moved the Action objects and which way you are facing, you may or may not be able to pick the MessageView, to put it back into inventory. The problem is that you are checking for distance to camera, and the MessageView object probably isn't in front of the First Person Controller's camera. Because you always know that active objects in layer 10, In View, are automatically sufficiently close, you can add a simple condition to fake the distance.

1. Open the Interactor script.

2. At the top of the DistanceFromCamera() function, add the following:

    ```
    //fake the distance for Camera View objects
    if(gameObject.layer == 10) return 1.0;
    ```

3. Save the script.

4. Click Play and test.

The message is now pickable.

Now the MessageView is read with the inventory hidden. The only problem is that the player can navigate the scene with it in front of the scene. Even if you consider that bonus functionality, you still will want to have the message go back into inventory, if the player picks anywhere else other than the object. In inventory mode, you had another object that covers the scene to catch picks, but it is associated with the Inventory layer. Rather than create another object and write code for it, you can simply increase the size of the MessageView's collider to cover the screen.

5. Select the MessageView object and enable Camera View's Camera component.

6. In the Game window, turn on Gizmos (next to the Maximize on Play toggle).

7. Increase the MessageView's collider's size until it is more than covering the screen, at the appropriate aspect ratio—8×5×0.05 should be plenty big enough.

8. Turn off Gizmos in the Game window and disable the camera component again.

9. Set Is Trigger to true, so it won't block the player in the game.

10. Click Play and test by clicking somewhere other than the MessageView object, to close it.

The message closes nicely with a pick, but if you open the inventory while the message is showing, you get the earlier problem of the inventory objects being active, even behind the message. This time, let's assume that if the player opens Inventory, any active objects from Camera View should be put back into Inventory first. It would be quick to hardcode in the two objects, but it would be better to create a little function that iterates though the action objects, looking for the Camera view, and handles things automatically. The code is partially borrowed from the CheckForActive function in the ObjectLookup script and then sends the info directly through the LookUpState function, as if the object were picked.

1. Open the InventoryManager script.

2. Add the following function to it:

    ```
    function StashViewObjects () {
        //load the actionObject array from the GameManager script
        var actionObjects : GameObject[] = controlCenter.GetComponent(GameManager).
                                                                    actionObjects;
        for (var y : int = 0; y < actionObjects.length; y++) { // iterate through the array
            if (actionObjects[y].gameObject.layer == 10 &&      //if it is in the In View layer
                actionObjects[y].gameObject.activeInHierarchy) { // and it is active in the scene
                // process it out of scene with ObjectLookup, currently state 1, default cursor
                actionObjects[y].gameObject.GetComponent(ObjectLookup).
                    LookUpState(actionObjects[y].gameObject,1,"default");
            } // close the if
        } // close the for loop
    }
    ```

And you can call the function every time the inventory screen is opened.

3. At the top of the ToggleMode function's else clause, add:

```
StashViewObjects (); // put away any view objects that are showing
```

4. Save the script.

5. Click Play and try opening inventory when the message is onscreen.

So now, the view object and inventory play nicely together. Later in the chapter, when you hook up the map, you will appreciate the generic code.

Here's the fun part. If you decide you want the message to be read as soon as it is picked up, all you have to do is change two lines in the ObjectLookup data.

1. Stop Play mode.

2. Select the Message object.

3. Change the Lookup State 1, as follows:

default,0,MessageView,1,s1_Camera Inventory,0

4. Change the Reply State 1 as follows:

You pick up the Message to see what it says

5. Click Play and test the rearranged functionality.

This time, the MessageView is activated, allowing the player to read it before stashing it into his pack.

Hiding the Message

With the functionality sorted out, it's time to hide the message in the locked chest.

1. Select the ChestLid and turn off its Mesh Renderer.

2. Select the Message object and move it into the bottom of the chest, scaling it to fit inside.

3. Turn on the ChestLid's Mesh Renderer and drag the Message into the AnimationObjects group.

4. While you're there, delete the Pedestal object.

5. In the Hierarchy view, drag the Message into the AnimationObjects group.

6. Turn on Maximize on Play.

7. Click Play and test.

The key is jumping directly into the lock, so now would be a good time to update the inventory object's initial states and finalize the key/lock functionality. See the StateManagement PDF for the full assignments. (See the Source Code/Downloads tab of the book's Apress product page www.apress.com/9781430248996.)

1. Set all of the Inventory Objects' Initial States to 0.

2. Select the Key At Rock.

3. Change the Lookup State 1 as follows:

   default,0,Iron Key Icon,1

4. Change the Reply State 1 as follows:

You drop the key carelessly into your pack

5. Select the LockPlate object.

6. Change the Lookup State 1, Element 1, as follows:

   Iron Key Icon,2, Iron Key Icon,0,KeyAtLock,1,b0_ChestLid,2

7. Change the Reply State 1, Element 1, as follows:

The key slips in and turns with a satisfying snick

8. Select the Key At Lock.

9. Change the Lookup State 1, as follows:

   default,0,b0_ChestLid,1,LockPlate,1,Iron Key Icon,1

10. Click Play and test the sequence.

11. Save the scene and save the project.

The CameraMatch script takes you nicely up to the chest, where you can see the message inside it (Figure 18-2).

Figure 18-2. *The Message in the chest*

Finding the Golden Sleeve

Because you have a means of positioning an object in the maze, you can make good use of it to hide the Golden Sleeve, the object necessary to activate the crystal. The message found in the locked chest provides a clue that tells the adventurer that the maze contains many things of use.

1. Move the First Person Controller up to the maze entrance.

2. Select the TrayCloth object from the NPC Assets, NPC Characters folder and position it in front of the First Person Controller.

3. Adjust its height, to about 0.8 units above the ground in the maze area, so that the First Person Controller has a good view of it (see Figure 18-3), approximately **55.655** for the Y position.

Figure 18-3. *The floating tray and Golden Sleeve, as seen by the First Person Controller*

4. Locate the Golden Sleeve in the Hierarchy view and position it on top of the tray in the scene.

5. Scale the tray size to match the sleeve—about **1.4** (see Figure 18-3).

6. Drag the Golden Sleeve onto the TrayCloth object in the Hierarchy view.

You will have to deactivate the tray after taking the Golden Sleeve, so let's give it a unique name, so it can be found.

7. Rename the TrayCloth to **TrayCloth Floating**.

8. Add a Box Collider to it.

9. Add the V_PositionCycler script to the tray.

10. Set the Up Range and Down Range to **0.03**.

11. Click Play and observe the effect.

Next, you will set up the Golden Sleeve and the TrayCloth Floating as ActionObjects. The tray is never accessed directly. It starts in scene but not pickable, 2, then goes to 1, when the sleeve is taken.

1. Exit Play mode.

2. Select the Golden Sleeve.

3. Add the Interactor (and ObjectLookup) scripts to it.

4. Fill them out as per the StateManagement PDF. (See the Source Code/Downloads tab of the book's Apress product page www.apress.com/9781430248996.)

5. Tag it as an ActionObject.

6. Repeat for the TrayCloth Floating.

7. Click Play and try taking the Golden Sleeve object.

The sleeve goes nicely into inventory, leaving the empty tray floating alone.

To dispose of the tray, you can add a clause to the MazeFX script. Because the player has to pass through it on the way out, that will be a good time to deactivate the tray, if the Golden Sleeve's state is 0, or out of scene.

1. Open the MazeFX script.

2. Add the following variables:

```
var trayClothFloating : GameObject;
```

3. Find the objects in the Start function.

```
function Start () {
    trayClothFloating = GameObject.Find("TrayCloth Floating");
}
```

4. In the OnTriggerExit function, add

```
// if the golden sleeve has been acquired, deactivate the tray
    if (trayClothFloating.GetComponent(Interactor).currentState == 2) {
        trayClothFloating.GetComponent(Interactor).ProcessObject(0);
}
```

5. Save the script.

6. Click Play.

7. Test by entering and leaving the maze.

The sleeve and tray should still be visible.

8. Now take the Golden Sleeve and enter and leave the maze again.

This time, the empty tray should disappear.

With the basic functionality working, you can go ahead and set the tray's location with the Transporter script.

1. Drop the Transporter script onto the TrayCloth Floating object.

2. Check Transport at Start.

3. Click Play and make sure the tray is randomly transformed in the maze.

The tray, as you set it up on the same level as the maze, can use its current Y position when being relocated.

4.   Being careful not to change the Y position, move the tray group inside the maze, on the off chance it can be seen at startup, before it is transformed.

The tray gets a nice random location on startup, but if the player begins to change the maze with the drawer at the music shrine, it could become trapped. To prevent this from happening, you will use the MusicDrawer, to tell any active objects to check for traps again. In this game, those objects will be the floating tray and the Gimbok character. The former can be repositioned, and the latter just has to have its position checked. If the gameObjects are not active, the message won't be a problem. You will uncomment the nPC lines later.

1.   Open the TriggerMusicDrawer script.

2.   Add a variable for the tray and the Gimbok Group.

```
var dropObject : GameObject; // the tray
//var nPC : GameObject;       // the Gimbok group
```

3.   At the bottom of the DoTheJob function, add the following:

```
//check objects currently in maze
dropObject.SendMessage("BeamMeUpScotty",SendMessageOptions.DontRequireReceiver);
//nPC.SendMessage("RecheckPosition",SendMessageOptions.DontRequireReceiver);
```

4.   Save the script.

5.   Assign the tray to the DrawerMusic's Drop Object parameter.

You will assign the Gimbok group later.

6.   Click Play and head down to pick the DrawerMusic a few times, to makes sure the tray is repositioned after each maze reset.

Raft Ride

One task the player can perform without solving any puzzles is to retrieve the vial from behind the waterfall. In this version of the game, he won't be able to swim or walk to the falls; he'll take a ride on the raft. The raft is self-propelled and goes back and forth from shore to falls.

In case you are thinking there is no challenge in this task, you will also be creating a "death zone" that transports the player if he falls into the water while attempting to get off and on the raft.

Let's start by putting the vial into the little basin behind the falls.

1.   Select the Water Basin object and focus in on it.

2.   Select the Vial of Elixir and use Move to View to position in the basin (Figure 18-4, left).

Figure 18-4. The Vial of Elixir in the basin, without the Glass ➤ Stained Bump Distort shader (left) and with it (right)

3. Add the Interactor (and ObjectLookup) scripts to the vial.

4. Set them up as per the StateManagement PDF. (See the Source Code/Downloads tab of the book's Apress product page [www.apress.com/9781430248996].)

5. Tag it as an ActionObject.

6. Set the Lookup State 1, as follows:

    default,0,Vial of Elixir Icon,1

7. Set the Reply State 1, as follows:

    You carefully fit the vial into your pack

If you have Pro, you might wish to experiment with Glass Refraction shader for the Water Basin object. You can see what refraction will look like with less adjustment than the Pro water shaders.

1. If you have Pro, Import the Glass Refraction (Pro Only) package.

2. Select the Water Basin object and locate its material, Simple Water Still.

3. Duplicate the material and name it **Simple Refractive Water**.

4. Change its shader to FX ➤ Glass ➤ Stained Bump Distort.

5. Add the WaterBumpLow normal map to it.

6. Add the new material to the Water Basin object.

7. Click Play and adjust its Distortion slider (Figure 18-4, right).

If you are using Deferred Lighting, the basin is rendered after the small waterfall, so you will have to move the water basin down.

Let's get the raft working next. To move the raft, you will alter the V_PositionCycler script to create a new version for horizontal cyclic movement. Let's make this one move in the global Z direction.

1.   Select and focus in on the Raft object.

2.   Select the V_Position Cycler script.

3.   Duplicate it and rename the new script **Hz_Position Cycler**.

4.   In the script editor, Search menu, highlight a y and use Replace to change y to z.

5.   Set both range variables to **0.0**.

6.   Save the script and drag it onto the raft.

7.   Click Play and adjust the Up Range value until the raft reaches the far shore (about **22**).

8.   Set the Speed to about **0.4**.

9.   When you are happy with the settings, stop Play mode and make them permanent.

To make it more interesting, you can also add some bobbing motion.

1.   Add the V_PositionCycler script to the raft.

2.   Set the Up Range to **0.2**, the Down Range to **0.05**, and the Speed to **0.35**.

3.   Move the First Person Controller into the area.

4.   Click Play and take a ride on the raft.

5.   Get off and take the vial from the basin behind the falls.

Death Zone

So now, you will handle the player falling or jumping into the water. An object with a Box Collider already exists for use as a "death zone."

1.   Select the Death Zone object.

2.   Turn on its MeshRenderer for a minute, to see where it is positioned.

Note that it is set to Is Trigger, so the player will be able to fall through it.

3.   Create a new script and name it **DeathZone**.

4.   Add the following two variables:

```
var spawnPoint: Transform[]; // array of possible positions
var blackout : GameObject;
```

5.   Add the following function:

```
function OnTriggerEnter () {

//Instantiate(blackout);                                // trigger a fade in/out
   var element : int = Random.Range(0, spawnPoint.length); // choose a position from the array
   yield new WaitForSeconds(1.5);
   gameObject.Find("First Person Controller").transform.position = spawnPoint[element].position;
}
```

6. Save the script.

7. Add it to the Death Zone object.

You don't have a blackout object yet, but you can decide on a "spawn point" for the character to be transported to. The array will allow you to make as many as you wish.

1. Click Play and drive the player to the point you want for the spawn point.

2. Select the First Person Controller.

3. From the GameObject menu, choose Align View to Selected.

4. Stop Play mode.

5. Create a new Empty GameObject.

6. From the GameObject menu, choose Align with View.

7. Name it **SpawnPoint**.

8. Select the DeathZone object and set the Spawn Point array Size to **1**.

9. Drag the SpawnPoint object into the Spawn Point Element 0 field on the DeathZone's DeathZone component.

10. Change the array size and add more positions, as desired.

11. Click Play and test the new death zone by jumping into the water.

12. Exit Play mode.

Blackout

Any time you want to transport the player, it will be useful to have him black out while the transform occurs. This can be a scene that fades in and out of black, white, or whatever color you wish. There are several ways to create the effect. For this one, you will use a texture with an animated opacity.

1. Select the Crossfade object in the Hierarchy view.

2. Duplicate it and name it **Generic Crossfade**.

GUI Texture objects must be in normalized screen space (0-1); therefore, this one must be removed from the GameEnvironment group, so you can position it correctly. For GUI Texture objects, 0,0 is in the upper right of the viewport.

3. Drag it out of the GameEnvironment group.

4. Set its X and Y Positions to **0**.

It should now cover the Game view, but you won't see it, unless you click Play, because its alpha value is 0.

5. In the Inspector, note that it consists of a GUI Texture object, using a small white texture.

For the Pixel Inset, the Width and Height are set to 2048. That's a bit of overkill, but easier than creating a script to set the width and height in a script with Screen.width and Screen.height.

6. Next, take a look at its Animation component.

It has three animations, with the crossfade assigned as the default. Play Automatically is checked. When the scene starts, or the prefab is instantiated, the animation plays.

7.   From the Window menu, open the Animation editor.

8.   Open the GUITexture drop-down and select the color.a track.

9.   Turn on Record, click Play, then click to stop, so the view will zoom to the curve.

The alpha value goes from 0 to 1 then back to 0, causing the screen to go black then clear again. The entire animation takes three seconds.

The last component is a simple script that destroys the prefab after a set time.

1.   Close the Animation editor.

2.   Open the TimedDestructor script.

It contains a variable for the time and a line to kill the object it resides on.

```
var time : float = 1.5;

Destroy (gameObject,time); //destroy object after the specified amount of seconds seconds
```

3.   In the Inspector, make sure the time is set to 3, for the Generic Crossfade object.

4.   Click Play to see the effect play out and the Generic Crossfade disappear from the Hierarchy view.

5.   Stop Play mode.

So far, you have used several different camera layers in your scene. To make sure the fade occurs above them, you will have to assign it to the In View layer.

6.   In the Project view, assign the Crossfade to the In View layer.

And now, having seen how it works, you can create a prefab with it, remove it from the scene, and assign the prefab to the Death Zone object.

1.   Create a new prefab in the Adventure Prefabs folder and name it **Crossfade**.

2.   Drag the Generic Crossfade object onto it from the Hierarchy view.

3.   Delete the Generic Crossfade from the scene.

4.   Assign the Crossfade prefab to the Death Zone's Blackout parameter.

5.   Open the DeathZone script and uncomment the Instantiate line.

6.   Save the script.

7.   Click play and test by jumping into the water.

8.   Save the scene and save the project.

Locating the Crystal

You've already created the functionality for the rockfall and crystal, so, next, you will move and adapt it to the earth shrine, to tie it nicely into the game.

When you move the rock zone, the prefab rocks and crystal will no longer fall in the correct place. Because you used the simple version of Instantiate, their prefabs must be updated with the new locations.

691

And, finally, you will require a means of triggering the rockfall. The trigger object will be inside the shrine, where the First Person Controller cannot intersect it. For this challenge, you will let the player try to take the shrine's glyph. When the player picks it, it will drop, triggering the rockfall and crystal reveal.

1. Update the Crystal's Lookup State 1, as follows:

   default,0,Crystal Icon,1

2. Move the Crystal near the Shrine Earth object.

3. Drag the rock prefabs into the Hierarchy view, near the earth shrine.

4. Select the Rock Zone and move it to the earth shrine.

5. Turn on the Rock Zone's Mesh Renderer, so you can see to adjust its size and location.

6. Adjust the Rock Zone, so that it is slightly below the earth glyph and does not extend beyond the odd-looking bench with the hole in it (Figure 18-5).

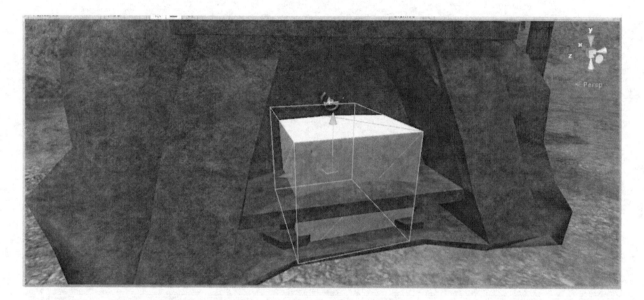

Figure 18-5. The Rock Zone positioned in the earth shrine

7. Position rock prefabs and the crystal between the ceiling and Rock Zone collider.

8. Update the prefabs at the top of the Inspector, as usual.

9. Turn off the Rock Zone's Mesh Renderer.

10. Click Play and watch the results.

11. Adjust the location of the crystal, if necessary, to increase the chances that it will fall forward into a pickable location.

12. Delete the rock prefabs from the scene.

The crystal can stay in scene, as it is at state 0, and the RockFall script transitions it to state 1.

Triggering the Rockfall

For this functionality, you will make the Earth Glyph an action object. This will provide the player with the clue that something must be done with it, as well as a means of remembering its state. The Earth Glyph will have three states, the third will be 2, in scene, but unpickable.

1. Select the Earth Glyph object in the shrine.

2. Add the Interactor [and ObjectLookup] scripts and set them up as per the StateManagement PDF. (See the Source Code/Downloads tab of the book's Apress product page [www.apress.com/9781430248996].)

3. Tag it as an ActionObject.

4. Set the Lookup State 1, as follows:

   default,2,s1_Earth Glyph,2

5. Set the Reply State 1, as follows:

   The glyph slips out of your hand as you pry it loose.

Its Mesh Collider is set to Convex, and the physics material is Wood.

To cause the glyph to fall on cue and intersect with the trigger, it will require a rigid body. But you don't want it until after the player picks the object, so you will add it during runtime, after the player picks the glyph.

To make sure all the distance checking is in place, you will initiate the action through the state machine with a call to DoTheJob. Read the comments to see what each line does.

6. Create a new script and name it **CueThePhysics**.

7. Add the following:

```
function DoTheJob () {

    gameObject.AddComponent (Rigidbody);    // adds the rigidbody component
    yield new WaitForSeconds(0.5);          // give it time to start falling
    rigidbody.AddForce(-50, 0, 0);          // push it away from the wall in the X direction

    yield new WaitForSeconds(10);           // wait for 5 seconds to let it play out and react
    rigidbody.isKinematic = true;           // disable physics

    yield;
    Destroy(this);                          // kill the script to prevent retriggering
}
```

8. Save the script.

9. Apply it to the Earth Glyph.

10. Click Play, pick the glyph, and watch as the Rigidbody component is added and the script removed.

11. Stop Play mode.

The crystal is now within reach of the player.

Access to the Temple

As you've seen, the temple steps must be lowered before the player will be able to go into the temple. Now that he is able to put the sleeve over the crystal to assemble the laser, it's time to give it a serious target.

1. Select the TempleStairs object and uncheck Play Automatically.

Defining a Target

2. Open the Laser script, add the following variables:

```
var target : GameObject;              // target for the lazer to do something when it
hits this
var actionObject : GameObject;        // object whose animation must be triggered
internal var triggered : boolean = false; // flag to prevent multiple triggers
```

3. In the Raycast conditional, change the if(hitParticles line to include a condition that it was also the correct target, as follows:

```
if (hitParticles && hit.transform.name == target.name) {
```

The target will be the StairLock object, the parent of the glyph in the middle of the wall. It conveniently has a sphere collider to enable the beam to identify it. The object that has the animation is the TempleStairs group. Because there will be several tasks related to hitting the target, and it should only trigger them once, you will create a function for them and use the triggered flag to monitor the action.

4. Just below the line that destroys the particle system prefabs, temp, add

```
if (!triggered) DoTheJob();
triggered = true; // set the flag to prevent more triggers
```

5. Now create the function that will handle all the details.

```
function DoTheJob () {

    actionObject.animation.Play(); // drop the stairs
}
```

6. Save the script.

7. Select the Crystal with Sleeve object.

8. Assign the two new parameters, StairLock, the Target, and TempleStairs, the Action Object.

As you saw earlier, TempleStairs already has the stair-drop animation ready to go. Now you will have to update the Crystal with Sleeve Icon pick to activate the object instead of the cursor. You will also be toggling the inventory mode off at the same time, through the Camera Inventory's DoTheJob function.

1. Change the Golden Sleeve Icon's Lookup State 1, Element 1 to

    default,0,Crystal with Sleeve,1,s1_Camera Inventory,0

2. Activate the Gear Handler and then select the Crystal with Sleeve object.

3. Add the Interactor and ObjectLookup scripts to it.

4. Fill them out as per the StateManagement PDF. (See the Source Code/Downloads tab of the book's Apress product page www.apress.com/9781430248996.)

5. Tag it as an ActionObject.

6. Click Play and test by manually activating the Crystal with Sleeve and hitting the target with the beam.

The stairs fall on cue! Once in the temple, you can put the laser back in inventory, by clicking on it, as with any of the other Action Objects.

7. Restart Play mode and gather the two component objects in the scene, then combine them in inventory to activate the laser device.

In the maze, you probably discovered the device was going through walls when you got too close. The usual solution for this issue is to create a camera exclusively for the weapon that draws on top of the other layers.

1. Change the Crystal with Sleeve's Initial State to 1 for a while.

2. Create a new layer in User Layer 11 and name it **Weapons**.

3. Duplicate the Main Camera and name it **Camera Weapons**.

4. Delete the children and remove the MouseLook script and Audio Listener from it.

5. Set its Clear Flags to Depth Only and its Culling Mask to Weapons.

6. Set its Depth to **1**.

7. Drag the new camera onto the Main Camera.

8. Uncheck Weapons on the Main Camera's Culling Mask.

9. Assign the Weapons layer to the Crystal with Sleeve object.

10. Click Play, turn the device on manually, and drive toward a wall.

This time the Crystal with Sleeve stays visible.

By now, you are probably starting to think about minor details, such as the First Person Controller being in the way of the stairs when they drop.

More on Layer Masks

To prevent an altercation between the First Person Controller and the stone staircase, a collider to prevent the player from getting too close, either from the front or climbing the sides, will be required. The problem will be to block the First Person Controller but not the raycast, as it also looks for a collider. The collider is already in place for you.

1. Select the TempleBlocker object.

2. Turn on its Mesh Renderer and Box Collider to see where it is in the scene.

3. Remove or disable the Mesh Renderer.

4. Set its Layer to Default for now.

5. Click Play and try running into it.

6. Now try Shooting the laser into it.

The laser and the First Person Controller are stopped by the object's collider. So now, you must find a way to have the physics raycast ignored, while the collider stops objects, such as the First Person Controller. It turns out there is a predefined layer you can use with no extra scripting—Layer number 2—Ignore Raycast.

1. Assign the Temple Blocker to the Ignore Raycast layer again.

2. Click Play and test the laser against it.

This time, the laser goes through, but the First Person Controller can't get close enough to be squashed. The only problem now is that he still can't get through the blocker to go up the steps. For that, you will have to turn the blocker's collider off.

You might also want to cause the player to bounce a bit when the stairs hit the ground, and it would be a good idea to decide whether the laser has used up its charge and should be shut down.

Most of these little extras will be dependent on the length of the animation. You can get that easily, as you already have contact with it.

1. In the Laser script, add a couple of new variables:

```
var templeBlocker : Collider;        // prevent player from standing under stairs
var fpc : Transform;                 // first person controller
```

2. And in the DoTheJob function, add

```
templeBlocker.collider.enabled = false; // disable blocker
// wait until the animation is almost done
yield new WaitForSeconds(actionObject.animation.clip.length - 0.05);
GetComponent(Laser).enabled = false;   // disable the laser script
hitLight.gameObject.SetActive(false);  // deactivate laser light
laser.gameObject.SetActive(false);     // kill the line renderer
fpc.position.y = fpc.position.y + 0.1; // "bump" the player up a bit
//animation.Play();                    // kill the crystal color
```

3. Assign the new parameters, the Temple Blocker and the First Person Controller, to the Crystal with Sleeve.

4. Click Play and test.

The final bit of functionality, a nice touch, is to change the crystal color to black, to show that it's spent. For that, you will animate the color of the crystal's shader.

1. Select the Crystal with Sleeve and open it in the Animation view.

2. Create New Clip in the Animation clips folder and name it **dead crystal**.

3. Open the Crystal (Material).

4. Turn on the Record button.

5. Select the Color.r, .g and .b tracks.

6. Move the time indicator to 2:00, click the Add Keyframe button.

7. Move the time indicator to 4:00 by panning the view (middle mousedown).

8. In the Inspector, change the material's Color to black.

9. At the bottom of the Animation view, set the wrap to Once (Figure 18-6).

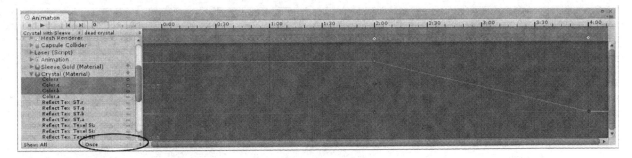

Figure 18-6. The dead crystal clip set to Once

10. Close the Animation view.

11. In the Inspector, in the newly added Animation component, uncheck Play Automatically and make sure dead crystal is set as the default Animation.

12. In the Laser script, uncomment the last animation line.

```
animation.Play(); // kill the crystal color
```

13. Save the script and click Play.

The sequence plays out nicely, and the player can go up the temple stairs as the laser crystal darkens and quits working.

1. Select the Crystal with Sleeve.

2. Change its ObjectLookup and Interactor metadata as per the StateManagement PDF to add the new state. (See the Source Code/Downloads tab of the book's Apress product page [www.apress.com/9781430248996].)

3. Set the Crystal with Sleeve's Lookup State 2, Element 0 to

    default,0,Spent Crystal Icon,1

4. Change the Crystal with Sleeve's Reply State 2, Element 0 to

You stuff the spent laser device carelessly into your pack.
Once the Crystal with Sleeve has been put into state 2, spent, you will use the Spent Crystal Icon in inventory. To make things simpler, you won't be able to take the laser in hand, once in inventory. There are several related states that must be notified, so you will require a small script to handle the work.

5. Create a new script and name it **QuickChange**.

6. Add the following to the Start function:

```
yield;
if (GetComponent(Interactor).currentState == 2){
   renderer.materials[1].color = Color.black;
   GameObject.Find("TempleBlocker").collider.enabled = false; // disable blocker
   GetComponent(Laser).enabled = false;                       // disable the laser script
   GameObject.Find("Laser Light").SetActive(false);           // deactivate laser light
   GameObject.Find("Laser").SetActive(false);                 // kill the line renderer
}
```

In case you're curious, to recharge the laser, you could set the animation clip speed to -1, to play it backward.

7.   Save the script and add it to the Crystal with Sleeve object.

Although triggering the stair animation directly was a quick way to implement functionality, later in the project, you will be saving and loading games, so you will want to know if the stairs are up or down. The action objects with the Interactor script have a lot of parameters to keep track of, but the State manages them all, so that only a single integer need be saved. For that reason, it is worth the extra effort to make the StairLock into an Action Object. It will require three states: out of scene, up/locked, and down.

1.   Select the StairLock object.

2.   Set its tag to Action Object.

3.   Add the Interactor (and ObjectLookup) scripts.

4.   Fill in the metadata as per the StateManagement PDF.

5.   Set the Name to Key Glyph.

6.   For the Animation Clip, Element 2, select the *Stair Drop* clip.

7.   Drag the TempleStairs into its Ani Object parameter.

At this point, you should be able to mouse over and pick the StairLock and obtain all of the usual action-object functionality. The interaction will not be initiated through a mouse pick, but it will still go through the usual code, so you will have to fill out the Object Lookup as well.

1.   Set Lookup State 1 and Reply State 1 to Size 1.

2.   For Lookup State 1, Element 0, add

      default,2,s0_Crystal with Sleeve,2

3.   For Reply State 1, Element 0, add

Hit by the laser, the glyph rotates and the stairs lower with a resounding thud

To reroute the code, the laser hit gets sent to the ProcessObject function on the StairLock object instead of the DoTheJob function. The DoTheJob function gets called from the special cases code in the ObjectLookup. It's an extra step, but keeps the Action Object functionality consistent.

1.   Open the Laser script.

2.   Replace:

```
if (!triggered) DoTheJob();
```

with:

```
if (!triggered) {
   // call the target's LookupState function, send its current state, 1, and tell it the default
cursor was the picker
   target.GetComponent(ObjectLookup).LookUpState(target,1,"default");
}
```

3.   Save the script.

4.   Click Play and make sure everything still works.

5. Select the Crystal with Sleeve and change the Initial State back to 0 in the
Interactor component.

6. Save the scene and save the project.

Meeting Gimbok

With the laser built, the player now has access to the temple. On reaching the balcony via the narrow passage,
he does what any normal adventurer does—he tries to take the golden topi fruit he finds in the bowl in the niche.
For his transgression, he finds himself transported to the maze, where he can have a conversation with Gimbok.

On the technical side, a lot happens with the pick. The topi fruit does not change states, but you will be creating
a DoTheJob function to trigger a blackout, cause the world to spin (if you have Pro), activate Gimbok, and, of course,
transport the player into the maze. And because the First Person Controller is in the temple, the terrain must be
moved back up too.

Topi Fruit

Let's start with the topi fruit in the temple, because it starts the whole sequence of events. It requires two states, but
will have to be picked by the Rock icon before it goes out of scene.

1. Select the Topi Fruit object.

2. Add the Interactor (and ObjectLookup) scripts and set them up as per the
StateManagement PDF. (See the Source Code/Downloads tab of the book's Apress product
page www.apress.com/9781430248996.)

3. Create a new script and name it **TopiMagic**.

4. Add the following variables to it:

```
var crossfade : GameObject;          // the crossfade prefab
var mazeCharacter : GameObject;      // want character not parent
var fpc : GameObject;                // the first person controller
var fpcWaypoint : GameObject;        // the placeholder
internal var maze : GameObject;      // object with MazeManager script, MazeWalls
var mazeSound : AudioClip;
var terrain : GameObject;            // to be able to reset the terrain
internal var terrainPosY : float;    // original y position
```

5. Add the following Start function:

```
function Start () {

   terrain = GameObject.Find("Terrain");
   terrainPosY = terrain.transform.position.y ; // get terrain y pos
}
```

6. Create the DoTheJob function:

```
function DoTheJob () {

}
```

7. Inside it, activate Gimbok and update his state.

```
// activate and update character's state
mazeCharacter.SetActive(true);
mazeCharacter.GetComponent(Interactor).currentState = 1;
```

8. Scramble the maze and check Gimbok's position.

```
// reset maze
var mazeManager : MazeManager = GameObject.Find("Maze Walls").GetComponent(MazeManager);
mazeManager.ResetMaze(); // scramble the maze
// make sure the way out from Gimbok character is open,
// 100 value is trapLimit to clear more than 4 wall trap
mazeManager.CheckDropPoint(mazeCharacter,100.00);
```

9. Move the terrain back up.

```
// raise terrain
terrain.transform.position.y = terrainPosY;
```

10. Cue an Image Effect (if you have Pro).

```
// cue the twirl effect
//GameObject.Find("Camera Weapon").camera.animation.Play();
```

11. Cue the Audio.

```
AudioSource.PlayClipAtPoint(mazeSound,fpc.transform.position); // play at character's position
```

12. Cue the crossfade and allow time for it to play a bit.

```
Instantiate(crossfade);
yield new WaitForSeconds(1.5);
```

13. And, finally, transport the character.

```
// move player
fpc.transform.position = fpcWaypoint.transform.position;
fpc.transform.rotation.eulerAngles.y = 130.0; // hard code to face npc
```

14. Save the script and add it to the Topi Fruit object.

Before testing the script, you will set up the locations for both Gimbok and the First Person Controller. Because finding your way around the maze can be tedious, Gimbok will always be in the center, DropPoint16, and the First Person Controller will always be transported in close proximity.

1. Change the Scene view to an iso top view.

2. Select DropPoint16, the maze center drop point.

3. Drag the Gimbok Prefab into the Hierarchy view.

4. Assign the First Person Controller as his Target in the Billboard Look At component.

5. Move the Gimbok Group to DropPoint16, being careful to center it on the point in the X and Z.

6. Set his Y Position to **56.3**.

7. Create a cube at DropPoint16's location and scale it to **5.1×1×5.1**.

This represents the area between the walls for each cell.

1. Move the First Person Controller to the same point, then back him away into the upper left corner (so Gimbok will be facing the light), about half a meter from the two sides of the cube (see Figure 18-7).

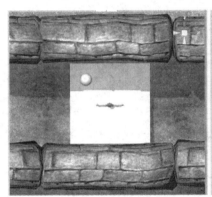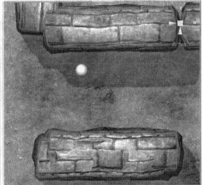

Figure 18-7. Positioning the First Person Controller

2. Set its Y rotation to 130 and check the Game view to make sure the First Person Controller is facing the Gimbok character. If not, adjust the Y rotation until you get a good forward view of the character. Replace the 130 value in the TopiMagic script with your new value and save the script.

3. Delete the cube.

4. Click Play several times and check the First Person Controller's position after the maze reset (Figure 18-7).

5. Make sure the First Person Controller is a little above the ground, so he'll fall a little after the transport.

6. Focus the view to him, then create an Empty GameObject and name it **FPC Waypoint**.

7. Make sure its position matches the First Person Controller's.

And now you should be ready to load the various objects into the Inspector.

8. Select the Topi Fruit.

9. Drag the appropriate objects into the Topi Magic component's various parameters (Figure 18-8).

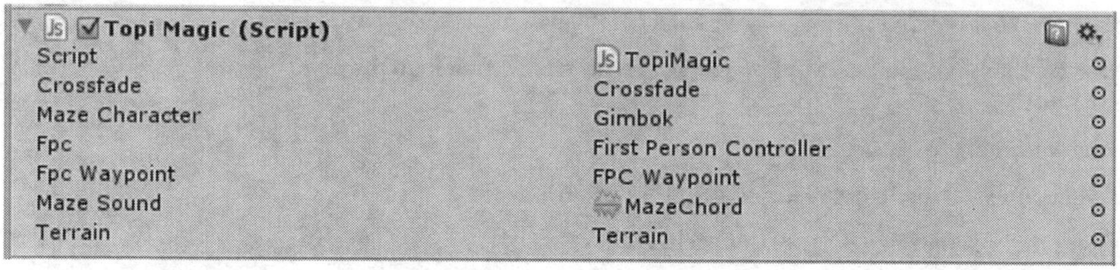

Js	✓ Topi Magic (Script)		🔲 ✿,
Script		Js TopiMagic	◎
Crossfade		Crossfade	◎
Maze Character		Gimbok	◎
Fpc		First Person Controller	◎
Fpc Waypoint		FPC Waypoint	◎
Maze Sound		MazeChord	◎
Terrain		Terrain	◎

Figure 18-8. *The Topi Fruit's TopiMagic parameters*

Making the World Spin (Pro Only)

If you have Unity Pro, you can use one of the Image Effects to make the view spin just before the player blacks out. Because the Camera Weapon layer is drawn after Camera Main, you will want to put the effect on it, rather than Camera Main. If you choose to use the Crossfade and Vortex together, you may have to set all cameras to Forward rending path. Be sure to save before testing.

1. If you have Pro, from the right-click menu or the Assets menu, Import Package, select the Image Effect (Pro Only) package and import it.

2. Select the Camera Weapon and set its Rendering Path to Forward, so it will play nicely with other effects.

3. From the Component menu, Image Effects, select Vortex.

4. Play with the Angle amount a bit to see what it does, then set it to **0**.

5. Open the Animation window and Create New Clip in the Animation Clips folder.

6. Name the new clip **twirly**.

7. Turn on Record and add Keyframe to the Vortex Effect's Angle track.

8. Set the Angle value to **0**.

9. Move the time indicator to 1:30 and set the Angle to **1422**.

The Game view twists into a vortex.

10. At 3:00, set the Angle back to **0**.

11. Scrub the time indicator to see the effect.

12. Close the Animation window and make sure the twirly clip is set as the Animation component's default.

13. Uncheck Play Automatically.

A few more steps, and you will be ready to test the transport.

1. Open the TopiMagic script.

2. If you've got Pro, uncomment the camera line.

```
GameObject.Find("Camera Weapon").camera.animation.Play();
```

3. Save the script.

4. Position the First Person Controller inside the temple, in front of the ledge with the topi fruit.

5. Click Play and pick the topi fruit.

After a brief blackout, the player is left in the maze, where he should be left facing the Gimbok character.

Acquiring the Rock

At this point, you are ready to have Gimbok conjure up a nice topi-size rock that the player will be able to substitute for the golden topi. The fun bit about this one is to let physics drop the rock for you. The tricky bit is that the drop location will vary, because Gimbok always turns to face the player. To account for that, you will create an empty gameObject that lives inside the Gimbok Group. When the rock is activated, it will use the current location as its drop point.

1. Select Gimbok and focus in on him in the maze.

2. Select the Rock from the Rock Group and duplicate it.

3. Rename it **Topi Rock** and remove it from the group.

4. Move it to the center of the tray.

5. Scale it to fit nicely on the tray, about **0.5~0.6** (Figure 18-9).

Figure 18-9. *The rock scaled to fit the tray*

6. Change the Sphere Collider to a Box Collider and add a Rigidbody component to it.

7. Remembering that Gimbok will be sitting, drag it up about even with his loincloth.

Before testing, you will have to deal with a couple of colliders.

8. Select the tray and add a Box Collider to it.

9. Select Gimbok and reduce his collider's Radius to **0.22**.

10. Click Play and check the drop.

Depending on where the First Person Controller is, the rock may or may not drop onto the tray. When you've got a good place from which to drop the rock, you'll have to make the location holder.

1. Stop Play mode and select the Topi Rock.

2. Drag it onto the Gimbok Group in the Hierarchy.

Next, you will have to set up the Topi Rock data and then create the script that handles everything that must be carried out. It will have two states and no animation.

3. Set up the Interactor and ObjectLookup as per the StateManagement PDF. (See the Source Code/Downloads tab of the book's Apress product page www.apress.com/9781430248996.)

4. For Lookup State 1, Element 0, add:

   default,0,TopiRock Icon,1

5. For Reply State 1, Element 0, add

You take the rock, barely managing to fit it into your pack.

Although the Rock is activated or transitioned into state 1 as part of the conversation, it can still be handled by the regular scripts. To make the rock more efficient, you will be doing most of the work in a DoTheJob function.

Right now, when the rock drops onto the moving tray, the physics are being constantly updated. If the player grabs the rock quickly, there's no problem; the rock is deactivated. But if he goes off without it, it will suck up resources needlessly. What you can do instead is turn on Is Kinematic, after it has landed on the tray. The trick here is that it will have to be made a child of the Gimbok Group, so that it will inherit the "floating" motion. Let's create the script that will manage the rock's transition.

1. Create a new script and name it **TopiRockHandler**.

2. Create a new function to handle the work.

```
function DoTheJob () {

}
```

3. After a short yield, update the Rigidbody and put the rock into the next state.

```
yield new WaitForSeconds(0.5); // allow the rock to drop and settle
rigidbody.isKinematic = true;  // turn off regular physics
```

4. Save the script.

5. Add it to the Topi Rock object.

6. Fill out the parameters (Figure 18-10).

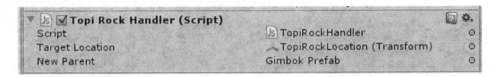

Figure 18-10. *The Topi Rock' Handler parameters*

To call the function, you will have to revisit the Dialogue Manager script's SpecialInstructions function.

1. Open the DialogueManager script.

2. Add the following variable:

```
var topiRock : GameObject;// the rock will require activating
```

3. Inside the SpecialInstructions function, above case "01"'s break statement, add the following:

```
topiRock.SetActive(true);                //activate the rock
topiRock.SendMessage("ProcessObject",1); //trigger the action
```

4. Save the script.

5. Assign the topi rock to the new parameter in the Dialogue Manager.

6. Assign Gimbok as Character, Element 1.

7. Click Play and test the sequence from picking the topi fruit in the temple to acquiring the topi rock.

Gimbok is beaned heavily on the head when the rock materializes above his Capsule collider. While it might be entertaining to have him yell "ouch" when hit, you should probably just solve the problem.

1. Open the TopiRockHandler script.

2. Add the following variable:

```
var gimbok : Collider; // required for collision ignore
```

3. Inside the Start function, add

```
// make sure the rock can drop to the tray
Physics.IgnoreCollision(this.collider, gimbok);
```

4. Save the script.

5. Assign Gimbok to the Gimbok parameter.

6. Click Play and test the sequence from topi fruit to rock.

With Gimbok functioning well, it's time to turn him off and make sure he is activated on cue.

7. Change Gimbok's Initial State to 0.

8. Click Play.

Meeting Kahmi

With the rock tucked safely in inventory, the player will now be able to swap it out for the golden topi fruit. But he doesn't yet know what to do with it in order to finish the game. For that, he'll have to talk to the other character, Kahmi, the second NPC. Not only does she provide clues, she will also clear the way into the tunnels for the player.

Like Gimbok, she will not appear until the player has completed a certain task—in this case, acquiring the Golden Topi Fruit object. Until she appears, she will reside in the passageway opposite the one that leads up to the balcony. That way, when the player comes down with the topi fruit, he will be looking straight at her, as he passes through the doorway, which will also trigger her to start moving toward him.

So, the first task will be to set the other passage door to an open state when the fruit is picked. It has three states, the third being in scene and not pickable, its initial state.

1. Add the Interactor (and ObjectLookup) scripts onto the Door Lower.

2. Fill in the settings for both as per the StateManagement PDF. (See the Source Code/Downloads tab of the book's Apress product page www.apress.com/9781430248996.)

3. In its Animation component, check Play Automatically.

4. Focus in on the Door Lower and click Play to make sure the animation works.

5. Stop Play mode and uncheck Play Automatically.

6. While you are positioning Kahmi, set the door's Z rotation to **-80**.

7. Drag the Kahmi prefab inside the doorway, but back far enough not to be hit by the opening door.

8. Drag the Collider Start prefab into the scene as well.

9. Assign the First Person Controller and Start Collider to Kahmi's Simple AI component.

10. Assign Kahmi as the Element 2 Character in the Dialogue Manager.

To prevent her from following the player around any corners and getting stuck, you will have to make a barricade.

1. Create a cube and scale it to about **30×1.5×0.3**.

2. Name it **NPC_Barricade**.

3. Position it so it blocks the two passages up to the exit and the doorway into the inner chamber (see Figure 18-11).

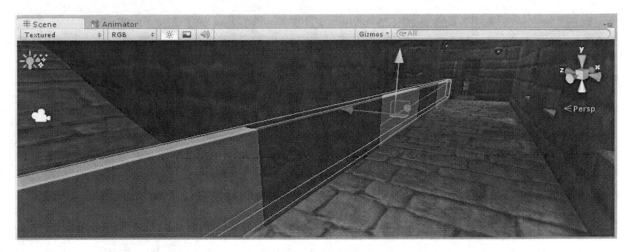

Figure 18-11. *The barracade in the temple*

4. From the NPC Assets, Scripts folder, drag the NPC_Barrier script onto the new object.

5. Disable its Mesh Renderer component.

6. Assign Kahmi as the Target.

7. Set the door's Z rotation back to **0**.

If you were to test the barricade now, you would discover a slight problem—it also blocks the First Person Controller. You will use the same IgnoreCollision you used for Gimbok and the rock. Because it can only be used on active objects, you will want to call it from an Awake function, so that it is run before the Kahmi character is deactivated in the Start function.

8. Add the following Awake function to the NPC_Barrier script:

```
function Awake () {

    var fpc : GameObject = GameObject.Find("First Person Controller");
    // make sure the fpc can get through the barrier
    Physics.IgnoreCollision(this.collider, fpc.collider);
}
```

9. Save the script.

Activating Kahmi

Here's the easy part: Kahmi and the door get activated through the regular scripts.

1. Check the Topi Fruit's ObjectLookup and change the Lookup State2, Element 0 is, as follows:

TopiRock Icon,1,TopiRock Icon,0,TopiRock Ledge,1,Topi Fruit,0,Topi Fruit Icon,1,Kahmi,1,Door Lower,1

When the Golden Topi is picked by the Topi Rock cursor, the Topi Fruit and TopiRock Icon-go out of scene, 0. The Topi Fruit Icon goes into inventory,1; the rock is left in the bowl; the Lower Door is opened,1; and Kahmi is activated,1. So, the only thing not yet covered is the replacement rock. For that, you can simply duplicate the original.

2. Select the TopiRock, duplicate it, and remove it from the Gimbok group.

3. Rename it **TopiRock Ledge**, and position it in the bowl where the topi fruit is.

4. Scale it up to be about the same size as the topi fruit.

5. Remove the Rigidbody and TopiRockHandler components.

6. Change its data as per the StateManagement PDF. (See the Source Code/Downloads tab of the book's Apress product page www.apress.com/9781430248996.)

7. Set the TopiRock Icon's Initial State to 1, for testing.

8. Click Play and test the sequence.

Once the player takes the topi fruit, Kahmi is activated and approaches the First Person Controller as soon as he is close enough.

9. Try escaping Kahmi by going through the invisible barricade.

The First Person Controller gets through, but Kahmi, after a few moments of useless effort, goes back to her start position.

Kahmi Magic

Once the player is able to talk to Kahmi, she will give him the information required to finish the quest. In addition to giving him the location, the tunnels, and a hint about a light source, she will unblock the entrance to the tunnel and create a path leading the player to it.

For the blocked entrance, it would seem a simple deactivate would work, but it's state is a critical one that must be saved and loaded, so it will be run through the action object system. This also lets the player identify it as an object that can be affected in the game.

1. Select the Rock Plug object.

2. Add the Interactor (and ObjectLookup) scripts.

3. Tag it as an Action Object.

4. Adjust the settings for both as per the StateManagement PDF. (See the Source Code/Downloads tab of the book's Apress product page www.apress.com/9781430248996.)

As well as removing the rock plug, Kahmi lights a path to the entryway. For this, you will be using a projector. If you were starting from scratch, you would import the Projector package, but in this case, the setup was fiddly, so you have been provided with one that is already in the correct place and has the correct settings. Before activating it, you will get a little practice to see how projectors work.

1. Focus in on the Dome object.

2. From the Standard Assets folder, Projector folder, drag a Blob Light Projector into the scene and over the dome.

3. Move it up and down until you can see the light pattern projected on the dome (Figure 18-12).

Figure 18-12. *The projector light shining on the dome*

The Material is using the Light texture as its "Cookie," a film term for a mask that lets the light show through in the cutout pattern. The falloff controls how the light fades as it approaches the projectors Far Clip Plane.

4. Replace the Falloff texture with the White texture and move the Blob Light Projector up and down.

This time, the light spot ends abruptly when the projector is raised beyond the Far Clip Plane.
One other important thing to know about projectors is that, generally, the texture is set to clamp rather than repeat.

5. Select the Cookie's Light texture.

6. In the Inspector, change its Wrap Mode to Repeat and click Apply.

7. Adjust the projector to see the result.

The light spots appear all across the dome (Figure 18-13).

Figure 18-13. *The projector light's texture set to Repeat*

8. Change the Wrap Type back to Clamp and Apply.

9. Replace the White Texture with the original Falloff Texture.

10. Delete the Blob Light Projector.

As you've probably realized by now, projectors are used to make simple blob shadows and glowing light spots under characters in a lot of overhead iso-view games. In this game, the usage is different but gives an interesting way to mark a path. When used with characters, you would use layers, to prevent the light from affecting the character it is over, just as you did earlier in the book with the blob shadow.

1. Select the Path to Tunnels object and enable the Projector component.

The light projector, coupled with the ChalkPath texture, gives the player a dotted line right up to the entrance to the tunnels (Figure 18-14). Because this is another state that should be tracked, you will have to do a bit more setup.

Figure 18-14. *The Path to Tunnels created by the projector light*

2. Add the Interactor (and ObjectLookup) scripts to the Path to Tunnels object.

3. Tag it as an Action Object.

4. Adjust the settings for both as per the StateManagement PDF.

With the Rock Plug and Path to Tunnels prepared, you can have Kahmi change their states. Because they only activate or deactivate the objects, they don't have to be run through the Object Lookup.

1. Open the DialogueManager script.

2. Inside the `SpecialInstructions` function, above case "02"s break statement, add the following:

```
var rock : GameObject = GameObject.Find("Rock Plug");
rock.SetActive(false);
rock.GetComponent(Interactor). currentState= 0;

path.SetActive(true);
path.GetComponent(Interactor). currentState= 1;
```

The path, like the topi rock, starts out deactivated and can't be "found" like the Rock Plug. Until now, you would have added a variable for it and dragged the correct object into it in the Inspector. But having had a taste of the Awake function and how it is called *before* the various action objects are deactivated in the `Start` function, you will be using it to find the path.

3. Add the following variable:

```
internal var path : GameObject;                 // the projector light
```

4. And "find" it in the `Awake` function.

```
function Awake () {
    path = GameObject.Find("Path to Tunnels");// find path before it is deactivated
}
```

5. Save the script.

Because it will now require you to play through almost all of the game to test the latest additions, you will want to change the states on inventory items once again, to bypass the regular sequence of events.

6. Click Play and work through the sequence and conversation with Kahmi.

After she has helped you, check the Scene view to make sure the path has been turned on and the rock plug removed.

Map of Tunnels

While you are still testing in the temple, you may as well set up the last clue. This one is not crucial to the game but makes an interesting addition.

1. Deactivate the Terrain while you set up the map.

2. Select the Map object and focus in on it.

It has a deactivated Interactive Cloth component. The cloth object has a couple of issues that pertain to using it as an action object. First, you can't pick it, so it must have a stand-in collider. Second, to get it to drape nicely for state one, you would have to fiddle with the friction, but then it wouldn't slide off into state two. To get control of it for both scenarios, you can simply turn the Interactive Cloth component off and on, as required.

3. Turn on the Cloth Renderer.

4. Click Play and turn on the Interactive Cloth Component.

The cloth slips down to the floor in a crumpled heap and continues to shiver, sucking up resources.

5. Click Play again, but this time, turn the component off and on a few times.

The map freezes in its current configuration whenever the component is turned off, then resumes its downward progress when the component is turned on again. So the answer becomes a means of setting timers to control where it stops. For that, you will create a little script that puts it into the start position, draped, and, when triggered, lets it slide to the floor and stop.

6. Create a new script and name it **ToggleCloth**.

7. Add the following variable:

```
var delay : float = 3; // time to allow cloth to get into draped configuration
```

8. Create the Start function as follows:

```
function Start () {

    yield new WaitForSeconds(delay);                    // let cloth fall
    GetComponent(InteractiveCloth).enabled = false; // freeze it
}
```

9. And next, create the familiar DoTheJob function.

```
function DoTheJob () { // drop cloth to crumpled state

    GetComponent(InteractiveCloth).enabled = true;
    yield new WaitForSeconds(5);
    GetComponent(InteractiveCloth).enabled = false;
}
```

10. Save the script and add it to the Map object.

The map will require three states: out of scene, draped, and crumpled.

1. Turn on its Interactive Cloth component.

2. Add the Interactor (and LookupState) scripts to the map and fill them out as per the StateManagement PDF. (See the Source Code/Downloads tab of the book's Apress product page www.apress.com/9781430248996.)

3. Tag it as an Action Object.

You'll require a Map Icon. Because it acts similarly to the Message Icon, it is a quick setup.

4. Duplicate the Message Icon and name it Map Icon.

5. Change its metadata as per the StateManagement PDF.

6. To see how the player will interact with the cloth object, select the Box Collider, so you can see its bounds and click play.

The cloth settles on the old grain sack, well within the collider. When it is triggered into the crumpled state by the player, it will still be within the collider, allowing the player to interact with it.

The map, just like the initial message, can be read when the player is finally able to take it. Having already worked out the technicalities of reading the message, you can just copy its metadata and make the changes necessary for the map.

1. Select the MessageView object.

2. Add it to the In View layer.

3. Click Play and watch it in the Scene view.

4. Turn on the Camera View.

You will create a collider to make the interactive cloth pickable, and it should fill the screen, just like the MessageView's collider.

1. Add a Box Collider to the MapView and set it to Is Trigger.

2. Turn on Gizmos in the Game view.

3. Set the collider's X, Y, and Z Centers to **0**.

4. Slowly set the collider scale to X, **35**, Y, **25,** and Z, **25**, watching the collider as you change its size.

Next, you can copy and paste action object scripts from the MessageView to the MapView.

1. Add the Interactor (and ObjectLookup) scripts to it.

2. Copy and paste the values from the Message View object's Interactor and ObjectLookup to it.

3. Adjust the metadata according to the StateManagement PDF.

4. Make sure Use Alpha is turned off, because the map uses the alpha channel.

5. Click Play and test the map functionality, starting at the grain sacks, adding it to inventory and then looking at it and putting it away again.

The player now has access to the tunnels and a map to guide him through them. If you are thinking that the task seems too simple, you'd be correct. There's one more obstacle you'll want to include in the mix. The tunnels should be dark, requiring the player to obtain a light source. Let's take care of that first.

Acquiring a Light Source

Remember that odd looking pollen ball that is revealed when the wilted plant is revived? It turns out that, in this strange place, it makes quite a decent light source. To provide a clue to its functionality, you will add a few more things to the plant sequence, when you are setting it up in the plant shrine, Shrine Flora.

1. Select the Flower object and move it to the Shrine Flora object

2. Position it on top of the center pedestal, as shown in Figure 18-15.

Figure 18-15. *The flower in Shrine Flora*

3.　Select the Glow Ball from inside the Flower hierarchy.

4.　Add a Light component to it from the Rendering submenu and set the Type to Point.

5.　Set the Range to **2.4**, the Color to a nice yellow, and the Intensity to **0**.

6.　Set LightMapping to Realtime Only.

The light's Intensity must be animated once the flower has revived. Because it is all part of the revive behavior, you can tack it onto that, after you duplicate the original clip.

1.　Select the Flower object and click on its lg flower revive clip, to select it in the Project view.

2.　Duplicate the clip and change its name to **flower revive new**.

3.　Move the new clip to the Animation Clips folder.

4.　Select the Flower and change its Animation Clip, Element 1 to the flower revive new clip.

5.　Make the change for the animation clip in the Interactor as well.

6.　Select the Pollen Ball object and open the Animation editor.

7.　Select the flower revive new clip.

8.　Click to open the Light component in the list and select the Intensity track.

9.　Turn on Record and move the time indicator to 2:20 in the time line.

10.　Click Add Keyframe.

11.　Move the time indicator to 4:00 and set the Intensity value up to **7.33**.

12.　Scrub through the time line to see the full animation.

13.　Select the Flower and load the new clip into the Interactor.

The light comes on as the flower opens.

1. Close the Animation editor.

2. Click Play and test the flower revive sequence.

3. Drive the First Person Controller back, to get a good view of the flower in its new position, and then match the Scene view to it.

4. Select the Target Flower and Target Flower Look and move them as one, to get a good view of the flower revive again.

5. Rotate the Target Flower Look, so that its local Z looks toward the flower again (Figure 18-16).

Figure 18-16. *The light in the Pollen Ball*

6. Add the Light Ball Icon to the Flower's Lookup State 1, Element 1.

   default,2,c0_Flower,0,p0_Flower,0,Light Ball Icon,1

7. Click Play and test the flower revive sequence, then collect the pollen ball.

When the pollen ball is collected, it is deactivated, turning off the light.

While you could decide the player must have the pollen ball in hand (as cursor) to explore the tunnels, it will be simpler just to have a light automatically turn on when required. For that, you will create a light that will reside on the player.

1. Focus in on the First Person Controller.

2. Create a new Point Light and name it **TorchLight**.

3. Drop it onto the Main Camera inside the First Person Controller.

4. Set the Range to **20**, the Color to a pale yellow, and the Intensity to **2**.

5. Disable the Light component.

The last detail that requires attention is the vial of elixir. It will have to activate the flower. You can see the full metadata for the flower in the StateManagemnt PDF. (See the Source Code/Downloads tab of the book's Apress product page [www.apress.com/9781430248996].) It will require two elements for Lookup State and Reply State 1, one for default, and one for the Vial of Elixir Icon. It already gets instantiated but has to have its location updated to the new flower position.

1. Select the Flower.

2. Change the Lookup State 1, Element 0, as follows:

   default,1

3. Change the Reply State 1, Element 0, as follows:

   The wilted flower doesn't respond to your prodding

4. Change the Lookup State 1, Element 1, as follows:

   Vial of Elixir Icon,2,c0_Flower,0,p0_Flower,0,Vial of Elixir Icon,0

5. Change the Reply State 1, Element 1, as follows:

   You pour the life-giving elixir over the wilted plant and watch the plant revive

6. Drag the Vial Animated prefab into the scene about halfway between the Flower and the ceiling of the shrine.

7. Click Apply to update the prefab, and then delete it from the scene.

The Tunnels

Any tunnel worthy of an adventurer's effort must be dark enough to require a light source to enable the player to navigate its passageways. This one is no exception. The problem is that, even if you turn off the scene light, ambient light is still around. And objects with baked light that contain a measure of self-illumination are still visible as well.

The other problem is that even if the player bumbles around fully in the dark, this tunnel is small enough that he could eventually find his way out merely by chance. To prevent that from happening, you will be using the Crossfade prefab with a relocation. Let's start by looking at the tunnel complex. Because the tunnels are an integral part of the dome, it will be challenging to see them.

1. Change the Scene view display mode to Wireframe.

2. Select the Terrain and disable it, so the view will not be so cluttered.

3. Select the Tunnel and focus in on it.

4. With the map in mind, examine the tunnel system (Figure 18-17).

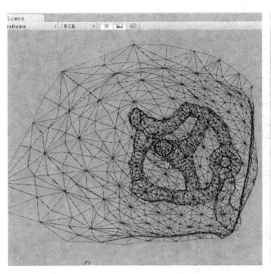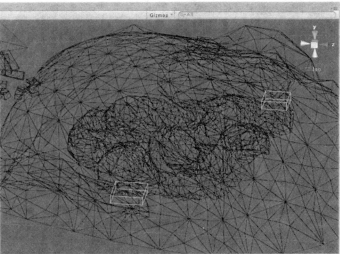

Figure 18-17. *The Dome object's tunnel system visible with the Wireframe display mode*

5. Toggle off the Overlay button to turn off lights and sky.

6. Select the Trigger Group to locate the two Fog Trigger objects.

To enter, the player falls into a small chamber from the hole at the top of the dome. From there, the only way to go is down, and he falls through a short shaft. Once inside the tunnels, he will be able to fall down a hole once again (Figure 18-17). To complete the game, instead of gaining access to the exit passage, he will be transported to the final level.

1. Set the Scene view back to Textured and turn the Terrain back on.

2. Focus in on the Rock Plug and deactivate it.

3. Move the First Person Controller to the top of the dome, near the hole, and click Play.

4. Spend a few minutes getting familiar with the layout of the tunnels from the player's point of view (don't forget about the map).

The tunnels will have two scenarios. If the player enters them without a light source, as soon as he falls to the main level, he should be given just enough time to see the openings before he blacks out. If he does have a light source, he is allowed to explore the tunnels, but as soon as he drops down the next hole, he will be transported to the final level to finish the game.

The colliders for triggering the two scenarios are already in place for you. All that's required is a bit of scripting to control the functionality. The fun part is the nice little technique you will be using to overcome the lightmapped tunnel. To keep the player from seeing too far ahead, you will be using fog, with its color set to black.

5. In Play mode, drive the player to the center intersection in the tunnels and turn on the TorchLight.

6. FromEdit ➤ Render Settings, turn on fog and set the color to black.

7. Set the Fog mode to Linear, the Linear Fog End to **30,** and the Linear Fog Start to **15**, and then experiment with the two values to see the effect.

8. Stop Play mode.

You will be using the default Exp2 fog mode to simplify things. In case you are already using fog in the scene, you will be storing the original values before turning on the black fog.

To start, let's create the script that will handle the fog settings.

1. Create a new script and name it **FogManager**.

2. Add the following variables:

```
//this script lives on control center
var lightSource : Light;              // so it can be turned off & on
var lightIcon : GameObject;           // to check inventory for the light source
var hasLight : boolean = false;       // flag for player light source
internal var originalState : boolean;  // state of fog in render settings
internal var originalColor : Color;    // save these to return to
internal var originalDensity : float;
```

The darkness of the fog when the player drops down into the tunnels will be set according to whether he has the light source. If not, he should still have a glimpse of the tunnels in reduced light, to motivate him to find light.

3. Add the following variables for the target fog settings:

```
internal var darkColor : Color = Color.black;
internal var darkDensity : float = 0.06;    // if player has light source
internal var darkerDensity : float = 0.2;   // if player doesn't, make it darker
internal var currentState : boolean = false; // darkness off
```

4. In the Start function, load the original settings.

```
originalState = RenderSettings.fog;        // is it off or on?
originalColor = RenderSettings.fogColor;
originalDensity = RenderSettings.fogDensity;
```

5. Create the function that does the work.

```
function InTheDark (state : boolean) { // pass in the fog state you want, true/on, false/off

}
```

6. Inside the new function, first check for a light source.

```
//check for light source in inventory
if(lightIcon.GetComponent(Interactor).currentState > 0) hasLight = true;
else hasLight = false;
```

7. Add the conditional to turn fog on if it isn't already.

```
if(state && !currentState){              // it's off & you want it on
   RenderSettings.fog = true;            // turn on fog
   RenderSettings.fogColor = darkColor;
   RenderSettings.fogDensity = darkerDensity;
   currentState = true;                  // dark fog is now on
```

```
    if (hasLight) {
        RenderSettings.fogDensity = darkDensity;// adjust density for light
        lightSource.enabled = true;              // turn on the light
    }
}
```

8. Add the else clause for returning to no fog.

```
else {
    if(!state && currentState){                  // it's on & you want it off
        RenderSettings.fog = originalState;
        RenderSettings.fogColor = originalColor;
        RenderSettings.fogDensity = originalDensity;
        currentState = false;                    // dark fog is now off
        lightSource.enabled = false;             // turn on the light
    }
}
```

9. Save the script.

10. Add the script to the Control Center object.

11. Assign TorchLight to the Light Source parameter and Light Ball Icon as the Light Source Icon.

To test the fog, you'll have to trigger the state changes from the trigger objects and another script.

1. Create a new script and name it **ToggleFog**.

2. Add the following variables:

```
var darkState : boolean;                         // which state to invoke
internal var controlCenter : GameObject;         // keeper of fog state
```

3. Assign the Control Center.

```
function Start () {
    controlCenter = GameObject.Find("Control Center");
}
```

4. Create the OnTriggerEnter function.

```
function OnTriggerEnter() {

    controlCenter.SendMessage("InTheDark", darkState);
}
```

5. Save the script.

6. Add it to both of the Fog Trigger objects.

7. In the Inspector, set Dark State to checked for Fog Trigger On and unchecked for Fog Trigger Off.

8. Toggle the Overlays button on in the Scene view to see the fog.

9. Click Play and go through the tunnels, noting the changes as the fog states are triggered.

If you were lucky, or maybe just tenacious, you found the way out and saw the fog triggered off again. Either way, without light, navigating the tunnels is challenging. This time, you will try it with the light source.

10. Select the Control Center and set Has Light to true.

11. Go through the tunnels again now that you "have" a light source.

With the fog working nicely, you can take care of the rest of the functionality for the tunnels.

1. Add the following variables to the ToggleFog script:

```
var fpc : GameObject;       // first person controller
var location : Transform;   // transport location
var blackout : GameObject;  // blackout crossfade prefab
var lightIcon : GameObject; // the light source icon
var newLevel : boolean;     // flag to send player to the next level
```

Location is the spot to transport the First Person Controller, fpc, if he enters the caves without a light source and blackout is the Crossfade prefab you used earlier. To check to see if the player has a light source, you will check to see if the pollen ball has been collected from the strange plant, lightIcon. And, finally, you will create a flag to send the player to the final level, newLevel. Everything will be handled in the OnTriggerEnter function.

2. Inside the OnTriggerEnter function, add the following:

```
//if player doesn't have a light source, blackout and relocate
if(lightIcon.GetComponent(Interactor).currentState == 0) { //check inventory for light source
    yield new WaitForSeconds(5);              // give him a few seconds to look around
    Instantiate(blackout);                    // start the blackout
    yield new WaitForSeconds(1);              // make sure its dark before changing anything
    controlCenter.SendMessage("InTheDark", false); // update the fog state
    fpc.transform.position = location.position;    // relocate the player

}
```

Before setting up the else clause, there's one more important thing to do. One of the topics the player has for the Kahmi character concerns the tunnels being dark and inquiring about the availability of a lantern. Obviously, until he (a), knows there are tunnels, and (b), knows they are too dark to investigate, he shouldn't be able to see the topic. Once he has blacked out in the tunnel, the topic should be made available.

3. Beneath the fpc line, add the following:

```
// activate the topic about light in the tunnels because he has now been there
var dm : DialogueManager = gameObject.Find("Dialogue Manager").
                                        GetComponent(DialogueManager);
dm.topics_2[7] = "107" + dm.topics_2[7].Substring(4);
}
```

4. And now, add the else clause, to send him on to the final level.

```
else {
    //turn off light & send player to the final level
    if(newLevel) {                                  // flag set in the Inspector
        Instantiate(blackout);
        yield new WaitForSeconds(1);
        //Application.LoadLevel ("FinalLevel");      // load the new level
        controlCenter.SendMessage("InTheDark", false); // temporary for testing
    }
}
```

The LoadLevel line is commented out until you have a level to load, so the line following will allow you to see if the rest is working.

5. Save the script.

Before testing, you will require another of those waypoints, so you can transport the player after a blackout. For this one, a location near the exit ledge of the tunnel will be perfect. You've already got one for the flower's camera match that you can duplicate and move.

6. Select Target Pollen Ball, duplicate it, and name it **Target Tunnel Wakeup**.

7. Move the new location point near the tunnel's exit ledge (Figure 18-18).

Figure 18-18. *The wake-up location, after blacking out in the tunnels*

8. Assign the new parameters to the Toggle Fog component in the Fog Trigger Off and Fog Trigger On objects (Figure 18-19).

721

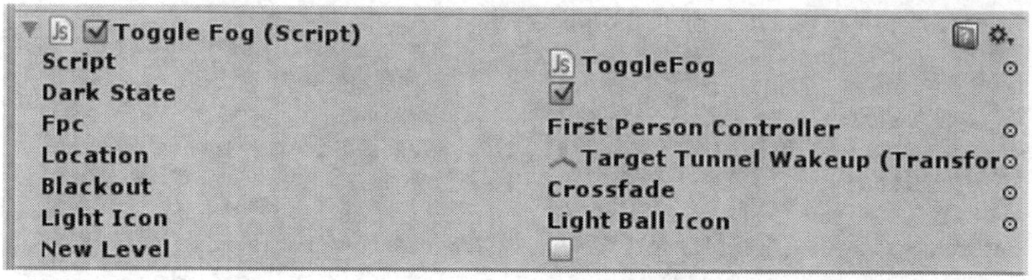

Figure 18-19. The ToggleFog's parameters

9. Select the Fog Trigger Off object and check its New Level parameter.

Finally, you will head back to the Dialogue Manager and disable the tunnel topic.

1. Open the DialogueManager script.

2. Change the topics_2[7] line to

    ```
    topics_2[7] = "007 I keep blacking out in the tunnels, any idea where I can find a
    lantern?"
    ```

3. Save the script.

4. Click Play and test the tunnels without a light source.

The player wakes up under the ledge. At this point, if you go back into the tunnel and talk to Kahmi again, the new topic about the light source will be present.

5. Save the scene and save the project.

The Final Level

The final level is short and quick, but takes a while to set up, so it has been provided to you as a UnityPackage. The only new code is the script to change levels, and that is called from the current level. There are, however, a few things you should know about levels in Unity.

In Unity, a level is a scene. In the Toggle Fog script, there is a line that reads "Application.LoadLevel ("FinalLevel")." Levels can be loaded by name, using the scene name, or by index number. The index number can be found in the Build settings dialog. It can also be adjusted there, as you will see when you add a start menu.

Menus, information, and player setup can all be separate scenes or levels. So, you are probably wondering what gets carried over between levels. If you were in a particular level and left it for another level or maybe a menu "level," the only thing Unity would remember is changes made by physics, such as your rockfall, and objects that were instantiated, in addition to objects that were destroyed. It also remembers the last location of the First Person Controller.

Unity does not remember the values assigned or changed during game play. To do that, you would have to add a simple line to any script or object you wished to be carried over to the next level, DontDestroyOnLoad(). In this game, you will want to limit your player to having only the topi fruit in inventory after he is transported, so nothing will be carried though.

Examining the Final Level

Any respectable Tree of Life ought to have a fancy place to grow, and yours is no exception. In this game, however, the quest will soon become apparent—the tree is blasted and dead, and the player must bring a new seed (the topi fruit) to replace it. Like the final few seconds of a fireworks display, a lot goes on as the game wraps up. Because Unity only allows one Audio Source per object, designing all of the events can become complicated. If you are curious, read the summary of the FinalLevel in the StateManagement PDF to see how it all fits together. (See the Source Code/ Downloads tab of the book's Apress product page www.apress.com/9781430248996.)

With the exception of the addition of a variable, end, to block all user navigation and input after the final sequence has been triggered, this level uses several scripts and assets that already exist in your current project. On import as a Unity package, Unity tends to get confused with duplicate assets in general, so to avoid a lot of reassigning of script, textures, and other assets, they've been given altered names. The exception is the Topi Fruit Icon, as its name is used as part of the functionality, so you will reassign it. Additionally, the original environment package already contains the standing stones, so you will begin by deleting those.

1. From the Structures folder, delete the existing StandingStones asset.

2. Import the FinalLevel.UnityPackage.

3. Load the FinalLevel from the Scenes folder.

The level contains little more than a small ring of standing stones and the Tree of Life in a twilight environment (Figure 18-20).

Figure 18-20. The FinalLevel's standing stones

1. Locate the Topi Fruit Icon in the Inventory group and reassign the Topi Fruit Icon texture.

Another new bit of functionality used in the FinalLevel is the Event marker used in the Final Group's animation.

2. Select the Final Group and open the Animation editor.

3. Zoom out until you can see the Event marker at 3:15 and click on it to see its contents.

723

Events are similar to SendMessage, in that they will call a function on any script on the object. They cannot pass an argument. Essentially, by adding an event to an animation time line, you save writing a few lines of code to delay using a regular SendMessage.

4. Click Play and finish the game. Refer to the StateManagement PDF for instructions, if necessary.

5. Press the Escape key to get your cursor back and stop Play mode when you are ready.

6. Activate the Fade Out from Black object in the Hierarchy and save the scene.

You will be adding one more level, a start menu, in the next chapter. Once you've added the MainLevel and FinalLevel to the Build Settings, you will be able to play through to the end of the game. When you exit Play mode, you will be returned to the Mail Level scene.

1. Open the Build Settings and select Add Current.

2. Uncheck the Cursor Control scene.

3. Click Build and name the new build **TheGame**.

4. Open the MainLevel scene and add it to the Build settings, moving it up above the FinalLevel.

5. Click Build, overwrite TheGame, and close the dialog.

6. Open the ToggleFog script and uncomment the `Application.LoadLevel ("FinalLevel")` line.

7. Save the script.

8. Play through to the end.

Summary

In this chapter, you incorporated the Action Object functionality into the game environment. With the use of a couple of stunt doubles and a camera layer, you allowed your player to read or examine objects outside of inventory to gain more information. You used the functionality created in the previous chapter to randomly place the Golden Sleeve somewhere in the maze, and then hooked up the rockfall sequence to the Earth Glyph once again, with the help of physics.

With the player able to construct the laser, you finalized its purpose to opening the temple, by activating the stair-lowering mechanism. As a nice touch, you animated the crystal into a spent state. Once in the Temple, when the player tried to take the Golden Topi Fruit, he blacked out and was transported to the center of the maze, where he had his first conversation with the Gimbok character. If he worked through the branch topic about what had just happened to him, he could obtain a rock that could be swapped for the topi fruit. Upon completing that task, the second character was activated inside the temple. Following that conversation, he could have the Kahmi character clear his way to the tunnels and offer him a suggestion for a light source.

Setting up the wilted flower in the flora shrine required the use of the Vial of Elixir, to bring the plant back to life. To do so and gain access to the Pollen Ball, an odd source of light, the player had to ride a raft to the falls, to find the vial. To make the task challenging, you created a "death zone" that served to relocate the player, in case he fell or jumped off the raft.

Without a light source, you used the Crossfade prefab and death zone functionality to prevent the player from going very far into the tunnels. With the Pollen Ball 'providing' a light source, however, you allowed him access to the final level. In changing levels or scenes, you learned that they must be loaded to the Build before use.

CHAPTER 19

■ ■ ■

Menus and Levels

So far, you have been working on your game's basic functionality and are now able to play through the entire game. Having gotten this far, it is time to create the graphical user interface (GUI) and menus for your game. As part of one of the menus, you will be creating the load/save functionality that makes use of the action object's current state. Along the way, you will add a few finishing touches to the scene. And, finally, you will add a third level that will serve as a start menu.

In the summer of 2012, Unity previewed a new GUI system, estimating a delivery of three to six months. The current GUI system will not be abandoned, but the new system, once implemented, will bring major changes. In light of the promise of the new system, you will keep the menus fairly simple, concentrating mainly on their contents' functionality.

Game Menus

With the advent of 3D, and especially real-time 3D environments, a useful goal is to keep non-environmental GUI objects hidden from the player, so as not to break the "suspension of disbelief." You can accomplish this with the use of key-activated or position-activated menus that will provide player access to instructions, settings, player preferences, and saved games.

Now that the rest of the game is locked down, you should have a list of some possible contents.

- Navigation/Instructions

- Resume/Quit

- Settings

- Load/Save/New Game

- Credits

Typically in Unity, one creates an entire level to hold a menu. In part, this avoids navigation and game-play conflicts, many of which you have already solved for your inventory system, but it also has the added benefit of breaking functionality down into bite-sized pieces, so that it is less overwhelming. The downside is load time to get back to the main game level and breaking suspension of disbelief. With that in mind, you will make use of both types of menus. Your Start menu will be a separate level or scene, and your other menus will be contained within your game.

Your previous GUI elements were manually placed into screen-space position. Because, at most, you would see only two elements at a time—the object name and its description—that was an acceptable solution. As soon as you start organizing several elements together, however, it makes sense to introduce the concept of a *GUI group*. This will allow for easier setup, because the controls' locations will become offsets of the group location.

The MenuManager Script

Most of the game's menu functionality will be contained within a single script. Menus will be activated by flags in the OnGUI function, so in addition to the main menu, you will need variables for a confirm dialog and a credits menu, as well as several settings-related variables. As expected in a menu, you will be adding a few buttons and, therefore, will also make use of a Rect type variable, so you won't have to enter the button size manually every time.

1. Open the MainLevel scene.

2. Create a new script.

3. Name it **MenuManager** and open it in the editor.

4. Add the following variables:

```
internal var groupWidth = 750;              // width of the main GUI group
internal var buttnRect = Rect(0,120,130,30); //default button size, x,y location, width and height

//menu management
internal var mainMenu = false;            // flag for main menu
internal var confirmDialog = false;       // flag for yes/no on quit dialog
internal var creditsScreen = false;       // flag for credits dialog
internal var end : boolean = false;       // flag for end sequence
```

The main menu will have four sections that will be contained within their own boxes. Because GUI Groups can be nested, the more complicated sections will have their own groups.

```
Block in the OnGUI function as follows: function OnGUI () {

    // *****  main menu  ******
    if(mainMenu) {
        // Make a master group on the center of the screen
        GUI.BeginGroup (Rect (Screen.width / 2 - 375 , Screen.height  / 2 - 270, 750, 500));

        //*** title and intro
        GUI.Box (Rect (0,0,750,80), "Main Menu");

        //*** navigation and instructions
        GUI.BeginGroup (Rect (0,90,370,340));
        GUI.Box (Rect (0,0,370,340), "General Information and Navigation");

        GUI.EndGroup (); // end navigation & instructions group

        //*** settings
        GUI.BeginGroup (Rect (380,90,370,340));
        GUI.Box (Rect (0,0,370,340), "Settings");

        GUI.EndGroup (); // end settings group

        //*** button options
        GUI.Box (Rect (0,440,750,40), "");
```

```
    // End the main group
    GUI.EndGroup ();

} // end the main menu if conditional

} // end the OnGui function
```

With the mainMenu flag in place, you should have at least one means of accessing the menu, so you will begin by setting up your main menu to toggle off and on with the F1 key.

5. Add the following inside the Update function:

```
//toggle the main menu off and on
if (Input.GetKeyDown("f1")) {
    if (end) Application.Quit(); // end now
    if(mainMenu) mainMenu = false;
    else mainMenu = true;
}
```

6. Save the script.

7. Add it to the Control Center object in the Hierarchy view.

8. Turn on Maximize on Play and set the Game window to the Standalone (1280×800) option.

9. Click Play, and test the menu, by pressing the F1 key and clicking in the scene.

The GUI Box appears in the middle of the game window (see Figure 19-1). But there is a problem. The cursor appears behind the menu, as the GameManager's GUI is drawn first.

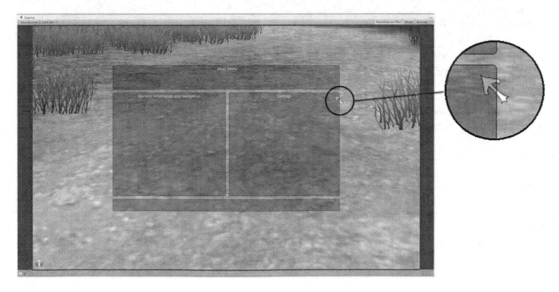

Figure 19-1. *The main menu, blocked in but showing half-covered cursor (callout)*

To fix the draw-order issue, you will set a draw-order depth on each of the conflicting scripts. A lower number is drawn last or on top of a higher numbered depth value. The GameManager draws the cursor, so it will get the lower number, so the cursor will get drawn last.

1. In the MenuManager script, at the top of the OnGUI function, add:

   ```
   GUI.depth = 1;
   ```

2. Open the GameManager script and, at the top of its OnGUI function, add

   ```
   GUI.depth = 0;
   ```

3. Save both scripts.

4. Click Play, press F1, and click and check to see that the cursor is drawn on top of the menu.

If you are wondering why you didn't have this problem with the inventory screen, it's because the inventory screen and items were GUI Textures—actual gameObjects. The scripted GUI Controls are always drawn on top of scene objects. If you had used a hardware cursor, it would have always been drawn on top of everything else.

The Main Menu

With the main menu roughed in, you can begin to add content to its various sections. The easiest is the top section. It contains a title and short description of the game. The navigation and instruction section contains a lot more text but also requires no functionality at the point. Note the use of \n to force a carriage return or new line.

1. Open the MenuManager and add the following variables:

   ```
   // misc menu text
   internal var introText = "Welcome to the Mystery of Tizzleblat... a simple world with a
   solvable problem.";
   internal var infoText = "Interactive objects- cursor changes color on \nmouse over,
   click to activate\nInventory- i key or pick on icon at lower left to \naccess\nGeneral-
   objects can be combined in scene or \nin inventory";
   internal var navText = "Navigation:\nUP/Down, W/S to move forward/Backward\n A/D to
   strafe left and right\nLeft and Right arrow keys to turn/look around, \nor <shift> or
   right mouse button \nand move mouse to turn and look around";
   ```

2. In the OnGUI function, title and intro section, below the GUI.Box line, add

   ```
   GUI.Label( Rect (30,0,650,100), introText); // intro text
   ```

3. In the navigation and instructions section, below its GUI.Box line, add

   ```
   GUI.Label( Rect (20,50,350,120), infoText);
   GUI.Label( Rect (20,160,350,350), navText);
   ```

4. Save the Script.

5. Click Play and check on the new additions to the main menu.

The default GUI Skin is pretty uninspiring. And there's no reason to attempt any fine-tuning of the layout until the final one is in place, so next, you will import a package with a GUI Skin ready to use.

1. From this chapter's Assets folder, Import Package, Custom Package and select the MenuSkin.unitypackage.

The Menu GUISkin can now be found in the GUI Skins folder, and the new textures have landed in the Structures, Textures folder.

The easiest way to see what the new skin looks like is to add it to the menu script. You will also want a GUI Style to override the rather flamboyant text style for the instructions, so you will add a couple of new variables to the MenuManager script.

2. Add the following variables:

```
var menuSkin : GUISkin;     // custom skin for the menus
var simpleText : GUIStyle; // text for nav and info
```

3. Near the top of the OnGUI function, below the depth line, add

```
GUI.skin = menuSkin;
```

Before testing, it will make sense to comment out the main menu conditional, so you won't have to keep pressing the F1 key to bring it up.

4. Comment out the main menu conditional, if(mainMenu) {, and its closing curly bracket.

5. Save the script and load the Menu GUISkin into the new Menu Skin parameter in the Inspector.

6. Click Play and check out the new skin.

The intro text is sorted out with the new skin, but the default is too much for the regular instructions.

7. Add the following custom style variable to the two navigation/instruction lines:

```
GUI.Label( Rect (20,50,350,120), infoText,simpleText);
GUI.Label( Rect (20,160,350,350), navText,simpleText);
```

8. As long as you're there, add the following lines to call the credits from a button:

```
if (GUI.Button (Rect (20,270,150,40), "Credits")) {
   mainMenu = false;     // turn off the main menu
   creditsScreen = true; // turn on the credits dialog
}
```

9. Save the script and exit Play mode to find out what happened to the rest of the text.

10. In the Inspector, change the Simple Text's Normal Text Color to a matching gold, **255,193,53**.

11. Set its Font to **Arial** and its Font Size to **15**.

12. Click Play and observe the changes.

The Credits button doesn't do anything yet, because you commented out the mainMenu conditional and haven't created the credits code, but you can see it has a mouseover state in keeping with the game.

Game Play Buttons

Next, you will add an assortment of buttons related to game play. This is where you will make use of the variable that stores the default button size, as well as create a temporary variable to make layout easier.

1. Under the button options' GUI.Box line, add the following:

```
//this is a local variable that gets changed after each button is added
var buttnRectTemp : Rect = Rect (20,445,buttnRect.width,buttnRect.height);

if (GUI.Button (buttnRectTemp, "New Game")) {
    Application.LoadLevel("MainLevel");  // Start the Main Level
}

buttnRectTemp.x += buttnRect.width + 15; //shift the starting position over for the next one
if (GUI.Button (buttnRectTemp, "Save Game")) {
    // save the current game
    //MenuMode(false);     // turn off menu mode
    //SaveGame(true);      // save the current game
}

buttnRectTemp.x += buttnRect.width + 15; //shift the starting position over for the next one
if (GUI.Button (buttnRectTemp, "Load Game")) {
    mainMenu = false;
    //LoadGame();          // load the saved game
    //MenuMode(false);     // turn off menu mode
}

buttnRectTemp.x += buttnRect.width + 15; //shift the starting position over for the next one
if (GUI.Button (buttnRectTemp, "Quit")) {
    confirmDialog = true; // turn on confirm menu
    mainMenu = false;     // turn off the menu
}

buttnRectTemp.x += buttnRect.width + 15; //shift the starting position over for the next one
if (GUI.Button (buttnRectTemp, "Resume")) {
    mainMenu = false;     // turn off the menu
    //MenuMode(false);     // turn off menu mode
}
```

2. Save the script.

3. Click Play and observe the new buttons.

The code for this batch of buttons is fairly minimal and doesn't do much yet. LoadGame and SaveGame will obviously be calling a lot of code to handle their tasks. The MenuMode function will manage what the player can and can't do when a menu is active. A few of the buttons simply manage which menus are active. You will be developing the new functions a little later.

The Settings Menu

The most complex part of the Main Menu is the Settings section. This is where you will let the player have some control over the visual and audio presentation of the game. Unlike the previous sections, which consisted mainly of buttons and labels, the settings will give you a chance to see how a few of the other more interactive GUI controls work. With the exception of the audio, you should also already have variables for several of the player preferences sitting in the GameManager script.

As before, you ought to have a list of what you require before you start coding.

- Navigation:
  - Walk Speed, slider
  - Turning speed, slider
- Text:
  - Use Text, Check Box
  - Use Object Description, Check Box
- Audio:
  - Sound FX Volume, Scrollbar
  - Ambient Sound Volume, Scrollbar
  - Music Volume, Scrollbar
  - Voice Volume, Scrollbar
- Cursor Options:
  - Cursor Color on Mouseover, four choices

Unlike the previous menu's buttons, most of the controls in the Settings menu return values other than just `true` or `false`. To utilize those values, you will assign them to variables, so they can be processed.

Another peculiarity of these controls is that you are better off checking for user changes in the GUI before you process changes, rather than processing the values of all of the controls every frame.

1. Add the following variables to the MenuManager script:

```
//Settings menu variables
internal var walkSpeed : float;              // element 0
internal var turnSpeed : float;              // element 1
internal var useText : boolean;              // element 2
internal var objectDescriptions : boolean;   // element 3
var fXVolume : float = 1;                     // element 4
var ambVolume : float = 1;                    // element 5
var musicVolume : float = 1;                  // element 6
var voiceVolume : float = 1;                  // element 7
internal var colorElement : int;             // element 8

internal var playerSettings  = new String[9]; // player settings array in string format

// cursor color
var colorSwatch : Texture;
var cursorColors = new Color[8];
var moColor : Color;                          // current mouseover color
```

The playerSettings variable is for the array where you will store the settings for easier managing. A regular JavaScript array could store data as is and return it in the correct format, but because mobile platforms can't use "non-typed" arrays, you will be converting the values to strings. At the other end, when the values are used to update the current variables, they will be converted back to their original types.

2. In the OnGUI function, settings section, under the GUI.Box line, add the following:

```
// fpc speeds
GUI.Label (Rect (25, 35, 100, 30), "Walk Speed");
walkSpeed = GUI.HorizontalSlider (Rect (150,40, 100, 20), walkSpeed, 0.0, 20.0);
GUI.Label (Rect (25, 60, 100, 30), "Turn Speed");
turnSpeed = GUI.HorizontalSlider (Rect (150,65, 100, 20), turnSpeed, 0.0, 40.0);
```

GUI sliders have their min and max values defined last. The variable used for the indicator also assigns itself as the player moves it. You will monitor the GUI for changes in those and other values near the end of the settings group.

3. Next, add the code for the text display options.

```
// text
var textY : int = 90;
useText = GUI.Toggle (Rect (30,textY, 120, 30), useText, "  Use Text");
objectDescriptions = GUI.Toggle (Rect (30,textY + 30, 120, 30), objectDescriptions,
" Use Descriptions");
The GUI Toggle, a.k.a check box, also assigns its current value to its variable.
```

4. Add the code for the various volume settings.

```
// audio
var audioY : int = 120;
audioY += 30;
GUI.Label (Rect (25, audioY, 100, 30), "FX Volume");
audioY += 10;
fXVolume = GUI.HorizontalSlider (Rect (150,audioY, 100, 20), fXVolume, 0.0, 1.0);
audioY += 14;
GUI.Label (Rect (25, audioY, 100, 30), "Ambient Volume");
audioY += 10;
ambVolume = GUI.HorizontalSlider (Rect (150,audioY, 100, 20), ambVolume, 0.0, 1.0);
audioY += 14;
GUI.Label (Rect (25, audioY, 100, 30), "Music Volume");
audioY += 10;
musicVolume = GUI.HorizontalSlider (Rect (150,audioY, 100, 20), musicVolume, 0.0, 1.0);
audioY += 14;
GUI.Label (Rect (25, audioY, 100, 30), "Dialog Volume");
audioY += 10;
voiceVolume = GUI.HorizontalSlider (Rect (150,audioY, 100, 20), voiceVolume, 0.0, 1.0);
```

5. And, finally, add cursor options.

```
// cursor
var cursorY = 260;
GUI.Label (Rect (30, cursorY, 140, 30), "Current Mouseover Color");
GUI.contentColor = moColor;
GUI.Box (Rect (180, cursorY, 20, 20),GUIContent (colorSwatch));
GUI.contentColor = Color.white;

cursorY += 25;
GUI.Label (Rect (20, cursorY , 120, 30),  "Mouseover Colors");
cursorY += 20;
var cursorX : int = 160;
// display color swatches
for (var i : int = 0;i < 8;i++) {
   GUI.color = cursorColors[i];
   if (GUI.Button (Rect (cursorX, cursorY - 15, 20, 40),colorSwatch,simpleText)) {
      moColor = cursorColors[i];
      colorElement = i;
   }
   cursorX += 25;
}
GUI.color = Color.white;// clear the color for the remaining GUI elements
```

Of interest here is the means of coloring the swatches. They all use the same white texture but are tinted with GUI.color, using the colors you will set up in an array. When the player picks one of the swatches, the color of that element is assigned to the current mouseover color, moColor.

The line below the last entry should be GUI.EndGroup (); // end settings group.

6. Save the script and exit Play mode.

7. Assign the White texture to the Color Swatch parameter.

8. Fill the eight Cursor Colors array elements with a selection of colors. Be sure to set the alpha to **255,** opaque. Element 0 will eventually be read in as the default color used for the game.

9. Click Play and check out the latest additions (see Figure 19-2).

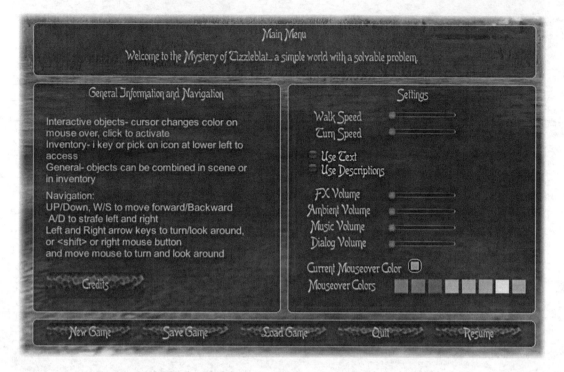

Figure 19-2. *The main menu, showing the new additions*

10. Try adjusting the sliders.

With the sliders sliding and the variables defined, you will have to find out when the values have changed, so that you can notify the appropriate scripts. To do so, you will use GUI.changed. Normally you would add it near the bottom of the OnGUI function, so it would report on any controls above it. In this case, however, the only controls that have to be checked are in the settings section, so you can put it inside the settings group, for easier reading.

1. Add the following above the GUI.EndGroup (); // end settings group line:

```
// track changes
if (GUI.changed) {

print (walkSpeed + " * " + turnSpeed);

}
```

2. Save the script.

3. Click Play and test the sliders, noting the output in the console.

The new values are reported as you move the knobs.

Now, you will update the values. Unfortunately, the GUI.changed does not report *which* control was changed, so you will update them all. Theoretically, you could keep track of the old values and update only the changed value, but because speed is not crucial, you will just update them all.

734

4. Change the print statement to call another function to handle the job.

```
UpdateSettings(); // process the changes
```

5. Create the following function:

```
function UpdateSettings() {

    playerSettings[0] = walkSpeed.ToString();
    playerSettings[1] = turnSpeed.ToString();
    playerSettings[2] = useText.ToString();
    playerSettings[3] = objectDescriptions.ToString();
    playerSettings[4] = fXVolume.ToString();
    playerSettings[5] = ambVolume.ToString();
    playerSettings[6] = musicVolume.ToString();
    playerSettings[7] = voiceVolume.ToString();
    playerSettings[8] = colorElement.ToString();

    // update the settings in the GameManager
    gameManager.NewSettings(playerSettings);

}
```

Before you can test the new code, you will have to "find" the Control Center object and its GameManager script. You may as well add access for a few others while you are there.

6. Add the following variables to the MenuManager script:

```
//Gain access to
internal var gameManager : GameManager;
internal var fPCamera : GameObject;
internal var fPController: GameObject;
```

7. Assign their objects in the Start function.

```
gameManager = GameObject.Find("Control Center").GetComponent(GameManager);
fPCamera= GameObject.Find("Main Camera");
fPController = GameObject.Find("First Person Controller");
```

Next, the GUI values must to be initialized at startup, using the values from a few of the other scripts.

8. In the Start function, add the following to initialize the settings values:

```
//initialize GUI
walkSpeed = fPController.GetComponent(CharacterMotor).movement.maxForwardSpeed;
turnSpeed = fPController.GetComponent(FPAdventurerInputController).rotationSpeed;
useText = gameManager.useText;
objectDescriptions = gameManager.useLongDesc;
moColor = gameManager.mouseOverColor; // get color, because there is no element;
UpdateSettings();                      // update the array that holds the settings
```

When you load saved games, you will require a means of updating the GUI controls to match the new values in the array. You will also require a function to convert Boolean values.

9. Create the following function:

```
function UpdateControls () { // update GUI from the settings array
        walkSpeed = parseFloat(playerSettings[0]);
        turnSpeed = parseFloat(playerSettings[1]);
        useText = parseBool(playerSettings[2]);
        objectDescriptions = parseBool(playerSettings[3]);
        fXVolume = parseFloat(playerSettings[4]);
        ambVolume = parseFloat(playerSettings[5]);
        musicVolume = parseFloat(playerSettings[6]);
        voiceVolume = parseFloat(playerSettings[7]);
        colorElement = parseInt(playerSettings[8]);
        moColor = cursorColors[colorElement]; // update current swatch
}
```

10. And you will want the parseBool function to convert the Boolean values.

```
function parseBool (psValue : String) {
    if (psValue == "True") return true;
    else return false;
}
```

11. Save the script.

And now, you can create the NewSettings function back in the GameManager, to receive and update the changes made in the Settings menu. The elements from the string array must be converted back to their original types, for immediate use. You will use the parseBool function here as well.

1. Open the GameManager script.

2. Add the following functions to update the non-audio settings:

```
function NewSettings(playerSettings: String[]) {
    var fpController = GameObject.Find("First Person Controller");
    //update the array and assign the individual vars
    fpController.GetComponent(CharacterMotor).movement.maxForwardSpeed =
parseFloat(playerSettings[0]);
    fpController.GetComponent(FPAdventurerInputController).rotationSpeed =
parseFloat(playerSettings[1]);
    useText = parseBool(playerSettings[2]);
    useLongDesc = parseBool(playerSettings[3]);
    // use the index number to get and assign the color swatch's color
    mouseOverColor = GetComponent(MenuManager).cursorColors[parseInt(playerSettings[8])];
}

function parseBool (psValue : String) {
    if (psValue == "True") return true;
    else return false;
}
```

Change the `mouseOverColor` var to `internal`, as it will now be handled by the MenuManager.

3. Save the script.

4. Click Play and experiment with the speed and text settings.

With the layout for the main menu taken care of, you can uncomment the conditional that wraps its code.

5. In the MenuManager, remove the `//` from the `//if(mainMenu)` line.

    ```
    if(mainMenu) {
    ```

6. Remove the `//` from the `// } // end the main menu if conditional` line.

    ```
    } // end the main menu if conditional
    ```

7. Save the script.

Confirm Dialog

Next, you will create a mini-menu with the Yes/No confirmation buttons, if the player chooses Quit. `Application.Quit()` does not stop the application in the editor or web player, so you will send a few print statements to the console, just to keep tabs on where you are.

1. Open the MenuManager script.

2. Below the `} // end the main menu if conditional`, add the following:

    ```
    // *******   confirmDialog dialog  *******
    if (confirmDialog) {
        // Make a group on the center of the screen
        GUI.BeginGroup (Rect (Screen.width / 2 - 100, Screen.height / 2 - 75, 200, 155));

        // make a box so you can see where the group is on-screen.
        GUI.Box (Rect (0,0,200,155), "Do you really want to quit?");

        // reset the  buttnRectTemp.y value
        buttnRectTemp = Rect (25,30,150,buttnRect .height);

        if (GUI.Button (buttnRectTemp, "No, resume game")) {
            // turn off the menu
            confirmDialog = false;
        }

        buttnRectTemp.y += 40;
        if (GUI.Button (buttnRectTemp, " Yes, quit without saving")) {
            // quit the game without saving
            confirmDialog = false;
            print ("closing");
            Application.Quit();
        }
    ```

```
        buttnRectTemp.y += 40;
        if (GUI.Button (buttnRectTemp, " Yes, but Save first")) {
            // turn off the menu, save the game, then quit
            confirmDialog = false;
            //SaveGame(true); // quit after saving
        }
        // End the confirmDialog group
        GUI.EndGroup ();

    } // end confirm
```

3. Save the script.

4. Press the F1 key, select the Quit option, and observe the results (see Figure 19-3).

Figure 19-3. Confirm dialog

Because you now have a yes/no menu for quitting the game, you can add the escape key to the Update function, in case the player tries to exit without going through the main menu, unless the end sequence is playing.

1. Add the following to the Update function:

```
// brings up the yes/no menu when the player hits the escape key to quit
if (Input.GetKey ("escape")) {
    if (end) Application.Quit(); // end now
    confirmDialog = true;        // flag to bring up yes/no menu
}
```

Before you save the changes, you will have to set up a placeholder for the LoadGame and SaveGame functions you will eventually write. Note that the SaveGame function will take an argument, quitAfter, so it will know whether to resume the game or quit, regardless of where it has been called from.

2. Block in the SaveGame function.

```
function SaveGame (quitAfter : boolean) {
    print ("saving");
    yield new WaitForSeconds(3);
```

```
     if (quitAfter) {
          Application.Quit();
        print ("closing");
     }
 }
```

3. Uncomment the SaveGame(true); // quit after saving lines in both the Confirm and the mainMenu sections of the OnGUI function.

4. Block in its counterpart, the LoadGame function, as follows:

```
function LoadGame () {
    print ("loading");
    yield new WaitForSeconds(3);
}
```

5. Uncomment the LoadGame() line in the mainMenu section of the OnGUI function.

6. Save the script.

7. Click Play and test each of the buttons from both the main menu and the confirm menu, to see if their message prints out.

An alternative method to bring up the main menu with the F1 key is to track the position of the cursor and bring up the menu, if the cursor is in the top section of the screen.

1. Add the following inside the Update function:

```
var pos = Input.mousePosition; //get the location of the cursor
print (pos);
```

2. Save the script.

3. Click Play and move the cursor toward the top and bottom of the Game view.

4. Resize the Game view and repeat.

The Input.mousePosition considers 0 at the bottom of the screen and Screen.height at the top of its y element.

5. Replace the print line with the following:

```
if (pos.y > Screen.height - 5.0) mainMenu = true;
```

6. Save the script.

7. Test by moving the cursor up to the top of the Game view.

8. Repeat the test in Maximize on Play mode.

Because the mouse is always beyond the location when you click the Play button, the menu will always turn up at the start. Another option is to use one side of the screen, say, the last five pixels, as an activation area. This could be a problem with players who prefer to mouse-turn rather than arrow-turn. A good compromise might be to bring the menu up when the cursor is in the top left corner of the screen. It is quick to get to and will rarely interfere with navigation or the Play button.

9. Change the line as follows:

```
if (pos.y > Screen.height - 5.0 && pos.x < 5.0 ) {
    mainMenu = true;
}
```

10. Save the script, click Play, and test, by moving the cursor over the top left area.

11. Save the scene and save the project.

Credits

The second of the auxiliary "menus" is the Credits dialog or screen. The Credits screen is very simple at this stage. It consists of a single GUI Label. To return to the game from the credits menu, however, you will try something new, the "anyKey" input. By putting this menu at the top of the OnGUI function, you can easily filter out the others during the game's final sequence.

1. Beneath the GUI.skin = menuSkin line, add the following:

```
// ********  credits screen  *************
if(creditsScreen) {
    // Make a group on the center of the screen
    GUI.BeginGroup (Rect (Screen.width / 2 - 150 , Screen.height  / 2 - 200, 300, 400));

    // make a box so you  can see where the group is on-screen
    GUI.Box (Rect (0,0,300,400), "Credits");

    // add labels here
    GUI.Label( Rect (20,20,250,100), "Your name here in lights!");

    // End the credits menu group
    GUI.EndGroup ();

} // end the credits screen conditional

if (end) return; // block any other GUI during the end sequence
```

Because the "anyKey" also includes mouse buttons, pretty much any input from the player will take him back to the game, making a text prompt unnecessary.

2. In the Update function, add the following:

```
if(creditsScreen && Input.anyKeyDown) {
    creditsScreen = false;
    //MenuMode(false);
}
```

3. Save the script.

4. Click Play and test the Credits screen, through its button on the main menu.

Tracking Menu Mode

While your menu now pops up on cue, your player is still free to wander around. The menu functionality should basically be the same as Inventory mode. The player should not be able to navigate the scene, and mouseover and picks outside the menu layer should be ignored.

Because you are likely to discover other things that must to be included in your "menu mode," you will make a function to toggle secondary functionality off and on. You've already blocked in a call to MenuMode, so now it's time to create the function and flesh out the functionality.

1. Open the MenuManager script.

2. Add a new variable to the //menu management section, to tell you if a menu is open.

```
internal var menuMode = false; // no menus are open
```

This will give you a means of preventing the main menu from being opened on top of a submenu.

3. In the Update function, change the if (Input.GetKeyDown("f1")) block as follows:

```
//toggle the main menu off and on
if (Input.GetKeyDown("f1") && !menuMode) {
if(mainMenu) {
        mainMenu= false;
        MenuMode(false);
    }
     else if (!menuMode ) { // if no other menus are open, open it
        mainMenu= true;
        MenuMode(true);
    }
}
```

Before you can test it, you will block in your MenuMode function. You will be passing in the state you want to be in as a Boolean (true/false) argument.

1. Create the following function:

```
function MenuMode (state : boolean) {
   if (end) return; // don't process menu mode

   if (state) { // go into menuMode
   menuMode = true;

   }
   else { // return from menuMode
   menuMode = false;
   }
}
```

Next, you will turn on menuMode from the two submenus, as soon as they are called.

2. Below the `confirmDialog = true` lines in the `OnGUI`, under the buttons section and in the Update function, add the following:

    `MenuMode(true);`

Whenever you turn off a menu and are not turning on another, you have to turn off `menuMode` as well.

1. Uncomment the calls to the `MenuMode` function in the `Save Game`, `Load Game` and `Resume` code in the buttons section.

All three of the options in the `confirmDialog` conditional leave no menus showing, so you must add the same line to each.

2. Add the following under each of the three `confirmDialog = false` lines:

    `MenuMode(false);`

Having set your `menuMode` flag off and on for the various buttons, you can now add the condition that `menuMode` is off, before you allow the F1 key press, the Esc (escape) key press, or the cursor position trigger to open the mainMenu or confirmDialog.

1. In the Update function, change `if (Input.GetKey ("escape")) {` to the following:

    `if (Input.GetKey ("escape") && !menuMode) {`

2. Change `if (pos.y > Screen.height - 5.0 && pos.x < 5.0) {` to the following:

    ```
    if (pos.y > Screen.height - 5.0  && pos.x <  5.0 && !menuMode) {
       mainMenu = true;
       MenuMode(true);
    }
    ```

3. In the Update function, uncomment `MenuMode(false)` in the `creditsScreen` conditional.

4. Save the script.

5. Click Play and test the buttons to make sure everything you have no errors.

The `MenuMode` function is set up and blocked in, so the next step is to add the code to manage non-menu-related input while the menus are showing.

Suspending Navigation and Scene Interaction

In the `MenuMode` function, you must be able to suppress player navigation and some types of interaction with the scene. The player must be able to interact with the menus, but should *not* be able to do anything with the action objects, including triggering any mouseover response. Because you've already got that type of functionality for inventory mode, iMode, it should be fairly quick to set this up.

You've already added the variables and identified the objects in the Start function.

1. Open the MenuManager script.

2. In the MenuMode function, under the `menuMode = true` line, add the following:

```
fPController.GetComponent(CharacterMotor).enabled = false;                    // turn off navigation
fPController.GetComponent(FPAdventurerInputController).enabled = false; // turn off navigation
fPController.GetComponent(MouseLookRestricted).enabled = false;               // turn off navigation
fPCamera.GetComponent(MouseLookRestricted).enabled = false;
```

3. In the MenuMode function, under the menuMode = false line, add the following:

```
fPController.GetComponent(CharacterMotor).enabled = true;              // turn on navigation
fPController.GetComponent(FPAdventurerInputController).enabled = true; // turn on navigation
fPController.GetComponent(MouseLookRestricted).enabled = true;         // turn on navigation
fPCamera.GetComponent(MouseLookRestricted).enabled = true;
```

4. Save the script.

5. Click Play and test, by bringing up the main menu and trying to move around the scene, then close the menu and make sure you can move again.

Navigation is disabled, but mouseovers and picks are still active. In the Interactor, you check for inventory mode, iMode. You will check for menuMode in the same way.

1. Open the Interactor script.

2. Add the following menuMode variable:

```
internal var menuMode : boolean; // menu mode flag
```

3. In the OnMouseOver function, below the if (processing) return line, add the following:

```
menuMode = controlCenter.GetComponent(MenuManager).menuMode; // check for active menus
if (menuMode) return;
```

4. In the OnMouseDown function, below the if (processing) return line, add the following:

```
if (menuMode) return;
```

5. Save the script.

6. Click Play and test, by stopping near an action object. Bring up the menu and mouseover and pick the object.

Mouseover and picks are safely disabled when the menus are up. But there is one more issue that requires attention. If you have a menu open, you can open the inventory and vice versa. Because neither scenario is desirable, each will have to check the other's state before being displayed.

Because OnGUI checks every frame, you must make sure the MenuManager is informed of changes in iMode, so it will not have to check for itself every frame. To do this, you will add a couple of lines to the InventoryManager's mastermind, the ToggleMode function. The MenuManager resides on the Control Center object, so you do not have to make any new "introductions."

1. Open the InventoryManager script.

2. In the ToggleMode function, duplicate the controlCenter.GetComponent(GameManager). iMode = false line in the if clause, and change the copy as follows:

```
controlCenter.GetComponent(MenuManager). iMode = false;   // inform the menu manager
```

3. Repeat for the same line in the else clause:

```
controlCenter.GetComponent(MenuManager). iMode = true;    // inform the menu manager
```

4. Save the script.

If any menus are active, you will prevent the inventory from displaying and vice versa.

5. Open the MenuManager script.

6. Add the following variable:

```
internal var iMode = false; // track inventory mode
```

7. At the top of the Update function, add the following:

```
if (iMode) return;            // the inventory screen is open
```

8. Add it to the top of the OnGUI function as well.

```
if (iMode) return;            // the inventory screen is open
```

9. Save the script.

10. Click Play, and test to make sure the menu will not appear if the inventory screen is up, either from the F1 key press or the cursor position.

The menus are not drawn when the inventory screen is active, and they automatically go away if inventory is opened, then return when it is closed. Next, you will prevent inventory from being opened if menuMode is true.

11. Open the InventoryManager script.

12. Add the following to the top of the ToggleMode function:

```
// if there is a menu open, inventory is not allowed
if(controlCenter.GetComponent(MenuManager).menuMode) return;
```

The menus and inventory displays now play nicely together.

Audio

To implement the volume sliders you blocked out in the main menu, you will want to devise a means of identifying each audio type. Because you have no way of tagging individual audio components, you will be creating tags for the audio types.

Sound FX

The sound effects used by the action objects are played using the objects' Audio Source component and are easily accessed through the ActionObject tag. Remember that some of them may not be active.

1. Open the MenuManager script.

2. In the UpdateSettings function, below the gameManager.NewSettings(playerSettings) line, add the following:

```
//Update Audio volumes
var gos = GameObject.FindGameObjectsWithTag ("ActionObject");
for (var go in gos) {
    print (go);
```

```
        if (go.activeSelf) {            // if it is active
           go.audio.volume = fXVolume; // adjust the volume
           }
        else { // wasn't active, so turn it on long enough to adjust sound
           go.SetActive(true);
           go.audio.volume = fXVolume; // adjust the volume
           go.SetActive(false);
        }
     }
```

3. Save the script.

4. Click Play.

If the console reports an error, the object from the line above the error will require an Audio Source. Most will have had it added automatically. You could also have objects mis-tagged as ActionObjects.

5. Open the console and see which object is causing the problem.

6. Fix any remaining action object problems and then comment out the print statement.

7. Save the script.

8. Test the sound effects adjustment, using the Chest Lid or other action object that has a sound effect assigned to it.

Ambient Sound

Before you can adjust the volume on ambient sounds, you will have to create at least one. The nice thing about the ambient sound is that it can go on its own GameObject, and you can create a Tag with which to access it.

1. Import the AmbientSounds.unitypackage from this chapter's Assets folder. (See the Source Code/Downloads tab of the book's Apress product page [www.apress.com/9781430248996].)

2. Drag the new prefab from the Adventure Prefabs folder into the Hierarchy view and inspect its Audio Source component.

Along with a Birds sound clip, it added a new tag, Ambient, to the scene.

▓ **Tip**   The birds in the clip are decidedly North American. If you have access to the Island demo that shipped with Unity 2.5, you may prefer to use the *jungle* clip.

---

3. Click Play and navigate to and from the prefabs location to test the sound.

You can reuse the sound prefab elsewhere in the scene for other sounds.

1. Drag one of the new prefabs over to the waterfall.

2. Name it **Ambient Falls** and position it at the waterfall.

3. After saving tour scene and project, load the Waterfall audio clip from the Bootcamp demo into it.

4. Because the waterfall is a very localized sound, change the Rolloff Mode to Logarithmic Rolloff.

By now, you are probably more than ready to be able to adjust the ambient sound. With a few small changes, you should be able to reuse the FX code.

1. Open the MenuManager script.

2. In the `//Update Audio volumes` section of the `UpdateSettings` function, add the following:

    ```
    gos = GameObject.FindGameObjectsWithTag ("Ambient");
    for (go in gos) go.audio.volume = ambVolume;
    ```

3. While you are there, add the code for music.

    ```
    gos = GameObject.FindGameObjectsWithTag ("Music");
    for (go in gos) go.audio.volume = musicVolume;
    ```

4. Create a new tag named **Music**.

5. Save the script and test changing the ambient volume.

Because you can hear it in the background, the instant feedback is quite useful.

Music

You do not yet have any music in the scene, but you can easily add some, using the same methods as before. In a more sophisticated system, you might want to attach the sound to the player and have it fade out and load different sound clips, according to location, but the following method will provide you with similar results for a lot less work.

■ **Note** The music was provided by Binary Sonata Studios and is a variation on a sample learning project found in the Garage Band app.

---

1. Import the TempleMusic.unity package from this chapter's book Assets folder.

2. Drop the new prefab into the Hierarchy view.

3. Click Play and navigate around the temple to test the sound.

There is a noticeable amount of distortion on the sound clip.

4. Set the Doppler Level to **0**.

The distortion goes away. If you wish, you can adjust the Audio Source's curve.

The keys for the Rolloff curve behave like the Animation keys. You can delete unwanted keys by hovering over them and using the right-click menu.

1. Stop Play mode and set the Max Distance down to **30** (full volume will be inside the temple).

2. With the Doppler issue solved, make any changes permanent and update the prefab.

Having tested the music in the scene and probably decided it should be turned down quite a bit, you should probably update the default value for the music in the GameManager and its component on the Control Center object in the Inspector.

1. Select the Control Center.

2. Lower the default value for the Music Volume to about **0.2**.

3. Save the scene and save the project.

Voice Volume

You have two NPC characters in your scene that are tagged as ActionObjects already. As such, their volumes will match the rest of the FX volumes, unless you change them *after* the FX updates. To identify them, you will use their CharacterID scripts. For disembodied voices, you will use a Voice tag.

1. Create a new tag named **Voice**.

2. Open the MenuManager script.

3. In the bottom of the UpdateSettings function, add the following:

```
gos = GameObject.FindGameObjectsWithTag ("Voice");
for (go in gos) go.audio.volume = voiceVolume;
For the NPCs, you will add a couple of lines to the //Update FX Audio volumes
section to override the FX volume. To identify them, you will look for the presence of
the CharacterID script.
Below the two go.audio.volume lines, add the following:
if(go.GetComponent(CharacterID)) go.audio.volume = voiceVolume; // readjust character's
volume
```

4. Save the script, the scene, and the project.

Final Level Menu

The final level will have the MenuManager added to its Control Center2 object. Because of all the name changes necessary for a reasonably painless import, you will import a version with the changes already in place. If you want to see what was done to it, you can consult the StateManagement PDF for this chapter. (See the Source Code/Downloads tab of the book's Apress product page www.apress.com/9781430248996.)

1. In the MainLevel scene, select the Control Center object and use Copy Component on the MenuManager.

2. Open the FinalLevel scene.

3. Add the MenuManager script to the Control Center2 object.

4. Use Paste Component Values on MenuManager to transfer the settings.

5. Use Import New Asset and import the MenuManager_F script from this chapter's Assets folder.

6. In the script parameter, load the MenuManager_F in place of the MenuManager script.

7. Open the MenuManager_F script and do a search for "###" to locate the new additions.

The end variable is used to block the menu and other functionality, once the FinalLevel has entered the end sequence. When the player has put the golden topi fruit inside the tree bole, navigation is suspended, and the menu is no longer available. After he has secured a new fruit and picked the tree once more, the cursor and inventory are no longer accessible. The restricted flag blocks navigation and menus, after the tree is resurrected. With the MenuManager_F in place, there are a few lines to uncomment in the new scripts.

8.   For the TreeEffects, FinalTask, and InventoryManager scripts, remove the //@ from any lines that are commented that way (5 lines).

9.   Save the scripts.

10. Add the AudioFX, Music, and Voice tags to the Audio Final FX, Audio Final Music, and Audio Final Voice objects.

11. Click Play and test the menu accessibility in the final scene.

Level Save and Load

Saving games can be quite involved, depending on platform and purpose. It is beyond the scope of this book to deal with anything other than a local save, so you will save your game in the same directory the application is being run from.

The next consideration is how and in what format to save the data. As usual, there are many options, with different pros and cons. A nice feature of adventure-type games is that the saved games don't have to be secure against the player breaking in and changing values. Unlike a first-person shooter, where the player is amassing points toward bragging rights, your player is more concerned with seeing and experiencing everything the game has to offer, while he pits his intellect, powers of observation, and problem-solving abilities against the game's end goal. He is more likely to go online to find vague hints when he is stuck and tries not to learn any more than he has to, so as to move forward in the game. With this in mind, you will write your saved values out to a simple text file, giving the file a cryptic name and extension, if you feel it is necessary.

Saving with PlayerPrefs

There are a few different methods that can be used to save games. Serious coders may use special classes to serialize and save their data. For a simple save, you can use PlayerPrefs. It saves the data in its native format as integers, floats, or strings. The syntax is similar to the parameters you used in Mecanim for the two characters. To save a value, you use the appropriate type for the data, SetFloat, SetInt, or SetString, followed by the parameter name, in quotation marks, and the value, separated by a comma. For example: PlayerPrefs.SetFloat("Player Score", 10.0). To retrieve the data, you would use: PlayerPrefs.GetFloat("Player Score"). Once your data gets complicated, such as different levels requiring different datasets, you would have to check for the existence of the key (the name representing that data), before trying to retrieve it.

Another drawback is that the PlayerPrefs only saves one file. Even if you plan on only allowing your player one save file, you will quickly discover that the option of keeping multiple save files while developing your game will make things exponentially easier. Keeping various saved games will allow you to check on target functionality, without having to "play through" every time you add or adjust things—especially as you get closer to the end of the game. Additionally, depending on the platform, the PlayerPrefs file may be saved to an obscure location in the registry. Be sure to check out PlayerPrefs in the Scripting help.

Saving to Text Files

After weighing the pros and cons, for the book project, you will be using a simple text file to load and save your data. Without the use of JavaScript arrays (which will happily store any data type), it gets a bit more complicated, as does reading and writing to a text file. The advantages are: you can store multiple saved games while you are developing; they are easy to inspect; and they can be moved between different computers. With some extra work, you could allow the player to save and load as many files as he chooses, providing you create a save/load screen to handle them. Even better, with a bit of research, you could include a screen-shot thumbnail for each.

Besides the player settings, you will want to save the state of all ActionObjects and Inventory objects, the current level, player location and orientation, and a few miscellaneous states.

You will begin by testing read/write functionality.

1. Save the FinalLevel scene and open the MainLevel scene.

2. Create a new script and name it **SaveLoad**.

3. Add the following code:

```
import System.IO;
internal var filePath : String;
internal var filename= "SavedGame";
internal var extension = ".txt";

function Start () {
    filePath = Application.dataPath + "/";
    print (filePath + filename+ extension);
}
```

4. Save the script.

The SystemIO gives you access to functions and variable types specific to the system's input and output. As expected, you must specify a path, along with a name for your file. Application.dataPath returns the path that is being used by your project, while you are authoring, and the application's data folder, after you have published, the game. In case you are not sure where this path is, you will have the Start function print it out to the console as soon as it gets it.

1. Create an empty GameObject and name it **SystemIO**.

2. Drag the new SaveLoad script onto it.

3. Click Play.

The console reports the path and name of the file you will be creating.

4. Add the following function to write (and create, if need be) your text file.

```
function WriteFile(filename : String) {

    var sWrite: StreamWriter = new StreamWriter(filePath + filename + extension);
    sWrite.WriteLine("This is a test");
    sWrite.WriteLine("We are in level " + Application.loadedLevel);
    sWrite.WriteLine("This will be some data");
    sWrite.Flush();
    sWrite.Close();
}
```

In your game, you will be saving and loading only one file, but breaking the path, file name, and extension apart allows for easy modification, if you wanted to increment save games by appending the name with sequential numbers or allow the players to name the files themselves.

5. Save the script.

You will call the function from the MenuManager.

6. Open the MenuManager script.

7. In the SaveGame function, above the yield line, add the following:

    ```
    GameObject.Find("SystemIO").SendMessage( "WriteFile", "MyNewSavedGame");
    ```
    SendMessage passes the name of the file as an argument to the WriteFile function in the SystemIO object's LoadSave function.

8. Save the script.

9. Click Play.

10. Open the main menu and click the Save button.

11. Find the newly created text in the Project view and look at it in the Inspector, but do not open it.

The contents of the file are exactly as you specified.

It is always useful to know if the game is actually saving—especially if the file is small and the save is fast. Next, you will create another GUI element to let your player know what is happening.

1. In the MenuManager's SaveGame function, change the yield line as follows:

    ```
    saving = true;
    yield new WaitForSeconds(2);
    saving = false;
    ```

2. Delete or comment out the print ("saving") line.

3. Add the new variable to the script.

    ```
    internal var saving = false; // flag for message for save function
    ```

4. And just above the closing curly bracket for the OnGui function line, add the following:

    ```
    // saving message
    if (saving) GUI.Label( Rect (20,20,250,100), "Saving game");
    ```

5. Save the script.

6. Open the SaveLoad script and change some of the text to make sure the file is updated the next time you save.

7. Save the script.

8. Click Play, open the main menu, and click the Save button.

9. Look for the "saving" message in the upper left area of the screen.

10. This time, open the text file to make sure it has updated the content.

11. Close the text file after you check it, or it will not update properly.

The Save function is working nicely—it creates a text file, if one does not exist, and updates it, if it already exists and the file is not open. Next, you will see about reading content back out of the file.

1. Open the LoadSave script.

2. Add the following function:

```
function ReadFile(fileName : String) {
    if (!File.Exists(filePath + fileName + extension)) return;// in case there is no file yet
    var sRead = new File.OpenText(filePath + fileName + extension);
    var input = ""; //
    while (true) {
        input = sRead.ReadLine();
        if (input == null) break;
        print ("Content: "+ input);
    }
    sRead.Close();
}
```

3. Save the file.

The ReadFile function is a bit more cryptic. It reads in lines of data until the input variable comes back as null or empty, then breaks out of the while loop. Because it checks for null, the input variable must be initialized as " ", which is a string with no characters, as opposed to a null value.

Now you will call the new function from MenuManager.

1. Open the MenuManager script.

2. In the LoadGame function, replace the print ("loading") line with the following:

```
GameObject.Find("SystemIO").SendMessage( "ReadFile", "MyNewSavedGame");
```

3. Delete the yield line.

4. Save the file.

5. Click Play, open the main menu, and click Load Game.

6. Open the console to see the content that was printed from the text file.

7. Open the LoadSave script.

8. For fun, change the extension name to .gme.

9. Change the content of the first line to a float number:

```
sWrite.WriteLine( 1.05);
```

10. Save the script.

11. Click Play, save, and then load the game.

12. Check the console.

The new extension was handled the same as the original .txt extension, and the float number was automatically converted to a string when written to the text file.

13. Save the script.

Saving the Game Data

With the mechanics of the load and save working, it's time to add the real data to the script. When organizing the game data, you will be relying on the order of the data when you read it back in, after it has been saved. The final level will not contain several of the objects, so the save will be designed accordingly.

1. Open the LoadSave script.

2. Delete the three sWrite.WriteLine lines in the WriteFile function and replace them with the following:

```
// level
var level = Application.loadedLevel; // the current level number
sWrite.WriteLine(level);

//First Person Controller transforms
var fpc = GameObject.Find("First Person Controller");
sWrite.WriteLine(fpc.transform.position);
sWrite.WriteLine(fpc.transform.localEulerAngles);

//Player Settings
var ps = GameObject.Find("Control Center").GetComponent(MenuManager).playerSettings;
sWrite.WriteLine(ps[0]); //walkSpeed
sWrite.WriteLine(ps[1]); //turnSpeed
sWrite.WriteLine(ps[2]); // useText
sWrite.WriteLine(ps[3]); //objectDescriptions
sWrite.WriteLine(ps[4]); //fXVolume
sWrite.WriteLine(ps[5]); //ambVolume
sWrite.WriteLine(ps[6]); //musicVolume
sWrite.WriteLine(ps[7]); // voiceVolume
sWrite.WriteLine(ps[8]); // mo color
```

3. Next, introduce the actionObject array:

```
//Action Objects- get the list generated by the GameManager on Awake
var ao = GameObject.Find("Control Center").GetComponent(GameManager).actionObjects;
```

Before you load the action objects from their array, you should think about how you are going to get the current state of the action objects that are temporarily disabled. To do so, you will identify the objects via the array, check to see if they are active, save the current state or activate, save the state, and then deactivate the object.

4. Add the following:

```
for (var x : int = 0; x < ao.length; x++) { // iterate through the array of action objects
    // save its current state
    print (ao[x]); // so you can see what objects are being processed
    if (ao[x].activeSelf == true) {
        sWrite.WriteLine(ao[x].GetComponent(Interactor).currentState);
    }
    else { // if inactive, wake it up long enough to save its current state
        ao[x].SetActive(true);  // activate it
        sWrite.WriteLine(ao[x].GetComponent(Interactor).currentState);
        ao[x].SetActive(false); // deactivate it
    }
}
```

The inventory objects are theoretically ActionObjects but have a tag of "InventoryObjects." Fortunately, you can reuse the same code with the inventoryObjects array to store their states.

5. Add the preceding block of code again, changing ao to io (seven places).

6. Add the following lines *between* the two:

```
//Inventory Objects- get the list generated by the GameManager on Awake
var io = GameObject.Find("Control Center").GetComponent(GameManager).inventoryObjects;
```

7. Remove var from in front of the x variable, because it was defined in the previous block of code.

The rest of the saved data will be specific to the main level, so you should make sure you aren't trying to save things that don't exist when you are in the final level.

8. Add the following:

```
// stop writing/saving data here if player is in FinalLevel
if (Application.loadedLevelName == "FinalLevel") {
    sWrite.Flush();
    sWrite.Close();
    return; // don't save any more data
}
```

Now, you can save the rest of MainLevel data, beginning with the dialogue arrays, as player interaction can change some of them.

9. Add the following to iterate through each of the dialogue arrays:

```
//save dialogue array contents
var dm : DialogueManager = GameObject.Find("Dialogue Manager").
GetComponent(DialogueManager);
var tempArray = new String[dm.topics_1.length];
tempArray = dm.topics_1;
for(var e : String in tempArray) sWrite.WriteLine(e);
tempArray = new String[dm.topics_2.length];
tempArray = dm.topics_2;
for(e in tempArray) sWrite.WriteLine(e);
tempArray = new String[dm.replies_1.length];
tempArray = dm.replies_1;
for(e in tempArray) sWrite.WriteLine(e);
tempArray = new String[dm.replies_2.length];
tempArray = dm. replies_2;
for(e in tempArray) sWrite.WriteLine(e);
```

And because the player might save the game from inside the maze, it will be important to save its current configuration.

10. Save the maze walls' z rotation:

```
// maze walls find them, save their local z rotation
var walls : Component[] = GameObject.Find("MazeWalls").GetComponentsInChildren(Transform);
for (var wall : Component in walls)
    if (wall.gameObject.GetComponent(MeshRenderer)) sWrite.WriteLine(wall. gameObject.
transform.localEulerAngles.z);
```

11. Save the script.

With the code in place, it's time to test the results.

12. Click Play, bring up the main menu, and save the game.

■ **Tip**   If you get a "NullReferenceException" error, check the last object listed in the console. If it has an ActionObject tag, but no Interactor script, it will have thrown an error. Stop Play mode and set the object to Untagged, or finish setting up the object, if it is supposed to be an action object. Edit problem objects until you no longer get errors.

---

13. Comment out the print statements in the SaveGame code and save the script.

14. Click Play and test the save in the MainLevel, but do not try to load it yet.

Loading the Saved Data

As you read the saved text file back into the scene, you will convert the data to the right type and reassign it to its original variables. Because you stored only the variable and not the object or variable type, you will have to be careful about keeping the read order exactly the same as the write order.

Before you add the code to read in the saved data, you will make a little function to process transforms. It takes the strings from the saved data, splits them and puts them into an array, then converts the elements to floats and updates the position and orientation of the object that was passed in.

1. Open the SaveLoad script.

2. Create a function to process transforms.

```
function ProcessTransforms (object :GameObject, theValue : String, transform : String) {
    //strip off parentheses
    theValue = theValue.Substring(1,theValue.length -2);
    //split the string into an array using the commas
    var readString : String[] = theValue.Split(","[0]);
    // feed the new elements into a Vector3
    var nt : Vector3 =
Vector3(parseFloat(readString[0]),parseFloat(readString[1]),parseFloat(readString[2]));
    if (transform == "position") object.transform.position = nt;
    else object.transform.localEulerAngles = nt;
}
```

Now you are ready to read-in the saved data. You will have to be aware of different levels, so that will be the first thing to check.

3. In the ReadFile function, beneath the var sRead = new File.OpenText(filePath + fileName + extension) line, add the following:

```
// level, if the level is different than the present level, load it
var level = parseInt( sRead.ReadLine());
if (level != Application.loadedLevel) {
   // more here later
   Application.LoadLevel(level);
}
```

Next, the transforms have to be processed before they can be used. You will send the object, the string version of the transforms, and which transform it is off to be processed.

4. Process the First Person Controller transforms next.

```
// First Person Controller transforms
var fpc = GameObject.Find("First Person Controller");
ProcessTransforms(fpc,sRead.ReadLine(),"position");
ProcessTransforms(fpc,sRead.ReadLine(),"rotation");
```

For the player settings, you will assign the settings into an array and then send the array off to both the MenuManager and GameManager scripts to be processed through their own functions.

5. In the ReadFile function, below the transforms section, add the following to load the settings array:

```
// read Settings into an array
var ps = new String[9];
for (var i : int; i<9; i++) {
   ps[i] = sRead.ReadLine();
}
var controlCenter : GameObject = GameObject.Find("Control Center");
controlCenter.GetComponent(GameManager).NewSettings(ps);      // update array in game manager
controlCenter.GetComponent(MenuManager).playerSettings = ps; // update the playerSettins array
controlCenter.GetComponent(MenuManager). UpdateControls();    // update GUI controls
```

Next, you will read-in the action objects and process them into their saved states. Once again you will be required to get the list of action objects before you start processing them. You will begin by using the ProcessObject function from the action object's Interactor script update the objects to their saved state.

6. Add the following:

```
//Process action objects- get the list generated by the GameManager on Awake
var ao = GameObject.Find("Control Center").GetComponent(GameManager).actionObjects;
for (var x : int = 0; x < ao.length; x++) { // iterate through the array of action objects
  // process it into the save's state
  ao[x].SetActive(true);                          // activate it
  ao[x].SendMessage("ProcessObject",parseInt(sRead.ReadLine()));
}
```

755

7. And add its InventoryObject counterpart.

```
//Process inventory objects- get the list generated by the GameManager on Awake
var io = GameObject.Find("Control Center").GetComponent(GameManager).inventoryObjects;
for (x = 0; x < io.length; x++) { // iterate through the array of inventory objects
   // process it into the save's state
   io[x].SetActive(true); // activate it
   io[x].SendMessage("ProcessObject",parseInt(sRead.ReadLine()));
}
```

Just as in the write/save function, you will check the level to find out if the MainLevel data should be processed.

8. Add the following:

```
// stop reading/loading data here if player is in FinalLevel
if (Application.loadedLevelName == "FinalLevel") {
   sRead.Close();
   return; // don't read any more data
}
```

9. Next, load the dialogue arrays.

```
//load dialogue array contents
var dm : DialogueManager = GameObject.Find("Dialogue Manager").GetComponent(DialogueManager);
for(i = 0; i < dm.topics_1.length; i++) dm.topics_1[i] = sRead.ReadLine();
for(i = 0; i < dm.topics_2.length; i++) dm.topics_2[i] = sRead.ReadLine();
for(i = 0; i < dm.replies_1.length; i++) dm.replies_1[i] = sRead.ReadLine();
for(i = 0; i < dm.replies_2.length; i++) dm.replies_2[i] = sRead.ReadLine();
```

10. Restore the maze wall rotations.

```
// maze walls find them, update their local z rotation
var walls : Component[] = GameObject.Find("MazeWalls").GetComponentsInChildren(Transform);
for (var wall : Component in walls)
   if (wall.gameObject.GetComponent(MeshRenderer)) wall.
gameObject.transform.localEulerAngles.z = parseFloat(sRead.ReadLine());
```

And, finally, you can delete the original code that read through the test contents and printed them out to the console.

11. Delete the following from the ReadFile function:

```
var input = ""; //
while (true) {
   input = sRead.ReadLine();
   if (input == null) break;
   print ("Content: "+ input);
}
```

Make sure you leave the sRead.Close() line.

12. Save the script.

13. Click Play and collect a couple of inventory objects and leave the chest open.

14. Save the game, then click New Game, or manually start a new game.

15. Focus in on the chest in the Scene view and load the previous saved game.

A few things are apparent. By using the ProcessObject function, the objects are forced to play their animations and sound effects while transitioning to their saved states.

To solve the issues, you will speed up the animation and skip the audio playback entirely. For the clips, an investigation of *animation* in the scripting reference shows you that normalizedTime will allow you to jump to the end of the animation when set to 0.

Rather than re-creating a stripped-down version of the Interactor's ProcessObject function, you will just be inserting a couple of flags to alter its functionality when you are using it to load states.

1. In the readFile function, above the ao[x].SendMessage("ProcessObject" line, add the following:

```
ao[x].GetComponent(Interactor).loading = true; // turn on the loading flag
```

The inventory objects neither animate nor have sound effects, so you can leave their code as is.

2. Save the script.

3. Open the Interactor script.

4. Add the new variable to the //Misc vars section.

```
internal var loading = false; // flag for alternate processing of object state
```

5. In the ProcessObject function, change the two ProcessAudio (currentSound) to the following:

```
if (!loading) ProcessAudio (currentSound);
```

6. At the bottom of the ProcessObject function, just above its closing curly bracket, turn off the loading flag.

```
loading = false;
```

7. Save the script.

8. Click Play and test.

The sound effects no longer play during load.

Next you will cause the animation clips to go immediately to their ends by setting normalizedTime to 0. Think of normalized time as 100% of the length of the animation.

1. In the ProcessObject function's if (animates) section, change the aniObject.animation.Play(currentAnimationClip.name) line to the following:

```
if (loading) {
    // set the animate time to 0, play the animation, then set it back to normal
    aniObject.animation[currentAnimationClip.name].normalizedTime = 0.0;
    aniObject.animation.Play(currentAnimationClip.name);
    aniObject.animation[currentAnimationClip.name].normalizedTime = 1.0;
}
else { // else it is not loading so process as usual
    aniObject.animation.Play(currentAnimationClip.name);
}
```

2. Save the script.

3. Click Play, and test by leaving a chest lid open, saving, closing it, and then loading; watch to make sure the lid opens instantly.

There is one more thing that must be addressed. The inventory objects are handled a bit differently than their 3D counterparts for visibility. If you opened the Inventory after a save and load, you will have seen a wad of "inactive" icons in the center of the panel because there is no code to deactivate objects that are already deactivated. You had to activate them, of course, to check their states to see if they required activation…

1. In the Interactor script, in the Handle2D function, at the bottom of the function, add:

    ```
    if(previousState == 0 && currentState == 0) gameObject.SetActive(false);
    ```

2. Save the script.

3. Click Play, save and load the game, then open Inventory to make sure the icons are behaving themselves.

Managing Nonaction Objects

With the load/save functionality in place, it's time to do some serious testing to see which objects are not handled by the regular ProcessObject code. Because you are only allowing one saved game, for testing purposes, you will require a practical way to test. For the preliminary test, follow the following procedure:

1. Save the game each time an action object is obtained or a task is completed.

2. Start a new game and then load the saved game.

3. Make note of any objects that will require special attention.

4. Rename the saved game immediately after the save and append the generic name with something meaningful.

5. Repeat until you have finished the game, manually handling any issues that appear.

At the end of the testing, you should have found several issues that should be addressed. Some will require a bit of thought as they may have several different solutions. The list should be more or less as follows:

- Decide how to handle rocks and crystal.

- Save the location of the floating tray after the golden sleeve has been collected.

- Figure out why KeyAtLock is invisible after load when it should be in the lock.

- Save and load Terrain's Y Position for player inside temple during load/save.

- Save and load Temple Blocker's collider state.

- Save and Load fog state for player inside tunnels during load/save.

The first of these is what to do about the rocks and crystal at the Earth shrine. The glyph will be reset, but it will be in 'location' 2, in scene, but no longer pickable. The crystal, if the player hasn't taken it into inventory, will drop down, triggering the rock fall again. Falling first, because of its rigid body, it could be unreachable after the rocks finish, so you will be destroying the Rockfall script on startup.

1. Open the Rockfall script.

2. Change the function OnTriggerEnter () { line to:

```
function OnTriggerEnter (object : Collider) {
    if( object == prize.collider) Destroy(this.gameObject); //prevent rock fall
```

3. Save the script and then test by triggering the rockfall, leaving the crystal, saving the game, starting a new game, and then loading the saved game.

A single rock will probably fall before the Rock Zone is deactivated, but the crystal will be easily available. It would be better, however, if the crystal "remembered"' where it was. Because you already created a little function to read in saved transforms, it will be useful to add that functionality. It will allow you to preserve the current transforms of an object, if it was moved by physics or randomly placed into the scene at some point, as with the TrayCloth Floating object.

4. Open the Interactor script and add the following variable:

```
var saveTransforms : boolean = false; // flag to save current transform for save/load
```

5. Save the script and set the new parameter to true for the Crystal object.

6. Open the SaveLoad script.

7. In the WriteFile function, below *both* sWrite.WriteLine(ao[x].GetComponent(Interactor).currentState) lines, add

```
if (ao[x].GetComponent(Interactor).saveTransforms == true){
    sWrite.WriteLine(ao[x].transform.position);
    sWrite.WriteLine(ao[x].transform.localEulerAngles);
}
```

8. In the ReadFile function, below the ao[x].SendMessage("ProcessObject", parseInt(sRead.ReadLine())) line, add

```
if (ao[x].GetComponent(Interactor).saveTransforms == true){
    ProcessTransforms(ao[x],sRead.ReadLine(),"position");
    ProcessTransforms(ao[x],sRead.ReadLine(),"rotation");
}
```

9. Save the script and set the Crystal's Save Transform parameter to true.

10. Click Play and test, by triggering the rockfall again, saving, restarting, and then loading again.

11. Set the Save Transforms parameter to true for the TrayCloth Floating object as well.

Next on the list is the KeyAtLock. The problem here is due to the way Unity saves animation clips. The key goes into state 2, after it was animated into position from state 1. On loading, it goes directly to state 2, so it never has a chance to animate into position.

1. Duplicate the key insert_copy clip and name it **key inserted**.

2. Select the KeyAtLock Group and increase its Animations array by 1.

3. Load the new clip into the new element.

4. Select the KeyAtLock and load the new clip into Animation Clip Element 2.

5. Open the Animation Editor, load the new clip, and turn on the Record button.

6. At the bottom left, toggle Show: All to Show: Animated

7. Select the Key material's Color.a track and change its value to **1** at frame 0.

8. Move the key at frame 26 to frame 1.

9. Select the Transform track and delete the keys at frame 15.

10. Move the indicator to frame 0 and click Add Keyframe.

11. At frame 1, click Add Keyframe again.

12. Delete the remaining keys.

The Terrain and Temple Blocker each have only one value to save, so they can easily be added as miscellaneous objects.

1. Open the SaveLoad script.

2. In the `WriteFile` function, above the `sWrite.Flush()` line, add the following:

```
// Misc single values
sWrite.WriteLine(GameObject.Find("Terrain").transform.position.y);
sWrite.WriteLine(GameObject.Find("TempleBlocker").collider.enabled);
```

3. In the `ReadFile` function, above the `sRead.Close()` line, add the following:

```
// Misc single values
 GameObject.Find("Terrain").transform.position.y = parseFloat(sRead.ReadLine());
 GameObject.Find("TempleBlocker").collider.enabled = parseBool(sRead.ReadLine());
```

And of course, you will use the little `parseBool()` function you added to the MenuManager.

4. Copy the `parseBool()` function from the MenuManager script and paste it into the SaveLoad script.

5. Save the script.

6. Click Play and test, by saving from far enough inside the temple to have dropped the Terrain.

The final problem, the tunnel state, involves the fog state and also what happens when the player drops down the last hole. Because it is dependent on several variables, you will send the new state off to a function for processing, instead of changing a value directly.

7. Open the SaveLoad script.

8. In the `WriteFile` function, above the `sWrite.Flush()` line, add the following:

```
sWrite.WriteLine(GameObject.Find("Control Center").GetComponent
(FogManager).currentState);
```

9. In the ReadFile function, above the sRead.Close() line, add the following:

```
GameObject.Find("Control
Center").GetComponent(FogManager).InTheDark(parseBool(sRead.ReadLine()));
```

10. Save the script.

11. Click Play and test the save from within the tunnels with the light source.

Traveling Between Levels

If you have been diligent in testing the load/save functionality, you will have discovered that load only works properly in the same level that the game was saved from. As soon as you try to load a saved game from a different level, the new level is loaded, but that is as far as it gets. For the final level, it's not much of an issue, as there isn't really anything to do before the final sequence is triggered. Going back to the main level from the final level, however, is a problem.

The solution seems simple. The new level is loaded from the previous level's SaveLoad script, so on startup, it must know whether or not to load the saved scene from *its* SaveLoad script. You might think that setting the Save/Load script to DontDestrotOnLoad is the solution, but the drawback would be that each time you traveled back and forth between levels, a new instance of the SystemIO, the object that houses the SaveLoad script, would be created. The challenge is to get data from one level to the next, without littering the levels with unwanted duplicate objects.

The solution will be to create a simple "courier service" to carry a value to the next level. Upon delivering the message, it will go away. In scripting terms, as soon as the code finds out it will be loading a new level, it instantiates a courier to deliver the message. Once a new level has been loaded, it looks to see if there is a courier. If there is, it will load the saved scene. In this game, there is only one saved file, but if you allowed multiple saves, the courier can pass the name of the file to the new level as a string.

Before you can test the FinalLevel, it will require its own version of the SaveLoad script.

1. Save the FinalLevel scene and load the FinalLevel scene.

2. Import the SaveLoad_F script from the chapter's Assets folder.

3. Add the SaveLoad_F script to the SystemIO_F object.

4. Save the scene.

Next, you will be creating the courier prefab.

1. Load the MainLevel scene.

2. Create an Empty GameObject and name it **Courier**.

3. Create a new script and name it **CourierBag**.

4. Add the following to the new script:

```
var fileName : String;

function Awake () {
    DontDestroyOnLoad(gameObject); // so it will persist to the next level
}

function Start () {
    Destroy(gameObject, 1); //allow the info 1 second to be harvested before killing courier
}
```

5. Save the script and drop it on the Courier object.

6. Create a new prefab named **Courier** and load the Courier object onto it.

7. Delete the Courier object from the Hierarchy view.

Next, you will instantiate the courier when a new level is loaded. Make the following changes to both the SaveLoad and SaveLoad_F scripts.

8. Open the SaveLoad script.

9. Add the following variable:

```
var courier : GameObject; // the prefab
```

10. In the ReadFile function, near the top, change the `// more here later` line to

```
// instantiate Courier to carry data to new level
var newCourier : GameObject =  Instantiate(courier);
// load the fileName into it
newCourier.GetComponent(CourierBag).fileName = fileName;
```

11. In the Start function, add

```
var tempCourier : CourierBag = GameObject.FindObjectOfType(CourierBag);
if(tempCourier) {
    yield;
    if(loadSavedGame) ReadFile(tempCourier.fileName); // load the saved game
}
```

To review the last couple of lines, when a saved game is loaded, and the saved level is different from the current one, a persistent object is instantiated and receives the name/path of the new game. The new level is loaded, and when it finds the persistent object, it loads the saved gave. This time, because it is already in that level, the loading continues.

12. Save the script.

13. Load the Courier prefab into the Courier parameter of the SaveLoad component.

14. Repeat for the SaveLoad_F script in the FinalLevel.

15. Click Play and test, by saving in the main level, playing through to the final level, and then loading the saved game before firing off the final sequence.

This time the saved scene is loaded in correctly.

Start Menu

With most of the game functional now, you can add one more level: the start menu. There is not much new in it, so you will be loading it in as a Unity package.

1. From the Book Assets folder, for this chapter, load the StartMenu.unitypackage file.

2. From the Scenes folder, open the StartScene.

3. Select the Main Camera and, in the Start Menu component, set the Simple Text's Font to Arial.

4.   Click Play, check out the Start menu, and try the "New Game" button.

5.   Stop Play Mode and open the StartMenu script from the Main Camera object.

6.   In the `LoadSavedGame` function, uncomment the `//var newCourier : GameObject` and `//newCourier.GetComponent` lines.

7.   Save the script.

Because it will always be opening a "new" level, it only requires the level number from the saved file. Once it has that, it instantiates the courier object and loads the new level. The presence of the Courier tells the level to load the saved game as designed. Before you can test, you will have to load the new scene to the build and identify the Courier prefab.

1.   From the Files menu, open the Build Settings.

2.   Add the current scene to the build and drag it to the top, so it becomes level 0.

3.   Save the build, overwriting TheGame.

4.   Load the Courier prefab into the Start Menu component's Courier parameter.

5.   Click Play and test, by loading the saved game.

The saved level loads.

Final Tasks

While you are now able to play through your game with all of the functionality in place, there are a few more things to do. First, you must finalize object placement and make any terrain adjustments you feel are necessary. Once those issues have been addressed, you will take care of a few publishing-related details, before doing your final game build.

If you kept all of the action objects within reach while you developed the game, you will want to move them to their final locations around the environment. Do not forget to move together the objects that came in with animations on the parent group (the Animation Objects).

The Chest sequence, for example, requires the following objects to be moved together:

•   Animation Objects (contains ChestLid, ChestBase, LockPlate, Message).

•   KeyAtRock Group, KeyAtLockGroup, and Rock Group.

•   Target Chest and Target Chest Look for the camera match. The Target Chest Look may have to be re-created, if you change the orientation of the objects.

Test the game after doing any rearranging. When you have finalized the locations and the terrain, bake the terrain shadows one last time.

After further testing, you will probably have a list of little things that could be fixed or improved. It is easy to get obsessed with fixing tiny details, if you are not constrained by time or budget. A good rule of thumb is to look for a few items that are quickly accomplished but give a major return for your time.

For this game, as navigation is suspended slightly when a new game loads—and the player might see a flash of objects transitioning to their correct states—it might be nice to have a crossfade on load or, to be more correct, a fade-out from the current scene, before `loadlevel` is called, and a fade-in on startup, as with the FinalLevel. The StartScene already has a couple of prefabs for a UnityGUI color change/fade.

1.   Drop the Fade in from Black prefab into the MainLevel scene and save the scene.

2.   Drop the Fade in from Black prefab into the FinalLevel scene and save the scene.

3. Add the following variable to the SaveLoad script:

```
var fadeOut : GameObject;      // prefab to fade out at end
var fadeIn : GameObject;       // prefab to fade in when not reloading scene
```

4. At the top of the ReadFile function, add

```
Instantiate(fadeOut);           // fade out current scene first
yield new WaitForSeconds(0.5); // let the fade finish
```

5. Under the if (level != Application.loadedLevel) line, add

```
else Instantiate(fadeIn);        // fade in to already scene
```

6. Save the script and load the two prefabs into the SystemIO's SaveLoad component.

7. Click Play and test, by loading saved games from both the MainLevel and FinalLevel.

The last thing to do before publishing is to set a better path for the saved games. Using Application.dataPath was handy for testing, keeping the saved game in the Assets folder, but Application.persistentDataPath provides a safer location for the published game.

1. Change Application.dataPath to Application.persistentDataPath in the SaveLoad, SaveLoad_F, and StartMenu scripts.

2. Save the scripts.

Publishing

Assuming you are calling the game "finished" now, there are a few things yet to do. While you have been doing some organization of assets along the way, feel free to organize further. Before you remove old, unused levels and assets, you will probably want to make a copy of the entire project folder elsewhere on your machine and give it an appropriate name.

One last thing you will do is disable the Player settings, so the player will not be able to change the screen size or make other changes that would mean extra work for you.

1. Go to Edit ➤ Project Settings ➤ Player.

2. Under Standalone Player Settings, set Display Resolution Dialog to Disabled.

To select the game icons, do the following:

3. Load the Key Glyph Icon as the Default Icon (at the top of the Inspector).

4. Open the Icon section.

An icon of each required size has been generated (see Figure 19-4).

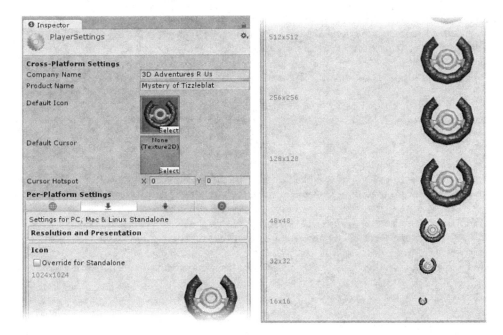

Figure 19-4. *Game Icon*

5. Save the scene and save the project.

You have already published several executables along the way. If you wish to distribute your game for Windows deployment, consider zipping both the .exe and the data folder together, along with the instruction that the two must reside in the same location.

While you have created this project as a desktop stand-alone application, it might be worth a few notes on stand-alone vs. publishing for a web browser–based delivery.

To publish for browser-based delivery, you will change the Platform to Web Player in the Build Settings dialog. Figure 19-5 shows the differences in build settings. Select Offline Deployment, then select the Build button. After compiling the build, you can find your game in a folder named Web Player. It contains three files: UnityObject.js, WebPlayer.html, and WebPlayer.unity3d.

Figure 19-5. *Build settings for stand-alone ,(left), and browser-based for web, (right)*

By its size, you can recognize your game as the last file. The first file contains instructions to check whether the Unity player is installed. The middle file contains the code to add your game to a web page. If you run the HTML file, the first thing you notice is that, despite your instructions to set the size to 1024×768, the window is too small for your text. It is correct on full screen, however.

If you open the HTML file in the script editor (or any HTML editor), you can see where the window size is set.

```
if (typeof unityObject != "undefined") {
   unityObject.embedUnity("unityPlayer", "WebPlayer.unity3d", 600, 450);
}
```

Change the window size to 1024×768 and save.

The other issue is that many browsers "sandbox" the application they are running, to prevent the application from executing malicious code on the player's machine. This means the load/save functionality may not work in the web player.

A third consideration is that the current version of your game may not play in the next version of Unity. A stand-alone executable ensures that future software changes will not affect your finished game. Even if you want to release your game with only web deployment, it is wise to save an .exe for reference, in case Unity updates cause problems. If you *are* interested in web delivery, the Unity manual has a good section on web- player streaming and web-player deployment.

Summary

In this chapter, you created a few menus and worked with the UnityGUI system a bit more. After learning how to use GUI groups and automating some of the button layout, you set up the main menu, so that it could be accessed by both keyboard and cursor position, allowing you to preserve "suspension of disbelief." In your menu script, you used flags to control the visibility of the various menus.

In the Settings menu, you went beyond GUIButtons and GUILabels and added toggles and sliders to control navigation speeds, audio volumes, and even cursor color, with the help of GUI.changed. Because you opted to keep the menu GUI in a separate script from your regular text and pointer, you required an economical means of passing the settings back and forth between the menu script and the game's main brain, the GameManager. By using a String array, you were able to store each of the settings, regardless of type, into a single easily accessed array. When it came time to implement the load/save functionality, the array was easily parsed and added to the simple text file, along with the First Person Controller transform, the current level, the current state of each of the action objects, and a few other worthwhile pieces of information. In addition to including the SystemIO class in your load/save script, you learned how to access the game's data path and add it to a file name and extension, in case you wanted to implement multiple saved games at a later date.

With the addition of the imported FinalLevel and StartScene levels, you learned how to order your scenes in the Build Settings, so the game would start with the correct scene when you created an executable.

Finally, with a fully working game to show for your tenacity, you considered the concept of "finished." After a short discussion about "feature creep," you made one final addition to your game, deeming it a quick addition for large visual gain.

Wrapping it up, you limited player choices, by disabling the application settings menu at the start of the game, because you had already decided on a set resolution and navigation keys.

Although you designed this game with the intent of creating a desktop stand-alone executable, you looked briefly at a few considerations for deploying via web players in browsers. Aside from the default window size, you discovered that loading and saving to the player's hard drive could be unrealistic.

Index

CPSIA information can be obtained at www.ICGtesting.com
Printed in the USA
LVOW06s0259061113

360185LV00016B/353/P